PLEASE HAND THE DISK IN SEPARATELY
KEPT BEHIND THE COUNTER → NO DISK
KB 4/7/05

BASIC
FINANCIAL
MANAGEMENT

WILLIAM H. MARSH
UNIVERSITY OF SOUTH CAROLINA, AIKEN

SOUTH-WESTERN College Publishing

An International Thomson Publishing Company

Acquisitions Editor: Christopher Will
Developmental Editor: Ann Sass
Production Editors: Marci Dechter, Rebecca Roby
Production House: TSI Graphics
Cover Design: Ben Ross Design
Internal Design: Ellen Pettengell Design
Cover Illustrator: Nickolai Punin
Photo Editor: Jennifer Mayhall
Photo Research: Debbie Leffert
Marketing Manager: Denise Carlson

FN64AA
Copyright © 1995
South-Western College Publishing
Cincinnati, Ohio

Library of Congress Cataloging–in–Publication Data

Marsh, William H.,
    Basic financial management / William H. Marsh. –– 1st ed.
        p.   cm.
    Includes index.
    ISBN 0–538–84170–2 ✔
    1. Corporations––Finance. 2. Business enterprises––Finance.
I. Title.
HG4026.M365   1994
658.15––dc20   94–2856
                                                                       CIP

ISBN: 0–538–84170–2
1 2 3 4 5 6 7 8 9 0 VH 3 2 1 0 9 8 7 6 5 4
Printed in the United States of America

 This book is printed on acid-free paper that meets Environmental Protection Agency standards for recycled paper.

I(T)P
International Thomson Publishing

South-Western College Publishing is an ITP Company. The ITP trademark is
used under license.

Preface

In writing *Basic Financial Management*, I wanted this text to be different. My goal was to create a readable, visual, useful, and friendly text for students taking financial management for the first time. As a result, the writing style is direct and the chapter structure is simple. As we all know, students must absorb a large amount of material in a small amount of time.

Today's students access new material most easily through visual images, partly the result of television's impact on the 20th century. In *Basic Financial Management* I've made every effort to acknowledge that reality by providing:

- An inviting four-color design;
- Color-coded cash flow diagrams, to help students visualize problems involving the time value of money; and
- *THE FINANCIAL MANAGER*, a spreadsheet program that furnishes a two-dimensional presentation of financial calculations.

Each chapter also includes the following pedagogical features to assist students in learning the material:

- A real-world, opening vignette to stimulate interest in the material to be covered,
- Highlighted examples to help reinforce new material,
- Boxed features, based on real-world situations, to lightly introduce international, ethical, quality, technological, competitive, and environmental issues,
- Color-coded graphs to provide a visual level of understanding,
- Learning objectives keyed to the chapter summary, to remind students of the key points covered,
- A finance case problem at the end of each chapter, to combine the "gray" real world with the "black and white" world of problems,
- A financial tables card that includes even years after year 30, and
- An Answers to Chapter Problems Appendix that provides answers to all of the end-of-chapter problems.

VALUATION ORIENTATION AS A UNIFYING THEME

The unifying theme of *Basic Financial Management* is a *valuation orientation*. As a result, time value of money, bond and stock valuation, and capital budgeting are introduced early in the text. This approach is consistent with the goal of the financial manager to maximize the price per share of stock. Since the emphasis is on adding value to the firm, each part of the text connects financial decision-making to common stock valuation.

- Part I, Basic Concepts. The student learns time value techniques and then applies this knowledge to bond and stock valuation.
- Part II, Financial Analysis and Planning. The student evaluates the relationships within a set of financial statements and prepares a financial plan for internal application or for use with various lenders.
- Part III, Capital Budgeting. The student studies cash flow estimation and project evaluation, with and without risk.
- Part IV, Leverage, Capital Structure Theory, Cost of Capital, and Dividend Policy. The student discovers how the determination of the marginal cost of capital relates to the optimal capital structure, the structure that maximizes shareholder wealth.
- Part V, Long-Term Financing. The student examines how to obtain securities, while making valuation choices that fit into a plan for minimizing the marginal cost of capital.
- Part VI, Working Capital Management. The student finds methods for minimizing the total costs of maintaining working capital, while studying the sources of financing required to support daily operations.
- Part VII, Special Topics. The student explores topics such as the formulation and evaluation of mergers, consolidations, and acquisitions, as well as business failure. In the final chapter, the student then relates the study of financial management to multinational organizations.

A COMPREHENSIVE SUPPLEMENTS PACKAGE

In coordinating the supplements package for *Basic Financial Management,* I have purposely taken a hands-on approach, writing and/or overseeing the preparation of all materials. In doing so, I have been able to exercise tighter quality control over the finished product.

- Instructor's Manual, prepared by William H. Marsh. *The Instructor's Manual* provides the instructor with a complete teaching resource. It includes teaching strategies, teaching summaries, answers to questions, solutions to problems, and solutions to the case problems.
- Transparencies, prepared by William H. Marsh. A set of transparencies displays the principal tables, figures, and problems from each chapter. The entire set of transparencies is available on Power Point Software. A selected number of these are also available as *Acetate Transparencies.*

- Test Bank, prepared by John Bowdidge and George Swales of Southwest Missouri State University. The *Test Bank* furnishes over 1,200 short discussion questions, multiple-choice questions, and problems. This material is available in three formats: in book form; on WordPerfect 5.1 disks; and on MicroExam disks. MicroExam is South-Western's automated testing program, which permits options such as random question selection.

- The Financial Manager, prepared by F. X. McGahee and William H. Marsh of the University of South Carolina at Aiken. *The Financial Manager* includes general models rather than presenting a solution to a specific text problem. Moreover, it does not require a commercial spreadsheet. Many end-of-chapter problems indicate that a particular model should be used. *The Financial Manager* includes the following spreadsheet models for solving problems:

  Interest Factor Table (TABLE) provides interest factors for combinations of term and interest rate;

  Equivalent Cash Flow (CASHFLOW) provides an equivalent cash flow for a given set of cash flows;

  Bond Valuation (BOND) provides bond valuation, yield to maturity, and yield to call;

  Ratio Analysis (RATIO) provides standard ratios;

  Cash Budgeting (BUDGET) provides cash budget;

  Miller-Orr Model (MILLORR) provides target level, upper limit, and average cash balance;

  Capital Budgeting (PROJECT) provides net present value, internal rate of return, modified internal rate of return, profitability index, payback period, discounted payback period, and accounting rate of return. Calculates depreciation, including MACRS;

  Basic Statistics (STAT) provides expected value, variance, standard deviation, and coefficient of variation;

  Expected Exchange Rate (RATE) provides expected exchange rate, N years in the future;

- CNBC Videos. This videotape series can help enhance your lectures and bring topics to life. These videos are composed of timely business topics and current news clips from CNBC, the cable news network, and are sure to invoke class discussion. Each video segment ranges from eight to twenty minutes. The complete videotape is available to adopters upon request.

- Study Guide, prepared by William H. Marsh and F. X. McGahee of the University of South Carolina at Aiken. The *Study Guide* includes an expanded summary of each chapter and additional problems with solutions. This manual also teaches the student how to use *The Financial Manager,* if additional instruction is desired, and presents the output of the spreadsheet models for many examples.

ACKNOWLEDGMENTS

Basic Financial Management was strongly influenced by the comments and suggestions of many individuals. To the following reviewers I offer my sincere thanks:

Stephen L. Avard
East Texas State University

Samuel Bulmash
University of South Florida

Richard M. Burns
University of Alabama at Birmingham

Kenneth J. Burns
Memphis State University

P.R. Chandy
University of North Texas

Robert E. Chatfield
University of Nevada, Las Vegas

Dean A. Dudley
Eastern Illinois University

Edwin H. Duett
Mississippi State University

David R. Durst
University of Akron

Robert S. Elliott
Northwestern State University of Louisiana

M. Andrew Fields
University of Delaware

Greg Filbeck
Miami University of Ohio

Asim Ghosh
Bloomsburg University

Marcus A. Ingram
Clark Atlanta University

Larry Johnson
New Hampshire College

James B. Kehr
Miami University of Ohio

Peppi M. Kenny
Western Illinois University

Daniel P. Klein
Bowling Green State University

George W. Kutner
Marquette University

Boyden E. Lee
New Mexico State University

David Louton
Bryant College

Wayne E. McWee
Longwood College

Dianne R. Morrison
University of Wisconsin-La Crosse

Don B. Panton
University of Texas at Arlington

Eugene O. Poindexter
West Georgia College

Daniel H. Raver
Geneva College

Robert J. Ryan, Jr.
Ithaca College

Robert Schweitzer
University of Delaware

Thomas O. Stanley
Nicholls State University

Amir Tavokkol
Kansas State University

Clifford F. Thies
Shenandoah College

George W. Trivoli
Jacksonville State University

Ben Uzoaru
Southeast Missouri State University

Paul A. Vanderheiden
University of Wisconsin-Eau Claire

Bernard W. Weinrich
St. Louis Community College

Tony R. Wingler
University of North Carolina at Greensboro

Daniel T. Winkler
University of North Carolina at Greensboro

Steve B. Wyatt
University of Cincinnati

Several other individuals also dedicated their time to the development of this text. Daniel T. Winkler of the University of North Carolina at Greensboro created the Kennedy example in Chapter 2. My student assistant, Deirdre Corley, spent countless hours checking the correctness of the chapters. Claire S. Bronson of Western New England College, Peppi M. Kenny of Western Illinois University, and the professionals at Mathematical Alternatives, Inc., had the painstaking task of checking the accuracy of the in-text examples and end-of-chapter problems.

The professionals at South-Western College Publishing are willing to try new things in an era of rapid change in publishing. Chris Will, Acquisitions Editor, has the vision to recognize new approaches that work. Ann Sass, the Developmental Editor, is willing to accept new ideas. Marci Dechter and Rebecca Roby, production editors, have the patience and understanding to work with me. Debbie Kokoruda, Art Director, has the artistic ability to create a new style of text. Jennifer Mayhall, Production/Photo Editor, has the creative capability to select and blend photographs into the text. Bill Wilson, Technical Editor, has the expertise to see our computer program from a new perspective.

Finally, I owe special thanks to my colleague, F.X. McGahee, for his dedication to this project and his development of *The Financial Manager* and the *Study Guide*.

William H. Marsh
University of South Carolina, Aiken

Brief Contents

Contents

Real-World Companies and References

Abitibi-Price Inc.
Advanced Micro Devices Inc.
Alcatel N.V.
Allied-Signal Corporation
Amerada Hess Corporation
Augusta Newsprint Company
Avery Dennison Corporation
Avery International Corporation
Bank of Japan
Barnett Bank
Bloomingdale's
Carolina Power & Company
Castle and Cooke
Chambers Development Company
Chrysler Corporation
Ciba-Geigy AG
Citibank
Coca-Cola
Collective Intelligence Inc.
Columbia Gas System Inc.
Coniston
Crowell, Weedon & Co.
CS Holding
David L. Babson & Company
Dean Witter Reynolds Inc.
Delaware Bay Company
Dennison Manufacturing Company
Donaldson Lufkin Jenrette
Federated Department Stores Inc.
Fidelity Investments
G.D. Searle and Company
General Electric
General Motors Acceptance Corporation
Georgia-Pacific Corporation
Goldman Sachs and Company
HSBC Holdings PLC
Illinois Superconductor Corporation
Industrial Bank of Japan
Ingersoll-Rand Company
Intel Corporation

ITT Corporation
Johnson and Johnson
Lehman Brothers
Levi Straus
Lloyds Bank PLC
LM Capital Management Inc.
Loomis, Sayles & Company
Mazda Motors
McCrory Corporation
McKinsey's Global Institute
Merck & Company
Microsoft
Midland Bank PLC
Monsanto
Morgan Stanley
Nestle S.A.
Neuberger & Berman
Nomura Research Institute
Omron Corporation
Phar-Mor
Procter and Gamble
Prudential Securities Research
PS Group Inc.
R.H. Macy & Company
Rich's
R.J. Reynolds Tobacco International
Rubbermaid
Salomon Brothers
Scudder, Stevens & Clark
Securities Data Company
Shearson Lehman Brothers Inc.
Southeast Research Partners
Storer Communications
Superconductivity Inc.
Tele-Communications
The Thomson Corporation
Uritski Tobacco
Wallace Company
Wal-Mart
Walt Disney Company

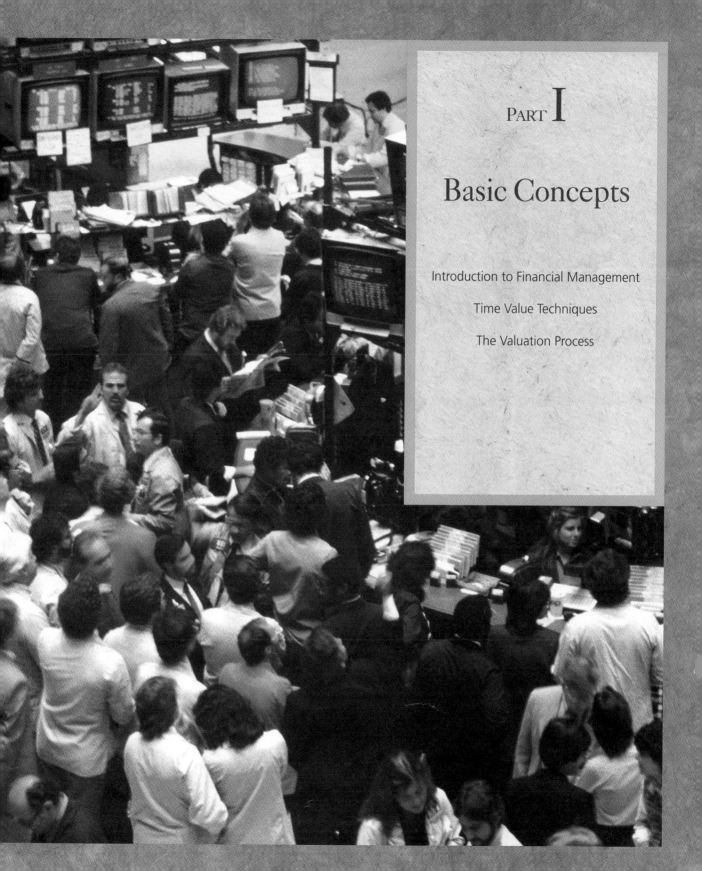

PART I

Basic Concepts

Introduction to Financial Management

Time Value Techniques

The Valuation Process

1 Introduction to Financial Management

AMERICA'S MOST ADMIRED CORPORATIONS

t's not listed in a 10K or proxy statement, and you won't find it on the balance sheet or income statement. But millions of consumers at home and in foreign countries, not to mention millions of potential customers, make a golden reputation more valuable than ever for U.S. companies. In their tenth annual Corporate Reputation Survey, FORTUNE polls more than 8,000 senior executives, outside directors, and financial analysts about the reputation of

307 companies in 32 industries. What constitutes reputation? According to the survey, the most acclaimed companies have worked their way to the top with excellent management, high-quality products, and superior financial performance. Quality management is cited by 82 percent of respondents as foremost to a golden reputation; 63 percent voted quality of product or services as the most important ingredient. Compared with a decade ago, twice as many respondents cited responsibility to the community and environment as the most important standard for judging a corporate reputation. Once at the top of the reputation ladder, companies find it difficult to stay there.

For the sixth year in a row, Merck, the pharmaceutical drug giant, has earned the highest rating among the 307 major companies. The secret to Merck's success lies in its ability to attract, develop, and keep good people. At Merck, senior executive promotions and salary increases are affected by how many people that person has recruited and trained. Quality of work force is clearly the catalyst of financial success.

A company's financial performance also has a halo effect on its reputation and vice versa. All of the most admired corporations have consistently produced first-rate returns for investors, while the least admired have not. Most of the top ten have consistent and enviable growth records. Rubbermaid, for example, has met or surpassed its corporate goal of 15 percent annual profit increases. Wal-Mart has expanded annual earnings at least 20 percent for the past five years; outselling and outgrowing its competitors. Says Robert Haas, CEO of Levi Straus: "Reputation definitely tilts in favor of financial success."

The most admired companies never stop innovating and improving their products. For example, Proctor and Gamble sells detergents in luggable detergent size in 30 countries. Their products show how the company is socially responsible as well as a financial success. Says Proctor and Gamble CEO Adwin Artzt: "Concentrate detergent is a real win for consumers. It's easy to carry, and it's good for the environment because it reduces the amount of packaging and chemicals per wash load." These products undergo continual refinement. Says Johnson and Johnson's CEO Wayne Colloway: "We start with the mind-set that innovation and continuous improvement are critical."

For small companies as well as big ones, the payoff from a good reputation is extensive. A solid reputation convinces a customer to be willing to pay more for your product or service. A highly-respected reputation helps attract and retain top employees in your industry, and in addition, steal talent away from competitors. Reputation can catapult new product innovations and help open doors more easily for international expansion.

When reading this chapter, keep in mind that few companies with poor reputations are financially successful. Conversely, companies with golden reputations seldom become bankrupt. The pressures of global competition demand that companies offer high-quality products, exercise social responsibility, and adhere to strict ethical standards. A quality work force stimulates ongoing product innovation and quality service to the customer. Social responsibility and strict ethical standards separate the most admired and profitable companies from their envious competitors.

Source: "America's Most Admired Corporations" FORTUNE, May 10, 1992 and May 11, 1991, and "The Payoff from a Good Reputation," FORTUNE, February 10, 1992 © 1991 and 1992 Time Inc. All rights reserved.

AN OVERVIEW OF FINANCIAL MANAGEMENT

Basic financial management is an interesting and challenging course, requiring a strong effort on your part. What is your payoff for responding to this challenge? The answer will lie in what happens after you graduate.

Opportunities in Finance

Finance students find many job opportunities after college[1]. This is a key reason why students majoring in other business administration concentrations often choose to take additional finance courses.

Financial Services Financial careers are divided into two categories: financial services and managerial finance. **Financial services** involve the delivery of financial products to all types of organizations. Banking, financial planning, investments, real estate, and insurance offer career opportunities in financial services. Table 1.1 lists opportunities in this area.

Barnett Bank, a multi-bank holding company in Florida, for example, places new college graduates in a 15 to 18 month training program. The program provides training in (1) commercial loan analysis, (2) loan compliance and documentation, and (3) bank operations. At the end of the program, the trainee becomes a lending assistant to commercial lenders for six months, and at that point is given limited authority.

TABLE 1.1 A Partial List of Opportunities in Financial Services

CAREER CLASSIFICATION	ORGANIZATIONAL OPPORTUNITIES
Banking	Banks, savings and loan associations credit unions, and finance companies.
Financial Planning	Banks, savings and loan associations, credit unions, finance companies, insurance companies, brokerage houses, and consulting firms.
Investments	Brokerage houses, insurance companies, banks, savings and loan associations, and consulting firms.
Real Estate	Real estate sales companies, real estate development companies, savings and loan associations, and insurance companies.
Insurance	Insurance companies, real estate development companies, and consulting firms.

---

[1] Finance involves the acquisition of resources and the allocation of funds to present and future operations.

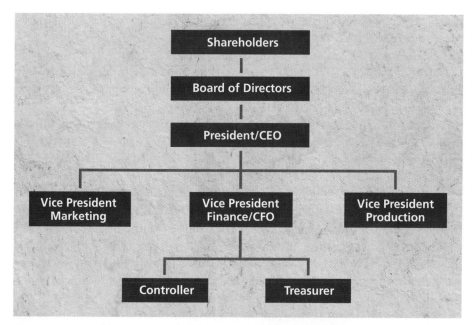

FIGURE 1.1 Typical Financial Management Organizational Structure

Managerial finance, the second career category, relates to duties of the financial manager in private companies, governmental operations, and not-for-profit institutions. This text focuses on managerial finance in middle-sized and large private companies. The chief financial officer in this type of organization is the vice president for finance. Figure 1.1 shows that the financial vice president reports directly to the president. The controller and treasurer, in turn, report to the vice president. The controller is primarily responsible for the accounting activities, including tax preparation, budgeting, and financial statements. The treasurer is primarily responsible for managing cash and marketable securities, acquiring external funds, and operating the credit department.

Prospective employees pursuing financial careers are typically rising college graduates from business schools. Achievement in these areas, however, often depends upon the ability to assess financial risks. As a result, demonstrating a knowledge of finance provides the graduate with an edge in landing a job and being successful.

What types of decisions do financial managers make? Before you can answer this question, you need to know the primary goal of management.

The Primary Goal

The **primary goal** of management in a public corporation, from the point of view of the shareholders, is to maximize the value of its common stock. This

Managerial Finance

Primary Goal

means that management should maximize the present value of future returns to its shareholders. Present value is the value today of a stream of future cash flows, using the proper discount rate. The future returns are the dividends shareholders will be paid and, in some cases, the future selling price of the stock. Chapter 2 discusses present value, and Chapter 3 applies the concept to bond, preferred stock, and common stock valuation.

Because of its great importance, the underlying theme of this text is maximization of the value of common stock. Maximizing stock value requires an understanding of the risk-return tradeoff faced by financial decision makers. In general, the higher the expected cash flows of a venture, the greater the risk; the greater the risk, the higher the required rate of return. To maximize the value of the company's stock, financial managers must balance risk and return in order to find the highest present value of cash flows. Chapter 3 applies this concept.

With private companies, the concept of maximizing shareholder value is more complex. When Microsoft went public in March of 1986, transaction fees were only 7.1 percent, a figure considered quite low. But Microsoft made a mistake in pricing the issue. The closing price on the day of the offering was $28, although the offering price was only $21. This represented underpricing of $22 million, not the way to maximize value.

Managers, left to their own devices, sometimes choose profit maximization or growth as a goal, instead of share-value maximization. Profit maximization involves a preference by management for increasing short-run profits. This approach may result in improper financial decisions since it does not account for the time value of money or the element of risk. Growth also may be selected as a goal, particularly if management compensation is tied to sales or total assets. Management can create growth by simply increasing assets, and that may not be in the best interests of the shareholders.

Agency Problems

Agency Problem

The tendency of management to choose goals other than share-price maximization is called the **agency problem**[2]. Agency problems exist because management has a tendency to place personal goals ahead of the goal of maximizing share value. Managers are naturally concerned with keeping their jobs, making more money, and certain perquisites such as fancy offices and country club memberships. These concerns may lead to decisions that are not in the best interests of shareholders. The costs of trying to minimize the agency problem are

---

[2] The root of the agency problem is the fact that most modern corporations have professional management who are not necessarily the owners. Research has shown that the greater the ownership stake, the lesser will be the potential agency costs. See G. William Trivioli, "Market Mechanisms For Restricting Corporate Discretionary Behavior," *Akron Business and Economic Review*, Fall 1972, Volume 2, Number 3.

referred to as **agency costs.** The most important **agency relationships** are be-tween management and shareholders and between shareholders and creditors.

Agency Costs

The relationship between management and shareholders produces a variety of agency costs. First, internal audits of company expenditures and managerial performance are carried out; the costs of these audits are called monitoring costs. Second, financial incentives are offered to employees to encourage them to max-imize the value of the company's common stock; the costs of these incentives are called structuring costs. Bell Atlantic, for example, allows employees to cham-pion new ideas on a full-time basis, while receiving full pay. Third, companies lose the chance for profitable business when agency problems cause inadequate organizational structures; the costs of losing business are called opportunity costs. Fourth, companies purchase surety bonds to prevent losses from dishonest man-agement; the costs of providing such bonds are called bonding costs.

Agency Relationship

Agency problems exist between shareholders and creditors when manage-ment makes decisions that attempt to shift wealth from creditors to sharehold-ers. Issuing bonds to pay a dividend to shareholders, for example, increases the value of shares at the expense of bondholders because of the increased riski-ness of the bonds. In the leveraged buyout of RJR, begun in 1988 and com-pleted in 1989, shareholders realized high rates of return, while bondholders suffered great losses. Creditors react to such actions by recruiting protective covenants in the bond indenture or by increasing the costs of bonds. This in-creases the costs of doing business and the cost of capital. As a result, manage-ment does not maximize the value of company stock.

A deeper understanding of agency relationships requires you to know the functions financial managers actually perform. How do they spend their time? What do they do to maximize the value of the common stock?

Functions of Managerial Finance

Managerial finance centers on the investment, financing, and dividend deci-sions. Financial mangers also become involved in strategic planning and con-trol of the company. Let's look more closely at each of these functions.

The **investment decision** involves determining the size and composition of company assets. We can see the results of previous investment decisions by looking at the left-hand side of a balance sheet. Table 1.2 shows a balance sheet for the Martin Corporation as of December 31, 19X4. This statement in-cludes current assets and fixed assets. (Chapter 4 describes the individual ac-counts in detail.) Financial managers must invest in new assets, as needed, and remove assets that are no longer productive.

Investment Decision

The **financing decision** determines how a company's assets are financed. The right-hand side of a balance sheet shows the results of previous financing decisions. For the Martin Corporation, accounts include current liabilities,

Financing Decision

TABLE 1.2 Martin Corporation: Balance Sheet as of December 31, 19X4 (in thousands)

ASSETS	
Current assets:	
Cash	$ 20,000
Marketable securities	5,000
Accounts receivable	80,000
Inventory	120,000
Total current assets	$225,000
Fixed assets:	
Property, plant, and equipment	$475,000
Less: Accumulated depreciation	200,000
Net property, plant, and equipment	275,000
Total assets	$500,000

LIABILITIES AND STOCKHOLDERS' EQUITY	
Current liabilities:	
Accounts payable	$ 40,000
Notes payable	60,000
Current maturities, long-term debt	5,000
Accrued expenses	15,000
Total current liabilities	$120,000
Long-term debt	40,000
Total liabilities	$160,000
Stockholders' equity:	
Preferred stock	$ 50,000
Common stock ($1 par)	50,000
Capital in excess of par	100,000
Retained earnings	140,000
Total stockholders' equity	340,000
Total liabilities and stockholders' equity	$500,000

long-term debt, and stockholders' equity. (Again, Chapter 4 describes the individual accounts in detail.) Financial managers must make financing decisions that result in the best mix of debt and equity.

Dividend Decision

The **dividend decision** determines how earnings after taxes are distributed to preferred and common shareholders, or retained for investment. Table 1.3 is an income statement for the Martin Corporation, and it shows how earnings after taxes were determined, the amount of preferred stock dividends, and the relationship between earnings per share and dividends per share.

Strategic Planning

Strategic planning is the design of strategies to meet the primary goal of maximizing the value of the common stock of the corporation. Plans must reflect

TABLE 1.3 Martin Corporation: Income Statement for the Year Ended December 31, 19X4
••••••• (in thousands)

Net Sales	$1,000,000
Cost of goods sold	700,000
Gross profit	$ 300,000
Selling and administrative expenses	$ 100,000
Depreciation expense	40,000
Earnings before interest and taxes (EBIT)	$ 160,000
Interest expense	10,000
Earnings before taxes (EBT)	$ 150,000
Taxes	60,000
Earnings after taxes (EAT)	$ 90,000
Preferred stock dividends	5,000
Earnings available to common shareholders	$ 85,000
Shares outstanding	50,000
Earnings per share	$1.70
Dividends per share	$0.85

this goal. As a financial manager, you must answer the question, "How do we set objectives that are consistent with the primary goal of the corporation?"

Control consists of the design of systems to ensure that the company achieves objectives that lead to attainment of the primary goal. As mentioned earlier, managers may choose other goals and set objectives that reflect these goals. Their objectives may be achieved at the expense of the shareholders.

Control

Before the Great Depression, financial management concentrated on the right-hand side of the balance sheet. It emphasized legal aspects of company formation and securities markets. During the 1930s and 1940s, because of the impact of the depression, finance focused more on business failure. In the 1950s, the accent shifted to include the left-hand side of the balance sheet as well. Capital budgeting became an important topic.

During the 1960s and 1970s, mathematical models were applied to cash, marketable securities, accounts receivables, and inventories in order to find their optimal levels. This trend continued into the 1980s, aided by advancements in the use of computers. This period also saw an increased interest in business combinations and new financial instruments, such as options and futures.

Financial management in the 1990s and beyond will show the impact of the globalization of business and the consequences of societal change. Competitiveness, quality, and technology will receive increased attention in this global climate. The interaction between business and social institutions will impose ethical and environmental restraints on management. Financial managers must consider the implications of these issues in their decision making.

Companies during the 1990s will flatten organizational charts while increasing sales, with fewer people. The winners during this period will be those companies that can bring ideas to the market fastest and are not necessarily the companies that create the ideas. In Crawfordsville, Indiana, the Nucor Corporation operates a mini-mill that rolls metal into steel slabs in a continuous process that is much more efficient than conventional processes. SMS Schloemann-Siemag of Germany developed the technology.

In light of these predictions, this text includes vignettes focusing on finance in practice and international business. These vignettes provide a vehicle for discussing issues that are not always easy to link to finance. Still, remember the primary goal of management remains the same.

The discussion of the functions of managerial finance applies not only to corporations, but also indirectly to other forms of business organization as well. As you study sole proprietorships and partnerships, think how you would apply what you have learned to each legal form of business, including the impact of taxes.

BUSINESS ORGANIZATION AND TAXES

Entrepreneurs beginning a new venture must choose the particular form the venture will take. Choices include the sole proprietorship, the partnership, and the corporation. Which form would you select? Of course, it depends in part on the particular type of business. To help you decide, Table 1.4 outlines the strengths and weaknesses of the three legal forms of business organization.

Sole Proprietorships

Sole Proprietorship

A **sole proprietorship** is a business owned by one person. About 75 percent of U.S. businesses are organized in this form Usually, these companies have few employees and are run by the proprietor. Many corporations begin as sole proprietorships.

The sole proprietor has unlimited liability. This means the owner is responsible for all liabilities of the company. Creditors can seize the personal assets of the sole proprietor to satisfy claims. No differentiation between company and proprietor's assets is made. A lawsuit brought against the company is a lawsuit against the owner.

The sole proprietor applies the net income or net loss of the company to his or her personal income tax return. The net loss application shelters other sources of income. For example, a $10,000 loss from a sole proprietorship allows $10,000 of other income to be sheltered from taxes. Losses from corporations,

TABLE 1.4   The Strengths and Weaknesses of the Legal Forms of Business Organization

SOLE PROPRIETORSHIP	
STRENGTHS:	**WEAKNESSES:**
Easy to establish.	Unlimited liability.
Income taxed to owner.	LImited skills.
Owner receives profits and losses.	Difficulty raising funds.
Easy to dissolve.	Ownership not easily transferred.
PARTNERSHIP	
STRENGTHS:	**WEAKNESSES:**
Raising funds easier.	Unlimited liability for some partners.
Income taxed to partners.	Partnership dissolved when partner dies.
More skills available.	Difficult to transfer ownership.
CORPORATION	
STRENGTHS:	**WEAKNESSES:**
Limited liability.	Taxation of income and dividends.
Easier to raise funds.	Most expensive form to organize.
Unlimited life.	More government regulation.
Easy to transfer ownership.	Greater disclosure of financial details.

unless they are taxed as S corporations (to be discussed later), are not passed along to the owners.

Sole proprietors report their income on their individual tax returns. As a result, their income tax liabilities and marginal tax rates depend in part on their taxable income outside of the businesses.

Sole proprietorships have difficulty raising funds as they grow since there is no market for ownership in the company. The owner does use retained earnings when possible, but ordinarily this is not enough. For this reason, sole proprietorships often become partnerships or corporations as they expand.

Partnerships

A **partnership** is a business operated by two or more persons working under a written or oral agreement. The partnership agreement states what each partner contributes, in terms of capital and effort. In a general partnership, the partners share gains and losses according to the agreement, and assume unlimited liability for partnership debts. In a limited partnership, one or more general partners operate the business and assume unlimited liability. The remaining limited partners risk only the capital they contribute to the partnership.

Partnership

A general partnership dissolves when a general partner withdraws or dies. This makes it difficult to transfer ownership of the partnership, since all the general partners must agree. With a limited partnership, the limited partners may sell their interests without dissolving the partnership.

Partnerships report their income on partnership returns. Since partnerships are not taxed, the partners' incomes are reported on their individual tax returns. As a result, the income tax liability and marginal tax rate depend in part on the taxable income outside of the partnership.

Partnerships, like sole proprietorships, have difficulty raising funds as they grow. The partnership must depend on the personal wealth of the partners or the addition of new partners. To avoid this problem, partnerships often convert to the corporate form of organization.

Corporations

Corporation

A **corporation** is a legal entity created by a state and is separate from the owners of the organization. This separation between existence and ownership enhances the ability of the corporation to attract capital and to survive indefinitely.

The shareholders of a corporation have limited liability. This means that shareholders risk only the amount they have invested in common stock and are under no personal obligation to corporate creditors. This doctrine follows from the concept of the corporation as a separate entity.

A corporation comes into existence when it is granted a charter, or certificate of incorporation, by a state. The charter includes the name of the company, the nature of its activities, the number of authorized shares of common stock, and the names and addresses of its directors. This document also details the rights and obligations of shareholders. The corporation also must have a set of by-laws—rules to direct the internal management of the company.

A stock certificate is used to represent ownership of the stock of the company. The authorized stock of a company is the maximum number of shares that can be issued without an amendment to the charter. This contrasts with the issued stock, the stock actually sold to shareholders. When companies repurchase stock on the open market or through a tender offer, the stock is called treasury stock. The outstanding stock of a company is the stock actually in the hands of shareholders, and it is equal to the amount of issued stock less the amount of treasury stock.

S Corporation

Corporations may elect to be treated for tax purposes as **S corporations**. To qualify for this status, several requirements must be met, the most restrictive being that the corporation have no more than 35 shareholders. The income of an S corporation is taxed to the individual shareholders, thereby avoiding the double taxation of the corporation. This is similar to the treatment of a partnership, although the business is still a corporation under state law.

Corporations that do not elect or are ineligible for S corporation status are treated for tax purposes as regular corporations, also known as **C corporations**. This results in a double taxation of income: corporate earnings are taxed and then dividends are taxed after they have been distributed to the individual shareholders.

C Corporation

The net operating loss of a corporation, like the net operating loss for an individual, may be carried back 3 years or forward 15 years. This results in lower taxes during those years. The tax savings for any year is equal to amount carried backward or forward multiplied by the marginal tax rate (to be covered in the next section).

Marginal Tax Rates

The **marginal tax rate** for sole proprietorships, partnerships, and corporations is the rate applied to each incremental amount of taxable income. The marginal tax rate is important in finance since it shows the marginal effect of a decision. This contrasts with the average tax rate, the total taxes paid divided by the total taxable income.

Marginal Tax Rate

> The Beringer Corporation has taxable income of $150,000. The first $50,000 is taxed at a rate of 15 percent; the next $25,000 at 25 percent; the following $25,000 at 34 percent; and the final $50,000 at 39 percent. What is the company's income tax liability, marginal tax rate, and the average tax rate?

The tax liability on income of $150,000 is determined as follows:

$$
\begin{aligned}
\$50,000(0.15) &= \$\ 7,500 \\
\$25,000(0.25) &= \quad 6,250 \\
\$25,000(0.34) &= \quad 8,500 \\
\$50,000(0.39) &= \underline{\quad 19,500} \\
&\quad\ \ \$41,750
\end{aligned}
$$

The marginal tax rate is 39 percent, the rate applied to the last increment. Divide the taxes paid, $41,750, by the taxable income, $150,000, to find the average tax rate of 27.83 percent. As you can see, the average tax rate is less than the marginal tax rate.

Taxes are important in making financial decisions since they affect cash flows, but other considerations are important as well. To make financing decisions, a financial manager must be familiar with the financial environment.

Partnership Structure Is Called in Question

The perils of partnership have become a hot issue, not merely among many accountants but also among attorneys, architects, investment bankers and others who once coveted a partner's perks, power and share of the profits. They are now asking: Do partnerships still make sense?

Many partnerships are scurrying to limit their shared liability. Others are abandoning the partnership setup altogether in favor of a corporate structure, even though corporations generally pay an income tax and partnerships do not. (Partnerships pay income taxes as individuals.)

The changes can mean clients are less able to get at partners' personal assets in suits over malpractice and bum advice. Clients could lose the reassurance of knowing that they've retained professionals willing to stake all they have on the work they and their partners do. It's possible the cost of professional services could go up as more partnerships incorporate and pass along the expense of their higher taxes.

On the other hand, if partnerships aren't able to somehow limit their liability, it will be tougher to find a lawyer or accountant willing to take on risky business. Some law and accounting firms may stop expanding in highly litigious states such as California. They also may stop handling business from some higher-risk banks, savings-and-loan associations, brokerage houses and real-estate operations.

Professional partnerships suffer from two threats at once. First, many accounting, law and architectural firms have grown much bigger in recent years and have lost much of their collegial atmosphere. At the same time, a slew of big court damage awards—$1 billion against U.S. accountants and attorneys in the past year alone—is raising some doubts about whether the nation's once-dominant form of business organization can survive.

Little wonder that professional partners are campaigning hard to reduce their personal vulnerabilities to litigation. Last January, members of the American Institute of Certified Public Accountants agreed to let accountants create professional corporations whose principals would have limited liability. The 300,000 member institute previously had resisted such state action because it believed that accountants should jointly stand behind their work.

Source: Lee Berton and Joann S. Lublin, "Partnership Structure Is Called in Question As Liability Risk Rises," *The Wall Street Journal*, June 10, 1992. Reprinted by permission of the Wall Street Journal, © 1992 Dow Jones & Company, Inc. All Rights Reserved Worldwide.

THE FINANCIAL ENVIRONMENT

The financing decision often requires the financial manager to obtain funds from sources outside the company. It is possible to secure these funds through direct sale to an investor or group of investors, but more often financial institutions and financial markets provide businesses with the money they need.

Financial Institutions

Financial Institutions   **Financial institutions** collect money from savers and use the funds to make loans or investments. The savers who deposit money in financial institutions are individuals, businesses, and governments. These financial intermediaries include depository institutions such as commercial banks, thrift institutions, and non-depository institutions like pension funds, insurance companies, investment companies, and finance companies. Let's look at each more closely.

Commercial banks receive demand deposits (checking accounts) and time deposits (certificates of deposit and savings accounts). Banks then loan this money to individuals, businesses, and governments. Loans to businesses may be short-term loans (less than a year), intermediate-term loans (one to five years), or mortgage loans (greater than five years). Businesses with seasonal needs—they require temporary current assets—use short-term financing to cover their peak cash requirements. Intermediate-term loans provide funds to finance current assets and fixed assets, and to repay debt. Mortgage loans finance real estate. Commercial banks also invest funds through their trust departments, perform stock brokerage services, and manage pension funds.

Thrift institutions, like commercial banks, receive demand deposits and time deposits. These organizations include savings and loan associations, mutual savings banks, and credit unions. Savings and loan associations primarily offer residential and commercial mortgages. Mutual savings banks lend predominantly to home buyers and consumers. Credit unions primarily make consumer loans. In recent years, thrift institutions have taken over some of the traditional functions of commercial banks. The differences between types of institutions has blurred as deregulation has lifted the limits on various activities.

Pension funds pool the contributions of employers and employees in order to provide income for the employees after retirement. Life insurance companies and commercial bank trust departments usually manage these funds, typically investing in corporate securities, mortgages, and real estate. Due to the long-term nature of pensions, most of these investments are for the long term.

Insurance companies receive premiums (payments) from policyholders and agree to make payments to policy beneficiaries. Life insurance companies make these payments upon death or disability of the insured. Property and casualty companies make payments to compensate losses from accident, illness, fire, and theft. Insurance companies use the premiums from policyholders to build reserves for future claims. They invest the reserves in corporate securities, mortgages, and real estate.

Investment companies accept money from savers and invest in a variety of assets. Mutual funds invest in specific types of financial assets, such as stocks, bonds, or short-term debt instruments. Real estate investment trusts invest their funds in real assets, such as real estate. Both types of investment companies offer professional management and the benefits of diversification.

Finance companies receive funds by issuing their own securities and through loans from commercial banks. This type of financial institution makes consumer installment loans, personal loans, and secured loans to businesses. Sales finance companies, the biggest of which is General Motors Acceptance

Corporation (GMAC), purchase installment contracts from the sellers of durable goods (such as vehicles and household appliances).

FINANCIAL MARKETS

Financial Markets

Financial markets are the markets in which financial assets are bought and sold. New securities are issued in the primary market, and existing securities are traded in the secondary market. Financial markets are also classified as short-term and long-term. Money markets are short-term markets, and capital markets are long-term markets.

The primary market makes possible the sale of new bonds, preferred stock, and common stock. In this market, the issuer receives cash, and the investor acquires a new security. The investment banker is the financial intermediary involved in raising these long-term funds. Investment bankers accomplish their role by advising the client, originating the issue, underwriting the issue, and distributing the securities. In pricing initial public offerings, studies show that unseasoned new issues are significantly underpriced on the average[3].

The secondary market includes the organized securities exchanges and the over-the-counter market. The organized exchanges consist of the New York Stock Exchange, the American Stock Exchange, smaller regional exchanges, and foreign exchanges. The over-the-counter market is an electronically connected network of dealers who trade stocks not listed on the organized exchanges.

The stock of large publicly owned corporations is traded in the secondary markets. In contrast, the stock of some small corporations, known as closely-held corporations, is not actively traded. These privately owned companies are typically owned by a few shareholders who play an active role in management.

Secondary markets provide two important functions. First, they allow purchasers of securities to sell when cash is needed. If no secondary market were available, investors would hesitate to buy in the primary market. Second, they determine the market price of the security. This is important in establishing the price of a new issue of securities.

Money markets, as noted, are short-term markets. Securities with maturities of one year or less are traded here. The major players in this market are corporations and governments. Individuals usually participate indirectly through money market funds. These highly marketable securities have little chance of not paying the interest or principal at the stated times.

The instruments most commonly found in money markets include treasury bills, federal funds, short-term municipal obligations, commercial paper,

---

[3] See Roger G. Ibbotson, Sindelar, Jody L., and Ritter, Jay R., "Initial Public Offerings," *Journal of Applied Corporate Finance*, Volume 1., No. 2, Summer, 1988, pp. 37–45.

negotiable certificates of deposit, bankers' acceptances, and repurchase agreements. Financial managers use these instruments to meet short-term financing needs and to invest temporary excess cash. Marketable securities are covered in greater detail in Chapter 16.

Capital markets involve securities with maturities greater than one year. The Treasury Department uses these markets to issue Treasury notes and

The Salomon Brothers Treasury Note Scandal

The U.S. Treasury note market is the enormous primary auction market for U.S. government securities. The U.S. Treasury awards the purchase to the highest bidders, and then it continues to fill orders until the auction is sold out. Treasury rules allow no more than 35 percent of an issue to be sold to a single bidder. In December 1990, Mr. Mozer, head of Salomon's government-bond trading desk, broke the rule by using a customer's account name together with the company name to bid for 46 percent of a four-year note issue. After that time, he repeated the violation in eight other auctions. In April 1991, the Treasury picked up the trail of the customer's account and informed it of the 35 percent rule. Then, Mr. Mozer advised Salomon Chairman John Gutfreund and three company officers of his illegal bid in the February auction. In June, the Securities and Exchange Commission and the Justice Department issued subpoenas to Salomon and its clients for records of the auctions during the period from December 1990 to May 1991.

The cost of impropriety exceeded almost everyone's expectations. On August 19, 1991, the Treasury announced that Salomon would be barred from bidding on government security auctions for customer accounts. Nine months later, Salomon settled with the government and agreed to pay $122 million to the Treasury and $68 million to the Justice Department. Salomon also established a $100 million restitution fund for private-damage claims and took a second quarter charge-off of $185 million. Mean-

while, The Federal Reserve Bank of New York suspended Salomon's authority to trade with the Bank for June and July 1992. This suspension is estimated to have cost $4 billion in trading volume.

The explicit costs are only a fraction of the costs imposed on Salomon. After the August 1991, announcement, the stock price of the firm dropped by one-third. A few days after the news release, Moody's Investor Service put the firm on its credit watch list. By the end of August 1991, it dropped Salomon's rating on their $7 billion long-term debt and $6.6 billion commercial paper issues. In addition, major customers suspended their trading with Salomon. Mr. Mozer was suspended by Salomon and has been named as a defendant in lawsuits filed by Salomon customers. The Chairman and corporate officers aware of the scandal were asked by the Board to resign.

The damage to Salomon's reputation from the Treasury note scandal reduced the expected value of its underwriting business and impaired its ability to certify new issues. In fact, the scandal raised concerns about Salomon's corporate survival.

The Salomon Treasury note scandal tarnished the firm's reputation as a Treasury securities dealer and proved very costly for Salomon in the long run. Despite the large influence of Salomon in the financial markets, Salomon quickly lost years of confidence it had built up.

Source: Clifford W. Smith, Jr., "Economics and Ethics: The Case of Salomon Brothers, *Journal of Applied Corporate Finance*, vol 5(2), Summer 1992, pp. 23–28.

Treasury bonds. Various government agencies, such as the Federal Housing Administration (FHA), employ capital markets to sell notes and bonds. States, counties, and municipalities utilize these markets to issue general obligation bonds and revenue bonds. Corporations use them to issue debt securities, preferred stock, and common stock.

Financial institutions and markets provide systems for transferring funds from savers to investors, at a cost[4]. It is important to know how this cost is determined.

Interest Rates

Rate of Interest

The **rate of interest, I,** is the compensation the demander of funds pays to the supplier. It is the actual rate charged by the supplier and paid for by the demander. This rate consists of a real risk-free rate of interest plus premiums reflecting inflation, risk, and marketability. We can state the relationships in equation form as follows:

$$I = I^* + IP + DP + LP + MP \tag{1.1}$$

where

$$I^* = \text{Real risk-free rate of interest}$$
$$IP = \text{Inflation premium}$$
$$DP = \text{Default premium}$$
$$LP = \text{Liquidity premium}$$
$$MP = \text{Maturity premium}$$

Let's look more closely at these elements. The real risk-free rate of interest is the interest rate on a riskless security in the absence of inflation. The inflation premium reflects inflationary expectations over the life of the security, not the level of inflation in the past. The default premium indicates the danger that the borrower will not make the interest and principal payments. The liquidity premium relates to the owner's ability to convert the security into cash; the more marketable the security, the lower the liquidity premium. The maturity premium generally increases with the term of the security, primarily due to higher interest rate risk, the variability in value with changes in interest rates. (Chapter 3 discusses interest rate risk in greater detail.)

Term Structure of Interest Rates

Yield Curve

The relationship between the interest rate and the time to maturity for a given class of securities is called the **term structure of interest rates. A yield curve**

[4] This cost could be reduced by a significant reform in our nationwide banking, payments, and regulatory systems. See Marcus W. Acheson, IV, "From Cash Management to Bank Reform," *Journal of Applied Corporate Finance*, Volume 4, No. 2, Summer, 1991, pp. 105–116.

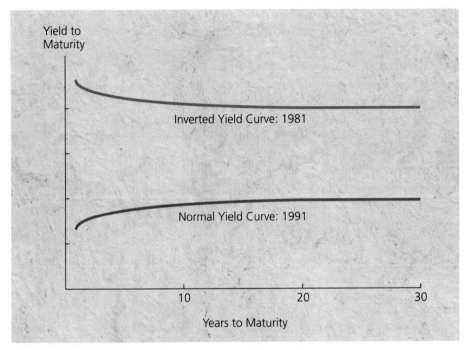

FIGURE 1.2 The Normal Yield Curve and the Inverted Yield Curve

shows the term structure of interest rates graphically. Figure 1.2 presents two yield curves, from the years 1981 and 1991. The bottom curve is a normal yield curve, indicating that short-term borrowing costs are less than long-term borrowing costs. This is a common situation since short-term securities are not as risky as long-term securities and usually require lower rates of return. The top curve is an inverted yield curve, and that represents the abnormal situation.

Three major theories attempt to explain the shape of the yield curve. The liquidity premium theory suggests the upward-sloping curve is the result of (1) the perception of investors that shorter-term securities are less risky and thus require a lower return, and (2) the willingness of borrowers to pay a higher rate for longer-term securities in order to secure a fixed rate for a long period of time. The expectations hypothesis states that the yield curve reflects investors' expectations about future interest rates; an upward sloping curve would indicate that rates will rise due to the expectation that inflation will increase. The third approach, market segmentation theory, suggests that the shape of the yield curve depends on the supply and demand conditions in the short-term and long-term markets. For example, an upward-sloping yield curve indicates a large supply of short-term funds and a relatively small supply of long-term funds.

There are, of course, other factors that affect interest rate levels. To stimulate the economy, the Federal Reserve Board increases growth in the money supply. In the short run, this may cause interest rates to decline. In the long run, it may lead to higher inflation and an increase in interest rates. In recent years, the federal government has run a deficit—that is, government outlays have been greater than revenues. The demand by the federal government for funds to finance the deficit tends to increase interest rates. U.S. trade deficits—caused by importing more than is exported—require financing, and this also may increase interest rates. Finally, the general state of the economy influences interest rates, with a tendency toward low rates during recessions and high rates during recovery.

The study of interest rates is one of the more complicated areas in finance and economics. It is important because we must relate interest rates to the financial environment, and the financial environment to the study of finance.

SUMMARY

This chapter focuses on the following learning objectives:

1. Explaining what job opportunities are available in finance.

    Financial careers are divided into two categories: financial services and managerial finance. Financial services consists of the delivery of financial products to all types of organizations, including banking, financial planning, investments, real estate, and insurance. Managerial finance relates to the duties of the financial manager in private companies, governmental operations, and not-for-profit institutions.

2. Specifying the primary goal of management in a corporation.

    The primary goal of management in a corporation, from the point of view of its shareholders, is to maximize the value of its common stock. Managers, left to their own devices, sometimes choose profit maximization or growth as a goal, instead of share value maximization. The tendency of management to choose goals other than share-price maximization is called the agency problem.

3. Describing the functions of managerial finance.

    Managerial finance centers on the investment, financing, and dividend decisions, and on strategic planning and control. The investment decision is the determination of the size and composition of company assets. The financing decision is the determination of how a company's assets are financed. The dividend decision is the determination of how earnings after taxes should be distributed to preferred and common shareholders or retained for investment. Strategic planning is the design of strategies to meet the primary goal of maximizing the value of the common stock of the corporation. Control consists of the design of systems to ensure that the company achieves objectives that lead to attainment of the primary goal.

4. Describing the three legal forms of business organization.
   Entrepreneurs must choose either the sole proprietorship, the partnership, or the corporation when beginning a new venture. A sole proprietorship is a business owned by one person. A partnership is a business operated by two or more persons, working under a written or oral agreement. A corporation is a legal entity created by a state and is separate from the owners of the organization.
5. Outlining financial institutions and markets.
   The financing decision requires the financial manager to obtain outside funds from financial institutions and financial markets. Financial institutions include commercial banks, thrift institutions, pension funds, insurance companies, investment companies, and finance companies. Financial markets are the markets in which financial assets are bought and sold.
6. Explaining the components of the rate of interest.
   The rate of interest is the compensation the demander of funds pays to the supplier. It is the actual rate charged by the supplier and paid for by the demander. This rate consists of a real risk-free rate of interest plus premiums reflecting inflation, risk, and marketability.

KEY TERMS

Agency costs, 7
Agency problem, 6
Agency relationship, 7
C corporation, 13
Control, 9
Corporation, 12
Dividend decision, 8
Financing decision, 7
Financial institutions, 14

Financial markets, 16
Financial services, 4
Investment decision, 7
Managerial finance, 5
Marginal tax rate, 13
Partnership, 11
Primary goal, 5
Rate of interest, 18
S corporation, 12

Sole
    proprietorship, 10
Strategic
    planning, 8
Term structure of
    interest rates, 18
Yield curve, 18

QUESTIONS

1.1   When you graduate, what job opportunities will be available to you in finance? How will you take advantage of these opportunities?

1.2   Describe the duties of the financial manager in middle-size and large private companies. How would you fit into this structure as a financial manager?

1.3   What are the traditional functions of managerial finance? What additional responsibilities would you have as a financial manager?

1.4 How do the investment, financing, and dividend decisions relate to a company's financial statements?

1.5 Briefly describe the history of financial management over the last 75 years. What changes do you see for business in general and finance in particular over the next 25 years?

1.6 What is the primary goal of management in a corporation? As a financial manager, how would you operate to achieve this goal?

1.7 Why would a manager have a goal other than share-value maximization? How would you, as a shareholder, prevent this type of behavior? As a creditor?

1.8 What are the legal forms of business an entrepreneur could use when starting up a new business? What form would you use when you start your business? Why?

1.9 What is the difference between the marginal tax rate and the average tax rate?

1.10 As a financial manager, where could you go for additional financing when retained earnings is not enough to finance growth in your business?

1.11 What is the nominal rate of interest? On what factors does this rate depend?

1.12 Explain the relationship between the interest rate and the time to maturity for a given class of securities.

1.13 What theories explain the shape of the yield curve? How do you explain the shape of the curve today?

1.14 As a financial manager, what ethical issues might you encounter in trying to ensure that the primary goal management in your company is to maximize the value of its common stock?

1.15 What are the characteristics of America's most admired corporations?

1.16 What are the perils of partnership?

1.17 What effects did the Salomon Treasury note scandal have on the reputation of the company.

PROBLEMS

1.1 **(Business Startup)** Your aunt has left you $100,000 which will be yours when you graduate. You decide to start a business and become rich. What form would the business take? Which financial principles would you use to ensure that the venture is a success? In the beginning, where would you go for additional financing? Where would you expect to go in the future? Why would you succeed when many others fail?

1.2 **(Tax Liability)** Susan Johnson is single, with taxable income of $60,000 from a sole proprietorship. A second job provides an additional $10,000 in taxable income. What is her income tax liability and marginal tax rate? (Assume rates of $0 to $22,100, 15%; $22,100 to $53,500, 28%; $53,500 to $115,000, 31%; $115,000 to $250,000, 36%; over $250,000, 39.6%.)

1.3 **(Tax Liability)** Jack and Elizabeth McDaniel are married filing jointly, with combined taxable income of $60,000 from their regular jobs. Elizabeth is also a partner in a small consulting firm, from which she earned $10,000 in taxable income. What is their income tax liability and marginal tax rate? (Assume rates of $0 to $36,900, 15%; $36,900 to $89,150, 28%; $89,150 to $140,000, 31%; $140,000 to $250,000, 36%; over $250,000, 39.6%.)

1.4 **(Tax Liability)** James and Jerrie Lane are married filing jointly, with joint taxable income of $95,000. Both are shareholders in an S corporation from which they made $75,000. What is their income tax liability and marginal tax rate? (Assume rates of $0 to $36,900, 15%; $36,900 to $89,150, 28%; $89,150 to $140,000, 31%; $140,000 to $250,000, 36%; over $250,000, 39.6%.)

1.5 **(Tax Liability)** Your corporation has taxable income of $150,000. What is its income tax liability and marginal tax rate? (Assume rates of 0 to $50,000, 15%; $50,000 to $75,000, 25%; $75,000 to $100,000, 34%; $100,000 to $335,000, 39%; $335,000 to $10,000,000, 34%; over $10,000,000, 35%.)

A Case Problem

The Walden Press was a leading supplier of printing and distribution services for catalog and other direct-mail marketers. These customers operated in a rapidly growing segment of the retail industry, reflecting the trend toward home shopping. Some of Walden's customers, such as Victoria's Secret, Brownstone Studios, and Coach Leatherware, used specialty catalogs to target consumers precisely.

The growth of demand for catalog and direct-mail printing placed great pressure on the company's printing capacity.

The growth of demand for catalog and direct-mail printing placed great pressure on the company's printing capacity. To respond, Walden made significant investments in technology and equipment—approximately $50 million over a five-year period. The company used $10 million of that amount to purchase a plant, the MacArthur facility, from a competitor that was under the protection of Chapter 11 of the Bankruptcy Act.

Walden planned a major expansion of the MacArthur facility requiring approximately $30 million. This expansion would provide a technologically advanced catalog printing and distribution plant, alleviate current production constraints, and provide a broader range of services to customers.

Henry J. Williams, the chief financial officer for Walden, was considering how to finance the expansion. He was also concerned with repaying $10 million in debt. To help generate a financing alternative, he studied balance sheet and statement of earnings data, present here in compact form.

Balance Sheet Data (in thousands):

Current assets	$ 52,200
Working capital	10,600
Total assets	104,200
Long-term debt	47,800
Stockholders' equity	8,500

Statement of Earnings Data (in thousands):

Net revenues	$174,800
Gross profit	24,500
Operating income	12,700
Net earnings	3,800

In the foreseeable future, Walden intended to retain its earnings and not pay cash dividends. The previous year, the company had paid a special dividend of $5 million to its shareholders. This was the only dividend paid since the company's establishment some ten years earlier.

Leading Questions

1. How would you determine if the new expansion should be undertaken?
2. How would you finance the expansion and repayment of debt?
3. What do you think of the dividend policy?

THE KENNEDY FAMILY FORTUNE

Joseph P. Kennedy, father to an American President, senior U.S. Senator, and the founder of the Special Olympics; grandfather to a U.S. Congressman, a state representative, and the woman who married Arnold Schwarzenegger, amassed one of America's greatest fortunes, conservatively estimated to be $100 million in 1957. At that time, his fortune supported his wife, Rose, and his seven surviving children, securing them social

2 Time Value Techniques

position, power, and prestige. Today [as of October 1991], the estate of the man who once controlled a movie studio, a chain of movie houses, a liquor distributing company with valuable franchises, and prime real estate is worth perhaps $350 million. As family fortunes go, that isn't a great deal of money. And most of it is in a single illiquid real estate property with no great future.

The illiquid real estate holding is a six million square foot Merchandise Mart/Apparel Center complex in Chicago. The Mart provides approximately $20 million free cash flow per year, after taxes, operating expenses, and improvements. This amount is divided among 53 family members, with each member receiving $377,358.49 per year, by no definition a paultry sum. So, do the Kennedy offspring need to worry about their financial future?

The answer is *yes*. If in 1957 they had invested the $100 million in the Dow Jones industrials, it would be worth well over $600 million today, instead of their present net worth of $350 million. This means that the Kennedys have been consuming capital at such a rate that the fortune will not last far into the next century.

How is such a conclusion reached? The answer—with time value techniques. Throughout this chapter we will return to the Kennedy plight, explaining the financial situation facing the family that produced a President who was said to have brought Camelot to the White House.

Source: "Shirtsleeves to shirtsleeves," *Forbes*, October 21, 1991, pp. 34–37. Reprinted by permission of FORBES magazine. © Forbes, 1991.

COMPOUNDING AND DISCOUNTING

A dollar today is worth more than a dollar in the future. A simple idea. Yet this is the one of the fundamental concepts of finance. The value of money depends on when it is collected or disbursed.

Future Value

How much money will you have in five years if you deposit $100 today at an annual interest rate of 10 percent? Financial managers know how to find that amount, and you will too after you understand future value.

> Lee Harris deposits $100 in a bank for one year at 10 percent annual interest. How much will she have at the end of that time?

The amount she will have after one year, V_1, is the **future value** at time 1.   **Future Value**

$$V_1 = \$100(1 + 0.10)$$
$$= \$110$$

The future value of $110 includes the beginning amount of $100, plus the $10 she will earn in interest.

27

Cash Flow Diagram

The $100 cash flow at time 0, V_0, is equivalent to the $110 cash flow at time 1, V_1. Because these cash flows are equivalent, we are indifferent between them. A convenient way to show this equivalence is by using a **cash flow diagram.**

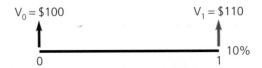

A cash flow diagram is a visual method of indicating the magnitude and timing of cash flows. It also shows the appropriate interest rate (10 percent in this case). Positive cash flows point up (as in this diagram), and negative cash flows point down.

> Lee decides to leave the $110 in the bank for another year. How much will she have at the end of the second year?

The amount she has after two years is V_2. This future value at time 2 can be calculated as follows:

$$V_2 = \$110(1 + 0.10)$$
$$= \$121$$

She can also find the result at time 2 with one equation.

$$V_2 = \$100(1 + 0.10)^2$$
$$= \$100(1.21)$$
$$= \$121$$

Notice that the bank pays interest during the second period on both the principal and the interest from the first period. The future value of $121 includes the $110 at time 1, plus the $11 she earns in interest. This is the principle of **compound interest.**

Compound Interest

> Suppose Lee leaves the original $100 for five years, instead of one or two years. How much will she have at that time?

Using the same approach—that is, multiplying by $(1 + 0.10)$ for each additional year—she can find the amount after five years:

$$V_5 = \$10\,0(1 + 0.10)^5$$
$$= \$100(1.6105)$$
$$= \$161.05$$

The $100 she invested for five years at 10 percent grows to $161.05. A cash flow diagram shows the equivalence of V_0 and V_5.

$V_0 = \$100$

$V_5 = \$161.05$

0

5

10%

We can generalize the equations above to derive an equation for the future value of any cash flow:

$$V_{t+n} = V_t(1 + k)^n \qquad (2.1)$$

where

$$V_{t+n} = \text{Cash flow at time } t + n$$
$$V_t = \text{Cash flow at time } t$$
$$k = \text{Annual interest rate}$$
$$n = \text{Number of periods from } V_t \text{ to } V_{t+n}$$

When the initial cash flow is at time 0, we can use the following simplified version of the equation:

$$V_n = V_0(1 + k)^n \qquad (2.1a)$$

where

$$V_n = \text{Cash flow at time } n$$
$$V_0 = \text{Cash flow at time } 0$$
$$n = \text{Number of periods from } V_0 \text{ to } V_n$$

To determine the future value of a single cash flow, we multiply the value V_t or V_0 by the term $(1 + k)^n$, the **future value factor.** We find future value factors by using either calculators or tables

Future Value Factor

Table 2.1 provides future value factors for various combinations of interest rate (k) and the number of periods (n). Appendix A contains a more complete listing. The values in the table were found using the formula $FVF_{k\%,n} = (1 + k)^n$.

We can apply the standard notation for the future value factor, $FVF_{k\%,n}$, to calculate the future value at time 5.

$$V_5 = \$100(FVF_{10\%,5})$$
$$= \$100(1.6105)$$
$$= \$161.05$$

TABLE 2.1 Future Value Factors

NUMBER OF PERIODS (n)	INTEREST RATE (k)		
	9%	10%	11%
1	1.0900	1.1000	1.1100
2	1.1881	1.2100	1.2321
3	1.2950	1.3310	1.3676
4	1.4116	1.4641	1.5181
5	1.5386	1.6105	1.6851
6	1.6771	1.7716	1.8704
7	1.8280	1.9487	2.0762

The Formula: $FVF_{k\%,n} = (1 + k)^n$

Here, the future value factor, 1.6105, comes from Table 2.1, the fifth row, the 10 percent column.

Equivalent Cash Flow   Future value factors allow us to find an **equivalent cash flow** in the future. This is important when we need to know the value of an amount of money after a number of years. We can also start with cash flows in the future and find an equivalent cash flow in the present.

> Returning to the Kennedy family, let's assume in 1957 that the family placed the $100 million in a bank account paying 5.4 percent compounded annually. Further, let's presume no member of the family added to or withdrew from the account over the period from 1957 to 1991. How large would the account be 34 years later?

We can find the answer by using the future value equation.

$$V_n = V_0(1 + k)^n$$
$$V_{34} = \$100,000,000(1 + 0.054)^{34}$$
$$= \$100,000,000(5.9783)$$
$$= \$597,830,000$$

This would be the amount after 34 years.

Present Value

Many finance problems require knowing the value today of future cash flows. In this section, we will learn how to make that type of calculation.

Lee Harris decides she would like to have $110 in the bank at the end of one year. How much must she deposit today if the bank pays 10 percent annual interest?

The amount she must deposit, V_0, is the **present value** of the amount she will have at time 1, V_1. She can calculate it as follows:

Present Value

$$V_0(1 + 0.10) = \$110$$

$$V_0 = \frac{\$110}{(1 + 0.10)}$$

$$= \$100$$

A cash flow diagram shows the equivalence of V_1 and V_0.

The diagram is the same as before; we're simply looking at it differently. This time we are looking from the future back to the present. The process of moving backward in time is called **discounting.** In contrast, moving forward in time, as was done with future value, is called **compounding.**

Discounting

Compounding

Suppose Lee decides she would like to have $121 after two years. How much must she deposit today if the bank continues to pay 10 percent interest?

She calculates that amount as follows:

$$V_0(1 + 0.10)^2 = \$121$$

$$V_0 = \frac{\$121}{(1 + 0.10)^2}$$

$$= \$100$$

How much should Lee deposit today in order to have $161.05 in five years, if the bank pays 10 percent annual interest?

Using the same approach, she finds the amount for five years.

$$V_0(1 + 0.10)^5 = \$161.05$$
$$V_0 = \frac{\$161.05}{(1 + 0.10)^5}$$
$$= \frac{\$161.05}{1.6105}$$
$$= \$100$$

Here is the cash flow diagram showing the equivalent cash flows.

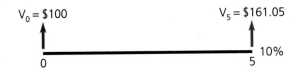

As with future value, we can state a general equation for present value:

$$V_t = \frac{V_{t+n}}{(1 + k)^n} \qquad (2.2)$$

where

$$V_t = \text{Cash flow at time t}$$
$$V_{t+n} = \text{Cash flow at time t+n}$$
$$k = \text{Annual interest rate}$$
$$n = \text{Number of periods from } V_t \text{ to } V_{t+n}$$

We also derive this equation by solving Equation 2.1 for V_t.

Again, we can use a simpler version of the equation if we are finding the cash flow at time 0. In that case, the present value is given by the following equation:

$$V_0 = \frac{V_n}{(1 + k)^n} \qquad (2.2a)$$

where

$$V_0 = \text{Cash flow at time 0}$$
$$V_n = \text{Cash flow at time n}$$
$$n = \text{Number of years from } V_0 \text{ to } V_n$$

TABLE 2.2 Present Value Factors

NUMBER OF PERIODS (n)	INTEREST RATE (k) 9%	10%	11%
1	0.9174	0.9091	0.9009
2	0.8417	0.8264	0.8116
3	0.7722	0.7513	0.7312
4	0.7084	0.6830	0.6587
5	0.6499	0.6209	0.5935
6	0.5963	0.5645	0.5346
7	0.5470	0.5132	0.4817

The Formula: $PVF_{k\%,n} = \dfrac{1}{(1+k)^n}$

To determine the present value of a single cash flow, we multiply the value V_{t+n} or V_n by the term $1/(1+k)^n$, the **present value factor.** As with future value **Present Value Factor** factors, we find present value factors by using either tables or calculators. Table 2.2 provides factors for various combinations of k and n. Appendix A contains a more complete listing. The values in the table were found using the formula.

The standard notation for a present value factor is similar to the notation for the future value factor.

$$PVF_{k\%,n} = \frac{1}{(1+k)^n} = \frac{1}{FVF_{k\%,n}}$$

Notice, the reciprocal relationship between the present value factor and the future value factor.

Using the standard notation, we can restructure the previous problem:

$$V_0 = \$161.05(PVF_{10\%,5})$$
$$= \$161.05(0.6209)$$
$$= \$100$$

The present value factor of 0.6209 comes from Table 2.2, the fifth row, the 10% column.

Let's examine the Kennedy situation again. Suppose the family wanted to have $350 million in 1991 to divide among the descendants. How much should Joseph deposit in 1957? Assume that no family member is allowed to add or withdraw from the account and that the interest rate of 5.4 percent does not change.

We can discover the answer by finding the present value of $350 million over the 34 years.

$$V_0 = \frac{V_n}{(1+k)^n}$$
$$= \frac{\$350,000,000}{(1+0.054)^{34}}$$
$$= \frac{\$350,000,000}{5.9783}$$
$$= \$58,545,071$$

So far, we have worked with a single cash flow. Next, we will work with a series of cash flows and find an equivalent cash flow in the future or in the present.

ANNUITIES

Many problems in finance require us to evaluate a series of cash flows. When the cash flows are identical and are spaced at equal intervals, the pattern is an **annuity.**

Annuity

Future Value of An Annuity

Future Value of an Annuity

The **future value of an annuity** is an equivalent cash flow located at the *end* of the last year of the annuity. In this section, we will find the future value of an annuity for three types of annuities: ordinary annuities, annuities due, and other annuities.

Ordinary Annuity

Ordinary Annuities. An **ordinary annuity** is a series of identical, equally spaced cash flows, with the cash flows received at the *end* of each period.

Joe Harris decides to deposit $100 per year for three years in a bank that pays 10 percent annual interest, with the first payment made at the end of year 1. How much will he have at the end of the third year?

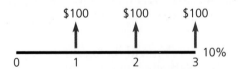

He calculates the future value at the end of the third year, time 3, by adding the future values of the individual cash flows. He does this by using the standard notation shown in the previous sections.

$$V_3 = \$100(FVF_{10\%,2}) + \$100(FVF_{10\%,1}) + \$100$$
$$= \$100(1.2100) + \$100(1.1000) + \$100$$
$$= \$121.00 + \$110.00 + \$100$$
$$= \$331.00$$

The first cash flow is moved two years forward, and the second cash flow is moved one year forward. The third cash flow is already at time 3 and need not be adjusted. The sum of the three equivalent cash flows, $331.00, is the future value of this annuity. At an interest rate of 10 percent, he is indifferent between receiving this amount at time 3 or receiving the $100 cash flows at time 1, time 2, and time 3.

Notice in the equation that the $100 is constant in each of the terms. Thus, we may factor out the $100 value:

$$V_3 = \$100[FVF_{10\%,2} + FVF_{10\%,1} + 1]$$
$$= \$100[(1 + 0.10)^2 + (1 + 0.10)^1 + 1]$$

This specific example leads to the general equation for the future value of an annuity:

$$V_t = A \sum_{i=1}^{N} (1 + k)^{N-i} \tag{2.3}$$

where

$$V_t = \text{Cash flow at time } t$$
$$A = \text{Amount of annuity}$$
$$k = \text{Annual interest rate}$$
$$N = \text{Number of cash flows}$$
$$i = \text{Number of the cash flow}$$

The equivalent cash flow, V_t, is located at the same point in time as the last of the equal cash flows, due to the way the equation is derived.

Equation 2.3 also may be expressed in the following notation:

$$V_t = A(FVFA_{k\%,N}) \tag{2.3a}$$

Table 2.3 provides future value factors of an annuity for combinations of k and N. As with future and present value factors, a more complete listing is found in Appendix A.

TABLE 2.3 Future Value Factors of an Annuity

NUMBER OF	INTEREST RATE (k)		
CASH FLOWS (N)	9%	10%	11%
1	1.0000	1.0000	1.0000
2	2.0900	2.1000	2.1100
3	3.2781	3.3100	3.3421
4	4.5731	4.6410	4.7097
5	5.9847	6.1051	6.2278
6	7.5233	7.7156	7.9129
7	9.2004	9.4872	9.7833

The Formula: $FVFA_{k\%,N} = \dfrac{(1+k)^N - 1}{k}$

Using Equation 2.3a, we can restructure the previous problem.

$$V_3 = \$100(FVFA_{10\%,3})$$
$$= \$100(3.3100)$$
$$= \$331.00$$

Future Value Factor of an Annuity

The **future value factor of an annuity** comes from the third row, the 10% column.

The equivalence of the $100 cash flows to the $331.00 cash flow is also shown by a cash flow diagram.

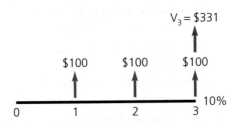

It is important to realize that the equivalent cash flow is at the same point in time, time 3, as the *last* of the series of cash flows.

Annuity Due

Annuities Due. An **annuity due** is a series of identical, equally-spaced cash flows with the cash flows received at the *beginning* of each period[1].

---

[1] In leasing, payments are normally made at the beginning of the year, the annuity due pattern.

Joe Harris decides to deposit $100 per year for three years in a bank that pays 10 percent annual interest, with the first deposit made today. How much would he have at the end of the third year?

Here is the cash flow diagram.

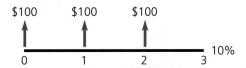

At this point, he may be tempted to use the future value of an annuity factor to find the future value at time 3. But its use would provide an equivalent cash flow at time 2, not time 3. Remember, a future value of an annuity factor *always* provides an equivalent cash flow at the same point in time as the *last* of the equal cash flows.

He can show this situation with a cash flow diagram:

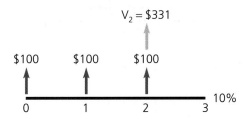

His objective is to find the future value at time 3, not time 2. He can, however, move the equivalent cash flow of $331.00 at time 2 forward one year simply by multiplying by a future value factor for one year.

$$V_3 = \$331.00(\text{FVF}_{10\%,1})$$
$$= \$331.00(1.1000)$$
$$= \$364.10$$

Here is the cash flow diagram.

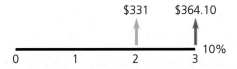

Of course, it is simpler to make this calculation with a single equation.

$$V_3 = \$100(\text{FVFA}_{10\%,3})(\text{FVF}_{10\%,1})$$
$$= \$100(3.3100)(1.100)$$
$$= \$364.10$$

Other Annuities. Many annuities begin a certain number of years from time 0. How do we bring these cash flows back to the present?

Joe Harris decides to deposit $100 per year for three years in a bank that pays 10 percent annual interest, with the first deposit made at time 3. How much would he have at the end of the fifth year?

Here is the cash flow diagram.

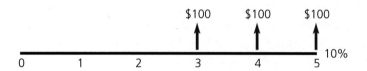

The future value factor of an annuity can be used to find the result.

$$V_3 = \$100(\text{FVFA}_{10\%,3})$$
$$= \$100(3.3100)$$
$$= \$331.00$$

The cash flow diagram shows the placement of the equivalent cash flow.

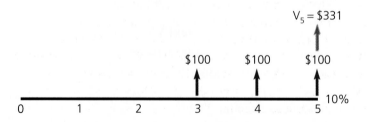

Again, the equivalent cash flow is at the same point in time, time 5, as the *last* of the series of cash flows.

In this section, we learned how to replace a series of cash flows with an equivalent cash flow in the future. Next, we will replace a series of cash flows with an equivalent cash flow in the present.

Present Value of an Annuity

The **present value of an annuity** is an equivalent cash flow located at the *beginning* of the first year of the annuity. In this section, we will find the present value of an annuity for three types of annuities: ordinary annuities, annuities due, and other annuities.

Present Value of an Annuity

Ordinary Annuities.   We have already examined an ordinary annuity of $100 per year for three years, with the cash flows at the end of each year, as shown in this cash flow diagram.

In some situations, we need to find an equivalent cash flow at time 0.

> Mary Valdez decides to deposit an amount of money today that will allow her to withdraw $100 per year at the end of each of the next three years. How large must the deposit be if the bank pays her 10 percent annual interest?

She can calculate the present value, V_0—the equivalent cash flow at time 0—by adding the present values of the individual cash flows.

$$
\begin{aligned}
V_0 &= \$100(\text{PVF}_{10\%,1}) + \$100(\text{PVF}_{10\%,2}) + \$100(\text{PVF}_{10\%,3}) \\
&= \$100(0.9091) + \$100(0.8264) + \$100(0.7513) \\
&= \$90.91 + \$82.64 + \$75.13 \\
&= \$248.68
\end{aligned}
$$

The first cash flow is moved one year backward, the second cash flow is moved two years backward, and the third cash flow is moved three years backward. The sum of the three equivalent cash flows, $248.68, is the present value of this annuity. At an interest rate of 10 percent, she is indifferent between having this amount at time 0 or receiving the $100 cash flows at time 1, time 2, and time 3.

Since in the previous equation the $100 is constant in each of the terms, we can factor it out.

$$
\begin{aligned}
V_0 &= \$100[\text{PVF}_{10\%,1} + \text{PVF}_{10\%,2} + \text{PVF}_{10\%,3}] \\
&= \$100\left[\frac{1}{(1+0.10)} + \frac{1}{(1+0.10)^2} + \frac{1}{(1+0.10)^3}\right]
\end{aligned}
$$

This specific example leads to the general equation for the present value of an annuity:

$$V_t = A \sum_{i=1}^{N} \frac{1}{(1+k)^i} \qquad (2.4)$$

where

$$V_t = \text{Cash flow at time t}$$
$$A = \text{Amount of annuity}$$
$$k = \text{Annual interest rate}$$
$$N = \text{Number of cash flows}$$
$$i = \text{Number of the cash flow}$$

The equivalent cash flow, V_t, is located one time period *before* the first of the equal cash flows, due to the way Equation 2.4 is derived.

Equation 2.4 may be expressed in the following standard notation:

$$V_t = A(PVFA_{k\%,N}) \qquad (2.4a)$$

Present Value Factor of an Annuity

Table 2.4 provides **present value factors of an annuity** for various combinations of k and N. As with the previous time value factors, a more complete listing is found in Appendix A.

Using Equation 2.4a, we can restructure the previous problem.

TABLE 2.4 Present Value Factors of an Annuity

NUMBER OF CASH FLOWS (N)	INTEREST RATE (k) 9%	10%	11%
1	0.9174	0.9091	0.9009
2	1.7591	1.7355	1.7125
3	2.5313	2.4869	2.4437
4	3.2397	3.1699	3.1024
5	3.8897	3.7908	3.6959
6	4.4859	4.3553	4.2305
7	5.0330	4.8684	4.7122

The Formula: $PVFA_{k\%,N} = \dfrac{1 - \dfrac{1}{(1+k)^N}}{k}$

$$V_0 = \$100(PVFA_{10\%,3})$$
$$= \$100(2.4869)$$
$$= \$248.69$$

This result agrees with our earlier answer using present value factors, except for a minor difference due to rounding. In this calculation, the present value of an annuity factor of 2.4869 comes from Table 2.4, the third row, the 10% column.

The equivalence of the $100 cash flows to the $248.69 cash flow is shown with a cash flow diagram.

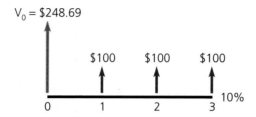

Notice the equivalent cash flow is located one time period *before* the first of the annuity cash flows. It occurs at time 0 *only* because the first cash flow of the annuity occurred at time 1.

Suppose in 1957 Joseph Kennedy made a deposit of $41,820,000 in a bank account paying 5.4 percent compounded annually. His goal was to provide his family with equal cash payments over the next 34 years. How much would he have each year to divide among the family members?

We find the answer by applying the present value of an annuity equation.

$$V_t = A(PVFA_{k\%,N})$$
$$\$41,820,000 = A(PVFA_{5.4\%,34})$$
$$\$41,820,000 = A(15.4209)$$
$$A = \$2,711,903.90$$

Annuities Due. Earlier, we calculated an annuity due of $100 per year for three years. Here is the cash flow diagram we used.

Sometimes, we need to find an equivalent cash flow at time 0.

Mary Valdez requires an amount of money that will allow her to make a payment of $100 now, deposit the remainder, and make $100 payments from the account at the beginning of years 2 and 3. How much must she have today if the bank pays 10 percent annual interest?

She uses the present value of an annuity factor to move backward in time. But this results in an equivalent cash flow at time −1, one period before the first of the annuity cash flows. She calculates that amount as follows:

$$V_{-1} = \$100(\text{PVFA}_{10\%,3})$$
$$= \$100(2.4869)$$
$$= \$248.69$$

She can show this equivalence using a cash flow diagram:

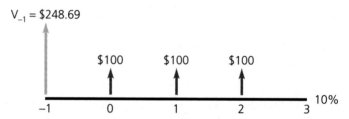

To find the value at time 0, she needs to multiply by the future value factor for one year.

$$V_0 = \$248.69(\text{FVF}_{10\%,1})$$
$$= \$248.69(1.1000)$$
$$= \$273.56$$

Show this with a cash flow diagram.

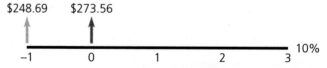

Of course, it is simpler to make this calculation with a single equation.

$$V_0 = \$100(\text{PVFA}_{10\%,3})(\text{FVF}_{10\%,1})$$
$$= \$100(\$2.4869)(1.1000)$$
$$= \$273.56$$

Another way to find the present value of an annuity due is to group the cash flows. Since the $100 at time 0 is already at the present, it comprises one group. The other group involves the two remaining cash flows. The resulting equation is as follows:

$$V_0 = \$100 + \$100(PVFA_{10\%,2})$$
$$= \$100 + \$100(1.7355)$$
$$= \$273.55$$

The answers are the same except for rounding error.

Other Annuities. Earlier, we examined an annuity of $100 per year for three years beginning in year three. We used the following cash flow diagram:

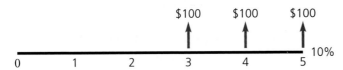

Many problems in finance require us to find an equivalent cash flow at time 0.

Mary Valdez decides to deposit an amount of money today that will allow her to withdraw $100 per year for three years, beginning three years from now. How large must the deposit be if the bank pays her 10 percent annual interest?

She can use the present value factor of an annuity to move backward in time. But this results in an equivalent cash flow at time 2, one period prior to the first of the annuity cash flows.

$$V_2 = \$100(PVFA_{10\%,3})$$
$$= \$100(2.4869)$$
$$= \$248.69$$

The equivalent cash flow at time 2 is shown by a cash flow diagram:

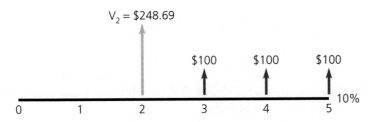

To find the present value, multiply by a present value factor for two years.

$$V_0 = \$248.69(\text{PVF}_{10\%,2})$$
$$= \$248.69(0.8264)$$
$$= \$205.52$$

A cash flow diagram shows the final result:

This calculation can be made with one equation.

$$V_0 = \$100(\text{PVFA}_{10\%,3})(\text{PVF}_{10\%,2})$$
$$= \$100(2.4869)(0.8264)$$
$$= \$205.52$$

An alternate approach involves restructuring the problem with an equivalent cash flow diagram.

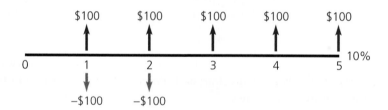

Adding +$100 and −$100 in years 1 and 2 yields net cash flows of 0. This scheme allows us to recognize two annuity groups with which we can easily work.

The resulting equation is as follows:

$$V_0 = \$100(\text{PVFA}_{10\%,5}) - \$100(\text{PVFA}_{10\%,2})$$
$$= \$100(3.7908) - \$100(1.7355)$$
$$= \$205.53$$

In both groups, the equivalent cash flow occurs at time 0 because the first cash flow of the annuity was at time 1. The result is the same as before except for rounding error.

TIME VALUE VARIATIONS

The calculations described so far have assumed annual compounding of a definite number of cash flows. Problems in finance, however, often involve other compounding periods and may include indefinite cash flows.

Other Compounding Periods

In addition to annual compounding, compounding on a semiannual, quarterly, monthly, daily, or even continuous basis is common. If we understand the concept of the cash flow diagram, making the changes to accommodate other periods is easy.

> John Allen decides to deposit $100 in an investment that pays 12 percent interest, compounded quarterly. How much would he have after five years? Would the amount be greater if the compounding were done monthly?

John calculates the result this way.

$$V_{20} = \$100(FVF_{3\%,20})$$
$$= \$100(1.8061)$$
$$= \$180.61$$

What did he do? He divided the annual interest rate by four (the number of compounding periods per year) and multiplied the number of years by four. John found the future value after 20 periods.

Show this by a cash flow diagram.

How would the calculation change for monthly compounding?

$$V_{60} = \$100(FVF_{1\%,60})$$
$$= \$100(1.8167)$$
$$= \$181.67$$

This time John divided the annual interest rate by 12, and multiplied the number of years by 12. The slightly larger amount with monthly interest reflects the more frequent compounding.

He can illustrate this with a cash flow diagram.

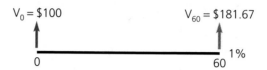

The results of this example can be generalized.

$$V_{m(t+n)} = V_t \left(1 + \frac{k}{m}\right)^{mn} \tag{2.5}$$

where

$$V_{m(t+n)} = \text{Cash flow at period } m(t + n), mn \text{ periods from } V_t$$
$$V_t = \text{Cash flow at time t}$$
$$k = \text{Annual interest rate}$$
$$m = \text{Compounding periods per year}$$
$$n = \text{Number of years}$$

Equation 2.5 simplifies when the initial cash flow is at time 0. In that case, the future value is given by the following equation:

$$V_{mn} = V_0 \left(1 + \frac{k}{m}\right)^{mn} \tag{2.5a}$$

where

$$V_{mn} = \text{Cash flow at period } mn, mn \text{ periods from } V_0$$
$$V_0 = \text{Cash flow at time 0}$$

The present value, future value of an annuity, and present value of an annuity factors are handled similarly. The annual interest rates are divided by and the number of years multiplied by the compounding periods per year.

Continuous compounding occurs when the number of compounding periods is unlimited. The equation for continuous compounding follows:

$$V_{t+n} = V_t(e^{kn}) \qquad (2.6)$$

where

V_{t+n} = Cash flow at time t + n
V_t = Cash flow at time t
e = 2.71828 ✓
k = Annual interest rate
n = Number of years from V_t to V_{t+n}

Equation 2.6 simplifies when the initial cash flow is at time 0. In that case, the future value, V_n, is given by the following equation:

$$V_n = V_0(e^{kn}) \qquad (2.6a)$$

where

V_n = Cash flow at time n
V_0 = Cash flow at time 0
n = Number of years from V_0 to V_n

Susan Singleton deposits $100 in a bank that pays 10 percent interest, compounded continuously. How much will she have after five years?

She calculates the result using Equation 2.6a:

$$V_5 = \$100e^{0.10(5)}$$
$$= \$100(2.71828)^{0.5}$$
$$= \$164.87$$

Notice the amount after five years with continuous compounding is greater than the $161.05 found earlier with annual compounding.

In a similar manner, the equation for continuous discounting is created.

$$V_t = \frac{V_{t+n}}{e^{kn}} \qquad (2.7)$$

The variables are defined in Equation 2.6.

Equation 2.7 simplifies when the initial cash flow is at time 0. In that case, the present value, V_0, is given by the following:

$$V_0 = \frac{V_n}{e^{kn}} \qquad (2.7a)$$

The variables are defined in Equation 2.6a.

Susan needs to know how much to deposit today at a stated interest rate of 10 percent in order to have $164.87 in five years, assuming continuous discounting.

She uses Equation 2.7a to make this calculation.

$$V_0 = \frac{\$164.87}{e^{0.10(5)}}$$

$$V_0 = \frac{\$164.87}{2.71828^{0.5}}$$

$$= \$100$$

The equivalence of the two cash flows can be shown with a cash flow diagram.

$V_0 = \$100$ $V_5 = \$164.87$

0   5   10%C

Perpetuities

Perpetuity

A **perpetuity** is an annuity that continues forever (an infinite sequence). The present value factor of an annuity for a perpetuity is given by the following equation:

$$PFVA_{k\%,Inf} = \frac{1}{k} \qquad (2.8)$$

where

$$Inf = \text{an infinite sequence}$$

Use of this notation leads to the following equation for the value of a perpetuity:

$$V_t = A(PVFA_{k\%,Inf}) = \frac{A}{k} \qquad\qquad (2.9)$$

The equivalent cash flow, V_t, is located one time period *before* the first of the equal cash flows.

> Keith Arrington purchases a bond that pays $100 per year indefinitely, beginning one year from today. How much is this cash flow stream worth if the interest rate is 10 percent?

He calculates the result using Equation 2.9.

$$V_0 = \$100(PVFA_{10\%,Inf})$$
$$= \frac{\$100}{0.10}$$
$$= \$1,000$$

Notice that if the interest rate decreases or increases, the value of the perpetuity will increase or decrease.

A cash flow diagram demonstrates how this works.

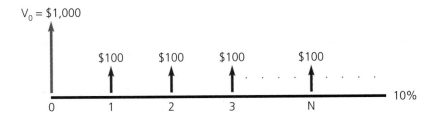

Now that we understand basic time value techniques, we are ready to apply our knowledge to more complicated problems.

TIME VALUE APPLICATIONS

Time value applications are numerous in managerial finance. In Chapter 3, for example, we will value bonds and stocks using time value techniques; and in Chapter 7, we will discount project cash flows to determine if a project should be accepted or rejected. This section supplies practice in applying time value techniques so we will be ready for what lies ahead.

Uneven Stream of Cash Flows

In the problems we worked earlier, cash flow patterns were fairly simple. We worked with a single cash flow or a uniform series of cash flows. Things are a bit more complicated when the stream of cash flows is uneven. We can, however, still use the same techniques if we group cash flows into simple patterns.

The industrial engineers at the Addison Company studied a new project and determined the following cash flow stream:

Year	Cash Flow	Year	Cash Flow
0	−$10,000	4	+$3,000
1	+$ 2,000	5	+$3,000
2	+$ 2,000	6	+$3,000
3	+$ 3,000	7	+$4,000

What is the present value of the cash flows assuming a 10 percent interest rate?

We can show this series with a cash flow diagram.

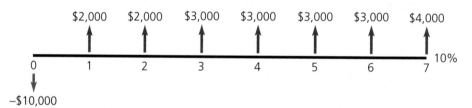

The simplest way to solve this problem is to *group* the cash flows. The first group, −$10,000 at time 0, is already at the present. The second group, +$2,000 at time 1 and 2, simply requires a present value of an annuity factor to bring the cash flows back to time 0.

$$V_0 = +\$2,000(\text{PVFA}_{10\%,2})$$

The third group, +$3,000 at time 3 through 6, an imbedded annuity, needs a present value of an annuity factor *and* a present value factor.

$$V_0 = +\$3,000(\text{PVFA}_{10\%,4})(\text{PVF}_{10\%,2})$$

The annuity factor brings the four cash flows back to time 2, one year before the first of the cash flows. The present value factor brings the equivalent cash flow back to time 0. The fourth group, +$4,000 at time 7, demands only a present value factor.

$$V_0 = +\$4,000(PVF_{10\%,7})$$

Including the present value in the cash flow diagram yields the following:

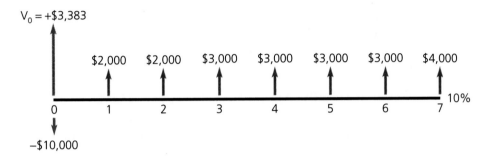

$V_0 = +\$3,383$

$2,000 $2,000 $3,000 $3,000 $3,000 $3,000 $4,000

0   1   2   3   4   5   6   7   10%

−$10,000

How did we find the present value?

To find the present value, we add the component parts.

$$V_0 = -\$10,000 + \$2,000(PVFA_{10\%,2}) + \$3,000(PVFA_{10\%,4})(PVF_{10\%,2}) + \$4,000(PVF_{10\%,7})$$
$$= -\$10,000 + \$2,000(1.7355) + \$3,000(3.1699)(0.8264) + \$4,000(0.5132)$$
$$= +\$3,382.62$$

In this problem the interest rate was known. How would we handle the calculation if we knew the cash flows, but we did not know the interest rate?

Finding the Interest Rate

The unknown interest rate goes by different names depending upon the application. With corporate bonds, it is the *yield to maturity;* with project evaluation, it is the *internal rate of return.* Those terms will be explained in Chapter 3 and Chapter 7.

Management at the Baxley Company analyzed a proposal and determined the following cash flow stream:

Year	Cash Flow	Year	Cash Flow
0	−$10,000	3	+$2,000
1	+$ 2,000	4	+$4,000
2	+$ 2,000	5	+$5,000

What rate of return will Baxley earn on its investments?

Here is the cash flow diagram.

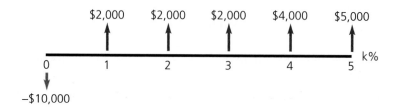

To solve this problem, we first write an expression for the present value.

$$V_0 = -\$10,000 + \$2,000(PVFA_{k\%,3}) + \$4,000(PVF_{k\%,4}) + \$5,000(PVF_{k\%,5})$$

Next, we try different values for k, a *trial and success* procedure[2]. Suppose we set k at 12 percent, for example.

$$V_0 = -\$10,000 + \$2,000(2.4018) + \$4,000(0.6355) + \$5,000(0.5674)$$
$$= +\$182.60$$

The definition of rate of return requires we find a value of 0. So, we try a different value for k.

To find a new value for k, consider Equation 2.2:

$$V_t = \frac{V_{t+n}}{(1 + k)^n}$$

Since k is in the denominator, making k larger reduces the values of the positive terms, making the present value smaller. If we set k at 13 percent, the present value would be smaller.

$$V_0 = -\$10,000 + \$2,000(2.3612) + \$4,000(0.6133) + \$5,000(0.5428)$$
$$= -\$110.40$$

The negative result indicates that we overshot our goal. Thus, the present value is 0 for an interest rate between 12 percent and 13 percent. With a financial calculator, we can find the precise answer, 12.6 percent.

---

[2] *Trial and success* is a learning tool, but it is not a good way to find the precise answer. Use an advanced calculator or THE FINANCIAL MANAGER for that purpose.

We can show all of this using a cash flow diagram.

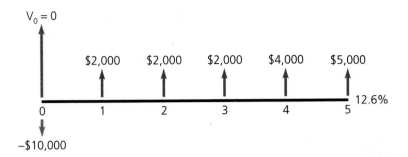

Using a trial and success procedure is useful in gaining an understanding of the time value of money, but learning to use a calculator or computer to find the exact answer is better.

Effective Rate of Interest

The **effective rate of interest** is the rate of interest for any compounding period compounded on an annual basis. The effective rate of interest, ER, can be found using the following formula:

Effective Rate of Interest

$$ER = \left(1 + \frac{k}{m}\right)^m - 1 \qquad (2.10)$$

Calculating the effective rate of interest allows us to compare interest rates using any compounding period with interest rates stated on an annual basis.

> John Allen, from an earlier example, decided to deposit $100 in an investment that paid 12 percent interest, compounded quarterly. What is the effective rate of interest? Would the effective rate be greater if the compounding were done monthly?

He can calculate the effective rate of interest for quarterly compounding.

$$ER = \left(1 + \frac{0.12}{4}\right)^4 - 1$$
$$= 1.1255 - 1$$
$$= 0.1255 \text{ or } 12.55\%$$

The calculation for monthly compounding follows:

$$ER = \left(1 + \frac{0.12}{12}\right)^{12} - 1$$
$$= 1.1268 - 1$$
$$= 0.1268 \text{ or } 12.68\%$$

Going from annual to quarterly to monthly compounding, the effective rate of interest increases.

Finding the effective rate of interest is important in finding the true rate of interest on loans. Finding the amount of interest is also an essential part of the loan process.

Loan Amortization

Amortized Loan

Amortization Schedule

An **amortized loan** includes equal loan payments over the life of the loan and provides a stated interest rate to the lender. An **amortization schedule** shows how each loan payment is divided between interest and principal.

The Cameron Company borrows $100,000, which it plans to repay in equal payments over five years. If the annual rate of interest is 10 percent, what is the amount of each payment? How are the payments divided each year between interest and principal?

We can describe this problem with a cash flow diagram

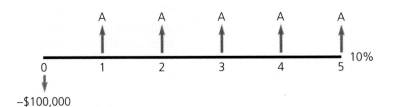

To find the annual payment, A, we must bring all of the cash flows to the same point in time and set the result equal to 0. The most convenient point is time 0 since −$100,000 is already at time 0.

$$-\$100,000 + A(PVFA_{10\%,5}) = 0$$
$$A(PVFA_{10\%,5}) = 100,000$$
$$A = \frac{\$100,000}{PVFA_{10\%,5}}$$
$$A = \frac{\$100,000}{3.7908}$$
$$A = \$26,379.66$$

We use an amortization schedule to divide the annual payments into interest and principal repayments.

Year	Payment	Interest	Principal Repayment	Balance
1	$26,379.66	$10,000.00	$16,379.66	$83,620.34
2	$26,379.66	$ 8,362.03	$18,017.63	$65,602.71
3	$26,379.66	$ 6,560.27	$19,819.39	$45,783.32
4	$26,379.66	$ 4,578.33	$21,801.33	$23,981.99
5	$26,380.19	$ 2,398.20	$23,981.99	$ 0.00

We calculate the interest for year 1 by multiplying the original loan amount of $100,000 by 0.10, the annual interest rate. In later years, we find this amount by multiplying the balance for the previous year by 0.10. We calculate the principal repayment by subtracting the interest for the year from the payment. We determine the balance by subtracting the principal repayment from the balance of the previous year. Notice that the last payment is $0.53 higher than the other payments due to rounding error.

Loan amortization requires that we use the present value factor of an annuity. What do we do when the interest rate is not found in the tables?

Calculators and Microcomputers

Calculators are useful in solving problems in finance. With simple calculators, we can perform the direct arithmetic computations shown in this chapter. With advanced calculators, the knowledgeable user can solve complex problems more efficiently. These calculators find present value, future value, and the interest rate, though some cannot handle uneven cash flows. Using calculators is easier if we can describe the problem in terms of a cash flow diagram.

Microcomputers have strengthened the practice of financial management over the last decade. Of special importance are electronic spreadsheet programs such as *Lotus 1-2-3* and *Microsoft Excel*. These programs allow financial problems to be shown on a spreadsheet of rows and columns. Formulas compute values in and between the cells of the spreadsheet. In the past, financial managers used paper worksheets and calculators to perform the same functions. Now, electronic spreadsheets allow managers to make changes easily, without having to recalculate the entire worksheet by hand.

Developing spreadsheets does require time and expertise. For this reason, financial analysts often use preprogrammed spreadsheets, called templates, to solve particular types of problems. The use of templates normally requires that the main spreadsheet program be used with the templates.

This text includes a spreadsheet program, THE FINANCIAL MANAGER, that solves a number of financial problems. It includes two models, Interest Factor Table (TABLE) and Cash Flow Equivalent (CASHFLOW), that are well suited to work the problems in this chapter. Interest Factor Table computes interest factors for combinations of time period and interest rate. Cash Flow Equivalent provides an equivalent cash flow, at any point in time, for a given set of cash flows.

> We have left open how we determined that the Kennedy fortune should be about $600 million instead of its estimated value of $350,000,000. By reading the Kennedy vignettes throughout the chapter, you may have answered the question yourself.

Let's review all of the material:

- In the future value section, we found the future value of $100 million at 5.4 percent for 34 years. That future value is close to the $600 million that the estate should be worth today.
- In the present value section, we found that the present value of $350 million, the estimate of the current value of the estate, is $58.55 million. By subtracting the present value of the estate from the original value of $100 million, we discover that $41.45 million of the original investment is gone.
- In the present value of an annuity section, we found that the family paid a $2.71 million annuity. This reduced the value of the estate by $2.71 million each year for 34 years.

Using the perpetuity equation, we can find the amount the family can withdraw each year indefinitely without dipping into their present capital of $350 million.

$$V_t = \frac{V}{k}$$

$$\$350,000,000 = \frac{V}{0.054}$$

$$V = \$18,900,000$$

To restate the original question, "Is the Kennedy family facing a financial crisis?" Considering the information we have collected throughout the chapter, we may be tempted to answer *no*. After all, the family members can withdraw $18.90 million each year, even though they have lost 41.45 percent of the original value of the estate. But have we considered all factors? What about growth of the family?

Of the nine children of Joseph and Rose, in 1957 seven of those children were alive. A few years later, the family tragically lost two members. Even so, the family grew by a factor of seven over the 34-year period, from eight to fifty-three. What could happen if this growth rate continues into the future?

At the present rate, the family will include 371 member in 34 years. This group cannot withdraw more than $18.90 million each year without dipping into the principal. If the family plans to maintain its present standard of living, it could be facing some hard choices in the near future.

SUMMARY

This chapter focuses on the following learning objectives:

1. Determining the future value of a single cash flow.

   A future value factor produces an equivalent cash flow n periods in the future. This equivalence of cash flows at different points in time is shown by a cash flow diagram. The process of moving forward in time is called compounding.

2. Determining the present value of a single cash flow.

   A present value factor creates an equivalent cash flow n periods toward the present. The process of moving backward in time is called discounting.

3. Determining an equivalent cash flow to represent the future value of an annuity.

   An annuity is a series of identical, equally spaced cash flows. A future value factor of an annuity allows replacement of an annuity with an equivalent cash flow at the end of the series. With an ordinary annuity, the cash flows are received at the end of each period.

4. Determining an equivalent cash flow to represent the present value of an annuity.

A present value factor of an annuity allows replacement of an annuity with an equivalent cash flow one time period before the first of the cash flows. With an annuity due, the cash flows are received at the beginning of each period.

5. Employing basic variations of the time value of money.

Time value factors are modified when semiannual, quarterly, monthly, daily, or even continuous compounding is used. To make this modification, the annual interest rate is divided by and the number of years multiplied by the compounding periods per year. The effective rate of interest is the rate under annual compounding that would have produced the same result as with other compounding periods, such as quarterly or monthly. Calculating the effective rate of interest allows comparisons with interest rates stated on an annual basis.

6. Applying the time value of money to financial problems.

An uneven stream of cash flows allows annuities and individual cash flows to be grouped separately. The equivalent cash flow is the sum of the group values. For a given set of cash flows, there is an interest rate for which the equivalent cash flow is 0. With a loan amortization, a series of equal payments reduces the loan balance to 0 after a given number of years.

KEY TERMS

Amortization schedule, 54	Equivalent cash flow, 30	Ordinary annuity, 34
Amortized loan, 54	Future value, 27	Perpetuity, 48
Annuity, 34	Future value factor, 29	Present value, 31
Annuity due, 36	Future value factor of an annuity, 36	Present value factor, 33
Cash flow diagram, 28	Future value of an annuity, 34	Present value of an annuity, 39
Compound interest, 28		Present value factor of an annuity, 40
Compounding, 31		
Discounting, 31		
Effective rate of interest, 53		

QUESTIONS

2.1 What is the relationship between present value and future value? How could you find a future value factor if you only had a present value table?

2.2 John Marsden was trying to find the present value of an ordinary annuity, and he used a future value of an annuity factor instead of a present value of an annuity factor. How could he modify the equation to get the right answer?

2.3 In evaluating a series of cash flows, Maria Stanley was interested in finding the interest rate where the equivalent cash flow is 0. Does it matter which point in time she chooses for the cash flow equivalent?

2.4 What effect would a decrease in the interest rate have on an equivalent cash flow? Does it matter which point in time is chosen for the cash flow equivalent?

2.5 Which is better for solving a financial problem, a computer or a calculator? Why?

2.6 In explaining the future value of an asset, what ethical problem might you have?

2.7 Do the Kennedy offspring need to worry about their financial future?

PROBLEMS

2.1 **(Present Value)** Angela Warren purchased a perpetuity that pays $1,000 per year beginning one year from today. What is the present value of the perpetuity if the interest rate is 10 percent?

2.2 **(Present Value or Future Value)** In buying a house, Harry Edwards can make a payment of $100,000 today or a single payment in five years. If the interest rate is 12 percent, what future payment makes the choices equally attractive?

2.3 **(Present Value)** Riley Corporation expects the salvage value of one of its plants to be $5,000,000 in five years. If the annual interest rate is 10 percent, what is the present value of the salvage value?

2.4 **(Other Compounding Periods)** Find the future value of a $1,000 deposit made today under each of the following conditions:

(a) 12 percent interest compounded annually for three years.

(b) 12 percent interest compounded semiannually for four years.

(c) 12 percent interest compounded monthly for five years.

2.5 **(Future Value of an Annuity)** Sally Kim plans to make bank deposits of $1,000 at the end of each year for 10 years. If the annual interest is eight percent, how much will she have at the end of the 10 years?

2.6 **(Effective Rate of Interest)** The First National Bank pays 12.46 percent interest on certificates of deposit. The Second National Bank pays 12 percent interest, compounded quarterly. Which bank pays the higher effective rate of interest?

2.7 **(Present Value of an Annuity)** Larry McNair just won a contest that included a prize of $50,000 per year for 20 years, with the first payment made today. What is the present value of his winnings if the interest rate is nine percent?

2.8 **(Present Value of Ordinary Annuity)** After filing a lawsuit, an insurance company offers to settle for $100,000 today plus an ordinary annuity of $10,000 per year for 20 years. If the appropriate interest rate is 10 percent, what is the present value of the settlement?

2.9 **(Finding the Interest Rate)** One of your relatives is planning a graduation gift: $3,000 a year from today or $3,300 two years from today. At what interest rate would you be indifferent between the two gifts?

2.10 **(Future Value of Uneven Stream)** If you invest $2,000 now, $1,500 in two years, and $1,000 in four years, at 10 percent interest, what is the future value in 10 years?

2.11 **(Making Equal Deposits)** Bill Ranson plans to make equal deposits in a bank at the end of each year for 30 years. How much must each deposit be in order to have $200,000 at the end of the time, given an interest rate of eight percent?

2.12 **(Finding Monthly Payments)** You could pay $100,000 in cash for a house or make monthly payments for five years. If the annual interest rate is 12 percent, how much should each monthly payment be in order to make the choices equally attractive?

2.13 **(Finding the Interest Rate)** The McLeod Corporation borrowed $100,000 over five years and makes annual payments of $25,708.92. What is the interest rate on the debt?

2.14 **(Rate of Return)** If you invest $1,000 today, you will receive $10,000 in 10 years. What is the rate of return on your investment?

2.15 **(Present Value of Uneven Stream)** Gorman, Inc. is evaluating a project and has estimated the following after-tax cash flows:

Year	0	1	2	3	4	5
Cash Flows	−$15,000	+$3,000	+$3,000	+$3,000	+$3,000	+$13,000

For an interest rate of 10 percent, what is the present value of the cash flows?

2.16 **(Higher Present Value)** Rainbow Electronics is considering two types of equipment for purchase. After making adjustments for taxes, the following cash flow streams were found:

Year	A	B
0	–$10,000	–$15,000
1	+$ 3,000	+$ 4,000
2	+$ 4,000	+$ 4,000
3	+$ 4,000	+$ 5,000
4	+$ 4,000	+$ 5,000
5	+$10,000	+$15,000

If the interest rate is 14 percent, which machine has the higher present value?

2.17 **(Growth Rate)** Last year, sales for the Land Company were $9,000,000, a $4,000,000 increase from five years earlier. To the nearest percent, what is the annual rate of growth in sales over the five year period?

2.18 **(Rate of Return)** You bought a note that will pay you $900 a year for four years, beginning one year from today. To the nearest percentage point, what rate of return will you earn if you purchased the note for $3,000? (CASHFLOW)[3]

2.19 Dickerson Corporation plans to invest $30,000 and to receive cash flows of $10,000 per year for five years, with the first cash flow starting a year from today. What is the present value for this project if the appropriate rate of interest is 10.5 percent? (TABLE or CASHFLOW)

2.20 **(Rate of Return)** Henderson Hydraulics, Inc. can purchase a new machine, including installation, for $67,000. This machine will reduce operating expenses to such a degree that after-tax cash flows are increased by $20,000 per year for five years. At the end of that time, the machine will be worthless. To the nearest percentage point, what is the rate of return on this investment? (CASHFLOW)

2.21 **(Present Value)** You will receive 10 payments of $1,000 per year beginning 10 years from today. If the interest rate is 10 percent, what is the present value of these cash flows?

2.22 **(Finding the Interest)** You borrow $50,000 from a bank at 13 percent interest and make annual payments at the end of each of four years. How much interest will you pay each year?

2.23 **(Rate of Return)** An investment of $100,000 today will yield cash flows of $14,000 per year for 15 years, beginning five years from now. To the nearest percent, what is the rate of return? (CASHFLOW)

2.24 **(Making Equal Deposits)** You have $9,834.62 in a bank account paying eight percent annual interest. You plan to make equal deposits at the end

---

[3] The CASHFLOW designation suggests which tool would be useful.

of each year for 10 years. Your goal is to have $100,000 at the end of that time. How much must you deposit each year?

2.25 **(Continuous Compounding)** If you deposit $1,000 in a bank account that pays eight percent annual interest compounded continuously, how much will you have in 10 years?

2.26 **(Making Equal Withdrawals)** A rich relative agreed to make deposits of $5,000 each year for four years beginning today so that you can go to graduate school. You will withdraw the total amount over three years beginning four years from now. If the annual interest rate is 10 percent, how much will you withdraw each year, assuming equal withdrawals?

2.27 **(Making Withdrawals Forever)** You plan to make 10 equal annual deposits in a bank beginning today. If the interest rate is 10 percent, how much would you have to deposit each year so that you could withdraw $1,000 for perpetuity beginning 10 years from today?

2.28 **(Making Equal Deposits)** The day a baby was born, the happy parents decided to open a bank account and make equal deposits beginning that day and each year through the child's 17th birthday. This would allow withdrawals of $5,000 per year on the 18th 19th, 20th, and 21st birthdays. If the account earns eight percent annual interest, how much should each deposit be?

2.29 **(Higher Present Value)** Hawkes, Inc. is considering the purchase of some new equipment, Type A or Type B. Type A will cost $50,000 and will produce after-tax cash flows of $15,000 per year for five years. Type B will cost $115,000 and will produce after-tax cash flows of $20,000 for 10 years. If the appropriate interest rate is 10 percent, answer the following:

(a) Which machine has the higher present value if neither project can be repeated?

(b) Which machine has the higher present value if project A can be repeated one time?

2.30 **(Continuous Rate of Return)** You invest $1,000 today and expect to receive $2,000 in 10 years. What is the continuously compounded rate of return?

2.31 **(Making Equal Withdrawals)** You inherited $75,000 and deposited $50,000 of it in an account guaranteed to earn eight percent indefinitely. You plan to retire at 65 and withdraw $100,000 per year until the money runs out. Assuming you live long enough, at what age will this occur?

2.32 **(Finding the Monthly Payments)** In 10 years, you plan to purchase a house for $250,000. You already have $5,000 in a savings account that pays and will continue to pay eight percent interest for 10 years. You plan to add to your savings $1,000 one year from today, $2,000 two years from today, continually increasing your yearly deposit by $1,000 per year, resulting in a $10,000 deposit in year ten. At year ten, you will use all of your savings as a down payment on your new house. If you finance the balance over 30 years at 12 percent annual interest, what is your monthly payment? (CASHFLOW)

2.33 **(The Range of Present Values)** James Alston was evaluating the following series of cash flows at interest rates of 11.0, 11.5, 12.0, 12.5, and 13.0 percent:

Year	Cash Flow	Year	Cash Flow
0	−$95,000	5	$19,000
1	15,000	6	20,000
2	16,000	7	21,000
3	17,000	8	22,000
4	18,000	9	23,000

What is the range of present values? (CASHFLOW)

2.34 **(Finding the Terminal Value)** Billy Marsh was born on February 26, 1970. On February 26, 1971, his father started a fund to finance his college education. He deposited $5,000 at that time and planned to deposit $2,500 on his birthday each year, with the last deposit made on his 17th birthday. On his 18th, 19th, 20th, and 21st birthdays, Billy would withdraw $10,000 a year for college. At age 25, Billy would receive the amount that is left. If the fund earns 5.5 percent annually, what would that amount be?

A Case Problem

andyTool Corporation was a manufacturer and marketer of consumer and home improvement products, including power tools, accessories, security hardware, and outdoor recreational products. The company operated 44 manufacturing facilities, 10 of which were in foreign countries. In the last fiscal year, international revenues accounted for 33 percent of total revenues.

HandyTool was best known for its power tools. The company manufactured a full line of corded and cordless power tools for home and commercial use. In connection with these products, Handytool sold workbenches, air pumps, buffers, hand-held vacuums, and related tools.

Engineers at the plant had contacted two vendors for quotes on the new equipment. Madison Machinery Company provided a quote of $175,000 dollars, while Richmond Industries produced a quote of $148,000. Engineers estimated that in both cases installation would add $5,000 to the cost.

The Goldsboro, North Carolina, plant of HandyTool planned to expand its capacity by adding a new machine used in the manufacture of a cordless drill.

The Goldsboro, North Carolina, plant of HandyTool planned to expand its capacity by adding a new machine used in the manufacture of a cordless drill. Lee Hardy, a financial analyst, calculated the cash flows resulting from acceptance of the project. In doing this, it was necessary to subtract the taxes paid on the increased earnings. The cash flows on an after-tax basis were as follows:

Year	Madison	Richmond
1	+$30,000	+$30,000
2	+$30,000	+$30,000
3	+$30,000	+$30,000
4	+$30,000	+$30,000
5	+$33,000	+$30,000
6	+$33,000	+$33,000
7	+$33,000	+$33,000
8	+$36,000	+$33,000
9	+$36,000	+$33,000
10	+$36,000	+$33,000

In addition, the net salvage value after taxes for each type of equipment was 10 percent of the original quote. Lee also found that the company used a discount rate of 12 percent on all projects.

Leading Questions

1. What are the cash flows for years 0 through 10?
2. What is the present value of these cash flows?
3. What is the incremental present value of the cash flows, subtracting the cash flows of one project from the cash flows of the other?
4. What decisions should be made? Why?

Despite a recent flood of money into stocks and stock mutual funds, individuals still have only about a fifth of their financial assets in the stock market, down from 45 percent in the late 1960s, according to David L. Babson & Company, a Cambridge, Massachusetts, investment adviser. Many financial experts contend that investors should be taking far more risk with money by owning more stocks.

3 The Valuation Process

The case for investing in stocks is based not on the market's short-term prospects, but on the superior returns that investors are likely to earn if they hold stocks for five years or longer. Since

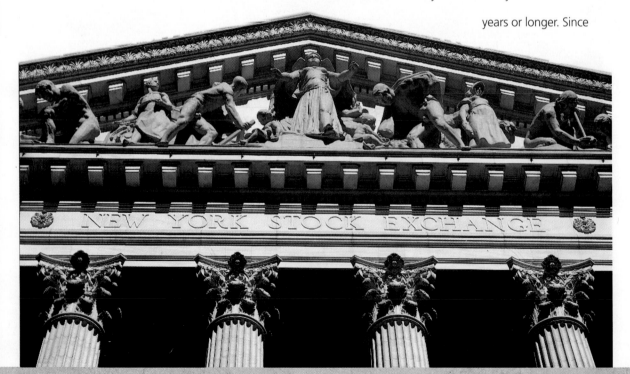

1926, long-term government bonds have had a total re-turn—bond-price changes plus interest payments—of 4.8 percent a year, and Treasury bills have gained 3.7 percent annually, according to Chicago's Ibbotson Associates. Those gains are barely ahead of inflation, which rose 3.1 percent a year during the same period. Figure in taxes, and investing your money with the government starts to look like legalized extortion.

And what about stocks? They handily outpaced infla-tion and taxes. Their pretax total return, which includes reinvested dividends, is 10.4 percent a year since 1926.

There have been 20 down years for the stock market since 1926, but the statistics are a lot more appealing if you look at longer time periods. The Ibbotson data, for in-stance, can be sliced up into 62 rolling five-year periods, beginning with the five years through December 1930, proceeding next to the five years through 1931, and so on, finishing up with the five years through December 1991. Out of these 62 five-year periods, there have been only seven occasions when stocks have posted a loss.

Investing in common stocks can be risky, especially in the short term. Dealing with this risk can be made eas-ier, however, by understanding the valuation process.

Source: Jonathan Clements, "Why It's Risky Not to Invest More in Stocks," *The Wall Street Journal,* February 11, 1992. Reprinted by permission of The Wall Street Journal, © 1992 Dow Jones & Com-pany, Inc. All Rights Reserved Worldwide.

THE VALUATION FRAMEWORK

The primary goal of management in a corporation, as we have seen, is to maxi-mize the value of its common stock. A corporation can do this by maximizing the present value of future cash flows to its shareholders. To fully understand this objective, you must understand the valuation framework. We begin our ex-amination of valuation by considering the rate of return investors require when making an investment.

The Required Rate of Return

The **required rate of return** is the minimum expected rate of return that would cause an investor to make an investment. This is true, however, only if assets are priced competitively. In this text, the required rate of return and the expected rate of return will be used interchangeably.

Required Rate of Return

The required rate of return is also the discount rate used in valuing assets. Three components determine what the required rate will be:

- The real rate of interest.
- The inflation premium.
- The risk premium.

The first component, the real rate of interest, is the rate earned on riskless investments in a noninflationary environment. The inflation premium and the risk premium are the extra returns necessary to compensate investors for inflation and risk.

Risk-Free Rate of Return

We can also define the **risk-free rate of return,** the real rate of interest plus the inflation premium. This definition allows us to restate the required rate of return as the risk-free rate of return plus the risk premium. We generally measure the risk-free rate of return by the rate on U.S. Treasury bills or U.S. Treasury bonds, since these securities are virtually risk free yet include an inflationary component. The capital asset pricing model (CAPM), to be studied in Chapter 8, supports the concept that the required rate of return is equal to the risk-free rate of return plus a risk premium.

The Valuation Model

The value of any asset, V, is the present value of its future cash flows. This concept can be described in equation form.

$$V = \frac{CF_1}{(1+k)^1} + \frac{CF_2}{(1+k)^2} + \ldots + \frac{CF_N}{(1+k)^N} \tag{3.1}$$

where

CF_n = Expected cash flow at the end of year n(n = 1,2,...,N)

k = Required rate of return

N = Number of periods

The cash flow diagram looks like this:

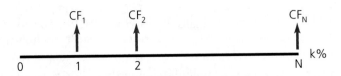

We will find out how to estimate expected cash flows in later chapters. For now, we will assume we have already determined these values.

Barbara Martin is interested in valuing an asset she purchased. She expects cash flows of $5,000 at the end of each of the next 10 years. She also knows that the required rate of return is 11 percent.

Using Equation 3.1 and time value techniques, she determines V, the value of the asset.

$$V = \$5,000(\text{PVFA}_{11\%,10})$$
$$= \$5,000(5.8992)$$
$$= \$29,496$$

A cash flow diagram shows the valuation relationships.

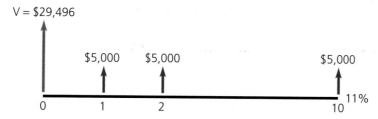

Exactly what does Barbara know when she has found V, the value of the asset? The value, $29,496, represents the maximum price she would pay to purchase the asset or the minimum price she would accept to sell it. In the marketplace, buyers and sellers make individual decisions based on their estimates of expected cash flows and the required rate of return.

Legality and Ethics: Arbs, Freeman, and Storer Communications

What is an "arb"? An "arb" is a person who exploits pricing differences in the market place; that is, purchases an asset in one market and sells it at a profit in another market. Arbitrage leads to price equilibrium between the market for assets of similar characteristics and risk. This activity is legal and ethical. Further, arbitrage is a natural human endeavor. Markets are made of humans engaging in financial activities: At the heart of the human make-up is the drive to acquire wealth. Individuals have motivation to trade on information they believe will result in the acquisition of wealth. Therein lies a natural conflict between motivation and resulting action.

What if you have privileged or confidential information that an individual entity is acquiring large amounts of stock in a specific company. The entity is acquiring the stock in hopes of mounting a takeover of that company. You know that until the entity files a disclosure to the Securities and Exchange Commission (SEC), required when any individual or company purchases (owns) five percent or more of a company's stock, the market at large is unaware of its actions and intentions. Your private information is not reflected in the stock price. Historically, when a SEC disclosure of this nature is filed, the stock price jumps. You are aware of history. Do you act on this information; buy now and sell at a profit at the announcement date? Our analysis of human nature tells us you would probably act.

Robert M. Freeman, head of the arbitrage department at Goldman Sachs and Company, did act. The entity was Coniston. The target was Storer Communications, a cable television and broadcast concern. The holder of the private information was Mr. Freeman.

Two weeks prior to the filing of a SEC disclosure to announce that Coniston possessed five percent of Storer stock, Mr. Freeman bought Storer stock and options for his personal portfolio. Mr. Freeman did not purchase Storer stock for Goldman Sachs at that time. Instead, he bought Storer stock for Goldman Sachs on the day of the filing. On that day, Storer Communications stock closed up $5.75.

Mr. Freeman spoke to insiders on the Storer deals, including the person who was executing all the buying for Coniston. Later, all employees were barred from trading in Storer stock by Goldman Sachs for personal or company portfolios. This is a common condition for an investment banking firm that becomes involved in any takeover activity. Mr. Freeman continued to trade in the stock for his personal portfolio. The end result was that both Freeman and Goldman Sachs earned large profits from his activity.

Was it arbitrage? Mr. Freeman bought an asset in one market and sold that asset at a large profit while acting as the head of the arbitrage department of Goldman Sachs and Company. He traded on non-public information, resulting in personal profit. He used information not in the public domain so that all investors are not equally able to evaluate it and make investment decisions. This is not arbitrage; this is insider trading, an activity that is unethical and illegal. Mr. Freeman spent four months in a federal prison for this and other insider trading activity.

Source: James B. Stewart, "Suspicious Trading," *The Wall Street Journal,* February 12, 1988, pg. 1; and James B. Stewart, *Den of Thieves,* New York: Simon and Schuster, 1991. Reprinted by permission of The Wall Street Journal, ©1988 Dow Jones & Company, Inc. All Rights Reserved Worldwide.

BOND VALUATION

People in business must understand valuation in order to manage the assets of their companies and to understand how investors value financial assets. We turn now to the valuation of one type of financial asset—bonds.

A bond is a long-term debt instrument which provides a fixed stream of interest payments and a lump sum at maturity.[1] To talk about bonds, we must first define several important terms.

Par Value

Coupon Interest Rate

Coupon Payment

Maturity Date

- The **par value,** or face value, is the amount to be repaid at maturity.
- The **coupon interest rate** is the percentage of par value that a company or governmental unit promises to pay the bondholder each interest period.
- The **coupon payment,** or interest payment, is the amount that must be paid each period.
- The **maturity date** is the time when the last payment and the lump sum are paid.

[1] Perpetual bonds and zero coupon bonds are exceptions. Perpetual bonds offer interest payments forever (an infinite sequence) and do not provide a lump sum at any point. Zero coupon bonds do not offer interest payments yet provide a lump sum at maturity.

Bond Valuation Model

The value of a bond, V_b, is the present value of its interest and principal payments when discounted at the discount rate. We can modify Equation 3.1 to reflect this definition.

$$V_b = \frac{I}{(1 + k_d)^1} + \frac{I}{(1 + k_d)^2} + \ldots + \frac{I}{(1 + k_d)^N} + \frac{P}{(1 + k_d)^N} \qquad (3.2)$$

where

I = Annual interest payment

k_d = Required annual rate of return

P = Par value (face value)

The annual interest payment is equal to the annual coupon interest rate times the par value.

A cash flow diagram shows the bond valuation model.

Jamie Richards is interested in finding the value of a 30-year McNair Corporation bond she recently purchased. The newly issued bond has a 12 percent annual coupon interest rate and a $1,000 par value. Bonds of similar risk have a 12 percent required annual rate of return. What is the value of the bond today?

She calculates the value of the newly issued bond using Equation 3.2.

$$V_b = \frac{\$120}{(1.12)^1} + \frac{\$120}{(1.12)^2} + \ldots + \frac{\$120}{(1.12)^{30}} + \frac{\$1,000}{(1.12)^{30}}$$

$$= \$120(PVFA_{12\%,30}) + \$1,000(PVF_{12\%,30})$$

$$= \$120(8.0552) + \$1,000(0.0334)$$

$$= \$966.62 + \$33.40$$

$$= \$1,000.02$$

Except for round-off error, the value of a bond is equal to its par value when-ever the coupon interest rate is equal to the required rate of return.

A cash flow diagram illustrates the cash flows of the bond.

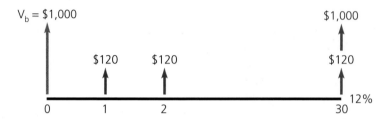

Jamie Richards decided to keep the McNair Corporation bond rather than sell it. After five years, the required annual rate of return on bonds of similar risk declined to 10 percent. What is the value of the bond after five years?

She recalculates the value of the bond after five years by again using Equation 3.2.

$$V_b = \frac{\$120}{(1.10)^1} + \frac{\$120}{(1.10)^2} + \dots + \frac{\$120}{(1.10)^{25}} + \frac{\$1,000}{(1.10)^{25}}$$
$$= \$120(\text{PVFA}_{10\%,25}) + \$1,000(\text{PVF}_{10\%,25})$$
$$= \$120(9.0770) + \$1,000(0.0923)$$
$$= \$1,089.24 + \$92.30$$
$$= \$1,181.54$$

Notice that the required annual rate of return is lower and the number of years to maturity is 25. Jamie is *interested in the number of years left until maturity, not in the number of years that have already gone by.*

A cash flow diagram shows this new relationship.

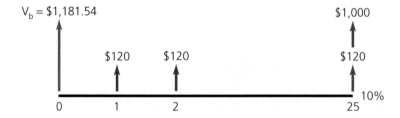

The value of a bond increases as the required rate of return decreases, *and* the value of a bond decreases as the required rate of return increases. In

How to Maximize Your Profits

Bond buyers should be wary of building castles based on the recent spectacular performance of fixed-income securities. The chin-high inflation of the late 1970s and early 1980s wreaked havoc in the bond market. When inflation rises, bond prices fall, pushing yields higher. The reaction occurs because investors demand a yield that is comfortably above the inflation rate. When inflation shot up into double digits in the late 1970s and early 1980s, bond prices collapsed. From 1977 to 1981, even before taking inflation into account, investors in 20-year Treasuries lost an average of one percent a year lending money to Washington. "But over the later part of the 1980s we essentially recouped that underperformance," says Eugene Chung, an analyst for Morgan Stanley. As inflation rates fell, the prices of long-term bonds shot up, producing some of the heftiest capital gains in the history of the bond market.

Gambling that interest rates will keep falling, some investors are buying 30-year Treasuries, which are most sensitive to any drop. But, Theresa Havell, director of fixed income at Neuberger & Berman, asks, why make the bet? Over the past three decades, 30-year Treasuries have tallied an average annual total return of just 5.9 percent, compared with 7.1 percent for five-year notes. And long bonds were almost twice as volatile. If you are hunting for capital gains, go after stocks. They pack a much bigger total return punch. After all, the real goal of investing in bonds is to preserve your principal and earn a rate of return that exceeds inflation in order to maintain or even increase your purchasing power. Intermediate bonds do that nicely.

this example, as the interest rate declined from 12 percent to 10 percent, the value of the bond increased from $1,000 to $1,181.54. As you work through the chapter problems, notice how the value of assets declines as the interest rate rises.

After a period of time most bonds sell at a price different from the par value. A bond selling below par value is a **discount bond,** and a bond selling above par value is a **premium bond.** When a bond sells at a discount, the required annual rate of return is *greater* than the coupon rate. When a bond sells at a premium, the required annual rate of return is *less* than the coupon rate.

Discount Bond

Premium Bond

Semiannual Interest Payments

The bond valuation model described by Equation 3.2 assumes that interest payments are made annually. Most bonds, however, pay interest semiannually. To find the value of these bonds, modify Equation 3.2 as follows:

$$V_b = \frac{I/2}{(1 + k_d/2)^1} + \ldots + \frac{I/2}{(1 + k_d/2)^{2N}} + \frac{P}{(1 + k_d/2)^{2N}} \qquad (3.3)$$

Jamie finds a 30-year semiannual bond that pays total interest of $120 each year and has a $1,000 par value. The bond was issued five years ago by the Cameron Corporation. What is the value of this bond if the required annual rate of return is now 10 percent?

She finds the value using Equation 3.3.

$$V_b = \frac{\$60}{(1.05)^1} + \frac{\$60}{(1.05)^2} + \ldots + \frac{\$60}{(1.05)^{50}} + \frac{\$1,000}{(1.05)^{50}}$$

$$= \$60(\text{PVFA}_{5\%,50}) + \$1,000(\text{PVF}_{5\%,50})$$

$$= \$60(18.2559) + \$1,000(0.0872)$$

$$= \$1,095.35 + \$87.20$$

$$= \$1,182.55$$

The interest of $120 each year is divided into two payments of $60 each. The required annual return of 10 percent is divided by two, to yield a semiannual rate of five percent. The 25 years that are left represent 50 periods.

A cash flow diagram shows the cash flows.

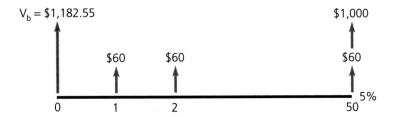

The value of the semiannual bond is higher than that of the similar annual bond, $1,182.55 to $1,181.54.[2] Under semiannual interest, the company disburses half of the coupon rate six months earlier. Cash flows received earlier have a higher present value. This makes the bond value under semiannual interest higher than under annual interest.

Time to Maturity

The semiannual bond just discussed is valued at $1,182.55 when the annual required rate of return is 10 percent and 25 years are left to maturity. By using THE FINANCIAL MANAGER (BOND), we can determine that the value of

---

[2] The value of the semiannual bond is less than that of the annual bond for bonds selling below par, however. If the coupon interest rate and the required annual rate of return are the same, the bond sells for par in both cases.

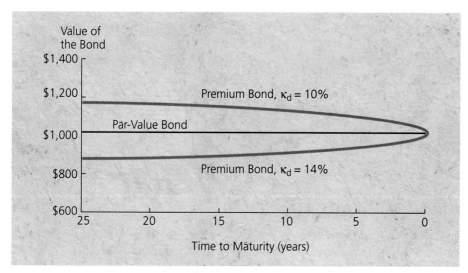

FIGURE 3.1 Time to Maturity Relationships When the Required Annual Rate of Return is Constant (12% Coupon)

the bond is $861.99 when the annual required rate of return is 14 percent and 25 years are left to maturity. If we revalued the bond at both interest rates—for 20, 15, 10, 5, and 0 years—we would notice that the value in each case approaches the par value. The value of a bond selling at par remains flat. Figure 3.1 demonstrates these relationships.

We have already seen that as the required rate of return (the market rate of interest) for a bond decreases, the value of a bond rises and, conversely, that as this rate increases, the value falls. This variability in value is called **interest rate risk.** The value of longer-term bonds changes more than the value of bonds of shorter maturity. As a result, longer-term bonds have a higher interest rate risk than shorter-term bonds.

Interest Rate Risk

Consider, for example, two annual bonds with 12 percent annual coupon rates and $1,000 par values. One bond has five years remaining to maturity while the other has 20 years. Using THE FINANCIAL MANAGER (BOND), we can easily value these bonds at different interest rates. The results are summarized in Table 3.1.

Notice that as the market rate of interest changes, the change in value is greater for the 20-year bond. For example, if the interest rate moves from 12 percent to 16 percent, the 20-year bond loses $237.15 ($1,000.00 – $762.85). In contrast, the 5-year bond loses $130.97 ($1,000 – $869.03).

Figure 3.2 graphically shows the relationship between the values of the 5-year and the 20-year bonds. As market interest rates approach the coupon interest rate, the difference in value is small. As the deviation between rates becomes greater, the deviation in value widens.

TABLE 3.1 Valuation of 12 Percent Bonds at Different Interest Rates

MARKET RATE OF INTEREST	20-YEAR BOND	5-YEAR BOND
8	$1,392.73	$1,159.71
10	1,170.27	1,075.82
12	1,000.00	1,000.00
14	867.54	931.34
16	762.85	869.03

This greater variability in the value of longer-term bonds is important to investors. They are particularly concerned with increases in interest rates, which cause a drop in the prices of bonds. As a result, investors avoid longer-term bonds unless higher yields justify the additional risk.

Reinvestment Rate Risk

While long-term bonds are subject to interest rate risk, short-term bonds are subject to **reinvestment rate risk.** This is the risk that interest rates will decline by the time the short-term bond matures. If interest rates do decline, short-term investors are forced to accept a lower rate of return. Long-term investors, in contrast, lock in the higher interest rate.

Yield to Maturity

Yield to Maturity

The **yield to maturity** of a bond is the interest rate that causes the cash flows, when discounted to time 0, to equal the current price. To find the yield to

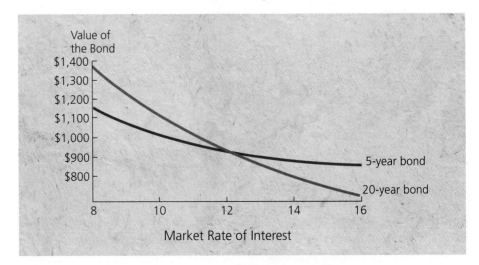

FIGURE 3.2 Valuation of 12 Percent bonds at Different Interest Rates

maturity, we use Equation 3.2 or Equation 3.3. In these formulas, V_b is the current price, and k_d is the annual yield to maturity.

John Franklin purchases a 12 percent, $1,000 par value, semiannual payment bond, with 25 years to maturity, for the current price of $1,182.55. What is the yield to maturity of the bond?

A cash flow diagram demonstrates the cash flows of the bond.

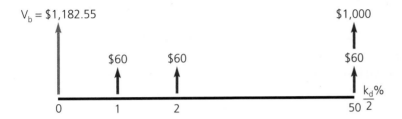

To find the yield to maturity, he discounts the cash flows of the bond back to time 0 and sets this amount equal to the current price. He does this by using Equation 3.3.

$$\$1,182.55 = \frac{\$60}{(1 + k_d/2)^1} + \ldots + \frac{\$60}{(1 + k_d/2)^{50}} + \frac{\$1,000}{(1 + k_d/2)^{50}}$$
$$= \$60(PVFA_{k_d/2,50}) + \$1,000(PVF_{k_d/2,50})$$

To find the value of $k_d/2$, he uses a *trial and success* procedure.[3] He starts by trying an interest rate less than 6 percent, the coupon interest rate divided by 2, since the current price of $1,182.55 is more than the $1,000 par value. If the bond were selling for less than $1,000, he would try an interest rate greater than 6 percent.

He tries 4 percent, an amount less than 6 percent.

$$\$1,182.55 = \$60(PVFA_{4\%,50}) + \$1,000(PVF_{4\%,50})$$
$$= \$60(21.4822) + \$1,000(0.1407)$$
$$= \$1,288.93 + \$140.70$$
$$= \$1,429.63$$

The right-hand side is too large. He can make it smaller by using a *larger* interest rate.

---

[3] *Trial and success* is a learning tool but is not a good way to find the precise answer. Use an advanced calculator or THE FINANCIAL MANAGER (BOND) for that purpose.

He then tries 5 percent.

$$\begin{aligned}
\$1,182.55 &= \$60(\text{PVFA}_{5\%,50}) + \$1,000(\text{PVF}_{5\%,50}) \\
&= \$60(18.2559) + \$1,000(0.0872) \\
&= \$1,095.35 + \$87.20 \\
&= \$1,182.55
\end{aligned}$$

The two sides are equal. The value of $k_d/2$ must be 5 percent, and the yield to maturity, k_d, is 10 percent.

The *trial and success* procedure works well when the value is an integer; but usually, this is not the case. Instead of this procedure, we generally use an advanced calculator or THE FINANCIAL MANAGER (BOND) to find the exact answer.

The yield to maturity (YTM) also can be approximated by the following formula:[4]

$$\text{YTM} = \frac{I + \dfrac{P - V_b}{N}}{0.4P + 0.6V_b} \tag{3.4}$$

Let's use the formula with the example we've already worked by *trial and success*.

$$\begin{aligned}
\text{YTM} &= \frac{\$60 + \dfrac{\$1,000 - \$1,182.55}{50}}{0.4(\$1,000) + 0.6(\$1,182.55)} \\
&= \frac{\$56.349}{\$1,109.53} \\
&= 0.0508 \text{ or } 5.08\%
\end{aligned}$$

This answer, 5.08 percent, contrasts with the exact semiannual value of 5.00 percent. Remember, Equation 3.4 is an approximation.

The yield to maturity (YTM) of a bond consists of a current yield (CY) and a capital gains yield (CGY).[5]

$$\text{YTM} = \text{CY} + \text{CGY} \tag{3.5}$$

We calculate the current yield by dividing the annual interest by the price. The capital gains yield is the yield to maturity less the current yield.

[4] See Gabriel A. Hawawini and Ashok Vora, "Yield Approximations: A Historical Perspective," *Journal of Finance*. Vol. 37, No. 1, pp. 145–156.
[5] A capital gain occurs when the selling price of a bond is more than the purchase price.

John Franklin purchased a bond from Aerobics Unlimited. The yield to maturity of the 10 percent, $1,000 par value, annual payment bond, with 30 years to maturity and a current price of $800, is 12.59 percent. What are the current yield and the capital gains yield?

Applying Equation 3.5 produces the following:

$$0.1259 = \frac{\$100}{\$800} + CGY$$

$$0.1259 = 0.1250 + CGY$$

$$CGY = 0.0009 \text{ or } 0.09\%$$

The yield to maturity is the rate an investor earns by buying a bond and holding it until maturity. But bonds are often called before that time.

Yield to Call

Corporations usually issue bonds with a call provision which allows the company to call the bonds before maturity. The process, discussed in detail in Chapter 14, is called refunding. Bondholders are paid a call premium when this occurs. The amount of the premium is normally one year's interest, but often declines after the initial call date. The **yield to call** is the market rate of return the bondholder receives when the bond is called at its earliest call date.

Yield to Call

Generally, corporations carry out refunding when there is a significant drop in interest rates. The bonds are redeemed when the present value of the cash flows is greater than or equal to zero. The cash flows result from the yearly interest savings and from the costs of the refunding.

John Franklin purchases a 12 percent annual coupon interest rate, $1,000 par value, semiannual payment bond, with five years remaining before the bond can be called. He pays the current price of $980.55 for the bond, knowing that if the bond is called, he will receive $1,100. What is the yield to call of the bond?

A cash flow diagram shows the cash flows associated with John's purchase under the assumption that the bond will be called at the earliest opportunity.

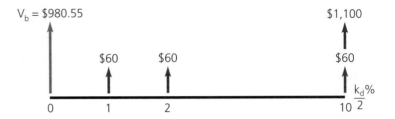

To find $k_d/2$, he discounts the cash flows of the bond back to time 0 and sets this amount equal to the current price. Using Equation 3.3, substituting the call price for the par value, he arrives at the following:

$$\$980.55 = \frac{\$60}{(1 + k_d/2)^1} + \ldots + \frac{\$60}{(1 + k_d/2)^{10}} + \frac{\$1,100}{(1 + k_d/2)^{10}}$$

$$= \$60(\text{PVFA}_{k_d/2,10}) + \$1,100(\text{PVF}_{k_d/2,10})$$

To find the value of $k_d/2$, he again uses a *trial and success* procedure. He knows that the current price is less than the $1,100 call price. Since the current price is less than the call price, he tries an interest rate greater than the coupon interest rate of 6 percent.

The Price of Redemption

A couple of months ago, I received a letter from an irate investor complaining about the call of his Carolina Power & Co. (CP&L) 10.5 percent first-mortgage bonds due May 15, 2009. Issued in 1979, these bonds were redeemed on April 1, 1991, at 100 percent of the principal amount and not at the regular redemption price of $106.52.

Our investor was burned by his own failure to thoroughly understand the ins and outs of bond calls. The fact is that many corporate issues, electric utilities in particular, have two sets of call prices, depending on the type of redemption.

The higher call price is for those happy occasions when a company finds itself with some extra cash on hand, say from better-than-expected earnings. But management has leeway since it can also satisfy its maintenance and replacement deficiency with credit taken for property and plant additions made in prior years. The lower special redemption price, normally par, is usually for redemptions the company is required to make. For example, in taking money from its bondholders, a utility is obligated to keep its plant and equipment in good repair. Those assets are the security for the loan, after all. If the utility fails to maintain and replace equipment as required, it must retire some of its bonds.

Source: Richard S. Wilson, "The Price of Redemption," *Financial World*, September 3, 1991, pg. 82.

He tries 7 percent.

$$\$980.55 = \$60(PVFA_{7\%,10}) + \$1,100(PVF_{7\%,10})$$
$$= \$60(7.0236) + \$1,100(0.5083)$$
$$= \$421.42 + \$559.13$$
$$= \$980.55$$

Since the two sides are equal, 7 percent is successful. Therefore, the yield to call is 14 percent, the semiannual rate multiplied by 2.

Zero Coupon Bonds

Up to this point, all bonds provided interest payments each year, either annually or semiannually. In recent years, corporations have issued **zero coupon bonds.** No interest is paid during the life of these bonds. At maturity, the bondholders receive the par value of the bonds. Corporations often use these bonds to avoid cash outflows over a certain time period. Buying zero coupon bonds allows the investor to lock in the yield over the life of the bond. With regular bonds, coupon interest payments must be reinvested at the prevailing rate.

Zero Coupon Bond

> John Franklin purchased a $1,000 par value, zero coupon bond, with 25 years to maturity, for the current price of $92.30. What is the yield to maturity of the bond, assuming annual discounting?

A cash flow diagram shows the cash flows of the bond.

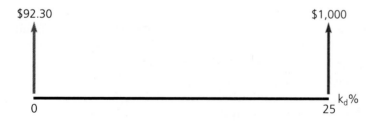

$92.30 $1,000

0   25 $k_d\%$

To find the yield to maturity, he first brings the $1,000 cash flow back to time 0 and sets this amount equal to the current price.

$$\$92.30 = \frac{\$1,000}{(1 + k_d)^{25}}$$
$$= \$1,000(PVF_{k_d\%,25})$$

He can obtain the same result by using Equation 3.2, with the annual interest payment equal to 0.

To determine the value of k_d, he divides both sides of the equation by $1,000. This isolates the present value factor.

$$(PVF_{k_d\%,25}) = 0.0923$$

Using a present value factor table, he can find that the value of k_d equals 10 percent.

Individuals sometimes buy zero coupon bonds in the mistaken belief that yearly income taxes can be avoided. But in the United States, individuals who purchase zero coupon bonds pay income taxes on the bonds each year. The original discount is amortized over the original life of the bond, and this amount is treated as ordinary income.[6] In contrast, the coupon interest payment on regular bonds is directly taxable as ordinary income.

Perpetual Bonds

Perpetual Bond

Perpetual Bonds offer annual or semiannual interest payments forever (an infinite sequence) and do not provide a lump sum at any point. They are *not* callable in the future.

The value of a perpetual bond is the present value of its expected cash flows and is given by the following equation:

$$V_b = \frac{I}{k_d} \tag{3.6}$$

The variables are defined as in Equation 3.3.

> John Franklin is interested in finding the value of a perpetual bond that he recently purchased. The bond provides $120 annual coupon payments, with the next payment due one year from today. The required annual rate of return is 10 percent.

With this information, he can calculate the value of the bond by using Equation 3.6.

$$V_b = \frac{\$120}{0.10}$$
$$= \$1,200$$

[6] The issuer of the zero coupon bond provides the purchaser, even if the bond is bought in the secondary market, with a Form 1099-OID, *Statement of Recipients of Original Issue Discount*, showing the interest that must be included as income.

A cash flow diagram shows the cash flows.

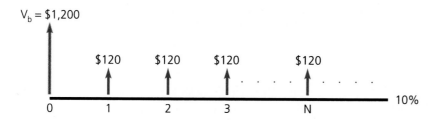

The value of perpetual bonds, like other bonds, depends on the required rate of return at the given point in time.

Bond Quotations

Most bonds are traded in the over-the-counter market, and as a result, information on trades is generally less available. Bonds are also listed in the bond section of the New York Stock Exchange (NYSE). Information on NYSE trades is contained in the financial section of newspapers such as *The Wall Street Journal.*

John Franklin learned from his broker that the Paxton Corporation issued $1,000 par value, semiannual interest bonds a few years ago. In today's newspaper, December 31, 1993, he found the following quotation in the financial section:

Bonds	Cur Yld	Vol	Close	Net Chg
Paxt 8¾ 05	9.1	5	96⅝	+ ½

What information does it contain?

This bond quote shows that the Paxton Corporation issued bonds maturing December 31, 2005 (05 in the quotation), with a coupon interest rate of 8.75 (8 3/4) percent. The close of 96 5/8, 1/2 higher than the previous trading day, indicates a price of $966.25 (96.625 percent of the $1,000 par value). Five of these bonds were traded on that date.

The current yield is defined as the annual interest divided by the closing price. John finds the annual interest, $87.50, by multiplying the coupon interest rate of 8.75 percent by the $1,000 par value. Therefore, he calculates the current yield by dividing $87.50 by $966.25. The result, 9.06 percent is rounded off to 9.1. This is the return he would receive from interest alone.

PREFERRED STOCK VALUATION

We turn next to the valuation of preferred stocks. This hybrid type of security pays a fixed dividend but, unlike most bonds, does not include a lump sum payment. Although preferred stocks are usually perpetuities, many preferred stocks have a call feature that allows the issuing company to retire the securities after a number of years. Preferred stocks are like bonds, since they have fixed cash flows, and are like common stocks, since they have no maturity date. Preferred stocks are, however, an equity—they represent ownership of the company. While they are preferred as to the receipt of dividends, payment is still dependent on the board of directors declaring a dividend each quarter.

Perpetual Preferred Stocks

Perpetual Preferred Stock

Perpetual preferred stocks pay a fixed dividend forever (an infinite sequence). The value of a perpetual preferred stock, V_p, is the present value of its expected dividends and is given by the following equation:

$$V_p = \frac{D_p}{k_p} \tag{3.7}$$

where

$$D_p = \text{Annual dividend payment}$$
$$k_p = \text{Required annual rate of return}$$

Carlos Ayala is interested in finding the value of 12 percent, $100 par value preferred stock that he recently purchased. The required annual rate of return is 10 percent.

With this information, he can calculate the value of the preferred stock using Equation 3.7.

$$V_p = \frac{\$12}{0.10}$$
$$= \$120$$

Notice that he determines the annual dividend payment of $12 by multiplying 12 percent by the $100 par value.

A cash flow diagram illustrates the cash flows.

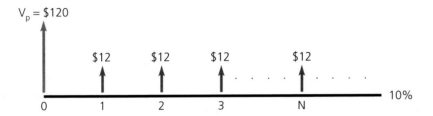

Quarterly Dividends

Most preferred stocks pay dividends every three months, not once a year. This suggests an effective rate of return higher than the stated rate.

> Carlos Ayala is interested in finding the effective rate of return on 12 per-cent, $100 par value preferred stock that he recently purchased for $120. How does he convert the implied rate of return of 10 percent, $12/$120, to an effective rate?

He finds the effective rate by using Equation 2.10.

$$\text{ER} = \left(1 + \frac{k}{m}\right)^m - 1$$
$$= \left(1 + \frac{0.10}{4}\right)^4 - 1$$
$$= 0.1038 \text{ or } 10.38\%$$

This is the annual rate of return that makes quarterly and annual dividends equally attractive.

COMMON STOCK VALUATION

The value of any asset is the present value of its expected cash flows. Earlier, we applied this principle to bonds and preferred stock. Now, we are ready to apply this same concept to common stock.

The value of a share of common stock, V_s, is the present value of its cash flows, in this case its future expected dividends.

$$V_s = \frac{D_1}{(1+k_s)^1} + \frac{D_2}{(1+k_s)^2} + \ldots + \frac{D_N}{(1+k_s)^N} \qquad (3.8)$$

where

$$D_n = \text{Expected annual dividend in year n } (n = 1,2,\ldots,N)$$

The required annual rate of return, k_s, may be estimated by use of the capital asset pricing model from Chapter 8 (page 240).

Equation 3.8 requires us to specify dividends indefinitely and bring each one back to time 0. Since this could become tiresome, we use several variations of the valuation model: (1) estimating stock price, (2) constant dividend growth, (3) supernormal dividend growth, and (4) nonconstant dividend growth. Let's look at each one of these variations.

Estimating Stock Price

We can modify the valuation model of Equation 3.8 by estimating the price of the stock at some point in the future.

$$V_s = \frac{D_1}{(1+k_s)^1} + \ldots + \frac{D_N}{(1+k_s)^N} + \frac{P_N}{(1+k_s)^N} \qquad (3.9)$$

Here, P_N equals the expected price of the stock at time N. When we are able to do this, bringing the cash flows back to time 0 is a fairly simple process.

> Ann Perneau purchases stock that she estimates will have a $1.00 dividend one year from today, a $1.10 dividend two years from today, and an estimated stock price two years from today of $24.20. She knows that the required annual rate of return is 15 percent. What is the value of the stock today?

With this information, she can calculate the value of the stock by using Equation 3.9.

$$
\begin{aligned}
V_s &= \frac{\$1.00}{(1+0.15)^1} + \frac{\$1.10}{(1+0.15)^2} + \frac{\$24.20}{(1+0.15)^2} \\
&= \$1.00(PVF_{15\%,1}) + \$1.10(PVF_{15\%,2}) + \$24.20(PVF_{15\%,2}) \\
&= \$1.00(0.8696) + \$1.10(0.7561) + \$24.20(0.7561) \\
&= \$0.87 + \$0.83 + \$18.30 \\
&= \$20.00
\end{aligned}
$$

A cash flow diagram demonstrates the cash flows.

Constant Dividend Growth

The second variation for valuing common stock assumes that dividends grow at a constant rate indefinitely. For example, if the dividend for time 1, D_1, is $1.00 and the dividend for time 2, D_2, is $1.10, the growth rate in year 2 is 10 percent. If this 10 percent growth rate continues for another year, we can calculate the dividend at time 3 by multiplying the dividend from the previous year by $(1 + 0.10)$.

$$
\begin{aligned}
D_3 &= \$1.10(1 + 0.10)^1 \\
&= \$1.10(1.10) \\
&= \$1.21
\end{aligned}
$$

We can easily find the dividend for any year by multiplying the dividend from the previous year by $(1 + g)$.

Myron J. Gordon used the assumption that dividends grow at a constant rate indefinitely to develop the **constant dividend growth model,** also known as the Gordon model.

Constant Dividend Growth Model

$$
V_s = \frac{D_0(1 + g)}{k_s - g} = \frac{D_1}{k_s - g} \tag{3.10}
$$

The equation for this model is valid only if k_s is greater than g.

Equation 3.10 allows us to value a share of common stock if we know D_0 or D_1, the required rate of return, and the constant growth expected in the future. Today's dividend is D_0. We can find next year's dividend by multiplying D_0 by $(1 + g)$. We estimate the future growth rate by projecting, or modifying, past growth rates. To estimate the required rate of return, we often use the capital asset pricing model from Chapter 8, but we may also use the required rate of return for similar stocks.

Ann Perneau owns stock in a company and expects a $1.00 dividend one year from today. She further believes that dividends will grow indefinitely at a rate of 10 percent per year. She finds that the required annual rate of return for similar stocks is 15 percent. What is the value of the stock today?

This information fits the Gordon model. The dividends are growing at a constant rate, and the required annual rate of return, 15 percent, is greater than the growth rate, 10 percent.

She substitutes these values into Equation 3.10.

$$V_s = \frac{D_1}{k_s - g}$$
$$= \frac{\$1.00}{0.15 - 0.10}$$
$$= \$20.00$$

The valuation process is shown using a cash flow diagram.

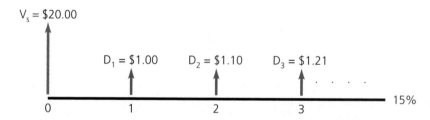

The equivalent cash flow, V_s, is always located one period *before* the first of the constant growth dividends. In this case it occurs at time 0, only because the first of the constant growth dividends occurs at time 1.

The two previous examples correctly suggest that the value of the stock does not depend on the holding period of the stock. Stock held indefinitely had the same value, $20.00, as did stock sold after two years.

Supernormal Dividend Growth

Now, we consider another sort of dividend growth—the case where the growth rate in dividends is temporarily high. Remember, the Gordon model equation is valid only if the required rate of return is greater than the growth rate. For some companies, though, the growth rate *exceeds* the required annual rate of return for a number of years. This is known as **supernormal dividend growth.** After that period, the company may return to dividend growth where the required rate of return is greater than the growth rate.

Supernormal Dividend Growth

William Perneau owns stock in a company and expects a $1.00 dividend one year from today. He further believes that dividends will grow at a rate of 20 percent for the next two years and then grow indefinitely at a rate of 10 percent per year. He finds that the required annual rate of return for similar stocks is 15 percent. What is the value of the stock today?

To find the value of the stock, V_s, he first calculates the dividends during the period when g is greater than k_s.

$$D_2 = \$1.00(1 + 0.20)^1 = \$1.20$$
$$D_3 = \$1.00(1 + 0.20)^2 = \$1.44$$

Then, he calculates D_4, the first dividend when k_s is greater than g.

$$D_4 = \$1.00(1 + 0.20)^2(1 + 0.10) = \$1.584$$

These dividends are shown by a cash flow diagram.

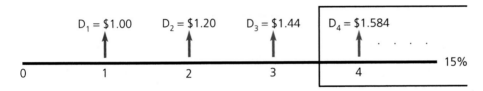

Notice that in the diagram the period of constant dividend growth is isolated.

To find the value of the stock, he first brings the three nonconstant growth dividends back to time 0.

$$V_0 = \$1.00(PVF_{15\%,1}) + \$1.20(PVF_{15\%,2}) + \$1.44(PVF_{15\%,3})$$
$$= \$1.00(0.8696) + \$1.20(0.7561) + \$1.44(0.6575)$$
$$= \$2.7237$$

Next, he uses the Gordon model to find an equivalent cash flow for the constant growth dividends. The equivalent cash flow is located at time 3, one period before the first constant dividend. He modifies Equation 3.10 for this purpose.

$$V_3 = \frac{D_4}{k_s - g}$$
$$= \frac{\$1.584}{0.15 - 0.10}$$
$$= \$31.68$$

Then, he brings this equivalent cash flow at time 3 back to time 0.

$$V_0 = \$31.68(PVF_{15\%,3})$$
$$= \$31.68(0.6575)$$
$$= \$20.8296$$

The value of the stock is the sum of the values of the nonconstant growth dividends and the constant growth dividends.

$$V_s = \$2.7237 + \$20.8296$$
$$= \$23.5533 \text{ or } \$23.55$$

A cash flow diagram shows the complete relationship.

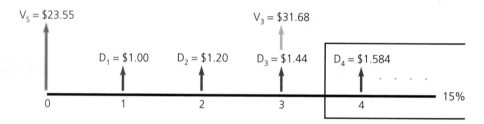

The equivalent cash flow, V_3, of $31.68 represents all dividends past time 3.

Nonconstant Dividend Growth

We have looked at situations in which dividend growth was constant and situations in which there was a period of supernormal growth. In practice, there are a wide variety of other possible assumptions about dividend growth. As a result, you should develop the technical expertise necessary to write the valuation equations for any situation.

> The dividend last year for the stock of the Ranson Company was $7.07, and no growth in dividends is predicted for the next two years. After that time, a 20 percent growth for two years is forecasted, with a 10 percent indefinite growth rate thereafter. As before, the required annual rate of return for similar stocks is 15 percent.

To find the value, V_s, we first identify the dividends before the period of constant dividend growth. The dividend for the first two years is expected to be $7.07, the same as last year's dividend:

$$D_1 = D_2 = \$7.07$$

The dividend for the third year is expected to increase by 20 percent:

$$D_3 = \$7.07(1.20)^1$$
$$= \$8.484$$

A 20-percent increase is expected for the fourth year as well:

$$D_4 = \$7.07(1.20)^2$$
$$= \$10.181$$

The fifth year begins the period of 10 percent growth.

$$D_5 = \$7.07(1.20)^2(1.10)$$
$$= \$11.199$$

These dividends can be shown in a cash flow diagram.

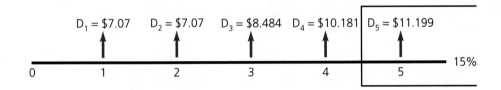

Notice in the diagram that the period of constant dividend growth is isolated.

To find the value of the stock, we bring the nonconstant growth dividends and the constant growth dividends back to time 0. This time we will use one equation.

$$V_s = \$7.07(PVF_{15\%,1}) + \$7.07(PVF_{15\%,2}) + \$8.484(PVF_{15\%,3})$$
$$+ \$10.181(PVF_{15\%,4}) + \frac{\$11.199}{0.15 - 0.10}(PVF_{15\%,4})$$
$$= \$7.07(0.8696) + \$7.07(0.7561) + \$8.484(0.6575)$$
$$+ \$10.181(0.5718) + \$223.98(0.5718)$$
$$= \$150.9652 \text{ or } \$150.97$$

The equivalent cash flow for the period of constant dividend growth is located at time 4, one period before the first constant dividend. A cash flow diagram shows the complete relationship.

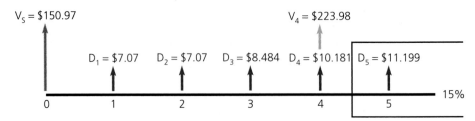

The equivalent cash flow, V_4, of $223.98 represents all dividends past time 4.

Using Growth Rates

To value stock, it is necessary to estimate dividend growth rates. One approach involves projecting past growth rates into the future.

Maria Evans has owned stock in the Richardson Corporation for the last 10 years. During that time, she has kept records of the dividends per share (DPS) each year.

Year	DPS	Year	DPS
1984	$3.00	1989	$4.75
1985	3.28	1990	5.25
1986	3.55	1991	6.00
1987	4.01	1992	6.40
1988	4.40	1993	7.07

What growth rate would she project for the future?

The growth rate of these dividends appears to be fairly stable over time. If Maria expects this growth rate to continue, she can use this data to estimate the future growth rate.

To calculate the growth rate, she must first select two dividends to represent future growth. Suppose she selects 1984 and 1993. This represents a nine year difference in time.

A cash flow diagram shows this 9-year period.

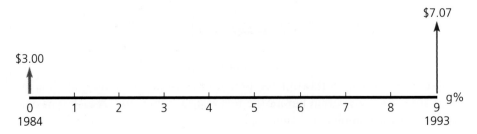

The dividends in the diagram are equivalent to each other at any point in time, when adjusted for growth rate. She chooses time 0 since the $3.00 dividend is already at time 0. Next, she writes the following equation, bringing the $7.07 to time 0:

$$\$7.07(\text{PVF}_{g\%,9}) = \$3.00$$
$$(\text{PVF}_{g\%,9}) = 0.4243$$

A present value table provides the growth rate of 10 percent, the average annual growth rate.

Stock Quotations

Since we are interested in valuing stocks, we are also interested in how the stock market values stocks. Stock quotations are found in the financial sections of newspapers.

John Franklin found the stock quotation for the Paxton Corporation in the financial section of the newspaper.

German Bonds Look Good To U.S. Money Managers

German bonds look like a delicious three-course dinner to some American money managers. For appetizers, Germany's interest rates are higher than America's. For the main course, German bonds could produce solid capital gains as the German economy sputters. And for dessert, some managers believe, the mark will rise against the dollar, offering American investors a currency gain as well. "You have not seen this kind of favorable difference (in yields) for Germany, ever," says Luis Maizel, president of LM Capital Management Inc. in La Jolla, California. One reason German rates are higher is that Germany's central bank has purposely kept them up, to prevent serious inflation from the absorption of the former East Germany. A bad economy is good for bonds because interest rates usually fall when the economy weakens. Falling interest rates are to bonds what water is to flowers. When interest rates fall, the value of existing bonds automatically rises: The older bonds are worth more because they still carry yesterday's comparatively generous interest rates. The trickiest part to predict is what the mark and the dollar will do. If the mark rises, it will provide a tasty dessert for U.S. investors, as the value of interest earned abroad will be worth more when translated into dollars. But if the dollar strengthens against the mark, U.S. investors will be reaching for their Alka-Seltzer.

Source: John R. Dorfman, "German Bonds Look Good To U.S. Money Managers," *The Wall Street Journal,* January 14, 1992. Reprinted by permission of The Wall Street Journal, © 1992 Dow Jones & Company, Inc. All Rights Reserved Worldwide.

52 weeks				Yld			Vol				Net
High	Low	Stock	Div	%	PE	100s	High	Low	Close	Chg
69¾	52½	Paxton	3.40	5.7	13	1720	60¼	59⅝	60	+½

What information does it contain?

The first two columns show the high and low stock prices over the last year. After the company name, the annual dividend rate—$3.40—appears. Next, the dividend yield, which is the dividend rate divided by the closing price, is shown as 5.7 percent. The next column provides the PE ratio, the price divided by the annual earnings; the PE ratio is 13. The daily volume of 1720 means that 1,720 round lots or 172,000 shares were traded. The next three columns present the high and low prices for the day, along with the closing price. The final column supplies the amount the stock price has changed from the close of the previous trading day. From this data, we can calculate the earnings per share (EPS) for Paxton Corporation, $60/13 = $4.62.

SUMMARY

This chapter focuses on the following learning objectives:
1. Explaining the valuation framework.
   The required rate of return is the minimum rate of return that would cause an investor to make an investment. The value of any asset is the present value of its future cash flows using the required rate of return.
2. Determining the value of a bond.
   A bond is a long-term debt instrument which provides a fixed stream of interest payments and an amount equal to the par value at maturity. The coupon interest rate is the percentage of par value that a company or governmental unit must pay the bondholder each period. The value of a bond is the present value of its interest and principal payments. Zero coupon bonds include no coupon interest during the life of the bond; the bondholder only receives the par value at maturity. Perpetual bonds offer interest payments forever and are not redeemable at any point in the future.
3. Calculating the yield to maturity of a bond.
   The yield to maturity of a bond is the discount rate that causes the cash flows when discounted to time 0 to equal the current price.
4. Calculating the yield to call of a bond.
   The yield to call is the rate of return the bondholder receives when the bond is called at its earliest call date. The call premium is the amount in excess of par paid to the bondholder when bonds are called.
5. Determining the value of preferred stock.
   A preferred stock pays a fixed dividend but, unlike most bonds, does not

include a lump sum payment. Although preferred stocks are perpetuities, some preferred stocks have a call feature, allowing the issuing company to retire the securities after a number of years. Preferred stocks are like bonds since they have fixed cash flows, and also are like common stocks since they have no maturity date.

6. Determining the value of common stock.

The value of a common stock is the present value of its dividends. The Gordon model provides the value of a common stock when the dividends grow indefinitely at a constant rate. Stocks may also be valued when dividends grow at a supernormal or nonconstant rate.

KEY TERMS

Constant dividend growth model, 87
Coupon interest rate, 70
Coupon payment, 70
Discount bond, 73
Interest rate risk, 75
Maturity date, 70
Par value, 70

Perpetual bond, 82
Perpetual preferred stock, 84
Premium bond, 73
Reinvestment rate risk, 76
Required rate of return, 67

Risk-free rate of return, 68
Supernormal dividend growth, 88
Yield to call, 79
Yield to maturity, 76
Zero coupon bond, 81

QUESTIONS

3.1 How is the required rate of return for an asset determined?

3.2 Describe the valuation model. How would you use it to value an asset?

3.3 How are perpetual bonds, preferred stocks, and common stocks with zero growth similar and different?

3.4 What happens to the value of a bond as the required rate of return increases and decreases?

3.5 If you owned a bond and the going rate of interest changed, would it matter if the bond was callable?

3.6 If the required rate of return for a bond remains constant, what happens to the value of the bond through time?

3.7 To use the Gordon model, what conditions must be met? What do you do if these conditions are not met?

3.8 Explain bond and stock quotations and terminology.

3.9 Which bonds are more risky, long-term or short-term? Why?

3.10 A client of yours plans to purchase zero coupon bonds to avoid taxes. From an ethical point of view, what should you tell the client?

3.11 Why is it risky *not* to invest in stocks?

3.12 What is an arb?

3.13 Why bet on stocks instead of bonds?

3.14 What is the danger of investing in foreign bonds?

PROBLEMS

3.1 (**Asset Valuation**) Janice Johnson is estimating the value of an asset she purchased. The required rate of return is 10 percent. Janice expects cash flows of $7,500 at the end of each of the next 15 years. What is the value of the asset?

3.2 (**Asset Valuation**) An asset owned by the Hoenshel Company provides after-tax cash flows of $1,000 for five years and $2,900 in the sixth year. What is the value of the asset if the required rate of return is nine percent?

3.3 (**Bond Valuation**) The McLain Corporation issued a 30-year bond five years ago. The bond has a 10 percent annual coupon interest rate and a $1,000 par value. The required annual rate of return for bonds of similar risk is nine percent. What is the value of the bond today?

3.4 (**Bond Valuation**) Miller Machinery, Inc., issued a 20-year, $1,000 par value bond three years ago. The bond pays $45 of interest semiannually ($90 per year). If the required annual rate of return is 10 percent, what is the value of the bond? (BOND)

3.5 (**Bond Valuation**) Poindexter Corporation has a $1,000 par value bond that matures in nine years. The coupon rate on this semiannual bond is seven percent. If the required annual rate of return is eight percent, what is the value of the bond today?

3.6 (**Yield to Maturity**) The 10 percent, semiannual payment bond of Robinson Sporting Goods, Inc., is selling for $1,200. What is the yield to maturity if the bond has 17 years left until it matures? (BOND)

3.7 (**Yield to Call**) The Rodriguez Company issued a 30-year, nine percent, semiannual payment bond two years ago. What is the yield to call if the bond could originally be called for $1,075 after five years and is now selling for $950? (BOND)

3.8 (**Yield to Call**) The Lawrence James Company issued a 25-year, six percent, semiannual payment bond one year ago. If the bond could originally be called for $1,100 after six years, and is now selling for par, what is the yield to call? (BOND)

3.9 **(Yield to Maturity)** You purchased a $1,000 par value, 30-year, zero coupon bond, two years after issue. If you paid $195.63 for the bond, what is the annual yield to maturity? (BOND)

3.10 **(Yield to Maturity)** The T.R. Rucker Company issued a $1,000 par value, 10 percent, semiannual bond several years ago. Today, with 10 years left until maturity, the bond is quoted at 90 3/8. Find the bond's yield to maturity. (BOND)

3.11 **(Perpetual Bond Valuation)** You inherited a $100 annual coupon payment, perpetual bond, with the next payment due one year from today. If bonds of similar risk are paying 12 percent, what is the value of your bond?

3.12 **(Interest Rate Risk)** You own two bonds, a five-year bond and a 10-year bond, each with a $1,000 par value and a 10 percent annual coupon rate. The required annual rate of return for bonds of similar risk is 12 percent. Show by calculation which bond increases more in value if the required annual rate of return for both bonds declines to eight percent.

3.13 **(Yield to Maturity)** The Browning Company issued a $1,000 par value, semiannual bond three years ago. The bond pays a total of $95 in interest each year, has 17 years left until maturity, and is selling for $1,208.21. What is the yield to maturity? (BOND)

3.14 **(Preferred Stock Valuation)** Modern Bathrooms issued nine percent, $100 par value preferred stock three years ago. The required annual rate of return is 10 percent. What is the value of the preferred stock?

3.15 **(Preferred Stock Valuation)** Westbury Retirement Homes issued perpetual preferred stock with a total annual dividend of $11 and a $100 par value. If the required annual rate of return is eight percent, what is the value of the preferred stock?

3.16 **(Preferred Stock Valuation and Effective Rate of Return)** The Billiard Ball, Inc. issued perpetual preferred stock with a total annual dividend of $15 and a $100 par value. If dividends are paid quarterly, what is the effective rate of return when the preferred stock is selling for $80? If the required annual rate of return is now 10 percent, what is the value of the preferred stock?

3.17 **(Common Stock Valuation)** Today, Kay Singley purchased stock in the Barenger Corporation. Yesterday, the company paid a dividend of $1.48 per share. Kay believes the dividends will grow at a rate of six percent indefinitely. If the required rate of return for stock in this risk class is 10 percent, what is the value of the stock today?

3.18 **(Common Stock Valuation)** You own stock in Johnston Properties, Inc. You expect a $2.00 dividend one year from today and an indefinite growth rate of eight percent. The required rate of return for stock in this risk class is 14 percent. What is the value of the stock?

3.19 **(Common Stock Valuation)** John Boynton purchased the stock of T.R. Major Corporation. He expects a $3.00 dividend one year from today and an indefinite negative growth rate of 10 percent. The required rate of return for stock in this risk class is 10 percent. What is the value of the stock?

3.20 **(Common Stock Valuation)** The stock of Hawkes Publishing Company is currently selling for $35 per share. A potential investor in the company expects the dividend to be $1.60 next year, with an indefinite growth after that time of five percent. If the required rate of return for stock in this risk class is 10 percent, should she purchase the stock?

3.21 **(Common Stock Valuation)** The Computer Shoppe, Inc., paid a dividend of $3.50 today. Because of increasing competition in the industry, earnings and dividends will decline by five percent per year. The required rate of return for similar companies is 15 percent. What is the value of the stock?

3.22 **(Common Stock Valuation)** Investors expect PrintoGraph, Inc., to pay a $2.00 dividend next year. Dividends will grow at a seven percent rate for three more years. The value of the stock four years from today will be $52.43. If the required rate of return for stock in this risk class is 12 percent, what is the value of the stock?

3.23 **(Common Stock Valuation)** You are evaluating the stock you own in the Lowe Company. You expect a $1.50 dividend one year from today and a $2.00 dividend in two years. Past that point, dividends will grow indefinitely at a nine percent rate. If the required rate of return is 13 percent, what is the value of the stock?

3.24 **(Common Stock Valuation)** The Morton Company just issued a dividend of $2.25 on its common stock. Management expects dividends to grow for the next two years at a 30 percent rate. After that time, the growth rate will be eight percent for the indefinite future. If the required rate of return is 14 percent, what is the value of the stock?

3.25 **(Estimating Growth Rate)** Brickle Construction Company paid a dividend today, 1992, of $1.75. Dividends per share (DPS) for the last five years are shown below:

Year	DPS
1988	$1.28
1989	1.40
1990	1.50
1991	1.60
1992	1.75

Estimate the growth rate of the stock.

A Case Problem

omputech, Inc., was a leading wholesale distributor of computer supplies and accessories. The company distributed over 3,000 products to more than 10,000 customers, who then resold to end-users. Brand names included Hewlett-Packard, IBM, NEC, Panasonic, and Digital. The principal products were laser toner, ink jet cartridges, printer ribbons, diskettes, and storage files. The final customers for these computer supplies and accessories were large and medium-sized institutions, rather than individuals and small businesses.

Net sales for Computech had increased from $30 million to $180 million over the previous five years. During the same period, operating income had risen from $690,000 to $4.9 million. This growth was the result of offering popular products at competitive prices while maintaining a high level of customer service.

The company believed that operating efficiency and cost control were critical factors in maintaining success. As a result, the organization assigned profit and cost center responsibilities to managers, with compensation tied to these objectives. To increase operating efficiency and improve cost control, Computech planned to invest in various management information systems. To attract new customers and expand its product line, the company also planned to start a software division with approximately 500 software titles.

> *Computech had historically relied upon bank borrowings, trade credit, and internally generated funds to finance its operations and expansion.*

Computech had historically relied upon bank borrowings, trade credit, and internally generated funds to finance its operations and expansion. Two years earlier the company had offered 1,000,000 shares of common stock and warrants to purchase additional shares. As a result of these transactions, the debt ratio was significantly lower than those of similar companies in the industry.

To finance the expansion and repurchase warrants, Computech planned the sale of $10.8 million in 10 percent, annual, sinking fund debentures. The net proceeds, after deducting $500,000 in underwriting expenses, were $10.3 million. The debentures were subject to redemption over the 30 years of the issue through a $360,000-per-year sinking fund. The debentures would be redeemed at 100 percent of their principal amount plus accrued interest.

Harry Alston, vice president and secretary of Computech, was interested in calculating the after-tax cost of the debentures. He knew by studying the previous year's corporate tax return that the marginal tax rate was 40 percent.

Leading Questions

1. What amount of interest would be paid each year, on a before-tax and on an after-tax basis?
2. What are the cash flows for years 0 through 30?
3. What is the discount rate that causes the equivalent cash flow to be 0?

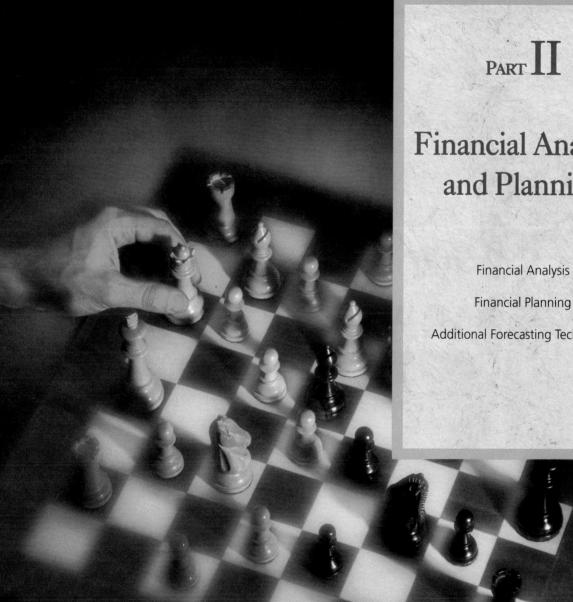

WHERE CREDIT IS DUE

The smart investor looks at both stock and bond investments. For either one, the investor has a lot of analysis to undertake. In the past, analyzing corporate bonds was mundane: calculate a few balance sheet ratios and check rating agencies such as Standard and Poor's or Moody's.

That simplistic approach isn't adequate in today's markets. Bond markets are volatile and are loaded with issues

4 Financial Analysis

that would not have found a market a generation ago. For instance, 55 to 60 percent of all industrial companies examined by S&P are rated below investment grade—the minimum rating for purchase by most financial institutions. At one time, debt had to be secured by tangible assets. Today, however, debt is often incurred to purchase businesses at prices in excess of the value of the physical assets. Therefore, cash flow is what really matters. Says Paul Ross, managing director of corporate bond research at Salomon Brothers, "Credit analysis has clearly moved away from the balance sheet and toward the income statement."

Standard and Poor's and Moody's are working to meet the changing needs of investors by emphasizing future cash flow and operating margins when arriving at their ratings. Unfortunately, rating agencies sometimes still react too slowly to changes in the risk level of bond issuers.

Mr. Marko Budgyk, a manager of credit analysis at a Los Angeles-based financial consulting firm, successfully examines relative credit quality based primarily on the interplay of market value, leverage, and volatility. He analyzes leverage by going beyond the traditional analysts who compute leverage in terms of debt versus historical cost of assets; he calculates leverage ratios based in what assets are worth today. The difference in the computation of leverage computed in the usual way versus using market values can be astounding. For example, Tele-Communications, the cable operator, has a scary seven-to-one leverage ratio using traditional methods and only a two-to-one ratio using equity market values.

Using traditional analysis, Castle and Cooke's bonds would show a lower rating than warranted by a market-value analysis. An expected rating of BBB- for one of Castle and Cooke's bonds understates the quality of their bonds. A traditional analysis might emphasize spotty but improving earnings. The stock prices, however, reflect

some excellent collateral held by the company. To supplement the financial analysis based on market value, leverage, and volatility, Mr. Budgyk takes into account other factors such as the terms of the bonds and callability. In addition, Mr. Budgyk examines risk by computing the volatility of changes in the firm's stock price. The more variable these changes, the riskier the bond.

How effective is Mr. Budgyk's financial analysis methods? A report published in March 1987 shows that of 24 issuers pegged as likely to run into trouble, 12 are in default, and three others escaped default by being acquired. The market-based analysis is not perfect, however. A takeover may cause the market value to become distorted. Mr. Budgyk said, "If the stock market misses something, we miss it, too."

Financial statement analysis is important to nearly all the stakeholders in a firm. Although this vignette focused on statement analysis from an investor's perspective, other stakeholders are intensely interested in information regarding the financial health of a firm. Decisions by management, creditors, suppliers, and even customers rely on an accurate financial picture of a firm's financial activities. This chapter will bridge your understanding of financial statements regardless of the particular perspective.

Source: "Where Credit Is Due," Forbes, June 27, 1992, pp. 224–229. Reprinted by permission of FORBES magazine. © Forbes, Inc. 1992.

Who is interested in the financial health of a company? The answer: investors, lenders, managers, employees, customers, and suppliers. All have an interest in seeing that the company prospers, but each stakeholder views the company differently. Stockholders and bondholders are especially interested in the generation of cash flows. Bankers are concerned with making sound lending decisions. Higher-level managers concentrate on the overall performance of the company, while lower-level managers focus on the operating performance of their units. Employees think about keeping their jobs. Customers and suppliers care about maintaining the company in the marketplace.

But as a financial manager, how should *you* view the company? Another answer: in such a way as to maximize the value of the common stock of the company. To do this, you need to understand how company cash flows result from the ownership of assets.

In this chapter, we will prepare a statement of cash flows. Preparation of this statement is part of the financial planning process and allows us to make better financial decisions. Since we will use information from the income statement and the balance sheet, let's look at the first of these two statements.

THE INCOME STATEMENT

Income Statement

The **income statement** for a company shows the total revenues and total expenses, including income taxes, over a stated period of time. The income statement is also called the earnings statement or the profit and loss statement. The statement shows the difference between total revenues and total expenses, which is called net income if positive and net loss if negative.

The reporting period for an income statement is the stated period of time over which the revenues and expenses are recognized. According to generally accepted accounting principles (GAAP), companies do not prepare income statements for more than 12 months. Companies sometimes prepare interim statements for periods of less than 12 months, typically for one, three, or six months. Companies also prepare year-to-date interim income statements, through the end of any month.

Income statements are normally prepared on an accrual basis, as opposed to a cash basis. With the accrual basis, revenues are recognized when sales are made, and expenses are recognized when they are incurred. With the cash basis, revenues are recognized when payment is received, and expenses are recognized when payment is made. Under the accrual basis, expenses are recognized in the reporting period they were incurred even though they may be paid in another period. Expenses paid in one period but not actually incurred until a later period are called prepaid expenses. Expenses incurred in one pe-

TABLE 4.1 Martin Corporation: Income Statement for the Year Ended December 31, 19X4
• • • • • • • (in thousands, components as a percentage of sales)

Net sales	$1,000,000	100.0%
Cost of goods sold	700,000	70.0
Gross profit	$ 300,000	30.0
Selling and administrative expenses	100,000	10.0
Depreciation expense	40,000	4.0
Earnings before interest and taxes (EBIT)	$ 160,000	16.0
Interest expense	10,000	1.0
Earnings before taxes (EBT)	$ 150,000	15.0
Taxes	60,000	6.0
Earnings after taxes (EAT)	$ 90,000	9.0
Preferred stock dividends	5,000	0.5
Earnings available to common shareholders	$ 85,000	8.5%
Actual shares outstanding		50,000,000
Earnings per share		$1.70
Dividends per share		$0.85
Market price per share		$26.125

riod and paid in a later period are called accruals. With accrual-based income statements, we must prepare the Statement of Cash Flows in order to understand the effect on cash flows.

Table 4.1 provides an example of an income statement of the Martin Corporation for the year ended December 31, 19X4[1]. The percentages in the rightmost column represent a **common-size income statement.** In such statements, all components are divided by sales and are expressed as percentages. This statement is quite valuable in comparing financial performance from year to year since it adjusts the components for the level of sales[2].

Common-Size Income Statement

Income Statement Components

Let's look more closely at the components of the income statement. Net sales, at the top, are gross sales less sales discounts and sales returns and allowances. Gross sales include all of the receipts over the reporting period, including credit sales. These receipts are lowered by discounts, which customers earn by prompt

[1] The financial statements and general approach in this chapter apply primarily to nonfinancial/industrial corporations. Analysis of financial/nonindustrial organizations is quite different.
[2] To reduce information to valuable form, see Lloyd Brandt, Jr., Joseph R. Danos, and J. Herman Brasseaux, "Financial Statement Analysis: Benefits and Pitfalls," *The Practical Accountant*, May 1989, pp. 35–47.

payment of their accounts or by purchasing large quantities of product; and by returns, which reflect cancellation of bills when merchandise is returned.

The next component, cost of goods sold, is the beginning inventory plus the net cost of purchases (or the cost of goods manufactured, for a manufacturer), less the ending inventory. The net cost of purchases includes transportation costs and adjustments for discounts and returns and allowances. The cost of goods manufactured consists of raw materials used, direct labor, and overhead expense. A service company has no cost of goods sold.

Gross profit is net sales less cost of goods sold. For a wholesaler or retailer, it reflects the markup on purchases. For a manufacturing company, gross profit represents the value added in the manufacturing process. For a service company, it is equal to net sales.

Any normal business expenses, except expenses that are a part of cost of goods sold, are called operating expenses. For the Martin Corporation, operating expenses comprise selling and administrative expenses and depreciation expenses. This general category of expenses often includes officers' salaries.

Earnings Before Interest and Taxes

Earnings before interest and taxes (EBIT), or operating profit, is gross profit less the various operating expenses. EBIT reflects how well management is doing in generating revenues and controlling expenses.

Earnings before taxes (EBT) are EBIT, plus other income less other expenses, less interest expense. This component includes earnings or expenses not incurred in the production of products or services. Other income may, for example, be rental income. Other expenses may include a variety of things, such as a loss from the sale of a fixed asset at less than book value. For the Martin Corporation, interest is the key component in determining earnings before taxes.

Earnings After Taxes

Earnings after taxes (EAT), or net income, are earnings before taxes less corporate income taxes. This is the bottom line of the income statement. Earnings after taxes are often expressed on a per share basis, as earnings per share. The income statement also frequently includes dividends per share.

Income Statement Analysis

The income statement means more when it can be compared with income statements from other years[3]. Table 4.2 provides income statements of the Martin Corporation for the year ended December 31, 19X4 and the next year, 19X5.

The net sales for the Martin Corporation increased 5.0 percent over the one-year period. To analyze the importance of this increase, we could compare it with what similar companies have done over this period. For example, if sales

[3] In this chapter, we are analyzing the company from the point of view of an outsider who is not familiar with company operations. As a result, we cannot make specific recommendations—the questions we would normally ask management cannot be answered.

TABLE 4.2 Martin Corporation: Income Statements for the Years Ended December 31
(in millions, components as a percentage of sales)

	19X4		19X5	
Net sales	$1,000	100.0%	$1,050	100.0%
Cost of goods sold	700	70.0	756	72.0
Gross profit	$ 300	30.0	$ 294	28.0
Selling and administrative expenses	100	10.0	105	10.0
Depreciation expense	40	4.0	42	4.0
Earnings before interest and taxes (EBIT)	$ 160	16.0	$ 147	14.0
Interest expense	10	1.0	21	2.0
Earnings before taxes (EBT)	$ 150	15.0	$ 126	12.0
Taxes	60	6.0	42	4.0
Earnings after taxes (EAT)	$ 90	9.0	$ 84	8.0
Preferrred stock dividends	5	0.5	5	0.5
Earnings available to common shareholders	$ 85	8.5%	$ 79	7.5%
Actual shares outstanding		50,000,000		50,000,000
Earnings per share		$1.70		$1.58
Dividends per share		$0.85		$0.85
Market price per share		$26.125		$25.250

in the industry decreased by 20.0 percent over the same period, then a 5.0 percent increase is good.

A company's net sales depend on the quantity of products sold and the selling price. It is useful to have unit sales figures for the two years, since price changes may mask changes in sales volume. For example, net sales for the Martin Corporation increased by 5.0 percent from 19X4 to 19X5. If the inflation rate is 5.0 percent and prices increased accordingly, then there is no real growth in net sales for the Martin Corporation. When unit sales figures are not available, it is especially important to use the inflation rate to estimate real growth in sales.

If we assume that the company has in fact sustained no real growth while competitors have experienced decreased sales, we should investigate the underlying causes. A steady sales volume for the company might reflect the introduction of new products or a more aggressive marketing strategy. For example, the Martin Corporation may have added a new product to its line and attracted new customers through a vigorous marketing campaign just to stay even.

The cost of goods sold has increased from 70.0 to 72.0 percent of sales. This is consistent with the introduction of a new product. Of course, we would need more information to confirm this conclusion. Other reasons for increased costs may exist. A new labor contract may cause a jump in costs, for example.

Gross Profit Margin

Gross profit must be large enough to cover the company's other operating expenses. The **gross profit margin**—gross profit divided by sales—for the company declined from 30.0 to 28.0 percent. To evaluate this decline, we should examine the trend of the gross profit margin for the company over a number of years, if this information is available. As with net sales, we can compare the gross profit margin with those of other companies in the same industry. We may find that the industry in general is experiencing similar problems.

Operating expenses—that is selling and administrative expenses and depreciation expenses—remained remarkably stable for the Martin Corporation. This does not mean that operating expenses are either high or low. To determine that, we would need to compare the percentage of 14.0 percent with the industry average.

To evaluate the job management is doing, we should examine a detailed breakdown of operating expenses. This includes an analysis of controllable and noncontrollable costs. Controllable costs include items such as travel, entertainment, and bonuses, all of which are subject to abuse (from the point of view of lenders and the IRS), especially in closely held corporations. Noncontrollable costs involve salaries, utilities, and lease payments—costs influenced by outside factors and thus not as easily controlled by management.

Earnings before interest and taxes, the operating profit for the company, reflects how efficiently the management of the Martin Corporation is using company resources in its operations. This figure shows how well the company is controlling costs in the generation of net sales. The decrease from 16.0 to 14.0 percent is the result of the cost of goods sold increasing by 2.0 percent. This reinforces our earlier indication to investigate the increase in the cost of goods sold.

Interest expense increased from 1.0 to 2.0 percent of net sales. Since the market rate of interest changes on a continual basis, market rate changes could be responsible for this increase. With the Martin Corporation, a probable cause for increased interest would be a greater need for borrowing due to the lower gross profit margin.

Income taxes declined from 6.0 to 4.0 percent of net sales. There are a number of possible reasons for this. First, the marginal tax rate may be lower because of the smaller earnings before taxes. Second, the company may have been able to use a number of tax credits in 19X5. Third, depreciation for tax purposes may be markedly different from the depreciation used for financial reporting. In Chapter 6, we will study Modified Accelerated Cost Recovery System (MACRS) depreciation. This type of depreciation is required for tax purposes yet is not used on financial statements.

Net Profit Margin

The **net profit margin**—earnings after taxes divided by sales—declined from 8.5 percent to 7.5 percent. The decline would have been greater had not the reduction in taxes partially offset the increases in cost of goods sold and in-

Ethical Considerations in Preparing Financial Statements

The primary goal of management is to maximize the value of its common stock. How does an investor know whether management is pursuing that goal? Financial statements provide an investor or potential investors with information to evaluate this question. To minimize the *garbage in, garbage out* phenomenon, firms follow certain reporting procedures uniformly recognized across the business and regulatory environment.

Enmeshed in the procedures are certain underlying principles which include the concept of materiality and the concept of conservatism. Their interpretation is regarded both in legal and ethical terms. Without these principles and attendance to reporting procedures, the rules of GAAP, financial reporting would be suspect to readers of a company's financials. When these procedures or principles are violated and the markets become aware of such violations, the intrinsic value of a company is reevaluated. The signal to the markets is that a company is not maximizing the wealth of its shareholders but indeed is pursuing some other unknown objectives—see agency problems. Shareholders can find themselves holding a share of stock whose value is questionable.

Shareholders of Chambers Development Company, a waste management concern, found themselves in such a situation after the company announced that it would have to revise their 1991 financial statements. This revision changed previously stated net income of $49.9 million to $1.5 million, the result of a change in the method of reporting expenses by Chambers. The central issue was the practice of putting off recognizing $37 million in indirect costs. Other companies in the industry recognize these costs immediately. The concept of accrual accounting plainly states that expenses are recognized when incurred, not at some later date. By deferring these expenses, Chambers overstated their earnings.

On the date of the announcement of the earnings change, the price of Chambers stock plunged 62 percent or $19 per share. Earnings before interest and taxes, the operating profit for a company, reflects how efficiently management is using company resources in its operations. With new operating profit information, the level of efficiency was reanalyzed.

Of further concern to investors was the apparent reason for the revision: The auditors refused to sign off on the reports unless Chambers revised its figures. To the financial markets this was a question of ethics. In essence, the company appeared to provide accurate information to the marketplace only when its hand was forced. Also, this matter raises questions regarding other reports made by Chambers. Is the information correct to the best of their knowledge? Is management pursuing the goal of shareholder wealth maximization? Can any reliable financial analysis be done involving the value of Chambers stock?

Source: Gabriella Stern and Laurie P. Cohen, "Chambers Development Switches Accounting Plan," *The Wall Street Journal*, May 19, 1992. Reprinted by permission of the The Wall Street Journal, © 1992 Dow Jones & Company, Inc. All Rights Reserved Worldwide.

terest expense. As with other components of the income statement, we should compare the net profit margin with what has occurred in the past and with similar businesses. In this way, we will gain perspective.

THE BALANCE SHEET

Balance Sheet

Balance sheet analysis is the next step after income statement analysis. Unlike the income statement, which displays how a company performed over a specified time period, the **balance sheet** provides a financial representation of the assets of and claims against a company at a given point in time. The balance sheet is based on the accounting equation:

$$\text{Assets} = \text{Liabilities} + \text{Stockholders' Equity}$$

This identity is always in balance. An increase or decrease in assets is accompanied by an increase (decrease) or decrease (increase) in liabilities and/or stockholders' equity.

The balance sheet records company investment and financing decisions. The asset segment shows the size and composition of company assets. The liabilities and stockholders' equity segment presents how a company's assets are financed. The balance sheet also is used in the preparation of the statement of cash flows.

The type of business in which a company engages influences the proportions of assets, liabilities, and stockholders' equity on its balance sheet. Manufacturing and farming demand a large quantity of raw materials and sizable fixed assets to operate, thereby requiring a high degree of long-term debt and equity. Wholesalers need smaller fixed assets, focusing their assets in accounts receivable and inventory, primarily financing with short-term liabilities. Retailers require more fixed assets than wholesalers, typically financing with a greater amount of short-term and long-term debt. Service companies are highly variable in the makeup of their balance sheets, since these companies include such diverse organizations as restaurants, utilities, and consulting firms.

The management philosophy of a company also affects the distribution of the balance sheet. Conservative companies have a high degree of stockholders' equity and a low amount of liabilities, and these companies tend to use a relatively lower level of receivables and a higher level of cash[4]. This approach may limit sales growth in the short run but may position the company for slow and steady growth in the future. In contrast, an aggressive company focuses on increasing sales and market share. This requires higher debt, receivables, and inventory, consequently reducing the amount of equity.

Table 4.3 provides an example of a balance sheet for the Martin Corporation on December 31, 19X4. The percentages in the rightmost column represent a

[4] The term *conservative* is relative to the industry. Utilities have a high degree of debt, yet are generally considered to be conservative as a group.

TABLE 4.3 Martin Corporation: Balance Sheet as of December 31, 19X4
(in thousands, accounts as a percentage of total assets)

ASSETS		
Current assets:		
Cash	$ 20,000	4.0%
Marketable securities	5,000	1.0
Accounts receivable	80,000	16.0
Inventory	120,000	24.0
Total current assets	$225,000	45.0
Fixed assets:		
Property, plant, and equipment	$475,000	95.0
Less: Accumulated depreciation	200,000	40.0
Net property, plant, and equipment	$275,000	55.0
Total assets	$500,000	100.0%
LIABILITIES AND STOCKHOLDERS' EQUITY		
Current liabilities:		
Accounts payable	$ 40,000	8.0%
Notes payable	60,000	12.0
Current maturities, long-term debt	5,000	1.0
Accrued expenses	15,000	3.0
Total current liabilities	$120,000	24.0
Long-term debt	40,000	8.0
Total liabilities	$160,000	32.0
Stockholders' equity:		
Preferred stock	$ 50,000	10.0
Common stock ($1 par)	50,000	10.0
Capital in excess of par	100,000	20.0
Retained earnings	140,000	28.0
Total stockholders' equity	$340,000	68.0
Total liabilities and stockholders' equity	$500,000	100.0%

common-size balance sheet in which all components are divided by total assets and are expressed as percentages.

Common-Size Balance Sheet

Balance Sheet Accounts

To analyze a balance sheet, we must become familiar with the balance sheet accounts. We begin our discussion with asset accounts and continue with liability and equity accounts.

Currency is usually deposited in checking accounts for use in operations. In examining the cash account, we must determine if the stated amount in the checking account is available for transactions. Banks often require a borrower to maintain a compensating balance, limiting the amount that can be withdrawn. Some businesses also need cash for daily transactions, and this cash is not accessible for other purposes.

Marketable securities are used for the temporary investment of excess cash. The value of this account is the current market value or the cost, whichever is lower. Companies invest in these short-term securities in order to earn income in the form of interest. On some balance sheets, cash and marketable securities are combined into one account because they are nearly the same.

Accounts receivable are credit sales that have not been collected. We need to check both the size and the quality of this account. The size of accounts receivable will be larger than competitors if credit terms are more liberal or if collection practices are lax. The quality of accounts receivable can be checked by an aging schedule. Aging is a method of analyzing the account by breaking down the receivables into how long they have been on the books. The higher the age of a receivable, the less likely it will be paid.

Inventory is an account whose definition depends on the type of business. For a manufacturing company, inventory includes raw materials, work-in-process, and finished goods inventories. A retailer or wholesaler considers products purchased for resale as inventory. A service company determines that supplies are inventory. In valuing inventory, we should decide if it is saleable or useable at its stated value. If it is not, we should reduce the value of inventory to its market value. Also, in checking inventory, we should find out how the inventory is being physically counted.

Total current assets equal cash plus those assets that can be turned into cash within a year. In the case of the Martin Corporation, this includes cash, marketable securities, accounts receivable, and inventory. The value of current assets is in their liquidity, their ability to be quickly turned into cash.

Fixed assets include tangible assets such as property, plant, and equipment, as well as intangible assets such patents and trademarks. The value of net fixed assets equals the original cost less depreciation—the book value of the fixed assets. In evaluating net fixed assets, we should be more concerned with the market value, or possibly liquidation value, not book value. In this regard, the valuation of land is especially important, since it often appreciates in value. Also, the flexibility of fixed assets should be considered because plant and equipment that are highly specialized may have a lower resale value.

Accounts payable are credit sales extended by suppliers. They provide a spontaneous source of financing that is interest-free. We should determine if the company is paying a high cost by not taking advantage of discounts. Some companies move in the other direction by paying late, but these companies take the chance of having suppliers refuse credit for new purchases. This type of behavior may signal liquidity problems, since companies with cash can take advantage of discounts.

Notes payable are a form of short-term financing from bankers or other creditors. The quantity of money borrowed is often based on a line of credit, an agreement between the company and a bank as to the maximum amount of credit allowed during the year. We should decide if the credit limit is adequate for the needs of the company, especially at those seasonal times when accounts receivable and inventory are high. In the next chapter, we will use the cash budget to help determine the credit limit.

Current maturities, long-term debt is the principal portion of long-term debt due over the next twelve months. Be cautious if this account includes a balloon payment, since it may require additional financing. Companies usually make these payments from after-tax profits, rather than using current assets, so we should see if adequate earnings are available for this purpose.

Accrued expenses are costs that have already been expensed through the income statement, yet have not been paid. They may include such items as wages, withholding taxes, sales taxes, and even utilities. We should be concerned if the amount in this account is relatively large. We may find, for example, that a company has failed to make required payments to the Internal Revenue Service. This would be especially important since the IRS may exact interest and penalties.

Total current liabilities are liabilities that may be paid off within a year, normally through the conversion of current assets to cash. In the case of the Martin Corporation, this includes accounts payable, notes payable, current maturities of long-term debt, and accrued expenses. We should be particularly interested in the relative size of total current assets compared with total current liabilities, since this relationship measures the ability of a company to pay its maturing obligations.

Long-term debt normally takes the form of term loans or bonds. A term loan is a loan agreement between a borrowing company and a lending financial institution. Typically, these loans range from 3 to 15 years. A bond (discussed in detail in Chapter 12) is an agreement between a borrowing company and the holder of the bond. Bonds usually range from 10 to 30 years in length.

Stockholders' equity is the difference between the total assets and total liabilities of a company. This section is divided into four accounts: preferred stock, common stock, capital in excess of par, and retained earnings. The preferred stock account gives the number of shares of preferred stock multiplied by the par value, normally $100. The common stock account gives the number of shares of common stock outstanding multiplied by the par value[5]. The par value for common stock is usually much smaller than the price for which the stock was originally sold. Capital in excess of par is the equity generated above

---

[5] This discussion assumes we are not dealing with no-par stock (stock without par value).

the par value. It is the selling price less the par value multiplied by the number of shares of common stock outstanding. Retained earnings represent all earnings that have been retained since the corporation was formed.

Balance Sheet Analysis

The balance sheet, like the income statement, means more when it is compared with balance sheets from other years. Table 4.4 provides balance sheets of the Martin Corporation as of December 31, 19X4, and the following year, 19X5.

TABLE 4.4 Martin Corporation: Balance Sheets as of December 31
(in millions, accounts as a percentage of total assets)

ASSETS	19X4		19X5	
Current assets:				
Cash	$ 20.0	4.0%	$ 21.0	4.5%
Marketable securities	5.0	1.0	5.2	1.1
Accounts receivable	80.0	16.0	85.0	18.1
Inventory	120.0	24.0	125.8	26.7
Total current assets	$225.0	45.0	$237.0	50.4
Fixed assets:				
Property, plant, and equipment	$475.0	95.0	$475.0	101.1
Less: Accumulated depreciation	200.0	40.0	242.0	51.5
Net property, plant, and equipment	$275.0	55.0	$233.0	49.6
Total assets	$500.0	100.0%	$470.0	100.0%

LIABILITIES AND STOCKHOLDERS' EQUITY	19X4		19X5	
Current liabilities:				
Accounts payable	$ 40.0	8.0%	38.5	8.2%
Notes payable	60.0	12.0	10.0	2.1
Current maturities,long-term debt	5.0	1.0	5.0	1.1
Accrued expenses	15.0	3.0	10.0	2.1
Total current liabilities	$120.0	24.0	$ 63.5	13.5
Long-term debt	40.0	8.0	30.0	6.4
Total liabilities	$160.0	32.0	$ 93.5	19.9
Stockholders' equity:				
Preferred stock	$ 50.0	10.0	$ 50.0	10.6
Common stock ($1 par)	50.0	10.0	50.0	10.6
Capital in excess of par	100.0	20.0	100.0	21.3
Retained earnings	140.0	28.0	176.5	37.6
Total stockholders' equity	$340.0	68.0	$376.5	80.1
Total liabilities and stockholders' equity	$500.0	100.0%	$470.0	100.0%

Total current assets increased by 5.3 percent from 19X4 to 19X5, 237.0 divided by 225.0 equals 1.053. Since we expect current assets to increase spontaneously with sales, the increase of 5.3 percent is in line with the 5.0 percent growth in sales we saw earlier. The expansion of current assets from 45.0 percent to 50.4 percent of total assets is of little consequence, since it is the result of the lower book value of net property, plant, and equipment.

There is no change in fixed assets over the two years. That means the company increased sales without adding fixed assets. This suggests the Martin Corporation was not operating at full capacity in 19X4. We should check to see if further increases in sales would cause capacity problems.

The book value of property, plant, and equipment decreased from $275.0 million to $233.0 million. We should investigate what plans have been made to replace equipment as it wears out.

Over the two-year period, Martin Corporation used $12.0 million to increase current assets, $10.0 million to decrease long-term debt, and $56.5 million to reduce total current liabilities. The total of $78.5 million is equal to the $42.0 million decrease in property, plant, and equipment plus the $36.5 million increase in retained earnings.

Purpose of the Statement of Cash Flows

The Financial Accounting Standards Board (FASB) was created in 1972 to establish financial accounting standards. In 1987, the FASB issued its new statement of cash flows. This statement provides information that enables credit professionals and others to assess an enterprise's liquidity, financial flexibility, profitability, and risk more easily.

The FASB suggested that the statement be used to: (1) assess an enterprise's ability to generate positive future net cash flows, (2) assess an enterprise's ability to meet its obligations and to pay dividends, and its needs for financing, (3) assess the effects of an enterprise's financial position of both its cash and noncash investing and financing during the reporting period, and (4) assess the reasons for differences between net income and associated cash receipts and payments. The statement of cash flows requires cash flow disclosure by functional areas of operating, investing, and financing. The most scrutinized area is likely to be cash from operating activities.

Although the statement of cash flows is valuable, users may believe that cash-basis net income is always a superior measure to accrual-based income from the income statement. An unsophisticated user, for example, may falsely conclude that cash flow per share of common stock is an accurate measure of cash available for stockholders. The FASB, keenly aware of this concern, has expressly prohibited reporting cash flow per share. Cash flow per share can be easily calculated, however, and is sometimes published.

Source: Linda H. Kistler and John G. Hamer, "Understanding the New Statement of Cash Flows," *Corporate Accounting*, Winter 1988, pp. 3–9; and Dennis F. Wasniewski, "Statement of Cash Flows," *Business Credit,* September 1988, pp. 26–28, published by the National Association of Credit Management.

STATEMENT OF CASH FLOWS

A statement of cash flows is constructed using information from the income statement and balance sheet. We will use the statements from the Martin Corporation for this purpose. What we need is two consecutive balance sheets and two consecutive income statements.

Statement of Cash Flows

The **statement of cash flows** shows over an accounting period the cash flows from operating, investing, and financing activities, as well as how these activities have affected liquidity. Before November 1987, the Financial Accounting Standards Board (FASB) allowed the use of the statement of changes in financial position. The new statement, the statement of cash flows, focuses on the importance of cash flow to the operations of a company.

We can prepare the statement of cash flows by either the direct method or the indirect method. The direct method deducts only those operating expenses that consumed cash from cash sales. The indirect method begins with net income and adjusts for items that affected net income that did not involve cash. This text includes the indirect method because it is the most commonly used approach in finance.

Preparation of the Statement

Table 4.5 shows the statement of cash flows for the Martin Corporation. To prepare this statement, we use the two income statements in Table 4.2 and the two balance sheets in Table 4.4. Any statement of cash flows includes three sections: (1) cash flows from operating activities, (2) cash flows from investing activities, and (3) cash flows from financing activities. These sections are combined to yield the net increase or decrease in cash.

The first section of the statement records cash flows from operating activities. Notice, we converted the items from millions to thousands of dollars. To prepare this section, we do the following:

1. List net income for the second year (net income of $84 million in 19X5).
2. Enter the amount of depreciation for the second year (depreciation of $42 million in 19X5).
3. Enter, except for financing items, each current asset component that increases as a negative number and each current asset component that decreases as a positive number (an increase in accounts receivable of $5.0 million and an increase in inventory of $5.8 million).
4. Enter, except for financing items, each current liability component that increases as a positive number and each current liability component that decreases as a negative number (a decrease in accounts payable of $1.5 million and a decrease in accrued expenses of $5.0 million).

TABLE 4.5 Martin Corporation: Statement of Cash Flows for the Year Ended December 31, 19X5 (in thousands)

Cash flows from operating activities:	
Net income	$ 84,000
Depreciation	42,000
Increase in accounts receivable	(5,000)
Increase in inventory	(5,800)
Decrease in accounts payable	(1,500)
Decrease in accrued expenses	(5,000)
Net cash flow from operating activities	$ 108,700
Cash flows from investing activities:	
Purchases of marketable securities	$ (200)
Cash flows from financing activities:	
Decrease in notes payable	$ (50,000)
Decrease in long term debt	(10,000)
Dividends paid	(47,500)
Net cash provided by financing activities	$(107,500)
Net increase (decrease) in cash	$ 1,000

Next, we determine the cash flows from investing activities as follows:

1. Enter increases in marketable securities as a negative number and decreases in marketable securities as a positive number (purchases of marketable securities of $0.2 million).
2. Enter increases in loans as a negative number and decreases in loans as a positive number (none).
3. Enter cash paid to acquire plant assets as a negative number and proceeds from the sale of plant assets as a positive number (none).

The second section of Table 4.5 records cash flows from investing activities.

Finally, to determine the cash flows from financing activities, we do the following:

1. Enter increases in short-term debt as a positive number and decreases in short-term debt as a negative number (decrease in notes payable of $50.0 million).
2. Enter increases in long-term debt as a positive number and decreases in long-term debt as a negative number (decrease in long-term debt of $10 million).

3. Enter increases in capital stock as a positive number and decreases as a negative number (none).
4. Enter common and preferred dividends paid as a negative number (dividends paid of $47.5 million).

The third section of Table 4.5 records cash flows from financing activities.

Interpreting the Statement

The statement of cash flows for the Martin Corporation shows that the company generated $108,700,000 from operating activities. This cash was used primarily to reduce notes payable ($50,000,000), decrease long-term debt ($10,000,000), and to pay dividends ($47,500,000). A relatively small amount of cash ($200,000) was used to purchase marketable securities.

The cash flows from operating activities came from net income ($84,000,000) and depreciation ($42,000,000). This amount was reduced by an increase in accounts receivable ($5,000,000) and an increase in inventories ($5,800,000) to yield the net cash flows from operating activities ($108,700,000).

The net increase in cash was $1,000,000. This agrees with the change in cash from $20,000,000 in 19X4 to $21,000,000 in 19X5.

RATIO ANALYSIS

Ratio analysis allows us to evaluate the financial condition of a company by examining its financial statements[6]. We do this by making comparisons within the company or with competitors, for a given year or through time.

Ratios are easy to calculate and even easier to misuse. They should form the basis for an investigation, but they are not conclusive proof of the cause of a particular problem. The value of ratio analysis is that it leads to questions whose answers may paint an accurate picture of the financial condition of the company.

There are two major limitations in the use of ratios. First, the information provided is basically historical in nature. It describes what has happened to a company over the preceding years but provides no definite indication as to future performance. Second, the significance of the ratios depends on the quality of the underlying numbers. The comparability of the accounting methods is important, especially for making industry comparisons.

Financial analysts normally group financial ratios into six categories: liquidity, activity, leverage, coverage, profitability, and market ratios. In the sections

---

[6] The ratios in this chapter may be calculated using THE FINANCIAL MANAGER (RATIO).

that follow, we will see how the individual ratios within each category are calculated for the Martin Corporation.

Liquidity Ratios

Liquidity ratios measure the ability of a company to meet its short-term obligations as they come due. If a company has sufficient liquidity, it avoids the distress of defaulting on its financial commitments. The level of liquidity required depends on the variability of the company's short-term funds flow and its need for financial flexibility. For example, a company may increase liquidity by stockpiling inventory to cover infrequent large purchases by customers.

Liquidity Ratios

One liquidity ratio is the *current ratio*, calculated by the following formula:

$$\text{Current ratio} = \frac{\text{Current assets}}{\text{Current liabilities}}$$

The Martin Corporation's current ratios are as follows:

$$\text{19X4 Current ratio} = \frac{225.0}{120.0} = 1.88$$

$$\text{19X5 Current ratio} = \frac{237.0}{63.5} = 3.73$$

The current ratio has increased greatly over the year. Although a low current ratio may show a lack of liquidity, a high current ratio may indicate idle cash, slow collection of accounts receivable, or excess inventory. In the case of Martin Corporation, the large current ratio is the result of the decrease in current liabilities.

The *quick ratio*, another liquidity ratio, is calculated by the following formula:

$$\text{Quick ratio} = \frac{\text{Cash} + \text{Marketable securities} + \text{Accounts receivable}}{\text{Current liabilities}}$$

The Martin Corporation's quick ratios are as follows:

$$\text{19X4 Quick ratio} = \frac{20.0 + 5.0 + 80.0}{120.0} = 0.88$$

$$\text{19X5 Quick ratio} = \frac{21.0 + 5.2 + 85.0}{63.5} = 1.75$$

The quick ratio, which includes only highly liquid current assets, also has increased over the year. Inventory and other less liquid assets are not included in this formulation, since they cannot be quickly converted to cash. As with the current ratio, this improvement reflects the decrease in total current liabilities.

Activity Ratios

Activity Ratios

Activity ratios measure how efficiently a company is using its assets. They accomplish this by relating sales to total assets, accounts receivable, and inventory. The *total asset turnover ratio* is calculated by the following formula:

$$\text{Total asset turnover ratio} = \frac{\text{Net sales}}{\text{Total assets}}$$

The Martin Corporation's total asset turnover ratios are as follows:

$$\text{19X4 Total asset turnover ratio} = \frac{1000.0}{500.0} = 2.00$$

$$\text{19X5 Total asset turnover ratio} = \frac{1050.0}{470.0} = 2.23$$

This ratio measures efficiency by showing the dollars in sales generated by each dollar of assets. You should understand that this ratio is based on the book value of assets, not the market value. This may cause the ratio to be higher for companies with older equipment and to drop when old equipment is replaced or when an expansion occurs. For the Martin Corporation, the increase in this ratio reflects the lower book value and an increase in asset utilization.

The *average collection period* is calculated by the following formula:

$$\text{Average collection period} = \frac{\text{Accounts receivable}}{\text{Net sales}/365}$$

The Martin Corporation's average collection periods are as follows:

$$\text{19X4 Average collection period} = \frac{80.0}{1000.0/365} = 29.2 \text{ days}$$

$$\text{19X5 Average collection period} = \frac{85.0}{1050.0/365} = 29.5 \text{ days}$$

This ratio measures the number of days it takes on the average to collect from customers on credit sales[7]. For the Martin Corporation, there is essentially no change. The credit terms of a company, discussed in detail in Chapter 17, have a strong impact on the size of this ratio.

The *days inventory*, or inventory turnover ratio, is calculated by the following formula:

[7] Sales are often used in this ratio instead of credit sales when information on credit sales is not available, even though this causes the average collection period to be understated.

$$\text{Days inventory} = \frac{\text{Inventory}}{\text{Cost of goods sold}/365}$$

The Martin Corporation's days inventory ratios are as follows:

$$\text{19X4 Days inventory} = \frac{120.0}{700/365} = 62.6 \text{ days}$$

$$\text{19X5 Days inventory} = \frac{125.8}{756/365} = 60.7 \text{ days}$$

This ratio measures selling, purchasing, and manufacturing efficiency. Significant changes in this ratio signal the analyst to ask *why*. The answer may lie in the makeup of the inventory or in the methods for calculating the cost of goods sold. For the Martin Corporation, there was a slight decline in this ratio.

Leverage Ratios

Leverage ratios measure the extent to which a company uses debt rather than equity to finance the company's assets. The higher the proportion of debt, the higher the chance of financial distress.

The *total debt to total assets ratio*, the debt ratio, is calculated by the following formula:

$$\text{Debt ratio} = \frac{\text{Total debt}}{\text{Total assets}}$$

The Martin Corporation's total debt to total assets ratios are as follows:

$$\text{19X4 Debt ratio} = \frac{160.0}{500.0} = 0.320 = 32.0\%$$

$$\text{19X5 Debt ratio} = \frac{93.5}{470.0} = 0.199 = 19.9\%$$

Total debt is total liabilities and stockholders' equity less stockholders' equity. The debt ratio declined significantly over the last year since both short-term and long-term debt were paid off. This would allow the company to finance a further sales expansion with new debt and retained earnings.

The *debt-to-net worth ratio* is calculated by the following formula:

$$\text{Debt-to-net worth ratio} = \frac{\text{Total liabilities}}{\text{Net worth}}$$

Leverage Ratios

The Martin Corporation's debt-to-net worth ratios are as follows:

$$\text{19X4 Debt-to-net worth ratio} = \frac{160.0}{290.0} = 0.552$$

$$\text{19X5 Debt-to-net worth ratio} = \frac{93.5}{326.5} = 0.286$$

This ratio measures the borrowing ability of a company. Like the debt ratio, the debt-to-net worth ratio showed strong improvement over the year.

Coverage Ratios

Coverage Ratios

Coverage ratios measure the extent to which the current debt obligations of a company are covered by the funds flowing from operations. Although a statement of cash flows provides a more complete analysis of funds flow, coverage ratios provide a quick indication of financial health.

The *times interest earned ratio* is calculated by the following formula:

$$\text{Times interest earned ratio} = \frac{\text{Earnings before interest and taxes}}{\text{Interest expense}}$$

The Martin Corporation's times interest earned ratios are as follows:

$$\text{19X4 Times interest earned ratio} = \frac{160}{10} = 16.0$$

$$\text{19X5 Times interest earned ratio} = \frac{147}{21} = 7.0$$

This ratio shows the extent to which current earnings cover current interest payments. The ratio dropped significantly during the year. The higher interest along with the $10 million reduction in long-term debt implies that the amount of long-term debt was low for much of 19X4 and was paid off late in 19X5.

The *cash flow-to-current maturities ratio* is calculated by the following formula:

$$\text{Cash flow-to-current maturities ratio} = \frac{\text{Earnings after taxes} + \text{Depreciation} - \text{Dividends}}{\text{Current maturities of long-term debt}}$$

The Martin Corporation's cash flow-to-current maturities ratios are as follows:

$$\text{19X4 Cash flow-to-current maturities ratio} = \frac{90 + 40 - 47.5}{5.0} = 16.5$$

$$\text{19X5 Cash flow-to-current maturities ratio} = \frac{84 + 42 - 47.5}{5.0} = 15.7$$

These ratios show that the cash flow for the Martin Corporation is about 16 times the amount necessary to pay the current maturities of long-term debt. This value demonstrates that cash flow could drop significantly without causing financial distress.

Profitability Ratios

Profitability ratios measure the ability of a company to grow and to repay debt. The common-size income statement already provides several useful profitability ratios, such as the gross profit margin and the profit margin. There are other profitability ratios that relate earnings to the levels of total assets and common equity.

The *net return on total assets (ROA)* is calculated by the following formula:

$$\text{Net return on total assets} = \frac{\text{Earnings available to common shareholders}}{\text{Total assets}}$$

The Martin Corporation's net return on total assets ratios are as follows:

$$\text{19X4 Net return on total assets} = \frac{85}{500} = 0.170 = 17.0\%$$

$$\text{19X5 Net return on total assets} = \frac{79}{470} = 0.168 = 16.8\%$$

This ratio measures profitability in terms of how efficiently a company uses its assets. In defining this ratio, we may prefer to use average total assets, if this information is available. Simply averaging year-end values for 19X4 and 19X5 does not provide the average total assets for the year. Due to seasonal variation, year-end values may be higher or lower than asset values averaged over the entire year.

The *net return on common equity (ROE)* is calculated by the following formula:

$$\text{Net return on common equity} = \frac{\text{Earnings available to common shareholders}}{\text{Common equity}}$$

The Martin Corporation's net return on total assets ratios are as follows:

$$\text{19X4 Net return on common equity} = \frac{85}{290.0} = 0.293 \text{ or } 29.3\%$$

$$\text{19X5 Net return on common equity} = \frac{79}{326.5} = 0.242 \text{ or } 24.2\%$$

This ratio measures the return earned on common equity. The reduction in the net return on common equity reflects a higher level of common equity more than it does lower earnings. Common equity is significantly higher due to the increase of $36.5 million in retained earnings.

Market Ratios

Market Ratios

Market ratios associate the market price of a share of stock with its earnings per share or its book value per share. High values for these ratios reflect investor confidence in the company.

The *price-to-earnings (P/E) ratio* is calculated by the following formula:

$$\text{Price-to-earnings ratio} = \frac{\text{Market price per share}}{\text{Earnings per share}}$$

The Martin Corporation's price-to-earnings ratios are as follows:

$$\text{19X4 Price-to-earnings ratio} = \frac{26.125}{1.70} = 15.4$$

$$\text{19X5 Price-to-earnings ratio} = \frac{25.250}{1.58} = 16.0$$

Companies with high growth potential tend to have higher P/E ratios, while riskier companies tend to have lower P/E ratios.

The *market-to-book value (M/B) ratio* is calculated by the following formula:

$$\text{Market-to-book value ratio} = \frac{\text{Market price per share}}{\text{Book value per share}}$$

Book value per share is calculated first.

$$\text{19X4 Book value per share} = \frac{50.0 + 100.0 + 140.0}{50} = 5.80$$

$$\text{19X5 Book value per share} = \frac{50.0 + 100.0 + 176.5}{50} = 6.53$$

The Martin Corporation's market-to-book value ratios are as follows:

$$\text{19X4 Market-to-book value ratio} = \frac{26.125}{5.80} = 4.5$$

$$\text{19X5 Market-to-book value ratio} = \frac{25.250}{6.53} = 3.9$$

The more the company is earning on its common equity, the higher this ratio will be. The lower market-to-book value ratio in 19X5 primarily reflects the increased level of common equity, which results in a higher book value per share[8].

Ratio Comparisons

We may graph company ratios and industry averages over time. This trend analysis shows whether the particular ratio is improving or deteriorating when compared on a company or industry basis. Table 4.6 summarizes Martin Corporation's ratios and provides industry averages. Figure 4.1 presents Martin Corporation's ratios and industry averages over five years for the net return on total assets.

There are a number of sources of **industry average ratios** to use for comparative purposes. Robert Morris Associates publishes *Annual Statement Studies*, which provides data on more than 150 industry classifications. Dun & Bradstreet's *Key*

Industry Average Ratios

TABLE 4.6 Martin Corporation and Industry Ratios for 19X4 and 19X5

RATIO/TYPE	MARTIN RATIOS		INDUSTRY RATIOS	
	19X4	19X5	19X4	19X5
I. Liquidity Ratios				
1. Current ratio	1.88	3.73	1.90	2.11
2. Quick ratio	0.88	1.75	0.90	1.12
II. Activity Ratios				
3. Total asset turnover ratio	2.00	2.23	2.10	2.09
4. Average collection period	29.2	29.5	30.2	31.0
5. Days inventory	62.6	60.7	58.0	54.9
III. Leverage Ratios				
6. Debt ratio	32.0%	19.9%	60.4%	58.3%
7. Debt-to-net worth ratio	.552	.286	1.500	1.400
IV. Coverage Ratios				
8. Times interest earned ratio	16.0	7.0	5.4	4.2
9. Cash flow-to-current maturities	16.5	15.7	12.8	13.0
V. Profitability Ratios				
10. Net return on total assets	17.0%	16.8%	11.2%	10.3%
11. Net return on common equity	29.3%	24.2%	28.1%	25.2%
VI. Market Ratios				
12. Price-to-earnings ratio	15.4	16.0	13.5	12.6
13. Market-to-book value ratio	4.5	3.9	2.1	1.9

---

[8] Book value depends on depreciation and inventory valuation methods, which differ from company to company. As a result, comparisons between companies may be misleading.

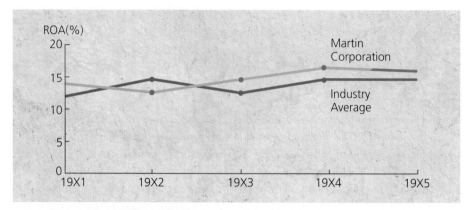

FIGURE 4.1 Martin Corporation Ratios and Industry Averages for the Net Return on Total Assets Over Five Years

Business Ratios gives 14 ratios for hundreds of groupings. The U.S. Commerce Department distributes *Quarterly Financial Report*, which furnishes ratios for manufacturing companies. In addition, there are financial services such as Moody's Investment Service, the Value Line Investment Survey, and Standard & Poor's Industry Surveys.

Business Fraud of the 90's: Falsifying Corporate Data

While fraud occurs in the biggest corporations, it is typically more damaging to the stock of small or midsized companies, which have become Wall Street favorites in the last two years. A case in point is Phar-Mor Inc., the drugstore chain in Youngstown, Ohio, that filed for bankruptcy in mid-August amid accusations by the company that a co-founder had embezzled money and hidden the fact behind a set of fake books. Phar-Mor had no publicly traded stock, but $61.2 million worth of its shares were held in nine mutual funds.

Harvey Pitt, a longtime Washington securities lawyer and former regulator whose firm has investigated several fraud cases, offered another possibility. "Maybe we've become more attuned to the scandals. Mr. Breeden, the S.E.C. chief, disagrees. His view is that today's spate of issuer fraud reveals that moral standards, far from rising, are slipping. "I think it's partly a function of the weakening of society's ethics," he said. "Less lying means less fraud."

Invariably, the best protection against issuer fraud is an alert, skeptical investor, said Robert A. Anderson, executive vice president at Southeast Research Partners, an institutional research and brokerage firm in Boca Raton. "But it's getting harder all the time to detect these things," he said. "If Phar-Mor had been publicly traded, I'd have had all my clients in it."

SUMMARY

This chapter focuses on the following learning objectives:

1. Describing the income statement.

   The income statement shows the total revenues and total expenses for a company over a stated reporting period. In a common-size income statement, all income statement components are divided by sales and are expressed as percentages.

2. Analyzing the income statement.

   The income statement should be compared with income statements from other years. This can be accomplished with a common-size income statement.

3. Describing the balance sheet.

   The balance sheet provides a financial representation of a company at a given point in time, showing what a company owns and how it is financed. In a common size balance sheet, all balance sheet accounts are divided by total assets and are expressed as percentages. The balance sheet is based on the accounting equation: total assets equals liabilities plus stockholders' equity.

4. Analyzing the balance sheet.

   The balance sheet should be compared with balance sheets from other years. This can be accomplished with a common-size balance sheet.

5. Preparing the statement of cash flows.

   The statement of cash flows shows over an accounting period the cash flows from operating, investing, and financing activities, as well as how these activities have affected liquidity. The statement of cash flows is calculated in this text by the indirect method.

6. Applying ratio analysis.

   Ratio analysis evaluates the relationships within a set of financial statements by comparing the company's position over time in relation to competitors. Financial ratios form the basis for an investigation but are not conclusive proof of the cause of a particular problem. Financial analysts normally group financial ratios into six categories: liquidity, activity, leverage, coverage, profitability, and market.

KEY TERMS

Activity ratios, 120

Balance sheet, 110

Common-size balance sheet, 111

Common-size income statement, 105

Coverage ratios, 122

Earnings after taxes, 106

Earnings before interest and taxes, 106

Gross profit margin, 108

QUESTIONS

4.1 Explain the purpose of an income statement.

4.2 Explain in detail the income statement's components.

4.3 What is a common-size income statement, and how is it used?

4.4 Explain the purpose of a balance sheet.

4.5 Explain in detail the balance sheet accounts.

4.6 What is a common-size balance sheet, and how is it used?

4.7 What factors influence the distribution of assets, liabilities, and stock-holders' equity on a balance sheet?

4.8 What is the purpose of the statement of cash flows?

4.9 Why would you use ratio analysis to evaluate financial statements?

4.10 What limitations are there in the use of financial ratios?

4.11 What are the six categories of financial ratios, and what do they measure?

4.12 What are some major sources of industry averages?

4.13 If you are presenting the results of your financial analysis of a company, what ethical questions might you encounter?

4.14 Why is financial statement analysis important to the stakeholders of a firm?

4.15 What is the best protection against issuer fraud?

PROBLEMS

4.1 (**Liquidity Ratios**) The balance sheet for the Williams Company included the following information:

	19X3	19X4	19X5
Inventory	$3,010	$3,320	$3,490
Total current assets	8,990	9,010	9,290
Net working capital	4,200	4,510	4,870

Analyze the liquidity of the company using the current ratio and the quick ratio.

4.2 **(Activity Ratios)** A financial analyst for Gorman Industries collected the following data:

	19X3	19X4	19X5
Net return on total assets	14.0%	15.4%	16.0%
Earnings available to common shareholders	$2,009	$2,079	$2,144
Average collection period	30.0 days	29.2 days	28.4 days
Accounts receivable	$2,520	$2,450	$2,414

Calculate the total asset turnover ratio for each of the three years.

4.3 **(Leverage Ratios)** The total debt to total assets ratio for Parnell Printing is 30 percent. If total assets amount to $500,000 and preferred stock is $50,000, what is the debt-to-net worth ratio?

4.4 **(Statement of Cash Flows)** Show in detail how the statement of cash flows in the chapter was prepared using the indirect method.

4.5 **(Coverage and Profitability Ratios)** The income statement for Hughes Electric Corporation follows:

HUGHES ELECTRIC CORPORATION: INCOME STATEMENT FOR THE YEAR ENDED DECEMBER 31, 19X4

Net sales	$5,000,000
Cost of goods sold	3,600,000
Gross profit	$1,400,000
Selling and administrative expenses	400,000
Depreciation expense	240,000
Earnings before interest and taxes (EBIT)	$ 760,000
Interest expense	45,000
Earnings before taxes (EBT)	$ 715,000
Taxes	275,000
Earnings after taxes (EAT)	$ 440,000
Preferred stock dividends	10,000
Earnings available to common shareholders	$ 430,000
Shares outstanding	100,000
Earnings per share	$4.30
Dividends per share	$1.72
Market price per share	$43.125

If total assets are $2,000,000, what are the times interest ratio and the net return on total assets.

4.6 **(Martin Corporation)** Prepare a report detailing the financial condition of the Martin Corporation. Use both the ratios and the industry averages presented in the chapter.

4.7 **(Ratio Analysis)** The income statements and balance sheets for the Harrison Corporation along with selected industry average ratios follow:

HARRISON CORPORATION: INCOME STATEMENTS FOR THE YEARS ENDED DECEMBER 31 (IN THOUSANDS)

	19X4	19X5
Net sales	$173,334	$164,552
Cost of goods sold	121,334	117,940
Gross profit	$ 52,000	$ 46,612
Selling and administrative expenses	24,018	24,810
Other expenses	11,366	11,644
Earnings before interest and taxes	$ 16,616	$ 10,158
Interest expense	2,320	2,608
Earnings before taxes (EBT)	$ 14,296	$ 7,550
Taxes	5,718	3,020
Earnings after taxes (EAT)	$ 8,578	$ 4,530
Depreciation expense	$1,692	$1,704
Shares outstanding	1,000,000	1,000,000
Market price per share	$73.50	$46.25

HARRISON CORPORATION: BALANCE SHEETS AS OF DECEMBER 31 (IN THOUSANDS)

ASSETS

	19X4	19X5
Current assets:		
Cash	$ 1,042	$ 188
Accounts receivable	27,450	27,474
Inventory	23,210	24,272
Prepaid expenses	898	832
Total current assets	$52,600	$52,766
Fixed assets:		
Land	$ 3,816	$ 3,816
Building, net	15,616	15,280
Equipment, net	14,712	14,776
Total fixed assets	$34,144	$33,872
Other assets	754	572
Total assets	$87,498	$87,210

LIABILITIES AND STOCKHOLDERS' EQUITY

	19X4	19X5
Current liabilities:		
Accounts payable	$21,044	$23,386
Accruals	810	792

	19X4	19X5
Notes payable	3,110	2,600
Current maturities, long-term debt	1,000	1,000
Taxes payable	2,046	720
Total current liabilities	$28,010	$28,498
Long-term debt	13,200	12,200
Total liabilities	$41,120	$40,698
Stockholders' equity:		
Common stock, $1 par	$ 5,900	$ 5,900
Retained earnings	40,388	40,612
Total stockholders' equity	$46,288	$46,512
Total liabilities and stockholders' equity	$87,498	$87,210

Industry average ratios follow:

	19X4	19X5
Liquidity:		
Current ratio	2.30	2.30
Quick ratio	0.80	1.00
Activity:		
Total asset turnover ratio	2.10	2.10
Average collection period	38.4	42.0
Days in inventory	101.4	104.3
Leverage:		
Debt ratio (%)	50.9	53.7
Debt-to-worth ratio	1.2	1.3
Coverage:		
Times interest earned ratio	2.0	2.0
Cash flow-to-current maturities ratio	4.0	4.0
Profitability:		
Net return on total assets (%)	5.2	5.0
Net return on common equity	12.7	11.9
Market:		
Price-to-earnings ratio	10.0	9.0
Market-to-book value ratio	1.6	1.5

(a) Calculate the ratios for which there are industry averages. (RATIO)

(b) Prepare a financial analysis of the Harrison Corporation.

4.8 **(Common-Size Statements, Statement of Cash Flows, and Numerous Ratios)** The income statements and balance sheets for the Singley Corporation along with selected industry average ratios follow:

SINGLEY CORPORATION: INCOME STATEMENTS FOR THE YEARS ENDED DECEMBER 31 (IN THOUSANDS)

	19X4	19X5
Net sales	$1,380	$1,318
Cost of goods sold	969	963
Gross profit	$ 411	$ 355
Selling and administrative expenses	229	248
Depreciation expense	36	41
Earnings before interest and taxes	$ 146	$ 66
Interest expense	16	18
Earnings before taxes (EBT)	$ 130	$ 48
Taxes	52	19
Earnings after taxes (EAT)	$ 78	$ 29
Preferred stock dividends	6	6
Earnings available to common shareholders	$ 72	$ 23
Shares outstanding	50,000	50,000
Earnings per share	$1.44	$0.46
Dividends per share	$0.80	$0.80
Market price per share	$18.750	$10.250

SINGLEY CORPORATION: BALANCE SHEETS AS OF DECEMBER 31 (IN THOUSANDS)

ASSETS

	19X4	19X5
Current assets:		
Cash	$ 24.0	$ 36.5
Marketable securities	6.0	9.1
Accounts receivable	220.2	188.3
Inventory	206.1	186.0
Prepaid expenses	9.3	7.0
Total current assets	$465.6	$426.9
Fixed assets:		
Property, plant, and equipment	$353.2	$376.8
Less: Accumulated depreciation	163.9	204.9
Net property, plant, and equipment	$189.3	$171.9
Total assets	$654.9	$598.8

LIABILITIES AND STOCKHOLDERS' EQUITY

	19X4	19X5
Current liabilities:		
Accounts payable	$149.6	138.5
Notes payable	40.0	20.0
Current maturities, long-term debt	10.0	10.0
Accrued taxes	20.2	21.4
Total current liabilities	$219.8	$189.9

	19X4	19X5
Long-term debt	129.8	120.6
Total liabilities	$349.6	$310.5
Stockholders' equity:		
Preferred stock	$ 60.0	$ 60.0
Common stock ($1 par)	14.0	14.0
Capital in excess of par	32.6	32.6
Retained earnings	198.7	181.7
Total stockholders' equity	$305.3	$288.3
Total liabilities and stockholders' equity	$654.9	$598.8

Industry average ratios follow:

	19X4	19X5
Liquidity:		
Current ratio	1.50	1.60
Quick ratio	0.80	0.90
Activity:		
Total asset turnover ratio	2.00	2.10
Average collection period	45.6	46.8
Days in inventory	49.3	48.0
Leverage:		
Debt ratio (%)	61.8	61.6
Debt-to-worth ratio	1.6	1.7
Coverage:		
Times interest earned ratio	2.4	2.1
Cash flow-to-current maturities ratio	5.0	4.9
Profitability:		
Net return on total assets (%)	9.0	8.8
Net return on common equity	15.0	13.3
Market:		
Price-to-earnings ratio	12.0	11.0
Market-to-book value ratio	1.8	1.7

(a) Calculate the ratios for which there are industry averages. (RATIO)

(b) Prepare a financial analysis of the Singley Corporation.

A Case Problem

Atlanta Scientific Corporation was a worldwide developer and marketer of medical devices. The company sold over 4,000 products used by physicians to perform less evasive medical procedures. These less evasive approaches reduced the overall cost of health care while providing important patient benefits. Sales growth for the company primarily had been a function of innovative product development.

The company's results of operations as a percentage of net sales and the percentage increases from the prior two years follows:

	Percentage of net sales for year ended December 31			Percentage increase from prior year	
	1991	1992	1993	1992	1993
Net sales	100%	100%	100%	37%	45%
Gross profit	56	62	64	52	51
Selling, general and administrative expenses	37	32	29	18	33
Research and development expenses	7	5	5	2	29
Total operating expenses	44	37	34	16	32
Income from operations	12	25	30	187	78
Net income	5	15	18	285	74

The improvement in gross profit resulted primarily from increased utilization of manufacturing facilities and increased labor productivity.

Net sales increased from $232.0 million in 1991 to $460.0 million in 1993. The increase was attributable to increased sales across all divisions of the company. The improvement in gross profit resulted primarily from increased utilization of manufacturing facilities and increased labor

productivity. Gross profit also benefited from higher profit margins on increased international sales and from selected price increases. This margin improvement was partially offset by a less profitable product mix during 1993.

The decrease in selling, general, and administrative expenses reflected economies of scale associated with a growing domestic and international sales force. Research and development expenses decreased over the period as a percentage of sales, but increased significantly in absolute terms.

Net income increased dramatically despite a higher tax rate of 38.8% in 1993 compared with 34.2% in 1991. All research and development tax carryforwards were used up in 1991. The company benefited from lower interest expense caused by declining interest rates.

Atlanta Scientific planned to expand its manufacturing capacity in 1995. The company estimated that it would incur capital expenditures of between $50 and $70 million in connection with the expansion. Capital expenditures were $19.4 million in 1992 and $32 million in 1993, and did not include expansion of manufacturing capacity.

Leading Questions

1. What are the financial strengths and weaknesses of Atlanta Scientific Corporation?
2. What pitfalls must management guard against?
3. What should you include in a memorandum to the chief financial officer regarding the details of your analysis?

declined. Observers of Japan view this recession not as just a cyclical downturn but as the beginning of an extended period of slow growth.

In the 1990s, steel producers are finding that their customers make buying decisions based on price. As a result, there is serious talk among top executives about prioritizing profit over market share. One Japanese company, Omron Corporation, has set a specific goal for return on shareholders equity. In essence, the Japanese are entering an era of cost cutting and downsizing. This is a most unfamiliar world, a concept in juxtaposition to their customs and culture.

In Japan, the idea of lifetime employment is woven into the corporate culture. The Japanese base this view on the belief that people with a sense of belonging work efficiently—they work as a family. Because the family in Japan is held in such high regard, the concept of laying off employees is nearly nonexistent.

Further complicating the labor issue is the misconception that corporate Japan is highly efficient. It is true that factories are efficient, but it is not true that offices work efficiently. Excess managers, clerks, receptionists, and other office workers are not easily dealt with in the Japanese corporate culture.

In this difficult environment, Japanese firms are beginning to downsize and cut costs incrementally. The manufacturing sector has already committed to 10 to 15 percent reductions in plant and equipment investments. Bonuses have also been slashed in an effort to reduce payroll costs. Mazda Motors will trim their dividend for the first time since 1975, while Omron Corporation will cut its product line by 30 percent. Value-added products are becoming popular since customers are no longer attracted to the bells and whistles available in wide-deep product lines.

What are the forecasting implications for a Japanese firm? One highly significant qualitative factor has been identified: The Japanese have entered an extended period of slow growth—not a cyclical downturn. Therefore, when preparing pro forma financial statements and cash budgets, sales projections must reflect this reality. In preparing a pro forma income statement, labor costs require special care, especially when layoffs are not an option. In preparing a pro forma balance sheet, the issue of excess capacity must be addressed.

Source: "Era of Slower Growth Brings a Strange Sight: Japan Restructuring," *The Wall Street Journal,* December 8, 1992, pg. A1. Reprinted by permission of The Wall Street Journal, © 1992 Dow Jones & Company, Inc. All Rights Reserved Worldwide.

SALES FORECASTING

Sales Forecast

Making a **sales forecast** is the first step in financial forecasting. Using this projection, a financial analyst can prepare the pro forma income statement, the pro forma balance sheet, and the cash budget. These statements are important as you make the investment, financing, and dividend decisions for your company. Two methods of forecasting are quantitative forecasting and qualitative forecasting.

Quantitative Forecasting

Quantitative Forecasting

Regression Analysis

Compound Growth Rate
Technique

The most common forms of **quantitative forecasting** are regression analysis and the compound growth rate technique. **Regression analysis** considers one or more independent variables to forecast the dependent variable. Usually, with sales forecasting, the dependent variable is sales, and the independent variable is time. The **compound growth rate technique** determines the compound growth rate of sales over a period of time and applies the growth rate to one or more future periods. This chapter uses the compound growth technique for forecasting. Regression analysis is discussed in Appendix 5A.

The Martin Corporation, from Chapter 4, recorded the following sales over the last five years:

Year	Sales
19X1	$ 850,000,000
19X2	875,000,000
19X3	975,000,000
19X4	1,000,000,000
19X5	1,050,000,000

Melissa Maxwell, a financial analyst for the company, plans to make a sales forecast for the next year. Using the compound growth rate technique, what is the compound growth rate in sales and her forecast for 19X6?

Melissa noticed that sales grew from $850,000,000 to $1,050,000,000 over the four year period from 19X1 to 19X5. We can show this with a cash flow diagram.

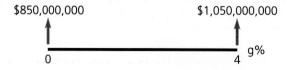

These two sales figures can be made equivalent at any point in time as long as we adjust for growth rate. If we choose time 4 (time 0 is just as good), the following equation applies.

$$\$850,000,000(FVF_{g\%,4}) = \$1,050,000,000$$
$$(FVF_{g\%,4}) = 1.2353$$

Since $(FVF_{g\%,4}) = (1 + g)^4$, then $(1 + g)^4 = 1.2353$. Using a basic calculator and taking the square root of 1.253 twice, we find $(1 + g)^4 = 1.054$. This implies a growth rate of 5.4 percent.

To find the forecast for 19X6, Y_{19X6}, Melissa assumes that the past growth rate of 5.4 percent will continue for another year. Therefore, she applies that growth rate to the 19X5 sales.[1]

$$Y_{19X6} = \$1,050,000,000(1.054)$$
$$= \$1,106,700,000$$

Melissa predicts sales of $1,106,700,000 for 19X6.

Qualitative Forecasting

The sales forecast above does not consider qualitative factors. **Qualitative forecasting** is based on judgments as to the factors that will cause sales, or any other financial variable, to be different in the future from what they were in the past. The methods used range from scientifically conducted opinion surveys to intuitive hunches about the future. For example, the Martin Corporation finds from market research that sales for a new product will be higher than those of the old product. Under these conditions, many companies use quantitative methods to arrive at an initial forecast and then modify the results based on qualitative approaches. More information about qualitative approaches is included in Appendix 5A.

The quantitative and qualitative forecasting methods eventually lead to a sales forecast. In the material that follows, management uses *executive consensus* (see Appendix 5A), to arrive at a sales forecast for the Martin Corporation during 19X6 of $1,113,000,000. The executives, after receiving input from many areas within the organization, felt that the quantitative forecast only mildly understated the demand for the company's products—women's wear.

Qualitative Forecasting

---

[1] Sales for 19X5 is obtained from Chapter 4 in the Martin Corporation income statement.

It Pays to Perform

A cross the United States, boards of directors are tying the compensation that executives receive to the financial results of the companies they manage. Companies are adopting new incentive plans, putting a higher percentage of income at risk, extending incentive plans lower in the organization and placing greater emphasis on stock and long-term incentives. The emphasis on incentive compensation has increased the importance of the financial measures used to evaluate company, departmental and individual performance, and this in turn has increased the role of senior financial executives in developing incentive programs.

The FASB is proposing new stock-option accounting rules that will undoubtedly encourage companies to shift away from simply using stock options as the primary long-term program, toward using long-term cash incentives and other vehicles. Ironically, shareholders always benefited as well as executives with option plans, but other types of long-term programs often yield payout whether or not the stock price has increased. And finally, both the press and the public

continue to be very interested in executive compensation to ensure a reasonable link between pay and performance.

As a result, companies have placed greater emphasis on the performance measures and more frequently use new and/or additional performance measures to evaluate company performance. Companies are increasingly using cash flow as a way to emphasize management for total cash generation, as opposed to simply for net income. Cash flow incorporates net income, but also emphasizes inventory minimization, accounts receivable collection and efficient use of fixed assets. Return on capital also emphasizes the importance of minimizing assets while achieving net income. Economic value added measures the adjusted after-tax profit.

Source: John D. McMillan, "It Pays To Perform," Financial Executive, pp. 48–51. Excerpted with permission from Financial Executive, Nov./Dec. 1993, copyright 1993 by Financial Executive Institute, 10 Madison Avenue, P.O. Box 1938, Morristown, New Jersey 07962-1939 201-898-4600.

PRO FORMA FINANCIAL STATEMENTS

After the sales forecast is made, pro forma income statements and balance sheets can be prepared. These financial statements are essential for financial planning and are especially useful in dealing with bankers and other lenders who make loan decisions based on financial performance. Some loan officers even require pro forma statements from prior years in order to highlight management's ability to forecast and plan for future events. Comparing financial statements to industry averages identifies positions of relative strength and weakness.[2]

---

[2] See Brenda Gilliam, "Can This Loan Be Repaid?," *The Bankers Magazine*, November-December 1990, pp. 74–79.

The Pro Forma Income Statement

Preparation of the **pro forma income statement** is easy when a common-size income statement is available from the previous year. The percentages for each item on the old income statement are applied to the forecast sales for the new year. If additional information is available for any item, the calculated amount may be changed to reflect the new estimated relationship.

Pro Forma Income Statement

> The Martin Corporation had sales in 19X5 of $1,050,000,000 and forecasts sales in 19X6 of $1,113,000,000. Melissa Maxwell plans to develop the pro forma income statement for 19X6. In preparing the statement, she knows that preferred dividends will remain constant.

The Martin Corporation pro forma income statement for 19X6 is based on the common-size income statement for 19X5. The 19X5 income statement from Chapter 4 is repeated here as Table 5.1.

Table 5.2 applies the percentages from the 19X5 income statement to the 19X6 forecast sales level of $1,113,000,000. The preferred stock dividends remain constant at $5,000,000.

With more information, we could make a more accurate pro forma income statement. The percentages for cost of goods sold as well as selling and admin-

TABLE 5.1 Martin Corporation: Income Statement for the Year Ended December 31, 19X5
(in thousands)

Net sales	$1,050,000	100.0%
Cost of goods sold	756,000	72.0
Gross profit	$ 294,000	28.0
Selling and administrative expenses	105,000	10.0
Depreciation expense	42,000	4.0
Earnings before interest and taxes	$ 147,000	14.0
Interest expense	21,000	2.0
Earnings before taxes (EBT)	$ 126,000	12.0
Taxes	42,000	4.0
Earnings after taxes (EAT)	$ 84,000	8.0
Preferred stock dividends	5,000	0.5
Earnings available to common shareholders	$ 79,000	7.5%
Actual shares outstanding		50,000,000
Earnings per share		$1.58
Dividends per share		$0.85
Market price per share		$25.250

TABLE 5.2 Martin Corporation: Pro Forma Income Statement for the Year Ended December
●●●●●●● 31, 19X6 (in thousands)

Net sales	$1,113,000	100.0%
Cost of goods sold	801,360	72.0
Gross profit	$ 311,640	28.0
Selling and administrative expenses	111,300	10.0
Depreciation expense	44,520	4.0
Earnings before interest and taxes (EBIT)	$ 155,820	14.0
Interest expense	22,260	2.0
Earnings before taxes (EBT)	$ 133,560	12.0
Taxes	44,520	4.0
Earnings after taxes (EAT)	$ 89,040	8.0
Preferred stock dividends	5,000	0.4
Earnings available to common shareholders	$ 84,040	7.6%
Actual shares outstanding		50,000,000
Earnings per share		$1.68
Dividends per share		$0.85

istrative expenses depend on how close to capacity the company is operating. Depreciation expense changes yearly and includes the depreciation on any new fixed assets.[3] Interest expense is related to interest rates and the amount of debt. The amount of taxes is determined by tax rates and available tax credits. Finally, dividends paid is declared by the board of directors. With all these complications, the simplest approach is to accept the pro forma income statement from Table 5.2 and proceed to the pro forma balance sheet.

The Pro Forma Balance Sheet

When sales increase, additional funds may be required to finance an increase in assets. There are two ways of estimating the funds required: (1) using the pro forma balance sheet, and (2) using the additional funds required equation. We will learn the balance sheet approach in this section and the funds required equation in the next section.

Pro Forma Balance Sheet

Percentage of Sales Forecasting Method

We develop the **pro forma balance sheet** using the **percentage of sales forecasting method.** This method assumes that certain balance sheet accounts are proportional to the level of sales and are currently optimal. For example, if we currently have the correct level of cash, not more than what is needed yet

---

[3] For depreciation to remain constant, new equipment is required while operating at full capacity.

enough to support operations, we can reasonably expect cash needs to rise at the same rate as sales. When this is not the case, adjustments must be made.

The Martin Corporation used its fixed assets at full capacity in 19X5, and the level of current assets is optimal. Melissa Maxwell plans to develop the 19X6 pro forma balance sheet and to indicate the level of additional financing required.

The Martin Corporation balance sheet for 19X6 is based on the balance sheet for 19X5. The 19X5 balance sheet from Chapter 4 is repeated as Table 5.3.

TABLE 5.3 Martin Corporation: Balance Sheet as of December 31, 19X5 (in thousands)

ASSETS	
Current assets:	
Cash	$ 21,000
Marketable securities	5,200
Accounts receivable	85,000
Inventory	125,800
Total current assets	$237,000
Fixed assets:	
Property, plant, and equipment	$475,000
Less: Accumulated depreciation	242,000
Net property, plant, and equipment	$233,000
Total assets	$470,000

LIABILITIES AND STOCKHOLDERS' EQUITY	
Current liabilities:	
Accounts payable	$ 38,500
Notes payable	10,000
Current maturities, long-term debt	5,000
Accrued expenses	10,000
Total current liabilities	$ 63,500
Long-term debt	30,000
Total liabilities	$ 93,500
Stockholders' equity:	
Preferred stock	$ 50,000
Common stock ($1 par)	50,000
Capital in excess of par	100,000
Retained earnings	176,500
Total stockholders' equity	$376,500
Total liabilities and stockholders' equity	$470,000

The first step in percentage of sales forecasting is to recognize which balance sheet accounts are proportional to sales. In the simplest case, all of the current asset items vary directly with sales: cash, marketable securities, accounts receivable, and inventory. We'll assume that this is the case for Martin Corporation. We'll also assume that net fixed assets (net property, plant, and equipment) increase proportionately since the company is operating at full capacity. Accounts payable and accrued expenses also increase spontaneously and proportionately with sales. The other liability and stockholders' equity items may change but are not directly related to sales.

The second step in percentage of sales forecasting is to find the new values for those balance sheet accounts that are proportional to sales. The easiest approach involves using the sales multiplier. The **sales multiplier (SM)** is found by dividing the forecast sales by the sales from the previous year.

Sales Multiplier

$$SM = \frac{\$1,113,000}{\$1,050,000} = 1.06$$

This procedure yields the following results for the 19X6 balance sheet items that are proportional to sales:

Current Assets:

Cash	$21,000(1.06) = 22,260$
Marketable securities	$5,200(1.06) = 5,512$
Accounts receivable	$85,000(1.06) = 90,100$
Inventory	$125,800(1.06) = 133,348$

Net Fixed Assets:

Net property, plant, and equipment	$233,000(1.06) = 246,980$

Current Liabilities:

Accounts payable	$38,500(1.06) = 40,810$
Accrued expenses	$10,000(1.06) = 10,600$

As noted, the sales multiplier is applied to *net* property, plant, and equipment. *This implies that the cash flows from depreciation are used to replace old equipment.*

We can find the property, plant, and equipment for 19X6 by working backwards—adding the accumulated depreciation for 19X6 to the net property, plant, and equipment for 19X6. Accumulated depreciation for 19X6 is equal to the 19X5 accumulated depreciation of $242,000 plus the 19X6 income statement depreciation expense of $44,520, a total of $286,520. The property, plant, and equipment for 19X6 is $533,500, $286,520 plus $246,980.

The third step in percentage of sales forecasting is to determine retained earnings in 19X6. This account is equal to the 19X5 retained earnings plus the 19X6 earnings available to common shareholders minus the 19X6 dividends paid to

TABLE 5.4 Martin Corporation: Pro Forma Balance Sheet as of December 31, 19X6, Including Additional Financing Required (in thousands)

ASSETS	
Current assets:	
Cash	$ 22,260
Marketable securities	5,512
Accounts receivable	90,100
Inventory	133,348
Total current assets	$251,220
Fixed assets:	
Property, plant, and equipment	$533,500
Less: Accumulated depreciation	286,520
Net property, plant, and equipment	$246,980
Total assets	$498,200

LIABILITIES AND STOCKHOLDERS' EQUITY	
Current liabilities:	
Accounts payable	$ 40,810
Notes payable	10,000 (unchanged)
Current maturities, long-term debt	5,000 (unchanged)
Accrued expenses	10,600
Total current liabilities	$ 66,410
Long-term debt	30,000 (unchanged)
Total liabilities	$ 96,410
Stockholders' equity:	
Preferred stock	$ 50,000 (unchanged)
Common stock ($1 par)	50,000 (unchanged)
Capital in excess of par	100,000 (unchanged)
Retained earnings	218,040
Total stockholders' equity	$418,040
Total liabilities and stockholders' equity	$514,450
Additional funds required	$(16,250)

common shareholders. Retained earnings is $218,040, $176,500 + $84,040 − $42,500. The 19X6 dividends paid is found by multiplying 50,000,000 shares by dividends of $0.85 per share, $42,500,000.

The fourth step is to construct the 19X6 pro forma balance sheet, indicating the level of additional financing required. Table 5.4 includes the accounts calculated in the previous steps, as well as the accounts that have not changed (See Table 5.3). The unchanged accounts may be increased but do not so spontaneously.

This pro forma balance sheet predicts that an increase in sales of six percent will cause additional funds required to be *negative*. This means that $16,250 may be used to reduce liabilities. If the value for additional funds required had been positive, notes payable would increase or new long-term debt, preferred stock, or common stock would be issued.

Additional Funds Required Equation

Another way to find additional funds required involves the use of a single equation. This approach is useful in finding that amount, but you learn more about the company by preparing the pro forma statements. Creditors prefer knowing more than the result from a formula.

The equation for finding the amount of additional funds required follows:

$$AFR = (SM - 1)(PA - PL) - PM(FS) + DV + AI - LI \qquad (5.1)$$

where

AFR = Additional funds required

SM = Sales multiplier

PA = Assets that increase in proportion to sales

PL = Liabilities that increase in proportion to sales

PM = Profit margin (EAT/Sales) for forecasted year[4]

FS = Forecasted sales

DV = Dividends paid

AI = Asset increase for nonproportional assets

LI = Liability increase for nonproportional liabilities[5]

The nonproportional increases reflect the amount of increase in assets or liabilities when the increase is not proportional. These amounts can be negative.

Let's work through this formula using the six percent increase in sales from the preceding section. For that situation, the variables take on the following values:

$SM = 1.06$

$PA = 21,000 + 5,200 + 85,000 + 125,800 + 233,000 = 470,000$

$PL = 38,500 + 10,000 = 48,500$

$PM = 8.0\% = 0.080$ (Common size EAT, 19X5 income statement)

---

[4] When the earnings after taxes are known from the pro forma income statement, this term can be replaced with the estimated earnings after taxes.

[5] This item does not include outside sources of financing.

$$FS = 1,050,000(1.06) = 1,113,000$$
$$DV = 50,000(0.85) + 5,000 \text{ (preferred dividends)} = 47,500$$
$$AI = 0$$
$$LI = 0$$

Substituting into Equation 5.1 yields the following:

$$
\begin{aligned}
AFR &= (SM - 1)(PA - PL) - PM(FS) + DV + AI - LI \\
&= (1.06 - 1)(470,000 - 48,500) - 0.080(1,113,000) + 47,500 \\
&= -16,250
\end{aligned}
$$

As we would expect, this is the same answer found by preparing the pro forma statements.

Assume that the sales forecast for 19X6 is incorrect and that sales increase by 25 percent. This implies actual sales of $1,050,000(1.25), or $1,312,500. How would this affect the level of additional financing required that Melissa Maxwell calculated?

Using Equation 5.1, finding the answer for a 25 percent increase in sales demands a change in the sales multiplier and in forecasted sales.

$$
\begin{aligned}
AFR &= (SM - 1)(PA - PL) - PM(FS) + DV + AI - LI \\
&= (1.25 - 1)(470,000 - 48,500) - 0.080(1,312,500) + 47,500 \\
&= 47,875
\end{aligned}
$$

This answer, of course, could be found by preparing the pro forma statements.

Equation 5.1 also allows you to find the break-even level of sales, the point at which the additional funds required is equal to zero. We simply set AFR at 0, using Equation 5.1.

$$
\begin{aligned}
AFR &= (SM - 1)(PA - PL) - PM(FS) + DV + AI - LI \\
0 &= (SM - 1)(470,000 - 48,500) - 0.080(SM)(1,050,000) + 47,500
\end{aligned}
$$

We then solve for SM.

$$SM = 1.108$$

This means that sales could increase by 10.8 percent without requiring additional financing.[6]

---

[6] Sustainable growth analysis shows how too much growth can be detrimental to a company. See Darrell M. Moore, "Growing Broke," *Business Credit*, September 1988, pp. 49–51.

THE CASH BUDGET
....

Cash Budget

The **cash budget** details the future cash inflows and cash outflows of a company over a specified period of time. It is prepared on a cash rather than on an accrual basis. Remember, as mentioned in Chapter 4, income statements are normally prepared on an accrual basis, as opposed to a cash basis. The financial manager, therefore, must take the accrual information and transform it to a cash format.

A cash budget may forecast cash flows on a monthly, weekly, or even daily basis. It includes inflows such as cash sales and the collection of accounts receivable and outflows such as purchases, labor costs, selling expenses, loan payments, and capital expenditures. By forecasting the timing of these cash flows, you determine the financing needs of your company.

After forecasting monthly sales, building a cash budget is a three-step process: (1) preparing the worksheet, (2) determining net cash flows, and (3) identifying financing requirements. Let's look at the first of these steps in the next section.

Cash Squeeze at R.H. Macy Causes Anxiety for Suppliers
....

Suppliers to R.H. Macy & Company, who expected payment last Friday, got an unpleasant surprise when they found out the company had delayed sending their checks for two weeks. News of Macy's cash squeeze spread quickly throughout the financial community, and prices on Macy's junk bonds responded, falling 20 percent by late in the day. A mix of bankers, trade creditors, and other lenders—owed more than $3.5 billion—expressed anxiety about being paid. Rumors spread that Macy would have to file for bankruptcy protection.

Macy was one of many department stores that borrowed heavily during the 1980s. As the result of a series of management missteps and an unexpectedly weak economy, Macy found itself short of cash. A week earlier, Macy executives made the difficult decision to ask its banking group and suppliers for more time. Macy borrows primarily through its $588 million revolving credit facility which it uses to buy new inventory. After purchasing for the Christmas season, Macy normally repays in January or February. After devising a repayment schedule to reduce its revolving credit borrowings, Macy believed its cash position was resolved.

Unfortunately, it didn't work out as planned. Macy did not have enough cash to pay vendors and reduce borrowings as promised. Although they considered asking for an amendment to the loan agreement, management felt that an amendment on short notice would have been "disruptive." Instead, Macy decided to delay payments to suppliers. With 20,000 suppliers, however, there was little chance of contacting them all.

As a result of not being able to pay, Macy's suppliers might discontinue shipment of product, though this decision may be beyond their control. Many smaller suppliers rely on selling their accounts receivable to a factor as collateral for loans. If the factor does not want to take the risk, smaller suppliers will not ship to Macy. The recession also compounds the problem since most suppliers are limited in their ability to absorb bad debts.

Macy bought time in late 1990 by selling its prized credit card business to General Electric for more than $100 million. It also raised more than $200 million from new and existing shareholders and used the proceeds to retire more than $550 million of its junk bond debt at a discount. But that cash is gone.

Edward Finkelstein, the chairman of Macy, disclosed the possibility of selling Macy stores to raise cash. He also proposed cutting advertising costs, renegotiating bank loans, and seeking new equity investors. Macy hired Goldman, Sachs and Company, the investment banker, to help find a way out of the financial squeeze.

Responding to growing concerns of liquidity, Mr. Finkelstein said, "I don't think it's in our best interest to file for Chapter 11. It runs against our grain. We know what we have to do. We have a comprehensive game plan."

Macy's cash pinch could have been avoided through less risky financing of additional funds requirements. The pro forma statements should have reflected a conservative financing posture. In the months preceding the cash pinch, an accurate sales forecast for the cash budget would have alerted Macy and its creditors to the impending liquidity problems.

Source: Jeffrey A. Trachtenberg and George Anders "Cash Pinch Leads Macy to Delay Paying Bills and Plan Other Steps," *The Wall Street Journal,* January 13, 1992, pg. A1. Reprinted by permission of The Wall Street Journal, © 1992 Dow Jones & Company, Inc. All Rights Reserved Worldwide.

Preparing the Worksheet

The **cash budget worksheet** represents the cash inflows from sales and the cash outflows from purchases. The cash inflows from sales occur as cash receipts during the month of sale and as payment of accounts receivable during the following months. The cash outflows from purchases also occur as cash purchases during the month of sale and as payment of accounts payable during the succeeding months.

Cash Budget Worksheet

Melissa Maxwell is interested in preparing a monthly cash budget worksheet for the first six months of 19X6, based on the following monthly sales forecast (in thousands):

Month	Sales	Month	Sales	Month	Sales
19X5 November	$73,500	19X6 February	$77,910	19X6 May	$100,170
December	63,000	March	77,910	June	111,300
19X6 January	66,780	19X6 April	89,040	19X6 July	122,430

(This monthly forecast is developed in Appendix 5A from the actual 19X5 sales and the pro forma 19X6 sales forecast of $1,113,000,000.) In studying old sales records, she finds that 30 percent of customers pay during the month of sale, 60 percent during the following month, and 10 percent two months later. She also discovers that each month, purchases amount to 60 percent of sales for the next month. The payment for the purchases is 10 percent by cash, with the remaining 90 percent paid the following month. Using a cash budget worksheet, Melissa wants to predict the total receipts and total payments for the company during the first six months of 19X6.

TABLE 5.5 Martin Corporation: Monthly Cash Budget Worksheet

	Nov	Dec	Jan	Feb	Mar	Apr	May	Jun	Jul
Sales	$73,500	$63,000	$66,780	$77,910	$77,910	$89,040	$100,170	$111,300	$122,430
Receipts:									
1st month (30%)	$22,050	$18,900	$20,034	$23,373	$23,373	$26,712	$ 30,051	$ 33,390	
2nd month (60%)		44,100	37,800	40,068	46,746	46,746	53,424	60,102	
3rd month (10%)			7,350	6,300	6,678	7,791	7,791	8,904	
Total receipts			$65,184	$69,741	$76,797	$81,249	$ 91,266	$102,396	
Purchases (60%)	$37,800	$40,068	$46,746	$46,746	$53,424	$60,102	$ 66,780	$ 73,458	
Payments:									
1st month (10%)	$ 3,780	$ 4,007	$ 4,675	$ 4,675	$ 5,342	$ 6,010	$ 6,678	$ 7,346	
2nd month (90%)		34,020	36,061	42,071	42,071	48,082	54,092	60,102	
Total payments			$40,736	$46,746	$47,413	$54,092	$ 60,770	$ 67,448	

Table 5.5 presents the monthly cash budget worksheet for 19X6. The receipts section of the cash budget worksheet records the amount and timing of the collection on sales. The first row under receipts reflects the normal 30-percent collection during the month of sale. For example, we find the figure of $22,050 under November by multiplying the November sales of $73,500 by 30 percent. The second row reflects the normal 60-percent collection in the month following the sale. The figure of $44,100 under December is computed by multiplying the November sales of $73,500 by 60 percent, for example. The third row reflects the 10-percent collection in the second month following the sale. The figure of $7,350 under January is determined by multiplying the November sales of $73,500 by 10 percent. The total receipts for each month are generated by adding the three components.

The remainder of the cash budget worksheet involves purchases. The amount of purchases is based on the sales for the next month. The figure of $40,068 under December is calculated by multiplying the sales of $66,780 by 60 percent, for example, and the other purchase figures are found in a similar fashion.

The payments section of the cash budget worksheet records the amount and timing of the disbursement for purchases. The first row reflects the 10-percent payment in the month of sale. The figure of $4,007 under December is computed by multiplying the December purchases of $40,068 by 10 percent, for example. The second row shows the 90-percent disbursement in the month following the sale. The figure of $36,061 under January is determined by multiplying the December purchases of $40,068 by 90 percent. The other disbursement figures are similarly found, with the total payments for each month generated by adding the two components.

Chapter 5 Financial Planning ● **151**

Determining Net Cash Flows

With the receipts and payments found on the worksheet and any other receipts or payments not included on the worksheet, we can determine the net cash flows for each month. This figure represents the gain or loss in cash for the month.

> Melissa has determined total receipts and total payments by preparing the cash budget worksheet. She also has collected information regarding other cash payments during the six-month period. How does she find the net cash flows for the company during the first six months of 19X6?

Table 5.6 includes the information on total receipts and total payments from the cash budget worksheet. It also contains the other payment information that Melissa collected for the six-month period.[7]

We find the net cash flow for each month by subtracting the total payments from the total receipts. Notice that the timing of payments causes the net cash flow to swing from $6,959 in January to ($30,586) in June.

Identifying Financing Requirements

With the net cash flows from the second part of the cash budget, the beginning cash, and the target cash balance, we can identify the monthly financing requirements. This figure represents the surplus of funds or the need for borrowing.

TABLE 5.6 Martin Corporation: 19X6 Cash Budget Net Cash Flows
● ● ● ● ● ● ●

	JAN	FEB	MAR	APR	MAY	JUN
Total receipts	$65,184	$69,741	$76,797	$81,249	$91,266	$102,396
Payments:						
Purchases	$40,736	$46,746	$47,413	$54,092	$60,770	$ 67,448
Labor expense	8,014	9,349	9,349	10,685	12,020	13,356
Selling and administrative	6,678	7,791	7,791	8,904	10,017	11,130
Working capital increase	942	943	942	943	942	943
Fixed asset acquisition			14,625			14,625
Interest expense	1,855	1,855	1,855	1,855	1,855	1,855
Taxes				8,904		12,020
Dividends			11,875			11,875
Total payments	$58,225	$66,684	$93,850	$85,383	$85,604	$133,252
Net cash flow	$ 6,959	$ 3,057	($17,053)	($ 4,134)	$ 5,662	($ 30,856)

---

[7] Depreciation is a noncash charge and does not appear on the cash budget.

> Melissa has determined the net cash flows in preparing the second part of the cash budget. The beginning cash for 19X6 is the cash from the December 31, 19X5, balance sheet, $21,000. Melissa also determined that the target cash balance, the cash needed to conduct business, should be $22,260. What are the financing requirements she finds for the first six months of 19X6?

Table 5.7 presents the computations leading to the monthly financing requirements. The net cash flows are from Table 5.6.

The cumulative cash figure for January is found by adding the cash (if no borrowing) to the net cash flow. The beginning cash figure is $21,000, the ending cash from the previous year, found in the December 31, 19X5, balance sheet. In subsequent months, the cash (if no borrowing) figure is equal to the cumulative cash from the previous month. The surplus or loan amount is determined by subtracting the target cash from the cumulative cash.

The Martin Corporation begins the first two months of the year with a surplus. The next four months the company must borrow, with peak borrowing of $37,625 occurring in June.

Table 5.8 shows the cash budget for January through April, 19X6. It shows the parts of the cash budget combined together.

You can also calculate the cash budget using THE FINANCIAL MANAGER (BUDGET). This allows you to experiment with different values for the variables, noting the effect of each on the financial requirements of your company.

SUMMARY

This chapter focuses on the following learning objectives:
1. Preparing a simple sales forecast.

TABLE 5.7 Martin Corporation: 19X6 Cash Budget Requirements

	JAN	FEB	MAR	APR	MAY	JUN
Net cash flow	$ 6,959	$ 3,057	($17,053)	($ 4,134)	$ 5,662	($30,856)
Cash (if no borrowing)	21,000	27,959	31,016	13,963	9,829	15,491
Cumulative cash	$27,959	$31,016	$13,963	$ 9,829	$15,491	($15,365)
Target cash	22,260	22,260	22,260	22,260	22,260	22,260
Surplus or (loan amount)	$ 5,699	$ 8,756	($ 8,297)	($12,431)	($ 6,769)	($37,625)

TABLE 5.8   Martin Corporation: January-April, 19X6 Cash Budget

	JAN	FEB	MAR	APR	MAY	JUN
Total receipts	$65,184	$69,741	$ 76,797	$ 81,249	$91,266	$102,396
Payments:						
Purchases	$40,736	$46,746	$ 47,413	$ 54,092	$60,770	$ 67,448
Labor expense	8,014	9,349	9,349	10,685	12,020	13,356
Selling and administrative	6,678	7,791	7,791	8,904	10,017	11,130
Working capital increase	942	943	942	943	942	943
Fixed asset acquisition			14,625			14,625
Interest expense	1,855	1,855	1,855	1,855	1,855	1,855
Taxes				8,904		12,020
Dividends			11,875			11,875
Total payments	$58,225	$66,684	$ 93,850	$ 85,383	$85,604	$133,252
Net cash flow	$ 6,959	$ 3,057	($ 17,053)	($ 4,134)	$ 5,662	($ 30,856)
Cash (if no borrowing)	21,000	27,959	31,016	13,963	9,829	15,491
Cumulative cash	$27,959	$31,016	$ 13,963	$ 9,829	$15,491	($ 15,365)
Target cash	22,260	22,260	22,260	22,260	22,260	22,260
Surplus or (loan amount)	$ 5,699	$ 8,756	($ 8,297)	($ 12,431)	($ 6,769)	($ 37,625)

The most common forms of quantitative forecasting are regression analysis and the compound growth rate technique. Regression analysis considers one or more independent variables to forecast the dependent variable. The compound growth rate technique determines the compound growth rate of sales over a period of time, while applying the growth rate to one or more future periods. Qualitative forecasting is based on judgments as to the factors that will cause sales, or any other financial variable, to be different in the future. The methods used range from scientifically conducted opinion surveys to intuitive hunches about the future.

2. Preparing a pro forma income statement.

Preparation of the pro forma income statement depends on a common-size income statement from the previous year. The percentages for each item on the old income statement are applied to the forecast sales for the new year. If additional information is available for any item, the calculated amount may be changed to reflect the new estimated relationship.

3. Preparing a pro forma balance sheet.

The pro forma balance sheet may be developed using percentage of sales forecasting. This method assumes balance sheet accounts are proportional to the level of sales and are currently optimal. The additional funds required for a sales increase may be calculated using a single equation. This approach is useful in finding that amount, but the analyst learns more about the company by preparing the pro forma statements.

4. Preparing a cash budget.

The cash budget details the future cash inflows and cash outflows of a company over a specified period of time. By forecasting the timing of these cash flows, the financial manager determines the financing needs of the company. The cash budget worksheet represents the cash inflows from sales and the cash outflows from purchases. The second part of the cash budget determines the net cash flows for each month. The third part of the cash budget determines the financing requirements over the planning period.

KEY TERMS

Cash budget, 148
Cash budget
   worksheet, 149
Compound growth rate
   technique, 138
Percentage of sales fore-
   casting method, 142

Pro forma balance
   sheet, 142
Pro forma income
   statement, 141
Qualitative
   forecasting, 139

Quantitative
   forecasting, 138
Regression
   analysis, 138
Sales forecast, 138
Sales multiplier, 144

QUESTIONS

5.1 If you were responsible for making a sales forecast, how would you combine quantitative and qualitative approaches to produce a result?

5.2 A financial analyst has a percentage of income statement available when preparing a pro forma income statement. What other information would be useful in preparing the statement?

5.3 In preparing a pro forma balance sheet, under what conditions are the items not proportional to the level of sales? What is the solution when this occurs?

5.4 What is the meaning when the additional funds required is negative? Positive?

5.8 What is the purpose of a cash budget?

5.9 Under what conditions would a monthly cash budget prove to be inadequate?

5.10 How would downsizing in Japan be reflected in pro forma financial statements?

5.11 Why are qualitative factors important in making forecasts?

5.12 How could the cash problems at R.H. Macy have been avoided?

PROBLEMS

5.1 **(Forecasting Sales)** The Gibson Corporation had the following sales over the last five years:

Year	Sales (in thousands)
19X1	1,023
19X2	1,275
19X3	1,495
19X4	1,767
19X5	1,974

Forecast the sales level in 19X6 by using the compound growth rate technique.

5.2 **(Forecasting Sales)** The Williams Company had the following sales over the last six years:

Year	Sales (in thousands)
19X1	914
19X2	922
19X3	1,016
19X4	1,112
19X5	1,215
19X6	1,302

Forecast the sales level in 19X7 by using the compound growth rate technique.

5.3 **(Forecasting Sales)** Vyas, Inc. had the following sales over the last ten years:

Year	Sales	Year	Sales
19X0	$5,100,000	19X5	$ 7,520,000
19X1	5,250,000	19X6	7,800,000
19X2	5,500,000	19X7	8,900,000
19X3	5,910,000	19X8	9,760,000
19X4	6,650,000	19X9	10,720,000

Raj Pandya, a financial analyst for the company, believes that sales growth since 19X2 is representative of future growth. Using the compound growth rate technique, what is his forecast for the next year?

5.4 **(Pro Forma Financial Statements)** Prepare a pro forma income statement and a pro forma balance sheet for the Martin Corporation for 19X6 assuming that sales grew 25 percent.

5.5 **(Pro Forma Financial Statements)** Rework Problem 5.4 with the following additional assumptions:

(a) Interest for 19X6 is $20,000,000.

(b) No additional fixed assets are required.

Check your answer with the additional funds required equation.

5.6 **(Pro Forma Financial Statements)** The income statements and balance sheets for the Singley Corporation follow:

SINGLEY CORPORATION: INCOME STATEMENT FOR THE YEAR ENDED DECEMBER 31, 19X5 (IN THOUSANDS)

Net sales	$1,318
Cost of goods sold	963
Gross profit	$ 355
Selling and administrative expenses	248
Depreciation expense	41
Earnings before interest and taxes (EBIT)	$ 66
Interest expense	18
Earnings before taxes (EBT)	$ 48
Taxes	19
Earnings after taxes (EAT)	$ 29
Preferred stock dividends	6
Earnings available to common shareholders	$ 23
Shares outstanding	50,000
Earnings per share	$0.46
Dividends per share	$0.80

SINGLEY CORPORATION: BALANCE SHEETS AS OF DECEMBER 31, 19X5 (IN THOUSANDS)

ASSETS	
Current assets:	
Cash	$ 36.5
Marketable securities	9.1
Accounts receivable	188.3
Inventory	186.0
Prepaid expenses	7.0
Total current assets	$426.9
Fixed assets:	
Property, plant, and equipment	$376.8
Less: Accumulated depreciation	204.9
Net property, plant, and equipment	$171.9
Total assets	$598.8

LIABILITIES AND STOCKHOLDERS' EQUITY

Current liabilities:	
Accounts payable	$138.5
Notes payable	20.0
Current maturities, long-term debt	10.0
Accrued taxes	21.4
Total current liabilities	$189.9
Long-term debt	120.6
Total liabilities	$310.5
Stockholders' equity:	
Preferred stock	$ 60.0
Common stock ($1 par)	14.0
Capital in excess of par	32.6
Retained earnings	181.7
Total stockholders' equity	$288.3
Total liabilities and stockholders' equity	$598.8

The sales forecast for 19X6 is $1,647,500. The company used its fixed assets at full capacity in 19X5, the level of current assets is optimal, preferred dividends remain constant and common stock dividends are half as much. Prepare a pro forma income statement and a pro forma balance sheet for 19X6.

5.7 **(Receipts and Payments)** Sales estimates for Richman Foods, Inc. for May through October are as follows: $2,400,000, $2,400,000, $2,000,000, $2,000,000, $3,000,000, and $6,200,000. In studying old sales records, you find that 10 percent of customers pay during the month of sale, 50 percent the following month, and 40 percent two months later. You also find that purchases amount to 70 percent of sales for the next month. The payment of the purchases is 20 percent by cash, with the remaining 80 percent paid the following month. Using a cash budget worksheet, what are the total receipts and total payments for the company during July, August, and September? (BUDGET)

5.8 **(Receipts and Payments)** Sales estimates for Burns Equipment Corporation, for November through April are as follows: $5,300,000, $4,800,000, $3,200,000, $3,500,000, $4,600,000, and $7,200,000. Old sales records indicate that 20 percent of customers pay during the month of sale, 50 percent the following month, and 30 percent two months later. Purchases amount to 80 percent of sales for the next month. Payment of purchases is 10 percent by cash, with the remaining 90 percent paid the following month. What are the total receipts and total payments for the company during January, February, March? (BUDGET)

5.9 **(Monthly Financing Requirements)** The monthly total receipts and total payments for the Art Woo Company are as follows:

Month	Total Receipts	Total Payments
April	$2,970,000	$2,590,500
May	$3,030,000	$3,087,600
June	$3,330,000	$3,027,600

In addition, a progress payment of $160,000 is due in April; a dividend payment of $189,000 is due in May; and an income tax payment of $332,000 is due in June. The beginning cash on March 31 is $310,000, and the target level of cash is $300,000. What are the monthly financing requirements for April, May, and June? (BUDGET)

5.10 **(Monthly Financing Requirements)** Madison Motors had the following monthly total receipts and total payments:

Month	Total Receipts	Total Payments
October	$540,000	$450,500
November	$502,300	$480,600
December	$530,000	$510,600

Also, a construction payment of $50,000 is due in October, and an income tax payment of $95,000 is due in November. The beginning cash on September 30 is $45,000, while the target level of cash is $50,000. What are the monthly financing requirements for October, November, and December? (BUDGET)

APPENDIX 5A

Additional Forecasting Techniques

As noted in Chapter 5, the compound growth rate technique or simple regression analysis may be employed in predicting future sales. By using one of these quantitative approaches along with qualitative factors, we can find the yearly forecast. We can then utilize the methods of this appendix to estimate monthly sales.

Simple Regression Analysis

The most common form of quantitative forecasting is simple regression analysis. Two variables are often used in this analysis, a dependent variable, such as sales, and an independent variable, such as time. The sales forecast uses sales over the last several years to predict sales for the next year.

The Martin Corporation had the following sales over the last five years:

Year	Sales (millions)
19X1	$ 850
19X2	875
19X3	975
19X4	1,000
19X5	1,050

Melissa Maxwell, a financial analyst for the company, decided to forecast the sales level in 19X6 using simple regression analysis.

The following equations are the formulas for simple regression analysis.

$$Y = a + bX$$

$$a = \frac{\sum x^2 \sum y - \sum x \sum xy}{n \sum x^2 - (\sum x)^2} \qquad b = \frac{n \sum xy - \sum x \sum y}{n \sum x^2 - (\sum x)^2}$$

where

$$Y = \text{Forecast value}$$
$$X = \text{Predictor value}$$
$$a = \text{Vertical axis intercept}$$
$$b = \text{Regression line slope}$$
$$x = \text{Independent values}$$
$$y = \text{Dependent values}$$
$$n = \text{Number of data points}$$

These forecast equations allow Melissa to predict sales for the next year.

Melissa's goal is to find the value of Y. To do so, she must first find the values of *a* and *b*. To find these values, she constructs the following table:

Year	Sales (y)	x	x²	xy
19X1	850	1	1	850
19X2	875	2	4	1,750
19X3	975	3	9	2,925
19X4	1,000	4	16	4,000
19X5	1,050	5	25	5,250
	$\Sigma y = 4{,}750$	$\Sigma x = 15$	$\Sigma x^2 = 55$	$\Sigma xy = 14{,}775$

Next, she substitutes values from the table into the formulas for a and b.

$$a = \frac{55(4{,}750) - 15(14{,}775)}{5(55) - (15)^2}$$
$$= 792.5$$
$$b = \frac{5(14{,}775) - 15(4{,}750)}{5(55) - (15)^2}$$
$$= 52.5$$

To forecast, Melissa uses the calculated values for a and b, and lets X equal 6, the X-value for the next year, 19X6.

$$Y = a + bX$$
$$= 792.5 + 52.5(6)$$
$$= 1{,}107.5$$

This compares with a result of 1,106.7 from the compound growth rate technique, discussed in Chapter 5. We can also perform simple regression analysis using THE FINANCIAL MANAGER.

Qualitative Approaches

Many companies use quantitative methods to arrive at an initial forecast, and then modify the results with one or more of the following qualitative approaches.

- **Survey of Customers.** Customers are asked what they plan to buy in the future. The sales estimate is determined by combining the responses.
- **Survey of Sales Force.** Salespersons are asked what customers plan to buy in their areas in the future. The sales estimate is determined by combining the responses.
- **Market Research.** Market surveys or market tests are performed. Market surveys use mail questionnaires, telephone interviews, or field interviews to determine the market. Market tests examine products in specific territories, with the results extrapolated to the total market.
- **Executive Consensus.** Key executives form a committee and provide input from various parts of the organization. This common forecasting method tends to prevent extreme forecasts.

Seasonality in Forecasting

The quantitative and qualitative forecasting methods eventually lead to a sales forecast. Let's assume, as in Chapter 5, that the assumed 19X6 sales level for the Martin Corporation, combining quantitative and qualitative approaches, is $1,113,000,000.

Financial managers are interested in taking yearly forecasts and breaking them into seasonal forecasts. Seasonal forecasts reflect the fact that sales usually are not uniform throughout the year. We can prepare seasonal forecasts with relatively simple procedures. We can then use the results as the first step in preparing a cash budget.

Melissa Maxwell has compiled the monthly sales data for the Martin Corporation for the five years ending 19X5. Table 5A.1 contains the information collected, as well as the monthly, yearly, and grand totals. The rightmost column, Index, represents the monthly total as a fraction of the grand total. Melissa wanted to know the monthly sales for 19X6 using a yearly sales forecast of $1,113,000,000.

The monthly sales for 19X6 are calculated by multiplying the yearly forecast by the monthly indexes. The results are compiled in Table 5.A2.

The sales of the Martin Corporation rise from a modest beginning, peak in midsummer, and fall as the end of the year approaches. The seasonality of the forecast is apparent.

TABLE 5A.1 Monthly Sales Data for the Martin Corporation (in millions)

MONTH	19X1	19X2	19X3	19X4	19X5	TOTAL	INDEX
Jan	51.2	56.4	57.8	58.6	61.0	285.0	0.06
Feb	56.1	60.0	67.0	71.2	78.2	332.5	0.07
Mar	58.5	63.5	70.0	72.3	68.2	332.5	0.07
Apr	71.3	72.1	81.0	79.7	75.9	380.0	0.08
May	82.4	77.3	88.0	90.1	89.7	427.5	0.09
Jun	95.6	85.0	99.0	96.1	99.3	475.0	0.10
Jul	102.0	96.1	99.1	103.9	121.4	522.5	0.11
Aug	85.5	90.3	87.9	102.9	108.4	475.0	0.10
Sep	82.6	87.4	87.7	106.0	111.3	475.0	0.10
Oct	68.9	72.9	87.6	93.6	104.5	427.5	0.09
Nov	50.7	60.6	80.0	64.8	76.4	332.5	0.07
Dec	45.2	53.4	69.9	60.8	55.7	285.0	0.06
	850.0	875.0	975.0	1,000.0	1,050.0	4,750.0	1.00

TABLE 5.A2 Martin Corporation Monthly Sales Forecast for 19X6 (in thousands)

MONTH	CALCULATION	RESULT
Jan	$1,113,000(0.06)	$ 66,780
Feb	$1,113,000(0.07)	$ 77,910
Mar	$1,113,000(0.07)	$ 77,910
Apr	$1,113,000(0.08)	$ 89,040
May	$1,113,000(0.09)	$ 100,170
Jun	$1,113,000(0.10)	$ 111,300
Jul	$1,113,000(0.11)	$ 122,430
Aug	$1,113,000(0.10)	$ 111,300
Sep	$1,113,000(0.10)	$ 111,300
Oct	$1,113,000(0.09)	$ 100,170
Nov	$1,113,000(0.07)	$ 77,910
Dec	$1,113,000(0.06)	$ 66,780
		$1,113,000

A Case Problem

RJ Software Corporation designed, developed, and marketed a family of data access and report writing products. The company believed that its products provided for productivity gains over traditional report creation technologies. The simple, intuitive menu system and visual interface would lead even a novice end user through report preparation quickly and easily. Revenues (in thousands) for 1989 through 1993 were $3,156, $5,536, $9,784, $14,388, and $20,718.

A new application due to be released in the second quarter of 1994 was an end-user tool that retrieved data from databases, reformatted the data, and allowed for its transfer and use in a variety of desktop applications, such as spreadsheets and word processors.

The goal of the company was to be the leading producer of data access and report writing software for both end users and computer professionals.

The goal of the company was to be the leading producer of data access and report writing software for both end users and computer professionals. The company's results of operations as a percentage of revenues and the percentage increases from the prior two years follows:

	Percentage of revenues for year ended December 31			Percentage increase from prior year	
	1991	1992	1993	1992	1993
Revenues:					
License fees	94.3%	89.4%	84.4%	39.3%	36.1%
Maintenance and support	5.7	10.6	15.6	175.5	110.3
	100.0	100.0	100.0	47.1	44.0
Operating expenses:					
Cost of revenues	8.4	9.5	11.0	66.7	67.2
Development	8.5	10.4	10.4	80.2	44.8
Selling	34.9	33.0	33.5	38.7	46.2
General and administrative	27.1	23.4	23.6	27.5	45.1
Total operating expenses	78.9	76.3	78.5	42.3	48.3
Operating income	21.1	23.7	21.5	64.8	30.3
Interest income (expense)	0.0	0.6	0.4	NA	15.0
Income from operations	21.1	24.3	21.9	69.0	30.0
Income taxes	7.3	7.7	7.5	54.8	41.6
Net income	13.8	16.6	14.4	76.5	24.6

RJ Software experienced an increase in license fees from both the United States and international operations during the previous two years. The increase in license fees from U.S. customers was due principally from sales to software companies, including pre-paid license fees from new customers and monthly per copy license fees from old customers. The increase in license fees from international customers was attributable primarily to the marketing and sales activities in the United Kingdom in 1992 and Germany in 1993. Maintenance and support service revenues increased principally as the result of the increase in the installed base of products.

Leading Questions

1. What is the forecasted revenue for 1994 using simple regression analysis?
2. What is the forecasted revenue for 1994 using the compound growth rate approach?
3. What is your estimate of revenues for 1994?

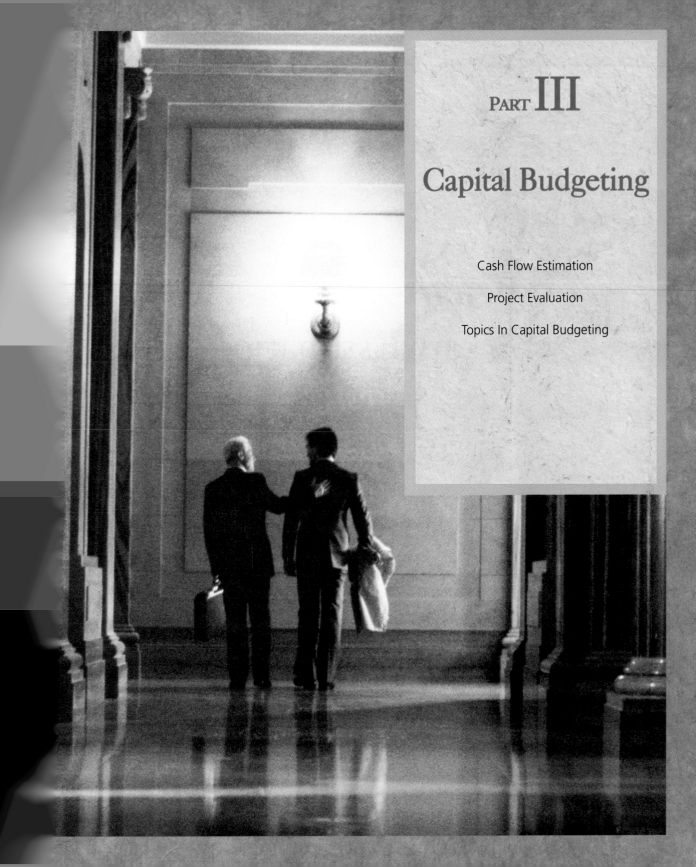

PART III

Capital Budgeting

Cash Flow Estimation

Project Evaluation

Topics In Capital Budgeting

6 Cash Flow Estimation

In their defense, airport officials say many U.S. airports facilities are wearing out. "Like many other infrastructure elements in the U.S.—roads, bridges and sewer systems—the airports are old, and many need to be upgraded," says Leonard Ginn, vice president for economic affairs at Airports Association Council International. Moreover, they say, domestic traffic, which has been flat in recent years, will pick up as the economy recovers, and if the airports can't accommodate it, the airlines themselves will suffer—and complain. "These projects have long lead times," says Spencer Dickerson, executive vice president of the American Association of Airport Executives. "You can't decide overnight to increase capacity."

Denver officials point out that at least some of the projected increase in the airlines' cost at the new airport will be offset by what is expected to be a drastic reduction in flight delays. The savings from cutting delays should be substantial. Chuck Cannon, senior public affairs officer for the airport, says that a loaded airplane waiting to take off racks up $25 a minute in fuel and crew expenses.

Cash flow estimation for airport capital projects is quite complex. In this chapter you will learn the basics of finding incremental cash flows. In doing so, imagine how you would apply this knowledge to the predicament at the nation's airports.

Source: Laurie McGinley, "Airlines Pressure Airports to Scale Back Expansion Plans in Bid to Reduce Costs," *The Wall Street Journal*, September 25, 1992. Reprinted by permission of The Wall Street Journal, © 1992 Dow Jones & Company, Inc. All Rights Reserved Worldwide.

Capital budgeting is the process of allocating funds among competing investment opportunities. In this process, cash flows are often used to determine which projects should be accepted and which should be rejected. In this chapter, we will learn how to estimate the cash flows necessary to make this determination. In the next two chapters, we will discover how to use these cash flows in project evaluation.

Capital Budgeting

INITIAL CASH FLOWS

With the valuation model, the value of any asset is the present value of its future cash flows. In capital budgeting, the value of any project is the present value of all of its cash flows[1]. In this chapter, we will learn specific techniques for finding project cash flows. This is important in deciding which projects to accept.

[1] Capital budgeting involves projects whose cash flows are expected to last more than one year.

The generation of investment proposals comes from new products, improved methods of production, replacement of equipment, acquisition of companies, or required expenditures such as environmental control. These proposals can originate from any employee in the organization. Many companies provide financial incentives for ideas that result in new projects.

The identification of specific projects requires a careful screening of investment proposals. This process often involves several levels of authority, the more money to be spent, the higher the level of authority. In identifying projects, more than one proposal may be included. This linkage is absolutely necessary when proposals are economically dependent on one another.

Incremental Cash Flows

Cash flow estimation demands **incremental cash flows.** This requires a determination of the *additional* after-tax cash flows expected when a project is accepted. These cash flows are positive when cash is flowing into the company and negative when cash is flowing out. Benefits produce positive cash flows and costs produce negative cash flows. For example, acceptance of a project requiring the purchase of equipment causes a negative incremental cash flow. This is usually followed by a series of incremental positive cash flows, the result of increasing revenues or decreasing expenses.

Initial Cash Flows

Initial cash flows are one-time expenditures made near the beginning of a project. While many cash flows occur at time 0, some projects, especially large projects, include cash outflows for several years. With any capital budgeting project, consider the following components in determining the initial cash flow:

1. Capital expenditures.
2. Sale of assets.
3. Operating expenditures.
4. Net working capital.
5. Investment tax credit.
6. Opportunity costs.
7. Sunk costs.

The initial cash flow is the sum of the incremental cash flows from these components.

Capital Expenditures

Capital Expenditures

Capital expenditures are expenditures that provide future benefits beyond the period in which they are incurred. As a result, capital expenditures are generally depreciated. The amount of depreciation for new equipment is not important in calculating initial cash flows but is critical when estimating after-tax operating cash flows.

Capital expenditures include not only the purchase price of the asset but also expenditures necessary to make the asset ready for use. These additional costs include freight, installation, site preparation, legal services, as well as any other expenditures that would be considered a betterment or improvement.

> Van Alstyne Industries purchased a replacement milling machine for $100,000. Freight amounted to $4,300. Removal of the old machine cost $700. What is the cash flow for the capital expenditure portion of the project?

To find the total cost, we sum the three component costs for a total of $105,000. The cash flow is –$105,000. The depreciable base used in calculating depreciation is $105,000.

Sale of Assets

The **sale of assets** involves selling old assets, where the sale is the result of the decision to purchase new assets. This action results in a positive cash flow, the net amount received from the sale.

Consider also the immediate tax effect of selling assets. If the assets are sold for an amount different from the book value, a tax effect normally results. When the assets sell for more than the book value, the difference is considered a gain. When the asset sells for less than the book value, the difference is considered a loss. This is a simplification of tax law but applies in most situations.

A gain or a loss normally results in a negative or a positive tax effect. The amount of the cash flow from taxes is determined by multiplying the marginal tax rate by the book value less the sales price. Multiplying in this manner produces the proper sign.

Sale of Assets

> As the result of the decision to purchase a replacement machine, Van Alstyne Industries sells an old machine purchased five years ago. The total capital expenditure for the old machine was $50,000. It is being depreciated on a straight line basis over 15 years toward a $5,000 salvage value. The old machine can be sold today for $40,000. The marginal tax rate for Van Alstyne is 40 percent. What is the cash flow resulting from the sale of the old machine?

To find the immediate tax effect of selling the old machine, first determine its book value. To find the book value, we must first know the yearly depreciation on the old machine.

The depreciation charge, using the accounting straight line method, is given as follows[2]:

$$DC = \frac{B - SV}{UL} \qquad (6.1)$$

where

$$DC = \text{Depreciation charge}$$
$$B = \text{Basis}$$
$$SV = \text{Salvage value}$$
$$UL = \text{Useful life}$$

To compute the yearly depreciation charge for the old machine, DC_{old}, we use Eq. 6.1.

$$DC_{old} = \frac{\$50,000 - \$5,000}{15}$$
$$= \$3,000$$

We find the book value after five years as follows:

$$\text{Book Value} = \$50,000 - 5(\$3,000)$$
$$= \$35,000$$

To find the amount of the cash flow from taxes, we multiply the 40 percent marginal tax rate by the $35,000 book value less the $40,000 sales price.

$$\text{Tax Cash Flow} = 0.40(\$35,000 - \$40,000)$$
$$= -\$2,000$$

The negative cash flow results from having to pay taxes on the gain.

To find the cash flow from the sale of the asset, we combine the positive cash flow from the sale with the negative cash flow from the taxes. The result is $38,000, $40,000 − $2,000.

Operating Expenditures

Operating Expenditures

Operating expenditures incurred at time 0 are outlays treated as expenses. They are not part of the depreciable base. Training expenses, for example, are

---

[2] For simplicity, the accounting definition of straight line depreciation is used. Later, accelerated cost recovery systems are discussed.

in this category. The IRS, under the Section 179 deduction, also allows certain qualifying capital expenditures to be treated as operating expenditures.

Operating expenditures produce negative cash flows but include a tax benefit as well. The cash flow resulting from the tax benefit is equal to the marginal tax rate multiplied by the amount of the operating expenditure. This action results in a positive cash flow. Combining the negative cash flow and the positive cash flow produces the cash flow from operating expenditures. The same result is found by multiplying the negative cash flow by one minus the marginal tax rate.

> Van Alstyne spends $5,000 to train machine operators for the replacement machine. What is the cash flow for this operating expenditure, assuming a 40 percent marginal tax rate?

To find the operating cash flow, we multiply –$5,000, the cash flow from training machine operators, by one minus the marginal tax rate of 40 percent.

$$\text{Operating Cash Flow} = -\$5000(1 - 0.40)$$
$$= -\$3,000$$

Also we can combine –$5,000 with the $2,000 tax effect, 0.40 ($5,000), a total of –$3,000.

Net Working Capital

Acceptance of a project usually increases current assets *and* current liabilities. Capital projects often require cash for transactions, accounts receivable for customer credit, and inventory for operations. Check these current assets to see if a change in the level required is anticipated. Capital projects also generate accounts payable for company credit, accrued wages for unpaid wages, and accrued taxes for outstanding taxes. Check these current liabilities to see if there is a change in the level expected.

The change in **net working capital** is the change in current assets minus the change in current liabilities. The net working capital cash flow is the negative of the change in net working capital.

Net Working Capital

> In order to purchase the replacement machine, Van Alstyne finds that inventories increase by $500 and accrued wages and taxes *decrease* by $200. All other working capital items remain the same. What s the cash flow from net working capital?

The change in net working capital is the increase in current assets minus the increase in current liabilities.

$$\text{Change} = \$500 - (-\$200)$$
$$= \$700$$

Notice that accrued wages and taxes increase by −$200.

The cash flow from the change in net working capital is −$700. Assume this cash flow returns at the end of the project, resulting in a positive cash flow of $700 at that time.

Investment Tax Credit

Investment Tax Credit

The **investment tax credit (ITC)** is an investment incentive from the federal government. It was first introduced in the early 1960s in order to stimulate business. Since that time, it has moved in and out of the tax code. In this text, we assume there is no investment tax credit, unless it is explicitly stated in a problem.

The ITC is calculated by multiplying the depreciable base of the asset by the applicable investment tax credit percentage. The resulting amount is a credit against federal income taxes. The cash flow from an ITC is always positive.

> Van Alstyne is eligible for a 10 percent investment tax credit when it purchases the replacement machine. What is the cash flow from the investment tax credit?

To find the cash flow from the investment tax credit, we multiply the depreciable base of $105,000 by the 10 percent credit.

$$\text{Credit} = \$105,000(0.10)$$
$$= \$10,500$$

The cash flow that results from the investment tax credit is $10,500.

Opportunity Costs

Opportunity Costs

The **opportunity costs** of a project are the cash flows foregone when a project is accepted. The cash flow for an opportunity cost is the negative of the opportunity cost.

> Van Alstyne must store new inventories when it purchases the replacement machine. Production management determines that no additional space is required to store the inventories. What is the cash flow from the opportunity costs?

It may seem obvious that the cash flow is zero. Be careful, however, to decide if there are additional space requirements during the life of the project. For example, growth in storage requirements in future years may cause additional space to be used, an opportunity cost if this space could otherwise be utilized. In that case, include the cash flows in the years they occur. (If you are using the cash flow worksheet or THE FINANCIAL MANAGER (PROJECT) from the next section, use the CF_{add} column for this purpose.)

A project that requires assets the company already owns includes an opportunity cost if the company could otherwise generate cash flows from the assets. For example, land that could be sold for $300,000 if not used for the project would represent an opportunity cost. Include it as an incremental cash flow.

Sunk Costs

Sunk costs are costs that do not depend on acceptance or rejection of the project. They are *not* incremental costs but are, instead, outlays made before the project begins.

Sunk Costs

> The engineering department at Van Alstyne Industries spends $1,000 studying the technical feasibility of operating the replacement machine. Does this result in an incremental cash flow?

The engineering department has already spent $1,000 for the feasibility study. It is a sunk cost, not an incremental cost and does not affect the initial cash flow.

The Initial Cash Flow

The initial cash flow for the project is −$60,200 at time 0. It consists of −$105,000 for the capital expenditure, +$38,000 for the sale of the asset, −$3,000 for the operating expenditure, −$700 for net working capital, +$10,500 for the investment tax credit, and $0 for opportunity cost. The $1,000 is a sunk cost and should not be included in the initial cash flow.

Show this with a cash flow diagram.

The next section covers after-tax operating cash flows. As with initial cash flows, we determine incremental cash flows for the project.

OPERATING CASH FLOWS

Operating Cash Flows

The calculation of **operating cash flows** is challenging. This section focuses on learning an approach that will handle both simple and complicated problems.

The Cash Flow Equation

The after-tax operating cash flows for a project represent the change in cash flows each period caused by acceptance of the project. Express this relationship with the following formula:

$$CF_n = (R_n - OC_n - DC_n)(1 - T) + DC_n \qquad (6.2)$$

where

$$CF_n = \text{Change in cash flow at time n}$$
$$R_n = \text{Change in revenue at time n}$$
$$OC_n = \text{Change in operating costs at time n}$$
$$DC_n = \text{Change in depreciation charge at time n}$$
$$T = \text{Marginal tax rate}$$

This definition of cash flow assumes after-tax cash flows for a company with no debt.

In Chapter 7, cash flows are discounted at the marginal cost of capital. This approach implies that the company returns interest to creditors and dividends to shareholders. To avoid double counting, Eq. 6.2 does *not* include interest expense.

Changes in Depreciation

The first term in Eq. 6.2 is an expression for the change in earnings after tax in period n. Thus, the equation is rewritten.

$$CF_n = EAT_n + DC_n \qquad (6.2a)$$

where

$$EAT_n = \text{Change in earnings after tax in period n}$$
$$= (R_n - OC_n - DC_n)(1 - T)$$

The industrial engineers at Van Alstyne Industries find the replacement machine (discussed in the previous section) reduces operating costs by $10,000 per year over the 10 year project life. The total cost of this machine is $105,000 and it is being depreciated on a straight line basis over 10 years toward a $20,000 salvage value. The total cost of the old machine—purchased five years ago—was $50,000, and it is being depreciated on a straight line basis over 15 years toward a $5,000 salvage value. The marginal tax rate for the company is 40 percent. What is the change in cash flows and the change in earnings after tax for each of the 10 years?

We calculate the depreciation charge for the replacement machine, DC_{new}, by using Eq. 6.1.

$$DC_{new} = \frac{\$105,000 - \$20,000}{10}$$

$$= \$8,500$$

This is the depreciation charge for the replacement machine, *not* the change in depreciation.

The change in depreciation charge, DC_n, is the difference in the two depreciation charges.

$$DC_n = DC_{new} - DC_{old} \qquad (6.3)$$

We calculate the change in depreciation charge for the project using Eq. 6.3.

$$DC_n = \$8,500 - \$3,000$$
$$= \$5,500$$

We find the change in cash flows for each of the 10 years using Eq. 6.2.

$$CF_n = (R_n - OC_n - DC_n)(1 - T) + DC_n$$
$$= [0 - (-\$10,000) - \$5,500](1 - 0.40) + \$5,500$$
$$= (\$10,000 - \$5,500)(0.6) + \$5,500$$
$$= \$2,700 + \$5,500$$
$$= \$8,200$$

The change in earnings after tax for each of the 10 years is $2,700, the amount of the first term in Eq. 6.2.

We show the after-tax operating cash flows with a cash flow diagram.

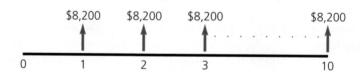

This is a relatively simple problem, for three reasons. First, the change in revenue and the change in operating costs is constant over the 10 years. Second, straight line depreciation is used for the new and the old assets. Third, the number of years of depreciation left for the old asset (ten years) is exactly equal to the number of years of depreciation for the new asset.

The Baldrige Boondoggle

A funny thing happened to the Wallace Co. on the way from the 1990 Malcolm Baldrige National Quality Award. The $90 million-a-year Houston pipe and valve manufacturer had just won the "small" business Baldrige Award. In recognition of that achievement, the company's senior management spent a few months lecturing the rest of the corporate world on the need for higher across-the-board quality at all costs. Eventually, however, people in the company began to notice that something wasn't quite right. The company, unfortunately, was swimming in red ink. Suddenly, quality at all costs didn't seem like such a good idea after all. As details of Wallace's troubles emerged, *Business Week* interviewed Curt W. Reimann, the civil servant in charge of the Baldrige program for the Commerce Dept.

Reimann noted that the Commerce Dept. has neither the expertise nor the resources to perform financial analysis on award candidates. The magazine also recounted the reasons for Wallace's fall from grace, as seen by an unnamed former senior Wallace executive. By investing heavily in new computers and operating systems, the company increased its on-time deliveries from 75% in 1987 to 92% in 1990. Market share also increases, from slightly more than 10% to 18%. But the cost was high, more than $2 million annually in extra overhead. And, although customers said they wanted more timely deliveries, they weren't willing to pay extra for that benefit.

Source: Jim Smith and Mark Oliver, "The Baldrige Boondoggle," *Machine Design,* August 6, 1992.

Worksheets and Spreadsheets

In estimating cash flows for complex problems, we should record the information on a **worksheet.** A format derived from Eq. 6.2 is included as Table 6.1. The simple case of the replacement project is illustrated. Notice that a new variable, CF_{add}, additional cash flow, is included. This represents cash flows not calculated according to Eq. 6.2. The initial cash flow from the previous section is in this category and is included at time 0. Other additional cash flows may be inserted in later years.   **Worksheet**

The easiest way to handle complex problems is to use THE FINANCIAL MANAGER (PROJECT). This **spreadsheet** model uses the same basic format as the worksheet in Table 6.1 and makes all of the calculations automatically.   **Spreadsheet**

TERMINAL CASH FLOWS

Terminal cash flows are those cash flows which result when a project is terminated. The cash flows occur at the end of the economic life of the project. This period does not have to be equal to the physical life of the equipment.   **Terminal Cash Flows**

TABLE 6.1 Partial Cash Flow Worksheet for the Replacement Project
● ● ● ● ● ● ●

PERIOD	CF_{add}	CF_n	R_n	OC_n
0	−$60,200	0	0	0
1	0	$8,200	0	−$10,000
2	0	$8,200	0	−$10,000
3	0	$8,200	0	−$10,000
4	0	$8,200	0	−$10,000
5	0	$8,200	0	−$10,000
6	0	$8,200	0	−$10,000
7	0	$8,200	0	−$10,000
8	0	$8,200	0	−$10,000
9	0	$8,200	0	−$10,000
10	0	$8,200	0	−$10,000

PERIOD	DC_n	DC_{new}	DC_{old}	EAT_n
0	0	0	0	0
1	$5,500	$8,500	$3,000	$2,700
2	$5,500	$8,500	$3,000	$2,700
3	$5,500	$8,500	$3,000	$2,700
4	$5,500	$8,500	$3,000	$2,700
5	$5,500	$8,500	$3,000	$2,700
6	$5,500	$8,500	$3,000	$2,700
7	$5,500	$8,500	$3,000	$2,700
8	$5,500	$8,500	$3,000	$2,700
9	$5,500	$8,500	$3,000	$2,700
10	$5,500	$8,500	$3,000	$2,700

Terminal Cash Flows Forms

Terminal cash flows are usually in two forms: (1) return of net working capital, and (2) after-tax cash flow from the sale of assets.

> Van Alstyne Industries terminates the replacement project after year 10. What is the terminal cash flow?

Remember from the section on initial cash flows that the change in net working capital is $700. At year 10, a cash flow of +$700 results from the return of that net working capital.

Also the sale of the replacement machine in year 10 results in a positive cash flow of $20,000. The immediate tax effect of selling the asset at that time must be considered.

To find out if there is a gain or a loss, we must know the book value of the machine at year 10. The book value is determined by subtracting the $8,500 per year depreciation on the new machine over 10 years:

$$\text{Book Value} = \$105,000 - 10(\$8,500)$$
$$= \$20,000$$

Since the book value is equal to the selling price, there is no tax effect for this relatively simple example. In using MACRS depreciation (to be discussed later), there normally is a tax effect.

The Terminal Cash Flow

The terminal cash flow for the project is $20,700 at time 10. It consists of $700 for the return of net working capital and $20,000 for the after-tax cash flow from the sale of the replacement machine.

The complete cash flow diagram, including the terminal cash flow at time 10, follows.

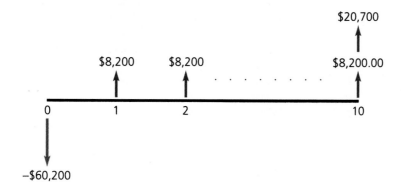

Table 6.2 presents the complete worksheet for the replacement project. The additional cash flow column includes both the initial cash flow and the terminal cash flow.

ACCELERATED COST RECOVERY SYSTEMS

In finance, the interest in depreciation often centers on how it will affect the incremental cash flows of a project. This contrasts with the accounting approach of considering depreciation as a means of cost allocation. Depreciation differences alter incremental cash flows by changing the amount of taxes that must be paid.

TABLE 6.2 Cash Flow Worksheet for the Replacement Project
● ● ● ● ● ● ●

PERIOD	CF_{add}	CF_n	R_n	OC_n
0	−$60,200	0	0	0
1	0	$8,200	0	−$10,000
2	0	$8,200	0	−$10,000
3	0	$8,200	0	−$10,000
4	0	$8,200	0	−$10,000
5	0	$8,200	0	−$10,000
6	0	$8,200	0	−$10,000
7	0	$8,200	0	−$10,000
8	0	$8,200	0	−$10,000
9	0	$8,200	0	−$10,000
10	$20,700	$8,200	0	−$10,000

PERIOD	DC_n	DC_{new}	DC_{old}	EAT_n
0	0	0	0	0
1	$5,500	$8,500	$3,000	$2,700
2	$5,500	$8,500	$3,000	$2,700
3	$5,500	$8,500	$3,000	$2,700
4	$5,500	$8,500	$3,000	$2,700
5	$5,500	$8,500	$3,000	$2,700
6	$5,500	$8,500	$3,000	$2,700
7	$5,500	$8,500	$3,000	$2,700
8	$5,500	$8,500	$3,000	$2,700
9	$5,500	$8,500	$3,000	$2,700
10	$5,500	$8,500	$3,000	$2,700

Depreciation methods for reporting purposes are unlike depreciation methods for tax purposes. For reporting purposes, depreciation methods match capital expenses of an investment against revenues. For tax purposes, depreciation methods depend on tax law and may not balance capital expenses and revenue.

Before 1981, the Internal Revenue Service allowed businesses to use accounting methods of depreciation. Beginning in 1981, the IRS, under the provisions of the Economic Recovery Tax Act of 1981, required a new depreciation system, the **Accelerated Cost Recovery System (ACRS)**. In 1987, the Tax Reform Act of 1986 replaced ACRS with the **Modified Accelerated Cost Recovery System (MACRS)**. This section explains the similarities between ACRS and MACRS.

Accelerated Cost Recovery System

Modified Accelerated Cost Recovery System

Recovery Period

Under both accelerated cost recovery systems, capital assets are grouped into property classes. For example, computers are classified as five-year property under both methods. The IRS requires that this specific **recovery period** be used. Before 1981, the useful life, which varied from company to company, could be used as the specified time period.

Recovery Period

Recovery Percentage

Under both accelerated cost recovery systems, the Internal Revenue Service requires that a **recovery percentage** be used for each year of the recovery period. For example, a computer purchased in 1985 under ACRS used the following percentages:

Recovery Percentage

Period	Recovery Percentage
1st year	15%
2nd year	22%
3rd–5th years	21%

Under MACRS, the IRS uses more complex procedures to determine the recovery percentages. This involves half-year, mid-quarter, and in some cases, mid-month conventions. Normally, the half-year convention is used, but if more than 40 percent of the company's assets are purchased in the last quarter, the mid-quarter convention is required. Mid-month applies primarily to real estate assets. These conventions specify when assets are put in service and taken out of service. The IRS also allows a switch to straight line as soon as that method yields a larger depreciation charge.

MACRS, like ACRS, requires recovery of the unadjusted basis over a specified time period. Assets are assigned to classes of property by recovery period:

- 3-year property (Example: tractor units for use over the road.)
- 5-year property (Examples: heavy general purpose trucks, computers and peripheral equipment, office machinery, any automobile, light general purpose trucks.)
- 7-year property (Examples: office furniture and fixtures, single purpose agricultural structures.)
- 10-year property (Examples: vessels, barges, tugs, similar transportation equipment.)
- 15-year property (Example: municipal wastewater treatment plant.)
- 20-year property (Examples: farm buildings, municipal sewers.)

- Residential rental property. (Example: Buildings such as apartments where 80 percent of rental income is from dwelling units.)
- Nonresidential real property. (Example: Buildings such as offices, warehouses, factories, and stores.)

Fortunately, MACRS depreciation recovery percentages may be found by using the optional tables found in IRS Publication 534, Depreciation. Table 6.3, which is adapted from those tables, provides the 200% or 150% declining balance switching to straight line percentages, assuming the half-year convention. Determination of recovery periods can be complicated. The practice in this text will be to provide the recovery percentages or the recovery period in problem applications.

TABLE 6.3 MACRS Depreciation Recovery Percentages, Assuming the Half-Year Convention

RECOVERY YEAR	3-YEAR	5-YEAR	7-YEAR	10-YEAR	15-YEAR	20-YEAR
1	33.33	20.00	14.29	10.00	5.00	3.750
2	44.45	32.00	24.49	18.00	9.50	7.219
3	14.81	19.20	17.49	14.40	8.55	6.677
4	7.41	11.52	12.49	11.52	7.70	6.177
5		11.52	8.93	9.22	6.93	5.713
6		5.76	8.92	7.37	6.23	5.285
7			8.93	6.55	5.90	4.888
8			4.46	6.55	5.90	4.522
9				6.56	5.91	4.462
10				6.55	5.90	4.461
11				3.28	5.91	4.462
12					5.90	4.461
13					5.91	4.462
14					5.90	4.461
15					5.91	4.462
16					2.95	4.461
17						4.462
18						4.461
19						4.462
20						4.461
21						2.231

Determining Depreciation

To find the yearly depreciation charges, multiply the unadjusted basis of the property by the recovery percentages. Unadjusted basis is usually the cost of the asset. Unlike the other depreciation calculations we have made up to now, the salvage value is not subtracted in finding the unadjusted basis.

Arthur Sanders, an employee of Van Alstyne Industries, purchased a computer in 1985 for $5,000, 5-year property under ACRS. The recovery percentages for IRS Publication 534, Depreciation, are 15, 22, 21, 21, and 21 percent. What are the allowable depreciation charges and book values?

Table 6.4 summarizes the depreciation charges and book values over the five-year period. Since no salvage value is used in determining the unadjusted basis, the final book value is zero.

Arthur Sanders purchased another computer in 1989 for $5,000. In studying IRS Publication 534, he determined that the recovery percentages are 20.00, 32.00, 19.20, 11.52, 11.52, and 5.76 percent. What are the allowable depreciation charges and book values?

Table 6.5 summarizes the depreciation charges and book value over a six-year period. Depreciation is calculated over six years due to the half-year convention.

Alternate Recovery Systems

Sometimes, it is useful to spread depreciation out over the years rather than using the accelerated methods of ACRS and MACRS. Under both accelerated

TABLE 6.4 Depreciation Charges and Book Values Using 5-Years ACRS

YEAR	DEPRECIATION CHARGE	BOOK VALUE
1985	$5,000(0.15) = $ 750	$4,250
1986	5,000(0.22) = 1,100	3,150
1987	5,000(0.21) = 1,050	2,100
1988	5,000(0.21) = 1,050	1,050
1989	5,000(0.21) = 1,050	0
	$5,000	

TABLE 6.5 Depreciation Charges and Book Values Using 5-Year MACRS

YEAR	DEPRECIATION CHARGE	BOOK VALUE
1989	$5,000(0.2000) = $1,000	$4,000
1990	5,000(0.3200) = 1,600	2,400
1991	5,000(0.1920) = 960	1,440
1992	5,000(0.1152) = 576	864
1993	5,000(0.1152) = 576	288
1994	5,000(0.0576) = 288	0

Alternate Method

cost recovery systems, an **alternate method** is allowed. This means straight line depreciation is applied over the recovery period, while using a half-year convention. The result is a half-year of allowable depreciation in the first year and in the year following the recovery period.

Marilyn Sanders purchased a computer in 1989 for $5,000. She knew this was five-year property under MACRS, that the half-year convention applies, *and* that she would choose the alternate method. What are the depreciation charges and book value?

A recovery period of five years implies a straight line value of 20 percent each year. Due to the half-year convention, years one and six each receive one-half of the calculated yearly percentage:

Period	Recovery Percentage
1st Year	10%
2nd Year	20%
3rd Year	20%
4th Year	20%
5th Year	20%
6th Year	10%

Table 6.6 summarizes the depreciation charges and book value over a six-year period. Depreciation is calculated over six years due to the half-year convention.

MACRS in the Replacement Project

In estimating the cash flows for the replacement project, we used accounting straight line depreciation. The calculations become more complicated when MACRS depreciation is used.

TABLE 6.6 Depreciation Charges and Book Values Using Alternate MACRS

YEAR	DEPRECIATION CHARGE	BOOK VALUE
1989	$5,000(0.1000) = $ 500	$4,500
1990	5,000(0.2000) = 1,000	3,500
1991	5,000(0.2000) = 1,000	2,500
1992	5,000(0.2000) = 1,000	1,500
1993	5,000(0.2000) = 1,000	500
1994	5,000(0.1000) = 500	0

Margaret Baxter, a financial analyst at Van Alstyne Industries, determined that MACRS depreciation should be used for the replacement project, not accounting straight line depreciation. The equipment for the project has a seven-year recovery period. The applicable percentages (for eight years) are as follows: 14.29, 24.49, 17.49, 12.49, 8.93, 8.92, 8.93, and 4.46. The marketing department also says that sales will increase by $10,000 each year. With this sales growth, there is an associated rise in operating costs of $6,000. The change in operating costs is –$4,000, –$10,000 + $6,000. What is the change in cash flows and the change in earnings after tax for each of the 10 years?

We determine the depreciation each year by multiplying the depreciable base by the percentages. Table 6.7 records the depreciation for the eight years.

TABLE 6.7 MACRS Depreciation for the Replacement Project

YEAR	DEPRECIATION CHARGE	BOOK VALUE
1	$105,000(0.1429) = $15,004.50	$89,995.50
2	105,000(0.2449) = 25,714.50	64,281.00
3	105,000(0.1749) = 18,364.50	45,916.50
4	105,000(0.1249) = 13,114.50	32,802.00
5	105,000(0.0893) = 9,376.50	23,425.50
6	105,000(0.0892) = 9,366.00	14,059.50
7	105,000(0.0893) = 9,376.50	4,683.00
8	105,000(0.0446) = 4,683.00	0.00
9	0.00	0.00
10	0.00	0.00

TABLE 6.8 Cash Flow Worksheet for the MACRS Replacement Project
• • • • • • •

PERIOD	CF_{add}	CF_n	R_n	OC_n
0	−$60,200	0	0	0
1	0	$13,201.80	$10,000	−$4,000
2	0	$17,485.80	$10,000	−$4,000
3	0	$14,545.80	$10,000	−$4,000
4	0	$12,445.80	$10,000	−$4,000
5	0	$10,950.60	$10,000	−$4,000
6	0	$10,946.40	$10,000	−$4,000
7	0	$10,950.60	$10,000	−$4,000
8	0	$ 9,073.20	$10,000	−$4,000
9	0	$ 7,200.00	$10,000	−$4,000
10	$12,700	$ 7,200.00	$10,000	−$4,000

PERIOD	DC_n	DC_{new}	DC_{old}	EAT_n
0	0	0	0	0
1	$12,004.50	$15,004.50	$3,000	$ 1,197.30
2	$22,714.50	$25,714.50	$3,000	−$ 5,228.70
3	$15,364.50	$18,364.50	$3,000	−$ 818.70
4	$10,114.50	$13,114.50	$3,000	$ 2,331.30
5	$ 6,376.50	$ 9,376.50	$3,000	$ 4,574.10
6	$ 6,366.00	$ 9,366.00	$3,000	$ 4,580.40
7	$ 6,376.50	$ 9,376.50	$3,000	$ 4,574.10
8	$ 1,683.00	$ 4,683.00	$3,000	$ 7,390.20
9	−$ 3,000.00	$0	$3,000	$10,200.00
10	−$ 3,000.00	$0	$3,000	$10,200.00

We record the information on a worksheet, as is done in Table 6.8. Determine CF_n by using Eq. 6.2. Since the change in depreciation varies each year, perform the calculation 10 times. For the first year, CF_1 is calculated as follows:

$$
\begin{aligned}
CF_1 &= (R_1 - OC_1 - DC_1)(1 - T) + DC_1 \\
&= [\$10,000 - (-\$4,000) - \$12,004.50](1 - 0.4) + \$12,004.50 \\
&= (\$1,995.50)(0.6) + \$12,004.50 \\
&= \$13,201.80
\end{aligned}
$$

The terminal cash flow changes with MACRS. Usually with this type of depreciation, the book value is not equal to the selling price. As shown in Table 6.6, the book value at time 10 is $0. Therefore, there is a gain on the sale of the replacement machine. The amount of the cash flow from taxes is determined by multiplying the marginal tax rate by the book value less the sales price.

$$\text{Tax Cash Flow} = 0.40(\$0 - \$20,000)$$
$$= -\$8,000$$

To find the cash flow from the sale of the replacement machine, we combine the $20,000 cash flow with the −$8,000 cash flow from taxes. The result is $12,000. The terminal cash flow for the project is $12,700 at time 10. It consists of $700 for the return of net working capital and $12,000 for the after-tax cash flow from the sale of the replacement machine.

The use of MACRS causes the changes in depreciation, earnings after tax, and cash flow to vary widely from year the year. This makes calculation by worksheet tedious. The FINANCIAL MANAGER (PROJECT) will calculate DC_{new}, DC_{old}, and DC_n, if the user supplies basic depreciation information. It computes CF_n and EAT after the values R_n and OC_n, are entered.

We use a cash flow diagram to show the newest change in cash flows.

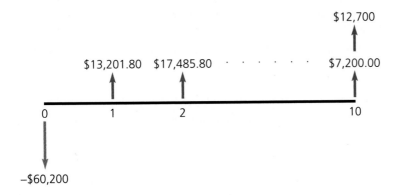

SUMMARY

This chapter focuses on the following learning objectives:

1. Determining the initial cash flow for a capital budgeting project.

    Initial cash flows involve seven elements: capital expenditures, sale of assets, operating expenditures, net working capital, investment tax credit, opportunity costs, and sunk costs. Capital expenditures include not only the purchase price of the asset but also the expenditures necessary to make the asset ready for use. The sale of assets produces a positive cash flow and normally a tax effect if the assets are sold for an amount different from the book value.

Operating expenditures are treated as expenses and include a tax benefit. The change in net working capital is the cash flow required at the beginning of a project and returned at the end. The investment tax credit is an investment incentive in the form of a credit against federal income taxes. The opportunity costs of a project are the cash flows foregone when a project is accepted. Sunk costs do not depend on whether the project is accepted or rejected and are not incremental costs.

2. Calculating the operating cash flows for a capital budgeting project.
   The after-tax operating cash flows for a project are the change in cash flows during each period caused by acceptance of the project. This cash flow may be divided into the change in earnings after tax and the change in depreciation.

3. Computing the terminal cash flow for a capital budgeting project.
   Terminal cash flows result when a project is completed. These cash flows occur at the end of the economic life of the project, not at the point when the equipment is useless.

4. Reporting cash flows using a worksheet/spreadsheet format.
   In estimating cash flows for complex problems, a worksheet or a spreadsheet can be used. The easiest way to handle complex problems is to use THE FINANCIAL MANAGER (PROJECT). The model uses the same basic format as the worksheet.

5. Explaining the basics of ACRS depreciation to cash flow determination.
   Beginning in 1981, the IRS, under the provisions of the Economic Recovery Tax Act of 1981, required a new depreciation system, the Accelerated Cost Recovery System (ACRS). In 1987, the Tax Reform Act of 1986 replaced ACRS with the Modified Accelerated Cost Recovery System (MACRS).

6. Applying the basics of ACRS and MACRS depreciation to cash flow determination.
   With ACRS and MACRS, the amount of depreciation is not constant over the project life. This causes cash flows to vary widely from year to year. Also, the book value and salvage value differ causing a gain or a loss for tax purposes.

KEY TERMS

Accelerated cost recovery system, 180

Alternate method, 184

Capital budgeting, 167

Capital expenditure, 168

Incremental cash flow, 168

Initial cash flow, 168

Investment tax credit, 172

Modified accelerated cost recovery system, 180

Net working capital, 171

Operating cash flows, 174

Operating expenditure, 170

Opportunity cost, 172

Recovery percentage, 181

QUESTIONS

6.1 If you were responsible for a capital budgeting project, what steps would you take to find the project cash flows?

6.2 What mistakes do managers make in determining the initial cash flow for a project?

6.3 How would the number of years of depreciation left on the replaced asset affect the change in depreciation charge?

6.4 Why are worksheets and spreadsheets useful in determining cash flows?

6.5 How are the calculations for a new project simpler than for a replacement project?

6.6 How does MACRS depreciation make cash flow calculations more difficult?

6.7 How is the estimation of cash flows for airports complicated?

6.8 How should South Korea control its industrial costs?

6.9 What happened after the Wallace Company won the Malcolm Baldridge National Quality Award?

PROBLEMS

6.1 **(Initial Cash Flow)** The O'Connell corporation is evaluating the purchase of a new machine costing $37,000 delivered and installed. Use of the new equipment requires $2,000 in net working capital. A 10 percent investment tax credit applies. What is the initial cash flow for the new project?

6.2 **(Initial Cash Flow)** Ruczko, Inc., a manufacturer of rubber products, is interested in purchasing a new tire mold in order to increase production. The equipment costs $85,000, including freight, and requires $5,000 to install. The company plans to expense an additional $5,000 in maintenance time in the installation phase of the project. Use of the equipment causes net working capital needs to increase by $3,000. A 10 percent investment tax credit is available. What is the initial cash flow for the new project, assuming a 40 percent marginal tax rate?

6.3 **(Initial Cash Flow)** Greene Transmissions, Inc. plans to order a new crankshaft machine to replace an older model. The older model, purchased 10 years ago for $50,000, is being depreciated on a straight line basis over 20 years toward a $10,000 salvage value. It can be sold today for $20,000. The new machine costs $75,000, delivered and installed. A three-week training course, costing $1,000, is required to learn the operation of the new machine. The company has a 40 percent marginal tax rate and does not qualify for the investment tax credit. No additional net working capital is required. What is the initial cash flow for the new project?

6.4 **(Initial Cash Flow)** The Fernandez Company, a manufacturer of non-woven fabrics, requires a replacement machine in its web bonding process. The new machine costs $240,000 and requires $10,000 for freight and installation. A 10 percent investment tax credit applies. Net working capital requirements decrease by $1,000, but the maintenance department must spend $2,000 to learn to use this equipment. The old machine, purchased five years ago for $100,000, is being depreciated over 10 years toward a $25,000 salvage value. An independent contractor has agreed to remove the old machine for its scrap value. If the company is in the 40 percent marginal tax bracket, what is the initial cash flow for the project?

6.5 **(Initial Cash Flow)** Gilbert Publishing plans to replace its bookbinding line at a cost of $400,000, including freight and installation. The equipment from the old process can be sold for $100,000 to an overseas buyer. It was purchased four years ago at a price of $250,000 and is being depreciated over 15 years toward a $40,000 salvage value. Acceptance of this project means that current assets would increase by $25,000 and current liabilities would increase by $10,000. The company has a 40 percent marginal tax rate and does not qualify for the investment tax credit. Purchase of the new equipment requires that a building currently owned be used for the expansion. This building could be sold today to net $100,000 after taxes. Gilbert spent $25,000 studying the feasibility of this expansion. What is the initial cash flow for the project?

6.6 **(Operating Cash Flows and Earnings After Tax)** The Phillips Pearson Paper Company is considering replacing one of its core machines. The new machine has a total cost of $150,000 and would be depreciated on a straight line basis over 10 years toward a $20,000 salvage value. The old machine was purchased five years ago for $75,000 and is being depreciated over 15 years toward a $15,000 salvage value. Purchase of the new machine will not change revenues, but it would decrease operating costs by $65,000 per year. The marginal tax rate is 40 percent. What is the change in cash flows and the change in earnings after tax for each of the 10 years? (PROJECT)

6.7 **(Operating Cash Flows and Earnings After Tax)** Ellis Electronics plans to purchase new equipment for its television camera line, a capital expenditure of $160,000. This new equipment will be depreciated toward a $40,000 salvage value over 12 years. The company is currently using equipment bought eight years ago for $70,000 that is being depreciated over 20 years toward a $20,000 salvage value. The new equipment will increase revenues by $20,000 while *decreasing* operating costs by $20,000. The marginal tax rate is 40 percent. What is the change in cash flows and the change in earnings after tax for each of the 12 years? (PROJECT)

6.8 **(Operating Cash Flows and Earnings After Tax)** The Stafford Steel Company is considering new nail manufacturing equipment to replace equipment purchased 10 years ago for $100,000. The total cost of the new equipment is $200,000. Like the old equipment, it is being depreciated on a straight line basis over 15 years toward a salvage value that is 25 percent of the original cost. The new equipment will increase revenues by $50,000 per year while keeping operating costs the same. The marginal tax rate is 40 percent. What is the change in cash flows and the change in earnings after tax for each of the 15 years? (PROJECT)

6.9 **(Operating Cash Flows and Earnings After Tax)** The Atlas Chemical Company plans to replace extruding equipment purchased 11 years ago for $275,000. The old equipment is being depreciated over 15 years toward a $50,000 salvage value. The new equipment costs $500,000 and is being depreciated over 10 years toward a $100,000 salvage value. While revenues remain constant, operating costs decline by $200,000. The marginal tax rate is 40 percent. What is the change in cash flows and the change in earnings after tax for each of the 10 years? (PROJECT)

6.10 **(Operating Cash Flows and Earnings After Tax)** Natural Foods, Inc. is replacing the fish processing equipment that it bought 10 years ago. The total cost at that time was $137,000. Straight line depreciation is being used over a 15 year life, with a salvage value of $17,000. The new equipment, costing $250,000, is depreciated using MACRS. Since the half-year convention applies, the applicable percentages (for 4 years) are as follows: 33.33, 44.45, 14.81, and 7.41. The economic life of the project is 10 years, and during that time, operating costs will be reduced by $60,000 per year. The marginal tax rate is 40 percent. What is the change in cash flows and the change in earnings after tax for each of the 10 years? (PROJECT)

6.11 **(Project Cash Flows)** Georgia Clay Products plans to replace one of its brick lines at a total cost of $900,000. The old line cost $300,000 to install 15 years ago. It is being depreciated over 25 years toward a $0 salvage value, the net amount it would bring today. The new process, which would be depreciated by the straight line method, would also be worthless at the end of 10 years. New operator training would cost $5,000. Net working capital requirements would increase by $4,000. The investment tax credit is 10 percent, and the marginal tax rate is 40 percent. The company spent $40,000 studying the feasibility of the project. If the project is accepted, revenues would increase by $150,000 per year while operating costs would decrease by $150,000. What is the change in cash flows and the change in earnings after tax over the life of the project? (PROJECT)

6.12 **(Project Cash Flows)** Portland Cement, Inc. plans to replace one of its cement lines at a cost of $1,300,000. The old line, installed 20 years ago, cost $350,000. It is being depreciated toward a $50,000 salvage value using straight line depreciation over 30 years and can be sold today for $20,000. The new line will be depreciated by the straight line method over 10 years toward a $300,000 salvage value. Installation of the new line allows revenues to increase by $500,000 per year while operating costs remain constant. Net working capital would increase by $50,000. The investment tax credit is 10 percent, and the marginal tax rate is 40 percent. What is the change in cash flows and the change in earnings after tax over the life of the project? (PROJECT)

6.13 **(Earnings After Tax and Project Cash Flows)** Butkus Iron and Steel will replace equipment in its molding operation. The old equipment cost $300,000 when purchased 20 years ago. It is being depreciated over 20 years on a straight line basis toward a $0 salvage value, but it can be sold today for $10,000. The new equipment cost $850,000 and requires $50,000 in freight and installation. It will be depreciated on a straight line basis over 10 years toward a $100,000 salvage value. Net working capital requirements will not change. Installation of the new equipment allows revenues to increase by $200,000 per year while operating costs decrease by $100,000. If the marginal tax rate is 40 percent, what is the change in cash flows and the change in earnings after tax over the life of the project? (PROJECT)

6.14 **(Earnings After Tax and Project Cash Flows)** Avery Aviation, Inc. plans to replace one of its old airplanes. The old plane was purchased 20 years ago at a cost of $95,000. It is being depreciated over 30 years by the straight line method toward a $5,000 salvage value. It can be sold today for $35,000. A replacement plane costs $500,000 and has a 15 year recovery period under MACRS. Since the half year convention applies in this case, the applicable percentage (over 16 years) are as follows: 5.00, 9.50, 8.55, 7.70, 6.93, 6.23, 5.90, 5.90, 5.91, 5.90, 5.91, 5.90, 5.91, 5.90, 5.91, and 2.95. Management estimates it could be sold in 20 years for $100,000. Over the 20 year economic life, the new plane increases revenues by $250,000 per year and increases operating costs by $50,000 per year. The investment tax credit is 10 percent, and the marginal tax rate is 40 percent. Net working capital increases by $25,000. What is the change in cash flows and the change in earnings after tax over the life of the project? (PROJECT)

A Case Problem

Magnetech, Inc. was a major producer of high performance scanning magnetic recording systems and magnetic tape media. The primary customers of the company were the television post-production and broadcasting industries. Secondary customers included government agencies and defense contractors involved in data recording and processing. As part of its company strategy, Magnetech focused on markets which required the highest levels of capability and reliability.

The company was founded during the Korean War and provided technical expertise to the U.S. Air Force during that conflict. To continue as a leader in technology, Magnetech had invested more than $250 million in new product research, development, and engineering since that time. As a result, the company held more than 1,000 patents from which it received significant royalty income.

The near-term strategy of Magnetech was to introduce products based on its current technology, which it would apply to new markets such as mass data storage.

The near-term strategy of Magnatech was to introduce products based on its current technology, which it would apply to new markets such as mass data storage.

This would allow the company to use designs and components that were proprietary in nature and not generally available to other competitors. The goal was to generate revenues necessary to return the company to profitability.

To support its introduction into the mass storage data market, Magnetech planned to invest $2,600,000 in new equipment. Robert Andrews, a financial analyst for the company, was evaluating the incremental cash flows that would result from the project. Since he was unsure of expected revenues and operating costs, he decided to direct his attention initially to comparing methods of depreciation.

In studying IRS Publication 534, Depreciation, Robert found that all of the required equipment was five-year property under MACRS and that the half-year convention applied. He further discovered that Magnetech could elect to use the alternate method under MACRS if this would benefit the company.

In examining past tax records, Robert determined that the marginal tax rates over the life of the project would not be constant. This was primarily the result of loss carryovers from previous years. He estimated the federal-plus-state marginal tax rate at zero percent the first year, 21 percent the second year, 31 percent the third year, and 40 percent over the remaining years of the 10-year project.

Leading Questions

1. What are the amounts of depreciation each year under accelerated MACRS and under the alternate method?
2. What are the resultant cash flows from depreciation under the two methods?
3. Which method of depreciation would you choose?

7 Project Evaluation

AUGUSTA NEWSPRINT EXPANDS

Augusta Newsprint Co., which manufactures newsprint for markets in Georgia, South Carolina, North Carolina and part of Virginia, has begun work on an expansion that will increase the amount of newspapers the company can recycle. The company, which is owned by Toronto-based Abitibi-Price Inc. and The Thomson Corp., became the first de-inking newspaper recycling plant in North America in

1990 when it spent $27 million to replace an existing stone ground wood pulp plant. Until that time, newsprint was made entirely from wood pulp.

John Weaver, general manager of Augusta Newsprint Co., said the decision to expand the plant's recycling process was twofold: "It was a combination of demand for increased recycling and the advantage for us cost-wise," said Mr. Weaver. "This way we don't have to buy as much (wood) pulp." Mr. Weaver said consumers are demanding more recycled products, with the environment in mind. More than 30 percent of the paper used to print *The Augusta Chronicle* and *Augusta Herald* is made from recycled newspaper.

The expansion allows the company to recycle 50 per-

cent more magazines and newspapers, or about 150,000 tons per year, turning them into 200,000 tons of newsprint containing 40 percent recycled papers and another 180,000 tons containing 20 percent recycled papers. While the 1990 expansion added 12 jobs at the plant, no additional employees will be taken on with the newest expansion, said Mr. Weaver.

The expansion at Augusta Newsprint required management to decide if the benefits of the project were greater than the costs. In this chapter, you will learn to make that kind of decision using techniques that will maximize the value of your company's common stock.

Source: Dale Hokrein, "Augusta Newsprint expands," *The Augusta Chronicle*, October 8, 1992.

FUNDAMENTAL SELECTION TECHNIQUES

The primary goal of financial management in a corporation is to maximize the value of its common stock. The project analysis techniques of net present value and internal rate of return, when properly used, help you as a financial manager to achieve this goal.

Net Present Value

The **net present value (NPV)** of a project is equal to the present value of its cash flows, discounted at the required rate of return. Chapter 9 shows that the required rate of return is the marginal cost of capital.

Net Present Value

NPV is expressed by the following formula:

$$NPV = CF_0 + \frac{CF_1}{(1+k)^1} + \ldots + \frac{CF_n}{(1+k)^n} \qquad (7.1)$$

where

$$CF_n = \text{Cash flow at year n, n} = 0,1,2, \ldots, N$$
$$k = \text{Marginal cost of capital}$$
$$N = \text{Terminal period}$$

Notice that the cash flows include the cash flow at time 0.

We can calculate the net present value for the basic replacement project from Chapter 6. The cash flow diagram follows:

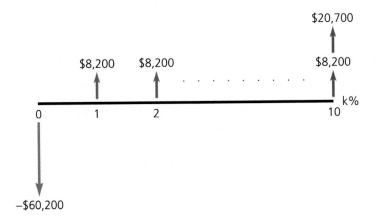

To write an expression for NPV, we use Equation 7.1, applying the time value techniques from Chapter 2.

$$NPV = -\$60,200 + \$8,200 \sum_{i=1}^{10} \frac{1}{(1+k)^i} + \frac{\$20,700}{(1+k)^{10}}$$
$$= -\$60,200 + \$8,200(PVFA_{k\%,10}) + \$20,700(PVF_{k\%,10})$$

We state the expressions for NPV as a function of k, the discount rate, in order to describe the general relationship.

We can compute the net present value for different values of k. For example, the following is the computation when k equals 10 percent.

$$NPV = -\$60,200 + \$8,200(PVFA_{10\%,10}) + \$20,700(PVF_{10\%,10})$$
$$= -\$60,200 + \$8,200(6.1446) + \$20,700(0.3855)$$
$$= -\$1,834$$

In Table 7.1, net present value is calculated for a range of values.

TABLE 7.1 NPV Calculations for Different Values of k, Basic Replacement Project

MARGINAL COST OF CAPITAL, K	NET PRESENT VALUE, NPV
0%	$42,500
5%	$15,826
10%	–$ 1,834
15%	–$13,929
20%	–$22,479

Net Present Value Profile

We can graph the relationship of the NPV to the discount rate used in the calculation. Such a graph is called a **net present value profile.** The profile for the basic replacement project is included as Figure 7.1.

Figure 7.1 demonstrates that the net present value decreases as the discount rate increases. The net present value is positive in the range from 0 percent to 9.38 percent. We find the point where the NPV is 0 by using a calculator or THE FINANCIAL MANAGER (PROJECT). Above 9.38 percent, the NPV is negative.

Net Present Value Profile

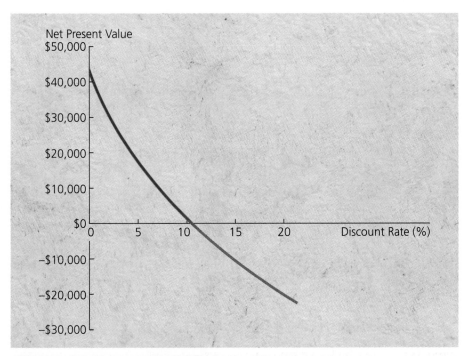

FIGURE 7.1 NPV Profile for the Basic Replacement Project

NPV Acceptance Criterion

A project is accepted when the NPV is greater than or equal to 0 and rejected when the NPV is less than 0[1]. The implication of this statement is that the value of the company's equity increases by the amount of the NPV if a project with a non-negative NPV is accepted. Accepting a project with a negative NPV would decrease the value of the company's equity by the amount of the negative NPV.

The basic replacement project should be accepted if the marginal cost of capital is less than or equal to 9.38 percent. For example, if the marginal cost of capital is five percent, the NPV is +$15,826. We accept the project, thereby increasing the value of the company's equity by that amount.

In a similar manner, we can calculate the net present value for the MACRS replacement project. The cash flow diagram based on Table 6.8 (page 186) follows:

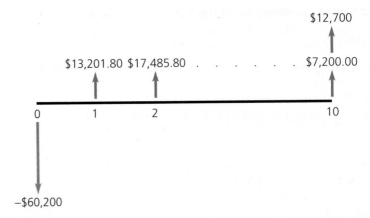

To find the NPV for the MACRS replacement project, we use Equation 7.1 over the 10 periods.

$$\text{NPV} = \begin{aligned} &-\$60,200 + \frac{\$13,201.80}{(1+k)^1} + \frac{\$17,485.80}{(1+k)^2} + \frac{\$14,545.80}{(1+k)^3} \\ &+ \frac{\$12,445.80}{(1+k)^4} + \frac{\$10,950.60}{(1+k)^5} + \frac{\$10,946.40}{(1+k)^6} + \frac{\$10,950.60}{(1+k)^7} \\ &+ \frac{\$9,073.20}{(1+k)^8} + \frac{\$7,200.00}{(1+k)^9} + \frac{\$19,900.00}{(1+k)^{10}} \end{aligned}$$

$$= \begin{aligned} &-\$60,200 + \$13,201.80(\text{PVF}_{k\%,1}) + \$17,485.80(\text{PVF}_{k\%,2}) \\ &+ \$14,545.80(\text{PVF}_{k\%,3}) + \$12,445.80(\text{PVF}_{k\%,4}) + \$10,950.60(\text{PVF}_{k\%,5}) \\ &+ \$10,946.40(\text{PVF}_{k\%,6}) + \$10,950.60(\text{PVF}_{k\%,7}) + \$9,073.20(\text{PVF}_{k\%,8}) \\ &+ \$7,200.00(\text{PVF}_{k\%,9}) + \$19,900.00(\text{PVF}_{k\%,10}) \end{aligned}$$

The FINANCIAL MANAGER (PROJECT) makes this calculation much easier.

[1] This chapter focuses on the independent project; the decision-maker accepts or rejects a single project.

TABLE 7.2 NPV Calculations for Different Values of k, MACRS Replacement Project

MARGINAL COST OF CAPITAL, K	NET PRESENT VALUE, NPV
0%	$66,500
5%	$38,568
10%	$19,238
15%	$ 5,407
20%	−$ 4,794

In Table 7.2, the net present value is calculated for different values of k.

Again, it is possible to graph the relationship of the NPV to the discount rate used in the calculation. The net present value profile for the MACRS replacement project is included as Figure 7.2. In Figure 7.2, the NPV is positive from 0 percent to 17.47 percent, and negative after that point. We accept the MACRS replacement project if the marginal cost of capital is less than or equal to 17.47 percent. This increases the value of the company's equity by the amount of the net present value.

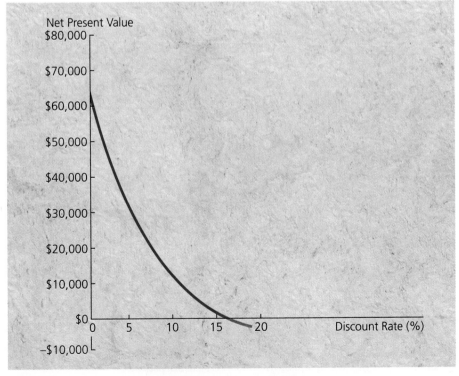

FIGURE 7.2 NPV Profile for the MACRS Replacement Project

Internal Rate of Return

Internal Rate of Return

The **internal rate of return (IRR)** of a project is the discount rate, r, which causes the present value of its cash flows to be equal to 0. It is thus the discount rate where the net present value is equal to zero, the point of intersection with the horizontal axis.

IRR is expressed by the following formula:

$$0 = CF_0 + \frac{CF_1}{(1+r)^1} + \ldots + \frac{CF_N}{(1+r)^N} \tag{7.2}$$

where

$$r = \text{Internal rate of return}$$

To determine the internal rate of return for the basic replacement project, we use Equation 7.2, applying the time value techniques from Chapter 2.

$$0 = -\$60,200 + \$8,200 \sum_{i=1}^{10} \frac{1}{(1+r)^i} + \frac{\$20,700}{(1+r)^{10}}$$

$$0 = -\$60,200 + \$8,200(PVFA_{r\%,10}) + \$20,700(PVF_{r\%,10})$$

We compute the internal rate of return, using either expression, by trying different values of r, a *trial and success* procedure[2]. We try a value of 9 percent for r.

$$0 = -\$60,200 + \$8,200(PVFA_{9\%,10}) + \$20,700(PVF_{9\%,10})$$

$$0 = -\$60,200 + \$8,200(6.4177) + \$20,700(0.4224)$$

$$0 = +\$1,169$$

To make the right side of the equation closer to 0, we try another value for r. Since r is in the denominator, using a larger r makes the net present value smaller. Let's try a value of 10 percent for r.

$$0 = -\$60,200 + \$8,200(PVFA_{10\%,10}) + \$20,700(PVF_{10\%,10})$$

$$0 = -\$60,200 + \$8,200(6.1446) + \$20,700(0.3855)$$

$$0 = -\$1,834$$

We conclude that the IRR is between 9 and 10 percent since the value on the right hand side went from positive to negative. With a financial calculator or

---

[2] "Trial and success" is a learning tool but is not a good way to find the precise answer. Use an advanced calculator or THE FINANCIAL MANAGER (PROJECT) for that purpose.

THE FINANCIAL MANAGER (PROJECT), the precise answer is 9.38 percent. Notice that this is the point on the net present value profile where the NPV is 0.

Similarly, we can find the IRR for the MACRS replacement project. Using a *trial and success* procedure, we can trap the value between 17 and 18 percent. The precise answer is 17.47 percent, the discount rate where the NPV is equal to 0.

IRR Acceptance Criteria

Conventional projects begin with one or more negative cash flows, followed by one or more positive cash flows (e.g. $-+++$ or $--+++$). One sign change is involved in the sequence. The basic and MACRS replacement projects are of this type. Conventional projects have net present value profiles that slope down and to the right. Figure 7.1 and Figure 7.2 illustrate the graphs of conventional projects.

Conventional projects are accepted if the internal rate of return is greater than or equal to the marginal cost of capital and are rejected when the internal rate of return is less than the marginal cost of capital. In Figure 7.1, notice this is equivalent to saying that the NPV is nonnegative, since all conventional projects have net present value profiles that slope down and to the right. For example, if the marginal cost of capital is 5 percent, we accept the basic replacement project since the IRR of 9.38 percent is greater than 5 percent. The NPV is positive at this discount rate, also indicating acceptance according to the NPV acceptance criterion.

Loan projects begin with one or more positive cash flows, followed by one or more negative cash flows (e.g. $+---$ or $++---$). One sign change is involved in the sequence. If we reverse the signs of the cash flows in the basic or MACRS replacement projects, the result is a loan project. Figure 7.3 illustrates the net present value profile for the reversed cash flows of the basic replacement project.

Loan projects are accepted if the internal rate of return is less than or equal to the marginal cost of capital and are rejected if the internal rate of return is more than the marginal cost of capital. This is equivalent to saying that the NPV is nonnegative, since all loan projects have net present value profiles that slope up and to the right. For example, we accept the loan project if the marginal cost of capital is 15 percent, since the IRR of 9.38 percent is less than 15 percent. The NPV is positive at this discount rate, also indicating acceptance according to the NPV acceptance criterion.

Nonconventional projects begin with either positive or negative cash flows, followed by no fixed order of cash flows (e.g. $-++-$ or $-++-+$). More than one sign change is involved in the sequence. The rule of Descartes says that the number of real roots of an equation (or rates of return) is, at most, equal to the number of sign changes. So, a nonconventional project with two sign changes will have zero, one, or two internal rates of return.

Conventional Projects

Loan Projects

Nonconventional Projects

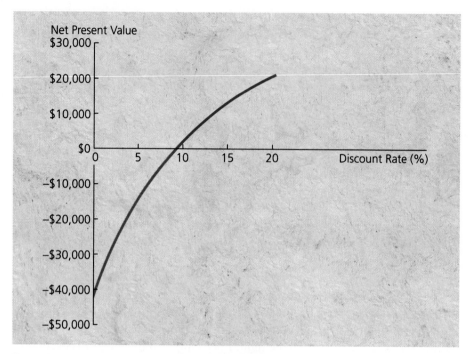

FIGURE 7.3 Net Present Value Profile for a Loan Project

There is no clear IRR acceptance rule for nonconventional projects since there may be zero, one, or more than one internal rates of return. Thus, the net present value may be equal to zero at one or more points in the net present value profile, or the net present value may never be equal to zero. The next two examples for Princeton Printers illustrate this point.

> Princeton Printers invests $10,000 in a project at time 0. The company expects an after-tax cash flow of $62,500 at time 1 and an after-tax cash flow of −$62,500 at time 2. What does the net present value profile look like for this project?

The net present values are calculated for different discount rates. The results are shown in Table 7.3. Next, graph the relationship of the NPV to the discount rate. The net present value profile is included as Figure 7.4.

The NPV is nonnegative between 25 and 400 percent. The nonconventional project should be accepted within this range. If the marginal cost of capital is less than 25 percent or greater than 400 percent, we reject the project.

TABLE 7.3 Net Present Values for a Nonconventional Project

MARGINAL COST OF CAPITAL, K	NET PRESENT VALUE, NPV	MARGINAL COST OF CAPITAL, K	NET PRESENT VALUE, NPV
0%	−$10,000	250%	2,755
25%	0	300%	1,719
50%	3,889	350%	802
100%	5,625	400%	0
150%	5,000	450%	−702
200%	3,889	500%	−1,319

Princeton Printers invests $17,500 in a project at time 0. The company expects an after-tax cash flow of $62,500 at time 1 and an after-tax cash flow of −$62,500 at time 2. What does the net present value profile look like for such a project?

We compute the net present value for different values of k, as shown in Table 7.4.

Next, we graph the relationship of the NPV to the discount rate. The net present value profile is included as Figure 7.5.

As shown in Figure 7.5, there is no discount rate where the NPV is equal to zero. At discount rates greater than 100 percent, the NPV in fact declines. This implies that the project is rejected regardless of the marginal cost of capital.

The IRR acceptance criteria in this section are valid for **independent** pro-   Independent
jects, projects whose cash flows do not depend on one another. If projects are

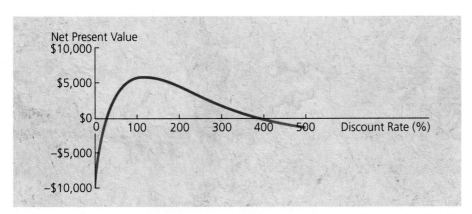

FIGURE 7.4 Net Present Value Profile, Nonconventional Project

TABLE 7.4 NPV Calculations for Different Values of k, Nonconventional Project with No IRR

MARGINAL COST OF CAPITAL, K	NET PRESENT VALUE, NPV
0%	−$17,500
25%	−7,500
50%	−3,611
100%	−1,875
150%	−2,500
200%	−3,611
250%	−4,745
300%	−5,781
350%	−6,698
400%	−7,500
450%	−8,202
500%	−8,819

Mutually Exclusive

mutually exclusive, acceptance of one project precludes acceptance of the other project. For example, a company chooses between Machine A and Machine B to replace an old machine. Machine A or Machine B could be chosen but not both. Chapter 8 studies the use of IRR for mutually exclusive projects.

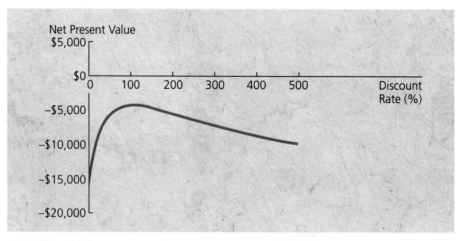

FIGURE 7.5 Net Present Value Profile for the Project with no IRR

A Comparison of Techniques

The NPV acceptance criterion conforms to the **value additivity principle.** This means that the net present value of a group of independent projects is the sum of the net present values of the individual projects. Since this is true, the value of a company's equity increases as projects with positive NPVs are accepted. For other investment criteria to be equally as good, they must deliver the same accept/reject decisions as net present value.

Value Additivity Principle

Internal rate of return provides the same accept/reject decisions as does NPV for conventional and loan projects, if properly used[3]. There is no clear IRR acceptance rule for nonconventional projects since there may be zero, one, or more than one internal rates of return. In that case, the financial manager must rely on net present value. Chapter 8 extends this discussion by examining the case of mutually exclusive projects.

America's Failing Capital Investment System

The internal capital market is the system by which corporations allocate available capital from both internal and external sources to investment projects within and across business units[4]. Corporate goals center on earning high returns on investment and maximizing current stock prices. Management exercises the dominant influence on corporate goals, interpreting signals about desired behavior from the external capital market. Boards, which have come to be dominated by outside directors with no other links to the company, exert only limited influence on corporate goals. The presence of knowledgeable owners, bankers, customers, and suppliers on corporate boards has diminished. Both as a cause and an effect, capital budgeting in the U.S system takes place largely through "by the numbers" exercises that require unit or functional managers to justify investment projects quantitatively. The system rarely treats investments such as R&D, advertising, or market entry as investments; rather they are negotiated as part of the annual budgeting process, which is primarily driven by a concern for current profitability. Both the Japanese and German systems are profoundly different from the American system. For both, the predominant aim is to secure the position of the corporation and ensure the company's continuity. Information flow is far more extensive, and financial criteria play less of a determining role in investment decisions than in the United States.

Source: Reprinted by permission of *Harvard Business Review.* Excerpts from "Capital Disadvantage: America's Failing Capital Investment System," by Michael E. Porter (September–October 1992). Copyright © 1992 by the President and Fellows of Harvard College.

[3] Profitability index, to be discussed later, also provides the same accept/reject decisions as does NPV for conventional and loan projects, if properly used.
[4] This vignette focuses on one section of this article.

ADDITIONAL SELECTION TECHNIQUES

Net present value and internal rate of return are powerful methods for evaluating projects. Businesspeople, however, use additional techniques in project selection, along with, or in place of, these methods.

Payback Period

Payback Period

The **payback period (PB)** is the number of years necessary to recover the initial investment of a project. It is also the time required for the cumulative cash flows from the project to equal zero. We use after-tax cash flows to make this determination. Managers evaluate payback period by setting a maximum number of years for acceptance.

We can calculate payback period for the basic replacement project. Here is the cash flow diagram.

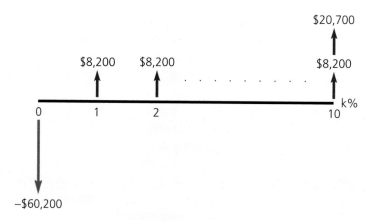

When cash flows are constant, we divide the yearly cash flow of $8,200 into the initial investment.

$$PB = \frac{\$60,200}{\$8,200}$$

$$= 7.34 \text{ years}$$

Since the $8,200 continued for at least eight years, the calculation makes sense.

We can also calculate payback period for the MACRS replacement project. When cash flows are *not* constant, accumulate the cash flows until the sum is equal to 0.

Period	Cash Flow	Cumulative Cash Flows
0	−$60,200.00	−$60,200.00
1	$13,201.80	−$46,998.20
2	$17,485.80	−$29,512.40
3	$14,545.80	−$14,966.60
4	$12,445.80	− $2,520.80
5	$10,950.60	+ $8,429.80

The payback period is between four and five years, since the cumulative cash flow went from negative to positive in year five. We need $2,520.80 of the $10,950.60 cash flow in year five.

$$PB = 4 + \frac{\$2,520.80}{\$10,950.60}$$
$$= 4.23 \text{ years}$$

It takes 4.23 years to recover the initial investment.

Payback period, although it is often used, has serious deficiencies:

- *It does not consider the time value of money.* During the payback period, early cash flows are treated the same as later cash flows, regardless of size.
- *It ignores cash flows beyond the payback period.* Cash flows after the payback period are not considered in making the accept/reject decision.

Therefore, in general, payback period cannot be used as a substitute for net present value.

Discounted Payback Period

The **discounted payback period (DPB)** uses the same definition as payback period, except that cash flows are discounted back to time 0, using the marginal cost of capital. In Table 7.5, for the basic replacement project, the cash flows, discounted cash flows, and cumulative cash flows are included. Assume a marginal cost of capital of five percent.

Discounted Payback Period

TABLE 7.5 Discounted Payback Period Calculations for the Basic Replacement Project

YEAR	CASH FLOW	DISCOUNTED CASH FLOW	CUMULATIVE CASH FLOW
0	−$60,200	−$60,200	−$60,200
1	$ 8,200	$ 7,810	−$52,390
2	$ 8,200	$ 7,437	−$44,953
3	$ 8,200	$ 7,083	−$37,870
4	$ 8,200	$ 6,746	−$31,124
5	$ 8,200	$ 6,425	−$24,699
6	$ 8,200	$ 6,119	−$18,580
7	$ 8,200	$ 5,828	−$12,752
8	$ 8,200	$ 5,550	−$ 7,202
9	$ 8,200	$ 5,286	−$ 1,916
10	$28,900	$17,742	+$15,826

To calculate discounted payback period, first we add the discounted cash flows until the sum is equal to 0. This is done in the rightmost column of Table 7.5. The discounted payback period is between 9 and 10 years, since the cumulative cash flow goes from negative to positive in year 10. We need $1,916 of the $17,742 cash flow for year 10.

$$DPB = 9 + \frac{\$1,916}{\$17,742}$$

$$= 9.11 \text{ years}$$

Notice that the NPV of the basic replacement project, from Table 7.1, is also $15,826 when the discount rate is five percent.

After computing discounted payback period, it is important to understand its application. *If there are enough positive cash flows for the DPB to be calculated, accept the project, unless there are negative cash flows after the discounted payback period.*

Discounted payback period delivers the same accept/reject decisions as net present value under the limited conditions of the previous paragraph. Otherwise, no definite decision is possible with DPB. Since it does not consider the time value of money, discounted payback period is preferable to payback period; since it ignores cash flows beyond the payback period, discounted payback period is *not* preferable to net present value.

Accounting Rate of Return

Accounting Rate of Return

The **accounting rate of return (ARR),** often called the average return on book value, is the average earnings after tax divided by the average book value.

TABLE 7.6 Earnings After Tax and Book Value for the Basic Replacement Project

PERIOD	EARNINGS AFTER TAX	BOOK VALUE
0	$ 0	$105,000
1	$2,700	$ 96,500
2	$2,700	$ 88,000
3	$2,700	$ 79,500
4	$2,700	$ 71,000
5	$2,700	$ 62,500
6	$2,700	$ 54,000
7	$2,700	$ 45,500
8	$2,700	$ 37,000
9	$2,700	$ 28,500
10	$2,700	$ 20,000

When this method is used for evaluating projects, the calculated value often is compared with the industry average accounting rate of return.

Table 7.6 shows the earnings after tax and book value for the basic replacement project. It is adapted from Table 6.2 (page 180). This information is readily available when using THE FINANCIAL MANAGER (PROJECT).

To calculate the accounting rate of return, first average the earnings after tax for the 10 periods. In the basic replacement project, the average is obviously $2,700 since the value is constant.

To find the average book value, use the following formula if constant depreciation is employed over the entire life of the project:

$$ABV_c = \frac{BV_0 - BV_N}{2} + BV_N \qquad (7.4)$$

where

ABV_c = Average book value (constant depreciation)

BV_0 = Book value at time 0

BV_N = Book value at end of project, period N

This formula represents a special situation where book value declines at a constant rate.

For the basic replacement project, we calculate the average book value using Equation 7.4.

$$\text{ABV}_c = \frac{\$105,000 - \$20,000}{2} + \$20,000$$
$$= \$62,500$$

We determine the accounting rate of return for the basic case as follows:

$$\text{ARR} = \frac{\text{Average Earnings After Tax}}{\text{Average Book Value}}$$
$$= \frac{\$2,700}{\$62,500}$$
$$= .0432 \text{ or } 4.32\%$$

The value of 4.32 percent is the average return on investment for the basic replacement project. If ARR is used as the investment criterion, this value would be compared to some predetermined standard.

Table 7.7 shows the earnings after tax and book value for the MACRS replacement project. It is adapted from Table 6.8 (page 186).

To calculate the accounting rate of return (ARR) for the MACRS replacement project, first average the earnings after tax for the 10 periods.

TABLE 7.7 Earnings After Tax and Book Value for the MACRS Replacement Project

PERIOD	EARNINGS AFTER TAX	BOOK VALUE
0	0	$105,000.00
1	$ 1,197.30	$ 89,995.50
2	-$ 5,228.70	$ 64,281.00
3	-$ 818.70	$ 45,916.50
4	$ 2,331.30	$ 32,802.00
5	$ 4,574.10	$ 23,425.50
6	$ 4,580.40	$ 14,059.50
7	$ 4,574.10	$ 4,683.00
8	$ 7,390.20	$ 0.00
9	$10,200.00	$ 0.00
10	$10,200.00	$ 0.00

$$\text{Average EAT}_n = \frac{\$1,197.30 - \$5,228.70 - \$818.70 + \ldots + \$10,200.00}{10}$$

$$= \$3,900.00$$

To find the average book value (ABV), we could use the following formula if the depreciation is not constant:

$$ABV = \frac{\dfrac{BV_0 - BV_N}{2} + \sum\limits_{n=1}^{N} BV_n}{N} \tag{7.5}$$

We can calculate the average book value for the MACRS project.

$$ABV = \frac{\dfrac{\$105,000 - \$0}{2} + \$275,163}{10}$$

$$= \$32,766.30$$

The $275,163 figure in the equation is the sum of the book values for periods 1 through 10.

We determine the accounting rate of return for the MACRS replacement project as follows:

$$ARR = \frac{\text{Average Earnings After Tax}}{\text{Average Book Value}}$$

$$= \frac{\$3,900.00}{\$32,766.30}$$

$$= 0.1190 \text{ or } 11.90\%$$

We can also use equation 7.5 to calculate the average book value for the basic case, although it is simpler to go with Equation 7.4.

$$ABV = \frac{\dfrac{(\$105,000 - \$20,000)}{2} + \$582,500}{10}$$

$$= \$62,500$$

The FINANCIAL MANAGER (PROJECT) employs Equation 7.5 in the average book value part of the accounting rate of return calculation.

ARR may be favored by some businesspeople, since managers often are evaluated by the ratio of net income to the total assets. Unfortunately, accounting rate of return has serious deficiencies.

- *It uses net income instead of cash flow.* Net income does not consider the investment possibilities of all of the benefits of a project. Since after-tax operating cash flows are the sum of net income plus depreciation, considering only net income may lead to incorrect decisions.
- *It does not consider the time value of money.* The timing of benefits is not considered. Early benefits are treated the same as later benefits.

Therefore, accounting rate of return cannot be used as a substitute for net present value.

Modified Internal Rate of Return

Modified Internal Rate of Return

The **modified internal rate of return (MIRR)** of a project is the discount rate, r_m, which causes the absolute value of the present value of the negative cash flows to equal the present value of the terminal value of the positive cash flows[5]. The terminal value (TV) is the future value of the positive cash flows at the end of the project, compounded at the marginal cost of capital. The rules for accepting a project with modified internal rate of return are the same as with the internal rate of return.

We can use the cash flows for the basic replacement project to calculate the modified internal rate of return, assuming a 10 percent marginal cost of capital. Here is the cash flow diagram.

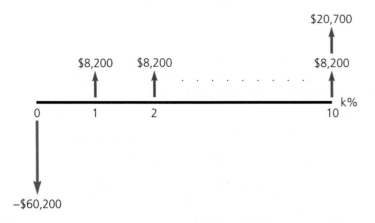

---

[5] Some project evaluators believe that modified internal rate of return avoids the reinvestment rate assumption. Most financial theorists disagree with this belief.

We bring the positive cash flows to time 10 with the following equation:

$$\begin{aligned} TV &= \$8,200(FVFA_{10\%,10}) + \$20,700 \\ &= \$8,200(15.937) + \$20,700 \\ &= \$151,383.4 \end{aligned}$$

The absolute value of the present value of the negative cash flows is +\$60,200. We show this with a cash flow diagram.

Using an advanced calculator or THE FINANCIAL MANAGER (PROJECT), the modified internal rate of return is 9.66 percent. We reject the project since 9.66 percent is less than the marginal cost of capital of 10 percent.

Profitability Index

The **profitability index (PI)** is the ratio of the present value of the positive cash flows of a project to the absolute value of the present value of the negative cash flows.

Profitability Index

$$PI = \frac{\text{Present Value of Positive Cash Flows}}{|\text{Present Value of Negative Cash Flows}|} \qquad (7.6)$$

The denominator includes negative cash flows at time 0, *or after.*

Calculate the profitability index (PI) for the basic replacement project, applying the time value techniques from Chapter 2.

$$\begin{aligned} PI &= \frac{\$8,200 \sum_{i=1}^{10} \dfrac{1}{(1+k)^i} + \dfrac{\$20,700}{(1+k)^{10}}}{|-\$60,200|} \\[2mm] &= \frac{\$8,200(PVFA_{k\%,10}) + \$20,700(PVF_{k\%,10})}{|-\$60,200|} \end{aligned}$$

Both expressions for PI are stated as a function of k, the discount rate, in order to describe the general relationship.

We can compute the profitability index for different values of k. For example, the following is the computation when k equals 10 percent:

$$PI = \frac{\$8,200(PVFA_{10\%,10}) + \$20,700(PVF_{10\%,10})}{|-\$60,200|}$$

$$= \frac{\$8,200(6.1446) + \$20,700(0.3855)}{\$60,200}$$

$$= 0.97$$

A value for profitability index less than 1.00 implies that the net present value is negative. Thus, the value of 0.97 indicates the project should be rejected.

In Table 7.8, the profitability index is calculated for different values of k.

Profitability Index Profile

Profitability Index Profile

It is possible to graph the relationship of the PI to the discount rate used in the calculation. Such a graph is called a **profitability index profile.** The profile for the basic replacement project is included as Figure 7.6.

In Figure 7.6, notice that the profitability index decreases as the discount rate increases[6]. The profitability index is greater than 1.00 in the range from 0 percent to 9.38 percent. We can find that point where the PI is equal to 1.00 by using a calculator or the FINANCIAL MANAGER (PROJECT)[7]. Above 9.38 percent, the PI is less than 1.00.

TABLE 7.8 Profitability Index Calculations for Different Values of k, Basic Replacement Project

MARGINAL COST OF CAPITAL, K	PROFITABILITY INDEX, PI
0%	1.71
5%	1.26
10%	0.97
15%	0.77
20%	0.63

[6] The profitability index profile and the net present value profile are similar, only the scale of the vertical axis has changed.

[7] The discount rate at which the PI is equal to 1.00 is equal to the internal rate of return.

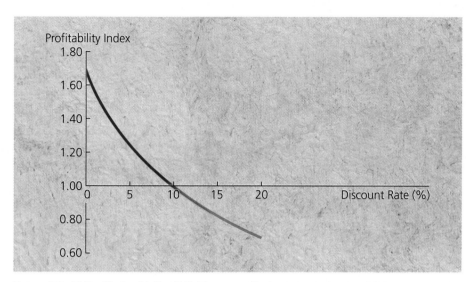

FIGURE 7.6 PI Profile for the Basic Replacement Project

PI Acceptance Criterion

A project is normally accepted when the NPV is greater than or equal to zero and rejected when the NPV is less than zero. *Using profitability index, this corre-*

Cost of Capital: The Japanese Way

Faced with an avalanche of investment by Japanese companies, U.S. managers may wonder how such investments are possible. . . . Japanese companies care about borrowing costs, of course, and they push their banks and brokers to get the best terms. They are also careful about investment decisions. But both the criteria and the constituencies Japanese managers must consider when making these decisions are different than those faced by U.S. managers. Japanese corporations sit in the midst . . . of interlocking relationships, some of them formal but more of them informal. . . . In such an environment, many different criteria guide investment decisions: the most important is the Japanese company's long-term goal of maintaining and, when possible, enhancing its posi-

tion in the Japanese power structure. Keeping and enhancing this status mandates a relentless drive for market share, cost reduction, meeting and beating the competition, and sheer size. . . . This does not mean that Japanese companies throw money away. Experts in the Japanese automobile industry, for example, say that auto companies do use financial criteria in making investment decisions but that those criteria are generally quantified in terms of a payback period.

sponds to accepting a project when the PI is greater than or equal to 1.00 and rejecting it when the PI is less than 1.00.

The basic replacement project should be accepted if the marginal cost of capital is less than or equal to 9.38 percent. For example, if the marginal cost of capital is five percent, the PI is 1.26, and the NPV is +$15,826. We accept the project, using PI to decide, thereby increasing the value of the firm by the amount of the NPV.

Profitability index, if properly used, provides the same accept/reject decisions as does NPV for conventional, loan, and nonconventional projects. Chapter 8 extends this discussion by examining the case of mutually exclusive projects.

SUMMARY

This chapter focuses on the following learning objectives:
1. Using net present value to decide if a project should be accepted or rejected.
   The net present value (NPV) of a project is equal to the present value of its cash flows, discounted at the required rate of return. A project is normally accepted when the NPV is nonnegative and rejected when the NPV is negative. The net present value profile is a graph showing the relationship between NPV and the discount rate used in its calculation. Conventional projects, projects that begin with one or more negative cash flows followed by positive cash flows, have net present value profiles that slope down and to the right.
2. Using internal rate of return to decide if a project should be accepted or rejected.
   The internal rate of return (IRR) of a project is the discount rate, which causes the present value of its cash flows to be equal to 0. In the case of independent projects, IRR produces the same accept/reject decisions as NPV. Conventional projects are accepted if the internal rate of return is greater than the marginal cost of capital.
3. Understanding of the basics of payback period.
   The payback period is the number of years necessary to recover the initial investment. It is also the time required for the cumulative cash flows to equal 0.
4. Understanding the basics of discounted payback period.
   The discounted payback period uses the same definition as payback period, except cash flows are discounted back to time 0 using the marginal cost of capital.
5. Understanding the basics of accounting rate of return.
   The accounting rate of return is the average earnings after tax divided by the average book value.
6. Understanding the basics of modified internal rate of return.

The modified internal rate of return of a project is the discount rate which causes the absolute value of the present value of the negative cash flows to equal the present value of the terminal value of the positive cash flows. The terminal value is the future value of the positive cash flows at the end of the project, compounded at the marginal cost of capital.

7. Understanding the basics of profitability index.

The profitability index is the ratio of the present value of the positive cash flows of a project to the absolute value of the present value of the negative cash flows. Conventional projects are accepted when the PI is greater than or equal to 1.00 and rejected when the PI is less than 1.00.

Key Terms

Accounting rate of return, 208	Loan project, 201	Nonconventional project, 201
Conventional project, 201	Modified internal rate of return, 212	Payback period, 206
Discounted payback period, 207	Mutually exclusive, 204	Profitability index, 213
Independent, 203	Net present value, 195	Profitability index profile, 214
Internal rate of return, 200	Net present value profile, 197	Value additivity principle, 205

Questions

7.1 Explain why net present value and internal rate of return give identical results when evaluating independent projects.

7.2 Why does the internal rate of return criterion depend on whether you are evaluating a conventional, loan, or unconventional project?

7.3 When would payback period work best, given its weaknesses?

7.4 How does discounted payback period attempt to correct for the weaknesses of payback period?

7.5 Why would managers use accounting rate of return even though it does not use cash flows and does not take into account the time value of money?

7.6 How does modified internal rate of return differ from internal rate of return?

7.7 How can you be sure that a project does not have multiple internal rates of return?

7.8 How is an expansion project a special case of a replacement project from a calculational point of view?

7.9 What factors caused Augusta Newsprint to expand?

7.10 How are the Japanese and German capital budgeting systems different from the American system?

7.11 Do the Japanese use different criteria in making investment decisions?

PROBLEMS

7.1 **(NPV, IRR, MIRR, and PI)** Diversified Industries, Inc. is studying a new project. The cash flows have been estimated as follows:

Year	Cash Flow
0	-$123,000
1	$ 30,000
2	$ 30,000
3	$ 30,000
4	$ 30,000
5	$ 30,000
6	$ 30,000

If the marginal cost of capital is 10 percent, what is the net present value, internal rate of return, modified internal rate of return, and profitability index? Explain whether or not the project should be accepted using each of the evaluation methods. (PROJECT)

7.2 **(NPV, IRR, MIRR, and PI)** Macon Sports Equipment plans to purchase a new slate machine for its pool table manufacturing line. Management has compiled the following cash flows for the project.

Year	Cash Flow
0	-$68,300
1	$15,000
2	$15,000
3	$15,000
4	$15,000
5	$25,000

If the marginal cost of capital is 12 percent, what is the net present value, internal rate of return, modified internal rate of return, and profitability index? Explain whether or not the project should be accepted using each of the evaluation methods. (PROJECT)

7.3 **(NPV, IRR, MIRR, and PI)** Bridgeport Mining is considering replacing equipment in its quarrying operation. A financial analyst working with the engineers has developed the following cash flow estimates for the project.

Year	Cash Flow
0	–$275,000
1	$ 58,000
2	$ 60,200
3	$ 70,400
4	$ 83,600
5	$144,000

If the marginal cost of capital is 11 percent, what is the net present value, internal rate of return, modified internal rate of return, and profitability index? Explain whether or not the project should be accepted using each of the evaluation methods. (PROJECT)

7.4 **(PB, ARR, NPV, IRR, MIRR, and PI)** Georgia Clay Products plans to replace one of its brick lines at a total cost of $900,000. The old line cost $300,000 to install 15 years ago. It is being depreciated over 25 years toward a $0 salvage value, the net amount it would bring today. The new process, which would be depreciated by the straight line method, would also be worthless at the end of 10 years. New operator training would cost $5,000. Net working capital requirements would increase by $4,000. The investment tax credit is 10 percent, and the marginal tax rate is 40 percent. The company spent $40,000 studying the feasibility of the project. If the project is accepted, revenues would increase by $150,000 per year while operating costs would decrease by $150,000. After calculating the change in cash flows and the change in earnings after tax over the life of the project, find the payback period, accounting rate of return, net present value, internal rate of return, modified internal rate of return, and profitability index, using a 10 percent marginal cost of capital.

7.5 **(PB)** American Hospitals, Inc. is installing new equipment in its radiology laboratory. Cash flows from this project are as follows:

Year	Cash Flow
0	−$50,000
1	$10,000
2	$15,000
3	$20,000
4	$25,000

What is the payback period for this project?

7.6 (**ARR**) The industrial engineers at the Benson Company have compiled the following information about a new project.

Period	Earnings After Tax	Book Value
0	$ 0	$100,000
1	$15,000	$ 85,000
2	$15,000	$ 70,000
3	$15,000	$ 55,000
4	$15,000	$ 40,000
5	$15,000	$ 25,000

What is the accounting rate of return?

7.7 (**ARR**) Smith Hastings, Inc. is planning a new project in one of its restaurants. So far they have compiled the following information:

Period	Earnings After Tax	Book Value
0	$ 0	$100,000
1	$ 3,426	$ 85,710
2	−$ 2,694	$ 61,220
3	$ 1,506	$ 43,730
4	$ 4,506	$ 31,240
5	$ 6,642	$ 22,310
6	$ 6,648	$ 13,390
7	$ 6,642	$ 4,460
8	$ 9,324	$ 0
9	$12,000	$ 0
10	$12,000	$ 0

What is the accounting rate of return?

7.8 **(PB, ARR, NPV, IRR, MIRR, and PI)** Portland Cement, Inc. plans to replace one of its cement lines at a cost of $1,300,000. The old line, installed 20 years ago, cost $350,000. It is being depreciated toward a $50,000 salvage value using straight line depreciation over 30 years and can be sold today for $20,000. The new line will be depreciated by the straight line method over 10 years toward a $300,000 salvage value. Installation of the new line allows revenues to increase by $500,000 per year while operating costs remain constant. Net working capital would increase by $50,000. The investment tax credit is 10 percent, and the marginal tax rate is 40 percent. After calculating the change in cash flows and the change in earnings after tax over the life of the project, find the payback period, accounting rate of return, net present value, internal rate of return, modified internal rate of return, and profitability index using an 11 percent marginal cost of capital. (PROJECT)

7.9 **(PB, ARR, NPV, IRR, MIRR, and PI)** Butkus Iron and Steel will replace equipment in its molding operation. The old equipment cost $300,000 when it was purchased 20 years ago. It is being depreciated over 20 years on a straight line basis toward a $0 salvage value, but it can be sold today for $10,000. The new equipment costs $850,000 and requires $50,000 in freight and installation. It will be depreciated on a straight line basis over 10 years toward a $100,000 salvage value. Net working capital requirements will not change. Installation of the new equipment allows revenues to increase by $200,000 per year while operating costs decrease by $100,000. After calculating the change in cash flows and the change in earnings after tax over the life of the project, find the payback period, accounting rate of return, net present value, internal rate of return, modified internal rate of return, and profitability index using a 12 percent marginal cost of capital. (PROJECT)

7.10 **(PB and DPB)** Ferguson Machine Company is considering new production equipment. The new equipment produces an initial cash flow of −$10,000, after-tax operating cash flows of $4,000 per year for six years, and no terminal cash flow. What is the payback period and the discounted payback period for a 10 percent marginal cost of capital? (PROJECT)

7.11 **(PB, ARR, NPV, IRR, MIRR, and PI)** Avery Aviation, Inc. plans to replace one of its old airplanes. The old plane was purchased 20 years ago at a cost of $95,000. It is being depreciated over 30 years by the straight line method toward a $5,000 salvage value. It can be sold today for $35,000. A replacement plane costs $500,000 and has a 15 year recovery period under MACRS. Since the half year convention applies in this case, the applicable percentages (over 16 years) are as follows: 5.00, 9.50, 8.55, 7.70, 6.93, 6.23, 5.90, 5.90, 5.91, 5.90, 5.91, 5.90, 5.91, 5.90, 5.91, and 2.95.

Management estimates it could be sold in 20 years for $100,000. Over the 20 year economic life, the new plane increases revenues by $250,000 per year and increases operating costs by $50,000 per year. The investment tax credit is 10 percent, and the marginal tax rate is 40 percent. Net working capital increases by $25,000. After calculating the change in cash flows and the change in earnings after tax over the life of the project, find the payback period, accounting rate of return, net present value, internal rate of return, modified internal rate of return, and profitability index using a marginal cost of capital of 13 percent. (PROJECT)

7.12 **(Marginal Cost of Capital Range)** West Virginia Mining plans to spend $2,000,000 for land to be used in mining operations. This will generate cash flows of $10,000,000 at the end of the first year and –$8,000,000 at the end of the second year. The negative cash flow in year two is caused by the need to clean up the environment. Describe the range of the marginal cost of capital over which the project would be acceptable. How would this change if the cash flow in year two was –$12,500,000?

A Case Problem

outheastern Wire Corporation (SWC) was a manufacturer of copper electrical wire for interior wiring in homes, apartments, and manufactured housing. The company began operations in 1991 and through expansions, tripled its production capacity by 1993. Producing more than 250,000 pounds of finished product per day, the plant was operating near its practical capacity. Sales over the last year exceeded $50 million.

SWC's strategy was to increase its market share by maintaining a low cost production capability while emphasizing responsiveness to its customers.

SWC's strategy was to increase its market share by maintaining a low cost production capability while em-

phasizing responsiveness to its customers. Management believed that speed in filling customers orders was the key to increasing sales. To avoid stockouts, the company maintained a relatively high level of finished goods inventory. Southeastern Wire used highly automated manufacturing equipment and a focused product line to insure low cost production.

The manufacturing process, which involved drawing copper rod into wire of varying diameters, used insulating and jacketing lines to produce finished wire products. Plant Engineering had designed a modification to a wire drawing machine in one of the insulating lines. The project, if accepted, would cost approximately $75,000, and it would be depreciated using 5-year MACRS. The modification would require an overhaul in five years costing $10,000. After the 10-year project life, the equipment could be sold for 20 percent of its original cost. The marginal tax rate for SWC was 35 percent, while the marginal cost of capital was 10 percent.

The principal benefits from the modification would come from savings in labor and materials. The Industrial Engineering Department estimated a reduction of one worker the second year and a total of two workers for the remainder of the project. Including fringe benefits, a labor savings of one worker would reduce costs by $27,400 per year. Savings in materials would amount to $8,400 for each of the 10 years. The operations manager needed to know if the project was economically justifiable.

Leading Questions

1. What are the cash flows in years zero through 10?
2. How would you convince the operations manager to accept or reject the project?

POWER GLITCHES BECOME CRITICAL AS WORLD COMPUTERIZES

Several times a month last year, workers at Georgia-Pacific Corporation's paper plant in Bellingham, Washington, suddenly found themselves listening to the sounds of silence. Brief power-line blips had made their sensitive electronic controls shut off, knocking down the whole mill. Days on which plants stand still due to power glitches cost more than $12 billion annually in the

8 Topics In Capital Budgeting

U.S., estimates Jane Clemmensen, president of Collective Intelligence Inc. of Santa Rosa, California.

If the problem has overtones of science fiction, so do emerging solutions based on superconductors, materials that conduct electricity without resistance. One is SMES, or superconducting magnetic energy storage, which Superconductivity Inc., a start-up company in Madison, Wisconsin, has developed to protect against voltage sags. Another company, Illinois Superconductor Corporation of Evanston, Illinois is developing superconducting devices to protect against surges.

Superconductivity Inc., whose systems start at about $700,000, will face stiff competition from the standard technology for dealing with power disturbances: battery powered uninterruptible power supplies, or UPS. The company claims that its devices are comparable in price but less trouble to maintain than UPS, which contain arrays of batteries whose electrolyte levels and interconnections must be continually monitored.

The choice between SMES and UPS is an interesting one for financial management. It involves making difficult cash flow estimates involving operating costs for the two systems, including the impact of risk. The methods for evaluating the systems are not simple to implement. Compounding the problem is the fact that the technology for SMES is not fully developed.

Source: David Stiff, "Power Glitches Become Critical as World Computerizes," *The Wall Street Journal,* May 18, 1992. Reprinted by permission of The Wall Street Journal, © 1992 Dow Jones & Company, Inc. All Rights Reserved Worldwide.

MUTUALLY EXCLUSIVE PROJECTS

In the previous chapter, only one capital budgeting candidate was available for acceptance or rejection. One independent project was evaluated without considering other possibilities. In this section, the accept/reject decision is made from mutually exclusive projects. Projects are **mutually exclusive** if acceptance of one project prevents acceptance of the other.

Mutually Exclusive

With independent projects, net present value and internal rate of return provide identical accept/reject decisions. If two projects are mutually exclusive, NPV and IRR *may* give conflicting results. This means that one project has the higher NPV while the other project has the higher IRR. To understand why the conflict exists, consider the situation a company faces when deciding between different types of equipment.

In Chapter 6, Van Alstyne Industries examined the purchase of a replacement milling machine, Project A. Since then, Plant Engineering spoke with several equipment vendors and identified a competing possibility, Project B. Project A requires automated equipment, while Project B is manually operated. Table 8.1 shows the cash flows for the two projects. Management needs to know which project, if either, to accept.

TABLE 8.1 Cash Flows for Mutually Exclusive Projects A and B
● ● ● ● ● ● ●

PERIOD	CF_A	CF_B
0	−$60,200	−$17,740
1	$ 8,200	$ 4,000
2	$ 8,200	$ 4,000
3	$ 8,200	$ 4,000
4	$ 8,200	$ 4,000
5	$ 8,200	$ 4,000
6	$ 8,200	$ 4,000
7	$ 8,200	$ 4,000
8	$ 8,200	$ 4,000
9	$ 8,200	$ 4,000
10	$28,900	$ 4,000

Evaluation by NPV

In Chapter 7, we learned how to evaluate independent projects using net present value. That discussion used net present value profiles to illustrate how correct capital budgeting decisions add value to a company. In this section, you will see that this approach applies to mutually exclusive projects as well.

The NPV of Project A may be expressed as a function of k, the discount rate, in order to describe the general relationship.

$$NPV_A = -\$60,200 + \$8,200 \sum_{i=1}^{9} \frac{1}{(1+k)^i} + \frac{\$28,900}{(1+k)^{10}}$$
$$= -\$60,200 + \$8,200(PVFA_{k\%,9}) + \$28,900(PVF_{k\%,10})$$

The NPV of Project B is expressed in a similar manner.

$$NPV_B = -\$17,740 + \$4,000 \sum_{i=1}^{10} \frac{1}{(1+k)^i}$$
$$= -\$17,740 + \$4,000(PVFA_{k\%,10})$$

Table 8.2 includes the net present value profile calculations for the two projects.

The NPV profile for each of the projects, using the information in Table 8.2, is shown in Figure 8.1. Notice that the two curves cross at 6.00 percent. To the left of this crossover point, the NPV of Project A is higher than the NPV of Project B; to the right, the NPV of B is higher. So, our choice as to which project has the higher NPV depends on the marginal cost of capital.

TABLE 8.2 NPV Profile Calculations for Projects A and B

MARGINAL COST OF CAPITAL, K	NET PRESENT VALUE, NPV_A	NET PRESENT VALUE, NPV_B
0%	$42,500	$22,260
5%	$15,826	$13,147
10%	-$ 1,834	$ 6,838
15%	-$13,929	$ 2,335
20%	-$22,479	-$ 970

For mutually exclusive projects, accept the project with the higher NPV, provided the higher NPV is greater than or equal to zero. Since NPV depends on the marginal cost of capital, accept Project A between 0 and 6.00 percent, and accept Project B between 6.00 and 18.37 percent. Reject both projects above 18.37 percent.

In studying Project A and Project B, Jessica Stewart, a financial analyst for Van Alstyne Industries, determined that the marginal cost of capital is 10 percent. Which project, if either, should she recommend?

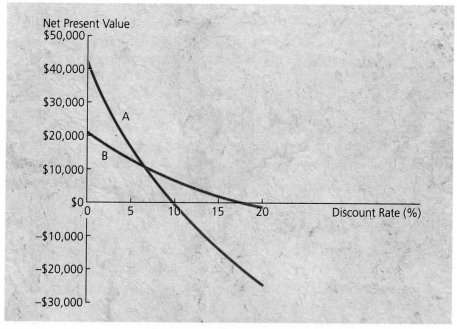

FIGURE 8.1 Net Present Value Profiles for Projects A and B

Jessica calculated that the NPV of Project A is −$1,834 and that the NPV of Project B is $6,838. These net present values are shown in Figure 8.1. Jessica chose the project with the higher NPV, Project B. As we can see from this example, the use of NPV for mutually exclusive projects is simple: We pick the project with the higher net present value.

Evaluation by IRR

The net present value rule provides a direct means for evaluating mutually exclusive projects. Even so, the majority of businesspeople prefer IRR to NPV. For this reason, it would benefit us to learn how to use internal rate of return for the mutually exclusive case.

In the previous chapter we discovered that independent, conventional projects are accepted if the internal rate of return is *greater* than or equal to the marginal cost of capital. The evaluation is more complicated when considering mutually exclusive projects. Examining Figure 8.1, we may be tempted to argue that since the IRR of B, 18.37 percent, is greater than the IRR of A, 9.38 percent, Project B should be accepted, assuming, of course, that the marginal cost of capital is less than or equal to 18.37 percent. On the surface, this argument seems plausible.

The NPV criterion provides the correct accept/reject decision. So, if IRR is to be used properly, it must be used in such a way as to give the same answers as NPV. It will, if handled skillfully. In the last section, we accepted Project A between 0 and 6.00 percent, and Project B between 6.00 and 18.37 percent. Table 8.3 shows that the NPV selection criterion provides results that disagree with simply selecting Project B as long as the marginal cost of capital is less than 18.37 percent.

The conflict between NPV and the simplified use of IRR, picking the higher IRR for mutually exclusive projects, centers around the opportunity cost assumption. NPV assumes that cash flows are reinvested at the marginal cost of capital, whereas IRR assumes that cash flows are reinvested at the internal rate of return.

In the case of two mutually exclusive projects, the magnitude and timing of cash flows affects which project has the higher IRR. For example, the present

TABLE 8.3 NPV Compared with IRR for Mutually Exclusive Projects

	MARGINAL COST OF CAPITAL		
Evaluation Technique	0.00–6.00%	6.00–18.37%	Above 18.37%
Net Present Value	Project A	Project B	Reject both.
Internal Rate of Return	Project B	Project B	Reject both.

value of a project with relatively high cash flows late in the project is more adversely affected by a high discount rate. The present value of its cash flows is driven to zero sooner as the discount rate increases; thereby, it has a lower IRR. On the other hand, a low discount rate affects this project less.

IRR can be used for mutually exclusive projects by first subtracting the cash flows of one project from the cash flows of the other project[1]. Subtract so that the resulting incremental project consists of one or more negative cash flows followed by at least one positive cash flow. Since this approach results in an independent project, the internal rate of return decision rules from the previous chapter apply[2]. In Table 8.4, the cash flows from Project B are subtracted from the cash flows of Project A.

The incremental project cash flows represent the additional costs and benefits that Project A provides over Project B. Project A costs $42,460 more than Project B, yet provides benefits of $4,200 per year for 9 years and a $24,900 benefit in year 10. The important question, "Is it worth it to spend the extra money now in order to receive the extra cash over 10 years?" Internal rate of return helps answer that question by reporting the rate of return the company will receive on the added investment. Our responsibility is to compare the IRR of the incremental project with the cost of money, the marginal cost of capital[3].

TABLE 8.4   Cash Flows for the Incremental Project, A – B
● ● ● ● ● ● ●

PERIOD	CF$_A$	CF$_B$	CF$_{A-B}$
0	–$60,200	–$17,740	–$42,460
1	$ 8,200	$ 4,000	$ 4,200
2	$ 8,200	$ 4,000	$ 4,200
3	$ 8,200	$ 4,000	$ 4,200
4	$ 8,200	$ 4,000	$ 4,200
5	$ 8,200	$ 4,000	$ 4,200
6	$ 8,200	$ 4,000	$ 4,200
7	$ 8,200	$ 4,000	$ 4,200
8	$ 8,200	$ 4,000	$ 4,200
9	$ 8,200	$ 4,000	$ 4,200
10	$28,900	$ 4,000	$24,900

[1]   See A. A. Alchian, "The Rate of Interest, Fisher's Rate of Return over Cost and Keynes' Internal Rate of Return," *American Economic Review*, December 1955, pp. 938–942, for further discussion of this approach.
[2]   The use of the incremental method is motivated by the fact that most businesspeople prefer internal rate of return to net present value.
[3]   Profitability index also requires an incremental approach when evaluating mutually exclusive projects.

We find the internal rate of return for the incremental project by applying Eq. 7.2.

$$0 = -\$42{,}460 + \$4{,}200 \sum_{i=1}^{9} \frac{1}{(1+r)^i} + \frac{\$24{,}900}{(1+r)^{10}}$$

$$0 = -\$42{,}460 + \$4{,}200(\text{PVFA}_{r\%,9}) + \$24{,}900(\text{PVF}_{r\%,10})$$

Using an advanced calculator, *trial and success*, or THE FINANCIAL MANAGER (PROJECT), the internal rate of return is 6.00 percent. This is the crossover point in Figure 8.1.

The incremental project is an independent, conventional project. Independent, conventional projects are accepted if the internal rate of return is greater than or equal to the marginal cost of capital. We accept the incremental project as long as the internal rate of return is greater than or equal to the marginal cost of capital.

Subtracting the cash flows of Project B from the cash flows of Project A reveals how much better Project A is than Project B. So, if we do accept the incremental project, it means that Project A is better than Project B. Conversely, if we reject the incremental project, it means that Project B is better than Project A.

Once we know which project is better using IRR, the selected project must still be acceptable on its own merits. Any project can appear to be acceptable if compared with a sufficiently bad alternative. For a conventional project, make sure that the IRR of the accepted project is greater than the marginal cost of capital[4].

Jessica Stewart wanted to evaluate the projects using internal rate of return. If she used a marginal cost of capital of five percent, which project, if either, should she accept?

Previously, it was determined that the IRR of the incremental project is 6.00 percent. The incremental project is accepted since the internal rate of return of 6.00 percent is *greater* than the marginal cost of capital, 5.00 percent. This simply means that Project A, the first project listed, is better than Project B.

Next, determine if Project A is acceptable on its own merits. The IRR of Project A is 9.38 percent. Therefore, Project A is *accepted* since the internal rate of return of 9.38 percent is greater than the marginal cost of capital, 5.00 percent.

---

[4] Making sure that a project minimally qualifies may be done before or after the incremental analysis. It is a matter of personal preference. When projects are sent to a higher corporate level to compete with other projects, obviously minimal qualification must come first.

> If Jessica used a marginal cost of capital of 10 percent, which project, if either, should be accepted?

By similar reasoning, the incremental project is rejected, and Project B is tentatively accepted. Since the IRR of B, 18.37 percent, is greater than the marginal cost of capital of 10 percent, Project B is finally accepted.

> If Jessica used a marginal cost of capital of 20 percent, which project, if either, should be accepted?

By more similar reasoning, the incremental project is rejected, and Project B is tentatively accepted. Since the IRR of B, 18.37 percent, is less than the marginal cost of capital of 20 percent, Project B is also rejected.

Table 8.5 summarizes the decision sequence for the incremental project. Make an initial decision by comparing the marginal cost of capital (MCC) with the internal rate of return of the incremental project. Based on the initial decision, tentatively accept one project, while rejecting the other. Make a final decision by comparing the marginal cost of capital with the internal rate of return of the tentatively accepted project.

In this section, we learned that the simplified use of IRR, picking the higher IRR for mutually exclusive projects, may lead to the wrong decision. But we also discovered that using IRR on an incremental basis will provide the same accept/reject decisions as NPV. In the examples presented, both projects had the same economic life. In the next section, we will find out what happens when projects have unequal lives.

PROJECTS WITH UNEQUAL LIVES

Previously, the two mutually exclusive projects had the same economic life, 10 years. In practice, lives differ. So how do we adjust? The answer depends on whether or not a project can be repeated. For example, if we have two projects,

TABLE 8.5 Incremental Project Decision Sequence for the IRR of 6%

MCC	INCREMENTAL PROJECT INITIAL DECISION	INDIVIDUAL PROJECT TENTATIVE DECISION	FINAL DECISION
5%	Accept Project	Accept A, Reject B	Accept A
10%	Reject Project	Accept B, Reject A	Accept B
20%	Reject Project	Accept B, Reject A	Reject B

with lives of 5 and 10 years, we must determine if the 5-year project can be repeated. It depends on the situation. When projects cannot be repeated, the evaluation methods we already learned apply. If projects can be repeated, there are two approaches for project selection: replacement chain or equivalent annual annuity.

In studying Project A and Project B, Jessica Stewart spoke with Plant Engineering. She discovered that they found other equipment which could do the job equally well. Project C, using less durable components, has an economic life of five years. Jessica already knew that Project B was preferred to Project A, at the marginal cost of capital of 10 percent. As a result, she only needed to compare Project B with Project C. The cash flows for these mutually exclusive projects are included in Table 8.6. Jessica had to decide which of these projects, if either, to accept.

Jessica must decide if Project C can be repeated. If it cannot, she simply calculates the NPV of Project C.

$$NPV_C = -\$20,100 + \$6,500(PVFA_{10\%,5})$$
$$= -\$20,100 + \$6,500(3.7908)$$
$$= \$4,540$$

Previously, she determined that the NPV of Project B is $6,838.

TABLE 8.6 Cash Flows for Mutually Exclusive Projects B and C
• • • • • • •

PERIOD	CF$_B$	CF$_C$
0	−$17,740	−$20,100
1	$ 4,000	$ 6,500
2	$ 4,000	$ 6,500
3	$ 4,000	$ 6,500
4	$ 4,000	$ 6,500
5	$ 4,000	$ 6,500
6	$ 4,000	
7	$ 4,000	
8	$ 4,000	
9	$ 4,000	
10	$ 4,000	

If Project C cannot be repeated, Jessica would select Project B, due to its higher NPV. But what would happen if Project C could be repeated for another five years? Would this change her decision? It might.

Replacement Chain Approach

The **replacement chain approach** compares projects over a common useful life and selects the project with the higher net present value. The common useful life is the lowest common multiple of the lives of the two projects. The lowest common multiple of the 10-year Project B and the five-year Project C is 10 years.

Replacement Chain Approach

Since project B already has a life of 10 years, it is only necessary to provide a replacement chain for Project C. When Project C is repeated, it is renamed Project C'. A cash flow diagram shows the timing of the cash flows for Project C'.

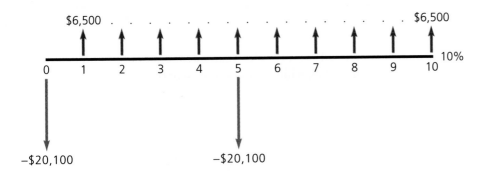

Notice that project C is repeated beginning at time 5.

Jessica then finds the NPV of project C', over the full 10 years of the project.

$$NPV_{C'} = -\$20,100 + \$6,500(PVFA_{10\%,10}) - \$20,100(PVF_{10\%,5})$$
$$= -\$20,100 + \$6,500(6.1446) - \$20,100(0.6209)$$
$$= \$7,360$$

Since the NPV of Project C', $7,360, is higher than the NPV of Project B, $6,838, Jessica would select Project C', Project C repeated for five more years.

The replacement chain method assumes that the projects can be repeated over the common useful life. For example, two projects with 7 and 9 year lives would have a common useful life of 63 years. Since it is unlikely that the projects would remain unchanged over this extended period, the replacement chain assumption would be violated. In practice, small differences in economic lives are ignored. Fortunately, a simpler method exists, the equivalent annual annuity approach.

Equivalent Annual Annuity Approach

Equivalent Annual Annuity

The **equivalent annual annuity approach** spreads the net present value over the life of each project, selecting the project which provides the greater yearly value increase. This method implies an infinite time horizon, in contrast to the common number of years with the replacement chain approach.

For project B, we previously found, with a 10 percent marginal cost of capital, that the NPV is $6,838 over a life of 10 years. Using a cash flow diagram, notice how this value can be spread over 10 years, the original life of the project.

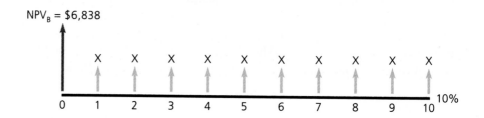

The equivalent annual annuity values can be brought back to time 0 and set equal to the NPV of $6,838, which is already at time 0.

$$X(PVFA_{10\%,10}) = \$6,838$$
$$X = \frac{\$6,838}{6.1446}$$
$$X = \$1,113$$

This is the yearly value increase if Project B is accepted.

For project C, we previously found, using a 10 percent marginal cost of capital, that the NPV is $4,540 over an economic life of five years. Using a cash flow diagram, notice how this value can be spread over five years, the original life of the project.

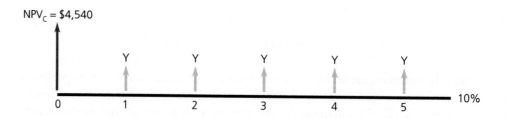

The equivalent annual annuity values can be brought back to time 0 and set equal to the NPV of $4,540, which is already at time 0.

$$Y(PVFA_{10\%,5}) = \$4,540$$
$$Y = \frac{\$4,540}{3.7908}$$
$$Y = \$1,198$$

This is the yearly value increase if Project C is accepted. Since the yearly value increase is greater for Project C, it is selected.

The equivalent annuity approach assumes that the projects are repeated indefinitely. Since this time horizon exceeds the common useful life under the replacement chain approach, the two methods provide the same accept/reject decision.

This brings up another important point: In all of the previous net present value and internal rate of return calculations, we implicitly assumed that projects were of average risk. What do we do if projects are more risky or less risky than normal? How do we adjust? The remainder of this chapter explores these questions.

RISK AND RETURN

The future is uncertain. Seems rather obvious. But in the problems up to this point, we have ignored the fact that actual future returns may deviate from expected returns. In capital budgeting projects, the actual rate of return may differ from the rate of return we expected. Still, as financial managers we must make decisions.

What, then, is risk? **Risk** is the probability of a loss when making an investment. Holding assets with highly variable returns increases the chance of that loss. Such assets are risky. When expected returns are equal, businesspeople prefer investments with a low variability of return.

Risk

Making decisions involves uncertainty and risk. With **uncertainty,** the probabilities of outcomes are not known (and cannot be estimated). With risk, the probabilities of outcomes are known (or can be estimated). And since probabilities are involved, it is important to understand the basics of probability theory in order to measure risk.

Uncertainty

The Measurement of Risk

The **probability** of an event is the likelihood the event will occur. If you flip a coin, the probability is 0.5 for a head and 0.5 for a tail. Similarly, we may list the probabilities for the internal rate of return of a project. A **probability distribution** is a description of all possible outcomes and probabilities.

Probability

Probability Distribution

Table 8.7 shows the internal rate of return probability distribution for the replacement project from Chapter 7. By investing in this project, management

TABLE 8.7 Probability Distribution for the Replacement Project

Scenario	Probability	Internal Rate of Return
Strong	0.25	13.40%
Normal	0.55	9.00%
Weak	0.20	5.40%

believes there is a 25 percent chance for a strong economy, a 55 percent chance for a normal economy, and a 20 percent chance for a weak economy over the life of the project. The internal rates of return are provided for each of these probabilities.

The actual internal rate of return for the replacement project is not known at the time of the investment. As a result, financial managers focus on the average return the project will bring, the **expected rate of return, E(r).** In mathematical terms, it is stated as follows:

Expected Rate of Return

$$E(r) = P_1 r_1 + P_2 r_2 + \ldots + P_n r_n \tag{8.1}$$

where

$$P_j = \text{Probability of earning return j, j} = 1,2,\ldots,n$$
$$r_j = \text{Rate of return for the } j^{th} \text{ outcome}$$
$$n = \text{Number of possible outcomes}$$

Jessica Stewart, a financial analyst for Van Alstyne Industries, was examining the information in Table 8.7. How does she calculate the expected rate of return for the replacement project?

Jessica uses Eq. 8.1.

$$E(R) = 0.25(13.40) + 0.55(9.00) + 0.20(5.40)$$
$$= 9.38\%$$

This is the expected rate of return for the replacement project.

The value of 9.38 percent will not be the actual return from the replacement project since it is not a possible outcome. The expected result will be 13.40, 9.00, or 5.40 percent. This variability from the expected rate of return reflects risk.

Jessica Stewart knows that the marginal cost of capital for Van Alstyne Industries is 10 percent. If the company accepts the replacement project, what percent of the time would this be a bad decision?

Accepting the replacement project is a bad decision whenever the actual rate of return is less than the marginal cost of capital. For rates of return of 9.00 and 5.40 percent, values less than the marginal cost of capital, the probabilities are 0.55 and 0.20, a total of 0.75. This means that accepting the replacement project is a bad decision 75 percent of the time.

One way to avoid making a bad decision is to create better alternatives to the project in question, Project A. Earlier in this chapter, Plant Engineering at Van Alstyne Industries did that by creating a competing possibility, Project B. Since the NPV of Project B is higher than the NPV of Project A, at a marginal cost of capital of 10 percent, it is less likely that choosing Project B will produce a bad decision. Managers in practice try very hard to avoid downside risk, in this case the risk of a negative net present value.

Managers like to quantify risk. The **standard deviation, σ,** measures the risk, or variability, of a probability distribution[5]. It is the square root of the sum of the squared deviations from the expected rate of return. In mathematical terms, the equation is stated as follows:

Standard Deviation

$$\sigma = \sqrt{[r_1 - E(r)]^2 P_1 + [r_2 - E(r)]^2 P_2 + \ldots + [r_n - E(r)]^2 P_n} \qquad (8.2)$$

Jessica Stewart is interested in measuring the variability of the internal rate of return for the replacement project. How does she calculate the standard deviation, given an expected rate of return of 9.38 percent?

Jessica applies Eq. 8.2.

$$\sigma = \sqrt{(13.40 - 9.38)^2 0.25 + (9.00 - 9.38)^2 .55 + (5.40 - 9.38)^2 0.20}$$
$$= 2.70\%$$

This is the standard deviation of the rate of return for the replacement project.

The replacement project example uses a **discrete probability distribution.** That implies a limited number of possible outcomes. In an actual situation, there are an unlimited number of possibilities, a **continuous probability distribution.**

Discrete Probability Distribution

Continuous Probability Distribution

---

[5] Another risk measure, the variance, is the standard deviation squared. Since, unlike the variance, the standard deviation is denominated in the same units as the expected rate of return, we will refer only to the standard deviation.

This allows a wider range of outcomes, ranging from negative values to values greater than the 13.40 percent identified for a strong economy.

The replacement project requires that cash flows be forecasted over 10 years. The riskiness of these cash flows may increase over that time due to factors such as changes in competition and technology. Since the cash flows of many projects are more and more risky as time passes, management may be tempted to use payback period to evaluate projects. Short payback periods tend to limit the increasing risk of a project over time.

Portfolio

In this section, we examined the replacement project as if it were the only asset held by Van Alstyne Industries. In practice, companies of this type hold a collection of assets, a **portfolio.** Measuring the risk of the replacement project under these conditions requires a different strategy.

Portfolio Risk and Return

Combining the replacement project with a second project creates a two-asset portfolio. We will examine the expected return and the risk of this portfolio. Later, we can extend the analysis to more than two assets.

Expected Return of a Portfolio

The **expected return of a portfolio,** r_p, is the weighted average of the expected returns of the individual assets in the portfolio.

$$r_p = w_1r_1 + w_2r_2 + \ldots + w_nr_n \tag{8.3}$$

where

w_i = Weights of the individual assets (i = 1,2,...n)
r_i = Expected returns of the individual assets (i = 1,2,...n)

The sum of the weights is equal to 1.00.

> Jessica Stewart is examining the effect of combining the replacement project, Project A, with a second project, Project D. Project A has an expected rate of return of 9.38 percent, while Project D has an expected rate of return of 11.62 percent. The two projects are equally weighted. What is the expected return of the project portfolio?

Eq. 8.3 provides the expected return for this two-asset portfolio.

$$r_p = 0.50(9.38\%) + 0.50(11.62\%)$$
$$= 10.50\%$$

The weights represent the proportions of the portfolio invested in each project.

The risk of a portfolio is more difficult to understand and to calculate since it is usually not a weighted average of the standard deviations of the individual projects. In the case of a two-asset portfolio, the **standard deviation of portfolio return**, σ_p, is given by the following expression:

Standard Deviation of Portfolio Return

$$\sigma_p = \sqrt{(w_1)^2(\sigma_1)^2 + (w_2)^2(\sigma_2)^2 + 2w_1w_2\rho_{12}\sigma_1\sigma_2} \qquad (8.4)$$

where

w_i = Weights of the individual assets (i = 1,2)
σ_i = Standard deviations of the individual assets (i = 1,2)
ρ_{12} = Correlation coefficient of returns between the assets

Correlation reflects the degree to which the returns on the two assets move together.

The **correlation coefficient** between two assets takes on values between +1 and −1. A positive correlation means that the returns tend to move in the same direction; a negative correlation means that the returns move in opposite directions. A correlation coefficient of zero indicates the returns are independent of each other.

Correlation Coefficient

Combining assets into portfolios normally produces a portfolio standard deviation less than the weighted average of the individual standard deviations. This effect is called **diversification.** The degree of risk reduction depends on the risk-return characteristics of the assets.

Diversification

> Jessica Stewart wonders what effect combining the replacement project, Project A, with a second project, Project D, would have on the risk of the two-asset portfolio. Project A has a standard deviation of 2.70 percent, while Project D has a standard deviation of 3.50 percent. Jessica plans to examine the projects assuming correlation coefficients of +1.0, +0.5, 0.0, −0.5, and −1.0.

Eq. 8.4 provides the standard deviation for this two-asset portfolio. For a correlation coefficient of +0.5, the following equation applies:

$$\sigma_p = \sqrt{(0.50)^2(2.70)^2 + (0.50)^2(3.50)^2 + 2(0.50)(0.50)(+.5)(2.70)(3.50)}$$
$$= 2.69\%$$

Table 8.8 includes the portfolio standard deviations for the full range of correlation coefficients. As we can see from the table, the portfolio standard deviation decreases as the correlation coefficient moves from +1 to −1. When the

TABLE 8.8 Portfolio Standard Deviations for Portfolio AD (%)
● ● ● ● ● ● ●

Correlation Coefficients	+1.0	+0.5	0.0	−0.5	−1.0
Portfolio Standard Deviation	3.10	2.69	2.21	1.59	0.40

Note: $\sigma_1 = 2.70\%$, $\sigma_2 = 3.50\%$, $w_1 = 0.50$, $w_2 = 0.50$

correlation coefficient is −1, we can eliminate risk entirely if the weights of the two projects are in the proper proportions.

International diversification can be used to significantly reduce the risk of portfolio returns. Countries whose economic cycles are not in phase with the U.S. will have lower correlation coefficients relative to the U.S. market. This also implies that the cash flows from foreign projects in these countries will have lower correlations with domestic projects. By investing in foreign plants, companies are able to reduce the variability of their returns.

The standard deviation of the two-project portfolio is less than the weighted average of the individual standard deviations for the two projects, unless the correlation coefficient is +1. And as more projects are added to the portfolio, risk should be reduced even further[6]. Unfortunately, the computations necessary to handle large portfolios of projects make it difficult to proceed with this line of attack. Fortunately, the methods in the next section are easier to use.

The Capital Asset Pricing Model

Capital Asset Pricing Model

The **capital asset pricing model (CAPM)** shows the relationship between diversification, risk, and the required rate of return of an asset[7]. Even though this model is often studied in the context of the stock market, it generally applies to other assets, including capital budgeting projects. We will study this model in more detail in a course on investment analysis[8].

Under the CAPM, the total risk of a portfolio consists of unsystematic and systematic risk. **Unsystematic risk** is the diversifiable risk that can be reduced by adding projects to the portfolio. **Systematic risk** is the nondiversifiable risk

Unsystematic risk

Systemic Risk

[6] When considering risk reduction, the covariance between the assets in a portfolio is much more important than the number of assets.

[7] See Harry Markowitz, *Portfolio Selection: Efficient Diversification of Investments* (New York, 1959); William F. Sharpe, "Capital Asset Prices: A Theory of Market Equilibrium Under Conditions of Risk," *Journal of Finance*, September 1964, pp. 425–442; and John Lintner, "The Valuation of Risk Assets and the Selection of Risky Investments in Stock Portfolios and Capital Budgets," *Review of Economics and Statistics*, February 1965, pp.13–37.

[8] Financial theorists recently have been casting doubt on the usefulness of the capital asset pricing model. See Eugene F. Fama and Kenneth R. French, "The Cross-Section of Expected Stock Returns," *The Journal of Finance*, June 1992, pp. 427–465.

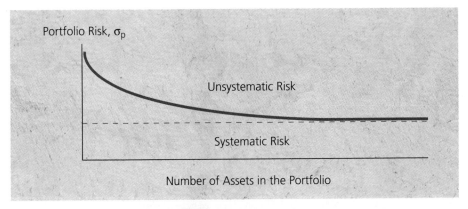

FIGURE 8.2   The Relationship of Portfolio Risk to Portfolio Size

that cannot be eliminated by having a diversified portfolio. In Figure 8.2, unsystematic risk is shown above the dotted line, and systematic risk below.

Unsystematic risk and systematic risk have different origins. Unsystematic risk results from circumstances within a particular company. Since internal outcomes are somewhat random, good effects in one company tend to offset bad effects in another. Systematic risk results from circumstances outside a particular company. Factors such as the economy affect all companies to varying degrees.

The **beta** of an asset measures the volatility of that asset relative to the market. An asset with a beta of 1.0 has risk equal to the market. An asset with a beta of 1.5 will be 1.5 times as volatile as the market. This means that if the return on the market goes up or down 10 percent, the return on the asset will on the average go up or down 15 percent. Similarly, an asset with a beta of 0.5 will go up or down at half the rate of the market.

Beta is estimated by using a **characteristic line,** the regression line of the returns of the asset and the market over time. Beta coefficients for individual stocks are calculated by Value Line, Merrill Lynch, and others. Table 8.9 provides betas for a selection of common stocks.

The **security market line (SML)** shows the relationship between an asset's required rate of return and its beta coefficient. As we can see in Figure 8.3, the greater the risk as measured by the beta coefficient, the higher the required rate of return.

Using the SML relationship, the required rate of return on an asset, k_S, is given by the following equation:

$$k_s = k_{rf} + (k_m - k_{rf})b_i \qquad (8.5)$$

Beta

Characteristic Line

Security Market Line

TABLE 8.9 Beta Coefficients for a Selection of Common Stocks

STOCK	BETA	STOCK	BETA
Newmont Mining	0.35	General Electric	1.15
Joslyn Corporation	0.55	Westinghouse	1.20
Tab Products	0.60	Zenith Electronics	1.25
Duplex Products	0.80	Microsoft Corporation	1.30
Wallace Computers	0.90	Ryder System	1.40
Cubic Corporation	1.00	Novell, Inc.	1.50
Bell Industries	1.05	Scientific Atlanta	1.70
Honeywell	1.10	Midlantic Corporation	1.80

Source: Copyright 1993 by Value Line Publishing, Inc. Reprinted by permission; all rights reserved.

where

$$k_{rf} = \text{Risk-free rate of return on treasury bonds}$$
$$k_m = \text{Required rate of return on the average asset}$$
$$b_i = \text{Beta coefficient (a measure of volatility)}$$

The term, $(k_m - k_{rf})b_i$ is the risk premium for the particular stock[9].

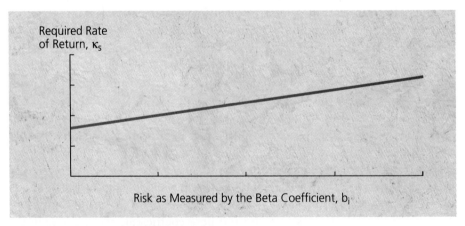

FIGURE 8.3 The Security Market Line (SML)

[9] Arbitrage pricing theory (APT) implies that the risk premium, $(k_m - k_{rf})$, in the capital asset pricing model, results from a number of factors, not simply the market return of the CAPM. This theory, derived by Stephen A. Ross, "The Arbitrage Theory of Capital Asset Pricing," *Journal of Economic Theory*, December 1976, pp. 341–360, suggests that investors make their decisions using multiple risk factors. The CAPM, therefore, can be thought of as a special case of arbitrage pricing theory. Since the risk factors of APT have not been clearly identified, this text will follow the CAPM.

Jessica Stewart is interested in finding the required rate of return for the stock of Van Alstyne Industries. She finds the risk-free rate of return is 8 percent, the required rate of return on the market is 12 percent, and that a beta of 1.99 applies. What is the required rate of return for the stock?

She calculates the required rate of return, k_s, using Eq. 8.5.

$$k_s = 8\% + (12\% - 8\%)1.99$$
$$= 15.96\%$$

This risk-return relationship is shown in Figure 8.4.

The required rate of return, k_s, is the rate necessary to compensate an investor for taking risk. This same investor could invest in bonds at the riskless rate, k_{rf}, at the market rate, k_m, or at a rate determined by the beta of the security. As with capital budgeting projects, the person making the investment has a choice.

RISK IN CAPITAL BUDGETING

In Chapter 6 and the beginning of this chapter, we learned how to use capital budgeting techniques when the cash flows of the project are known. In the previous section, we investigated the relationship of risk and return. Now we are ready to apply these concepts in the evaluation of capital budgeting projects.

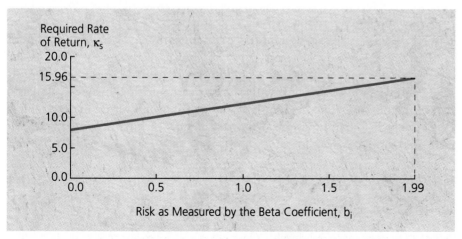

FIGURE 8.4 The Security Market Line and Van Alstyne Industries

Two important ways to incorporate risk in capital budgeting are the risk-adjusted discount rate approach and sensitivity analysis[10]. In practice, companies use these quantitative methods more often than any others[11]. Risk-adjusted discount rates are often determined subjectively, while the use of sensitivity analysis is more objective.

Risk-Adjusted Discount Rates

Risk Adjusted Discount Rate

The **risk-adjusted discount rate (RADR)** approach allows for risk by controlling the discount rate used for capital budgeting decisions. The simplest way to do this is to use the marginal cost of capital for projects of average risk, and to raise or lower the discount rate for projects of greater or lesser risk. Although this approach is subjective, it does not necessarily lead to incorrect decisions.

> After further study, Jessica Stewart determines that Project B is more risky than average. She believes the project requires a discount rate greater than the 10 percent marginal cost of capital but no more than 15 percent. Earlier, she calculated the internal rate of return of Project B, 18.37 percent. With this additional knowledge, should she recommend acceptance of that project?

Using the internal rate of return criterion, Jessica would still recommend Project B. The internal rate of return is greater than the discount rate even if the rate is 15 percent. Knowing a discount rate range often permits an analyst to advise a particular course of action. Further complicating the decision-making process is the fact that the decision maker often is aware of other considerations that are not quantified in the analysis.

Another approach to risk-adjusted discount rates involves using different rates for the separate divisions of a company. This is necessary since companies often have divisions with widely varying costs of capital. Finding the RADR under these conditions begins with finding a company in a business similar to that of the division. The beta from the proxy company is used to determine a cost of capital for the division. The exact details of this procedure are a bit complex for this text[12].

---

[10] Other advanced techniques include simulation analysis, decision tree analysis, and the certainty-equivalent method.

[11] See Suk H. Kim, Trevor Crick, and Seung H. Kim, "Do Executives Practice What Academics Preach?" *Management Accounting*, November 1986, pp. 49–52.

[12] See "Divisional Hurdle Rates and the Cost of Capital," *Financial Management* Spring 1989, pp. 18–25.

Jessica Stewart is evaluating a project similar to the replacement project for another division of Van Alstyne Industries. Using the Hoffman Corporation as a proxy, she determined that the appropriate risk-adjusted discount rate is eight percent. Earlier she determined that the internal rate of return for the replacement project is 9.38 percent. Should she reconsider her position and recommend this project for the new division?

Using the lower discount rate, the replacement project is acceptable for the other division. The lower discount rate implies that this division as a whole is less risky than Van Alstyne Industries. The evaluation of the project reflects this fact.

Sensitivity Analysis

Sensitivity analysis is used to determine the effect on the output variable of increasing or decreasing one input variable, all other input variables held constant. When using NPV for project evaluation, the output variable is NPV and the input variables are items such as the change in revenues, the change in operating costs, and the marginal cost of capital.

Sensitivity Analysis

Jessica is studying the replacement project under the assumption that revenues will increase by $10,000 each year and operating costs will increase by $6,000 each year. She collects the information shown in Table 8.10, and calls it Project S. Jessica is still using a marginal cost of capital of 10 percent. How sensitive is Project S to changes in revenues, operating costs, and the marginal cost of capital?

Jessica begins the analysis by determining the base NPV for the project.

$$NPV = -\$60,200 + \$10,600(PVFA_{10\%,10}) + \$20,700(PVF_{10\%,10})$$
$$= -\$60,200 + \$10,600(6.1446) + \$20,700(0.3855)$$
$$= \$12,913$$

Next, she increases one of the input variables, the change in revenues, by a given percentage, say 10 percent. In Table 8.11, R_n is increased by 10 percent, from $10,000 to $11,000. This modification alters CF_n. (In this example, the simplifying assumption is made that operating costs do not change.)

Using the new cash flows, she finds the NPV is $16,600. Similarly, she calculates the net present values for increases and decreases of 10 percent in the other input variables. The results are summarized in Table 8.12.

TABLE 8.10 Cash Flow Worksheet for Project S
· · · · · · · · ·

PERIOD	CF_{add}	CF_n	R_n	OC_n
0	–$60,200	0	0	0
1	0	$10,600	$10,000	–$4,000
2	0	$10,600	$10,000	–$4,000
3	0	$10,600	$10,000	–$4,000
4	0	$10,600	$10,000	–$4,000
5	0	$10,600	$10,000	–$4,000
6	0	$10,600	$10,000	–$4,000
7	0	$10,600	$10,000	–$4,000
8	0	$10,600	$10,000	–$4,000
9	0	$10,600	$10,000	–$4,000
10	$20,700	$10,600	$10,000	–$4,000

PERIOD	DC_n	DC_{new}	DC_{old}	EAT_n
0	0	0	0	0
1	$5,500	$8,500	$3,000	$5,100
2	$5,500	$8,500	$3,000	$5,100
3	$5,500	$8,500	$3,000	$5,100
4	$5,500	$8,500	$3,000	$5,100
5	$5,500	$8,500	$3,000	$5,100
6	$5,500	$8,500	$3,000	$5,100
7	$5,500	$8,500	$3,000	$5,100
8	$5,500	$8,500	$3,000	$5,100
9	$5,500	$8,500	$3,000	$5,100
10	$5,500	$8,500	$3,000	$5,100

Jessica discovers that Project S is the most sensitive to changes in revenues and least sensitive to changes in operating costs, as measured by the range of NPVs. Changes in the marginal cost of capital also produce relatively large changes in net present value. In going through this process, Jessica develops a feel for the risk involved.

THE FINANCIAL MANAGER (PROJECT) is well suited for sensitivity analysis. After changing revenues, operating costs, or the marginal cost of capital, the program calculates the new operating cash flows as well as net present value, internal rate of return, modified internal rate of return, payback period, discounted payback period, accounting rate of return, and profitability index.

TABLE 8.11 Cash Flow Worksheet with Revenue Changes

PERIOD	CF_{add}	CF_n	R_n	OC_n
0	–$60,200	0	0	0
1	0	$11,200	$11,000	–$4,000
2	0	$11,200	$11,000	–$4,000
3	0	$11,200	$11,000	–$4,000
4	0	$11,200	$11,000	–$4,000
5	0	$11,200	$11,000	–$4,000
6	0	$11,200	$11,000	–$4,000
7	0	$11,200	$11,000	–$4,000
8	0	$11,200	$11,000	–$4,000
9	0	$11,200	$11,000	–$4,000
10	$20,700	$11,200	$11,000	–$4,000

PERIOD	DC_n	DC_{new}	DC_{old}	EAT_n
0	0	0	0	0
1	$5,500	$8,500	$3,000	$5,700
2	$5,500	$8,500	$3,000	$5,700
3	$5,500	$8,500	$3,000	$5,700
4	$5,500	$8,500	$3,000	$5,700
5	$5,500	$8,500	$3,000	$5,700
6	$5,500	$8,500	$3,000	$5,700
7	$5,500	$8,500	$3,000	$5,700
8	$5,500	$8,500	$3,000	$5,700
9	$5,500	$8,500	$3,000	$5,700
10	$5,500	$8,500	$3,000	$5,700

SUMMARY

This chapter focuses on the following learning objectives:
1. Evaluating mutually exclusive projects using net present value.
   Projects are mutually exclusive if acceptance of one project prevents accep-

TABLE 8.12 Net Present Value Sensitivity Analysis for Project S

BASE CHANGE	R_n	OC_n	MCC
+10%	$16,600	$11,438	$ 9,516
0%	$12,913	$12,913	$12,913
–10%	$ 9,226	$14,388	$16,571

tance of the other. For mutually exclusive projects, accept the project with the higher NPV, provided the higher NPV is greater than or equal to zero.

2. Evaluating mutually exclusive projects using internal rate of return.
   Internal rate of return can be used for mutually exclusive projects by treating the projects on an incremental basis. Since this procedure results in an independent project, the internal rate of return decision rules for independent projects apply.

3. Evaluating mutually exclusive projects with unequal lives.
   Mutually exclusive projects with unequal lives are evaluated on the basis of the stated lives, unless the project or projects can be repeated. If that is possible, either the replacement chain approach or the equivalent annual annuity approach is used.

4. Measuring risk and return for individual assets using standard deviation and expected rate of return.
   Risk is the probability of a loss when making an investment. Holding assets with highly variable returns increases the chance of that loss. Financial managers focus on the average return an investment will bring, the expected rate of return, and the standard deviation, a measure of the risk of the investment.

5. Measuring risk and return for a portfolio using standard deviation of portfolio returns and expected return of a portfolio.
   Combining assets into portfolios normally produces a portfolio standard deviation less than the weighted average of the individual standard deviations. The degree of risk reduction depends on the risk-return characteristics of the assets. The expected return of a portfolio is the weighted average of the expected returns of the individual assets in the portfolio.

6. Incorporating risk into capital budgeting using risk-adjusted discount rates and sensitivity analysis.
   The risk-adjusted discount rate approach allows for risk by controlling the discount rate used for capital budgeting decisions. Sensitivity analysis is used to determine the effect on the output variable of increasing or decreasing one input variable, all other input variables held constant.

KEY TERMS

Beta, 241
Capital asset pricing model, 240
Characteristic line, 241
Continuous probability distribution, 237

Correlation coefficient, 239
Discrete probability distribution, 237
Diversification, 239

Equivalent annual annuity approach, 234
Expected rate of return, 236
Expected return of a portfolio, 238

QUESTIONS

8.1 What are mutually exclusive projects? In your answer provide a specific example of two projects that are mutually exclusive.

8.2 In evaluating mutually exclusive projects, the project with the higher NPV is accepted, provided the higher NPV is greater than or equal to zero. Could two mutually exclusive projects be evaluated on an incremental basis using NPV?

8.3 How are mutually exclusive projects evaluated using internal rate of return when more than two projects are involved?

8.4 What is a replacement chain? In your answer provide a specific example of two mutually exclusive projects that require a replacement chain.

8.5 Suppose you won $1,000,000 in the Georgia lottery, and you were offered the chance to double your money by flipping a coin. Heads, $2,000,000; tails, nothing. Would you take the flip? What is the most amount of money you would risk to win the $2,000,000? How does your answer relate to risk?

8.6 How is risk reduced by combining projects into portfolios? Does adding projects always lower the risk of the portfolio?

8.7 Using the risk-adjusted discount approach to capital budgeting, do you always need a precise discount rate to determine if a project should be accepted or rejected? Provide an example.

8.8 How does sensitivity analysis cause a financial manager to think about risk? Provide an example.

8.9 What problems are involved for financial management in making the choice SMES and UPS?

PROBLEMS

8.1 **(Mutually Exclusive Projects with NPV)** The McCartland Corporation plans to replace machinery used in the manufacture of vegetable oils. Two alternatives have been studied, Project A and Project B. The after-tax cash flows are as follows:

Year	CFA	CFB
0	−$96,000	−$66,000
1	$28,900	$23,200
2	$28,900	$23,200
3	$28,900	$23,200
4	$28,900	$23,200
5	$28,900	$23,200

For a 10 percent marginal cost of capital, which project, if either, should be accepted using net present value to decide?

8.2 **(Mutually Exclusive Projects with IRR and NPV)** The SucreSweet Company produces sugar and sugar products. A machine designed to extract raw sugar from sugar cane will be replaced with Model 3402 or Model 3581 from Autin Machinery Corporation. The industrial engineers have calculated the after-tax cash flows for both models.

Year	CF$_{3402}$	CF$_{3581}$
0	−$167,000	−$244,000
1	$ 39,100	$ 57,900
2	$ 39,100	$ 57,900
3	$ 39,100	$ 57,900
4	$ 39,100	$ 57,900
5	$ 39,100	$ 57,900
6	$ 39,100	$ 57,900
7	$ 39,100	$ 57,900

The marginal cost of capital for this company is 12 percent. Determine which model to accept, if either, using incremental internal rate of return analysis. Show that your answer agrees with the net present value method.

8.3 **(Mutually Exclusive Projects with IRR and NPV)** Hospital Products, Inc. will install new specialty needle equipment. Two types are available, R and S. Management has studied the situation and has determined the after-tax cash flows for each type of equipment.

Year	CF$_R$	CF$_S$
0	−$35,400	−$42,800
1	$10,500	$10,700
2	$10,500	$10,700

3	$10,500	$10,700
4	$10,500	$10,700
5	$10,500	$10,700
6	$10,500	$10,700
7	$10,500	$10,700
8	$17,900	$18,800

The marginal cost of capital for this company is 10 percent. Determine which model to accept, if either, using incremental internal rate of return analysis. Show that your answer agrees with the net present value method.

8.4 **(Mutually Exclusive Projects with IRR and NPV)** Fabricated Metal Products, Inc. plans to purchase and install one of two metal stamping machines. Engineers at the plant have identified the after-tax cash flows.

Year	Machine 1	Machine 2
0	−$128,000	−$156,000
1	$ 26,900	$ 30,800
2	$ 26,900	$ 30,800
3	$ 26,900	$ 30,800
4	$ 26,900	$ 30,800
5	$ 26,900	$ 30,800
6	$ 26,900	$ 30,800
7	$ 26,900	$ 30,800
8	$ 26,900	$ 30,900
9	$ 26,900	$ 30,900
10	$ 53,800	$ 60,500

The marginal cost of capital for this company is 12 percent. Determine which model to accept, if either, using incremental internal rate of return analysis. Show by a net present value profile that your answer agrees with the net present value method.

8.5 **(Replacement Chain and Equivalent Annual Annuity)** Engineers for the McCartland Corporation, Problem 8.1, have found a third type of machinery, which they call Project C. This equipment has an initial cash flow of −$172,000 and yearly cash flows of $31,200 for 10 years. The engineers believe that Project A and Project B can be repeated. Show which project should be accepted using the replacement chain approach and the equivalent annual annuity approach.

8.6 **(Replacement Chain and Equivalent Annual Annuity)** A project with the Fitzmorris Company, Project Z, produces cash flows over 10 years. An alternative project, Project K, produces cash flows over five years and can be repeated. Cash flows are as follows:

Year	CF$_Z$	CF$_K$
0	−$60,200	−$28,900
1	$13,200	$11,000
2	$17,500	$11,250
3	$14,500	$11,500
4	$12,400	$11,250
5	$11,000	$11,000
6	$10,900	
7	$11,000	
8	$ 9,100	
9	$ 7,200	
10	$19,900	

For a 10 percent marginal cost of capital, show which machine should be accepted using the replacement chain approach and the equivalent annual annuity approach.

8.7 **(Expected Rate of Return and Standard Deviation)** John Carter, a financial analyst for Allied Industries, was examining the internal rate of return probability distribution for a new project:

Probability	Internal Rate of Return
0.15	25.20%
0.65	9.80%
0.20	−5.50%

Calculate the expected rate of return and standard deviation for this project. John Carter knows that the marginal cost of capital for Allied Industries is 9 percent. If the company accepts the project, what percent of the time would this be a bad decision?

8.8 **(Expected Rate of Return and Standard Deviation)** The Smallwood Boat Company is examining two mutually exclusive projects. The net present value probability distributions follow:

Project A		Project B	
Probability	NPV	Probability	NPV
0.15	$10,000	0.25	$15,000
0.70	$20,000	0.50	$20,000
0.15	$30,000	0.25	$25,000

Calculate the expected value and standard deviation for each project. Which project would you choose?

8.9 **(Expected Rate of Return and Standard Deviation)** Project M has the following cash flows under three states of the economy:

		Cash Flow in Years		
Scenario	Probability	0	1–10	10
Strong	0.20	–$40,000	$8,000	$17,000
Normal	0.60	–$40,000	$7,000	$14,000
Weak	0.20	–$40,000	$6,000	$11,000

Calculate the expected return and standard deviation for the internal rate of return distribution.

8.10 **(Portfolio Risk and Return)** Nina Griffin plans to combine Project X with Project Y. Project X has an expected rate of return of 10.42 percent, while Project Y has an expected rate of return of 13.16 percent. The projects are equally weighted and have the same standard deviation, 4.32 percent. If the correlation coefficient between the two projects is 0.25, what is the expected return and standard deviation of the project portfolio?

8.11 **(Risk-Adjusted Discount Rates)** The industrial engineers from the SucreSweet Company, Problem 8.2, now believe that Model 3402 is of average risk, while Model 3581 requires a 3 percent higher discount rate. Determine which model to accept, if either, using the risk-adjusted approach.

8.12 **(Sensitivity Analysis)** Diversified Industries, Inc. is studying a new project. The cash flows have been estimated as follows:

Year	Cash Flow
0	–$123,000
1	$ 30,000
2	$ 30,000
3	$ 30,000
4	$ 30,000
5	$ 30,000
6	$ 30,000

The marginal cost of capital is calculated to be 10 percent. Perform a sensitivity analysis using 8, 9, 10, 11, and 12 percent as the marginal cost of capital.

8.13 **(Sensitivity Analysis)** The Hopkins Company is evaluating a new project. A worksheet has been completed.

Period	CF_{add}	CF_n	R_n	OC_n
0	−$196,000	0	0	0
1	0	$60,000	$200,000	$120,000
2	0	$60,000	$200,000	$120,000
3	0	$60,000	$200,000	$120,000
4	0	$60,000	$200,000	$120,000
5	$ 60,000	$60,000	$200,000	$120,000

Period	DC_n	DC_{new}	DC_{old}	EAT_n
0	0	0	0	0
1	$30,000	$30,000	$0	$30,000
2	$30,000	$30,000	$0	$30,000
3	$30,000	$30,000	$0	$30,000
4	$30,000	$30,000	$0	$30,000
5	$30,000	$30,000	$0	$30,000

Operating costs are 60 percent of revenues, the marginal tax rate is 40 percent and the marginal cost of capital is 10 percent. Perform a sensitivity analysis, plus or minus 10 percent, on revenues, operating costs, and the marginal cost of capital.

A Case Problem

airyland Corporation was a manufacturer and marketer of refrigerated specialty food products. With manufacturing facilities throughout the United States, the company was strongly positioned to compete with a small number of rival companies.

The company was founded in 1985 to acquire regional dairy operations. In 1988, after acquiring several companies, Dairyland changed its strategy by moving toward refrigerated specialty food products. The goal was to increase share price by moving away from low profit margin fluid milk and ice cream. By 1990, the company began divesting itself of its regional dairy operations.

Larry Hegland joined Dairyland Corporation as a financial analyst in June of 1992 shortly after graduating with a degree in business administration from the University of Wisconsin. He was assigned to the home office in Madison, Wisconsin. Larry planned to work on a graduate degree. As part of his training program, he was temporarily assigned to the Memphis, Tennessee, manufacturing plant. That put his education plans on hold.

Plant Engineering had previously identified two alternatives that were equally attractive from a technical point of view.

Memphis management was considering a refrigeration expansion to increase plant capacity. As a first assignment, Larry was asked by the plant manager to study the economic feasibility of the project. Plant Engineering had previously identified two alternatives that were equally attractive from a technical point of view.

Egland Corporation would provide the refrigeration equipment. Using older technology, the equipment cost $800,000 installed, and would last 10 years. Using newer technology, the installed cost was $1,200,000, but it would last 15 years. In either case, the net salvage value would be 10 percent of the cost of the equipment.

Using Publication 534, Larry determined that the refrigeration equipment was 7-year property under MACRS, and the half-year convention applies. This required percentage rates of 14.29, 24.49, 17.49, 12.49, 8.93, 8.92, 8.93, and 4.46, over *eight* years.

Yearly revenues in the first year were $2,000,000 for both types of equipment but would grow at a compound rate of five percent. Yearly operating costs in the first year were $1,770,000 for the older technology and $1,700,000 for the newer technology. Due to anticipated methods improvements, operating costs would grow at a four percent compound rate after the first year. The marginal cost of capital was 10 percent for the 2 projects, while the marginal tax rate was 40 percent. In discussing the two alternatives with Plant Engineering, Larry discovered that either technology was appropriate for at least thirty years.

Larry wondered what to recommend to the plant manager.

Leading Questions

1. Over how many years should each project be evaluated?
2. What are the yearly revenues and operating costs over the life of the project?
3. What are the equipment costs for later years if the projects are repeated?
4. What is the amount of depreciation each year?
5. What are the salvage values on an after-tax basis?
6. What is the net present value for each project?

PART IV

Cost of Capital, Leverage, Capital Structure, and Dividend Policy

Cost of Capital

Leverage and Capital Structure

Dividend Policy

HESS TO RAISE $412.5 MILLION IN STOCK OFFER

Amerada Hess Corporation plans a stock offering to help pay for development of a large North Sea oil field and the upgrade of its refinery in the Virgin Islands. In a filing with the Securities and Exchange Commission, Hess said it will sell eight million shares in the U.S. and two million abroad in offerings managed by Goldman, Sachs & Co. Despite the stock sale, Hess said that it expects completion of the projects to increase its debt.

9 Cost of Capital

The offering would be the biggest by a U.S. oil company since January 1990 and the third largest ever by an oil company, according to Securities Data Co. of Newark, New Jersey. It may also reflect a change in strategy by the industry. In recent years many big oil companies have been aggressively buying back their shares but that trend has slowed substantially.

"Its not a bad time" for the stock offering, said Eugene Nowak, a securities analyst at Dean Witter Reynolds Inc. in New York. "The oils have perked up a little bit," noting that oil industry stocks rallied last week.

He expects industry earnings, currently depressed, to improve by the second half. In the SEC filing, Hess, based in New York, said it will use the proceeds of the sale to repay a portion of its sizable debt that was accrued to fund major projects totaling more than $2.2 billion.

The stock offering by Amerada Hess Corporation and the subsequent repayment of its debt reflects an attempt by management to minimize its cost of capital. This is accomplished by reducing the component costs of capital whenever possible and by moving toward the optimal capital structure.

Source: Caleb Solomon, "Hess to Raise $412.5 Million In Stock Offer," *The Wall Street Journal,* May 5, 1992. Reprinted by permission of The Wall Street Journal, © 1992 Dow Jones & Company, Inc. All Rights Reserved Worldwide.

CALCULATING CAPITAL COMPONENT COSTS

Why are we as managers interested in calculating capital component costs? Why do we care? It would be easier to find the cost of the latest source of capital and use it as the cost of capital. But would this approach maximize the value of the common stock of the company? The answer is *no*.

The **cost of capital** is the rate of return a company must earn on its average-risk investments in order to leave the market value of its equity unchanged. For an investment to be acceptable to the shareholders of a company, it must provide cash flows to the suppliers of capital in proportion to the amounts and the costs of the capital supplied. This implies that we must find a weighted average cost of capital.

Cost of Capital

The **weighted average cost of capital, k_a,** is the weighted average of the capital component costs. The capital components are debt, preferred stock, and common equity. When retained earnings is used to supply the equity capital component, the following equation applies:

Weighted Average Cost of Capital

$$k_a = w_d k_d (1 - T) + w_p k_p + w_s k_s \qquad (9.1)$$

When the company issues new common stock to supply common equity, the last term of the equation changes.

$$k_a = w_d k_d (1 - T) + w_p k_p + w_s k_e \qquad (9.1a)$$

In supplying common equity for the capital budget, retained earnings is used up before new common stock is issued.

As we move through the chapter, we will use the following variables found in Equation 9.1 and Equation 9.1a:

$$w_d = \text{Weight of debt}$$
$$k_d = \text{Before-tax cost of debt}$$
$$T = \text{Marginal tax rate}$$
$$w_p = \text{Weight of preferred stock}$$
$$k_p = \text{Cost of preferred stock}$$
$$w_s = \text{Weight of common equity}$$
$$k_s = \text{Cost of retained earnings}$$
$$k_e = \text{Cost of new common stock}$$

Each of these variables requires more discussion.

Cost of Debt

After-Tax Cost of New Debt

The cost of the debt component, given by the following equation, is the **after-tax cost of new debt (ATCD):**

$$\text{ATCD} = k_d(1 - T) \tag{9.2}$$

We multiply by the term $(1 - T)$ because interest from debt is tax deductible. The before-tax cost of debt, k_d, is usually the yield to maturity of new bonds after adjustment for flotation costs.

> Henderson Hydraulics issued a 12 percent, $1,000 par value, annual payment bond, with 30 years to maturity at a price of $990.00. Flotation costs were $10.00 per bond and the marginal tax rate was 40 percent. What is the after-tax cost of debt?

A cash flow diagram shows the cash flows from issuing the bond.

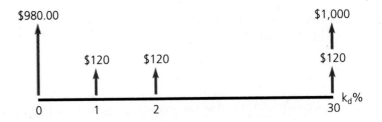

The net proceeds to the company is $980.00 ($990.00 − $10.00).

To find the before-tax cost of debt, we bring the cash flows of the bond back to time 0 and set this amount equal to the net proceeds. We do this by using Equation 3.3.

$$\$980.00 = \frac{\$120}{(1+k_d)^1} + \ldots + \frac{\$120}{(1+k_d)^{30}} + \frac{\$1,000}{(1+k_d)^{30}}$$
$$= \$120(PVFA_{k_d,30}) + \$1,000(PVF_{k_d,30})$$

Using THE FINANCIAL MANAGER (BOND), the before-tax cost of debt is 12.25 percent.

To find the after-tax cost of debt, for a marginal tax rate of 40 percent, we use Equation 9.2.

$$\text{Cost of Debt} = 12.25\%(1 - 0.40)$$
$$= 7.35\%$$

This is the after-tax cost of debt.

Cost of Preferred Stock

The cost of the preferred stock component, given by the following equation, is the **cost of perpetual preferred stock, k_p**:

Cost of Perpetual Preferred Stock

$$k_p = \frac{D_p}{P_n} \qquad (9.3)$$

where

D_p = Annual dividend on preferred stock
P_n = Preferred stock price, net of flotation costs

Since preferred stock dividends are not tax deductible, there is no adjustment for taxes.

Henderson Hydraulics, Inc. issued 12.5 percent perpetual preferred stock with a $100 par value. The amount received by the company after flotation costs was $98.04. What is the cost of the preferred stock?

Equation 9.3 provides the cost of preferred stock.

$$k_p = \frac{\$12.50}{\$98.04}$$
$$= 0.1275 \text{ or } 12.75\%$$

We find the annual dividend on preferred stock by multiplying the dividend percentage, 12.5 percent, by the par value of $100.

Cost of Common Equity

Cost of Retained Earnings

Cost of New Common Stock

The cost of the common equity component is either the **cost of retained earnings, k_s,** or the **cost of new common stock, k_e.** We find the cost of retained earnings by using the Gordon model or the capital asset pricing model. To find the cost of new common stock, we adjust the retained earnings equation for flotation costs.

In Chapter 3, using Equation 3.10, we studied the constant dividend growth model, also known as the Gordon Model.

$$V_s = \frac{D_0(1 + g)}{k_s - g} = \frac{D_1}{k_s - g}$$

Solving the Gordon Model for k_s yields the following formula:

$$k_s = \frac{D_0(1 + g)}{P_0} + g = \frac{D_1}{P_0} + g \qquad (9.4)$$

This equation provides one way for finding the cost of retained earnings.

For the common stock of Henderson Hydraulics, the dividend, paid today is $2.00, the indefinite growth rate is 7 percent, and the price is $26.75. What is the cost of retained earnings?

The information fits the Gordon model and allows us to use Equation 9.4.

$$k_s = \frac{\$2.00(1 + 0.07)}{\$26.75} + 0.07$$
$$= 0.08 + 0.07$$
$$= 0.1500 \text{ or } 15.00\%$$

This approach assumes dividends are growing at a constant rate.

We also calculate the cost of retained earnings using the capital asset pricing model (CAPM). With this model, the required rate of return on common stock, k_s, is given by Equation 8.5:

$$k_s = k_{rf} + (k_m - k_{rf})b_i$$

We use the required rate of return to estimate the cost of retained earnings.

Susan Sanderson, a finance trainee at Henderson Hydraulics, found out that the current risk-free rate on Treasury bonds is 9 percent, the required rate of return for an average stock is 14 percent, and the beta coefficient for the stock of Henderson is 1.20. What is the cost of retained earnings?

The information in this example fits the capital asset pricing model and allows Susan to use Equation 7.9.

$$k_s = 9.00\% + (14.00\% - 9.00\%)1.20$$
$$= 9.00\% + 6.00\%$$
$$= 15.00\%$$

The two estimates give the same answer, 15.00 percent, but in practice they may differ.

Finding the cost of new common stock requires an adjustment for flotation costs. These costs include underwriting costs as well as the cost of having to underprice the stock in order to sell the issue[1]. The cost of new common stock, k_e, is provided by the following equation:

$$k_e = \frac{D_0(1 + g)}{P_0(1 - f)} + g = \frac{D_1}{P_0(1 - f)} + g \qquad (9.5)$$

This equation may be rewritten.

$$k_e = \frac{D_0(1 + g)}{P_n} + g = \frac{D_1}{P_n} + g \qquad (9.5a)$$

where

f = Flotation costs (as a fraction of market price)

P_n = Common stock price, net of flotation costs

---

[1] See Jay R. Ritter, "The Costs of Going Public," *Journal of Financial Economics*, Volume 19, 1987, pp. 269–282, for a further discussion of flotation costs.

The second form of the equation, Equation 9.5a, is useful when we know the amount the company actually receives for each share.

> Susan determined that the estimated dividend a year from today is $2.14, the indefinite growth rate is 7 percent, the price of the stock is $26.75, and the flotation costs on new common stock is 11.11 percent. What is the cost of new common stock for the company?

The information in this example fits the modified form of the Gordon model and allows Susan to use Equation 9.6.

$$k_e = \frac{\$2.14}{\$26.75(1 - 0.1111)} + 0.07$$
$$= 0.0900 + 0.07$$
$$= 0.1600 \text{ or } 16.00\%$$

The practice in this text is to round percentage component costs to two decimal places.

In finding the cost of common equity, Susan used dividend and price information that is generally available only to publicly owned corporations. Estimating the cost of this component for private corporations, partnerships, and sole proprietorships is difficult even though the basic principles are the same. In finding the after-tax cost of debt, the differing tax structures of the three forms of business organization also makes estimating the cost of this component troublesome.

THE MARGINAL COST OF CAPITAL

Marginal Cost of Capital

The **marginal cost of capital, MCC,** is the cost of the last dollar of capital that a company raises for its capital budget[2]. Since component costs increase as more and more capital is raised, the marginal cost of capital will also increase as more and more capital is raised. The component costs used to calculate the marginal cost of capital are the required returns on new capital, not the costs of raising capital in the past.

Book Versus Market Value Weights

Target Capital Structure

The weights used in Equation 9.1 and Equation 9.1a reflect the **target capital structure,** the proportions of debt, preferred stock, and common equity the

---

[2] This definition of marginal cost of capital is widely used in finance. Others define the MCC as the increase in total capital cost resulting from issuing one more dollar of capital.

company will use in the future. The target capital structure should be the optimal capital structure. The **optimal capital structure,** which we will study in the next chapter, is the capital structure that maximizes the value of the common stock of the company. In practice, financial managers accept some variation about the target capital structure from one year to another because of the costliness of issuing new equity.

Optimal Capital Structure

In calculating the marginal cost of capital, book value or market value weights may be used. **Book value weights** are based on historical costs, the book values found on company balance sheets. **Market value weights** are based on the market values of the securities of a company. Financial managers prefer market value weights since they reflect the way investors value the company.

Book Value Weights

Market Value Weights

> Henderson Hydraulics uses long-term debt, preferred stock, and common equity in its capital structure. The long-term debt consists of 50,000 semiannual coupon bonds, each with a par value of $1,000. The bonds have a coupon rate of 12 percent, mature in 15 years, and include a going rate of interest of 14 percent. The preferred stock consists of 100,000 shares, each with a stated value of $100 and a market value of $90. The common equity consists of 1,000,000 shares of common stock, each with a book value of $40 and a market value of $50. What are the book value and market value weights if the current capital structure is considered to be optimal?

We find the book value of each capital component by multiplying the book value on a per-unit basis by the number of units. The book value of the bonds is the par value of each bond times the number of bonds.

$$\text{Book Value (bonds)} = \$1,000(50,000) = \$50,000,000$$

The book value of the preferred stock is the stated value of each share times the number of shares of preferred stock.

$$\text{Book Value (preferred)} = \$100(100,000) = \$10,000,000$$

The book value of the common equity is the book value per share times the number of shares of common stock.

$$\text{Book Value (common equity)} = \$40(1,000,000) = \$40,000,000$$

The total book value is $100,000,000, the sum of $50,000,000, $10,000,000, and $40,000,000.

In a similar manner, we find the market value of each component by multiplying the market value on a per-unit basis by the number of units. Before finding the market value of the bonds, we must find the value of each bond using Equation 3.3.

$$
\begin{aligned}
V_b &= \frac{\$60}{(1.07)^1} + \frac{\$60}{(1.07)^2} + \ldots + \frac{\$60}{(1.07)^{30}} + \frac{\$1,000}{(1.07)^{30}} \\
&= \$60(PVFA_{7\%,30}) + \$1,000(PVF_{7\%,30}) \\
&= \$60(12.4090) + \$1,000(0.1314) \\
&= \$744.54 + \$131.40 \\
&= \$875.94
\end{aligned}
$$

The market value of the bonds is the market value of each bond times the number of bonds.

$$\text{Market Value (bonds)} = \$875.94(50,000) = \$43,797,000$$

The market value of the preferred stock is the market value of each share times the number of shares of preferred stock.

$$\text{Market Value (preferred)} = \$90(100,000) = \$9,000,000$$

The market value of the common equity is the market value per share times the number of shares of common stock.

$$\text{Market Value (common equity)} = \$50(1,000,000) = \$50,000,000$$

The total market value is $102,797,000, the sum of $43,797,000, $9,000,000, and $50,000,000.

Table 9.1 provides a comparison of book value and market value weights. There is a dramatic difference in using book value weights versus market value weights. As stated previously, market value weights are preferred.

TABLE 9.1 A Comparison of Book Value and Market Value Weights

COMPONENT	BOOK VALUE		MARKET VALUE	
	AMOUNT	WEIGHT	AMOUNT	WEIGHT
Long-term debt	$ 50,000,000	50.0%	$ 43,797,000	42.6%
Preferred stock	10,000,000	10.0%	9,000,000	8.8%
Common equity	40,000,000	40.0%	50,000,000	48.6%
	$100,000,000	100.0%	$102,797,000	100.0%

Marginal Cost of Capital Schedule

Earlier in this section, it was pointed out that the marginal cost of capital increases as more and more capital is raised. This is caused by financial managers making the rational decision to use cheaper funds before more expensive funds. With this in mind, we will learn how to calculate the marginal cost of capital, given specific information about the costs and availability of the various capital components.

There is a jump in the cost of common equity when retained earnings is used up and new common stock is required. New common stock costs more than retained earnings. This causes a break point in the **marginal cost of capital (MCC) schedule,** the schedule showing the relationship between the size of the capital budget and the cost of capital. We can show the MCC schedule with a tabular presentation or with a MCC curve. (If you would like to look ahead, Figure 9.2 shows a MCC curve.)

Marginal Cost of Capital Schedule

Henderson Hydraulics has a $600,000 increase in retained earnings. The company includes 30 percent debt, 10 percent preferred stock, and 60 percent common equity in its optimal capital structure. The cost of retained earnings is 15 percent, and the cost of new common stock is 16 percent. How large a capital budget would the increase in retained earnings support?

We find this common equity break point, BP_{CE}, by multiplying the common equity weight by BP_{CE} and setting it equal to the amount of retained earnings.

$$0.60(BP_{CE}) = \$600,000$$
$$BP_{CE} = \$1,000,000$$

Retained earnings would support a capital budget of $1,000,000, consisting of 30 percent debt, 10 percent preferred stock, and 60 percent common equity in the form of retained earnings.

Debt	$ 300,000
Preferred stock	100,000
Retained earnings	600,000
	$1,000,000

To maintain the optimal capital structure, $300,000 in debt and $100,000 in preferred stock would be issued.

There is an increase in the cost of debt whenever cheaper debt is used up. This also causes a break point in the marginal cost of capital curve.

Henderson Hydraulics can borrow $450,000 at 12 percent, with higher amounts of debt costing 14 percent. The marginal tax rate is 40 percent. How large a capital budge could the lower-costing debt support?

We find this debt break point, BP_{DT}, by multiplying the debt weight by BP_{DT}, and setting it equal to the maximum amount of the lower costing debt.

$$0.30(BP_{DT}) = \$450,000$$
$$BP_{DT} = \$1,500,000$$

Lower costing debt would support a capital budget of $1,500,000, consisting of 30 percent debt, 10 percent preferred stock, and 60 percent of common equity in the form of retained earnings and new common stock.

Debt	$ 450,000
Preferred stock	150,000
Retained earnings	600,000
New Common Stock	300,000
	$1,500,000

To maintain the optimal capital structure, $50,000 in additional preferred stock and $300,000 in new common stock would be issued.

There is a jump in the cost of preferred stock whenever less expensive stock is used up. This also causes a break point in the marginal cost of capital curve.

Henderson Hydraulics can issue $200,000 of preferred stock at 12.5 percent with higher amounts costing 13.5 percent. How large a capital budget could the lower costing preferred stock support?

We find this preferred stock break point, BP_{PS}, by multiplying the preferred stock weight by BP_{PS}, and setting it equal to the amount of the lower costing preferred stock.

$$0.10(BP_{PS}) = \$200,000$$
$$BP_{PS} = \$2,000,000$$

Lower costing preferred stock would support a capital budget of $2,000,000, consisting of 30 percent debt, 10 percent preferred stock, and 60 percent common equity in the form of retained earnings and new common stock.

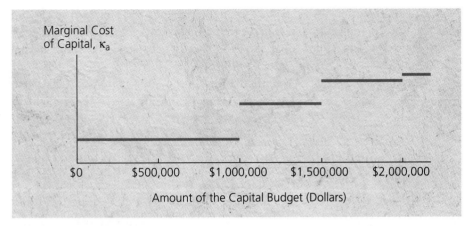

FIGURE 9.1   Partial Marginal Cost of Capital Curve (Henderson Hydraulics)

Debt (12%)	$ 450,000
Debt (14%)	150,000
Preferred stock	200,000
Retained earnings	600,000
New Common Stock	600,000
	$2,000,000

To maintain the optimal capital structure, $150,000 in 14 percent debt and $600,000 in new common stock would be issued.

As shown in Figure 9.1, there are three break points in the marginal cost of capital schedule: $1,000,000, $1,500,000, and $2,000,000. It is only a partial marginal cost of capital curve since it does not display the marginal cost of capital percentage for each interval.

The number of intervals in a marginal cost of capital schedule is equal to the number of break points plus one. In this example, there are three break points and, therefore, four intervals. The intervals represent the amount of the capital budget from $0 to $1,000,000, from $1,000,000 to $1,500,000, from $1,500,000 to $2,000,000, and $2,000,000$^+$. Each interval requires a calculation of the marginal cost of capital. The simplest way to make these calculations is with a tabular presentation.

The first table provides the calculations in the interval from $0 to $1,000,000.

$0 to $1,000,000				
Capital Component	**Weight**	× **Cost**	=	**Weighted Cost**
Debt (12%)	0.30	7.20		2.16
Preferred stock	0.10	12.50		1.25
Retained earnings	0.60	15.00		9.00
				12.41%

Notice that we start off with the cheapest debt, the cheapest preferred stock, and the cheapest common equity, retained earnings. The cost of debt, $12\%(1 - 0.40) = 7.20\%$, is the after-tax cost of debt. The marginal cost of capital in the interval from $0 to $1,000,000 is 12.41%.

The second table provides the calculations in the interval from $1,000,000 to $1,500,000.

$1,000,000 to $1,500,000

Capital Component	Weight	×	Cost	=	Weighted Cost
Debt (12%)	0.30		7.20		2.16
Preferred stock	0.10		12.50		1.25
New common stock	0.60		16.00		9.60
					13.01%

Notice that the capital component that changes is the one that causes the break, at $1,000,000 in this case. Looking back at the breakeven equations, we see $BP_{CE} = \$1,000,000$. The common equity component will change. It changes from retained earnings to new common stock. The marginal cost of capital in the interval from $1,000,000 to $1,500,000 is 13.01%.

The third table provides the calculations in the interval from $1,500,000 to $2,000,000.

$1,500,000 to $2,000,000

Capital Component	Weight	×	Cost	=	Weighted Cost
Debt (14%)	0.30		8.40		2.52
Preferred stock	0.10		12.50		1.25
New common stock	0.60		16.00		9.60
					13.37%

Notice that the capital component that changes is based on the break point $BP_{DT} = \$1,500,000$. The debt component will change. The cost of debt, $14\%(1 - 0.40) = 8.40\%$, is the after-tax cost of debt. The marginal cost of capital in the interval from $1,500,000 to $2,000,000 is 13.37%.

The fourth table provides the calculations in the $2,000,000$^+^ interval.

$2,000,000$^+^

Capital Component	Weight	×	Cost	=	Weighted Cost
Debt (14%)	0.30		8.40		2.52
Preferred stock	0.10		13.50		1.35
New common stock	0.60		16.00		9.60
					13.47%

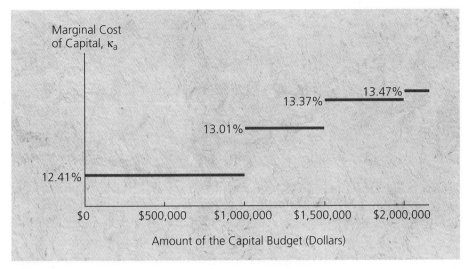

FIGURE 9.2   Complete Marginal Cost of Capital Curve (Henderson Hydraulics)

Notice that the capital component that changes is based on the break point $BP_{PS} = \$2,000,000$. The marginal cost of capital in the $\$2,000,000^+$ interval is 13.47%.

Figure 9.2 is a complete marginal cost of capital curve and includes the MCC for each interval.

COST OF CAPITAL AND CAPITAL BUDGETING

The marginal cost of capital schedule is used along with the company's investment opportunities to determine which investments to choose. This selection process also defines the amount of the optimal capital budget.

Projects are selected as long as the internal rate of return of the project is greater than the marginal cost of capital for that particular project. As we learned in the previous section, the MCC increases as more and more capital is required. At the same time, the IRRs of available projects decrease as more and more capital is invested. Financial managers accept projects until the marginal return on investment is equal to the marginal cost of capital.

Investment Opportunity Schedule

The **investment opportunity (IO) schedule** arranges the investment opportunities from the highest to the lowest ranking (using IRR) while summing the required initial investments. We can show the IO schedule with a tabular presentation or with an IO curve.

Investment Opportunity Schedule

Peterson Pumping has the following investment opportunities for next year:

Project	Initial Investment	Internal Rate of Return
A	$ 900,000	15%
B	$1,100,000	16%
C	$ 700,000	18%
D	$ 900,000	14%
E	$1,200,000	12%

Dave Hamilton, a financial manager at Peterson Pumping, plans to plot the investment opportunity curve for this set of investments.

Dave plots the IO curve in a series of steps. First, he arranges the projects in descending order according to internal rate of return. The order is C-B-A-D-E. Second, he finds the cumulative investment required. The results follow:

Project	Cumulative Investment	IRR
C	$ 700,000	18%
B	$1,800,000	16%
A	$2,700,000	15%
D	$3,600,000	14%
E	$4,800,000	12%

Finally, he plots the investment opportunity curve as Figure 9.3.

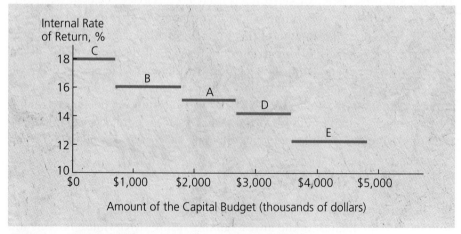

FIGURE 9.3 Investment Opportunity Curve (Peterson Pumping)

Combining MCC and IO Curves

The investment opportunity curve is combined with the marginal cost of capital curve to determine which investments to choose and to define the amount of the optimal capital budget. In this segment, we prepare a new marginal cost of capital curve and combine it with the previously graphed investment opportunity curve.

Peterson Pumping has a target capital structure of 40 percent debt, no preferred stock, and 60 percent common equity. The company expects net income of $2,500,000 and will pay out 40 percent of earnings as dividends. The before-tax cost of debt depends on the amount borrowed.

Amount Borrowed	Before-Tax Cost
$0 to $600,000	12%
$600,000 to $1,400,000	14%
$1,400,000$^+$	16%

The marginal tax rate is 40 percent. The common stock of the company sells for $30.00 per share, and new common stock can be sold to net the company $27.50 per share. Today's dividend is $1.50, and it will grow at a rate of 10 percent indefinitely. Dave Hamilton is preparing the marginal cost of capital tables.

Dave begins by finding the break points in the marginal cost of capital schedule. There are two debt break points and one break point caused by using up retained earnings.

He finds the first debt break point, BP_{DT1}, by multiplying the debt weight by BP_{DT1} and setting it equal to the maximum amount of the lower costing debt.

$$0.40(BP_{DT1}) = \$600,000$$
$$BP_{DT1} = \$1,500,000$$

The capital budget will have one break at $1,500,000.

Dave finds the second debt break point, BP_{DT2}, by multiplying the debt weight by BP_{DT2} and setting it equal to the maximum amount of the middle-costing debt.

$$0.40(BP_{DT2}) = \$1,400,000$$
$$BP_{DT2} = \$3,500,000$$

The capital budget will have another break at $3,500,000.

He finds the break point caused by using up retained earnings, BP_{CE}, by multiplying the common equity weight by BP_{CE} and setting it equal to the amount of retained earnings. The amount of retained earnings is the net income times the retention ratio, $2,500,000(1 - 0.40) = $1,500,000.

$$0.60(BP_{CE}) = \$1,500,000$$
$$BP_{CE} = \$2,500,000$$

The capital budget will have a break at $2,500,000.

Dave next calculates capital component costs. This includes finding the after-tax costs of debt, the cost of retained earnings, and the cost of common equity for both retained earnings and new common stock.

He finds the after-tax costs of new debt using Equation 9.2:

$$ATCD_{12\%} = 12\%(1 - 0.40) = 7.20\%$$
$$ATCD_{14\%} = 14\%(1 - 0.40) = 8.40\%$$
$$ATCD_{16\%} = 16\%(1 - 0.40) = 9.60\%$$

These are the after-tax costs of debt to be used in the MCC tables.

Dave finds the cost of retained earnings by using Equation 9.4.

$$k_s = \frac{D_0(1 + g)}{P_0} + g$$
$$= \frac{\$1.50(1 + 0.10)}{\$30.00} + 0.10$$
$$= 0.1550 \text{ or } 15.50\%$$

He finds the cost of new common stock by using Equation 9.5a.

$$k_e = \frac{D_0(1 + g)}{P_n} + g$$
$$= \frac{\$1.50(1 + 0.10)}{\$27.50} + 0.10$$
$$= 0.1600 \text{ or } 16.00\%$$

Dave then creates the MCC tables. In this example, there are three break points, resulting in four tables. The four tables represent the intervals $0 to $1,500,000, $1,500,000 to $2,500,000, $2,500,000 to $3,500,000, and $3,500,000[+].

The first table provides the calculations in the interval from $0 to $1,500,000.

$0 to $1,500,000

Capital Component	Weight	×	Cost	=	Weighted Cost
Debt (12%)	0.40		7.20		2.88
Retained earnings	0.60		15.50		9.30
					12.18%

Notice that he starts off with the cheapest debt and the cheapest common equity, retained earnings. The marginal cost of capital in the interval from $0 to $1,500,000 is 12.18%

The second table provides the calculations in the interval from $1,500,000 to $2,500,000.

$1,500,000 to $2,500,000

Capital Component	Weight	×	Cost	=	Weighted Cost
Debt (14%)	0.40		8.40		3.36
Retained earnings	0.60		15.50		9.30
					12.66%

Notice that the capital component that changes is the component that causes the break, at $1,500,000 in this case. Looking back at the breakeven equations, he sees $BP_{DT1} = \$1,500,000$. This suggests the debt component will change from the cheapest debt to the middle-costing debt. The marginal cost of capital in the interval from $1,500,000 to $2,500,000 is 12.66%.

The third table provides the calculations in the interval from $2,500,000 to $3,500,000.

$2,500,000 to $3,500,000

Capital Component	Weight	×	Cost	=	Weighted Cost
Debt (14%)	0.40		8.40		3.36
New common stock	0.60		16.00		9.60
					12.96%

Notice that the capital component that changes is based on the break point $BP_{CE} = \$2,500,000$. The common equity component will change from retained earnings to new common stock. The cost of new common stock is 16.00%. The marginal cost of capital in the interval from $2,500,000 to $3,500,000 is 12.96%.

The fourth table provides the calculations in the $3,500,000^+$ interval.

$3,500,000^+$

Capital Component	Weight	×	Cost	=	Weighted Cost
Debt (16%)	0.40		9.60		3.84
New common stock	0.60		16.00		9.60
					13.44%

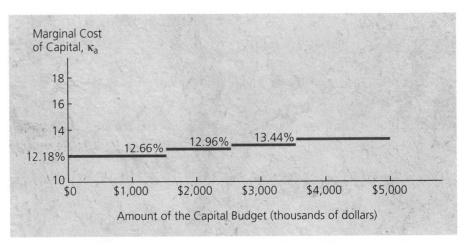

FIGURE 9.4 Marginal Cost of Capital Curve (Peterson Pumping)

Notice that the capital component that changes is based on the break point $BP_{DT2} = \$3,500,000$. The debt component will change from the middle-costing debt to the highest costing debt. The marginal cost of capital in the $3,500,000^+$ interval is 13.44%.

Figure 9.4 includes a complete marginal cost of capital curve, including the marginal cost of capital for each interval.

Japan's Woes Stir Talk Firms May Modify Time-Honored Ways

The sharp slowdown in Japan's economic growth and a collapse in its stock and real estate prices have hit Japanese industry with a double whammy. At issue are some basic management practices such as the penchant for pursuing market share at the expense of profits and for planning for the distant future with scant regard for the near term. Now, the problems in Japan's financial markets, says Richard Koo, senior economist at Nomura Research Institute, will force Japanese companies to behave more like overseas rivals, abandoning unprofitable product lines and offering higher returns to investors. Yoshio Suzuki, a former Bank of Japan director, concedes that Japan's big companies may change the way they raise capital, but he doubts that they will ever stop planning 10 to 15 years into the future. Among other distressing effects, depressed stock prices will prohibit Japanese companies from floating new shares to reduce the amount of equity linked bonds. "From now on, Japan's companies will have to make investment decisions on the basis of the true cost of capital," says Hideo Ishihara, deputy president of Industrial Bank of Japan. "They will have to be more careful."

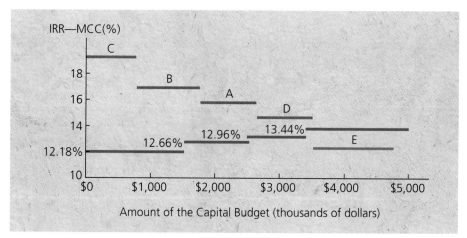

FIGURE 9.5 Combining Investment Opportunity and Marginal Cost of Capital Curves (Peterson Pumping)

In Figure 9.5, Dave combines the investment opportunity and marginal cost of capital curves. The graph indicates the projects to be accepted and rejected as well as the optimal capital budget. Projects C, B, A, and D have IRRs greater than the marginal cost of capital and are accepted. Project E has an IRR less than the marginal cost of capital and is rejected. The amount of the optimal capital budget is the amount of funds required to support the accepted projects, a total of $3,600,000.

THE EFFECT OF RATIONING

Up to this point, we have assumed there was no limit to the availability of capital to fund capital budgeting projects. For example, with Peterson Pumping we determined that $3,600,000 would be available to fund projects C, B, A, and D. But what if Peterson decides to spend less than $3,600,000 on capital projects?

To answer this question, we must understand the two types of rationing: external rationing and internal rationing. **External rationing** (credit rationing) occurs when lenders restrict the amount of borrowing a company can do by making the cost of credit prohibitively high. **Internal rationing** (capital rationing) occurs when company management chooses not to accept all projects indicated by the optimal capital budget.

External Rationing

Internal Rationing

External Rationing

External rationing is consistent with common stock value maximization. When lenders raise the cost of debt to prohibitively high levels, the company's marginal cost of capital is also raised. What may appear to be capital rationing is actually a reduction in the level of the optimal capital budget.

> Peterson Pumping, from the previous section, finds that the cost of debt after $1,400,000 of borrowing is prohibitively high. Dave Hamilton determines that the marginal cost of capital increases to 16.00 percent after the capital budget reaches $3,500,000, the associated debt break point. Under these conditions, what is the optimal capital budget?

Figure 9.6 shows the old investment opportunity curve combined with the new marginal cost of capital curve. Projects C, B, and A have IRRs greater than the marginal cost of capital and are accepted. Project D would be rejected assuming it is an all-or-nothing project. Project E has an IRR less than the marginal cost of capital and is rejected. The new optimal capital budget, the amount of funds required to support the accepted projects, is $2,700,000. The reduction in the optimal capital budget from $3,600,000 to $2,700,000 is not capital rationing but represents share-maximizing behavior.

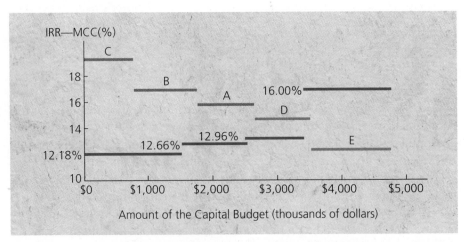

FIGURE 9.6 Investment Opportunity Curve Combined with the New Marginal Cost of Capital Curve (Peterson Pumping)

Internal Rationing

Using the marginal cost of capital curve in Figure 9.5, management may decide to accept Projects C, B, and A and to reject Projects D and E. Under normal conditions, the rejection of Project D is capital rationing.

George Trivoli and William McDaniel argue that this is not necessarily the case[3]. During periods of increased economic uncertainty—approaching or during recessionary times—managers add an uncertainty premium to the marginal cost of capital curve[4]. By raising the MCC curve, the optimal capital budget is reduced, in a manner not unlike the preceding external-rationing example.

The Real Key To Creating Wealth

What if you could look up almost any business operation and see immediately whether it was becoming more valuable or less? What if you as a manager could use this measure to make sure your operation—however large or small—was increasing in value? What if you as an investor could use it to spot stocks that were far likelier than most to rise high? What if using this measure would give you a marked competitive advantage, since most managers and investors aren't using it?

So what is it? Simply stated, Economic Value Added (EVA) is just a way of measuring an operation's real profitability. What makes it so revealing is that it takes into account a factor no conventional measure includes: the total cost of the operation's capital. The capital is all the money tied up in such things as heavy equipment, real estate, computers, and other stuff that's expected to be productive for a while after it has been purchased, plus so-called working capital, mainly cash, inventories, and receivables. EVA is sim-

ply after-tax operating profit, a widely used measure, minus the total annual cost of capital.

Here's how Coca-Cola CEO Roberto Goizueta, a champion wealth creator, explains it: "We raise capital to make concentrate, and sell it at an operating profit. Then we pay the cost of that capital. Shareholders pocket the difference." This turns out to be profound. Incredibly, most corporate groups, divisions, and departments have no idea how much capital they tie up or what it costs. True, the cost of borrowed capital shows up in a company's interest expense. But the cost of equity capital, which the shareholders have contributed, typically appears nowhere in any financial statements—and equity is extraordinarily expensive capital. Until managers figure all this out, they can't know whether they're covering all their costs and adding value to a company.

---

[3] See George W. Trivoli and William R. McDaniel, "Uncertainty, Capital Immobility and Capital Rationing in the Investment Decision," *Journal of Business Finance and Accounting*, Vol. 14, No. 2, Summer 1987, pp. 215–229.

[4] See Chapter 8 for a discussion of the differences between risk and uncertainty.

Trivoli and McDaniel point out that the uncertainty premium depends on two factors: (1) changes in the level of credit tightness in the firm's respective market, and (2) the impact of changing market conditions. The greater the level of uncertainty caused by a decline in economic activity or credit tightness, the larger the uncertainty premium.

What appears to be irrational behavior is quite logical. This is not capital rationing per se but instead a sensible approach for setting investment levels in the face of uncertainty. Under these conditions, limiting the level of the capital budget is consistent with the primary goal of management in a corporation.

SUMMARY

This chapter focuses on the following learning objectives:

1. Calculating capital component costs.

   The before-tax cost of debt is usually the yield to maturity of new bonds after adjustment for flotation costs. The cost of preferred stock is the preferred dividend divided by the net amount received. The cost of common equity is either the cost of retained earnings or the cost of new common stock. The cost of retained earnings is found using the Gordon Model or the capital asset pricing model. The cost of new common stock is found by adjusting for flotation costs.

2. Determining book value and market value weights.

   In calculating the marginal cost of capital, book value or market value weights may be used. Book value weights are based on historical costs, the book values found on company balance sheets. Market value weights are based on the market values of the securities of a company. Financial managers prefer market value weights.

3. Computing the marginal cost of capital schedule.

   The marginal cost of capital is the cost of the last dollar of capital that the company raises. There are jumps in the cost of common equity, preferred stock, and debt when lower costing components are used up. This causes break points in the marginal cost of capital schedule. The number of intervals in a marginal cost of capital schedule is equal to the number of break points plus one.

4. Computing the investment opportunity schedule.

   The investment opportunity schedule arranges the investment opportunities from the highest to the lowest (using IRR) while summing the required initial investments. This schedule is shown with a tabular presentation or with an investment opportunity curve.

5. Combining the marginal cost of capital curve with the investment opportunity curve.
   The marginal cost of capital curve is combined with the investment opportunity curve to determine the optimal capital budget. Projects are selected as long as the internal rate of return of the project is greater than the marginal cost of capital for that particular project.

6. Explaining the effect of rationing on the capital budgeting process.
   External rationing (credit rationing) occurs when lenders restrict the amount of borrowing a company can do by making the cost of credit prohibitively high. Internal rationing (capital rationing) occurs when company management chooses not to accept all projects indicated by the optimal capital budget. During periods of increased economic uncertainty—approaching or during recessionary times—managers add an uncertainty premium to the marginal cost of capital curve, thereby raising the marginal cost of capital curve and reducing the optimal capital budget.

KEY TERMS

After-tax cost of new debt, 260

Book value weights, 265

Cost of capital, 259

Cost of new common stock, 262

Cost of perpetual preferred stock, 261

Cost of retained earnings, 262

External rationing, 277

Internal rationing, 277

Investment opportunity schedule, 271

Marginal cost of capital, 264

Marginal cost of capital schedule, 267

Market value weights, 265

Optimal capital structure, 265

Target capital structure, 264

Weighted average cost of capital, 259

QUESTIONS

9.1 What is meant by the marginal cost of capital?

9.2 How are the marginal cost of capital and investment opportunity graphs used to determine which investments to choose?

9.3 Why is the cost of debt calculated on an after-tax basis? What changes in the tax code would affect the cost of this component?

9.4 Why are retained earnings used up before new common stock is issued?

9.5   Why are market value weights used instead of book value weights when computing the marginal cost of capital?

9.6   What is capital rationing? Give an example that appears to be capital rationing but in fact is not.

9.7   What steps does Amerada Hess Corporation take to minimize its cost of capital?

9.8   Why might Japan change the way it raises capital?

9.9   What is the Economic Value Added concept?

PROBLEMS
● ● ● ● ● ● ● ● ● ● ● ●

9.1   **(After-Tax Cost of Debt)** The before-tax cost of debt for the Hall Company is 12 percent. The marginal tax rate is 40 percent. What is the after-tax cost of debt?

9.2   **(After-Tax Cost of Debt)** Hillcrest Corporation issued a 10 percent, $1,000 par value, annual payment bond, with 20 years to maturity, at a price of $1,050.00. Flotation costs are $15.00 per bond. The marginal tax rate is 40 percent. What is the after-tax cost of debt? (BOND)

9.3   **(After-Tax Cost of Debt)** Hines Sports Equipment issued a 12 percent, $1,000 par value, semiannual payment bond, with 30 years to maturity, at a price of $980.00. Flotation costs are $20.00 per bond. The marginal tax rate is 40 percent. What is the after-tax cost of debt? (BOND)

9.4   **(Cost of Preferred Stock)** Indiana Industries issued 12 percent preferred stock with a $100 par value. The amount received by the company after flotation costs was $97.00. What is the cost of the preferred stock?

9.5   **(Cost of Retained Earnings)** The McLaughlin Corporation will pay a dividend a year from today of $3.21. The indefinite growth rate for the company is 7 percent, and the price of the stock is $40.125. What is the cost of retained earnings?

9.6   **(Cost of Retained Earnings)** White House Furnishings paid a dividend today of $1.50. The expected growth rate for the company is 10 percent, and the price of the stock is $33.00. What is the cost of retained earnings?

9.7   **(Cost of Retained Earnings)** Poole Products, Inc. has a beta coefficient for its stock of 1.40. The risk-free rate on Treasury bonds is 8 percent, and the required rate of return for an average stock is 13 percent. What is the cost of retained earnings?

9.8   **(Cost of Retained Earnings)** The Porter Luggage Company has a beta coefficient of 0.8. The average return on the market is 12 percent, and the risk-free rate is 9 percent. What is the cost of retained earnings?

9.9 **(Cost of New Common Stock)** Singley Machine Company will pay a dividend a year from today of $3.00. The future growth rate is 9 percent, the price of the stock is $45.00, and the flotation cost is 10 percent. What is the cost of new common stock?

9.10 **(Cost of New Common Stock)** Trulock Development Corporation (TDC) has an expected growth rate in earnings and dividends of 12 percent. The company can sell stock to net the company $27.00 per share. TDC paid a dividend today of $2.16 per share. What is the cost of new common stock?

9.11 **(Book and Market Value Weights)** Kirkland Construction Company uses long-term debt, preferred stock, and common equity in its capital structure. The long-term debt consists of 10,000 semiannual coupon bonds, each with a par value of $1,000. The bonds have a coupon rate of 13 percent, mature in 20 years, and include a going interest rate of 12 percent. The preferred stock consists of 25,000 shares, each with a par value of $100 and a market value of $95. The common equity consists of 500,000 shares of common stock, each with a book value of $30 and a market value of $40. What are the book value weights and the market value weights, if the capital structure is considered to be optimal? (BOND)

9.12 **(Investment Opportunity Curve)** Parker Publishing has the following investment opportunities for next year:

Project	Initial Investment	Rate of Return
A	$ 600,000	12%
B	$1,000,000	18%
C	$ 500,000	15%
D	$ 800,000	13%

Plot the investment opportunity curve for this set of investments.

9.13 **(Marginal Cost of Capital Table and Curve)** Parker Publishing has a target capital structure of 40 percent debt, no preferred stock, and 60 percent common equity. The company expects net income of $3,000,000 and will pay out 40 percent of earnings as dividends. The before-tax cost of debt depends on the amount borrowed.

Amount Borrowed	Before-Tax Cost
$0 to $500,000	10%
$500,000 to $1,500,000	12%
$1,500,000+	14%

The marginal tax rate is 40 percent. The common stock of the company sells for $50.00 per share, and the new common stock can be sold to net the company $45.00 per share. Today's dividend is $3.00 and will grow at a rate of 9 percent indefinitely. Prepare the marginal cost of capital tables and plot the marginal cost of capital curve.

9.14 **(Finding the Optimal Capital Budget)** Combine the investment opportunity curve from Problem 9.12 with the marginal cost of capital curve from Problem 9.13. Determine which projects should be accepted and the size of the optimal capital budget.

A Case Problem

The National Oil and Gas Company (NOGC) was engaged in the business of gathering, processing, transporting, and marketing natural gas and natural gas liquids. The company owned the principal intrastate pipeline system in Texas, gas processing plants, and a gas storage reservoir.

The profitability of the company depended to a large degree upon its ability to respond to changing market conditions in negotiating gas purchase and sales agreements.

The price of natural gas and natural gas liquids depended upon the level of domestic production, availability of imported oil, marketing of competitive fuels, seasonal demand, and governmental regulation. The profitability of the company depended to a large degree upon its ability to respond to changing market conditions in negotiating gas purchase and sales agreements. These decisions involved judgments about future events and market conditions.

William Connelly was Senior Vice President and Chief Financial Officer for National Oil and Gas Company. In July of 1993, he was gathering information in order to determine the next year's capital budget. NOGC used long-term debt and common equity in its capital structure. The long-term debt consisted of 73,500 semiannual coupon bonds, each with a par value of $1,000. The bonds had a coupon rate of 12 percent, matured in 15 years, and included a going interest rate of 10 percent. The common equity consisted of 16,000,000 shares of common stock, each with a market value of $7.50. William Connelly considered the market value capital structure to be optimal.

National Oil and Gas Company expected net income of $7,000,000 and planned to pay out 40 percent of earnings as dividends. The before-tax cost of debt depended

on the amount borrowed: 10 percent for less than $6,000,000; 12 percent for more. The marginal tax rate was 35 percent. William Connelly determined that the beta coefficient for NOGC stock was 1.50, the risk-free rate on Treasury bonds was 7 percent, and the required rate of return for an average stock was 11 percent. Flotation costs on new issues amounted to 9 percent.

In the new capital budget, National Oil and Gas Company had three investment opportunities. A pipeline improvement proposal cost $10,000,000 and had a 19 percent rate of return. A gas processing plant proposal cost $8,000,000 and had a 15 percent rate of return. A gas storage reservoir proposal had a cost of $5,000,000 and had a 10 percent rate of return.

William Connelly had to decide which proposals to accept.

Leading Questions

1. What are the market value weights?
2. What are the component costs for the marginal cost of capital?
3. Determine which projects would be accepted/rejected by combining the investment opportunity curve with the marginal cost of capital curve?

10 Leverage and Capital Structure

ITT PROPOSES NEW BUY-BACK OF ITS SHARES

ITT Corporation authorized a new stock-repurchase program as part of a continuing effort to boost shareholder value. The new buy-back is for common and convertible preferred shares, as many as 25 million equivalent common shares. The repurchase plan is part of ITT's goal to bring its return on equity to 15 percent by 1996 and improve its share price. Analysts expected more news from ITT about restructuring after the company announced its sale of Alcatel N.V. The analysts expected difficulty for ITT in reaching its goal without further restructuring efforts. As Alcatel performed above average in return on equity, the share-repurchase plan would compensate on return on equity by reducing the shares outstanding.

Rand V. Araskog, ITT chairman and chief executive officer, assured shareholders that "the coming years will see a good deal of action intended to accomplish our goal of a better share price." He said prospects are good for reaching the 15 percent return-on-equity goal. "We're in a down economy, but we are still doing quite well." Mr. Araskog declared that the company's highest priority is building shareholder value.

The repurchase of shares is one method for changing the capital structure at ITT. By reducing the number of shares outstanding, the debt ratio is increased. This may increase the return-on-equity but will increase financial risk as well.

Source: Michael Selz, "ITT Proposes New Buy-Back Of Its Shares," *The Wall Street Journal,* May 6, 1992. Reprinted by permission of The Wall Street Journal, © 1992 Dow Jones and Company, Inc. All Rights Reserved Worldwide.

LEVERAGE

In Chapter 9, we studied how to find the cost of capital. In that discussion, we assumed an optimal capital structure—the capital structure that maximizes the value of the common stock of a company. In this chapter, we go a step further: We examine how to find the proper mix of debt and equity.

In studying capital structure, we investigate leverage. In everyday usage, this term involves the mechanical advantage gained by using a lever. But in finance there are three types of leverage—operating, financial, and total. **Operating leverage** is the extent to which operating costs are fixed as opposed to variable. **Financial leverage** is the extent to which debt is used in the capital structure. **Total leverage** is the combined effect of using operating and financial leverage. Before we study the first type of leverage, operating leverage, let's examine a related topic—breakeven analysis.

Operating Leverage

Financial Leverage

Total Leverage

Breakeven Analysis

Breakeven analysis is used to find the output or sales level which generates earnings before interest and taxes (EBIT) of 0. At this point, total revenues are equal to total costs. This is part of a general approach to planning known as cost-volume-profit (CVP) analysis. CVP is involved with examining the impact of changes in prices, costs, and volume and their effect on profit.

Costs are classified as either fixed or variable. Fixed costs do not change over a relevant range of output. They include items such as salaries, advertising, property taxes, insurance, and depreciation. Rent is usually considered fixed, unless the company expands. Variable costs change directly with the level of

Breakeven Analysis

production. These costs include items such as labor, materials, freight, sales commissions, and energy.

If we subtract fixed costs and variable costs from sales revenue, the result is earnings before interest and taxes (EBIT). For a company with a single product, EBIT is given by the following formula:

$$EBIT = PQ - VQ - F \qquad (10.1)$$

where

$$P = \text{Sales price per unit}$$
$$Q = \text{Units of output}$$
$$V = \text{Variable cost per unit}$$
$$F = \text{Fixed costs}$$

The term PQ represents sales revenue, and the term VQ represents total variable costs.

Breakeven conditions occur when earnings before interest and taxes are equal to 0. Using Eq. 10.1, we set EBIT equal to 0 and let Q_{BE} represent the breakeven quantity in units.

$$EBIT = PQ - VQ - F$$
$$0 = PQ_{BE} - VQ_{BE} - F$$

We can then solve this equation for the breakeven quantity, Q_{BE}, with the following result:

$$Q_{BE} = \frac{F}{(P - V)} \qquad (10.2)$$

This equation provides the breakeven point in units, Q_{BE}.

Barry Friedman, a financial analyst for Mobley Manufacturing Corporation, is analyzing two other companies. Company A, an aggressive company, has fixed costs of $50,000, a $2.00 sales price per unit, and a $1.00 variable cost per unit. Company C, a conservative company, has fixed costs of $15,000, a $2.00 sales price per unit, and a $1.50 variable cost per unit. He needs to know the breakeven point in units for each company.

He can calculate the breakeven points in units for Company A and for Company C using Eq. 10.2.

$$Q_{BE(A)} = \frac{\$50,000}{(\$2.00 - \$1.00)}$$
$$= 50,000 \text{ units}$$
$$Q_{BE(C)} = \frac{\$15,000}{(\$2.00 - \$1.50)}$$
$$= 30,000 \text{ units}$$

Figure 10.1 shows the breakeven points in units for the two companies. For Company A, the breakeven point is 50,000 units, and for Company C, the breakeven point is 30,000 units. Above each breakeven point is profit, and below each breakeven point is loss. Both profit and loss are larger for Company A when compared with Company C.

In analyzing companies, we may wish to calculate the breakeven point in sales dollars rather than in units. We can modify Eq. 10.1 for this purpose.

$$EBIT = S - V_T - F \tag{10.3}$$

where

$$S = \text{Sales (in dollars)}$$
$$V_T = \text{Total variable costs (for a given level of sales)}$$

Again, breakeven conditions occur when earnings before interest and taxes are equal to 0. Using Eq. 10.3, we set EBIT equal to 0 and let S_{BE} represent the breakeven quantity in dollars.

$$EBIT = S - V_T - F$$
$$0 = S_{BE} - V_T - F$$

We can then solve this equation for the breakeven quantity, S_{BE}, with the following result:

$$S_{BE} = \frac{F}{1 - \dfrac{V_T}{S}} \tag{10.4}$$

This equation provides the breakeven point in dollars, S_{BE}.

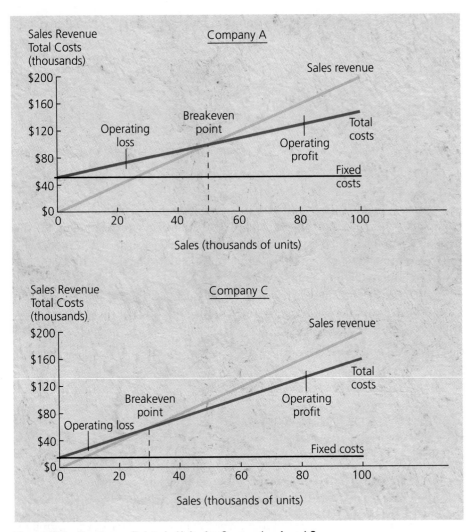

Figure 10.1 Breakeven Points in Units for Companies A and C

Barry Friedman is again analyzing Company A and Company C. Table 10.1 provides basic sales/cost information over a period of time for the two companies. This time he needs to know the breakeven point *in dollars* for each company.

He can calculate the breakeven points in dollars for Company A and for Company C using Eq. 10.4.

TABLE 10.1 Basic Sales/Cost Information for Companies A and C

	COMPANY A	COMPANY C
Sales Revenue	$200,000	$200,000
Total Variable Costs	$100,000	$150,000
Fixed Costs	$ 50,000	$ 15,000

$$S_{BE(A)} = \frac{\$50,000}{1 - \dfrac{\$100,000}{\$200,000}}$$

$$= \$100,000$$

$$S_{BE(C)} = \frac{\$15,000}{1 - \dfrac{\$150,000}{\$200,000}}$$

$$= \$60,000$$

[handwritten margin notes:]
∴ $S_{BE} = V + F$
$F = 50K$
$\frac{V}{S} = \frac{100K}{200K}$
$\frac{1}{2} F = \frac{1}{2} \Rightarrow V = \frac{1}{2}S$
∴ $S_{BE} = \frac{1}{2}S + 50K$
$\frac{1}{2}S = 50K$
$S = 100K$

Figure 10.2 shows the breakeven points in dollars for the two companies. For Company A, the breakeven point is $100,000, and for Company C, the breakeven point is $60,000. We can find the same results with these one-product companies by multiplying the breakeven points in units, 50,000 and 30,000, by the sales price per unit, $2.00. But Eq. 10.4 also works for a company with more than one product if the company has a product mix that is fairly constant and a steady ratio of variable costs to sales.

Operating Leverage

Operating leverage is the extent to which operating costs are fixed as opposed to variable. As a result of operating leverage, a change in sales has a magnified effect on the level of earnings before interest and taxes (EBIT). This is true for an increase or for a decrease in sales.

> Barry Friedman is studying Company A and Company C to determine the effect a 10 percent increase or decrease in sales would have on EBIT, at a base of 60,000 units of sales. He has summarized his results in Table 10.2. What does he conclude from this summary?

At 60,000 units, a 10 percent change in sales affects Company A more than it does Company C. For Company A, a 10 percent increase or decrease in sales

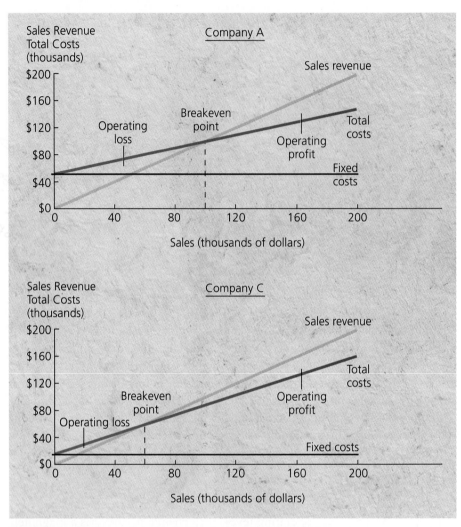

Figure 10.2 Breakeven Points in Dollars for Companies A and C
● ● ● ● ● ● ● ● ●

results in a 60 percent increase or decrease in EBIT. For Company C, a 10 percent increase or decrease in sales results in a 20 percent increase or decrease in EBIT.

This type of analysis works, but we can estimate changes in EBIT easier by defining a new term: The **degree of operating leverage (DOL)** is the percentage change in EBIT for a given percentage change in sales.

**Degree of Operating
Leverage**

$$\text{DOL} = \frac{\text{Percentage Change in EBIT}}{\text{Percentage Change in Sales}} \qquad (10.5)$$

TABLE 10.2 The Effect of a 10 Percent Increase or Decrease in Sales on the EBIT of Company A and Company C

	COMPANY A		
	−10 PERCENT	**BASE SALES**	**+10 PERCENT**
Sales (in units)	54,000	60,000	66,000
Sales revenue	$108,000	$120,000	$132,000
Less: Variable costs	54,000	60,000	66,000
Fixed costs	50,000	50,000	50,000
Earnings before interest and taxes (EBIT)	$ 4,000	$ 10,000	$ 16,000
	60% decrease	60% increase	

	COMPANY C		
	−10 PERCENT	**BASE SALES**	**+10 PERCENT**
Sales (in units)	54,000	60,000	66,000
Sales revenue	$108,000	$120,000	$132,000
Less: Variable costs	81,000	90,000	99,000
Fixed costs	15,000	15,000	15,000
Earnings before interest and taxes (EBIT)	$ 12,000	$ 15,000	$ 18,000
	20% decrease	20% increase	

$$= \frac{\frac{\Delta EBIT}{EBIT}}{\frac{\Delta Q}{Q}} \qquad (10.5a)$$

We can use Eq. 10.5 or Eq. 10.5a directly, but fortunately a simpler equation exists for calculating the degree of operating leverage.

$$DOL = \frac{Q(P - V)}{Q(P - V) - F} \qquad (10.6)$$

The variables are defined at Eq. 10.1.

Barry Friedman is now interested in finding the degrees of operating leverage for Company A and for Company C at 60,000 units by using the information from the previous examples. What is the meaning of these calculations?

He calculates the degree of operating leverage for each company at 60,000 units by using Eq. 10.6.

$$DOL_A = \frac{60,000(\$2.00 - \$1.00)}{60,000(\$2.00 - \$1.00) - \$50,000}$$

$$= 6.0$$

$$DOL_C = \frac{60,000(\$2.00 - \$1.50)}{60,000(\$2.00 - \$1.50) - \$15,000}$$

$$= 2.0$$

We previously found that a 10 percent change in sales revenue causes a 60 percent change in EBIT for Company A and a 20 percent change in EBIT for Company C. To find these answers using DOL, we simply multiply the change in sales by the degree of operating leverage. For example, a 10 percent increase in sales multiplied by 6.0 provides the 60 percent increase in EBIT for Company A. Also notice that Company A has a higher operating leverage than Company C at 60,000 units, since the degree of operating leverage and the change in EBIT are greater for Company A. This indicates the effect on EBIT from a change in sales will be greater for Company A than for Company C.

Another version of Eq. 10.6 uses sales in dollars and total variable costs.

$$DOL = \frac{S - V_T}{S - V_T - F} \qquad (10.6a)$$

The variables are defined at Eq. 10.4.

Barry Friedman plans to find the degrees of operating leverage for Company A and for Company C at a sales level of $120,000 by using the information from the previous examples.

A sales level of $120,000 is equivalent to 60,000 units since the sales price per unit is $2.00 for both companies. He can calculate the degree of operating leverage at $120,000 by using Eq. 10.6a.

$$DOL_A = \frac{\$120,000 - \$60,000}{\$120,000 - \$60,000 - \$50,000}$$

$$= 6.0$$

$$DOL_C = \frac{\$120,000 - \$90,000}{\$120,000 - \$90,000 - \$15,000}$$

$$= 2.0$$

Multiplying 60,000 units by the variable cost per unit yields the total variable costs, V_T.

Financial Leverage

Financial leverage is the extent to which debt is used in the capital structure. As a result of financial leverage, a change in earnings before interest and taxes has a magnified effect on the level of earnings per share (EPS). This is true for an increase or for a decrease in EBIT.

Barry Friedman is again studying Company A and Company C, this time to find out how financial leverage affects each company. Company A has $6,000 of interest and Company C has $9,000. The marginal tax rate is 40 percent, and each company has 1,000 shares of common stock. In Table 10.3, he used the EBIT information from Table 10.2 to find earnings per share (EPS). What does he conclude about financial leverage?

TABLE 10.3   The Effect of a Change in EBIT on the EPS of Company A and Company C

	COMPANY A		
	−60 PERCENT	BASE EBIT	+60 PERCENT
Earnings before interest and taxes (EBIT)	$ 4,000	$10,000	$16,000
Interest	6,000	6,000	6,000
Earnings before taxes	$ (2,000)	$ 4,000	$10,000
Taxes (40%)	(800)	1,600	$ 4,000
Earnings after taxes	$ (1,200)	$ 2,400	$ 6,000
Earnings per share (EPS)	($1.20)	$2.40	$6.00
		150% decrease 150% increase	

	COMPANY C		
	−20 PERCENT	BASE EBIT	+20 PERCENT
Earnings before interest and taxes (EBIT)	$12,000	$15,000	$18,000
Interest	9,000	9,000	9,000
Earnings before taxes	$ 3,000	$ 6,000	$ 9,000
Taxes (40%)	1,200	2,400	$ 3,600
Earnings after taxes	$ 1,800	$ 3,600	$ 5,400
Earnings per share (EPS)	$1.80	$3.60	$5.40
		50% decrease 50% increase	

The change in earnings per share depends on the change in EBIT. For Company A, a 60 percent change in EBIT causes a 150 percent change in EPS. For Company C, a 20 percent change in EBIT causes a 50 percent change in EPS. In both cases, the change in EPS is 2.5 times the change in EBIT.

As with operating leverage, this type of analysis works, but we can estimate changes in EPS easier by defining a new term: The **degree of financial leverage** **(DFL)** is the percentage change in EPS for a given percentage change in EBIT.

Degree of Financial Leverage

$$DFL = \frac{\text{Percentage Change in EPS}}{\text{Percentage Change in EBIT}} \qquad (10.7)$$

It is easier to use the following equation derived from Eq. 10.7:

$$DFL = \frac{Q(P - V) - F}{Q(P - V) - F - I} \qquad (10.8)$$

In this equation, I is the interest expense on all of the debt of the company.

The term in the numerator of Eq. 10.8 is an expression for EBIT. As result, we can restate the equation as follows:

$$DFL = \frac{EBIT}{EBIT - I} \qquad (10.8a)$$

Barry Friedman is interested in finding the degree of financial leverage at an EBIT of $10,000 for Company A and $15,000 for Company C. Using the information from the previous example, would this change his previous results?

He can calculate the degree of financial leverage for each company using Eq. 10.8a.

$$DFL_A = \frac{\$10,000}{\$10,000 - \$6,000}$$
$$= 2.5$$

$$DFL_C = \frac{\$15,000}{\$15,000 - \$9,000}$$
$$= 2.5$$

To find the change in EPS, we multiply the change in EBIT by the degree of financial leverage—2.5 in both cases. For Company A, an EBIT change of 60 percent results in an EPS change of 150 percent. For Company C, an EBIT change of 20 percent results in an EPS change of 50 percent.

The two companies have the same degree of financial leverage, but these numbers should not be compared. The degrees of financial leverage for two companies can be compared if, and only if, they have the same EBIT base.

Total Leverage

Total leverage is the combined effect of using operating and financial leverage. As a result of total leverage, a change in sales has a magnified effect on the level of earnings per share. This is true for an increase or for a decrease in sales.

Barry Friedman continues to study Company A and Company C, this time to determine the effect a 10 percent increase or decrease in sales would have on EPS at a base of 60,000 units of sales. He has summarized his results in Table 10.4. What does he conclude from this summary?

At 60,000 units, a 10 percent change in sales affects Company A more than it does Company C. For Company A, a 10 percent increase or decrease in sales results in a 150 percent increase or decrease in EPS. For Company C, a 10 percent increase or decrease in sales results in a 50 percent increase or decrease in EPS.

This type of analysis works, but we can estimate changes in EPS easier by defining a new term. The **degree of total leverage (DTL)** is the percentage change in EPS for a given percentage change in sales.

Degree of Total Leverage

$$DTL = \frac{\text{Percentage Change in EPS}}{\text{Percentage Change in Sales}} \qquad (10.9)$$

It is easier to use the following equation derived from Eq. 10.9:

$$DTL = \frac{Q(P - V)}{Q(P - V) - F - I} \qquad (10.10)$$

Barry wants to know the total leverage for Company A and for Company C at 60,000 units. Would this change the results from the previous example?

TABLE 10.4 The Effect of a 10 Percent Increase or Decrease in Sales on the EPS of Company A and Company C

	COMPANY A		
	−10 PERCENT	**BASE SALES**	**+10 PERCENT**
Sales (in units)	54,000	60,000	66,000
Sales revenue	$108,000	$120,000	$132,000
Less: Variable costs	54,000	60,000	66,000
Fixed costs	50,000	50,000	50,000
Earnings before interest and taxes (EBIT)	$ 4,000	$ 10,000	$ 16,000
Interest	6,000	6,000	6,000
Earnings before taxes	$ (2,000)	$ 4,000	$ 10,000
Taxes (40%)	(800)	1,600	4,000
Earnings after taxes	$ (1,200)	$ 2,400	$ 6,000
Earnings per share (EPS)	($1.20)	$2.40	$6.00
	150% decrease	150% increase	

	COMPANY C		
	−10 PERCENT	**BASE SALES**	**+10 PERCENT**
Sales (in units)	54,000	60,000	66,000
Sales revenue	$108,000	$120,000	$132,000
Less: Variable costs	81,000	90,000	99,000
Fixed costs	15,000	15,000	15,000
Earnings before interest and taxes (EBIT)	$ 12,000	$ 15,000	$ 18,000
Interest	9,000	9,000	9,000
Earnings before taxes	$ 3,000	$ 6,000	$ 9,000
Taxes (40%)	1,200	2,400	3,600
Earnings after taxes	$ 1,800	$ 3,600	$ 5,400
Earnings per share (EPS)	$1.80	$3.60	$5.40
	50% decrease	50% increase	

He calculates the degree of total leverage by using Eq. 10.10.

$$DTL_A = \frac{60,000(\$2.00 - \$1.00)}{60,000(\$2.00 - \$1.00) - \$50,000 - \$6,000}$$

$$= 15.0$$

$$DTL_C = \frac{60,000(\$2.00 - \$1.50)}{60,000(\$2.00 - \$1.50) - \$15,000 - \$9,000}$$

$$= 5.0$$

To find the change in EPS, we multiply the 10 percent change in sales by the degree of total leverage for each company. For Company A, this results in an EPS change of 150 percent. For Company C, this results in an EPS change of 50 percent.

Another version of Eq. 10.10 uses sales in dollars and total variable costs.

$$DTL = \frac{S - V_T}{S - V_T - F - I} \qquad (10.10a)$$

Barry Friedman plans to find the degrees of total leverage for Company A and for Company C at a sales level of $120,000 by using the information from the previous examples. Would this change his previous results?

A sales level of $120,000 is equivalent to 60,000 units since the sales price per unit is $2.00 for both companies. We can calculate the degree of total leverage at $120,000 by using Eq. 10.10a.

$$DTL_A = \frac{\$120,000 - \$60,000}{\$120,000 - \$60,000 - \$50,000 - \$6,000}$$
$$= 15.0$$

$$DTL_C = \frac{\$120,000 - \$90,000}{\$120,000 - \$90,000 - \$15,000 - \$9,000}$$
$$= 5.0$$

If we multiply Eq. 10.6 by Eq. 10.8, we obtain the following result:

$$(DOL)(DFL) = \left[\frac{Q(P - V)}{Q(P - V) - F} \right] \left[\frac{Q(P - V) - F}{Q(P - V) - F - I} \right]$$

We then cancel the terms $Q(P - V) - F$, leaving us with the following equation.

$$(DOL)(DFL) = \frac{Q(P - V)}{Q(P - V) - F - I}$$

Since this is the equation for total leverage, Eq. 10.10, we conclude that the degree of total leverage is equal to the degree of operating leverage times the degree of financial leverage.

$$DTL = DOL(DFL) \qquad (10.11)$$

Is Big Still Good?

n America, big has always been beautiful. As a nation we revel in being a superpower and having the biggest economy. But these days something very un-American is happening in the corporate world. Big is becoming bad. According to much new thinking, big means complex, and complexity results in inefficiencies, bureaucratic bloat, and strangled communications. Tomorrow's big company, according to the emerging wisdom, will consist of tens or hundreds of small, highly decentralized units, each one with a laserlike focus on a market or a customer.

In many businesses, economies of scale, once a principal reason for getting big, are no longer an effective competitive weapon. The world of mass production is giving way to flexible manufacturing systems making smaller batches of a wider array of products. The day is over when a big company can thrive by producing more of a standard product at a lower cost than its rivals.

Source: Brian Dumaine, "Is Big Still Good?" FORTUNE, April 20, 1992, pp. 50–59. © 1992 Time Inc. All rights reserved.

This identity allows us to check our previous results.

$$DTL_A = 6.0(2.5) = 15.0$$
$$DTL_C = 2.0(2.5) = 5.0$$

The results agree.

CAPITAL STRUCTURE

In Chapter 9, we studied the target capital structure—the proportions of debt, preferred stock, and common equity the company will use in the future. In that discussion, we found financial managers accept some variation about the target capital structure because of the costliness of issuing new equity. When the debt proportion is below the target level, management raises new capital by issuing new debt; and when the debt proportion is above the target level, management raises new capital by issuing new common stock. The target capital structure should be the same as the optimal capital structure.

The optimal capital structure is the capital structure that maximizes the value of the common stock of the company. Finding that optimal capital structure requires that we understand the tradeoff between risk and return: In general, as we use more debt in the capital structure, risk as measured by the required annual rate of return on company stock increases but also return in the form of future expected dividends increases. Higher risk reduces the price of the stock, while higher return increases the price of the stock. Given this conflict between risk and return, the purpose of capital structure management is to find the debt level where the price of company stock is maximized.

Capital Structure Theory

The evolution of modern capital structure theory began in the early 1950s with work by David Durand. He presented two extreme positions regarding the effect of financial leverage on the value of the company: the net income approach and the net operating income approach[1]. Franco Modigliani and Merton H. Miller (MM) in the late 1950s and 1960s added to the body of knowledge by offering a number of theories and conclusions about capital structure.

The **Modigliani and Miller (MM) model without corporate taxes** states that the value of the company and the cost of capital are independent of its capital structure. In presenting the proof of their propositions, MM made a number of assumptions, including a world without taxes, market imperfections, and transaction costs.

> **Modigliani and Miller Model Without Corporate Taxes**

MM state that the value of the company, V, without corporate taxes, is given by the following:

$$V = \frac{EBIT}{k_a} = \frac{EBIT}{k_{su}} \qquad (10.12)$$

where

$$k_a = \text{Cost of capital}$$
$$k_{su} = \text{Cost of equity for a company with no debt}$$

For Eq. 10.12 to be true, k_a must equal k_{su}. This means that the cost of capital for any company, even levered companies, is equal to the cost of capital for an unlevered company if both are in the same risk class. The value of both levered and unlevered companies is also equal.

MM show that the cost of equity for a company with debt, k_{sl}, without corporate taxes, is given by the following:

$$k_{sl} = k_{su} + (k_{su} - k_d)\frac{D}{S} \qquad (10.13)$$

---

[1] See David Durand, "Cost of Debt and Equity Funds for Business: Trends and Problems of Measurement," *Conference on Research in Business Finance*, New York: National Bureau of Economic Research, 1952.

where

$$k_d = \text{Interest rate on debt}$$
$$D = \text{Market value of debt}$$
$$S = \text{Market value of equity}$$
$$V = \text{Market value of debt} + \text{Market value of equity}$$

This means that the use of leverage increases the cost of equity. The second term in Eq. 10.13 is the risk premium associated with using debt.

MM confirm that a company without corporate taxes cannot increase its value by adding debt to its capital structure. The benefits of using cheaper debt are offset by the increased cost of equity. Figure 10.3 illustrates how the cost of capital and the value of the company vary with changes in the capital structure. In this illustration, k_e is the market value of common stock.

> The Mobley Manufacturing Corporation (MMC) has earnings before interest and taxes of $1,000,000, a cost of equity of 12.5 percent when no debt is used, and an interest rate on debt of nine percent. What is the value of MMC and its cost of equity, assuming that the market value of debt and equity are equal?

The value of the company is given by Eq. 10.12.

$$V = \frac{\text{EBIT}}{k_a} = \frac{\text{EBIT}}{k_{su}}$$
$$= \frac{\$1,000,000}{0.125}$$
$$= \$8,000,000$$

The cost of equity for the company is given by Eq. 10.13.

$$k_{sl} = k_{su} + (k_{su} - k_d)\frac{D}{S}$$
$$= 12.5\% + (12.5\% - 9\%)\left(\frac{\$4,000,000}{\$4,000,000}\right)$$
$$= 16.0\%$$

The risk premium for using leverage is 3.5 percent.

Modigliani and Miller Model With Corporate Taxes

The **Modigliani and Miller (MM) model with corporate taxes** states that the value of the company increases and the cost of capital of the company de-

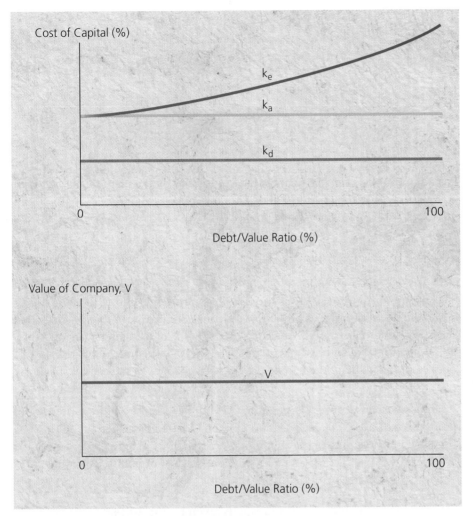

Figure 10.3 Effects of Leverage, MM Model Without Corporate Taxes

creases as debt is added to the capital structure. The changes in the model are caused by the fact that interest payments are deductible when calculating taxes.

The value of the unlevered company, V_u, is found with the following formula:

$$V_u = \frac{EBIT(1 - T)}{k_{su}}$$

(10.14)

The unlevered company has no tax advantage.

MM state that the value of the levered company, V_l, with corporate taxes, is given by the following:

$$V_l = V_u + TD \qquad (10.15)$$

where

$$V_u = \text{Value of the unlevered company}$$
$$T = \text{Marginal tax rate}$$

The added value is the marginal tax rate multiplied by the market value of debt.

MM show that the cost of equity for a company with debt, k_{sl}, with corporate taxes, is given by the following:

$$k_{sl} = k_{su} + (k_{su} - k_d)(1 - T)\frac{D}{S} \qquad (10.16)$$

The second term in Eq. 10.16 is the risk premium associated with using debt.

MM demonstrate that a company with corporate taxes can increase its value by adding debt to its capital structure. The benefits of using debt are caused by the deductibility of interest payments. Figure 10.4 illustrates how the cost of capital and the value of the company vary with changes in the capital structure.

Mobley Manufacturing Corporation (MMC) has earnings before interest and taxes of $1,000,000, a cost of equity of 12.5 percent when no debt is used, an interest rate on debt of nine percent, and a marginal tax rate of 40 percent. What is the value of MMC and its cost of equity, assuming that the market value of debt is $4,000,000?

The value of the unlevered company is given by Eq. 10.14.

$$V_u = \frac{\text{EBIT}(1 - T)}{k_{su}}$$
$$= \frac{\$1,000,000(1 - 0.40)}{0.125}$$
$$= \$4,800,000$$

The value of the levered company is given by Eq. 10.15.

$$V_l = V_u + TD$$
$$= \$4,800,000 + 0.40(\$4,000,000)$$
$$= \$6,400,000$$

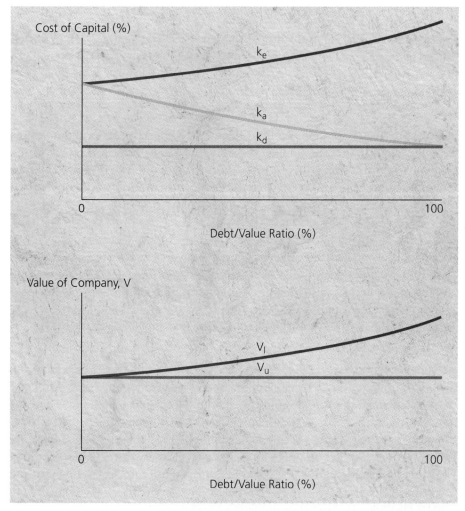

Figure 10.4   Effects of Leverage, MM Model With Corporate Taxes
● ● ● ● ● ● ● ● ●

Since $V = D + S$, the market value of equity is \$2,400,000.

The cost of equity for the company is given by Eq. 10.16.

$$k_{sl} = k_{su} + (k_{su} - k_d)(1 - T)\frac{D}{S}$$

$$= 12.5\% + (12.5\% - 9\%)(1 - 0.40)\left(\frac{\$4,000,000}{\$2,400,000}\right)$$

$$= 16.0\%$$

The risk premium for using leverage is 3.5 percent.

Other Capital Structure Factors

Other factors affecting the optimal capital structure include: (1) the costs caused by managers having more information than investors, (2) the probability of bankruptcy caused by increased debt, and (3) the agency costs associated with the lender controlling management.

Information Costs. Modigliani and Miller assumed that managers and investors have the same information about the operations and future prospects of the company—**symmetric information.** But managers often have more and better information than investors—**asymmetric information**—and this affects the capital structure decision.

Symmetric Information

Asymmetric Information

> Engineers from Constantini Corporation have developed a new, secret, and highly-profitable product that requires significant capital for an expansion of manufacturing facilities. To raise the needed funds, management has a choice: equity or debt. If the current capital structure is nearly optimal, which source of financing should they choose?

If management selects new common stock, the amount received from the sale would not reflect the favorable prospects of the new product. After the issue, the price of the stock would rise, benefiting the old shareholders and the new shareholders. By using debt, only the current shareholders would benefit from the new product. As a result, management would choose debt. If management selects equity when other financing alternatives are available, investors view this action as a **signal** that company prospects are not very good, causing the price of the stock to decline. A signal is any method management uses to convey information about the company's prospects.

Signal

Bankruptcy Costs. The probability of bankruptcy depends on the level of both business risk and financial risk. But for a given level of business risk, the more a company borrows, the higher the expected **bankruptcy costs** and the lower the value of its common equity. This cost tends to limit the amount of debt that a company uses in its capital structure.

Bankruptcy Costs

Business Risk

   Business risk is measured by the variability in earnings before interest and taxes (EBIT) for a company. The degree of this risk depends on the particular industry. Cyclical industries, such as steel, have high business risk. Producers of food products and utilities have relatively low business risk. Large diversified companies have lower risk than small one-product companies. Companies with relatively high fixed costs find it difficult to reduce fixed costs when sales decline and, as a result, suffer from high business risk. Companies with little competition have low business risk, since they are better able to adjust sales prices to changes in operating costs. Product choice also affects business risk. The manufacture of some products uses technology that requires high fixed costs. This results in high operating leverage and, as a result, high business risk.

High operating leverage for a company implies that the company has high business risk. But operating leverage is not the only source of business risk. Revenue stability and cost stability also determine the level of business risk. Companies with stable demand and sales prices have low business risk as do companies with stable input prices.

Financial risk is the additional risk, above business risk, resulting from substituting debt into the capital structure. For example, an all-equity company has $5,000,000 in assets and 50,000 shares each worth $100. If the company replaces half of the equity with debt, then the company's risk is increased due to the possibility of not being able to pay the principal and interest payments.

Financial Risk

Agency Costs.   In Chapter 1, we learned that the costs of trying to minimize the agency problem are referred to as agency costs. In that discussion, we pointed out that agency problems exist between shareholders and creditors when management makes decisions that attempt to shift wealth from creditors to shareholders. Creditors react to such actions by requiring protective covenants in the bond indenture or by increasing the costs of bonds.

The interest rate a creditor charges depends on the assessment of the company's business risk and financial risk. Management could take advantage of this relationship by increasing risk after acquiring the debt. If the risky approach pays off, the shareholders and not the creditors benefit; if the risky approach fails, both the creditors and the shareholders share in the loss. To avoid this type of behavior, creditors limit the ability of management to increase the business or financial risk of the company, often by using protective covenants. The cost of this protection is an agency cost.

The Target Capital Structure

The **traditional approach** to finding the target capital structure assumes that the cost of debt and the cost of equity remain fairly constant up to a point and then begin to rise at higher levels of debt. This means that the amount of debt in the capital structure is, in fact, relevant.

Traditional Approach

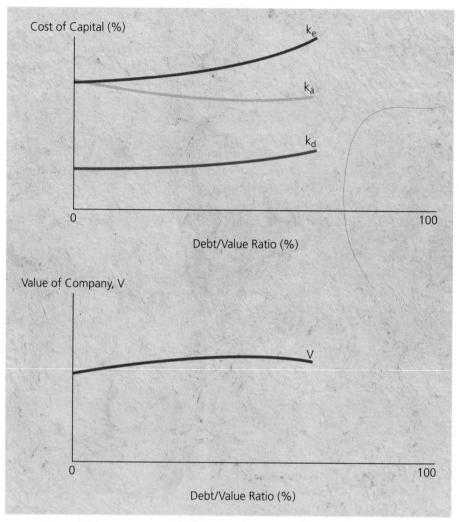

Figure 10.5 Effects of Leverage Under the Traditional Approach

Since debt is less costly than equity, increasing the use of debt will at first lower the cost of capital. As the costs of debt and equity begin to rise, the advantage of the cheaper debt is lost, and the cost of capital increases. The implication of this theory is that there is an optimal capital structure, the point where the cost of capital is at a minimum. With this amount of debt, the value of the company is at its maximum. Figure 10.5 illustrates how the cost of capital and the value of the company vary with changes in the capital structure.

SUMMARY

This chapter focuses on the following learning objectives:

1. Calculating the breakeven point for a company.
   Breakeven analysis is used to find the output or sales level which generates earnings before interest and taxes (EBIT) of 0. At this point, total revenues are equal to total costs.

2. Measuring the degree of operating leverage for a company.
   Operating leverage is the extent to which operating costs are fixed as opposed to variable. As a result of operating leverage, a change in sales has a magnified effect on the level of earnings before interest and taxes.

3. Measuring the degree of financial leverage for a company.
   Financial leverage is the extent to which debt is used in the capital structure. As a result of financial leverage, a change in earnings before interest and taxes has a magnified effect on the level of earnings per share.

4. Measuring the degree of total leverage for a company.
   Total leverage is the combined effect of using operating and financial leverage. As a result of total leverage, a change in sales has a magnified effect on the level of earnings per share.

5. Explaining capital structure theory as proposed by Modigliani and Miller.
   The Modigliani and Miller model without corporate taxes states that the value of the company and the cost of capital are independent of its capital structure. The Modigliani and Miller model with corporate taxes states that the value of the company increases and the cost of capital of the company decreases as debt is added to the capital structure.

6. Explaining how other factors affect capital structure.
   Managers often have more and better information than investors—asymmetric information—and this affects the capital structure decision. Also, for a given level of business risk, the more a company borrows, the higher the expected bankruptcy costs and the lower the value of its common equity. In addition, creditors limit the ability of management to increase the business or financial risk of the company, often by using protective covenants.

7. Explaining the traditional approach to finding the target capital structure.
   The traditional approach to finding the target capital structure assumes that the cost of debt and the cost of equity remain fairly constant up to a point and then begin to rise at higher levels of debt. Since debt is less costly than equity, increasing the use of debt will at first lower the cost of capital. As the costs of debt and equity begin to rise, the advantage of the cheaper debt is lost, and the cost of capital increases.

KEY TERMS

Asymmetric information, 306
Bankruptcy costs, 306
Breakeven analysis, 287
Business risk, 306
Degree of financial leverage, 296

Degree of operating leverage, 292
Degree of total leverage, 297
Financial leverage, 287
Financial risk, 307
MM model with corporate taxes, 302
MM model without

corporate taxes, 301
Operating leverage, 287
Signal, 306
Symmetric information, 306
Total leverage, 287
Traditional approach, 307

QUESTIONS

10.1 How could a capital budgeting decision change the operating leverage of a company?

10.2 How would a change in operating leverage affect the breakeven point?

10.3 Why might a change in operating leverage cause management to change the degree of financial leverage?

10.4 Discuss the relationship between operating, financial, and total leverage.

10.5 Distinguish between business risk and financial risk.

10.6 Compare the MM model without corporate taxes and the MM model with corporate taxes.

10.7 Is it ethical to keep information about a promising product away from investors?

10.8 How would you determine the capital structure of your company?

10.9 What does ITT accomplish by buying back its shares?

10.10 Why are companies less likely today to employ mass production?

PROBLEMS

10.1 **(Breakeven Point)** The Hanson Company produces mailboxes that sell for $25 each. The variable cost per unit is $8.00, and fixed costs are $10,200. Compute the breakeven point in units and the number of units necessary to make a profit of $17,000.

10.2 **(Breakeven Point)** Breakaway Bicycle Company manufactures racing bikes selling for $850 each. Fixed costs for the operation amount to $250,000, and variable costs are $350 each. Find the breakeven point in units and in sales dollars.

10.3 **(Breakeven Point and Degree of Operating Leverage)** Patterson Corporation has fixed costs of $200,000, variable costs per unit of $10.00, and a selling price of $30.00. Calculate the breakeven point in units and the degree of operating leverage at 15,000 units.

10.4 **(Degree of Operating Leverage)** Bush Bearing, Inc. has sales of $600,000 and total variable costs of $200,000. Fixed costs are $250,000. Find the degree of operating leverage for sales of $600,000.

10.5 **(Breakeven Point and Degrees of Operating, Financial, and Total Leverage)** Franklin Heating & Cooling has the following income statement:

Sales revenue	$850,000
Less: Variable costs	250,000
Fixed costs	300,000
Earnings before interest and taxes	$300,000
Interest	100,000
Earnings before taxes	$200,000
Taxes (40%)	80,000
Earnings after taxes	$120,000

At this level of sales, find the degree of operating leverage, the degree of financial leverage, the degree of total leverage, and the breakeven point in dollars.

10.6 **(Earnings Per Share, Degrees of Leverage, and Breakeven Point)** The Thomas Oldham Company is a manufacturer of furniture. Sales this year amounted to $10,000,000, while total variable costs were $8,000,000 and fixed costs were $1,000,000. The company has $3,000,000 of debt outstanding at a 10 percent interest rate. There are 100,000 shares of common stock outstanding. Oldham has a 40 percent marginal tax rate and a dividend payout ratio of 40 percent. The company plans to invest $5,000,000 in new machinery. This would not affect sales but would cause the ratio of variable costs to sales to decline to 65%. Fixed costs would increase by $500,000. The company could raise the $5,000,000 by selling debt at an interest rate of 12 percent or common stock at $50 per share.

a. Calculate the EPS under the present plan, under the new plan with debt, and under the new plan with common stock.

b. Calculate the DOL, DFL, and DTL under each of the three plans.

c. Calculate the breakeven point in dollars for the present plan and the new plans.

10.7 **(Modigliani and Miller Without Taxes)** The MacDonald Company and the McDonald Company are quite similar except that McDonald has $5,000,000 of 10 percent debt while MacDonald has no debt. Both companies have EBIT of $1,000,000 and pay no taxes. The MacDonald Company has a cost of equity of 14 percent. Under these conditions, what value would Modigliani and Miller estimate for each company? What is the cost and market value of equity for the McDonald Company?

10.8 **(Modigliani and Miller With Taxes)** The Smith Company and the Smyth Company are very much alike except that Smyth has $6,000,000 of 8 percent debt while Smith has no debt. Both companies have EBIT of $2,000,000 and pay taxes at a 40 percent rate. The Smith Company has a cost of equity of 12 percent. Under these conditions, what value would Modigliani and Miller estimate for each company? What is the cost and market value of equity for the Smyth Company?

A Case Problem

Handy Electronics Corporation was the second largest industrial distributor of electronic components and systems products in the United States. The company distributed approximately 110,000 different products to more than 30,000 customers, including industrial firms and original equipment manufacturers. The electronics distribution industry had become an increasingly important marketing channel for electronics products, permitting manufacturers to market their products economically to end-users.

The electronics industry had been affected by general economic downturns that have had an adverse economic effect on most manufacturers, including Handy. The industry was also highly competitive, with respect to price, product availability, number of locations, and promptness of service. In addition, Handy had agreements with its suppliers, but these contracts could be terminated on relatively short notice under certain conditions.

The company planned to improve the profitability of its operations through aggressive inventory management, an emphasis on higher margin profits and services, enhanced management information systems, and the continuation of the total quality management program.

Handy's strategy was to maintain its leadership position in the central and southern regions of the United States and to expand catalog operations. The company planned to improve the profitability of its operations through aggressive inventory management, an emphasis on higher margin profits and services, enhanced management information systems, and the continuation of the total quality management program.

Scott Summers was Treasurer and Chief Financial Officer for the company. In August of 1993, he was compiling the list of funds requirements for the new fiscal year. In conversations with Brad Phillips, Director of Operations, it was agreed that a total of $95,000,000 was required. Scott Summers estimated that $25,000,000 would come from internal sources, leaving $70,000,000 to be financed by either a bond or a stock issue.

Scott Summers contacted several investment bankers concerning the prospective terms of each type of issue. Since long-term interest rates had declined, the company could borrow over 25 years at a 10 percent rate. This would require a sinking fund payment of $3,500,000 from the sixth year until maturity. The investment bankers also indicated that the company could market common stock at $70 per share. Currently, yearly interest charges amounted to $12,000,000, and 4,000,000 common shares were outstanding.

Scott Summers forecasted sales for the next fiscal year at $600,000,000. He believed that variable costs would remain at 60 percent of sales and fixed operating costs would increase to $180,000,000. The marginal federal-plus-state tax rate would stay at 40 percent.

Scott wondered which financing plan, stock or bonds, would be better for Handy Electronics Corporation.

Leading Questions

1. What are the degree of operating leverage, the degree of financial leverage, and the degree of total leverage under the bond plan and under the stock plan?
2. What is the earnings per share under the bond plan and under the stock plan?

PROCTER & GAMBLE SETS STOCK SPLIT, BOOSTS ITS DIVIDEND

Procter & Gamble Company, citing "progress" this year and long-term confidence, raised its dividend 10 percent and declared a 2-for-1 common stock split. The dividend, increased to 55 cents a share from 50 cents, is payable May 15 to shareholders of record April 24. The stock split, in the form of a 100 percent stock dividend, is payable to shareholders of record May 15, with stock to be issued on or after June 12.

11 Dividend Policy

In New York Stock Exchange composite trading, P&G stock jumped $4.50 to $104.50 on the announcement. Analysts were divided about whether the dividend increase signaled more robust results ahead. "The stage is set for

Procter to record a series of better-than-expected results," says Andrew Shore, analyst at Prudential Securities Research. "When this company turns, it really turns. Analysts were surprised by the stock split, which P&G said was designed to make the stock more attractive to investors.

Several blue-chip companies, including Merck & Co. and Walt Disney Co., have announced stock splits in the past few months. "A lot of companies are trying to get more backing by individual investors, which is a more consistent base and cuts down on the volatility," says Doug Christopher of Crowell, Weedon & Co.

Does the announcement of the increased dividends by P&G lead to an increase in the price of the stock? Some observers conclude that this is true, because investors prefer dividends to capital gains. Others believe that an increase in dividends is a signal from management, since management normally has better access to information.

Source: "Procter & Gamble Sets Stock Split, Boosts Its Dividend," *The Wall Street Journal,* April 15, 1992. Reprinted by permission of The Wall Street Journal, © 1992 Dow Jones & Company, Inc. All Rights Reserved Worldwide.

THE BASICS OF DIVIDENDS

In Chapter 1, we learned that the dividend decision determines how earnings after taxes are distributed to preferred and common shareholders or retained for investment. If the dividend decision does not depend on the investment decision, then dividend policy reflects the way a company plans to finance its assets. When a company pays higher dividends, it tends to issue more new common stock. But by issuing more costly new common stock, the capital budget may be smaller.

The question then is: Does the dividend policy of a company affect the value of its common stock? In this chapter, we will try to provide an answer or at least to stimulate your thinking on this important subject. But first let's look at how dividends are paid.

Payment Procedures

The board of directors of a company decides on the amount and timing of dividend payments. Even though the amount may be stated on an annual basis, the payments are usually, but not always, on a quarterly basis. For example, Consolidated Can Corporation paid quarterly dividends of $0.95 per share in

315

1992. This translates into a $3.80 per share annual dividend. Since the stock is selling for $95.00 per share, the annual dividend yield is four percent, $3.80/$95.00.

There are four important dates associated with announcing a dividend:

Declaration Date

- **Declaration date.** The board of directors meets on the **declaration date** to declare the regular dividend. For example, Consolidated Can Company, on July 19, 1992, announced the amount of the quarterly dividend, the holder-of-record-date, and the payment date.

Holder-of-Record Date

- **Holder-of-record date.** The company pays dividends to shareholders who are registered on the **holder-of-record date** as the owners of the stock. Consolidated Can Company must be notified by 5:00 p.m. on August 7, 1992, the holder-of-record date, regarding the date of the sale and transfer of the stock.

Ex-Dividend Date

- **Ex-dividend date.** The major stock exchanges have decided that the right to the dividend remains with the stock until four business days before the holder-of-record date. This **ex-dividend date** is determined to allow time to process transactions. For example, the ex-dividend date for Consolidated Can Company is August 3, 1992, since August 7, 1992, is a Friday. The stock sells *ex-dividend* on August 3, 1992. This means that the new owner must buy the stock before August 3, 1992, in order to receive the dividend.

Payment Date

- **Payment date.** This is the date when the dividend checks are mailed out. For example, on September 4, 1992, the **payment date,** the company mails checks to the holders of record.

Legal and Contractual Constraints

A company is usually limited by various legal and contractual constraints as to the amount of dividends it pays. Let's look at the various ways this happens:

Protective Covenants

Covenants

- **Protective covenants.** The legal agreement between bondholders or preferred shareholders and the issuing company is called the indenture. The indenture carries **covenants** that limit the risk to the bondholder or preferred shareholder. For example, if certain financial ratios do not reach prescribed levels, dividend payments may be limited or disallowed.

Capital Impairment Rule

- **Capital impairment.** The **capital impairment rule** prevents a company from paying dividends out of its shareholder capital. Shareholder capital is defined here, as it is in some states, as the par value of common stock plus the capital in excess of par. This means that a company cannot pay dividends in excess of its retained earnings. For example, a company in financial difficulty might be tempted to pay large dividends by simply selling its assets. This would be detrimental to the financial position of its creditors.

- **Improper earnings accumulation.** A company may also be constrained if it pays too small a dividend. If the Internal Revenue Service finds that a company has an **improper earnings accumulation,** it may exact a penalty tax. The purpose of this tax is to discourage closely held corporations from limiting dividends in order to allow shareholders to defer personal taxes on the dividends. For example, a wealthy shareholder may try to avoid paying taxes by simply leaving his/her earnings in the corporation. The Internal Revenue Service would then force the company to pay an accumulated earnings tax.

Improper Earnings Accumulation

- **Cash Availability.** Cash dividends may only be paid with cash. This sometimes limits the amount of the dividend payments. Companies can improve their cash position, however, by borrowing.

Stock Dividends and Stock Splits

Instead of paying a cash dividend, a company can choose to make a dividend payment in the form of additional shares of stock to its common shareholders. This distribution is called a **stock dividend.** For example, shareholders in a company receive 10 new shares for each 100 shares owned. This proportion of new to old shares is typical of stock dividends.

Stock Dividend

A **stock split** represents a proportionate increase in the number of common shares owned. For example, a company splits its stock two-for-one. This means that the shareholders, as of the holder-of-record date, receive two new shares for each old share previously held. From this example, we can see stock splits and stock dividends are quite similar.

Stock Split

The primary difference between stock splits and stock dividends is with the accounting treatment of the two transactions. With a stock dividend, there is a transfer of retained earnings to the capital stock account. With a stock split, there is a reduction in the par value of each share of stock. For accounting purposes, a distribution of stock of 25 percent or more is generally considered a stock split. Lesser distributions are termed stock dividends.

The Anderson Company and the Baker Company have the same financial position. The Anderson Company plans a stock dividend of 10 percent. The Baker Company plans a stock split of two-for-one. The current market price of both types of stock is $15 per share. The initial capital accounts, the same for both companies, is shown in Table 11.1. What is the financial position of each company after the transactions? If each company had earnings after taxes of $2,200,000, what is the earnings per share for each company before and after the stock distribution?

TABLE 11.1 Capital Accounts of Anderson Company and Baker Company

Common stock (1,000,000 shares at $1 par)	$ 1,000,000
Capital in excess of par	4,000,000
Retained earnings	5,000,000
	$10,000,000

The 10 percent stock dividend by the Anderson Company causes the number of shares to increase by 100,000. Since the stock is selling for $15 per share, transfer $1,500,000, $15(100,000), from retained earnings into the other two accounts. Common stock receives $100,000, $1(100,000), and capital in excess of par receives $1,400,000, ($15 − $1)(100,000). Table 11.2 reflects the financial position of the Anderson Company after the stock dividend.

A two-for-one stock split by the Baker Company doubles the number of shares outstanding, from 1,000,000 to 2,000,000. The par value decreases from $1 to $0.50 per share. Table 11.3 shows the accounting adjustments. Notice that all of the account values remain the same.

The earnings per share for the Anderson Company changes with the 10 percent increase in the number of shares. Before the stock dividend, calculate earnings per share as follows:

$$EPS = \frac{\$2,200,000}{1,000,000}$$
$$= \$2.20$$

After the stock dividend, recalculate the earnings per share as follows:

$$EPS = \frac{\$2,200,000}{1,100,000}$$
$$= \$2.00$$

The old EPS is 10 percent more than the new EPS, the same percentage that the number of shares increased.

TABLE 11.2 Anderson Company Capital Accounts After Stock Dividend

Common stock (1,100,000 shares at $1 par)	$ 1,100,000
Capital in excess of par	5,400,000
Retained earnings	3,500,000
	$10,000,000

TABLE 11.3 Baker Company Capital Accounts After Stock Split

Common stock (2,000,000 shares at $0.50 par)	$ 1,000,000
Capital in excess of par	4,000,000
Retained earnings	5,000,000
	$10,000,000

The earnings per share for the Baker Company reflects the two-for-one increase in the number of shares. Before the stock split, calculate earnings per share as follows:

$$EPS = \frac{\$2,200,000}{1,000,000}$$
$$= \$2.20$$

After the stock split, recalculate the earnings per share as follows:

$$EPS = \frac{\$2,200,000}{2,000,000}$$
$$= \$1.10$$

The old EPS is twice the new EPS, the same multiple as the stock split.

Stock dividends allow a company to conserve cash while still appearing to pay dividends. Also, stock dividends and, to a greater degree, stock splits are used to keep the price of a stock in a particular trading range. For example, if management of the Baker Company wants the price of its stock below $10 per share, it announces a two-for-one stock split. This causes the stock to sell for about $7.50, $15 divided by two. Some financial managers believe that the lower price will make the stock more appealing to small investors and thereby will increase its value, above the $7.50 calculated in this example[1].

Stock Repurchases

A company that has excess cash may repurchase its own stock instead of paying a cash dividend. Companies may also use a **stock repurchase** to change the degree of financial leverage. If a company issues bonds and uses the proceeds to repurchase stock, this increases the weight of debt in the capital structure.

Stock Repurchase

[1] One study on stock splits indicates this effect is only temporary. See Eugene F. Fama, Lawrence Fisher, Michael Jensen, and Richard Roll, "The Adjustment of Stock Prices to New Information," *International Economic Review*, February 1969, pp. 1–21.

PS Group Inc. Suspends Quarterly Dividend Payments

P S Group Inc., San Diego, suspended quarterly dividend payments for at least the remainder of 1992 as part of a proposed amendment in its bank credit agreement covering debt of about $120 million. The aircraft leasing and hazardous waste recycling concern's last dividend of 15 cents a share was paid in February. PS Group said the amendments would bring the company back into compliance with its loan covenants. Without the amendments, the lenders could declare a default, accelerate all outstanding debt and require cash collateral for outstanding letters of credit. PS Group agreed to suspend dividends for the next three quarters as a condition for the bank's revising the covenant levels. Beginning in 1993, dividends will be paid only if cumulative net income exceeds the amount of any future dividend payments. In recent years, dividends have been paid out of retained earnings. In addition, PS Group agreed to a higher rate of interest, a limitation on the level of capital expenditures through the first quarter of 1993, a reduction in available credit to the amount currently outstanding, and accelerated principal payments. In the previous year, PS Group reported a net loss of $23.9 million, or $4.38 a share, on revenue of $297.8 million. The losses stemmed largely from a large write-down of aircraft and problems with a new recycling plant in Illinois.

Source: "Corporate Dividend News," *The Wall Street Journal*, April 6, 1992. Reprinted by permission of The Wall Street Journal, © 1992 Dow Jones & Company, Inc. All Rights Reserved Worldwide.

Repurchased stock is called treasury stock. A stock repurchase may have the effect of driving up the stock price. Increasing the price causes a gain when the stock is sold.

Stock repurchases were quite popular after Black Monday, October 19, 1987, the day the New York Stock Exchange lost almost 20 percent in value. After the fall in prices, many executives still had confidence in their companies and believed their stocks were undervalued. For those undervalued stocks, repurchase ultimately increased their price, more than simple calculations suggest.

Companies primarily use three methods to repurchase stock: (1) The company can buy stock on the open market. (This is the method most often used.) (2) The company can announce a tender offer. (This means that it will buy a specified number of shares at a stated price above the current market price. If the offer is oversubscribed, the company may buy more than the number of shares originally specified.) (3) The company can negotiate with a major shareholder to buy a large block of stock. (If the company is buying stock from an unwanted suitor, the practice is known as greenmail.)

Dividend Reinvestment Plans

Dividend Reinvestment Plans

Dividend reinvestment plans allow shareholders to reinvest their dividends in the stock of the company paying the dividends. There are two basic types of plans:

1. plans that sell treasury or unissued shares. (This method raises new capital for the company.)
2. plans that use a trustee, such as a bank, to purchase shares in the open market. (This method does not add cash to the company, but it does provide a service to the shareholders at a low cost.)

DIVIDEND THEORY AND POLICY

There are several approaches a company can take toward dividend policy. The best approach is the one that maximizes shareholder wealth. Alternatives are based on the residual dividend theory, the constant dividend payout ratio policy, the constant dividends with growth policy, and the constant dividends with extras policy. In studying this material, keep in mind that choices about dividends will impact not only the cost of capital but the capital structure as well.

Residual Dividend Theory

The **residual dividend theory** requires that earnings be used to provide the amount of equity needed for capital budgeting purposes. The company uses any residual earnings to pay dividends.

Residual Dividend Theory

This policy is based on the idea that investors prefer that earnings be retained and reinvested if the company can produce a higher return, given the level of risk. In this favorable situation, if dividends are paid, the individual expects only an average return, a return less than the company is expected to receive.

The residual dividend theory is implemented by using a four step procedure: (1) determine the amount of the optimal capital budget, (2) calculate the quantity of equity needed to support that capital budget, (3) set the level of retained earnings equal to the quantity of equity needed or the earnings available, whichever is smaller, and (4) pay out residual earnings, if any, as dividends. Chapter 9 covers the first two steps of this procedure.

> The Carson Company has the investment opportunity graph shown previously in Figure 9.3 (page 272) and repeated in Figure 11.1. It has a target capital structure of 40 percent debt, no preferred stock, and 60 percent common equity. Also assume, for simplicity, a marginal cost of capital of 13 percent over the entire range of the capital budget. The investment opportunity and marginal cost of capital graphs are combined in Figure 11.1. The Carson Company is interested in finding the amount of dividends using the residual dividend theory under two scenarios: Net income of $1,500,000 and net income of $2,500,000.

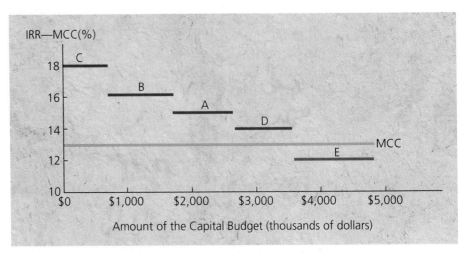

Figure 11.1   Carson Company Investment and MCC Graphs Combined
● ● ● ● ● ● ● ● ●

The first step in the procedure is to determine the amount of the optimal capital budget. This is the amount of funds required to support the accepted projects. Projects C, B, A, and D require a total of $3,600,000.

The second step in the procedure is to calculate the quantity of equity needed to support that capital budget. Since we know the company has 60 percent common equity, the calculation is easily made.

$$\text{Equity Needed} = \$3,600,000(0.60)$$
$$= \$2,160,000$$

The third step in the procedure is to set the level of retained earnings equal to the quantity of equity needed or the earnings available, whichever is smaller. There are two answers, depending on the amount of net income: (1) If net income is $1,500,000, the level of retained earnings is set at $1,500,000. The additional equity of $660,000 comes from new common stock. (2) If net income is $2,500,000, the level of retained earnings is set at $2,160,000.

The fourth step in the procedure is to pay out residual earnings, if any, as dividends. Again, there are two answers, depending on the amount of net income: (1) If net income is $1,500,000, there are no dividends. All of the net income is retained. (2) If net income is $2,500,000, the level of retained earnings is $2,160,000, and the residual amount of dividends is $340,000.

Constant Dividend Payout Ratio

Constant Dividend Payout Ratio

The **constant dividend payout ratio** policy requires a company to pay out a fixed percentage of earnings each year. Since the amount of earnings varies each year, *employing this policy causes the amount of dividends to vary widely.*

The Davis Company had the following earnings per share over the period from 1984 through 1993:

Year	EPS	Year	EPS
1984	$2.00	1989	$3.00
1985	2.20	1990	3.00
1986	2.80	1991	2.80
1987	3.20	1992	3.20
1988	4.00	1993	3.60

If the company employs a constant 60 percent payout ratio, how does this affect dividends per share for the 10 year period?

Earnings per share and dividends per share are plotted in Figure 11.2. As we can see, dividends per share is as erratic as earnings per share. Shareholders, as a result, cannot depend on receiving a constant stream of dividends.

Companies rarely follow a constant dividend payout ratio policy. When management cuts a dividend as earnings go down, investors interpret that action as a signal that future earnings will also be lower. This may cause the value of the stock to decline.

Constant Dividends With Growth

A **constant dividends with growth** policy requires a company to pay low dividends, increasing the amount of the dividends when it appears that the increase

Constant Dividends With Growth

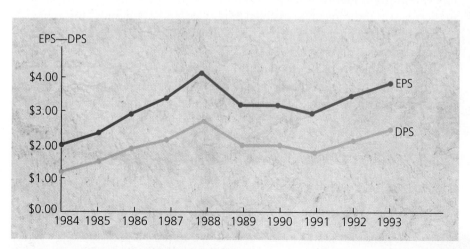

Figure 11.2 EPS and DPS with a Constant 60 Percent Payout Ratio

can be sustained. This approach is taken to avoid sending the negative indication caused by erratic dividends.

We can illustrate this policy using the 10-year EPS figures from the previous section. This time the amount of dividends is not tied to a constant payout ratio. As earnings increase, dividends conservatively increase. As earnings decrease, dividends remain fairly constant.

Year	EPS	DPS	Year	EPS	DPS
1984	$2.00	$1.20	1989	$3.00	$1.60
1985	2.20	1.30	1990	3.00	1.60
1986	2.80	1.40	1991	2.80	1.60
1987	3.20	1.50	1992	3.20	1.70
1988	4.00	1.60	1993	3.60	1.80

The dividends per share shown above reflects only one possible response in applying this policy.

Earnings per share and dividends per share are plotted in Figure 11.3. This curve shows that dividends per share are not so erratic as earnings per share. Shareholders, as a result, can depend on receiving a reasonably constant stream of dividends. But big differences and changing differences between EPS and DPS suggests a changing capital structure as more or less equity is available from internal sources.

Constant Dividends With Extras

Constant Dividends With Extras

The **constant dividends with extras** policy requires a company to pay a small quarterly dividend plus an occasional extra year-end dividend. This approach is taken to signal investors that a high dividend, when it occurs, may not continue.

Again this policy can be illustrated by using the 10-year EPS figures from the previous sections. This time the amount of dividends on a quarterly basis is fairly constant, while the extra year-end dividend is variable.

Year	EPS	Quarterly DPS	Extra DPS	Year	EPS	Quarterly DPS	Extra DPS
1984	$2.00	$1.20	$0.00	1989	$3.00	$1.50	$0.00
1985	2.20	1.30	0.00	1990	3.00	1.50	0.00
1986	2.80	1.40	0.00	1991	2.80	1.50	0.00
1987	3.20	1.50	0.00	1992	3.20	1.60	0.00
1988	4.00	1.50	0.50	1993	3.60	1.70	0.00

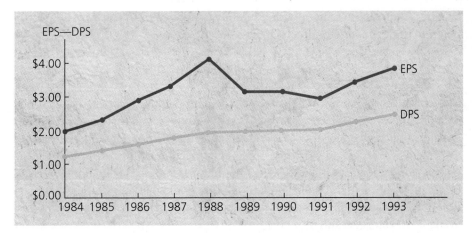

Figure 11.3 EPS and DPS, Constant Dividends with Growth Policy

Using the approach, the company could offer a fairly constant dividend being careful to offer the extra dividend only on an occasional basis.

Earnings per share and dividends per share are plotted in Figure 11.4. As shown, dividends per share on a quarterly basis are quite stable.

DIVIDENDS CONTROVERSIES

The question of the best dividend policy remains unresolved. Some financial theorists believe that dividends should be paid only after the equity needs of the company are met. A second group believes that dividends should be quite

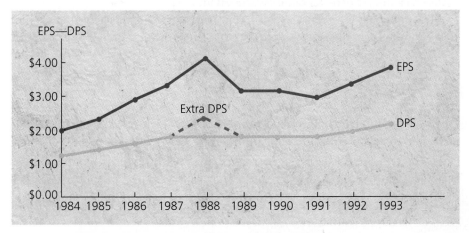

Figure 11.4 EPS and DPS, Constant Dividends with Extras Policy

steady. Others believe that dividend policy is irrelevant. In this section we will begin to understand why theorists take these positions.

Dividend Irrelevance

Merton Mill and Franco Modigliani concluded in a theoretical article that dividend policy is irrelevant[2]. They argue that the value of a company depends upon its earnings ability, given its risk class, and not upon the distributions of its earnings.

Miller and Modigliani base their arguments on a number of assumptions: (1) no personal or corporate income taxes, (2) no transaction costs, (3) no flotation costs, (4) no effect of dividend policy on cost of equity, (5) no relationship between investment policy and dividend policy, and (6) no difference between information available to managers and investors.

Acceptance of the MM proposition depends upon acceptance of the assumptions. An important part of the MM proof is the assumption that investment policy is independent of dividend policy. If this is so, then investment policy determines earnings ability. Thus, the value of a company is simply the present value of its future cash flows.

BIRD-IN-THE-HAND THEORY

Bird-in-the-Hand Approach

John Lintner concludes in another article that investors prefer the certainty of dividends to the uncertainty of receiving income in the form of capital gains[3]. This **bird-in-the-hand approach** implies that investors will discount the dividend stream at a lower discount rate than the future capital gains stream. This results in a higher present value for the dividends.

MM argue that investors are indifferent between dividends and capital gains. They contend that investors reinvest in similar companies, thereby not decreasing the riskiness of the cash flows.

Dividend Signaling

Increases in dividends often lead to increases in stock prices. This fact leads some observers to conclude that investors prefer dividends to capital gains.

---

[2] See Merton H. Miller and Franco Modigliani, "Dividend Policy, Growth, and the Valuation of Shares," *Journal of Business*, October, 1961, pp. 411–433.
[3] See John Lintner, "Dividends, Earnings, Leverage, Stock Prices, and the Supply of Capital to Corporations," *Review of Economics and Statistics*, August 1962, pp. 243–269.

Miller and Modigliani suggest this is not the reason for the price increases. They believe that an increase in dividends is a **signal** from management that better earnings are forecast. This signaling is important to shareholders since management normally has better access to information.

Signal

Dividend Clientele Effect

The tax position of shareholders may affect which dividend policy is preferred. Investors with low marginal tax rates may prefer dividends since taxes are not that great a consideration. Investors with high marginal tax rates may wish to delay taxes by having company earnings reinvested. The Tax Reform Act of 1986 moved dividend policy in the direction of paying dividends by taxing dividends at the same rate as capital gains.

Miller and Modigliani believe that certain dividend policies attract a particular **dividend clientele.** They suggest, for example, that a company which increases dividends attracts investors who prefer immediate income. This increases the demand for the stock and pushes prices upward. Like **dividend signaling,** the dividend clientele effect is difficult to prove empirically[4].

Dividend Clientele

Dividend Signaling

Dividends and Stock Offerings

At the beginning of this chapter, we pointed out that when a company pays higher dividends, it tends to issue more new common stock causing a smaller capital budget. This does not appear to be value-maximizing behavior.

Guy Charest, in one study, and Joseph Aharony and Itzhak Swary in another, however, show that dividend increases or decreases before a stock offering lead to stock-price appreciation or depreciation[5]. This implies that increasing dividends before a new issue is beneficial.

A study by Claudio Loder and David Mauer does not support the previous findings[6]. They contend that linking dividend and stock offering announcements results in few if any benefits. There are two explanations offered for this conclusion: (1) Increased earnings expectations from the dividend announcement may be dampened by the stock offering, and (2) Issuing firms may have more valuable investment opportunities.

---

[4] See R. Richardson Pettit, "Taxes, Transactions Costs, and the Clientele Effect of Dividends," *Journal of Financial Economics*, December 1977, pp. 419–436.

[5] See G. Charest, "Dividend Information, Stock Returns and Market Efficiency," *Journal of Financial Economics*, 1978, Vol. 6, pp. 297–330; and J. Aharony and I. Swary, " Quarterly Dividend and Earnings Announcements and Stockholders' Returns: An Empirical Analysis," *Journal of Finance*, 1980, Vol. 35, pp. 1–12.

[6] See Claudio F. Loderer and David C. Mauer, "Corporate Dividends and Seasoned Equity Issues: An Empirical Investigation," *Journal of Finance*, 1992, Vol. 47, pp. 201–225.

SUMMARY

This chapter focuses on the following learning objectives:

1. Explaining procedures for paying cash dividends.

    The board of directors meets on the declaration date to declare the regular dividend. The company pays dividends to shareholders who are registered on the holder-of-record date. Payment of the dividend on the ex-dividend date allows time to process transactions. The payment date is the time when dividend checks are mailed out.

2. Describing the constraints that limit the amount of dividends a company can legally and contractually pay.

    The legal agreement between bondholders or preferred shareholders and the issuing company is called the indenture. A company may also be constrained if it pays too small a dividend and has improper earnings accumulation. Cash dividends may only be paid with cash.

3. Reporting alternatives to paying cash dividends.

    Instead of paying a cash dividend, a company may choose to provide a stock dividend or create a stock split. The primary difference between the two transactions is with the accounting treatment. A company that has excess cash may repurchase its own stock instead of paying a cash dividend. Dividend reinvestment plans allow shareholders to reinvest their dividends in the stock of the company paying the dividends.

4. Describing the residual dividend theory.

    The residual dividend theory requires that earnings be used to provide the amount of equity that is needed for capital budgeting purposes. This policy is based on the idea that investors prefer earnings to be retained and reinvested if the company can produce a higher return, given the level of risk. In this favorable situation, if dividends are paid, the individual expects only an average return, a return less than the company is expected to receive.

5. Outlining alternative dividend policies.

    The constant dividend payout ratio policy requires a company to pay out a fixed percentage of earnings each year. A constant dividends with growth policy requires a company to pay low dividends, increasing the amount of the dividends when it appears that the increase can be sustained. The constant dividends with extras policy requires a company to pay a small quarterly dividend plus an occasional extra year-end dividend.

6. Summarizing the controversy in dividend policy.

    Merton Miller and Franco Modigliani state that under certain conditions dividend policy is irrelevant. John Lintner concludes that investors prefer the certainty of dividends to the uncertainty of receiving income in the form of capital gains, the bird-in-the-hand approach. A study by Claudio

Loder and David Mauer contends that linking dividend and stock offering announcements results in few in any benefits.

KEY TERMS

Bird-in-the-hand
  approach, 326
Capital impairment
  rule, 316
Constant dividend
  payout ratio, 322
Constant dividends
  with extras, 324
Constant dividends
  with growth, 323
Covenants, 316

Declaration date, 316
Dividend
  clientele, 327
Dividend reinvestment
  plan, 320
Dividend
  signaling, 327
Ex-dividend
  date, 316
Holder-of-record
  date, 316

Improper earnings
  accumulation, 317
Payment date, 316
Protective
  covenants, 316
Residual dividend
  theory, 321
Signal, 327
Stock dividend, 317
Stock split, 317
Stock repurchase, 319

QUESTIONS

11.1   What are the four important dates associated with announcing a dividend?

11.2   Explain the various legal constraints as to the amount of dividends a company pays.

11.3   What are the differences between stock dividends and stock splits?

11.4   Discuss stock repurchases.

11.5   What are the two basic types of stock reinvestment plans?

11.6   Explain the residual dividend theory.

11.7   How does the constant dividend payout ratio policy operate?

11.8   Contrast the policies of constant dividends with growth and constant dividends with extras.

11.9   Explain the argument of dividend irrelevance.

11.10   What is meant by the bird-in-the-hand theory of dividends?

11.11   How does dividend signaling lead to increases in stock prices?

11.12   How does the tax position of shareholders affect which dividend policy is preferred?

11.13   What would be the effect of announcing a stock dividend just before issuing new common stock?

11.14 Would the announcement of the increased dividends by P&G lead to an increase in the price of the stock?

11.15 What restrictions did the PS Group, Inc. consent to in order to maintain its bank credit agreement?

PROBLEMS

11.1 **(Retention and Payout Ratios)** Last year, the Provenzano Corporation retained $6,600,000 from earnings of $16,500,000. What is the retention ratio? What is the payout ratio?

11.2 **(Retention Ratio and Retained Earnings)** Last year, Shumpert Heating & Air Conditioning had a profit margin of 5 percent on sales of $900,000. The company has a policy of paying out 40 percent of its earnings as dividends. What is its retention ratio? What is the amount of retained earnings?

11.3 **(Dividend Yield)** The Howle Company recently paid a quarterly dividend of $0.50 per share. If the stock is selling for $50 per share, what is the annual dividend yield?

11.4 **(Ex-dividend Date)** The board of directors of Kuper Insurance met on November 16, 1992, to declare the regular quarterly dividend. They set the holder-of-record date as December 11, 1992. What is the ex-dividend date?

11.5 **(Ex-dividend Price)** The common stock of the Van Hook Corporation sold for $50 the day before the stock went ex-dividend. The annual dividend is $10.00. If dividends are distributed on a quarterly basis, what is the ex-dividend price of the stock?

11.6 **(Dividend Estimation)** Today, the Johnson Company announced earnings per share of $4.00. Management projects steady growth, with earnings expected to grow indefinitely at a rate of 10 percent. The company plans to continue its constant dividend payout ratio of 40 percent. Estimate the dividend in 5 years.

11.7 **(Earnings Distribution)** The Elizabeth Richardson Company published the following information in its annual report:

Earnings after taxes	$2,900,000
Price-earnings ratio	10
Common shares outstanding	1,000,000
Preferred shares outstanding	100,000
Common dividends per share	$1.40
Preferred dividends per share	$1.00

Determine earnings available to common shareholders, earnings per share of common stock, the dividend yield, the payout ratio, and the retention ratio.

11.8 **(Amount of Dividends)** H.J. Hodge, Inc. has the following balance sheet.

Cash	$ 600,000	Accounts payable	$ 700,000
Other current assets	1,200,000	Long-term debt	500,000
Total current assets	$1,800,000	Common stock, $1 par	200,000
		Paid-in capital	1,000,000
Fixed assets	1,500,000	Retained earnings	900,000
Total assets	$3,300,000	Total claims	$3,300,000

Legally, what is the maximum dividends per share the company can pay out? Based on available cash, what is the maximum dividends per share the company can pay out? If return on total assets is 5 percent and the payout ratio is 40 percent, what is the total amount of dividends that the company will pay?

11.9 **(Price After Stock Dividend)** Key Executives, Inc. stock currently sells for $25.00. If the company declares a 20 percent stock dividend, what is the approximate price of the new shares?

11.10 **(Price After Stock Split)** The stock of the Marley Tree Company is currently selling for $75.00. If the board of directors declares a three-for-one stock split, what is the approximate price of the new shares?

11.11 **(Stock Dividend EPS)** Green Nurseries, Inc. plans a stock dividend of 10 percent. The current market price of the stock is $50. The capital accounts for the company are shown below:

Common stock (2,000,000 shares at $1 par)	$ 2,000,000
Capital in excess of par	10,000,000
Retained earnings	18,000,000
	$30,000,000

How is the balance sheet affected after the transactions? If earnings after taxes are $4,400,000, what is the earnings per share (EPS) before and after the stock distribution?

11.12 **(Stock Split EPS)** The Black Company plans a stock split of three for one. The current market price of the stock is $28.50. The capital accounts for the company are shown as follows:

Common stock (1,000,000 shares at $0.60 par)	$ 600,000
Capital in excess of par	5,000,000
Retained earnings	3,400,000
	$9,000,000

What is the financial position of the company after the transactions? If earnings after taxes are $1,500,000, what is the earnings per share (EPS) before and after the stock distribution?

11.13 **(Stock Dividend Pro Forma Balance Sheet)** The board of directors of the Carling Company examined its latest balance sheet to determine the form and quantity of its next quarterly dividend.

Current		Current liabilities	$ 15,000,000
assets	$ 50,000,000	Long-term debt	185,000,000
Fixed		Common stock ($1 par)	10,000,000
assets	350,000,000	Paid-in capital	35,000,000
		Retained earnings	155,000,000
Total		Total	
assets	$400,000,000	claims	$400,000,000

The board decided to pay a 5 percent stock dividend and a cash dividend, on old and new shares, of $0.10 per share. The stock of the company is currently selling for $20 per share. Construct a pro forma balance sheet which reflects the stock dividend *and* the cash dividend.

11.14 **(Declaring Dividends)** The Hensley Construction Company had the following earnings per share over the period from 1984 through 1993.

Year	EPS
1984	$1.00
1985	1.20
1986	1.30
1987	2.00
1988	1.20
1989	1.40
1990	1.40
1991	1.50
1992	2.00
1993	1.60

For the last several years, the company paid out 40 percent of earnings as dividends. Calculate or suggest the amount of dividends each year under the following dividend policies:

a. Constant dividend payout ratio policy.
b. Constant dividends with growth policy.
c. Constant dividends with extras policy.

11.15 **(Payout and Retention Ratios)** Mills Corporation expects earnings next year of $20,800,000. The optimal capital budget for the company amounts to $15,600,000. Mills plans to maintain its 40 percent debt ratio. Determine the amount of dividends under the residual dividend theory. Calculate the effective payout and retention ratios.

11.16 **(Residual Theory of Dividends)** Paschal Products, Inc. has the following investment opportunities for next year:

Project	Initial Investment	Internal Rate of Return
A	$400,000	19%
B	$900,000	16%
C	$600,000	10%
D	$600,000	13%

The target capital structure includes 40 percent debt, no preferred stock, and 60 percent common equity. The company expects net income of $2,000,000 and follows the residual theory of dividends. The before-tax cost of debt is 12 percent, and the marginal tax rate is 40 percent. The cost of retained earnings is 14 percent, and the cost of new common stock is 16 percent. Determine which projects should be accepted, the size of the optimal capital budget, the amount of dividends, and the effective payout ratio.

11.17 **(Residual Theory of Dividends)** Parker Publishing has the following investment opportunities for next year:

Project	Initial Investment	Internal Rate of Return
A	$ 600,000	12%
B	$1,000,000	18%
C	$ 500,000	15%
D	$ 800,000	13%

The target capital structure contains 40 percent debt, no preferred stock, and 60 percent common equity. The company expects net income of $3,000,000 and will follow the residual theory of dividends. The before-tax cost of debt depends on the amount borrowed.

Amount Borrowed	Before-Tax Cost
$0 to $500,000	10%
$500,000 to $1,500,000	12%
$1,500,000+	14%

The marginal tax rate is 40 percent. The cost of retained earnings is 15.54 percent, and the cost of new common stock is 16.27 percent. Determine which projects should be accepted, the size of the optimal capital budget, the amount of dividends, and the effective payout ratio.

A Case Problem

The Dayton Corporation was one of the largest manufacturers of fleece fabrics sold to the domestic manufacturing industry. The company purchased fiber, spun it into yarn, knitted yarn into fabric, and dyed and finished the fabric. Dayton Corporation also produced jersey fabrics used in women's lightweight apparel, such as tops and shorts.

Dayton Fabrics was purchased in 1990 by members of management and a group of individual investors. In a recapitalization completed in 1991, the shareholders of Dayton Fabrics exchanged their shares for shares of the Dayton Corporation. Dayton Fabrics became a wholly owned subsidiary of the company. In the acquisition process, Dayton Fabrics incurred a significant amount of debt.

In 1992, 7,000,000 shares of common stock of Dayton Corporation were sold to the public, 4,600,000 by the company and 2,400,000 shares by selling shareholders. The company planned to use the proceeds to help retire the indebtedness of Dayton Fabrics and to pay a $5,000,000 dividend to holders of common stock prior to the offering. No dividends had been paid since Dayton Corporation was incorporated in Tennessee in 1991. After the offering, 13,500,000 shares were outstanding.

Jeffrey Walker was chief financial officer and treasurer of Dayton Corporation. He was examining dividend policy for fiscal 1993 in order to recommend a policy to the board of directors. Jeffrey knew that long-term debt, even after the stock issue, was 50 percent of total capitalization. The directors wanted to reduce the debt percentage by approximately 1 percent per year over the next 10 years. This amounted to about $2,000,000 per year.

In recent years, production facilities had operated near the limits of capacity, requiring the company to operate twenty-four hours a day, seven days a week.

The company also planned a plant modernization program begun in the late 1980s. The purpose was to maintain its industry position as a high-quality, cost-efficient manufacturer through the addition of technologically advanced equipment. In recent years, production facilities had operated near the limits of capacity, requiring the company to operate twenty-four hours a day, seven days a week. Total capital expenditures for fiscal 1993 amounted to $8,250,000. The company expected net income during that period of $9,850,000.

Jeffrey believed that an appropriate dividend policy would be to pay out the remainder of net income as dividends after paying for debt reduction and capital expenditures. He knew a director was planning to suggest a cash dividend of $.10 per share with any excess funds to be invested on a short-term basis.

Leading Questions

1. How much equity is required to support capital expenditures and debt reduction?
2. What is the amount of dividends per share under Jeffrey's plan.
3. What are the advantages and disadvantages of the two plans?

PART V

Long-Term Financing

Security Markets

Common and Preferred Stock

Long-Term Debt and Leasing

Options, Warrants, and Convertibles

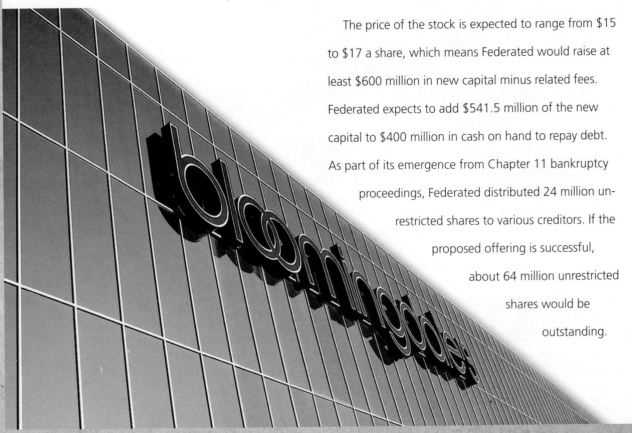

FEDERATED DEPARTMENT STORES PLANS STOCK OFFERING

Federated Department Stores Inc. announced it intends to issue 40 million common shares as part of a plan to repay $941.5 million of debt. Federated, which operates chains such as Bloomingdale's and Rich's, also disclosed that it is negotiating to establish a $300 million line of credit with a group of banks led by Citibank. Because the retailer intends to draw on its large amount of cash as part of its debt repayment plan, it wants to establish working capital lines.

12 Security Markets

The price of the stock is expected to range from $15 to $17 a share, which means Federated would raise at least $600 million in new capital minus related fees. Federated expects to add $541.5 million of the new capital to $400 million in cash on hand to repay debt. As part of its emergence from Chapter 11 bankruptcy proceedings, Federated distributed 24 million unrestricted shares to various creditors. If the proposed offering is successful, about 64 million unrestricted shares would be outstanding.

Federated disclosed the size of its proposed stock offering, the retailer's first direct public offering, in a registration statement filed with the Securities and Exchange Commission. Lehman Brothers is lead manager of the U.S. underwriting syndicate. Andrew Herenstein, an analyst at Delaware Bay Company, which specializes in distressed securities, said the proposed stock offering could significantly reduce Federated's leverage.

The situation at Federated Department Stores is complicated for the underwriters. In offering this stock, there are a number of risks to be considered. The company will use the net proceeds to increase equity but will still have a high level of debt. The debt instruments also contain a number of restrictive covenants, including limits to capital expenditures and sale of assets, as well as financial ratio requirements. With all of the risk factors involved, setting the offering price is difficult.

Source: Jeffrey A. Trachtenberg, "Federated Posts Mixed Results, Plans Stock Offering and Seeks Line of Credit," *The Wall Street Journal,* April 2, 1992. Reprinted by permission of The Wall Street Journal, © 1992 Dow Jones & Company, Inc. All Rights Reserved Worldwide.

CAPITAL MARKETS

In order to maximize the share price of its stock, corporations frequently must raise new capital in the security markets. In this framework, short-term markets are **money markets,** while long-term markets are **capital markets.** As is the case with Federated Department Stores, companies have a variety of needs for new funds.

Money Markets

Capital Markets

Money markets involve securities with maturities of one year or less (an arbitrary line of demarcation). The major participants in this market are corporations, institutions, and governments. Individuals tend to participate indirectly through money market funds. These highly marketable securities have little risk that the issuer will not pay interest or principal at the proper time.

The instruments most commonly traded in these markets include Treasury bills, federal funds, short-term municipal obligations, commercial paper, negotiable certificates of deposit, bankers' acceptances, and repurchase agreements. Financial managers use these instruments to meet short-term financing needs and to invest temporary excess cash. These markets are covered in greater detail in Chapter 16.

Capital markets involve securities with maturities greater than one year. Corporations draw on these markets to issue debt securities, preferred stock, and common stock. Individuals, financial institutions, and other organizations also purchase these securities. The Treasury Department uses these markets to issue Treasury notes and Treasury bonds. Various government agencies, such as the Federal Housing Administration (FHA), employ these markets to sell notes and bonds. States, counties, and municipalities utilize these markets to issue general obligation bonds and revenue bonds. In the material that follows, we will discuss these capital market participants and the securities they use.

Corporate Securities

Corporate securities are issued in two basic forms: debt and equity. Bonds represent the debt of the corporation while common stock and preferred stock represent equity. Preferred stock combines both debt and common stock characteristics. We will study these securities in greater detail in this chapter and the next chapter.

The bond market includes debentures, subordinated debentures, convertible debentures, mortgages, income bonds, collateral trust bonds, and equipment trust certificates. Debentures are unsecured corporate bonds. Subordinated debentures are debentures that are paid only after the claims of secured debt and senior unsecured debt are satisfied. Convertible debentures are debt securities that can be converted into shares of common stock at the option of the bondholder. Mortgages are secured loans backed by real estate or other real property. Income bonds are similar to municipal revenue bonds in that interest is paid only to the extent it is earned. Collateral trust bonds are backed by financial assets. Equipment trust certificates are issued by transportation industries and include specified equipment as collateral.

Preferred stock is like debt in that the amount of payment is stated in its contract. Preferred stock is unlike debt in that the dividend is not a liability until the board of directors declares it. Preferred stock enjoys a superior position to common stock in the case of liquidation. Preferred stock never matures. Bonds, in contrast, have a stated maturity.

Common stock ownership represents ownership of the company. As a result, common shareholders have the residual claim to earnings and assets of the company after all prior claims have been paid. The earnings after taxes of a corporation, less preferred stock dividends, are paid out as dividends or kept in the form of retained earnings.

Government Securities

Treasury Notes

Treasury Bonds

The Treasury Department issues securities to finance the federal government. **Treasury notes** have maturities greater than one year and less than ten years. **Treasury bonds** have maturities of more than ten years. Treasury notes and bonds have virtually zero default risk.

Treasury notes and bonds are issued in denominations of $1,000, $5,000, $10,000, $100,000, and $1,000,000. The sale of notes and bonds is announced in Treasury newsletters and daily newspapers. These securities are registered in the owner's name as opposed to bearer form whereby the holder is assumed to be the owner. Prospective buyers may obtain new Treasury securities through either a competitive or noncompetitive bid. The noncompetitive bid price is a weighted average of the accepted competitive bids.

Treasury notes and bonds are bought and sold through government security dealers. Figure 12.1 is an example of note and bond quotations from *The Wall Street Journal*. *Rate* is the yearly coupon, even though payments are on a semi-annual basis. *Bid* (what the buyer wants to pay) and *Asked* (what the seller wants to receive) prices appear to be in the decimal form, but the decimal amount is actually in 32nds of a dollar. On the third line, for example, an asked price of 100:17 means that issue could be bought at 100 17/32 percent of face value. The yield to maturity, *Yld*, using asked prices is shown as 1.93 percent. If the bonds are callable, those with two maturity dates listed and are selling above face value, the yield is actually the yield to call.

Government Agencies and Enterprises

Government agencies and government-sponsored enterprises raise funds to finance operations by selling notes and bonds. Their debt is not guaranteed by the federal government, but these securities are considered as safe as Treasury securities since they have a strong implicit guarantee [1]. Government agency securities include the Federal Housing Administration (FHA) and the Government National Mortgage Association (GNMA), popularly known as *Ginnie Mae*. Government-sponsored enterprise securities include the Federal Home Loan Banks (FHLB) and the Federal National Mortgage Association (FNMA), popularly known as *Fannie Mae*.

These securities are usually issued in denominations between $1,000 and $50,000. Interest on these obligations is normally paid semiannually, with principal due at maturity. Some issues are subject to state and local income taxes while others are tax-exempt. The interest rate paid on a particular security depends upon the tax status of the interest. Figure 12.2 is an example from *The Wall Street Journal* of price quotations on U.S. Agency issues.

Municipal Bonds

States, counties, cities, and other political units issue municipal bonds. An attractive feature of these securities is that interest is not subject to federal income taxes. Municipal bonds also avoid taxation in the state in which the bonds are issued. For example, the interest on Georgia Port Authority bonds is not taxable to Georgia residents. Because of their income tax-exempt status,

[1] There is an important exception to this. Ginnie Mae (GNMA) securities are guaranteed by the full faith and credit of the U.S. Treasury.

TREASURY BONDS, NOTES & BILLS

Thursday, October 7, 1993

Representative Over-the-Counter quotations based on transactions of $1 million or more.

Treasury bond, note and bill quotes are as of mid-afternoon. Colons in bid-and-asked quotes represent 32nds; 101:01 means 101 1/32. Net changes in 32nds. n-Treasury note. Treasury bill quotes in hundredths, quoted on terms of a rate of discount. Days to maturity calculated from settlement date. All yields are to maturity and based on the asked quote. Latest 13-week and 26-week bills are boldfaced. For bonds callable prior to maturity, yields are computed to the earliest call date for issues quoted above par and to the maturity date for issues below par. *-When issued.

Source: Federal Reserve Bank of New York.

U.S. Treasury strips as of 3 p.m. Eastern time, also based on transactions of $1 million or more. Colons in bid-and-asked quotes represent 32nds; 101:01 means 101 1/32. Net changes in 32nds. Yields calculated on the asked quotation. bp-Treasury bond, stripped principal. ci-stripped coupon interest. np-Treasury note, stripped principal. For bonds callable prior to maturity, yields are computed to the earliest call date for issues quoted above par and to the maturity date for issues below par.

Source: Bear, Stearns & Co. via Street Software Technology Inc.

GOVT. BONDS & NOTES

Rate	Maturity Mo/Yr	Bid	Asked	Chg.	Ask Yld.
7 1/8	Oct 93n	100:02	100:04	....	0.00
6	Oct 93n	100:06	100:08	....	1.12
7 3/4	Nov 93n	100:15	100:17	....	1.93
8 5/8	Nov 93	100:18	100:20	− 1	1.79
9	Nov 93n	100:18	100:20	− 1	2.14
11 3/4	Nov 93n	100:28	100:30	− 1	1.52
5 1/2	Nov 93n	100:11	100:13	....	2.41
5	Dec 93n	100:13	100:15	....	2.79
7 5/8	Dec 93n	100:01	100:02	− 1	2.65
7	Jan 94n	101:00	101:02	....	2.81
4 7/8	Jan 94n	100:17	100:19	....	2.86
6 7/8	Feb 94n	101:09	101:11	....	2.88
8 7/8	Feb 94n	101:31	102:01	....	2.84
9	Feb 94	102:01	102:03	....	2.79
5 3/8	Feb 94n	100:28	100:30	....	2.89
5 3/4	Mar 94n	101:07	101:09	....	2.96
8 1/2	Mar 94n	102:16	102:18	....	2.93
7	Apr 94n	101:29	101:31	− 1	3.07
5 3/8	Apr 94n	101:05	101:07	....	3.13
7	May 94n	102:06	102:08	....	3.14
9 1/2	May 94n	103:22	103:24	....	3.07
13 1/8	May 94n	105:26	105:28	− 1	3.05
5 1/8	May 94n	101:06	101:08	+ 1	3.12
5	Jun 94n	101:07	101:09	+ 1	3.18
8 1/2	Jun 94n	103:22	103:24	+ 1	3.18
8	Jul 94n	103:16	103:18	....	3.21
4 1/4	Jul 94n	100:23	100:25	....	3.26
6 7/8	Aug 94n	102:29	102:31	....	3.28
8 5/8	Aug 94n	104:12	104:14	....	3.25
8 3/4	Aug 94	104:15	104:19	....	3.19
12 5/8	Aug 94n	107:24	107:26	....	3.16
4 1/4	Aug 94n	100:25	100:27	....	3.27
4	Sep 94n	100:19	100:21	....	3.31
8 1/2	Sep 94n	104:28	104:30	....	3.27
9 1/2	Oct 94n	106:00	106:02	....	3.34
4 1/4	Oct 94n	100:27	100:29	....	3.37
6	Nov 94n	102:23	102:25	+ 1	3.39
8 1/4	Nov 94n	105:04	105:06	....	3.38
10 1/8	Nov 94	107:04	107:06	....	3.37
11 5/8	Nov 94n	108:24	108:26	....	3.35
4 5/8	Nov 94n	101:09	101:11	....	3.41
4 5/8	Dec 94n	101:11	101:13	+ 1	3.44
7 5/8	Dec 94n	104:30	105:00	+ 1	3.40
8 5/8	Jan 95n	106:07	106:09	....	3.48
4 1/4	Jan 95n	100:28	100:30	....	3.51
3	Feb 95	100:00	100:02	....	2.24
5 1/2	Feb 95n	102:16	102:18	+ 1	3.53
7 3/4	Feb 95n	105:15	105:17	+ 1	3.50
10 1/2	Feb 95	109:01	109:03	....	3.51

Rate	Maturity Mo/Yr	Bid	Asked	Chg.	Ask Yld.
9 1/8	May 99n	120:30	121:00	+ 1	4.80
6 3/8	Jul 99n	107:17	107:19	+ 1	4.85
8	Aug 99n	115:26	115:28	+ 1	4.85
6	Oct 99n	105:20	105:22	+ 1	4.90
7 7/8	Nov 99n	115:16	115:18	+ 2	4.89
6 3/8	Jan 00n	107:21	107:23	....	4.93
7 7/8	Feb 95-00	105:18	105:22	+ 3	3.50
8 1/2	Feb 00n	119:07	119:09	+ 1	4.92
5 1/2	Apr 00n	103:11	103:13	+ 1	4.88
8 7/8	May 00n	121:25	121:27	+ 1	4.95
8 3/8	Aug 95-00	108:04	108:08	− 1	3.70
8 3/4	Aug 00n	121:15	121:17	+ 1	5.00
8 1/2	Nov 00n	120:10	120:12	+ 1	5.05
7 3/4	Feb 01n	116:04	116:06	....	5.08
11 3/4	Feb 01	140:22	140:26	− 1	5.03
8	May 01n	117:29	117:31	+ 1	5.11
13 1/8	May 01.	150:05	150:09	− 1	5.07
7 7/8	Aug 01n	117:11	117:13	+ 2	5.15
8	Aug 96-01	110:02	110:06	− 2	4.16
13 3/8	Aug 01	152:27	152:31	+ 2	5.10
7 1/2	Nov 01n	115:02	115:04	+ 1	5.19
15 3/4	Nov 01	169:20	169:24	+ 2	5.12
14 1/4	Feb 02	161:03	161:07	+ 2	5.14
7 1/2	May 02n	115:12	115:14	+ 2	5.25
6 3/8	Aug 02n	107:14	107:16	+ 13	5.30
11 5/8	Nov 02	145:03	145:07	+ 1	5.30
6 1/4	Feb 03n	106:11	106:13	+ 1	5.37
10 3/4	Feb 03	139:09	139:13	+ 1	5.34
10 3/4	May 03	139:30	140:02	+ 2	5.36
5 3/4	Aug 03n	103:08	103:10	+ 1	5.31
11 1/8	Aug 03	143:16	143:20	+ 1	5.36
11 7/8	Nov 03	149:27	149:31	+ 1	5.39
12 3/8	May 04	155:21	155:25	+ 3	5.39
13 3/4	Aug 04	167:22	167:26	+ 5	5.40
11 5/8	Nov 04	150:18	150:22	+ 2	5.47
8 1/4	May 00-05	116:28	117:00	− 1	5.17
12	May 05	155:00	155:04	+ 3	5.50
10 3/4	Aug 05	144:25	144:29	+ 3	5.53
9 3/8	Feb 06	133:21	133:25	+ 4	5.56
7 5/8	Feb 02-07	113:18	113:22	+ 2	5.55
7 7/8	Nov 02-07	116:07	116:11	+ 5	5.56
8 3/8	Aug 03-08	120:24	120:28	+ 3	5.59
8 3/4	Nov 03-08	123:30	124:02	+ 3	5.60
9 1/8	May 04-09	127:21	127:25	+ 3	5.61
10 3/8	Nov 04-09	138:25	138:29	+ 3	5.62
11 3/4	Feb 05-10	150:24	150:28	+ 4	5.62
10	May 05-10	136:23	136:27	+ 3	5.63
12 3/4	Nov 05-10	161:23	161:27	+ 4	5.63
13 7/8	May 06-11	173:09	173:13	+ 3	5.65
14	Nov 06-11	176:09	176:13	+ 3	5.66

Mat.	Type	Bid	Asked	Chg.	Ask Yld.
May 01	ci	67:16	67:21	+ 2	5.22
May 01	np	67:14	67:19	+ 2	5.22
Aug 01	ci	66:12	66:17	+ 2	5.26
Aug 01	np	66:10	66:15	+ 2	5.28
Nov 01	ci	65:05	65:10	+ 1	5.34
Nov 01	np	65:02	65:07	+ 1	5.36
Feb 02	ci	63:31	64:04	+ 2	5.39
May 02	ci	63:03	63:08	+ 2	5.41
May 02	np	63:03	63:08	+ 2	5.41
Aug 02	ci	62:01	62:06	+ 2	5.45
Aug 02	np	62:03	62:08	+ 1	5.43
Nov 02	ci	60:30	61:03	+ 2	5.49
Feb 03	ci	59:25	59:30	+ 1	5.55
Feb 03	np	59:28	60:01	+ 2	5.53
May 03	ci	58:24	58:29	....	5.59
Aug 03	ci	57:24	57:30	− 1	5.63
Nov 03	ci	56:25	56:31	....	5.66
Feb 04	ci	55:21	55:27	+ 2	5.72
May 04	ci	54:17	54:23	....	5.78
Aug 04	ci	53:19	53:25	....	5.80
Nov 04	ci	52:23	52:29	....	5.82
Nov 04	bp	53:04	53:09	....	5.76
Feb 05	ci	51:22	51:27	....	5.88
May 05	ci	50:30	51:03	+ 4	5.88
May 05	bp	51:16	51:22	+ 4	5.78
Aug 05	ci	49:31	50:05	+ 2	5.91
Aug 05	bp	50:18	50:23	+ 4	5.82
Nov 05	ci	48:29	49:02	− 2	5.97
Feb 06	ci	48:01	48:06	+ 2	6.00
Feb 06	bp	49:09	49:15	+ 3	5.78
Aug 06	ci	47:07	47:12	+ 2	6.02
Aug 06	ci	46:13	46:18	+ 2	6.04
Nov 06	ci	45:17	45:22	+ 2	6.07
Feb 07	ci	44:20	44:25	+ 4	6.11
Aug 07	ci	43:27	44:00	+ 4	6.13
Aug 07	ci	43:00	43:06	+ 2	6.16
Feb 08	ci	42:06	42:11	+ 4	6.19
Feb 08	ci	41:12	41:17	+ 4	6.22
May 08	ci	40:18	40:23	+ 6	6.25
Aug 08	ci	39:24	39:30	+ 6	6.28
Nov 08	ci	38:31	39:05	+ 4	6.31
Feb 09	ci	38:05	38:10	+ 6	6.35
May 09	ci	37:12	37:18	+ 6	6.38
Aug 09	ci	36:22	36:27	+ 9	6.40
Nov 09	ci	36:02	36:07	+ 8	6.41
Nov 09	bp	36:27	37:01	....	6.27
Feb 10	ci	35:07	35:12	....	6.46
May 10	ci	34:19	34:24	+ 2	6.47
Aug 10	ci	33:30	34:03	+ 2	6.49
Nov 10	ci	33:11	33:16	+ 2	6.50
Feb 11	ci	32:24	32:29	+ 6	6.51
May 11	ci	32:00	32:06	+ 2	6.55
Aug 11	ci	31:14	31:19	+ 4	6.56
Nov 11	ci	30:26	31:00	+ 4	6.58
Feb 12	ci	30:07	30:12	....	6.60
May 12	ci	29:20	29:25	....	6.62
Aug 12	ci	29:06	29:12	+ 2	6.61
Nov 12	ci	28:23	28:28	+ 4	6.61
Feb 13	ci	28:05	28:10	+ 4	6.63
May 13	ci	27:21	27:26	+ 4	6.64
Aug 13	ci	27:06	27:11	+ 4	6.64
Nov 13	ci	26:24	26:29	+ 4	6.64
Feb 14	ci	26:05	26:10	....	6.67
May 14	ci	25:24	25:28	....	6.67
Aug 14	ci	25:08	25:13	....	6.68
Nov 14	ci	24:27	25:00	+ 2	6.68
Feb 15	ci	24:13	24:17	+ 2	6.69
Feb 15	bp	24:17	24:22	....	6.66
May 15	ci	24:01	24:06	+ 2	6.68
Aug 15	ci	23:21	23:26	+ 2	6.68
Aug 15	ci	23:13	23:30	+ 2	6.65
Nov 15	ci	23:10	23:15	+ 2	6.67

Figure 12.1 Treasury Bond and Note Quotations

GOVERNMENT AGENCY & SIMILAR ISSUES

Thursday, October 7, 1993

Over-the-Counter mid-afternoon quotations based on large transactions, usually $1 million or more. Colons in bid-and-asked quotes represent 32nds; 101:01 means 101 1/32.

All yields are calculated to maturity, and based on the asked quote. * -- Callable issue, maturity date shown. For issues callable prior to maturity, yields are computed to the earliest call date for issues quoted above par, or 100, and to the maturity date for issues quoted below par.

Source: Bear, Stearns & Co. via Street Software Technology Inc.

FNMA Issues

Rate	Mat.	Bid	Asked	Yld.
7.75	11-93	100:11	100:19	0.11
7.38	12-93	100:21	100:29	1.69
7.55	1-94	101:00	101:04	2.86
9.45	1-94	101:16	101:24	2.20
7.65	4-94	102:04	102:12	2.81
9.60	4-94	103:03	103:11	2.78
9.30	5-94	103:12	103:16	3.12
8.60	6-94	103:14	103:22	2.91
7.45	7-94	102:30	103:02	3.26
8.90	8-94	104:11	104:19	3.22
10.10	10-94	106:12	106:20	3.29
9.25	11-94	105:19	105:27	3.66
5.50	12-94	101:23	101:27	3.89
9.00	1-95	106:11	106:19	3.53
11.95	1-95	109:30	110:10	3.40
11.50	2-95	109:29	110:09	3.50
8.85	3-95	107:04	107:12	3.44
11.70	5-95	112:01	112:13	3.54
11.15	6-95	111:23	112:03	3.60
4.75	8-95	101:18	101:22	3.80
10.50	9-95	112:03	112:15	3.69
8.40	11-95*	100:15	100:19	0.74
8.80	11-95	109:22	109:30	3.78
10.60	11-95	113:09	113:17	3.77
9.20	1-96	111:01	111:09	3.90
7.00	2-96	106:04	106:12	4.10
7.70	2-96*	101:13	101:17	3.02
9.35	2-96	111:10	111:18	4.10
8.00	4-96*	102:06	102:10	3.25
8.05	6-96*	102:26	102:30	3.50
8.50	6-96	110:14	110:22	4.21
8.75	6-96	111:01	111:09	4.22
4.41	7-96*	100:12	100:16	3.71
8.00	7-96	109:14	109:22	4.22
7.90	8-96	109:11	109:19	4.27
8.15	8-96	110:00	110:08	4.27
8.20	8-96*	103:27	103:31	3.32
7.70	9-96	109:00	109:04	4.33
8.63	9-96	111:16	111:24	4.29
7.05	10-96	107:18	107:22	4.29
8.45	10-96	111:19	111:27	4.24
6.90	11-96*	103:18	103:22	3.40
7.70	12-96	109:18	109:26	4.34
8.20	12-96	111:04	111:12	4.35
6.20	1-97*	103:22	103:30	2.95
7.60	1-97	109:06	109:14	4.44
7.05	3-97*	104:29	105:01	3.37
7.00	4-97*	104:22	104:26	3.66
9.25	4-97*	102:31	103:03	2.90
6.75	4-97	106:16	106:20	4.69
9.20	6-97	114:28	115:04	4.66
8.95	7-97	114:05	114:13	4.70
8.80	7-97	113:25	114:01	4.71
9.15	9-97*	104:29	105:05	3.35
9.55	9-97	116:12	116:20	4.83
5.70	9-97*	102:07	102:11	4.41
5.35	10-97*	101:26	101:30	4.32
6.05	10-97*	103:20	103:26	4.08
6.05	11-97	104:07	104:11	4.86
9.55	11-97	117:02	117:08	4.88
7.10	12-97*	108:11	108:19	4.80
8.60	12-97*	116:13	116:21	2.73
9.55	12-97	117:28	118:04	4.70
6.30	12-97*	105:02	105:06	3.78
6.05	1-98	105:00	105:04	4.70
8.65	2-98	114:26	115:02	4.76
8.20	3-98	113:09	113:13	4.79
5.30	3-98*	101:16	101:20	4.58
5.25	3-98	102:00	102:04	4.72
9.15	4-98	117:03	117:11	4.81
8.38	4-98*	107:30	108:02	2.95
8.15	5-98	113:21	113:25	4.76
5.25	5-98*	101:08	101:16	4.63

Rate	Mat.	Bid	Asked	Yld.
8.63	4-01*	111:01	111:05	3.89
8.70	6-01*	111:17	111:21	4.04
8.88	7-01*	113:27	113:31	3.49
7.80	12-01*	104:28	105:04	3.20
7.20	1-02*	107:26	108:02	4.50
7.50	2-02	113:11	113:19	5.45
7.90	4-02*	112:23	112:31	3.89
7.55	4-02	113:19	113:27	5.49
7.80	6-02*	111:26	112:02	4.21
7.30	7-02*	109:01	109:09	4.57
7.00	8-02*	107:06	107:14	4.85
6.95	9-02*	106:22	106:30	4.97
7.30	10-02*	109:16	109:24	4.63
6.80	10-02*	105:30	106:11	3.53
7.05	11-02	110:09	110:17	5.56
6.80	1-03	109:01	109:05	5.52
6.40	3-03*	103:27	103:31	5.39
6.63	4-03*	105:16	105:20	5.20
6.45	6-03*	104:19	104:23	5.29
6.20	7-03*	102:30	103:02	5.46
6.25	8-03*	103:05	103:09	5.47
5.45	10-03	100:00	100:02	5.44
12.35	12-13*	100:29	101:13	3.43
12.65	3-14*	102:29	103:13	4.18
0.00	7-14	24:04	24:12	6.93
10.35	12-15	148:09	148:25	6.25
8.20	3-16	122:28	123:04	6.26
8.95	2-18	132:12	132:20	6.31
8.10	8-19	121:23	121:31	6.36
0.00	10-19	17:00	17:08	6.88
9.65	8-20*	119:06	119:14	2.39

Federal Home Loan Bank

Rate	Mat.	Bid	Asked	Yld.
6.09	10-93	100:04	100:06	0.87
7.88	10-93	100:06	100:12	0.00
8.80	10-93	100:08	100:14	0.00
9.13	11-93	100:24	100:30	1.39
7.38	12-93	100:26	101:00	2.50
7.50	12-93	100:27	100:31	2.76
12.15	12-93	101:27	102:01	2.27
5.00	1-94	100:14	100:18	2.98
7.30	1-94	101:03	101:09	2.74
7.55	1-94	101:06	101:08	3.09
9.30	2-94	102:00	102:06	2.80
7.45	2-94	101:14	101:20	2.97
9.60	2-94	102:09	102:15	2.81
12.00	2-94	103:04	103:16	2.40
7.58	3-94	101:28	101:30	3.23
5.48	4-94	101:02	101:06	3.21
7.28	4-94	102:01	102:05	3.16
9.55	4-94	102:22	102:28	3.00
9.55	4-94	103:08	103:14	3.00
7.20	5-94	102:11	102:15	3.12
7.50	6-94	102:25	102:29	3.29
8.60	6-94	103:18	103:24	3.17
8.63	6-94	103:19	103:25	3.15
8.30	7-94	103:21	103:27	3.28
6.70	8-94	102:21	102:23	3.48
8.60	8-94	104:09	104:15	3.32
6.58	9-94	102:26	102:30	3.42

Rate	Mat.	Bid	Asked	Yld.
8.00	7-96	109:18	109:26	4.22
7.70	8-96	108:28	109:04	4.29
8.25	9-96	110:25	111:01	4.23
7.10	10-96	107:26	107:30	4.28
8.25	11-96	111:06	111:14	4.29
6.85	2-97	107:00	107:08	4.50
7.65	3-97	109:12	109:20	4.60
9.15	3-97	114:04	114:12	4.60
6.99	4-97	107:09	107:13	4.69
9.20	8-97	114:18	114:26	4.94
5.26	4-98*	101:08	101:12	4.33
9.25	11-98	119:04	119:12	4.92
9.30	1-99	118:04	118:12	5.27
8.60	6-99	117:07	117:15	5.03
8.45	7-99	116:21	116:29	5.04
8.60	8-99	117:24	118:00	5.02
8.38	10-99	116:16	116:24	5.11
8.60	1-00	118:27	119:03	5.02
9.50	2-04	126:29	127:13	5.92

Federal Farm Credit Bank

Rate	Mat.	Bid	Asked	Yld.
11.80	10-93	100:08	100:14	0.00
3.13	11-93	100:00	100:02	1.92
3.21	11-93	100:00	100:02	2.01
3.48	11-93	100:00	100:02	2.26
3.07	12-93	100:00	100:02	2.60
3.31	12-93	100:00	100:02	2.82
3.80	12-93	100:01	100:03	3.07
7.38	12-93	100:26	100:28	3.08
3.00	1-94	99:31	100:01	2.86
3.30	1-94	100:00	100:02	2.99
3.63	1-94	100:01	100:05	2.90
3.36	2-94	100:01	100:03	3.03
3.43	2-94	99:30	100:00	3.41
7.19	2-94	101:06	101:10	3.04
3.19	3-94	100:00	100:02	3.02
3.34	3-94	99:30	100:00	3.33
12.35	3-94	103:14	103:26	2.35
3.33	4-94	99:30	100:00	3.33
3.15	4-94	100:01	100:03	2.95
5.80	4-94	101:05	101:09	3.08
14.25	4-94	105:22	106:02	2.44
3.32	5-94	99:29	100:01	3.26
3.56	6-94	100:04	100:08	3.15
3.60	7-94	100:01	100:05	3.37
3.64	8-94	100:05	100:09	3.28
3.40	9-94	100:00	100:02	3.33
4.31	9-94	100:20	100:24	3.44
8.63	9-94	104:13	104:19	3.30
13.00	9-94	108:07	108:19	3.07
3.43	10-94	100:01	100:03	3.33
11.45	12-94	108:19	108:27	3.43
8.30	1-95	105:18	105:26	3.58
6.38	4-95	103:24	103:28	3.65
5.50	12-95	103:08	103:12	3.85
5.08	1-96	102:09	102:13	3.95
4.49	3-96*	100:12	100:16	3.16
6.65	5-96	105:27	105:31	4.16
5.75	11-96*	100:00	100:08	0.99
11.90	10-97	125:02	125:14	4.86

World Bank Bonds

Rate	Mat.	Bid	Asked	Yld.
11.63	12-94	108:24	108:28	3.82
8.63	10-95	108:18	108:22	3.99
7.25	10-96	107:28	108:04	4.30
8.75	3-97	113:02	113:10	4.47
5.88	7-97	104:07	104:15	4.57
9.88	10-97	116:08	116:16	5.22
8.38	10-99	117:02	117:10	4.99
8.13	3-01	117:04	117:06	5.28
6.75	1-02	111:01	111:05	5.08
12.38	10-02	146:04	146:12	5.72
8.25	9-16	122:30	123:06	6.32
8.63	10-16	127:15	127:19	6.33
9.25	7-17	135:01	135:09	6.35
7.63	1-23	117:19	117:27	6.28
8.88	3-26	133:15	133:23	6.39

Financing Corporation

Rate	Mat.	Bid	Asked	Yld.
10.70	10-17	151:04	151:16	6.45
9.80	11-17	140:15	140:27	6.44
9.40	2-18	135:19	135:31	6.45
9.80	4-18	140:19	140:31	6.45
10.00	5-18	143:03	143:19	6.44
10.35	8-18	147:17	147:29	6.45
9.65	11-18	139:04	139:16	6.45
9.90	12-18	142:08	142:24	6.44
9.60	12-18	138:19	139:03	6.44
9.65	3-19	139:11	139:27	6.44
9.70	4-19	139:17	139:29	6.48
9.00	6-19	131:18	132:02	6.43
8.60	9-19	127:05	127:21	6.40

Inter-Amer. Devel. Bank

Rate	Mat.	Bid	Asked	Yld.
13.25	8-94	108:01	108:05	3.32
11.63	12-94	108:11	108:15	3.91
11.38	5-95	111:11	111:15	3.70
7.50	12-96	108:16	108:24	4.51
9.50	10-97	116:20	116:28	4.82
8.50	5-01	118:24	119:00	5.40
12.25	12-08	161:25	162:01	5.97
8.50	3-11	124:25	125:01	6.14

GNMA Mtge. Issues   a-Bond

Rate	Mat.	Bid	Asked	Yld.
6.00	30Yr	99:12	99:20	6.14
6.50	30Yr	101:10	101:18	6.34
7.00	30Yr	103:10	103:18	6.40
7.50	30Yr	104:26	105:02	6.36
8.00	30Yr	105:21	105:29	6.22
8.50	30Yr	105:30	106:06	6.14
9.00	30Yr	106:24	107:00	6.23
9.50	30Yr	107:31	108:07	6.20
10.00	30Yr	110:05	110:13	5.80
10.50	30Yr	112:02	112:10	5.82
11.00	30Yr	113:20	113:28	6.46
11.50	30Yr	115:05	115:13	6.56
12.00	30Yr	116:10	116:18	6.54
12.50	30Yr	117:10	117:18	6.01

Tennessee Valley Authority

Rate	Mat.	Bid	Asked	Yld.
8.25	10-94	104:14	104:18	3.41
4.38	3-96*	100:06	100:10	3.56
8.25	11-96	110:20	110:24	4.49
6.00	1-97*	101:08	101:16	5.49
6.50	1-99*	101:18	101:26	6.09
6.25	8-99*	104:25	104:29	4.98
8.38	10-99	117:07	117:11	4.98

Figure 12.2 Quotations on U.S. Agency Issues

the yield to maturity is less on municipal bonds. The tax equivalent yield, however, is equivalent to other securities in the same risk class.

> John Latham purchases a tax-free municipal bond yielding 8.00 percent. If he pays tax at a 40 percent marginal tax rate, what is the equivalent tax yield?

Find the tax equivalent yield (TEY) by dividing the before-tax yield by one minus the marginal tax rate of the investor.

$$\text{TEY} = \frac{8.00\%}{(1 - 0.40)}$$
$$= 13.33\%$$

This means that a taxable security yielding 13.33 percent produces the same return as a tax-free municipal bond yielding 8.00 percent.

There are two types of municipal bonds: general obligation bonds and revenue bonds. General obligation bonds are backed by the taxing power of the issuing municipality. If a state issues this type of bond, it obligates itself, if necessary, to pay the interest or principal. Revenue bonds are backed by the revenue generated from specific projects. As a result, these bonds have more risk than general obligation bonds and, therefore, pay a higher return to investors. In both cases, municipal bonds involve risk.

U.S. Has Wider Probe In Treasurys

The government's investigation into possible collusion in the Treasury-securities market is much broader than acknowledged earlier, a document released by the Justice Department shows. In newly disclosed specifics of its civil settlement with Salomon Brothers Inc., the department's Antitrust Division said it is taking a hard look at whether there have been "pre-auction conversations and related conduct" among major dealers in the Treasury market "that violated the antitrust laws." In one auction, for two-year notes sold on May 22, 1991, the department alleged that Salomon and certain unnamed "co-conspirators" manipulated the market. Salomon settled civil charges with the Justice Department and the Securities and Exchange Commission without admitting or denying wrongdoing. The firm agreed to pay $290 million in fines and restitution. In 1979, Treasury Department officials investigated the bidding process after complaints of dealer collusion on a sale of 52-week Treasury bills. No charges were brought as a result of that review, although the Treasury changed some of its bidding rules.

Source: Kevin G. Salwen and John Connor, "U.S. Has Wider Probe in Treasurys," *The Wall Street Journal,* June 15, 1992. Reprinted by permission of The Wall Street Journal, © 1992 Dow Jones & Company, Inc. All Rights Reserved Worldwide.

General obligation bonds are different from revenue bonds in that they are normally issued on a serial basis. This means that the debt is paid off over the life of the issue. In contrast, revenue bonds are usually term issues, with the principal paid on or near the final maturity. Some revenue bonds, however, amortize a small portion of the principal.

Industrial development bonds are a special type of revenue bond. These bonds are sold by a municipality to build new industrial plants. To pay the interest and principal on the industrial development bonds, the plants are leased to corporations. Although this approach attracts new businesses by passing the tax advantages of municipal bonds to the corporation, federal regulations limit their use by states and their municipal authorities.

THE PRIMARY MARKET

We can classify security markets by the market in which the securities are sold, either the primary market or the secondary market. The **primary market** is the market for the issuance of new securities. This includes the sale of bonds, preferred stock, and common stock. In this market, the issuer receives cash, an entry of assets on its balance sheet, and the investor acquires a new security. The secondary market, to be discussed later in this chapter, is the market for existing securities. This market includes the New York Stock Exchange, the American Stock Exchange, regional exchanges, foreign exchanges, and the over-the-counter market. This section focuses on the primary market and the role of investment banking in that market.

Primary Market

One of the major participants which makes the primary markets work is the **investment banker.** These bankers, as distinct from the local banker, serve as financial middlemen in the process of raising long-term funds for businesses and government. Investment bankers can provide any or all of the following services for their customers: (1) Advisement of the client, (2) Origination of the issue, (3) Underwriting of the issue, and (4) Distribution of the securities. Each of these areas requires further explanation.

Investment Banker

Advisement

Advisement of the client is the consulting function of investment banking. Some companies that wish to issue securities may engage an investment banker for this purpose only and may not use an investment banker for the other functions. Other companies, for a variety of reasons, have the necessary expertise to make their own financial decisions and do not require outside advice.

Advisement

Advisory services, when used, are normally greater in scope than the selling of a particular issue. The investment banker gives advice on long-term financial matters involving types of securities, the quantity of distribution, and the timing of sale. Advisory services can be as extensive as counsel on mergers and acquisition, leverage buyouts, refinancing, long-term planning, corporate restructuring, and foreign financial connections. Members of investment banking firms often serve on the board of directors of client companies.

Origination

Origination

The **origination** of the issue begins with preliminary discussions as to the amount of new capital to be raised. The timing of the offering, the type of securities to be issued, the characteristics of the issue, and the price of the security are usually integral aspects of these discussions. During this process, the investment banker gets to know the issuing company to make sure that this is the type of company it wishes to represent. This is important in protecting the reputation of the investment banking firm and later in registering the issue.

The Securities and Exchange Commission (SEC) requires formal disclosure of the financial condition and future plans of the issuing company. According to the Securities Act of 1933, new interstate securities must be registered with the

Registration Statement

SEC. This is done in the form of a **registration statement.** The SEC also requires that the documents are not misleading or incomplete. These disclosure requirements do not imply any substantive safeguard for the investor, only a procedural safeguard. Larger corporations sometimes bypass SEC regulations by issuing debt through foreign subsidiaries.

Prospectus

Included with the registration statement is a **prospectus,** the purpose of which is to provide investors with enough information to make an informed buying decision. This document provides the names of the principal officers and directors in the company, including their stock options, salaries, and shareholdings. The prospectus also gives the purpose and use of the funds that result from the sale of the securities.

A preliminary prospectus is usually issued to potential buyers before the offering date. Issuance of a preliminary prospectus requires filing but not approval of the registration statement. It is called a *red herring* due to the color of the words *preliminary prospectus* on the cover. Unlike the prospectus, the preliminary prospectus does not state the price of the security or the date of the offering. The offering price is determined on the day of the offering.

The SEC permits large corporations, under Rule 415, to file a master registration statement covering a period of up to two years. The corporation can then update this statement with a short-form statement prior to offering new securities. This procedure is called shelf registration. The purpose of this is to provide greater flexibility in the sizing and timing of issues and gives large companies somewhat of an advantage.

The Securities and Exchange Commission allows advertising of issues in newspapers and journals. The advertisement shown in Figure 12.3, called a

*This announcement is neither an offer to sell nor a solicitation of an offer to buy these securities.
The offer is made only by the Prospectus.*

September 29, 1993

1,480,000 Shares

SOUTHWEST SECURITIES GROUP, INC.

Common Stock

Price $10.50 Per Share

*Copies of the Prospectus may be obtained in any State in which this announcement is circulated only
from such of the undersigned as may legally offer these securities in such State.*

Raymond James & Associates, Inc.

Southwest Securities, Inc.

D. A. Davidson & Co.
INCORPORATED

Robert W. Baird & Co. INCORPORATED	**J. C. Bradford & Co.**	**First of Michigan Corporation**
Gruntal & Co., Incorporated	**Interstate/Johnson Lane** CORPORATION	**Edward D. Jones & Co.**
Legg Mason Wood Walker INCORPORATED	**McDonald & Company** SECURITIES, INC.	**Morgan Keegan & Company, Inc.**
Piper Jaffray Inc.		**The Principal/Eppler, Guerin & Turner, Inc.**
Rauscher Pierce Refsnes, Inc.		**Stephens Inc.**
Anderson & Strudwick INCORPORATED	**Barre & Co., Inc.**	**Calton & Associates, Inc.**
Empire Securities Inc. of Washington	**Ernst & Co.**	**Fechtor, Detwiler & Co., Inc.**
First Southwest Company	**Fox & Company**	**John G. Kinnard and Company** INCORPORATED
Scott & Stringfellow, Inc.		**William K. Woodruff & Company** INCORPORATED

Source: The Wall Street Journal, October 5, 1993.

Figure 12.3   The Tombstone Advertisement

tombstone advertisement, gives some brief facts about the issue. It includes the company offering the securities, the number of securities to be issued, and the syndicate members (to be discussed in the next section). The higher the listing of an underwriter in the tombstone, the greater the role of that underwriter in the offering. Since the tombstone advertisement does not give complete information, investors must receive a copy of the final prospectus before actually purchasing securities.

Underwriting

Underwriting

Underwriting Syndicate

The **underwriting** of the issue initially involves formation of the **underwriting syndicate**. This syndicate is composed of an originating house, or manager, and a group of investment bankers. The syndicate may include as few as two or as many as 200 members. These underwriters agree to purchase the issue by signing the underwriting contract. In this document, each investment banker promises to pay for its portion of the issue on a specified date. The syndicate members hope for a quick resale, but in signing the contract, they actually assume the risk of loss or gain.

The underwriter and the issuer normally strike a deal through direct negotiation. If the underwriter purchases the full amount of the issue at an agreed-upon price, this is a firm commitment. With this arrangement, the underwriter assumes all of the market risk—they guarantee the price.

In certain situations, particularly with regulated industries, competitive bidding is used in the underwriting of the issue. For example, the Federal Power Commission mandates competitive bidding on issues offered by public utility holding companies and their subsidiaries. This bidding approach requires specification of all details of the issue except price. The apparent advantage of competitive bidding is that the issuer receives the issue at the lowest cost. The obvious disadvantage is that the investment banker is forced to bid a firm price, exposing it to a high amount of risk.

In the underwriting process, the underwriter may sign a standby agreement, usually for 30 days, agreeing to help sell the security. After that time, the underwriter buys unsold securities at a given price. Some investment houses handle the more speculative issues on a best efforts basis and do not underwrite them. This means that the investment banker provides no guarantees that the entire issue will be sold. Only a small percentage of issues are managed in this manner. Normally, with this arrangement, the amount per share to the issuer is lower, since these issues are difficult to sell at a given price.

The underwriting spread is the difference between the price paid to the issuer and the price at which it is sold to the investing public. For example, if the price to the public is $26.50 and the price to the issuer is $25.00, the spread is

$1.50. This amount represents compensation for participation in the distribution process. The underwriting spread of $1.50 is 5.66 percent of the price to the public. It is payment for originating and distributing the issue and payment for assuming risk. Generally speaking, the higher the value of an issue, the lower the percentage spread. More risky securities demand higher spreads. In setting the price to the public, a discount from the market price must be offered in order to attract the larger number of buyers necessary to sell the issue.

A public offering may be avoided by selling the issue directly to the current shareholders, called a rights offering, or by negotiating a private placement with insurance companies, pension funds, or even possibly some wealthy individuals. A rights offering is mandatory when shareholders have a preemptive right—the right to purchase new common stock issues in proportion to current ownership. Rights offerings are discussed in greater detail in the next chapter.

A private placement of a security involving 25 or fewer investors does not require registration with the SEC. This avoids the high cost of preparing the registration statement. There is a cost of finding buyers for the issue (the finder's fee), but this cost is usually less than the underwriting spread. Another advantage of private placement is the reduction in delays and legal complications. This allows more flexible contract provisions and greater speed than with the public placement of securities. The primary disadvantage of private placement is that the security is less marketable in the future.

Distribution

The **distribution** of the securities requires the participation of a number of parties. The lead investment banker is the investment banker with the initial responsibility for issuing the security. The underwriting syndicate members are other investment bankers that have agreed to sell the newly issued security. The dealers group is a collection of investment houses that participate by selling only a small portion of the total issue. In this process, the investing public has contact only with the brokers. Some investment bankers are vertically integrated in that they act as underwriter, dealer, and broker. Figure 12.4 shows the structure of the distribution network.

The actual purchase of the securities cannot take place until the *opening of the books*. This occurs when market conditions are favorable and after legal requirements are met. At this point, the underwriter may stabilize the offering by repurchasing the securities. This is a legal form of security price manipulation. This period of stabilization may last from a couple of days to as long as a month. Investment bankers insist that this control is necessary in order to insure an orderly market.

Distribution

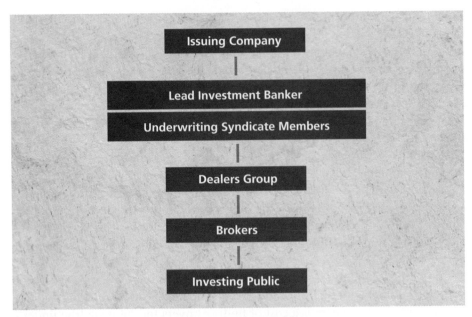

Figure 12.4 The Distribution Process in Investment Banking

THE SECONDARY MARKET

Secondary Market

The **secondary market** is the market for the purchase and sale of existing securities. This includes the organized exchanges and the over-the-counter (OTC) market. The organized exchanges consists of the New York Stock Exchange (NYSE), the American Stock Exchange (AMEX), smaller regional exchanges, and foreign exchanges. The over-the-counter market is an electronically connected network of dealers who trade stocks not listed on the organized exchanges.

The stock of large publicly owned corporations is traded in the secondary markets. In contrast, the stock of some small corporations is not actively traded. **Closely Held Corporations** These privately owned companies are known as **closely held corporations.** Typically, these companies are owned by a few shareholders who play an active role in management.

Secondary markets provide two important functions. First, they give liquidity to the purchasers of securities. If no secondary market were available, investors would hesitate to buy in the primary market. Second, they determine the market price of the security. This is important in establishing the price of a new issue of outstanding securities.

The New York Stock Exchange

The **New York Stock Exchange (NYSE)** is the largest and most important stock exchange in the United States, dominating the American Stock Exchange and the regional exchanges such as the Midwest Stock Exchange and the Pacific Stock Exchange. It accounts for about 80 percent of the volume on the organized exchanges. The NYSE was founded in 1792, with the organizational meeting taking place on Wall Street. The name *New York Stock and Exchange Board* was chosen in 1817. In 1863, the name was changed to the *New York Stock Exchange.* Today, securities of more than 1,500 companies are traded on the NYSE. **New York Stock Exchange**

A stock that is traded on the NYSE is a listed security. In order for a security to be listed, the company must show that it meets certain standards and it will continue to meet those standards. The standards relate to size, ownership distribution, and the record of earnings. A company may be delisted if trading declines significantly. Securities may also be involved in a trading halt, which is a temporary suspension from trading, if circumstances warrant that action. Since the rules for listing on the NYSE are quite stringent, the turnover of securities is less than with other exchanges.

The number of members of the NYSE has been fixed at 1,366 since 1933. A new membership, therefore, requires that the applicant buy a *seat* from an existing member. These seats have sold for as little as $17,000 in 1942 to as much as several hundred thousand dollars in recent years. Even then, the prospective member must be approved by the board of directors of the exchange. A company may become a member of the NYSE if at least one partner or stockholding employee is an exchange member. Approval of members and companies is possible if and only if strict standards of conduct and financial responsibility are met.

Members of the New York Stock Exchange assume particular roles as follows.

- **Commission brokers** act as agents for brokerage firms and execute orders on the floor of the exchange. For this service, the clients of the firm pay brokerage commissions. A firm often has more than one broker executing orders at different posts on the floor. **Commission Brokers**
- **Floor traders** buy and sell for their own accounts and do not handle public orders. Floor traders make money by speculating on trading imbalances. They take advantage of temporary low prices when the number of sell orders is high, and they take advantage of temporary high prices when the number of buy orders is high. While this action may reduce price volatility, the speculative side of floor trading has drawn criticism. This has led to restrictions on floor traders and, as a result, a reduction in their number. **Floor Traders**

- **Floor brokers** assist commission brokers when there are too many orders to handle. The floor broker receives part of the commission paid to the commission broker.
- **Specialists** perform two functions. First, they execute orders for other brokers, receiving part of the customer commission. This often happens when a limit order cannot be executed immediately. Second, they act as dealers, buying and selling stocks in which they specialize, accepting the risk of price changes. In this process, specialists give precedence to orders that are not their own.

The procedure for a normal market order begins when an investor asks the broker for the price of a particular stock. The broker's quotation machine provides the bid and asked prices, along with the number of shares for which these prices are valid. If the investor wishes to buy, he or she instructs the broker to buy a stated number of shares at the asked price. The broker then sends the order to the New York headquarters of the brokerage firm. The order is then sent to the floor of the exchange where the commission broker deals with specialists to execute the sale.

Security transactions on the NYSE are shown on consolidated tape. Other exchanges, such as the American Stock Exchange, the Pacific Coast Stock Exchange, and the Midwest Stock Exchange, participate in the consolidated tape listings. More than 80 percent of tape volume is the result of NYSE transactions.

Stock orders are normally placed in round lots, units of 100 shares or multiples of 100 shares. A fraction of a round lot is called an odd lot. The sale of lots of stock at 10,000 or more shares is called a block trade. The commission on odd lot sales is higher as a percentage of the total transaction than with round lots since an odd-lot broker is involved. At the other end of the scale, the commission for a block trade is much less. This accounts for the high volume of stock sales through block trades, almost 50 percent in some years.

Requests to buy securities reflect the bid price, and requests to sell reflect the asked price. A market order is a request to buy or sell a security at the current bid or asked price. A limit order is a request to buy or sell a security at a price at least as advantageous as the stated price. For example, a limit order to buy Allied Corporation at $50 means that the purchase must take place at $50 or less. Similarly, a limit order to sell the same company for $50 means that the sale must take place at $50 or more. The disadvantage of limit orders is that market orders are executed first. Therefore, it is possible for a limit order not to be executed, even though many transactions occur at that price.

A stop order, or a stop-loss order, is kept in the specialist's book—a record that includes the specialist's inventory of securities as well as limit and stop orders. This type of order specifies at what price it becomes a market order. For example, you purchase a stock at $40, and the price rises to $50. To protect yourself against a large drop in price, you place a stop order at $47. If the price drops to $47, the stop order becomes a market order. If the price drops quite rapidly, the order may be executed at less than $47, even with the stop order.

The American Stock Exchange

The **American Stock Exchange (AMEX)**, also known as the *Little Big Board*, began operations in 1850 with a group trading issues at the corner of Wall and Hanover Streets in New York. At that time it was referred to as the Outdoor Curb Market, and this is why today it is called *The Curb*. In 1910 the name was changed to the New York Curb Market Association, and in 1953 the name was changed again to the American Stock Exchange.

American Stock Exchange

The American Stock Exchange is similar in operation to the NYSE, although the AMEX has characteristics that differentiate it from the NYSE. First, most of its listed firms are smaller and newer since listing requirements are less stringent. Second, the AMEX has a large number of foreign securities, encompassing about 25 percent of total market value. Third, the AMEX includes numerous warrants and options to buy stock[2]. Today, no stocks are simultaneously listed on the NYSE and AMEX.

Regional Exchanges

The **regional exchanges** list popular NYSE and AMEX securities as well as securities of regional interest. The number of securities traded at each of these exchanges ranges from 100 to 900. The largest regional exchanges are the Pacific Coast Stock Exchange (PCSE), located in San Francisco and Los Angeles, and the Midwest Stock Exchange (MSE), located in Chicago.

Regional Exchanges

Dual listing of stocks on national and regional exchanges makes for a more price competitive situation for the investor. Brokers at the large and the small exchanges follow the prices and volume at the other exchange, allowing for more aggressive pricing. The importance of lower commissions on transactions at regional exchanges has diminished in recent years with the abandonment of a fixed rate schedule by the national exchanges.

The Over-the-Counter Market

The **over-the-counter market (OTC)** is a network of securities dealers linked by computer terminals, telephones, and teletypes. The name of this market refers to the time in history when banks literally sold stocks and bonds *over-the-counter*. Today, the *National Association of Security Dealers Automated Quotations*

Over-the-Counter Market

---

[2] These terms are discussed in Chapter 15.

(NASDAQ) system instantly provides the terms offered by security dealers. These dealers own the securities they trade, in contrast to brokers who act as agents for investors.

Only members of the *National Association of Security Dealers* (NASD) are allowed to trade on the OTC market. The individual over-the-counter investor, therefore, requires a broker and a brokerage account. The actual OTC transaction involves negotiation between a broker and a dealer. In the process, the investor is charged a commission. Figure 12.5 is an example of quotations from *The Wall Street Journal*.

Foreign Exchanges

Throughout the world there are national securities exchanges that compete with the New York Stock Exchange and the American Stock Exchange. The most important exchanges outside the United States are the Tokyo Stock Exchange (TSE) and the London Stock Exchange (LSE).

The Tokyo Stock Exchange (TSE) is the largest exchange in Japan, enjoying a similar position to the NYSE in the United States. Although there are 8 securities exchanges in the country, the TSE is responsible for more than 80 percent of total trading in Japan in terms of the market value of its listed securities. In 1987, the Tokyo Stock Exchange became the largest exchange in the world.

The TSE lists domestic and foreign stocks. The most active domestic stocks are bought and sold on the trading floor, but the less active stocks are traded by computer. The number of foreign stocks on the TSE has increased sharply in recent years with the decline of the U.S. dollar relative to the yen.

The London Stock Exchange (LSE), known as *The Stock Exchange*, is the largest exchange in the United Kingdom. Listed and unlisted securities are traded on this exchange. Stocks listed on the LSE are divided into Alpha, Beta, and Gamma groupings, from most actively traded to least actively traded. Firm bid/ask quotations of the most actively traded stocks must be available to members of the LSE.

Regulation of Security Markets

The first major legislation affecting the securities industry was the Glass-Steagall Act, the Banking Act of 1933. This act prohibited commercial banks from underwriting security offerings. This separation of investment banking and commercial banking is not practiced in countries outside the United States. For example, in Japan the leading investment bankers are the commercial banks.

NASDAQ NATIONAL MARKET ISSUES

Quotations as of 4 p.m. Eastern Time
Friday, October 8, 1993

-A-A-A-

	52 Weeks Hi	52 Weeks Lo	Stock	Sym	Div	Yld %	PE	Vol 100s	Hi	Lo	Close	Net Chg
s	24 1/2	15	A&W Brands	SODA	.32	1.3	21	286	24 1/2	24 3/8	24 1/2	+ 1/8
s	13 1/4	5 5/8	ABS Ind	ABSI	.20	1.7	19	358	12	11 3/8	11 3/4	+ 1/2
n	21 1/2	15	ABT BldgPdt	ABTC		...	...	67	20 1/4	20	20 1/4	...
s	21	10 1/8	ACC	ACCC	.12	.6	66	382	19 1/4	18 3/4	19	...
n	46 3/4	10 3/4	ACX Tch	ACXT		...	...	179	36	35	35 3/4	+ 1/4
s	41	16 1/4	ADC Tel	ADCT		...	35	363	38 3/4	38	38 3/4	...
	17 1/4	4 7/8	ADESA	SOLD		...	26	56	15 1/4	14 3/4	15	+ 1/4
	7 1/2	5	AEL Ind A	AELNA		...	dd	155	6 7/8	6 3/4	6 7/8	− 1/8
	19 1/2	9 3/4	AEP Ind	AEPI	.05e	.3	15	108	15 3/4	15 1/2	15 3/4	...
n	9 1/4	7	AER EngyRes	AERN		...	...	129	9 1/4	8 1/2	9 1/4	...
▲	33 1/4	21	AES Cp	AESC	1.00f	3.0	20	2083	33 3/8	32 1/2	32 7/8	− 1/8
	26	5	AGCO Cp	AGCO	.04	.2	28	306	25 1/2	24 3/4	25 1/2	+ 5/8
n	38	24 1/2	AGCO pf		.46p	1.2	...	42	37 3/4	37	37 5/8	− 1/8
	18	12	AgSvcAm	AGSV		...	14	9	16 3/4	16 3/4	16 3/4	+ 3/4
n	25 1/4	20 1/8	AMCOR Ltd	AMCRY	.51e	2.1	...	5gg				...
n	16 1/4	15 1/2	APS Hldg	APSI		...	...	3910	15 5/8	15 1/2	15 5/8	+ 1/8
n	12 3/4	11 3/4	A PealnPod	APOD		...	...	64	12 1/4	11 3/4	11 7/8	+ 1/8
n	17 3/4	14	A+ Comm	ACOM		...	...	930	16 1/2	16	16 1/2	...
	6	1 7/8	ARI Netwk	ARIS		...	dd	58	4 5/8	4 3/8	4 1/2	+ 1/8
	28 1/8	9 1/2	ASK Grp	ASKI		...	dd	4687	14 1/4	13 1/8	13 5/8	− 1/2
	24 1/4	12 3/4	AST Rsrch	ASTA		...	dd	2200	17 1/4	16 3/4	17 1/8	+ 1/8
	9	5 1/4	ATSMed	ATSI		...	dd	300	6 1/8	5 7/8	6 1/8	...
	6 1/8	2 5/8	AW Cptr A	AWCSA		...	9	103	3 3/4	3 3/8	3 3/4	+ 1/8
s	13 1/8	5 5/8	AamesFnl	AAMS	.30	3.4	8	1352	9 1/4	8 1/2	8 7/8	− 1/8
s	14	7 3/8	AaronRents	ARONA	.06	.5	13	77	13	11 7/8	11 7/8	−1 1/8
	8	3 3/4	Abaxis	ABAX		...	...	337	7 3/4	7	7	− 1/2
	24 3/4	11	AbbeyHlthcr	ABBY		...	17	1499	23	22 1/8	22 1/2	+ 3/4
	12	6 1/4	AbingtnSav	ABBK		...	14	34	11	10 1/2	11	− 1/2
	15 1/2	7	Abiomed	ABMD		...	dd	551	10 1/4	8 3/4	9 1/4	− 1/4
	6 1/2	3 3/4	AbramsInd	ABRI	.12f	2.0	8	1	6	6	6	− 7/16
n	16 1/2	4 1/2	AbsolutEntn	ABSO		...	...	824	7 3/4	6 5/8	7 5/8	+ 7/8
	4 3/4	2 3/4	AccelInt	ACLE		...	dd	3	3 1/8	3 1/8	3 1/8	− 3/8
	12 1/8	3 1/4	AccessHlth	ACCS		...	35	407	8 1/8	7 5/8	7 3/4	− 1/4
s	31 3/4	7 9/16	AcclmEntn	AKLM		...	44	36573	30 7/8	28	28 1/4	−3 1/8
n	17 1/2	6 3/4	AceCashExp	AACE		...	29	49	11	10 3/4	11	...
s	17 1/2	12 5/8	Aceto	ACET	.28	2.2	36	36	13	12 3/4	12 3/4	...
	20 3/4	11	AcmeMetals	ACME		...	cc	2	15	15	15	...
n	20 1/2	10 1/2	Actel	ACTL		...	...	877	14 1/2	14	14 1/2	+ 3/8
n	7	4 1/2	ActionPerf	ACTN		...	...	78	4 13/16	4 11/16	4 13/16	− 1/16
n	1 3/4	9/16	ActionPerf wt			...	...	10	15/16	15/16	15/16	− 1/16
s	23 1/2	11 3/4	Acxiom	ACXM		...	39	59	23 1/2	22 3/4	23 1/2	+ 1/2
s	16 7/8	9 1/4	AdacLabs	ADAC	.48	3.8	12	532	13 1/4	12 1/2	12 3/4	...
	7 1/2	3 1/4	Adage	ADGE		...	37	22	7 1/8	6 5/8	6 5/8	− 1/2
	33 1/4	18 1/2	Adaptec	ADPT		...	15	5722	30	29 1/4	30	+ 1/2
	18 1/4	12 1/4	AddintnRes	ADDR		...	cc	380	17	16 1/2	17	+ 1/2
	22	11 1/2	AdelphiaComm	ADLAC		...	dd	342	19 1/4	18	18 1/2	+ 7/8
	26 1/2	15	AdiaSvcs	ADIA	.16	.7	18	8	24	23 3/4	23 3/4	...
s	37	12 5/8	AdobeSys	ADBE	.20	1.0	18	5859	19 3/4	18 1/2	19 1/4	− 1/4
	8 1/2	1 1/4	AdvaCare	AVCR		...	dd	411	2 3/8	2 1/8	2 3/8	+ 1/8
	15	6	AdvCircuit	ADVC		...	9	777	10 7/8	10 1/4	10 1/2	− 3/8
	20 1/8	9 5/8	AdvRoss	AROS		...	22	30	18 1/2	18 1/2	18 1/2	− 1/2
	5 7/8	1 15/16	AdvIntrvnt	LAIS		...	dd	2679	3 1/4	3	3 1/16	− 1/8
	5 9/16	2 1/2	AdvLogicRsrch	AALR		...	dd	360	3 1/2	3 1/8	3 5/32	− 3/32
	9 3/4	4 7/8	AdvMktg	ADMS		...	12	310	6 3/4	6 1/2	6 3/4	...
	10 1/8	5 1/8	AdvPolymer	APOS		...	dd	1246	5 5/8	5 3/8	5 5/8	...
n	8 1/4	4 1/4	AppldSignal	APSG		...	...	11	5 3/4	5 1/4	5 1/4	...
	5 3/8	2 1/8	ArabShld	ARSD		...	...	507	2 5/8	2 1/2	2 1/2	...
n	25 3/4	22 3/4	Aramed	ARAM		...	...	110	25	25	25	...
	23 3/4	15 1/2	ArborDrug	ARBR	.20	1.1	17	171	18 1/4	17 3/4	17 3/4	− 1/2
n	15 1/4	12 3/4	ArborHlth	AHCC		...	...	45	15 1/4	15	15	+ 1/4
	19 1/2	8 3/4	ArborNtl	ARBH		...	14	52	19 1/2	19	19 1/4	+ 1/8
	18 3/4	7	ArchComm	APGR		...	dd	916	17 3/4	17 1/4	17 1/4	− 3/8
	5 11/16	3 1/2	ArchPete	ARCH		...	25	392	4 1/2	4 1/4	4 1/2	...
s	27	11 1/8	Arctco	ACAT	.21	.8	25	349	26	25	25 1/4	− 1/2
n	16 3/8	9 5/8	Arethusa	ARTHF		...	...	712	14 5/8	14 1/8	14 1/2	− 1/8
s	27	13 1/2	ArgentBk	ARGT	.48	1.9	10	4	25	23	25	+2
	35 1/2	27	ArgonautGp	AGII	1.00	3.2	10	384	32 3/4	31	31	−1 1/4
n	36 3/4	15 1/4	ArgosyGaming	ARGY		...	...	796	27 3/4	26 1/2	27 1/4	+ 3/4
	10 3/4	3 1/4	ArgusPharm	ARGS		...	...	241	5 3/8	5 1/4	5 1/4	...
	29/32	1/16	AristotleCp	ARTL	.45j	...	dd	52	11/16	11/16	11/16	− 3/32
	7	3 1/2	Aritech	ARIT		...	10	288	5 1/4	4 15/16	4 15/16	
	17 1/8	8 1/8	ArkansBest	ABFS	.04	.3	16	143	11 1/2	11 1/8	11 1/2	+ 3/8
n	52 5/8	36 1/2	ArkansBest pfA		2.88	6.5	...	23	44	43 7/8	44	...
	21	12 3/4	ArmorAll	ARMR	.64	3.2	21	202	20	19 1/4	20	+ 1/4
	40 1/2	26 3/4	ArnoldInd	AIND	.68	1.7	20	27	39 7/8	39 1/4	39 7/8	...
	13 3/4	6 5/8	ArrowFnl	AROW	.05e	.4	15	13	13 3/4	13	13 3/4	...
	29 1/2	17 1/2	ArrowInt	ARRO	.10	.4	22	109	23 1/8	23	23	− 3/4
n	7	5	ArrowTransp	ARRW		...	...	37	7	6 1/2	7	+ 3/8
	13 1/2	5 3/4	ArtsWayMfg	ARTW		...	24	1	11 1/4	11 1/4	11 1/4	...
	19 3/4	5 3/4	Artisoft	ASFT		...	17	595	9 1/4	8 7/8	8 7/8	− 3/8
	11 1/2	3 7/8	ArtGreetg	ARTG	.05e	1.1	15	52	4 3/4	4 1/4	4 3/4	+ 1/8
n	14 1/2	9 1/2	Aseco	ASEC		...	...	101	10 3/4	10 5/8	10 3/4	+ 1/4
	35 3/4	9	AspectTel	ASPT		...	53	944	34 3/4	33 1/4	34 5/8	+1 3/8
	18 1/4	8 1/4	AspenBcsh	ASBK	.20	1.1	18	28	18 1/4	17 3/4	17 7/8	+ 1/8
s	40	27 1/4	AssocBcp	ASBC	1.00b	2.6	14	1	37 3/4	37 3/4	37 3/4	...
	27 1/2	13	AssocComm B	ACCMB		...	...	344	26 3/4	26	26	−1 1/2
	27 1/2	13	AssocComm A	ACCMA		...	cc	32	27 1/2	27	27 1/4	− 1/4
s	14 7/8	5	AstecInd	ASTE		...	12	127	13 7/8	13 1/4	13 1/4	− 5/8
	17	10	AstroMed	ALOT	.12	1.1	17	8	11 1/8	11	11	− 5/8
	3	2	Astronic	ATRO		...	8	4	2 3/8	2 3/8	2 3/8	− 1/4
	5 3/8	3 7/8	Astrosys	ASTR		...	24	14	4 1/8	4 1/8	4 1/8	− 5/32
n	12 1/2	10	AsystTech	ASYT		...	...	481	10 1/2	10	10	− 1/2
n▲	14 5/8	13 5/8	AtchisonCast	ACCX		...	...	3179	15 1/4	14 1/2	14 7/8	+ 5/8
	9 3/4	6 1/2	AthenaNeuro	ATHN		...	...	594	9 1/2	8 3/4	8 3/4	− 1/4
	7 3/4	5	AtheyPdts	ATPC		...	dd	30	7 1/4	7 1/4	7 1/4	...
	10 1/4	7 1/2	AtkinsnGuy	ATKN		...	38	126	9 3/4	9	9 3/8	− 1/8
	2 3/4	5/8	AtlanAm	AAME		...	11	16	2	1 7/8	1 7/8	...
n	17	10	AtlCoast	ACAI		...	...	116	12 7/8	12 1/4	12 1/4	− 5/8
	7 1/4	4 1/4	AtlGulf	AGLF		...	dd	331	7	6 3/4	7	+ 3/16
s	39	14 3/4	AtlanSEAir	ASAI	.28	1.0	25	1575	29 3/4	29	29	− 3/4
	25 3/4	9 3/4	AtlTeleNtwk	ATNI	.40	3.1	16	149	13	12 1/2	13	+ 1/2
	38 5/8	11 1/2	Atmel	ATML		...	28	5985	35 1/2	33 3/4	35	− 1/8
	10 1/2	5 3/4	AtrixLabs	ATRX		...	...	174	6 1/2	6	6 1/2	− 1/4
	12	8 1/2	AtwoodOcn	ATWD		...	dd	1	11 1/2	11 1/2	11 1/2	− 1/2
	29	17 1/2	AuBonPain A	ABPCA		...	39	1619	18 3/4	18	18 1/2	+ 1/8
	6 7/8	2 15/16	AuraSystems	AURA		...	dd	2082	6 5/8	6 1/8	6 7/16	+ 1/4
n▼	15 1/2	9 1/2	AuspexSys	ASPX		...	...	2827	10	9	9	− 3/4
	16 1/2	9 1/4	Autocam	ACAM	.52t	3.4	17	8	16 1/4	15 1/2	15 1/2	−1
	8 3/4	6 7/8	AutoclvEngr	ACLV	.24	2.8	77	7	8 1/2	8 1/2	8 1/2	+ 1/8
	56 3/4	38 3/4	Autodesk	ACAD	.48	1.1	20	3180	44 3/4	44	44 1/8	− 3/8
	11 3/4	4 1/2	AutoFinGp	AUFN		...	42	76	11 1/4	10 3/4	11	+ 1/4
n	15	4 3/4	AutoImmune	AIMM		...	...	1606	8	7	7 3/4	+ 1/2
	5	3 1/4	AutoInfo	AUTO		...	14	110	3 7/8	3 3/4	3 7/8	− 1/8
	30 3/4	13	AutoIndus A	AIHI		...	27	1164	28 1/2	28	28	− 1/2
s	50	7 1/8	Autotote A	TOTE		...	66	1051	47	45 1/2	46	−1
	17 1/2	11 3/4	AutotrolCp	AUTR	.59t	4.0	dd	44	14 3/4	14 5/8	14 5/8	− 1/4

Source: The Wall Street Journal, October 11, 1993. Reprinted by permission of The Wall Street Journal,

Figure 12.5 Over-the-Counter Price Quotations

In recent years, the restrictions of the Banking Act of 1933 have been reduced with the passage of Depository Institutions Deregulation and Monetary Control Act of 1980 and the Depository Institution Act of 1982. Now, banks may offer security brokerage services and are attempting to obtain more investment banking powers.

The Securities Act of 1933 was a reaction to the abuses surrounding the securities markets in the 1920s and the subsequent market crash of 1929. During this period, there were fraudulent trading practices, excessive speculation with borrowed funds, and insider trading. This act was the first major legislation directed at the securities industry. It is essentially a *truth in securities* law, in that it requires registration of new issues and disclosure of relevant information through a prospectus. It also prohibits misrepresentation and fraud in security sales.

The Securities Exchange Act of 1934 extended federal regulation to the organized exchanges of the secondary market. This act created the Securities Exchange Commission (SEC) and required that exchanges, brokers, and dealers be registered. It also prohibited corporate insiders from making speculative profits based on inside information. The Securities Exchange Act of 1934 established margin requirements to determine the amount of credit available to purchasers of securities.

The Securities Exchange Commission administers other federal laws. The Public Utility Holding Company Act of 1935 brought public utilities, such as gas and electric companies, under the jurisdiction of the SEC. This allowed the SEC to control the accounting practices and to determine the types of securities the utilities can issue.

The Bankruptcy Act of 1938 required the SEC to advise the bankruptcy court when there is a high degree of public interest involving the securities of the company. The Maloney Act of 1938 brought the over-the-counter markets under the control of the SEC. This act also provides for self-regulation of the industry by the National Association of Security Dealers (NASD).

The Trust Indenture Act of 1939 gave the SEC the power to make sure that bond trustees are independent of the bond issuer. This allowed the trustee to enforce the terms of the indenture. The Investment Company Act of 1940 extended registration and disclosure requirements to investment companies. The purpose was to prevent the management manipulation and speculative abuses of the 1920s.

The Investment Advisors Act of 1940 brought investment advisors under the regulation of the SEC. This act does not require that the investment advisor have any special knowledge or ability. The Securities Investor Protection Act of 1970 created the Securities Investor Protection Corporation (SIPC). This government corporation acts as an insurance company to pay for losses investors would incur if their brokers became insolvent.

The Securities Act Amendments of 1975 required the Securities Exchange Commission to move toward the development of a single nationwide securities market. This act prohibits fixed commission rates but permits the NYSE to require its members to trade listed securities on the NYSE. It also mandates that the SEC establish minimum capital requirements for brokers.

SUMMARY

This chapter focuses on the following learning objectives:

1. Explaining the use of capital markets by corporations to issue debt securities, preferred stock, and common stock.

   Corporate securities are issued in two basic forms: debt and equity. Bonds represent the debt of the corporation while common stock and preferred stock represent equity. Preferred stock combines both debt and common stock characteristics. Common stock ownership represents ownership of the company.

2. Explaining the use of capital markets by governments to issue debt instruments.

   The Treasury Department issues securities to finance the federal government. Government agencies and government-sponsored enterprises raise funds to finance operations by selling notes and bonds. States, counties, cities, and other political units issue municipal bonds.

3. Detailing the advisement, origination, underwriting, and distribution functions in the issuance of new securities.

   One of the major participants that makes the primary markets work is the investment banker. These bankers serve as financial middlemen in the process of raising long-term funds for businesses and government. Investment bankers can provide advisement, origination, underwriting, and distribution services for their customers.

4. Describing the purchase and sale of existing securities in the organized exchanges and in the over-the-counter market.

   The secondary market is the market for the purchase and sale of existing securities. This includes the organized exchanges and the over-the-counter market. The organized exchanges consist of the New York Stock Exchange, the American Stock Exchange, smaller regional exchanges, and foreign exchanges. The over-the-counter market is an electronically connected network of dealers who trade stocks not listed on the organized exchanges.

5. Describing the regulation of securities markets.

   The first major legislation affecting the securities industry was the Glass-Steagall Act, the Banking Act of 1933. The Securities Act of 1933 was a reaction to the abuses surrounding the securities markets in the 1920s and the subsequent market crash of 1929. The Securities Exchange Act of 1934 extended federal regulation to the organized exchanges of the secondary market. The Securities Exchange Commission administers other federal laws.

KEY TERMS

Advisement, 345
American Stock Exchange, 353
Capital market, 339
Closely held corporation, 350
Commission broker, 351
Distribution, 349
Floor broker, 352

Floor trader, 351
Investment banker, 345
Money market, 339
New York Stock Exchange, 351
Origination, 346
Over-the-counter market, 353
Primary market, 345
Prospectus, 346

Regional exchanges, 353
Registration statement, 346
Secondary market, 350
Specialist, 352
Treasury bond, 340
Treasury note, 340
Underwriting, 348
Underwriting syndicate, 348

QUESTIONS

12.1 Explain money markets and list the instruments most commonly traded in these markets.

12.2 Explain capital markets and specify what groups are involved in these markets.

12.3 Discuss Treasury notes and Treasury bonds.

12.4 Explain how government agencies and government-sponsored enterprises raise funds to finance operations.

12.5 What are the attractive features of municipal bonds?

12.6 What is the difference between general obligation bonds and revenue bonds?

12.7 Explain how preferred stock relates to debt and common stock.

12.8 What is the difference between the primary market and the secondary market?

12.9 Explain the advisement, origination, underwriting, and distribution functions of the investment banker.

12.10 What is included in a registration statement and a prospectus?

12.11 Explain a master registration statement and a short-form statement as they relate to shelf registration.

12.12 What is a preliminary prospectus and a tombstone advertisement?

12.13 What is an underwriting syndicate and how does it operate?

12.14 What is a firm commitment and what is a standby agreement?

12.15 Explain how an underwriting spread works.

12.16 List the major worldwide organized exchanges.

12.17 What are the differences between publicly held corporations and closely held corporations?

12.18 What functions do secondary markets provide?

12.19 What are roles of commission brokers, floor brokers, floor traders, and specialists on the New York Stock Exchange?

12.20 What is the consolidated tape?

12.21 What is meant by a round lot, an odd lot, and a block trade?

12.22 How does the American Stock Exchange differ from the New York Stock Exchange?

12.23 What is the makeup of the regional exchanges?

12.24 Describe the two largest foreign exchanges.

12.25 What is the over-the-counter market and how does it operate?

12.26 What is the significance of the Glass-Steagall Act of 1933 and the Securities Act of 1934?

12.27 What other laws does the Securities Exchange Commission administer?

12.28 Why was Federated Department Stores interested in offering common stock?

12.29 Why did the Justice Department investigate the actions of Salomon Brothers in the Treasury market?

PROBLEMS

12.1 **(Equivalent Yield)** John Rafferty purchased a municipal bond yielding 10 percent. If he is in the 40 percent marginal tax bracket, what is his tax equivalent yield?

12.2 **(Number of shares)** Fernandez Sporting Goods, Inc., plans to raise $10,000,000 from the sale of common stock. After talks with the underwriters, management believes that the stock must be priced at $25.00 per share. The underwriters will receive 10 percent of the issue price as compensation while the company will incur an additional $125,000 in flotation expenses. How many shares must the company sell to net $10,000,000?

12.3 **(New Stock Issue)** You are responsible for a new issue of common stock. Explain in detail how you would handle this assignment.

A Case Problem

The Computer Shoppe, Inc., sold, installed, and serviced desktop computer equipment manufactured and supplied by more than 30 vendors. The company's customers were small and medium-sized businesses located throughout the southeastern United States. The business strategy was to provide customers with advanced microcomputer products along with high level services and support. The company believed that its ability to deliver equipment competitively priced along with higher margin services allowed it to compete effectively against alternative distribution channels.

The Computer Shoppe planned to offer 1,000,000 shares of common stock at a price of $9.00 per share. Prior to the offering, there had been no public market for the stock. The initial public offering price was determined by negotiation between the company and the underwriter, First Georgia Corporation. Since the stock market had experienced extreme price fluctuations in the computer hardware industry, the offering price might differ greatly from the market price of the stock.

The offering price was based on a number of factors: the business potential of the company, its earnings history and prospects, the present state of development, an assessment of company management, the market valuations of comparable companies, the condition of the industry, and the state of the economy. After the initial public offering, the price was subject to change by First Georgia.

The Computer Shoppe purchased a substantial portion of its inventory from a company that made large purchases from manufacturers.

The prospectus advised prospective investors to weigh certain investment considerations in determining whether or not to invest in the stock. The Computer Shoppe purchased a substantial portion of its inventory from a company that made large purchases from manufacturers. That company had the right to terminate the agreement with little notice. The microcomputer industry was highly competitive and was characterized by rapid technological change. The company had experienced significant growth primarily though its marketing programs. In the future, The Computer Shoppe planned to enter the mail order distribution of hardware and software. By custom building computer equipment, it would serve customers whose primary motivation to buy was price. The company was also considering growth through acquisition.

In the Underwriting Agreement, First Georgia Corporation had agreed to purchase the 1,000,000 shares of common stock. Subject to the terms and conditions of the agreement, the underwriters were committed to pay for all shares if any shares were taken and purchased. The underwriters proposed to offer the shares to the public at the offering price included on the front cover of the prospectus. First Georgia retained the right to select dealers who were members of the National Association of Securities Dealers.

Leading Questions

1. What functions does the investment banker perform in this stock offering?
2. How should the initial offering price be determined?
3. What information would you need as an investor to decide whether or not to purchase this stock?

PREFERREDS' RICH YIELDS BLIND SOME INVESTORS TO RISKS

Attracted by high yields and a conservative reputation, individual investors are snapping up huge amounts of preferred stock. But while preferred stocks can be solid additions in a well-rounded portfolio, investment advisors say they can also be much trickier and riskier than they may appear at first glance.

13 Common and Preferred Stock

Preferred stock is a hybrid investment, containing some characteristics of stocks and some of bonds. That can cushion the impact

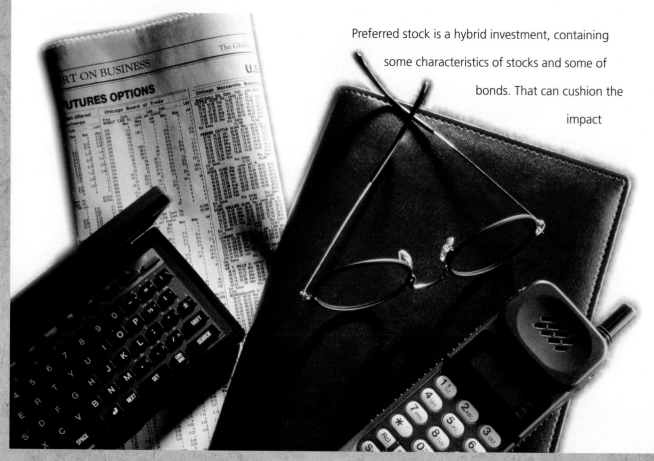

when stock prices tumble. But that also means preferred stock "doesn't have the upside potential of common stock if a company does well," says Robert Boyden Lamb, a professor of finance and management at New York University. The high dividend can also cause preferred stock prices to rise and fall as interest rates fluctuate. A company also can eliminate its preferred dividends any time without triggering a default, as would happen if it didn't make timely payments on a bond.

Individuals seeking the security of a fixed-income investment often would do better buying a company's bonds, says Daniel Fuss, an executive vice president of Loomis, Sayles & Co. in Boston. Dividends on ordinary preferred stock would be even higher if it weren't for a special tax break corporate investors get when they buy preferreds. Mr. Fuss says that "the issuer typically doesn't have to pay as high a dividend to attract buyers. That's a powerful reason for individuals to avoid" most straight preferreds.

The argument as to the pros and cons of common stock and preferred stock continues. It focuses on the risk-return tradeoffs of the two types of securities. With many types of preferreds available, it is up to the individual investor to decide.

Source: Tom Herman, "Preferreds' Rich Yields Blind Some Investors to Risks," *The Wall Street Journal,* March 24, 1992. Reprinted by permission of The Wall Street Journal, © 1992 Dow Jones & Company, Inc. All Rights Reserved Worldwide.

THE BASICS OF COMMON STOCK

Both common stock and preferred stock represent an ownership, or equity, position in a company. The ownership by common shareholders brings with it the right to control the enterprise, at least in the long run. Preferred stockholders exert far less managerial control. Nevertheless, they enjoy a superior position in the assignment of dividends and priority in the settlement of claims during liquidation.

Organizing a corporation requires a fundamental knowledge of the basics of common stock. This includes incorporation of the company, the nature of stock certificates, the operation of clearinghouses, the types of common stock, the classes of common stock, the measures of common stock value, and stock market averages and indexes.

Incorporation

A corporation comes into existence when it is granted a **charter,** or certificate of incorporation, by a state. The charter includes the name of the company, the

Charter

nature of its activities, the number of authorized shares of common stock, and the names and addresses of its directors. This document also details the rights and obligations of its shareholders. It may be amended, usually by either a majority or two-thirds vote, with each share owned providing one vote. The charter, and any subsequent amendments, must be approved by the issuing state.

Incorporation also requires preparation of a set of bylaws. This is a set of rules to direct the internal management of the company. It includes the specifics of electing directors, the makeup of committees, preemptive rights of current shareholders, and procedures for changing the bylaws. The initial bylaw format is fairly standard for new corporations.

Stock Certificates

Stock Certificate

A **stock certificate** represents ownership of the stock of the company. The certificate shows the name of the company, the state of incorporation, the number of shares owned by the shareholder, and the signatures of the corporate president and secretary. Stock certificates are usually registered on the company's books and include essential information about the investor. This is necessary for the investor to receive dividend payments, annual reports, and voting materials.

The transfer of stock from an old owner to a new owner is handled by a transfer agent who cancels the old stock certificate and issues the new one. The registrar is responsible for maintaining the official list of shareholders. Banks and trust companies often act as transfer agents and registrars.

Clearinghouses

Clearinghouse

To avoid the procedures of transfer agents and registrars, **clearinghouses** use computerized records instead of embossed certificates. The National Securities Clearing Corporation handles trades on the New York Stock Exchange, the American Stock Exchange, and the over-the-counter market. Use of centralized clearinghouses greatly reduces the cost of transfer operations.

The Depository Trust Company (DTC) maintains computerized records of the securities owned by member firms. With this arrangement, stock certificates are kept by issuing corporation in the name of the DTC. Bookkeeping entries indicate the security holdings of the member firms. Dividends paid to DTC are simply credited to the member accounts. As mentioned in the previous chapter, the Securities Act Amendments of 1975 requires the Securities Exchange Commission to move toward the development of a single nationwide securities market, including a central system to eliminate the movement of stock certificates.

Types of Common Stock

The **authorized stock** of a company is the maximum number of shares that can be issued without an amendment to the charter. To avoid the costs of amending the charter, companies set the number of authorized shares at a high level and initially issue only a small percentage of the shares. Part of the remainder of the authorized shares may be set aside for outstanding options and convertible securities (as discussed in Chapter 15).

There are other terms that relate to authorized stock. The issued stock of a company is the stock actually bought by shareholders, usually an amount less than the number of authorized shares. The treasury stock of a company is stock repurchased on the open market or through a tender offer, a formal offer to purchase a specified number of shares at a set price. Treasury stock does not have voting rights or pay dividends. The outstanding stock of a company is the stock actually in the hands of shareholders. Therefore, the outstanding stock is the amount of issued stock less the amount of treasury stock.

Authorized Stock

Classes of Common Stock

Some companies issue more than one class of common stock. In the past, Class A stock was nonvoting and Class B was voting. This allowed companies to be controlled by individuals who owned Class B stock. Today, Class A stock usually includes voting rights and pays dividends. Class A stock is held by the public while Class B stock is kept by the company organizers and does not receive dividends until the company reaches a certain level of earnings. Under these conditions, Class B shares are known as founders shares.

Companies sometimes offer more than two classes of common stock. In 1984, General Motors (GM) acquired Electronic Data Systems (EDS) for Class E common stock plus cash. In 1985, General Motors acquired Hughes Aircraft for Class H common stock plus cash. The Class E and the Class H common stock receive 1/4 and 1/2 votes respectively, in contrast to the full one vote of regular GM common stock. The amount of dividends for the Class E and Class H stock is based on the adjusted earnings of the Electronic Data Systems and Hughes Aircraft subsidiaries. The Class E and Class H shares are listed on the New York Stock Exchange.

Measures of Value

The common equity section of a balance sheet provides information about the common stock of that company. Table 13.1 focuses on the stockholders' equity accounts of the Hardeman Corporation as of December 31, 1992. The **par value** is an arbitrary amount set by the organizers of the corporation in the

Par Value

TABLE 13.1 Hardeman Corporation Stockholders' Equity Accounts as of December 31, 1992

Common stock (10 million shares authorized, 5 million shares outstanding, $1 par)	$ 5,000,000
Capital in excess of par	45,000,000
Retained earnings	50,000,000
Total stockholders' equity	$100,000,000

charter. Corporations cannot pay dividends that would reduce the value of the stockholders' equity below the total shown in the common stock account[1]. This is the reason the par value is set at a low value. In this example, the par value of $1 is multiplied by the five million shares outstanding to produce a common stock account of $5,000,000.

Common stock is normally sold for more than the par value. When this happens, the difference between what the new shareholders paid and the par value is added to the **capital in excess of par** account. In Table 13.1, the common stock has sold at various times for $45,000,000 more than the par value.

Capital in Excess of Par

The final stockholders' equity account is for retained earnings. It is equal to total earnings of the corporation over the years less total dividends paid. Each year additional retained earnings are added to this account. In Table 13.1, the total amount of retained earnings of the corporation throughout its history is $50,000,000.

> In 1993, the Hardeman Corporation sold 1,000,000 new shares of common stock at a price of $25.00 per share. The company earned $15,000,000 during the year, of which it paid out 40 percent in dividends. Under these conditions, Ricardo Estrada, a financial analyst, had to construct the stockholders' equity accounts of the Hardeman Corporation as of December 31, 1993.

These changes are recorded in the accounts of Table 13.2. The number of shares outstanding increases from 5,000,000 to 6,000,000. Common stock is found by multiplying 6,000,000 shares by the par value of $1. To find capital in excess of par, first subtract the par value of $1 from the price paid of $25 per share, $25 − $1 = $24. Then, multiply $24 by 1,000,000 new shares, 1,000,000($24) = $24,000,000. Finally, add $24,000,000 to the old value, $24,000,000 plus $45,000,000 = $69,000,000.

[1] In recent years, state laws have allowed corporations to issue no-par value stock. However, in some states the board of directors is permitted to establish a stated value for the stock.

TABLE 13.2   Hardeman Corporation Stockholders' Equity Accounts as of December 31, 1993

Common stock (10 million shares authorized, 6 million shares outstanding, $1 par)	$ 6,000,000
Capital in excess of par	69,000,000
Retained earnings	59,000,000
Total stockholders' equity	$134,000,000

The addition to retained earnings is calculated by multiplying the retention ratio of 0.60 by the earnings of $15,000,000, 0.60($15,000,000) = $9,000,000. This amount is added to the old retained earnings, $50,000,000 + $9,000,000 = $59,000,000. The new total stockholders' equity is $134,000,000.

The **book value** of the Hardeman Corporation was $100,000,000 on December 31, 1992, and $134,000,000 one year later. Book value per share is calculated by dividing the book value by the number of shares outstanding. For 1992, book value was $20.00, $100,000,000/5,000,000, and for 1993, book value was $22.33, $134,000,000/6,000,000. The common stock of the Hardeman Corporation may trade above or below the book value per share for the following reason: Book value is based on accounting methods, while market value depends on investors' assessments of the value of future cash flows.

Book Value

Liquidation value is the current market value of company assets less the total of liabilities, preferred stock, and liquidating expenses. Liquidation value per share is calculated by dividing the liquidation value by the number of shares outstanding. This represents a floor value for the common stock of the company since it is the actual amount received per share upon liquidation. The market value per share is the price at which a share of stock is currently trading in the market. Organizational value per share is the market value per share less the liquidation value per share. Organizational value is the result of synergy, the whole being more than the sum of its parts.

Liquidation Value

Stock Market Averages and Indexes

Many investors monitor the behavior of stock prices by using stock market averages and indexes. A **stock market average** is the arithmetic average of the market prices of a given set of stocks at a specified point in time. A **stock market index** is often defined as the ratio of the market prices of a given set of stocks to a base value set at an earlier point in time. An upward trend in these indexes is called a bull market, and a downward trend a bear market.

Stock Market Average

Stock Market Index

Dow Jones & Company, the publisher of *The Wall Street Journal*, furnishes four stock averages: the Industrial Average, the Transportation Average, the

Dow Jones Industrial Average

Public Utility Average, and the Composite Average. The **Dow Jones Industrial Average (DJIA)** is an average of the market prices of 30 industrial common stocks. This list of stocks, including General Motors, IBM, Westinghouse, and other large companies, changes from time to time. If this happens, or if a stock dividend or stock split occurs, an adjustment must be made to the divisor used in making the calculation. The Dow Jones Transportation Average is based on 20 transportation stocks. The Dow Jones Public Utility Average is calculated using 15 public utility stocks. The Dow Jones Composite Average is made up of 30 industrials, 20 transportation, and 15 public utilities.

Standard & Poor's Corporation, a large financial publisher, produces six common stock indexes: the 500 Index, the Industrial Index, the Public Utility Index, the Transportation Index, the Financial Index, and the MidCap index. Each of these indexes relates the current market prices of a group of stocks to a base value for the years 1941–1943 (multiplied by 10). These indexes are further adjusted by weighting each company in the index by the number of shares outstanding for that day. An index with a value of 150 indicates that the index has increased by a factor of 15, 150 divided by the constant 10.

Standard & Poor's 500 Index

The **Standard & Poor's 500 Index (S&P 500)** is made up of 400 industrials, 40 public utilities, 20 transportations, and 40 financial stocks. The Standard & Poor's Industrial Index includes the 400 industrial stocks; the Standard & Poor's Public Utility Index contains the 40 public utility stocks; the Standard & Poor's Transportation Index involves the 20 transportation stocks; the Standard & Poor's Financial Index incorporates the 40 financial stocks. In 1991, the company unveiled the Standard & Poor's MidCap Index, which includes 400 medium-size stocks.

Federal Jury Deliberates Long Battle

An important legal dispute involves the copyright infringement lawsuit between Intel Corporation and Advanced Micro Devices Inc. The case centers around whether or not Advanced Micro illegally used Intel-copyrighted software in a clone of an Intel chip called the 287. The verdict will make it easier, or much harder, for Advanced Micro to design and sell future Intel clones. While the verdict on the 287 chip won't immediately affect the Silicon Valley rivals' businesses, it will probably impact their stock prices. Despite the general expectations among Wall Street analysts the Advanced Micro has the edge in the suit, the company's stock is depressed because investors are worried about the verdict's potential impact, says analyst Drew Peck of Donaldson Lufkin Jenrette. If Advanced Micro wins, company lawyer Richard Lovgren says it will clear the way for the company to use Intel microcode in clones of future Intel chips, including chips code-named P-5 and P-6. A positive verdict could also boost Advanced Micro's stock, which had been selling below what analysts expect based on earnings.

Source: Stephen Kreider Yoder, "Federal Jury Deliberates Long Battle Between Intel and Advanced Micro Devices," *The Wall Street Journal*, June 10, 1992. Reprinted by permission of The Wall Street Journal, © 1992 Dow Jones & Company, Inc. All Rights Reserved Worldwide.

There are other widely reported indexes of U.S. stocks. The New York Stock Exchange computes a composite index of all listed stocks, along with subindexes for industrials, utilities, transportations, and financial stocks. The American Stock Exchange publishes a similar index of its listed stocks. The National Association of Securities Dealers calculates indexes based on the market value of 5,000 over-the-counter stocks. Figure 13.1 includes stock indexes published daily in *The Wall Street Journal*.

STOCK MARKET DATA BANK   10/1/93

MAJOR INDEXES

HIGH	LOW (†365 DAY)		CLOSE	NET CHG	% CHG	†365 DAY CHG	% CHG	FROM 12/31	% CHG
DOW JONES AVERAGES									
3652.09	3136.58	30 Industrials	3581.11 +	25.99 +	0.73	+ 380.50	+ 11.89	+ 280.00 +	8.48
1683.08	1219.56	20 Transportation	1638.82 +	10.69 +	0.66	+ 392.07	+ 31.45	+ 189.61 +	13.08
256.46	214.76	15 Utilities	249.41 −	0.39 −	0.16	+ 31.71	+ 14.57	+ 28.39 +	12.84
1358.57	1107.47	65 Composite	1332.06 +	7.52 +	0.57	+ 202.59	+ 17.94	+ 127.51 +	10.59
439.93	380.79	Equity Mkt. Index	438.84 +	2.06 +	0.47	+ 51.46	+ 13.28	+ 25.55 +	6.18
NEW YORK STOCK EXCHANGE									
256.88	222.11	Composite	256.29 +	1.06 +	0.42	+ 30.48	+ 13.50	+ 16.08 +	6.69
304.74	273.18	Industrials	302.50 +	1.39 +	0.46	+ 24.33	+ 8.75	+ 8.11 +	2.75
246.95	198.98	Utilities	c243.24 +	0.52 +	0.21	+ 39.56	+ 19.42	+ 33.58 +	16.02
255.27	182.66	Transportation	c253.42 +	1.67 +	0.66	+ 66.92	+ 35.88	+ 38.70 +	18.02
232.75	177.91	Finance	232.40 +	0.84 +	0.36	+ 52.30	+ 29.04	+ 31.57 +	15.72
STANDARD & POOR'S INDEXES									
463.56	402.66	500 Index	461.29 +	2.36 +	0.51	+ 50.82	+ 12.38	+ 25.58 +	5.87
524.99	471.36	Industrials	519.56 +	2.84 +	0.55	+ 38.72	+ 8.05	+ 12.10 +	2.38
409.36	307.94	Transportation	403.43 +	2.79 +	0.70	+ 87.20	+ 27.57	+ 39.68 +	10.91
189.49	148.88	Utilities	186.04 +	0.65 +	0.35	+ 31.06	+ 20.04	+ 27.58 +	17.41
48.40	35.17	Financials	48.17 +	0.21 +	0.44	+ 12.37	+ 34.55	+ 7.28 +	17.80
175.74	140.50	400 MidCap	175.73 +	0.13 +	0.07	+ 33.69	+ 23.72	+ 15.17 +	9.45
NASDAQ									
763.66	565.21	Composite	763.23 +	0.45 +	0.06	+ 191.60	+ 33.52	+ 86.28 +	12.75
781.73	598.56	Industrials	779.82 −	0.31 −	0.04	+ 175.21	+ 28.98	+ 54.88 +	7.57
946.00	701.03	Insurance	941.24 −	4.76 −	0.50	+ 235.00	+ 33.27	+ 137.33 +	17.08
701.66	453.28	Banks	701.66 +	2.85 +	0.41	+ 242.70	+ 52.88	+ 168.73 +	31.66
337.87	250.33	Nat. Mkt. Comp.	337.43 +	0.16 +	0.05	+ 84.31	+ 33.31	+ 36.87 +	12.27
312.88	239.80	Nat. Mkt. Indus.	311.90 −	0.19 −	0.06	+ 69.74	+ 28.80	+ 20.50 +	7.04
OTHERS									
461.59	364.85	Amex	461.59 +	1.20 +	0.26	+ 90.35	+ 24.34	+ 62.36 +	15.62
288.21	238.81	Value-Line (geom.)	288.21 +	0.42 +	0.15	+ 45.96	+ 18.97	+ 21.53 +	8.07
253.00	186.50	Russell 2000	253.00 +	0.05 +	0.02	+ 63.51	+ 33.52	+ 31.99 +	14.47
4619.87	3899.31	Wilshire 5000	4619.87 +	18.03 +	0.39	+ 660.45	+ 16.68	+ 330.13 +	7.70

†-Based on comparable trading day in preceding year.

Figure 13.1 Stock Market Indexes from The Wall Street Journal

THE LEGAL RIGHTS OF SHAREHOLDERS

The most important legal rights of shareholders involve the right to earnings, the right to vote, and the preemptive right. Each of these rights will be discussed in detail.

The Right to Earnings

After paying creditors interest, common shareholders have the right to the after-tax earnings not paid out to preferred stockholders. These residual earnings are disbursed in the form of dividends or are retained for the future benefit of the shareholders. For example, a corporation has net income of $5,000,000, after paying creditors $2,000,000 in interest. If preferred stockholders receive $1,000,000 in dividends, common shareholders have the right to $4,000,000 in earnings.

The board of directors may declare any portion of the $4,000,000 as a dividend, but if they do not do so, the shareholders have no legal recourse[2]. The shareholders may, however, vote to change management when they are unhappy with the dividend policy. When dividends are not paid out, shareholders benefit indirectly from the retained earnings, as long as these funds are reinvested in profitable assets. Under these conditions, the price of the common stock will rise.

The Right to Vote

Ownership of common stock entitles a shareholder to one vote for each share held. Election of the board of directors is the most important use of these votes, but there are other ways to exercise this power. Voting is utilized in amending the company charter or bylaws, in approving mergers or consolidations, in making changes in company policy, and in authorizing different classes of stock.

Common shareholders elect the board of directors, who then select the management of the company. This election normally takes place once a year, usually at the annual meeting. Some shareholders are present at this event, but in most cases they transfer their voting rights to someone else. In some companies, a portion of the directors are elected each year in order to frustrate unfriendly takeover attempts.

The document giving power of attorney to another person to vote is called a proxy. Management solicits shareholder proxies in order to retain control of the

---

[2] There is no necessary connection between dividends and current earnings since companies may pay dividends out of earnings retained in the past.

company. If shareholders are generally satisfied with the management of the company, there will be only one slate of candidates for the board of directors. When this is not the case, an outside group may solicit proxies in order to take control of the company.

The attempt to take control of a company is known as a proxy fight. Proxy fights typically include accusations that the other side is not acting in the best interests of the shareholders.

Corporations under the jurisdiction of the Securities and Exchange Commission must follow set procedures in soliciting proxies, including a proxy statement. This document outlines the background of nominees to the board of directors and provides information on subjects to be voted on at the annual meeting. In recent years, proxy fights as a part of takeovers have increased.

The method of voting is important in determining who has control of the corporation. With majority voting, shareholders cast one vote for each director position for each share of stock owned. This allows a group owning more than 50 percent of the outstanding common stock to elect all directors and to assume total control of the company. With cumulative voting, shareholders have one vote for each share of stock owned, but they may cast the votes for one director or divide the votes among the directors. This often permits shareholders who own less than 50 percent of the outstanding stock to elect at least one director. Thus, cumulative voting lets minority shareholders voice their concerns and challenge management on certain issues.

> Ricardo Estrada owns 2,100 shares of stock in a company with 12,000 shares of stock outstanding . The shareholders will elect a slate of five directors. How many directors could he elect under majority and under cumulative voting?

The number of directors he could elect under majority voting is zero, unless he happens to be on the side of the majority of shareholders. This means that he really has no control of the situation, owning only 17.5 percent of the outstanding stock.

The number of directors he could elect under cumulative voting depends on how he casts his votes. Assuming he casts all of his votes for the director of his choice, he would be guaranteed of electing that person since he has 10,500 votes, (2,100)5. The other shareholders control 49,500 votes, (12,000 − 2,100)5, but must split their votes over five candidates, 49,500/5 = 9,900. He wins, 10,500 is greater than 9,900.

To find the number of shares necessary under cumulative voting to elect a given number of directors, use the following formula:

$$SR = \frac{DD(SO)}{TD + 1} + 1 \qquad\qquad (13.1)$$

where

$$SR = \text{Number of shares required}$$
$$DD = \text{Desired number of directors}$$
$$SO = \text{Number of shares outstanding}$$
$$TD = \text{Total directors to be elected}$$

Eq. 13.1 confirms that 2,100 shares is more than enough to elect one director.

$$SR = \frac{1(12,000)}{5 + 1} + 1$$
$$= 2,001$$

To elect 2 directors, a minimum of 4,002 shares are needed.

The Preemptive Right

Preemptive Right

The corporate charter often gives common shareholders the **preemptive right,** the right to purchase any new shares sold by the corporation. Most states do not specifically require its inclusion, but all permit the preemptive right in the charter.

Shareholder Rights In Other Economies

Complaints of stockbroker "churning" of client accounts is a fact of life wherever there are financial markets, but in Japan the plight of the victims is especially severe. In many countries, investors can recover all or most of their losses by taking legal action. In Japan, mores and legal roadblocks discourage victims from going to court and prevent them from recovering much if they do. This is the downside of Japan's conflict-avoidance society, which favors harmony over individual rights. Japanese are taught from childhood that they aren't a litigious people—and they aren't. The stock market's image in Japan also discourages action. Investors are "ashamed to reveal their conduct (playing the mar-

ket) in public" says Toshiro Ueyanagi, who has handled a number of securities cases for small investors. Japanese society also values compromise, even when people think they've been wronged. The assumption of shared responsibility makes it hard for people to contemplate legal action. And what of new laws on churning, punitive damages for securities fraud against customers, or stronger court command of internal documents? That would be "disruptive to society," ministry officials say.

The preemptive right serves two purposes. First, it allows current shareholders to retain the same level of control in the corporation. If this were not the case, management could issue additional shares, purchase them, and assume a higher level of control. Second, it prevents management from issuing shares of stock at prices below the current market price, thus diluting the value of the stock. For example, a company has 12,000 shares of stock outstanding, each share selling at $100. Management decides to issue an additional 3,000 shares at $50 per share. The old total market value was $1,200,000, but with the addition of $150,000 from the new shares, the new total market value is $1,350,000. The new market value per share is $90, $1,350,000/15,000, a loss to the old shareholders of $10 per share, unless the new shares are purchased.

THE RIGHT TO PURCHASE COMMON STOCK

New common stock may be sold in five different ways: (1) to the public through investment bankers, (2) to a large investor through a private placement, (3) to employees through stock purchase plans, (4) to shareholders through a dividend reinvestment plan, and (5) to shareholders through a rights offering. This section focuses on the last of these methods.

The Nature of Rights Offerings

The preemptive right, when present in the charter, gives shareholders the right to buy a proportion of new shares based on current holdings issued by the corporation. Even if the company is not required to sell to this group, it is a good idea to sell to the current shareholders since they are likely buyers of additional shares. In either case, the transaction is called a **rights offering,** or sometimes a privileged subscription.

Rights Offering

Under a rights offering, each shareholder receives an option to purchase a certain number of new shares. The document authorizing the holder to subscribe to the new shares, according to the terms of the offering, is called a stock purchase right, or simply a **right.** Shareholders receive one right for each share of stock owned.

Right

The board of directors must approve a rights offering before a letter including a subscription warrant is sent to current shareholders announcing the new stock issue. The subscription warrant contains the terms of the issue, including the subscription price, the subscription date, and the issue date for the new stock. The subscription price is the price that must be paid for one new share. The subscription date is the last date the right may be exercised. The issue date is the date that the new stock will be issued.

TABLE 13.3 Key Dates Associated with a Rights Offering

May 1	Rights Offering Announcement
May 19	Ex-Rights Date
May 23	Date of Record
June 15	Mailing Date
June 26	Subscription Date
July 14	Issue Date

Table 13.3 is an example of the key dates associated with a rights offering. On May 1 the board of directors makes the rights offering announcement and designates May 23 as the date of record. This is the date when names of shareholders eligible to participate in the rights offering are compiled. The list includes those shareholders who owned the stock four days prior to the date of record. Therefore, shareholders who owned the stock on May 18, or before, held the stock during the rights-on period. Stock purchased during this period is purchased rights on. If the stock is sold on or after May 19, it is sold ex-rights, without rights attached. On June 15, subscription warrants are mailed to eligible participants. The last day to exercise the rights is June 26. The company issues the new stock on July 14.

The Value of a Right

The board of directors sets the subscription price when it announces the rights offering. In order to induce holders to exercise the right, it must set the price below the minimum probable price on the subscription date. The subscription price, along with the amount of funds to be raised by the issue, determines the number of new shares.

> The Hardeman Company plans to raise $1,000,000 through a rights offering. The common stock is currently selling for $30 per share, and the subscription price is set at $20 per share. Ricardo must calculate how many new shares the company must issue.

The number of new shares under a rights offering is determined by the following formula:

$$\text{New Shares} = \frac{\text{Funds required}}{\text{Subscription Price}}$$
$$= \frac{\$1,000,000}{\$20}$$
$$= 50,000 \text{ shares}$$

The company must issue 50,000 shares to raise $1,000,000.

A preemptive rights offering requires that each shareholder be give an option to participate on a pro rata basis in the sale of new shares. This is accomplished by specifying the number of rights necessary to purchase one new share of stock.

> The Hardeman Company has 200,000 shares of common stock outstanding. Ricardo must determine how many rights are required to purchase one new share of common stock.

The number of rights required to purchase a new share is given by the following formula:

$$\text{Number of Rights} = \frac{\text{Outstanding Shares}}{\text{New Shares}}$$
$$= \frac{200,000}{50,000}$$
$$= 4 \text{ rights}$$

Since shareholders receive one right for each share of stock owned, shareholders may purchase one new share for every four old shares owned.

A right has value because it allows the holder to purchase a share of stock at a price below the market. The value of this right is equal to the decline in value of the stock after the ex-rights date.

> Ricardo Estrada wants to find the value of his company's stock after the rights offering. He needs to know the total market value after the issue and the theoretical market value per share.

The total market value (TMV) is given by the following formula:

$$\text{TMV} = \text{Market Value (Old)} + \text{Market Value (New)}$$

He can find the total market value for this example.

$$TMV = 200,000(\$30) + 50,000(\$20)$$
$$= \$6,000,000 + \$1,000,000$$
$$= \$7,000,000$$

The theoretical market value per share, the stock price ex-rights (P_{ex}), is determined by the following formula:

$$P_{ex} = \frac{\text{Total Market Value}}{\text{Shares Outstanding}}$$
$$= \frac{\$7,000,000}{200,000 + 50,000}$$
$$= \$28 \text{ per share}$$

The decline in value of $2.00, $30 – $28, is equal to the value of the right.

The value of a right (R) when the stock is trading ex-rights is also given by the following formula:

$$R = \frac{P_{ex} - S}{N} \tag{13.2}$$

where

$$S = \text{Subscription Price}$$
$$N = \text{Number of Rights Required}$$

He can find the value of a right.

$$R = \frac{\$28 - \$20}{4}$$
$$= \$2$$

This equals the decline in value of the stock.

The value of a right when the stock is trading rights-on is determined by the following formula:

$$R = \frac{P_{ro} - S}{N + 1} \tag{13.3}$$

Here P_{ro} is the stock price rights-on. He can find the value of the right using the information from the example.

$$R = \frac{\$30 - \$20}{4 + 1}$$
$$= \$2$$

The theoretical value of the right, $2, may be a bit less than the actual market value of the right due to the speculative attraction of the stock increasing in price.

A few of the shares offered during a rights offering, perhaps one or two percent, will not be subscribed. In this case, the company uses an oversubscription privilege, allowing old shareholders the right to purchase unsubscribed shares on a pro rata basis. Under these conditions, shareholders are truly gaining by buying shares at below market value.

CLASSIFICATIONS OF COMMON STOCK

The stock market is made up of a wide range of common stocks, from extremely conservative to highly speculative. It is possible, then, to classify stocks according to their risk-return characteristics. Investors require such knowledge in order to select the securities that satisfy their overall investment objectives. This section examines the five major classifications of common stock.

Blue Chip Stocks

Blue chip stocks are stocks of highly regarded, established corporations such as General Motors, IBM, and Xerox. The 30 stocks included in the Dow Jones Industrial Average are blue chip stocks. These companies have dominant industry positions and sound balance sheets, as well as stable records of earnings and dividends.

Even though the blue chip companies are not necessarily alike, they are generally regarded by investors as conservative investments. These stocks offer reasonable dividends and moderate growth potential and, as a result, are particularly attractive during times of financial crisis. Investors showed a strong interest in blue chip stocks after the market crash of October 19, 1987.

Blue Chip Stocks

Growth Stocks

Growth stocks are stocks that are expected to experience a substantial growth in earnings per share and price in the future while retaining a high proportion of earnings. This definition is in contrast to the explanation by some writers

Growth Stocks

that growth stocks are stocks that have experienced growth in the past. Growth stocks must also be differentiated from growth companies. The latter category applies to companies that have simply increased in size.

Growth stocks suggest that management will successfully invest in projects that yield rates of return greater than the marginal cost of capital. For example, a company with a marginal cost of capital of 12 percent plans to invest in projects yielding 20 percent. This allows the company to grow faster.

Income Stocks

Income Stocks

Income stocks are stocks that have a long-term record of steady, large cash dividends. Utility stocks fit this classification since they have a reputation for paying dividends in this manner. Other stocks, such as high technology stocks, may not stress cash dividends, focusing instead on retaining earnings in order to take advantage of growth opportunities. With their approach to dividends, income stocks have limited growth potential but may have strong earnings possibilities.

Income stocks appeal to a certain investor clientele. They are ideal for investors who want a high level of current income with relative safety. Selection of this type of stock, however, does not guarantee their stock prices will not be volatile.

Defensive and Cyclical Stocks

Defensive Stocks

Cyclical Stocks

Defensive stocks are stocks with prices that remain stable, or possibly increase, during periods of recession. Thus, these stocks are less sensitive to economic cycles. This contrasts with **cyclical stocks,** which experience price changes greater than the overall market. Public utilities and grocery chains are examples of defensive stocks, and machine tool manufacturing is an example of a cyclical stock.

In terms of the capital asset pricing model (CAPM), defensive stocks are stocks with low systematic risk, indicating low betas, and cyclical stocks are stocks with high systematic risk, indicating high betas. Defensive stocks, those stocks with betas less than 1.0, have below average nondiversifiable risk. The most extreme example of defensive stocks, perhaps to the point of being countercyclical, are gold mining stocks. These stocks do particularly well during economic downturns. In contrast, cyclical stocks have betas greater than 1.0.

Speculative Stocks

Speculative Stocks

Speculative stocks are stocks with high risk and high potential return. This includes the stocks of newly established companies as well as the stocks of older companies that are beginning to experience financial problems. Earnings for speculative stocks are uncertain and unstable, and usually they sell at a high price-earnings ratio. Investors who deal in speculative stocks tend to do so on a short-term basis, getting in and getting out as the situation dictates.

PREFERRED STOCK FINANCING

Preferred stock is a hybrid security, sharing characteristics of both debt and common stock. The dividends on preferred stock are similar to the coupon payments of perpetual bonds. Unlike bonds, however, missed dividends do not permit preferred stockholders to seek legal relief against the company. Preferred stock also differs from debt in that preferred dividends are not tax-deductible as is the interest on bonds.

Preferred stock is normally issued with a stated par value, usually $100. The dividends on preferred stock are expressed as a dollar amount or as a percentage of the par value. For example, an annual dividend may be stated as $10 or as 10 percent of the $100 par value. The actual payments may be in quarterly installments of $2.50 each.

Types of Preferred Stock

Cumulative preferred stock requires that all unpaid preferred dividends be paid before dividends are paid on common stock. This feature puts pressure on the board of directors to keep dividends current. When a company misses a certain number of preferred dividend payments, it may be required to provide representation on the board of directors or, in some cases, to offer new common stock in place of the missed dividends.

Callable preferred stock may be retired at the discretion of the issuing corporation by paying the preferred stockholder a stated amount, usually a sum slightly higher than the par value. This additional amount is designated as the call premium. Since this provision does not favor the preferred stockholder, the yield is normally higher for issues of this type. As is the case with corporate bonds, preferred stock cannot be called for a set number of years. When a preferred stock issue is called, the refunding decision is similar to the bond refunding decision. This process is studied in the next chapter.

Convertible preferred stock is convertible into a fixed number of shares of common stock at the discretion of the preferred stockholder. Almost half of the preferred stock issued in recent years has this feature. For example, the Martin Corporation issues 10 percent preferred stock at $100 par, callable at $110, and convertible into 2.0 shares of common stock. If the common stock is selling at $60, the preferred stockholders should convert before the first call date, since two shares of common stock are worth $120.

Cumulative Preferred Stock

Callable Preferred Stock

Convertible Preferred Stock

Participating Preferred Stock

Participating preferred stock, although somewhat rare, allows preferred stockholders to receive dividends above the stated rate of the preferred stock. Participating plans vary, but generally common stockholders receive an amount equal to preferred dividends. Any funds left over for dividends are divided equally between common shareholders and preferred stockholders. For example, the Morris Company issued 10 percent participating preferred stock with a $100 par value. Under this arrangement, common shareholders must be paid $10 in dividends before there is any sharing. Then, each class of stock must be paid the same amount per share.

During the 1980s, adjustable rate and market auction preferred stocks were introduced. In 1982, adjustable rate preferred stock (ARPS) was issued by a number of companies. The dividends of these preferred stocks are not fixed, but are instead tied to Treasury rates. This security is attractive as a short-term corporate investment since the floating rate reduces price volatility. In 1984, market auction preferred stocks were issued for the first time. The dividends for these preferred stocks depend upon auctions of the preferred shares conducted every seven weeks to determine the amount of the dividend.

Tax Issues With Preferred Stock

As is the case with common stock, dividends from preferred stock must be paid from after-tax income. In contrast, the interest from corporate bonds is paid from pre-tax income. This unfavorable tax treatment tends to make preferred stock an unattractive alternative to corporate bonds.

> The financial managers of the Hardeman Corporation are trying to decide whether to issue $1,500,000 of preferred stock or $1,500,000 of corporate bonds. The dividend rate of preferred stock and the coupon rate on corporate bonds are both 10 percent. Expected earnings before interest and taxes (EBIT) for next year is $1,000,000, and the marginal tax rate is 40 percent. Management wants Ricardo to find the earnings available to common shareholders under each plan.

Table 13.4 presents the calculations of available earnings under both the preferred stock and corporate bonds plans. Under these conditions, earnings available to common shareholders are $450,000 for preferred stock and $510,000 for corporate bonds. The $150,000 deduction for interest under the bond plan results in a tax savings of $60,000, 0.40($150,000).

Most preferred stock is bought by corporations, insurance companies, and pension funds. This results from the tax advantage of preferred stock over corporate bonds from the investment point of view. The tax laws allow corporate

TABLE 13.4 Earnings Available to Common Shareholders Under Preferred Stock and
Corporate Bond Plans

	PREFERRED STOCK	CORPORATE BONDS
Earnings before interest and taxes	$1,000,000	$1,000,000
Interest expense	0	150,000
Earnings before taxes	$1,000,000	$ 850,000
Income taxes	400,000	340,000
Earnings after taxes	$ 600,000	$ 510,000
Preferred stock dividends	150,000	0
Earnings available to common shareholders	$ 450,000	$ 510,000

investors to exclude a high percentage of preferred dividends from taxation. This may make after-tax preferred yield attractive.

> The Hardeman Corporation is considering investing in either preferred stock or corporate bonds, each of which has a before-tax yield of 10 percent. For this company, 80 percent of preferred dividends may be excluded from taxation. If the marginal tax rate for the corporation is 40 percent, what is the after-tax yield in each case.

Interest on corporate bonds receives no tax break, so the after-tax bond yield (ATBY) is calculated as follows:

$$ATBY = BTBY[1 - \text{tax rate}]$$
$$= 10\%(1 - 0.40)$$
$$= 6.00\%$$

BTBY is the before-tax bond yield.

Dividends on the preferred stock receives an 80 percent exclusion, so the after-tax preferred yield (ATPY) is determined as follows:

$$ATPY = BTPY[1 - (\text{tax rate})(1 - \text{exclusion rate})]$$
$$= 10\%[1 - (0.40)(0.20)]$$
$$= 9.20\%$$

BTPY is the before-tax preferred yield.

SUMMARY

This chapter focuses on the following learning objectives:

1. Explaining the basics of common stock.

   A corporation comes into existence when it is granted a charter by a state. A stock certificate is used to represent ownership of the stock of the company. A stock market average is the arithmetic average of the market prices of a given set of stocks, while a stock market index is the ratio of the market prices of a given set of stocks to a base value.

2. Specifying the legal rights of shareholders.

   Common shareholders have the right to earnings not paid out to creditors or preferred stockholders. Common shareholders elect the board of directors, who then select the management of the company. The corporate charter often gives common shareholders the preemptive right, the right to purchase new shares sold by the corporation.

3. Describing rights offerings.

   Under a rights offering, each shareholder receives an option to purchase a certain number of new shares. The document authorizing the holder to subscribe to the new shares is called a stock purchase right, or simply a right.

4. Determining the value of a right.

   In order to induce holders to exercise the right, it must set the price below the minimum probable price on the subscription date. A right has value because it allows the holder to purchase a share of stock at a price below the market. The value of this right is equal to the decline in value of the stock after the ex-rights date.

5. Classifying stocks according to their risk-return characteristics.

   Blue chip stocks are stocks of highly regarded, established corporations. Growth stocks are stocks that are expected to experience growth in earnings per share in the future. Income stocks are stocks that have a long-term record of stable dividends. Defensive stocks are stocks with prices that remain stable or increase during periods of recession. Speculative stocks are stocks with high risk and high potential return.

6. Detailing the basics of preferred stock.

   Preferred stock is a hybrid security, sharing characteristics of both debt and common stock. Like common stock, dividends from preferred stock must be paid from after-tax income.

KEY TERMS

Authorized stock, 365	Blue chip stock, 377	Book value, 367

QUESTIONS

13.1   Explain the basics of incorporation.

13.2   Explain the basics of stock certificates.

13.3   Explain the basics of clearinghouses.

13.4   Discuss the types of common stock.

13.5   Discuss the classes of common stock.

13.6   Explain the common equity section of the balance sheet.

13.7   What is meant by book value, book value per share, liquidation value, and liquidation value per share?

13.8   What is the difference between stock market averages and stock market indexes?

13.9   Discuss the right to earnings with common stock.

13.10 How is the board of directors of a typical corporation elected?

13.11 What is the difference between majority voting and cumulative voting?

13.12 Explain the purposes of the preemptive right.

13.13 List the five ways of selling common stock.

13.14 What is a rights offering, and how does it work?

13.15 What are the key dates associated with a rights offering?

13.16 Explain the six classifications of common stock.

13.17 How does preferred stock differ from common stock?

13.18 Discuss the types of preferred stock.

13.19 How is preferred stock treated from a tax point of view?

13.20 What are the pros and cons of common stock versus preferred stock ownership?

13.21 How would the verdict in the copyright infringement lawsuit between Intel Corporation and Advanced Micro Devices affect company stock prices?

13.22 Why might investors in Japan avoid taking legal action?

PROBLEMS

13.1 **(Stockholders' Equity Accounts)** The stockholders' equity accounts of Madison, Inc., as of December 31, 1993, are as follows:

Common stock (1,000,000 shares authorized,	
500,000 shares outstanding, $1 par)	$ 500,000
Capital in excess of par	3,500,000
Retained earnings	6,000,000
Total stockholders' equity	$10,000,000

In 1994, the corporation sold 100,000 new shares of common stock at a price of $15.00 per share. It earned $1,000,000 during the year, of which it paid out 40 percent in dividends. Construct the stockholders' equity accounts of Madison, Inc., as of December 31, 1994.

13.2 **(Stockholders' Equity Accounts)** On December 31, 1993, the stockholders' equity accounts of Champion Corporation were as follows:

Common stock ($1 par)	$ 750,000
Capital in excess of par	2,250,000
Retained earnings	5,000,000
Total stockholders' equity	$8,000,000

Champion sold 150,000 new shares of common stock at a price of $10.00 per share during the next year. During that time, the company earned $800,000, of which it paid out 30 percent in dividends. Construct the stockholders' equity accounts of Champion, as of December 31, 1994.

13.3 **(Electing Directors)** You own 175,000 shares of stock in a company with 465,000 shares of stock outstanding. The shareholders will elect a slate of 6 directors. How many directors could you elect under majority and under cumulative voting?

13.4 **(Electing Directors)** Jane Robinson owns 375,000 shares of the 950,000 shares of Blanding Corporation. The shareholders elect a slate of seven directors. How many directors could she elect under majority and under cumulative voting?

13.5 **(Rights and Value)** The Vyas Company plans to raise $2,000,000 through a rights offering. The common stock is currently selling for $25 per share, and the subscription price is set at $20 per share. How many new shares must the company issue? Vyas has 200,000 shares of common stock outstanding. How many rights are required to purchase one new share of common stock? What is the total market value after the issue and the theoretical market value per share?

13.6 **(Rights and Value)** Turner Tools, Inc., issued rights to shareholders. Five rights are needed along with the subscription price of $25 to purchase one of the new shares. The stock is selling for $30 rights-on. What is the value of the right? What is the new price of the stock after the stock goes ex-rights?

13.7 **(Earnings Available to Common Shareholders)** The financial managers of the Qualitool Corporation are trying to decide between issuing $1,000,000 of preferred stock or $1,000,000 of corporate bonds. The dividend rate on preferred stock and the coupon rate on corporate bonds are both 11 percent. Expected earnings before interest and taxes (EBIT) for next year is $750,000, and the marginal tax rate is 40 percent. What are the earnings available to common shareholders under each plan?

13.8 **(Earnings Available to Common Shareholders)** Advanced Systems, Inc., will issue either $6,000,000 of preferred stock or corporate bonds. The dividend rate on preferred stock is 9 percent, and the coupon rate on corporate bonds is 11 percent. Expected earnings before interest and taxes (EBIT) for next year is $1,900,000 while the marginal tax rate is 40 percent. What are the earnings available to common shareholders under each plan?

13.9 **(After-Tax Yield)** New Brunswick Corporation is considering investing in either preferred stock or corporate bonds, each of which has a before-tax yield of 12 percent. For this company, 80 percent of preferred dividends may be excluded from taxation. If the marginal tax rate of the corporation is 40 percent, what is the after-tax yield in each case?

13.10 **(After-Tax Yield)** The marginal tax rate of Hoenshel Manufacturing Corporation is 40 percent. The bonds of the corporation yield 11 percent while the preferred stock yields 12.5 percent. For this company, 70 percent of preferred dividends may be excluded from taxation. What is the after-tax yield for each type of security?

A Case Problem

Trimatic Corporation was a leading manufacturer of high quality interior trim systems, including complete door panel assemblies, arm rests, consoles, and head rests. Trimatic sold to North American car, mini-van, and light truck manufacturers.

The company planned to offer 5,000,000 shares of Class A common stock at an initial offering price of $15.00 per share. Prior to the offering, the company had five classes of common stock outstanding, Class A through Class E. Upon consummation of the offering the company would have two classes: Class A (voting) and Class B (nonvoting). Class B stock would be convertible into Class A stock at the option of the holder, subject to certain limitations. The outstanding shares of the old Class A, B, C, and D common stock would be convertible into the new Class A common stock and the old Class E common stock would be convertible into the new Class B common stock.

Trimatic had previously issued Series A Cumulative Redeemable Exchangeable Preferred Stock with a face value of $24 million. The preferred stock had a stated annual dividend rate of 9.5% payable quarterly and must be redeemed by April 4, 2001. The company could, at its option, exchange the preferred stock for junior subordinated notes upon cash payment of 5% of the outstanding face amount of the preferred stock. The junior subordinated notes would have an interest rate of 9.5% and would mature in 2001. The dividends on the preferred stock and interest on the junior subordinated notes would not be paid in cash unless Trimatic met certain financial requirements. In the past, preferred dividends had been paid only in additional shares of preferred stock.

In connection with the issuance of senior subordinated debt, the company had also issued warrants to purchase 34,000 shares of its Class A common stock. The warrants were exercisable after April 3, 1997, at an exercise price of $210.00 per share. At any time after April 3, 2000, unless there was a public offering by Trimatic, a warrant holder could elect to put to the company all of his/her warrants. Trimatic could call the warrants after April 3, 2001.

Prior to the stock offering, substantially all of the existing stockholders of Trimatic agreed to vote their shares in the manner of the largest stockholder.

After the sale of the new Class A common stock, the existing stockholders as a group would control approximately 64 percent of the Class A stock. Prior to the stock offering, substantially all of the existing stockholders of Trimatic agreed to vote their shares in the manner of the largest stockholder. They would thereby be able to control the election of the board of directors and generally would be able to direct the affairs of the company.

Trimatic had not declared or paid any cash dividends on its common stock since it acquired another company two years earlier. The company planned to continue this policy of retaining all earnings in order to support its growth strategy. Any future payments are within the discretion of the board of directors.

Leading Questions

1. Why would the company change its classes of common stock?
2. What is cumulative redeemable exchangeable preferred stock?
3. How would the warrants work?
4. How would you classify the common stock of this company?
5. What rights would you have as a new Trimatic stockholder?

I n the U.S. bond market, traders and money managers were convinced that President Clinton would
pull out a victory for Nafta. That helped steady the
price of the 30-year Treasury, whose price had tumbled
as investors feared that inflation was heating up. It is
not that investors believed that Nafta would have a
powerful effect on bond prices. But they believed its
passage would bode well for other international trade

14 Long-Term Debt and Leasing

agreements, including important European ones. These
traders and investors say globalization of trade will hold
down inflation.

"Liberalization of trade means efficiency, and efficiency means less
inflationary pressures over

time," said John Lipsky, chief economist at Salomon Brothers. The upside for the U.S. bond market from Nafta's passage "is limited, but the downside" from its rejection "is significant," said Adam Greshin, a portfolio manager at Scudder, Stevens & Clark, a money-management firm. Before passage of Nafta, some money managers were arranging to be in touch with Tokyo traders to begin unloading long-term Treasurys in the event the treaty were rejected. Robert Beckwitt,

a portfolio manager at Fidelity Investments, predicted that passage of Nafta would prompt an upgrade of Mexico's credit rating to investment grade.

The circumstances of Nafta illustrate the effect a free-trade pact has on the global bond market. In this chapter, you will learn more about the intricacies of that market.

Source: Thomas T. Vogel, Jr. and Leslie Scisml, "Bond Markets in U.S. and Mexico Were Tranquil In Anticipation of Vote on Free Trade Accord," *The Wall Street Journal,* November 18, 1993. Reprinted by permission of The Wall Street Journal, © 1993 Dow Jones & Company, Inc. All Rights Reserved Worldwide.

LONG-TERM DEBT FINANCING

Long-term debt is usually in the form of notes or bonds. Notes have maturities of from one to ten years. Bonds have maturities of over ten years. This section focuses on the bond indenture, types of bonds, and bond ratings.

The Bond Indenture

The **bond indenture** is a contract between the company issuing the bonds and the bondholder. The document, complete with legal terminology, may be as long as several hundred pages. A bond trustee, usually the trust department of a major commercial bank, ensures that the terms of the bond indenture are met. The trustee, who is appointed under the provisions of the Trust Indenture Act of 1939, is paid by the issuer of the bonds. The more important sections of the bond indenture involve protective covenants and methods for repayment of the bonds.

Bond Indenture

Protective covenants are provisions in bond indentures designed to reduce the possibility that the company will default on the bonds. Virtually all indentures require proper records, maintenance of assets, payment of taxes, and adequate insurance. Indentures also include an acceleration clause, a provision that allows the trustee to declare the interest and principal due when the interest is not paid within a set number of days after the payment date.

Protective Covenants

Protective covenants often limit the ability of the company to issue additional debt, thereby protecting the quality of the outstanding bonds. Bond indentures also include restrictions on asset management. This may involve constraints on the current ratio, prohibitions on the assignment of accounts receivable, or limitations on the sale of fixed assets. Finally, indentures sometimes include a limitation on dividends, tying the payment to current earnings.

There are basically five methods for repaying bonds: (1) a call feature, (2) serial bonds, (3) a sinking fund, (4) conversion, and (5) payment at maturity.

Call Feature

A **call feature** specifies conditions under which a bond may be retired by the issuer prior to its stated maturity. A freely callable bond may be called with notice of 30 to 60 days. Noncallable bonds are prevented by the indenture from being called at any time. Deferred callable bonds allow the bonds to be called after a specified length of time, such as five years. At that point, they become freely callable bonds. A refunding provision is a type of call feature that allows an issue to be retired, *except* when the reason for retirement is replacement by a lower-coupon bond. With the refunding provision, the company must have another reason, such as excess cash, for calling in the bonds.

Sinking Funk Provision

A **sinking fund provision** requires that bonds be retired in a systematic fashion. For example, a company retires 5 percent of the bonds each year in years 11 through 30. Most bond indentures allow the company to use the cheapest method in retiring the bonds. If the going rate of interest is above the coupon rate, the bonds sell below par, and management buys bonds in the market. If the going rate of interest is below the coupon rate, bonds sell above par, and management uses a lottery to determine which bonds to redeem at par. Notice that this method reduces the life of the issue; the average bond is outstanding only 20.5 years

Serial Bonds

Serial bonds and sinking funds are similar in nature. With serial bonds, each bond has its own maturity. This method of payment has the advantage of allowing investors to choose the maturity of the bond, apparently reducing the cost of debt. Because of their differentiated nature, making out of one issue many small issues, serial bonds are less liquid and may not enjoy an active secondary market.

Bonds can also be repaid by conversion or simply by waiting until maturity. Convertible bonds may be exchanged for a specified number of shares of common stock. This subject will be covered in detail in the next chapter. Waiting until maturity to pay off bonds is a risky process. The company is gambling that the market will be right for the company at that specific point in time.

Types of Bonds

Secured Bonds

Secured bonds have specific assets pledged to protect the bondholder in the event of default. This prevents the company from disposing of the pledged assets without obtaining the consent of the bondholders. There are three principal types of secured bonds: mortgage bonds, collateral trust bonds, and equipment trust certificates. Figure 14.1 shows the breakdown of unsecured and secured bonds.

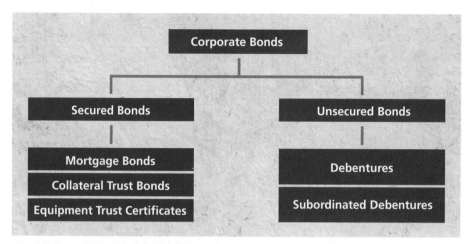

Figure 14.1   Types of Unsecured and Secured Bonds

Unsecured bonds are backed by the general credit of the company issuing them and are not secured by any specific property. Most companies issue only this type of debt. A **debenture** is an unsecured bond and normally has a life of more than 15 years. Debenture holders in liquidation are general creditors. If specific assets are pledged for secured bonds, debenture holders occupy a secondary position to these secured issues. Debentures often include a negative pledge clause which prevents pledging of additional assets. Issuing debentures is advantageous to the company in that new general creditors worry less about extending credit when assets are not tied up.

Unsecured Bonds

Debenture

Subordinated debentures are debentures that are subordinate to other creditors named in the bond indenture. This debt is honored after unsubordinated creditors, such as bank loans and unsubordinated debentures, are satisfied. Placing subordinated debentures in this position raises the cost of this type of financing.

Subordinated Debentures

Junk bonds are high-risk, high-yield subordinated debentures rated BB or lower by Standard & Poor's and Ba by Moody's. These bonds are categorized into two groups: (1) bonds classified as risky at the time of issue, and (2) bonds that have become risky through time. Junk bonds of the first type are often used to finance a leveraged buyout. More on this subject is found in Chapter 20. Since these high-risk bonds are more difficult to sell than investment-grade bonds, junk bonds in the 1980s produced high underwriting fees for investment bankers such as Drexel Burnham.

Junk Bonds

Income bonds are unsecured bonds which pay interest with income from the projects they finance. Coupon interest for these bonds is paid from earnings before interest and taxes (EBIT). If EBIT is positive and less than the stated interest, only the amount of the EBIT will be paid. If the EBIT is nega-

Income Bonds

tive, the company pays no interest on the income bonds that year but may pay later if the bonds have a cumulative feature. These characteristics make income bonds similar to preferred stock; they are not the same since interest on income bonds is tax deductible.

Mortgage Bonds

Mortgage bonds are secured by liens on real property, such as buildings and land. Under this arrangement, the value of the property comfortably exceeds the value of the mortgage bonds. Companies often issue first mortgage bonds and second mortgage bonds against the same real property. When this happens, the second mortgage holders require a higher yield on their bonds, due to the more risky position in default.

The bond indenture of mortgage bonds may prohibit issuance of additional bonds against the property. If this is the case, it is a closed-end mortgage. With an open-end mortgage, no such restrictions apply. Blanket mortgage bonds are not secured by specific real property, instead by all of the assets of the company. As further protection for bondholders, the company may insert an after-acquired clause, which includes property acquired after the original mortgage as collateral.

Collateral Trust Bonds

Collateral trust bonds are bonds secured by financial securities, such as stocks and bonds, deposited with the trustee. On these pledged securities, the company receives the interest and dividends and retains the voting privilege. Holding companies often use the stock of their subsidiaries as collateral since the holding companies are able to issue the bonds at a lower rate. To prevent the subsidiaries from then issuing additional debt, at the disadvantage of the collateral trust bondholders, the bond indenture often includes restrictions on borrowing by the subsidiaries.

Equipment Trust Certificates

Equipment trust certificates are bonds secured by equipment, such as railroad rolling stock. Historically, these securities have been of high quality, since the underlying equipment retains its market value due to interchangeability with other pieces of equipment. The title to new equipment is normally held by a trust company until the certificates are retired, with ownership then passing to the user of the equipment. The financing of the equipment by the trust company is based on a down payment from the user and the sale of the equipment trust certificates. Curiously, the payment to the bondholder is called a dividend, even though the security is actually a bond.

Bond Ratings

Bond Ratings

Bond ratings reflect the probability that the issuing corporation will default on the bond. There are a number of companies that publish this information, with Standard & Poor's Corporation and Moody's Investors Service, Inc. being the two largest. Figure 14.2 and Figure 14.3 provide interpretations of the rating scales for these agencies.

AAA Debt rated 'AAA' has the highest rating assigned by Standard & Poor's. Capacity to pay interest and repay principal is extremely strong.

AA Debt rated 'AA' has a very strong capacity to pay interest and repay principal and differs from the higher rated issues only in small degree.

A Debt rated 'A' has a strong capacity to pay interest and repay principal although it is somewhat more susceptible to the adverse effects of changes in circumstances and economic conditions than debt in higher rated categories.

BBB Debt rated 'BBB' is regarded as having an adequate capacity to pay interest and repay principal. Whereas it normally exhibits adequate protection parameters, adverse economic conditions or changing circumstances are more likely to lead to a weakened capacity to pay interest and repay principal for debt in this category than in higher rated categories.

BB, B, CCC, CC, C Debt rated 'BB', 'B', 'CCC', 'CC' and 'C' is regarded, on balance, as predominantly speculative with respect to capacity to pay interest and repay principal in accordance with the terms of the obligation. 'BB' indicates the lowest degree of speculation and 'C' the highest degree of speculation. While such debt will likely have some quality and protective characteristics, these are outweighed by large uncertainties or major risk exposures to adverse conditions.

BB Debt rated 'BB' has less near-term vulnerability to default than other speculative issues. However, it faces major ongoing uncertainties or exposure to adverse business, financial, or economic conditions which could lead to inadequate capacity to meet timely interest and principal payments. The 'BB' rating category is also used for debt subordinated to senior debt that is assigned an actual or implied 'BBB –' rating.

B Debt rated 'B' has a greater vulnerability to default but currently has the capacity to meet interest payments and principal repayments. Adverse business, financial, or economic conditions will likely impair capacity or willingness to pay interest and repay principal. The 'B' rating category is also used for debt subordinated to senior debt that is assigned an actual or implied 'BB' or 'BB –' rating.

CCC Debt rated 'CCC' has a currently identifiable vulnerability to default, and is dependent upon favorable business, financial, and economic conditions to meet timely payment of interest and repayment of principal. In the event of adverse business, financial, or economic conditions, it is not likely to have the capacity to pay interest and repay principal. The 'CCC' rating category is also used for debt subordinated to senior debt that is assigned an actual or implied 'B' or 'B–' rating.

CC The rating 'CC' is typically applied to debt subordinated to senior debt that is assigned an actual or implied 'CCC' rating.

C The rating 'C' is typically applied to debt subordinated to senior debt which is assigned an actual or implied 'CCC –' debt rating. The 'C' rating may be used to cover a situation where a bankruptcy petition has been filed, but debt service payments are continued.

CI The rating 'CI' is reserved for income bonds on which no interest is being paid.

D Debt rated 'D' is in payment default. The 'D' rating category is used when interest payments or principal payments are not made on the date due even if the applicable grace period has not expired, unless S&P believes that such payments will be made during such grace period. The 'D' rating also will be used upon the filing of a bankruptcy petition if debt service payments are jeopardized.

Plus (+) or Minus (–): The ratings from 'AA' to 'CCC' may be modified by the addition of a plus or minus sign to show relative standing within the major categories.

NR indicates that no public rating has been requested, or that there is insufficient information on which to base a rating, or that S&P does not rate a particular type of obligation as a matter of policy.

Source: Reprinted by permission of Standard & Poor's, a division of McGraw-Hill, Inc.

Figure 14.2   Interpretation of Standard and Poor's Bond Ratings

Bonds may also be grouped as either investment grade or speculative grade. **Investment grade bonds** require a rating in the top four classifications, AAA through BBB for Standard & Poor's, and Aaa through Baa for Moody's. **Speculative grade bonds,** called junk bonds, are assigned the other ratings. A drop in classification increases the interest rate on new issues and reduces the market prices on the company's outstanding bonds. Moving from investment to speculative grade may be disastrous, since many banks and other institutional investors are not allowed to hold junk bonds.

Investment Grade Bonds

Speculative Grade Bonds

Aaa

Bonds which are rated **Aaa** are judged to be of the best quality. They carry the smallest degree of investment risk and are generally referred to as "gilt edge." Interest payments are protected by a large or by an exceptionally stable margin and principal is secure. While the various protective elements are likely to change, such changes as can be visualized are most unlikely to impair the fundamentally strong position of such issues.

Aa

Bonds which are rated **Aa** are judged to be of high quality by all standards. Together with the **Aaa** group they comprise what are generally known as high grade bonds. They are rated lower than the best bonds because margins of protection may not be as large as in **Aaa** securities or fluctuation of protective elements may be of greater amplitude or there may be other elements present which make the long term risks appear somewhat larger than in **Aaa** securities.

A

Bonds which are rated **A** possess many favorable investment attributes and are to be considered as upper medium grade obligations. Factors giving security to principal and interest are considered adequate but elements may be present which suggest a susceptibility to impairment sometime in the future.

Baa

Bonds which are rated **Baa** are considered as medium grade obligations, i.e., they are neither highly protected nor poorly secured. Interest payment and principal security appear adequate for the present but certain protective elements may be lacking or may be characteristically unreliable over any great length of time. Such bonds lack outstanding investment characteristics and in fact have speculative characteristics as well.

Ba

Bonds which are rated **Ba** are judged to have speculative elements; their future cannot be considered as well assured. Often the protection of interest and principal payments may be very moderate and thereby not well safeguarded during both good and bad times over the future. Uncertainty of position characterizes bonds in this class.

B

Bonds which are rated **B** generally lack characteristics of the desirable investment. Assurance of interest and principal payments or of maintenance of other terms of the contract over any long period of time may be small.

Caa

Bonds which are rated **Caa** are of poor standing. Such issues may be in default or there may be present elements of danger with respect to principal or interest.

Ca

Bonds which are rated **Ca** represent obligations which are speculative in a high degree. Such issues are often in default or have other marked shortcomings.

C

Bonds which are rated **C** are the lowest rated class of bonds and issues so rated can be regarded as having extremely poor prospects of ever attaining any real investment standing.

Source: Moody's Bond Record, November 1993, p. 8.

Figure 14.3 Interpretation of Moody's Bond Ratings

Profits And Perils Of Global Bonds

t's no wonder that many income-minded investors are turning to global bond funds—those that put their funds either partly or wholly in higher-yielding securities issued outside the U.S. Global funds can help you diversify your fixed-income portfolio, reduce its overall risk, and boost your returns. As always, when investments sound so good, there's a catch: In this case, it is currency risk. A rising U.S. dollar erodes a fund's foreign profits as surely as a falling greenback enhances them. And a strengthening economy could drive the dollar even higher.

Most international bond funds try to guard against currency risks by using the foreign exchange markets to hedge their bets. Their strategies are complex, though: A simple hedge alone won't work. Fund managers instead employ strategies like the so-called cross hedge that is used to cut the risk of European bonds. It takes advantage of the fact that currencies tied together through the European Monetary System fluctuate against one another only within a limited range. There's another problem too. In addition to sales charges, most international bond funds impose steep annual expenses of 1.5 percent or so, half a point higher than those of domestic bond funds.

Source: Ruth Simon, "The Profits And Perils Of Global Bonds." Reprinted from the April 1992 issue of MONEY by special permission; copyright 1992, Time Inc.

BOND REFUNDING

Bond refunding is the replacement of all or part of a bond issue with another bond issue. Companies consider refunding when interest rates decline. Naturally, this saves interest expense. But the question for the financial manager is: Are the benefits of refunding greater than the costs? To answer this question, it is necessary to perform a capital budgeting-type analysis.

Bond Refunding

The Richardson Corporation has outstanding $10,000,000 of 12 percent bonds, originally issued 10 years ago. The old flotation costs of $500,000 were amortized on a straight line basis over the 25-year life of the issue. Richardson is considering refunding the old issue with $10,000,000 of 10 percent bonds. This requires payment of a 10 percent call premium. The new flotation costs of $450,000 will be amortized on a straight line basis over the 15-year life of the issue. The new bonds will be sold one month before the old issue is called, and during this month the proceeds from the new issue will be invested in short-term securities at an interest rate of nine percent. If the marginal tax rate of the company is 40 percent, should the refunding take place?

We solve this problem by determining the incremental cash flows and then finding the present value. The procedure for finding the initial cash flow and the yearly cash flows employs methods similar to those in Chapter 6. The approach for using present value is like the capital budgeting methods from Chapter 7.

The Initial Cash Flow

The initial cash flow is the sum of the after-tax cash flows from four sources: (1) the call premium on the old issue, (2) the flotation costs on the new issue, (3) the tax savings from the immediate writeoff of the unamortized flotation costs, and (4) the net extra interest from the overlap period. Each of these cash flows will be considered separately.

The after-tax cash flow ($ATCF_1$), resulting from the *call premium on the old issue*, is calculated as follows:

$$ATCF_1 = -\$10,000,000(0.10)(1 - 0.40)$$
$$= -\$600,000$$

The cash flow from the call premium is −$1,000,000. This amount is tax deductible and results in a tax savings of 0.40($1,000,000) = $400,000. Combining the cash flows from the call premium and the tax savings results in −$600,000, but it is easier to write it all in one equation.

The after-tax cash flow resulting from the *flotation costs on the new issue* is calculated as follows:

$$ATCF_2 = -\$450,000$$

There is no tax treatment on the new flotation costs at time zero. Taxes are calculated on the new flotation costs on a yearly basis, as they are amortized over the 15-year life of the new issue.

The after-tax cash flow resulting from the *tax savings from the immediate write-off of the unamortized flotation costs* is calculated as follows:

$$ATCF_3 = +\$500,000(15/25)(0.40)$$
$$= +\$120,000$$

The unamortized portion of the old flotation costs is $500,000(15/25) = $300,000. This means the company will receive a tax deduction of $300,000. The deduction will reduce company taxes by $300,000(0.40) = $120,000, the amount calculated using one equation.

The after-tax cash flow resulting from the *net extra interest from the overlap period* is calculated as follows:

$$\text{ATCF}_4 = -\$10,000,000(0.12 - 0.09)(1/12)(1 - 0.40)$$
$$= -\$15,000$$

The company will be paying interest on the old issue for one month at a rate of 12 percent. The proceeds are being invested on a short-term basis at nine percent, resulting in a cash flow from the net interest of $-\$10,000,000(0.12 - 0.09)(1/12) = -\$25,000$ for the month. This amount is tax deductible and results in a tax savings of $0.40(\$25,000) = \$10,000$. Combining the cash flows from the net interest and the tax savings results in $-\$15,000$.

The initial cash flow for the refunding is found by combining the after-tax cash flows from the four sources.

$$\text{CF}_0 = \text{ATCF}_1 + \text{ATCF}_2 + \text{ATCF}_3 + \text{ATCF}_4$$
$$= -\$600,000 - \$450,000 + \$120,000 - \$15,000$$
$$= -\$945,000$$

The Yearly Cash Flows

The after-tax operating cash flows for a project are the change in cash flows during each period caused by acceptance of the project. For refunding, the changes in interest and yearly amortization determine the change in cash flows.

The after-tax cash flows for years 1 through 15 resulting from the changes in interest are calculated as follows:

$$\text{ATCF}_{1,1-15} = \$10,000,000(0.12 - 0.10)(1 - 0.40)$$
$$= \$120,000$$

The yearly interest savings is $\$10,000,000(0.02) = \$200,000$. Richardson must pay taxes on this increase in earnings before taxes, in the amount of $\$200,000(0.40) = \$80,000$. The after-tax cash flow would be $\$200,000 - \$80,000 = \$120,000$, the same result found using the equation.

The after-tax cash flows for years 1 through 15, resulting from the changes in yearly amortization, are calculated as follows:

$$\text{ATCF}_{2,1-15} = (\$450,000/15 - \$500,000/25)0.40$$
$$= \$4,000$$

The increase in yearly amortization is $30,000 − $20,000 = $10,000. This increase in tax deductions lowers taxes by $10,000(0.40) = $4,000.

The after-tax cash flows for years 1 through 15 are found by combining the after-tax cash flows from the two sources.

$$CF_n = ATCF_{1,1-15} + ATCF_{2,1-15}$$
$$= \$120,000 + \$4,000$$
$$= \$124,000$$

Calculating Present Value

The discount rate used in refunding is the after-tax cost of the new debt. This rate is used because the after-tax cash flows are not risky. They are the result of contractual obligations in the bond indentures.

The after-tax cost of new debt is given by Eq. 9.2. Substituting the cost of the new bonds into that equation yields the following:

$$ATCD = k_d(1 - T)$$
$$= 10\%(1 - 0.40)$$
$$= 6\%$$

The previous information may be summarized in a cash flow diagram.

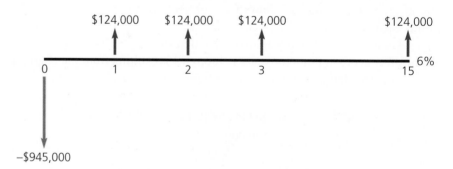

To find the present value, apply the six percent discount rate to the cash flows.

$$PV = -\$945,000 + \$124,000(PVFA_{6\%,15})$$
$$= -\$945,000 + \$124,000(9.7122)$$
$$= \$259,313$$

The positive PV is comparable to NPVs of capital projects and suggests that refunding should take place.

TABLE 14.1 Cash Flow Worksheet for Refunding

PERIOD	CF_ADD	CF_N	R_N	OC_N
0	-$945,000	0	0	0
1	0	$124,000	$200,000	0
2	0	$124,000	$200,000	0
3	0	$124,000	$200,000	0
4	0	$124,000	$200,000	0
5	0	$124,000	$200,000	0
6	0	$124,000	$200,000	0
7	0	$124,000	$200,000	0
8	0	$124,000	$200,000	0
9	0	$124,000	$200,000	0
10	0	$124,000	$200,000	0
11	0	$124,000	$200,000	0
12	0	$124,000	$200,000	0
13	0	$124,000	$200,000	0
14	0	$124,000	$200,000	0
15	0	$124,000	$200,000	0

PERIOD	DC_N	DC_NEW	DC_OLD	EAT
0	0	0	0	0
1	$10,000	$30,000	$20,000	0
2	$10,000	$30,000	$20,000	0
3	$10,000	$30,000	$20,000	0
4	$10,000	$30,000	$20,000	0
5	$10,000	$30,000	$20,000	0
6	$10,000	$30,000	$20,000	0
7	$10,000	$30,000	$20,000	0
8	$10,000	$30,000	$20,000	0
9	$10,000	$30,000	$20,000	0
10	$10,000	$30,000	$20,000	0
11	$10,000	$30,000	$20,000	0
12	$10,000	$30,000	$20,000	0
13	$10,000	$30,000	$20,000	0
14	$10,000	$30,000	$20,000	0
15	$10,000	$30,000	$20,000	0

Table 14.1 shows how to use the cash flow worksheet from Chapter 6, page 178. This format is not especially helpful unless you use THE FINANCIAL MANAGER (PROJECT). This model allows you easily to recalculate the PV, while varying the assumptions.

The previous example included a simplifying circumstance: The number of years left on the old issue is exactly equal to the number of years on the new issue. In most cases, the remaining life of the old issue is less than that of the new issue. When this is the case, include only the cash flows until the end of the old issue.

> Assume from the Richardson Corporation example that the old bonds were originally issued *15* years ago and that everything else remains the same. How does this affect the analysis?

The after-tax cash flow resulting from the *tax savings from the immediate write-off of the unamortized flotation costs* is recalculated as follows:

$$ATCF_3 = +\$500,000(10/25)(0.40)$$
$$= +\$80,000$$

The other after-tax cash flows in year zero remain the same.

The yearly after-tax cash flows are now for years 1 through 10.

Bond Deals Pinch Taxpayers

While taxpayers pinch pennies to make ends meet, local government officials across the country are on a credit-based spending spree—borrowing billions behind taxpayers' backs. Moreover, it is expensive borrowing, with higher interest rates and higher fees. An investigation by The Atlanta Journal-Constitution shows that local public officials waste millions of dollars each year by avoiding competitive bidding on local bond deals. Government officials are bypassing local taxpayers by turning to a select group of Wall Street financiers, underwriters and lawyers who benefit most from higher fees and interest on negotiated bond deals. They design bond issues that do not require voter approval. . . . And in Georgia, local governments routinely pay bond attorneys more than 10 times what the state would pay.

. . . Wall Street investment firms and underwriters seeking to profit from bond issues are contributing millions of dollars annually to political campaigns across the country—so much that Florida banned contributions from those doing state bond work because the money had corrupted financial judgments. These bond merchants sell debt . . . through town councils, commissions and public authorities so obscure that few local taxpayers even know they exist. . . .

Source: Richard Witt, "Bond deals pinch taxpayers," *The Atlanta Journal-Constitution,* June 21, 1992. Reprinted with permission from the Atlanta Journal and The Atlanta Constitution.

$$CF_n = ATCF_{1,1-10} + ATCF_{2,1-10}$$
$$= \$120,000 + \$4,000$$
$$= \$124,000$$

To find the present value, apply the six percent discount rate to the new cash flows

$$PV = -\$945,000 + \$124,000(PVFA_{6\%,10})$$
$$= -\$945,000 + \$124,000(7.3601)$$
$$= -\$32,348$$

The new calculations suggest that the refunding should *not* take place.

LEASING

A **lease** is a contract between a lessor and a lessee. The owner, called the lessor, grants to the user, called the lessee, the right to use the asset for a given time, in return for periodic payments. The lessee usually chooses the asset to be leased and then negotiates with the lessor as to terms. With traditional leases, the lessor retains legal ownership of the asset.

Lease

Types of Leases

An **operating lease,** or service lease, is a traditional lease with the following typical features:

Operating Lease

- The lease is not fully amortized, and thus does not cover the useful life of the asset. (This implies the lessor must either renew the lease or sell the asset for a reasonable amount.)
- The lessor is responsible for maintenance, property taxes, and insurance.
- The lease is cancelable at the option of the lessee. (This option is valuable to the lessee since it shifts the risk of obsolescence to the lessor.)

A **financial lease,** or capital lease, usually has the following characteristics:

Financial Lease

- The lease is fully amortized.
- The lessee is responsible for maintenance, property taxes, and insurance.
- The lease is noncancelable.
- The lessee may renew the lease at expiration.

Financial leases come in two forms: sale-and-leaseback arrangements and leveraged leases.

Sale-and-Leaseback Arrangement

A **sale-and-leaseback arrangement** normally has the following properties:

- The lessee sells an asset to the lessor for cash and immediately leases it back.
- The lessee keeps the asset and makes periodic payments to the lessor.

Leveraged Lease

A **leveraged lease** usually has the following characteristics:

- The lessee makes periodic payments for use of the assets.
- The lessor purchases the assets but only provides 20 to 50 percent of the capital necessary for the purchase.
- A lender, possibly an insurance company or pension fund, provides the remainder of the financing. (For protection in case of default, the lender has a first lien on the assets.)

Accounting for Leases

Off-Balance-Sheet Financing

Before November 1976, a financial, or capital, lease allowed **off-balance-sheet financing.** This means that financial leases did not appear as debt on the right hand side of the balance sheet. Instead, accountants reported the leases in footnotes to the financial statements. As a result, some companies leased assets instead of using debt in order to improve their debt ratios, believing that this would actually lower the cost of new debt.

The Financial Accounting Standards Board (FASB) in November 1976 issued FASB Statement No. 13, "Accounting for Leases." This statement requires financial leases, as defined by the FASB, to be capitalized on the balance sheet. Capitalization requires accountants to report the value of the asset on the left hand side of the balance sheet and the present value of the lease payments on the right hand side.

FASB Statement No. 13 defines a lease as a financial, or capital, lease if one or more of the following criteria are met:

- The lessee owns the asset at the end of the lease period.
- The lease gives the lessee the option to purchase the asset at below fair market value at the end of the lease period.
- The present value of the lease payments is equal to or greater than 90 percent of the fair market value at the beginning of the lease.
- The term of the lease is at least 75 percent of the estimated economic life of the asset.

The Financial Accounting Standards Board defines all other leases as operating leases.

Leases and Taxes

The key question with leases and taxes is whether or not the lease is an operating lease (a true lease) or a financial lease (a conditional sale lease). Unfortunately, the definitions that accountants use for the two types of leases are not necessarily valid for tax purposes.

The Internal Revenue Service (IRS) regards a true lease, a tax-oriented lease, as a lease in which the lessor assumes the risk of ownership. With a true lease, the lessor receives the benefits of depreciation and the investment tax credit, if available.

The IRS considers a lease a conditional sale if one or more of the following criteria are met:

- The term of the lease is for more than 30 years.
- The lease gives the lessee the option to purchase the asset at below fair market value at the end of the lease period.
- The lessee owns the asset at the end of a stated number of payments.
- The lease includes a number of high payments near the beginning of the lease.
- The lessor does not receive a fair rate of return on the investment.
- The lease includes a penalty clause for early termination.

This list is not exhaustive, so the leasing parties should consult the IRS before entering into a significant lease.

Designation of a lease as a conditional sale requires lease payments to be treated as purchase price installments. This allow the lessee to deduct depreciation and the imputed interest, not the full lease payment. The lessor is taxed on the interest and receives no other tax benefits.

The IRS is concerned if leases are set up simply to shift expenses or income. High payments near the beginning of the lease allow equipment to be depreciated faster than is allowed under MACRS. This causes the present value of the tax savings to be higher with leasing than with depreciation, resulting in a gain for the lessee and a loss for the IRS.

Evaluation by the Lessee

The evaluation of a lease by the lessee is similar to bond refunding in that it requires a capital budgeting-type analysis. The question for the financial manager is: How does the present value of the net cash flows from leasing compare with the present value of the net cash flows from borrowing and buying?

> The Richardson Corporation is considering leasing or borrowing and buying some new equipment. The charge for leasing is $300,000 per year for five years, payable at the end of each year. The equipment, if purchased, costs $1,000,000 and has a $100,000 salvage value at the end of five years. Richardson, which has a marginal tax rate of 40 percent, will depreciate the equipment on a straight line basis. The purchase amount of $1,000,000 may be borrowed at an interest rate of 10 percent. The lease contract does not require Richardson to pay for maintenance, but if the equipment is purchased, a maintenance charge of $40,000 must be paid at the end of each year. Should Richardson lease or borrow and buy the equipment?

We can solve this problem by determining the incremental cash flows for leasing and finding the present value for each method of financing. It is not necessary in this analysis to consider cash flows that are the same for leasing and for borrowing and buying. For example, changes in revenues and operating costs need not be included.

The after-tax cash flows from leasing ($ATCFL_i$) for years 1 through 5 are calculated as follows:

$$ATCFL_{1-5} = -\$300,000(1 - 0.40)$$
$$= -\$180,000$$

This lease payment is tax deductible and results in a tax savings of $0.40(\$300,000) = \$120,000$. Combining the cash flows from the lease payment and the tax savings results in −$180,000.

The after-tax cash flow from borrowing and buying ($ATCFO_i$) for year zero is simply stated as follows:

$$ATCFO_0 = -\$1,000,000$$

This is the only cash flow occurring at time zero. If the maintenance charges occur at the beginning of the year, then a second term is added to the equation.

The after-tax cash flows from borrowing and buying ($ATCFO_i$) for years 1 through 5 are calculated as follows:

$$ATCFO_{1-5} = [(\$1,000,000 - \$100,000)/5]0.40 - \$40,000(1 - 0.40)$$
$$= \$72,000 - \$24,000$$
$$= \$48,000$$

The first term is the depreciation tax savings. The second term is the maintenance charge combined with the tax savings from deducting the maintenance expense.

The after-tax cash flow from borrowing and buying ($ATCFO_i$) for year five is simply stated as follows:

$$ATCFO_5 = \$100,000$$

There is no tax effect since the book value at year five is the same as the salvage value.

The discount rate used in leasing versus borrowing and buying is the after-tax cost of the debt. As with refunding, the cash flows are essentially riskless. They are the result of contractual obligations.

The after-tax cost of debt is given by Eq. 9.2. Substituting the cost of borrowing into that equation yields the following:

$$\begin{aligned} ATCD &= k_d(1 - T) \\ &= 10\%(1 - 0.40) \\ &= 6\% \end{aligned}$$

The previous information for leasing may be summarized with a cash flow diagram.

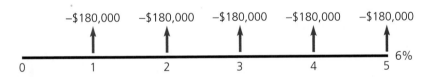

Similarly the information for borrowing and buying may be summarized.

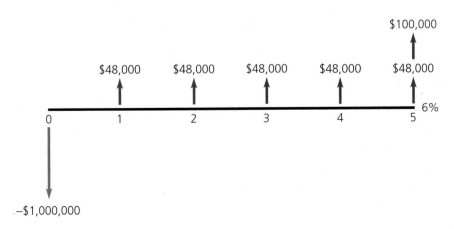

Find the present value for leasing, PV_L, with the following equation:

$$PV_L = -\$180{,}000(PVFA_{6\%,5})$$
$$= -\$180{,}000(4.2124)$$
$$= -\$758{,}232$$

Find the present value for borrowing and buying PV_O, with the following equation:

$$PV_O = -\$1{,}000{,}000 + \$48{,}000(PVFA_{6\%,5}) + \$100{,}000(PVF_{6\%,5})$$
$$= -\$1{,}000{,}000 + \$48{,}000(4.2124) + \$100{,}000(0.7473)$$
$$= -\$723{,}075$$

The calculations suggest that borrowing and buying is better than leasing since the present value of the cash flows is less negative.

This example could be altered slightly by requiring that lease payments and maintenance charges be paid at the beginning of the year. This changes the cash flow diagram for leasing.

The cash flow diagram for borrowing and buying is also changed.

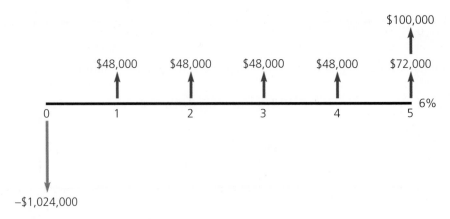

The new present value calculations for leasing are as follows:

$$PV_L = -\$180{,}000 - \$180{,}000(PVFA_{6\%,4})$$
$$= -\$180{,}000 - \$180{,}000(3.4651)$$
$$= -\$803{,}718$$

The new present value calculations for borrowing and buying are as follows:

$$PV_O = -\$1,024,000 + \$48,000(PVFA_{6\%,4}) + \$172,000(PVF_{6\%,5})$$
$$= -\$1,024,000 + \$48,000(3.4651) + \$172,000(0.7473)$$
$$= -\$729,140$$

Even with the change, borrowing and buying is favored.

Evaluation by the Lessor

The evaluation of a lease by the lessor also requires a capital budgeting-type analysis. The relevant question is: What is the present value of the lease, given the opportunity cost of the lessor? The opportunity cost is the after-tax yield the lessor receives on investments of similar risk.

Assume the conditions from the Richardson Corporation example remain the same and that the following conditions apply: (1) the marginal tax rate of the lessor is 40 percent, (2) the before-tax yield on bonds of similar risk to the lease is 8 1/3 percent, and (3) the lessor uses straight line depreciation and perceives the same salvage value as the lessee. Should the lessor invest in the lease?

We can solve this problem by determining the incremental cash flows from the point of view of the lessor and then finding the present value using the after-tax yield the lessor receives on investments of similar risk. A positive PV implies the lessor should invest in the lease.

The lessor after-tax cash flow ($LATCF_i$) for year zero is stated as follows:

$$LATCF_0 = -\$1,000,000$$

This is the only cash flow occurring at time zero. If the maintenance charges or the lease payments occur at the beginning of the year, then one or two more terms are added to the equation.

The lessor after-tax cash flows ($LATCF_i$) for years 1 through 5 are calculated as follows:

$$LATCF_{1-5} = [(\$1,000,000 - \$100,000)/5]0.40 - \$40,000(1 - 0.40)$$
$$+ \$300,000(1 - 0.40)$$
$$= \$72,000 - \$24,000 + \$180,000$$
$$= \$228,000$$

The first term is the depreciation tax savings. The second term is the maintenance charge combined with the tax savings from deducting the maintenance expense. The third term is the revenue from the lease payment less the taxes that are due.

The lessor after-tax cash flow (LATCF$_i$) for year five, the result of the salvage value, is stated as follows:

$$LATCF_5 = \$100,000$$

There is no tax effect since the book value at year five is the same as the salvage value.

This information is summarized with a cash flow diagram.

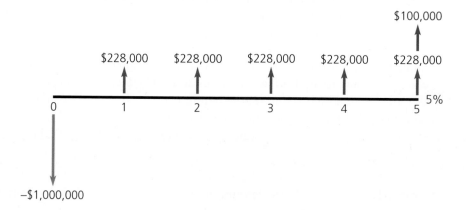

The after-tax yield (ATY) the lessor receives on investments of similar risk is given by the following:

$$ATY = 8\ 1/3\%(1 - 0.40)$$
$$= 5\%$$

This is the discount rate used in the PV calculation.

To find the present value, apply the five percent discount rate.

$$PV = -\$1,000,000 + \$228,000(PVFA_{5\%,5}) + \$100,000(PVF_{5\%,5})$$
$$= -\$1,000,000 + \$228,000(4.3295) + \$100,000(0.7835)$$
$$= \$65,476$$

The positive PV implies that the lease is a good investment.

In this example, it is easy to find the amount of the lease payment at which the lessor is indifferent to investing in the lease. First, replace the $228,000 cash flow with X and set the PV equal to zero.

$$0 = -\$1,000,000 + X(PVFA_{5\%,5}) + \$100,000(PVF_{5\%,5})$$
$$= -\$1,000,000 + X(4.3295) + \$100,000(0.7835)$$

After some manipulation, we find the value of X.

$$X = \$212,876.77$$

Moving back to the lessor after-tax cash flows (LATCF$_i$) for years 1 through 5 suggests a new equation, with Y the indifferent lease payment.

$$\$212,876.77 = [(\$1,000,000 - \$100,000)/5]0.40 - \$40,000(1 - 0.40)$$
$$+ Y(1 - 0.40)$$
$$= \$72,000 - \$24,000 + Y(0.6)$$

Bond Insurers Nearing Their Capacity

Bond insurance companies are running out of the capacity to insure bonds from several of the municipal bond market's most popular issuers. Investors say it is nearly impossible to find insurance for tax-free bonds issued by New York City and New York State, which are among the municipal market's biggest borrowers. The difficulty insuring their bond offerings translates into higher borrowing costs and—when its available—more expensive insurance fees for some frequent municipal borrowers.

For a fee, often paid by the municipality selling the bonds, bond insurance companies will guarantee to make principal and interest payments in the event that the issuer of the bonds defaults. And because all bonds insurers are rated triple-A by the credit rating agencies, any bonds that carry their guarantee are assigned the credit agencies' top rating. This is the main reason municipalities buy insurance: Essentially, borrowers are buying a triple-A credit rating, which lets them issue bonds much more cheaply than they could with their own credit rating.

A group that may look favorably on the bond insurance capacity squeeze is big institutional investors who buy tax-free bonds. They have complained that the huge volume of newly issued insured debt is reducing yields in the overall municipal market. That's because yield on insured bonds are much lower than on uninsured bonds.

Yields are quite important in bond selection, but are only one basis for judging. Investors must also consider characteristics such as time to maturity, call features, protective covenants, and sinking fund provisions. These and other attributes must be weighed in the light of specific investment objectives.

Solving, we find the value for Y.

$$Y = \$274{,}794.61$$

At this point, the lessor is indifferent about investing in the lease.

The calculation of the indifference point is more difficult when the cash flows are not constant. This occurs when you see MACRS depreciation. In such a case, use THE FINANCIAL MANAGER (PROJECT). This model allows you easily to recalculate the PV while varying the amount of the lease payment.

SUMMARY

This chapter focuses on the following learning objectives:

1. Describing long-term debt financing in terms of the bond indenture, types of bonds, and bond ratings.

   Long-term debt is usually in the form of notes or bonds. The bond indenture is a contract between the company issuing the bonds and the bondholder. A call feature specifies the conditions under which a bond may be retired by the issuing company. With serial bonds, each bond has its own maturity. A sinking fund provision requires that bonds be retired in a systematic fashion. Protective covenants are provisions in bond indentures designed to reduce the possibility that the company will default on the bonds. Unsecured bonds are backed by the general credit of the company issuing them, and are not secured by any specific property. Subordinated debentures are debentures that are subordinate to other creditors named in the bond indenture. Secured bonds have specific assets pledged to protect the bondholder in the event of default. Bond Ratings reflect the probability that the issuing corporation will default on the bond.

2. Performing a bond refunding analysis to determine if an old bond issue should be replaced with a new issue.

   Bond refunding is the replacement of all or part of a bond issue with another bond issue. Companies consider refunding when interest rates decline. The question for the financial manager is: Are the benefits of refunding greater than the costs?

3. Detailing the types of leases, the accounting for leases, and the effect of taxes on leases.

   A lease is a contract between a lessor and a lessee. Leases are generally classified as operating leases or financial leases. The Financial Accounting Standards Board (FASB) in November 1976 issued FASB Statement No. 13, "Accounting for Leases," requiring financial leases, as defined by the FASB, to be capitalized on the balance sheet. The key question with leases and taxes is whether or not the lease is an operating lease (a true lease) or a financial lease (a conditional sale lease).

4. Evaluating leases from the point of view of the lessee and the lessor.
   The evaluation of a lease by the lessee or by the lessor requires a capital budgeting-type analysis. The question for the lessee: How does the present value of the net cash flows from leasing compare with the present value of the net cash flows from borrowing and buying? For the lessor: What is the present value of the lease, given the opportunity cost of the lessor?

Key Term

Bond indenture, 389	Investment grade bond, 393	Sale-and-leaseback arrangement, 402
Bond rating, 392	Junk bond, 391	Secured bond, 390
Bond refunding, 395	Lease, 401	Serial bond, 390
Call feature, 390	Leveraged lease, 402	Sinking fund provision, 390
Collateral trust bond, 392	Mortgage bond, 392	Speculative grade bond, 393
Debenture, 391	Off-balance-sheet financing, 402	
Equipment trust certificate, 392	Operating lease, 401	Subordinated debenture, 391
Financial lease, 401	Protective covenant, 389	Unsecured bond, 391
Income bond, 391		

Questions

14.1   Explain the bond indenture and the role of the bond trustee in ensuring that its terms are met.

14.2   What are the five methods for repaying bonds?

14.3   Discuss the role of call features in the bond indenture.

14.4   Contrast serial bonds and sinking funds.

14.5   Explain how protective covenants are designed to reduce the possibility that a company will default on its bonds.

14.6   Explain the nature of unsecured bonds.

14.7   What is meant by subordinated debentures?

14.8   What are junk bonds? Income bonds?

14.9   Explain secured bonds, and discuss the major types.

14.10 Explain how bonds are rated.

14.11 Discuss the differences between investment grade and speculative grade bonds.

14.12 What are the positives and negatives of refunding?

14.13 What are the differences between operating leases and financial leases?

14.14 What is the significance of FASB Statement No. 13, "Accounting for Leases?"

14.15 What are the differences between an operating lease, a true lease, and a financial lease, a conditional sale lease, from the point of view of the Internal Revenue Service?

14.16 How might the passage of Nafta affect bond prices?

14.17 What are the perils of global bonds?

14.18 How might municipal bonds deals pinch taxpayers?

14.19 How do bond insurers protect investors?

PROBLEMS

14.1 **(Bond Refunding)** Golden Foods, Inc., outstanding $50,000,000 of 13 percent bonds, originally issued 10 years ago. The old flotation costs of $2,000,000 were amortized on a straight line basis over the 25-year life of the issue. The company is considering refunding the old issue with $50,000,000 of 10 percent bonds. This requires payment of a 10.5 percent call premium. The new flotation costs of $1,500,000 will be amortized on a straight line basis over the 15-year life of the issue. The new bonds will be sold one month before the old issue is called, and during this month, the proceeds from the new issue will be invested in short-term securities at an interest rate of eight percent. If the marginal tax rate of Golden Foods is 40 percent, should the refunding take place?

14.2 **(Bond Refunding)** The Singhal Company has outstanding $20,000,000 of 11 percent bonds, originally issued 20 years ago. Singhal is considering refunding the old issue with $20,000,000 of nine percent bonds. The old flotation costs of $900,000 were amortized on a straight line basis over the 30-year life of the old issue. The new flotation costs of $960,000 will be amortized on a straight line basis over the 30-year life of the new issue. Refunding requires payment of a 10 percent call premium. The new bonds will be sold one month before the old issue is called, and during this month the proceeds from the new issue will be invested in short-term securities at an interest rate of eight percent. If the marginal tax rate of Singhal is 40 percent, should the refunding take place?

14.3 **(Bond Refunding)** Monet Publishing is considering refunding $100 million of 12 percent, 30-year bonds issued 5 years ago. Investment bankers indicate Monet could sell a new 25-year issue at an interest rate of 10 percent. The old flotation costs amounted to $3,000,000, while the new flotation costs will be $4,000,000. The company amortizes flotation costs on a straight line basis. The new bonds will be sold one month before the old issue is called, and during this month the proceeds from the new issue will be invested in short-term securities at an interest rate of nine percent. If the marginal tax rate of Monet is 40 percent and a 10.5 percent call premium is required, should the refunding take place?

14.4 **(Lease or Borrow and Buy)** The Miller Corporation is considering leasing or borrowing and buying some new equipment. The charge for leasing is $450,000 per year for five years, payable at the end of each year. The equipment, if purchased, costs $1,400,000 and has a $200,000 salvage value at the end of five years. The Miller Corporation has a marginal tax rate of 40 percent, and it will depreciate the equipment on a straight line basis. The purchase amount of $1,400,000 may be borrowed at an interest rate of 10 percent. The lease contract does not require Miller to pay for maintenance, but if the equipment is purchased, a maintenance charge of $75,000 must be paid at the end of each year. Should Miller lease or borrow and buy the equipment?

14.5 **(Investor Leasing)** The marginal tax rate of the leasing company from the previous problem is 40 percent. It can invest in bonds of similar risk to the lease at 8 1/3 percent. The leasing company uses straight line depreciation and perceives the same salvage value as the Miller Corporation. Should it invest in the lease?

14.6 **(Lease or Borrow and Buy)** Dernian Dumpsters, Inc. is considering either leasing or borrowing and buying some new equipment. The equipment, if purchased, costs $3,000,000 and has a $500,000 salvage value at the end of five years. Dernian has a marginal tax rate of 40 percent and will depreciate the equipment on a straight line basis. The purchase amount of $3,000,000 may be borrowed at an interest rate of 10 percent. The charge for leasing is $800,000 per year for five years, payable at the beginning of each year. The lease contract does not require Dernian to pay for maintenance, but if the equipment is purchased, a maintenance charge of $100,000 must be paid at the beginning of each year. Should Dernian lease or borrow and buy the equipment?

14.7 **(Investor Leasing)** A wealthy investor, with a marginal tax rate of 40 percent, is considering leasing this equipment from the previous problem. Her before-tax yield on bonds of similar risk to the lease is 8 1/3 percent. She uses straight line depreciation and expects the same salvage value as Dernian. Should she invest in the lease? What must the leasing payment be for the investor to be indifferent to leasing?

A Case Problem

entral Area Rapid Transit (CART) provided an express bus service and a fixed rail system for a large metropolitan area. In 1970, CART was formed and immediately acquired the privately owned bus company serving the area. The rail system consisted of 39 miles of operational double track and 30 functioning stations. Future plans called for a total of 62 miles of double track and 46 stations.

In 1993, CART offered $307,000,000 of Sales Tax Revenue Bonds, Refunding Series K. The Series K Bonds were being issued to refund portions of Refunding Series G, H, and I. The Series K Bonds were dated May 1, 1993, and included interest from that date payable on July 1, 1993, and semiannually thereafter. The bonds were issued in fully registered form in denominations of $5,000 or any multiple thereof. Interest would be paid by check or draft to the owner of record as of June 15 or December 15 preceding the payment date. Payment of the principal and interest on the Series K Bonds was guaranteed by a municipal bond insurance policy issued by AMAC Indemnity Corporation. As a result, Standard & Poor's Corporation and Moody's Investors Service, Inc., assigned municipal bond ratings of "AAA" and "Aaa", respectively, to the Series K Bonds.

Several stock and bond brokerage firms agreed, subject to certain conditions, to purchase all of the Series K

Bonds at a price representing an aggregate underwriting discount from the initial public offering prices. These underwriters also agreed to make a bona fide public offering of the Series K Bonds at prices not in excess of such public offering prices, plus accrued interest. The bonds could also be offered to certain dealers (including the underwriters) at prices lower than the initial public offering prices.

Under a contract with counties that CART served, sales tax collected at the maximum rate for rapid transit purposes would be allocated to CART. These payments would be further assigned to the trustee, NationsBank. The bond indenture established a sinking fund, to be held by the trustee, and provided that so long as any bonds were outstanding, revenues from the sales tax would be deposited into a sinking fund. Any monies in the sinking fund were for the benefit of the bondholders.

CART was a party to a number of litigation matters relating to disputes with the union, breaches of contract, condemnation of property, personal injuries during construction.

CART was a party to a number of litigation matters relating to disputes with the union, breaches of contract, condemnation of property, personal injuries during construction. The outcome of this litigation was not determinable, although counsel for CART believe these matters would not materially affect the Series K Bonds.

Leading Questions

1. What factors would lead you to purchase the Series K Bonds?
2. What factors would lead you *not* to purchase the Series K Bonds?

15 Options, Warrants, and Convertibles

of holders of the company's common stock was more muted. If Chrysler sells $1 billion of preferred, holders of the common would see their investments diluted by 18% to 20% when the preferred is converted into common shares.

Industry analysts generally lauded Chrysler's plans to sell as much preferred stock as it can. Several analysts said Chrysler's need for a quick cash injection far outweighs concerns about dilution. It isn't clear how Chrysler will use proceeds from the preferred stock. But it faces a number of drains on its reserves including heavy product spending in a weak economy and a $4.4 billion unfunded pension deficit. And, among the most immediate problems facing the company: The need to replace $3.7 billion in debt this year at its Chrysler Financial subsidiary.

The convertible preferred stock offering at Chrysler creates an interesting question: Who wins and who loses? The bondholders seem happy and the common stockholders seem unhappy. As we shall see in this chapter, it is not quite that simple.

Source: Bradley A. Stertz, "Chrysler May Offer $1 Billion Of Its Preferred," *The Wall Street Journal,* February 12, 1992. Reprinted by permission of The Wall Street Journal, © 1992 Dow Jones & Company, Inc. All Rights Reserved Worldwide.

OPTIONS

Most investment and financing alternatives include options embedded in them. For example, spending money on new technology allows a company to expand the amount of the investment if that action increases stock value. If the project appears not to be beneficial, the embedded option is allowed to expire.

Options appear in many different forms—options on land, options with leases, and options with securities, but all share the following definition: An **option** is a contract giving the holder the right, but not the obligation, to buy or sell an asset at a fixed price on or before a specified expiration date. A **European option** can only be exercised on the expiration date, whereas an **American option** can be exercised at any time until, but not after, the expiration date. The **striking price,** or exercise price, is the price at which the underlying asset is sold. It can be fixed or variable according to a schedule, as is the call premium for a bond. **Exercising the option** involves buying or selling the asset through the option contract.

Option
European Option
American Option

Striking Price

Exercising the Option

Call and Put Options

A **call option** gives the holder the right to *buy* an asset at a fixed price for a specified period of time. For example, you are given the option until Decem-

Call Option

417

ber 31, 1999, to buy a building for $500,000. You have the right to buy, but you are not obligated to do so.

Put Option

A **put option** gives the holder the right to *sell* an asset at a fixed price for a specified period of time. For example, you are given the option until the last day of this year to sell your boat for $10,000. You have the right to sell, but you are not obligated to do so.

This chapter focuses on stocks as the underlying assets for the call and put options. These are the options commonly found on the exchanges. Initially, the discussion is restricted to the simpler European option.

> John MacDonald purchased a European call option to buy 100 shares of common stock in the Martin Corporation with an exercise price of $25 and an expiration date of October 15, 19X4. What is the value of the contract on the expiration date?

On the expiration date, the value of the contract depends upon the value of the underlying stock. Figure 15.1 illustrates the value of the call option on a per share basis. If the value of the common stock is less than $25, he would not exercise the option, and the value is $0. The option is said to be *out of the money*. If the value of the common stock is more than $25, the option is *in the money*, and he would exercise it. For example, if the common stock sold for $30, he would gain $5 per share ($30 – $25), or $500 for the 100 shares. Similarly, at $35 he would gain $1,000. This is a limited liability instrument, the most he can lose is the amount paid for the option.

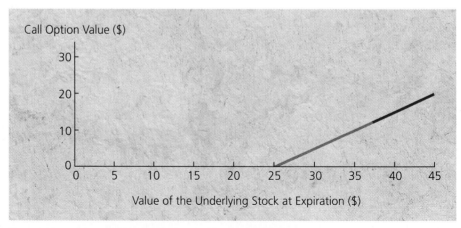

Figure 15.1　Value of a Call Option to the Buyer at Expiration

Lisa MacDonald purchased a European put option to sell 100 shares of common stock in the Martin Corporation with an exercise price of $25 and an expiration date of October 15, 19X4. What will be the value of the contract on the expiration date?

On the expiration date, the value of the contract again depends upon the value of the underlying stock. Figure 15.2 illustrates the value of the put option on a per share basis. If the value of the common stock is more than $25, she would not exercise the option, and the value is $0. The option is said to be *out of the money*. If the value of the common stock is less than $25, the call is *in the money*, and she would exercise the option. For example, if the common stock sold for $20, she would gain $5 per share ($25 – $20), or $500 for the 100 shares. Similarly, at $15 she would gain $1,000. This is also a limited liability instrument, the most she can lose is the amount paid for the put option.

Selling Calls and Puts

The investor who writes (sells) a call is obligated to provide the shares of common stock if the call holder exercises the option. In order to accept this potential liability, the writer receives cash when the option is purchased. If an investor enters into a contract and owns the underlying stock, the investor is selling a **covered option.** If the stock is not owned, the investor is selling a **naked option.**

Covered Option
Naked Option

The amount of the writer's liability in the previous call option example depends upon the value of the underlying stock on the expiration date. Figure 15.3

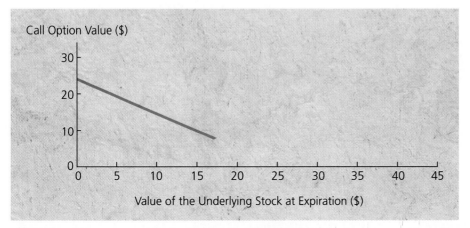

Figure 15.2   Value of a Put Option to the Buyer at Expiration

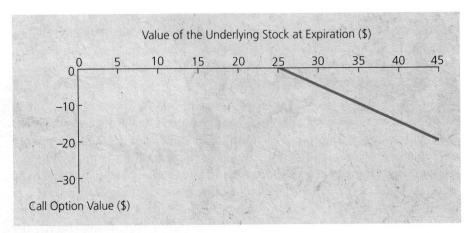

Figure 15.3 Value of a Call Option to the Writer at Expiration

illustrates the value of the call option to the writer on a per share basis. If the value of the common stock is less than $25, the option would not be exercised, and the value is $0. If the value of the common stock is more than $25, the option would be exercised, and the writer would lose money. For example, if the common stock sold for $30, the writer would lose $5 per share ($30 − $25), or $500 for the 100 shares. The loss, however, would be reduced by the proceeds from the sale.

The amount of the writer's liability in the previous put option example also depends upon the value of the underlying stock on the expiration date. Figure 15.4 illustrates the value of the put option to the writer on a per share basis. If the value of the common stock is greater than $25, the option would not be exercised, and the value is $0. If the value of the common stock is less than $25, the option would be exercised, and the writer would lose money. For example,

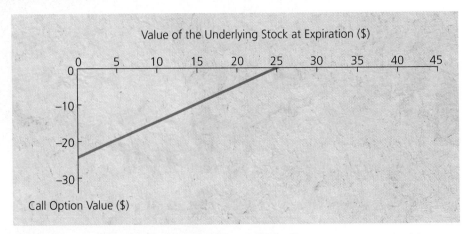

Figure 15.4 Value of a Put Option to the Writer at Expiration

if the common stock sold for $20, the writer would lose $5 per share ($25 – $20), or $500 for the 100 shares.

The Wall Street Journal provides quotations on calls and puts. Figure 15.5 includes the options traded on November 23, 1993, from the November 24, 1993, issue. Reading down the first column, you find that the stock of A M D closed at 18 1/2 the previous day. Moving across, notice that for a striking price of $20, you could purchase a call option maturing near the end of April for $2. The cost for a 100-share contract, not including commissions is $200, the per share cost multiplied by 100. Similarly, you can purchase a put option maturing at the end of April for $3 1/4, or $325 for a 100-share contract.

Option Valuation

In the previous section, you considered the value of European call options at expiration. This segment expands the discussion by considering the value of the American call option.

MOST ACTIVE CONTRACTS

Option/Strike			Vol	Exch	Last	Net Chg	a-Close	Open Int
A M R	Dec	70	6,034	AM	1/2	– 7/8	65 1/8	9,438
ParaCm	Dec	80	4,181	CB	2 5/16	+ 1/16	76 1/2	32,353
I B M	Dec	55	3,649	CB	13/16	+ 1/8	53 1/8	17,741
TelMex	Dec	60	3,494	XC	1/4	– 1/4	55	33,779
Intel	Dec	60	3,245	AM	2	+ 3/8	58 7/8	13,304
Hewlet	Dec	70	p 3,017	CB	1 1/2	– 3/8	71 1/2	2,324
F P L	Jan	35	3,000	PB	1 1/8	...	36 3/8	...
BellAtl	Apr	60	2,844	CB	2 1/16	– 3/16	58 1/8	4,352
Citicp	Dec	35	p 2,692	CB	15/16	– 13/16	35	4,343
BellAtl	Jul	60	2,691	CB	2 7/8	– 1/8	58 1/8	60
TelMex	Feb	60	2,548	XC	1 11/16	– 7/16	55	10,449
ParaCm	Dec	65	p 2,446	CB	1 5/8	– 5/8	76 1/2	12,822
ParaCm	Dec	70	2,341	CB	8 3/8	+ 5/8	76 1/2	18,877
TelMex	Dec	55	2,210	XC	1 3/4	– 5/8	55	38,481
Merck	Jan	35	2,188	CB	15/16	+ 3/16	34 1/4	30,576
ParaCm	Dec	75	2,146	CB	4 7/8	– 1/2	76 1/2	22,458
USWst	Dec	50	2,060	AM	1/8	+ 1/16	45	2,336
A M R	Dec	100	p 2,000	AM	33 3/8	+ 3	65 1/8	...
PallCp	Mar	17 1/2	p 2,000	CB	7/8	+ 3/8	18 1/2	9
PallCp	Mar	20	2,000	CB	5/8	– 7/8	18 1/2	5,916
A M R	Dec	60	p 1,991	AM	5/8	+ 3/8	65 1/8	1,070
ParaCm	Dec	85	1,955	CB	15/16	...	76 1/2	28,711
A M R	Dec	65	p 1,933	AM	1 13/16	+ 13/16	65 1/8	3,056
EKodak	Jan	50	1,911	CB	12 1/2	+ 5/8	62 1/4	1,244
I B M	Dec	50	1,870	CB	3 3/8	+ 7/8	53 1/8	14,082
I B M	Dec	50	p 1,735	CB	5/16	– 3/16	53 1/8	7,983
EKodak	Jan	40	1,697	CB	22 1/4	+ 1 3/4	62 1/4	1,103
Compaq	Dec	65	p 1,685	XC	1	– 1/2	68 3/4	2,454
Merck	Dec	35	1,636	CB	5/8	+ 1/16	34 1/4	17,001
Motrla	Dec	100	1,636	AM	2	+ 5/8	95 7/8	8,234
I B M	Jan	55	1,521	CB	1 3/4	+ 5/16	53 1/8	21,747
Motrla	Dec	95	1,494	AM	4	+ 1	95 7/8	3,446
I B M	Jan	50	1,488	CB	4 3/8	+ 3/4	53 1/8	24,804
Motrla	Jan	95	1,460	AM	6	+ 1 1/4	95 7/8	2,927
Citicp	Jan	35	1,414	CB	1 3/4	+ 1/2	35	17,816
I B M	Jan	45	1,393	CB	8 3/8	+ 7/8	53 1/8	21,870
I B M	Jan	45	p 1,361	CB	1/4	– 1/8	53 1/8	10,626
Ph Mor	Dec	60	1,352	AM	5/16	– 1/16	54 7/8	36,089
ParaCm	Jan	80	1,345	CB	3 1/4	+ 3/8	76 1/2	3,481
FstUSA	Feb	27 1/2	p 1,300	AM	1 3/4	...	31 1/8	40

Option/Strike		Exp.	Call Vol.	Call Last	Put Vol.	Put Last
A Hess	50	Jan	46	1	...	...
A M D	15	Dec	...	...	90	1/8
18 1/2	15	Jan	30	4 1/8	...	...
18 1/2	15	Apr	40	4 1/2	20	1
18 1/2	17 1/2	Dec	13	1 3/4	131	9/16
18 1/2	17 1/2	Jan	117	2 1/8	64	1
18 1/2	20	Dec	561	1/2	10	2
18 1/2	20	Jan	690	1 1/8	...	...
18 1/2	20	Apr	25	2	22	3 1/4
18 1/2	22 1/2	Dec	50	3/16	6	3 7/8
18 1/2	22 1/2	Jan	356	5/8	...	...
18 1/2	22 1/2	Apr	35	1 5/8	...	...
18 1/2	25	Jan	60	5/16	30	6 3/4
18 1/2	30	Jan	215	1/8	...	...
A M P	60	May	572	13/16	...	...
A M R	55	Dec	...	...	75	1/8
36 1/2	40	Dec	45	9/16	...	...
Biomet	10	Dec	49	1	50	1/4
10 3/8	10	Jan	14	15/16	30	7/16
10 3/8	10	Apr	25	1 3/8	...	...
10 3/8	15	Jan	50	1/8	...	...
BkBost	22 1/2	Dec	30	3/8	...	...
21 5/8	25	Jan	125	5/16	...	...
BkrsLH	20	Dec	66	13/16	...	...
BkrsTr	75	Jan	25	3 3/8	30	2 7/8
75 5/8	80	Dec	150	1/2	...	...
Blk Dk	20	Feb	50	1 1/2	...	...
Blkbst	30	Dec	145	2	76	1/2
31 1/2	30	Jan	34	2 1/4	24	1
31 1/2	35	Dec	25	3/16	15	4 3/8
31 1/2	35	Jun	1003	1 1/2	...	...
Block	35	Jan	125	3 1/2	...	...
40	35	Jul	411	8 3/8	...	...
40	40	Dec	295	1 7/8	54	1 3/4
40	40	Jan	445	3	...	...
40	45	Dec	1078	9/16	...	...
CmpUSA	20	Dec	...	...	100	1/4
25 5/8	25	Dec	54	2 1/4	33	1 1/4
25 5/8	25	Feb	29	3 3/8	...	...
25 5/8	30	Jan	59	3/4	...	...
25 5/8	30	Feb	26	1 1/8	...	...
CmprsL	12 1/2	Dec	60	15/16	...	...
13 1/4	15	Jan	35	5/8	8	23/16
13 1/4	17 1/2	Jan	25	3/8	...	...
Cmptrx	5	Feb	142	5/8	...	...
4 3/8	5	May	35	3/4	...	...
Cmw Ed	30	May	27	7/8	...	...
Cnseco	50	Dec	21	6	68	1 3/8

Source: The Wall Street Journal, November 24, 1993. Reprinted by permission of the Wall Street Journal,

Figure 15.5 Listed Options from The Wall Street Journal

Figure 15.1 provides the value of the European call option for the example given in that section. The graph also represents the lower bound for the value of an American call option with the same basic information.

> John MacDonald purchased an American call option to buy 100 shares of common stock in the Martin Corporation with an exercise price of $25 and an expiration date of October 15, 19X4. If the underlying stock is selling for $35, what is the lowest possible value of the option before the expiration date?

The lower bound value of the call is $10 ($35 – $25), on a per share basis. To see what would happen if the option were selling for less than $10, pretend he is lucky enough to buy it for $8. Under these conditions, he would buy the call for $8, exercise the call at $25, and sell the share of stock for $35. The profit per share is $2 (–$8 – $25 + $35). For the full contract, the profit is $200, assuming zero trading expenses.

This example illustrates how to make a riskless trade with funds invested for only a brief period. If markets are efficient, prices adjust rapidly, and the opportunity for such profits disappears. In this example, a price of $8 would create high demand for the option, forcing the price upward to at least $10. This is the lower bound.

The upper bound for the value of an American call option is the price of the underlying stock. No investor is willing to pay more for an option on the stock than the price of the stock. Even here, the investor would require a zero exercise price and an infinite time until maturity. Figure 15.6 shows the upper and lower bounds for the value of the call option.

Figure 15.6 places limits on the value of the particular American call option, but more information is necessary to determine the market price. There are five variables that are important: (1) The value of the underlying stock, (2) The exercise price, (3) The time until expiration of the option, (4) The interest rate, and (5) The variability of the underlying stock price. The dotted line in Figure 15.7 suggests that the market price lies somewhat above the lower bound for the value of the call option.

The value of the underlying stock is positively related to the market price of the call option: As the value of the stock increases, the price of the option increases. Figure 15.7 shows that the market-price curve is convex; the increase in price is greatest when the value of the underlying stock is high. Notice also that the market premium, the difference between the market price of the option and the lower bound, declines as the value of the underlying stock increases. This occurs because of the decreasing leverage effect and the increasing chance of losses.

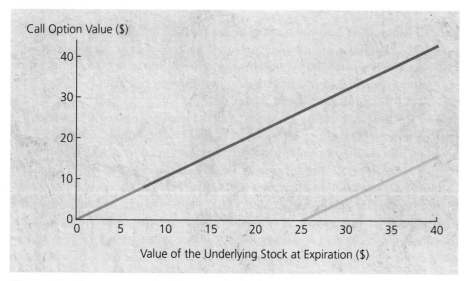

Figure 15.6 Upper and Lower Bounds for the Call-Option Value

The market price of the call option is inversely related to the exercise price; as the exercise price increases, the price of the option decreases. Keep in mind, however, that the market price cannot be negative. An American option always will have value prior to maturity, as the value of the underlying stock may be greater than the exercise price before the option expires.

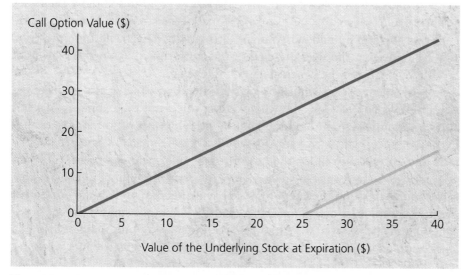

Figure 15.7 The Market Price for the American Call Option

The time until expiration is directly related to the market price of the option: As the time to maturity decreases, the price of the option decreases. Two American call options on the same stock, with identical exercise prices and different expiration dates, have market prices that are not the same. The option with the greater time until expiration allows greater opportunity for price increases and demands the higher market price.

The risk-free rate of interest is positively related to the market price of the option; as the interest rate increases, the price of the option increases. For a given length of time until maturity, the present value of the exercise price decreases as the interest rate increases. Therefore, the buyer of the option pays less for the stock when interest rates are relatively high.

The variability of the underlying stock price is positively related to the market price of the option; as the price of the stock becomes more volatile, the price of the option increases. With greater volatility, there is a greater chance for gain on the upside of the stock price distribution. The large downside potential of the stock is of no consequence to the call option holder. Stock prices below the exercise price, regardless of how far below, have a zero value.

WARRANTS

Warrant

A **warrant** is an option that gives the holder the right to *buy* a share of common stock at a fixed price for a specified period of time. Warrants are often attached to bond and preferred stock issues as *sweeteners* in order to sell these securities at lower yields. Warrants are also sold as new issues or distributed to shareholders instead of a dividend. Warrants are usually detachable from the issue and are traded on the over-the-counter market, as well as on the New York Stock Exchange and the American Stock Exchange.

A warrant agreement, similar to a bond indenture, contains the terms of the warrant. This contract specifies the exercise price and the expiration date. It also protects the warrant holder by limiting the number of warrants outstanding and by specifying what happens should a merger or acquisition occur.

A warrant typically allows the holder to buy one share of stock at the exercise price. If a stock split or stock dividend occurs, the number of shares that can be purchased and the exercise price are changed to protect the position of the warrant holder. For example, the company announces a two-for-one stock split. Originally, the warrant authorizes the purchase of one share of common stock at an exercise price of $50. After the split, the warrant holder may purchase two shares of common stock at an exercise price of $25.

Differences With Call Options

Warrants generally have longer lives than call options. Some warrants have a time to expiration of five years or more. Companies also issue perpetual warrants, with no expiration date.

Warrants are issued by companies, while call options are issued by individuals. Call options do not affect the number of shares the company has outstanding. But with warrants, the company issues a new share of stock at the time the warrant is exercised. The company receives cash for the share of stock, in contrast to no cash for call option transactions.

Changing the number of shares outstanding by exercising warrants affects the value of the company. For example, a company with $10,000 in assets and 10 shares of stock issues a warrant with an exercise price of $1,000. By the expiration date, the value of the assets has increased to $12,200. The holder exercises the warrant and pays the company $1,000. The company issues one new share of stock, increasing the number of outstanding shares to 11. The new value of the company is $13,200 ($12,200 + $1,000).

The holder of the warrant makes more money by owning a similar call option. By owning and exercising the warrant, the new share is worth $1,200 ($13,200/11). The warrant holder gains $200 ($1,200 − $1,000). After buying a call option with the same exercise price and expiration date, the value of the company is $12,200, while the number of shares remains at 10. Exercising the call option, the holder receives one share worth $1,220 ($12,200/10). The call option holder gains $220 ($1,220 − $1,000). The dilution caused by issuing the warrant causes the call option to be more valuable.

Warrant Valuation

The value of a warrant when compared with its underlying stock is similar to the call-option relationship studied earlier in this chapter. The value of underlying stock is positively related to the market price of the warrant; as the value of the stock increases, the price of the warrant increases. The value of the warrant also depends on the exercise price, the time until expiration, the risk-free rate of interest, and the variability of the underlying stock price. Figure 15.8 places upper and lower bounds on the value of the warrant and shows the market value of the warrant.

The value of the warrant may be calculated using the Black-Scholes model (Appendix 15A), provided the exercise price is constant and no dividends are paid. Under these conditions, the warrant holder will not exercise the warrant before the expiration date. This causes the warrant to function as a European call option, thus satisfying one of the key assumptions of the OPM.

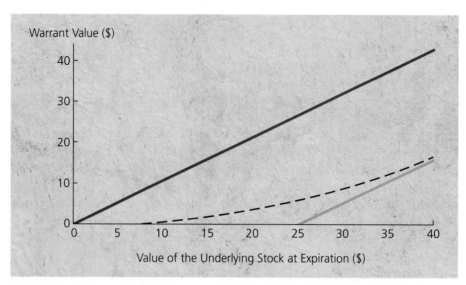

Figure 15.8   Upper and Lower Bounds and Market Price for Warrants
• • • • • • • • •

Accounting for Warrants

Primary EPS

Fully Diluted EPS

Simple EPS

The Securities and Exchange Commission and generally accepted accounting principles require the company income statement to disclose **primary EPS** and **fully diluted EPS,** if material dilution could occur. This applies not only to warrants, but to rights and convertible securities as well.

Simple EPS is earnings available to common shareholders divided by the average number of shares outstanding. Primary EPS is adjusted earnings available to common shareholders divided by the average number of shares outstanding, based on warrants, rights, and convertible securities *likely* to be exercised or converted. Fully diluted EPS is adjusted earnings available to common shareholders divided by the average number of shares outstanding, based on *all* warrants, rights, and convertible securities being exercised or converted. Adjusted earnings available to common shareholders are earnings that have been adjusted for the interest of convertible securities.

In calculating the primary EPS and the fully diluted earnings per share, the accountant first determines the adjusted number of common shares that would be added if the warrants were exercised. The adjusted number of common shares is equal to the new shares created less the number of shares that could be bought with the money received from exercising the warrants. To find the EPS, the accountant then divides the old shares plus the adjusted number of common shares into the adjusted earnings available to common shareholders.

Meffe Manufacturing Corporation has $5,500,000 in adjusted earnings available to common shareholders and 1,000,000 common shares outstanding. Warrants to purchase 200,000 shares of common stock, with an exercise price of $25, are outstanding. The stock is currently selling for $50 per share. What is the primary EPS for the company?

The number of shares that could be bought with the money received from exercising the warrants is calculated as follows:

$$\text{New Shares} = \frac{200,000(\$25)}{\$50}$$

$$= 100,000 \text{ shares}$$

The adjusted number of common shares is 100,000 (200,000 − 100,000).

The primary EPS is found by dividing the adjusted earnings available to common shareholders by the old shares plus the adjusted number of common shares.

$$\text{Primary EPS} = \frac{\$5,500,000}{1,000,000 + 100,000}$$

$$= \$5.00$$

Since the exercise of the warrants is likely, the primary EPS and the fully diluted EPS are the same.

CONVERTIBLES

The conversion privilege is often included with a bond issue as a *sweetener* in order to sell these securities at lower yields. This makes the convertible bond issue similar to a straight bond issue with warrants added. The primary difference between the two is that warrants are usually detachable from the convertible bonds and thus have a life and value of their own.

The Basics of Convertibles

A **convertible security** is a bond or preferred stock that can be exchanged at the option of its holder for a specified number of common shares of the company. The **conversion ratio** is the number of common shares into which the convertible security converts. The **conversion price** is the par value of the

Convertible Security

Conversion Ratio

Conversion Price

Conversion Premium Ratio   convertible security divided by the conversion ratio. The **conversion premium ratio** is the conversion price less the current stock price, divided by the current stock price.

> Lisa MacDonald purchased a convertible bond with a par value of $1,000 and a conversion ratio of 20. The stock is currently selling for $42. What are the conversion price and the conversion premium ratio?

The conversion price is the par value of $1,000 divided by the conversion ratio of 20.

$$\text{Conversion Price} = \frac{\$1,000}{20}$$
$$= \$50$$

The conversion price may also be stated in the contract of the convertible security.

The conversion premium ratio is the conversion price of $50 less the current stock price of $42, divided by the stock price.

$$\text{Conversion Premium Ratio} = \frac{\$50 - \$42}{\$42}$$
$$= 0.19 \text{ or } 19\%$$

This value is typical of new issues.

The conversion privilege on a convertible issue may be delayed until a certain number of years have passed or may be terminated after a fixed period of time. For example, the holder of a convertible bond may have to wait 4 years to convert or may even lose the conversion privilege after 15 years on a 20-year bond.

Convertible bonds are usually callable after a fixed amount of time, such as five years. This is equivalent to the company selling a straight bond and buying a call option from the holder of the bond. It requires the company to provide a higher yield for including this feature. This is accomplished by market forces lowering the price of the bond.

Convertible bonds are usually protected against stock splits and stock dividends. This protection is achieved by changing the conversion ratio, and thereby the conversion price. For example, a company announces a two-for-one stock split. Originally, the conversion ratio was 20, implying a conversion price of $50. After the split, the conversion ratio is 40, suggesting a conversion price of $25.

Conversion ratios are established by the company so that conversion is not attractive unless the underlying stock increases substantially in value. This is also the approach used with warrants in setting the exercise price. The conversion ratio may change through the life of the bond. Generally, when that happens, the conversion ratio declines, causing the conversion price to increase.

A company can force conversion of convertible securities by means of the option to call the issue early before expiration. Ideally, a company calls its bonds when the value of the bonds equals the call price. Many companies wait until the value is much higher. When a company announces a call, bond holders have a choice of accepting the call price or converting the bond into common shares. Normally when companies call convertible bonds, the value of the stock is higher than the call price, and the bond holder takes that option.

The *Standard & Poor's Bond Guide* provides information on a long list of convertible bonds. *Moody's Bond Record* also contains material on convertibles, as does Merrill Lynch's *Convertible Securities. Value Line Options and Convertibles* furnishes more in-depth analysis.

Convertible Valuation

The **conversion value** is the market value of the common stock if the convertible bond is converted. The market value is calculated by multiplying the conversion ratio by the market price of the common stock.

Conversion Value

> John MacDonald purchased a convertible bond with a conversion ratio of 20 and a market price of shares of $42. What is the conversion value?

The conversion value is found by multiplying the conversion ratio by the market price.

$$\text{Conversion Value} = 20(\$42)$$
$$= \$840$$

As the market price changes, the conversion value changes.

The **straight bond value** of a convertible bond is the value of the bond without the conversion privilege. Straight bond value is estimated using the methods of Chapter 3, applying the discount rate of a nonconvertible bond with the same risk and maturity.

Straight Bond Value

> The convertible bond John MacDonald purchased is an 8 percent, 25-year, $1,000 par bond with semiannual interest payments. What is its straight bond value if the required annual rate of return for similar nonconvertible bonds is 10 percent?

Find the value using Eq. 3.3.

$$V_b = \frac{\$40}{(1.05)^1} + \frac{\$40}{(1.05)^2} + \ldots + \frac{\$40}{(1.05)^{50}} + \frac{\$1,000}{(1.05)^{50}}$$

$$= \$40(PVFA_{5\%,50}) + \$1,000(PVF_{5\%,50})$$

$$= \$40(18.2559) + \$1,000(0.0872)$$

$$= \$730.24 + \$87.20$$

$$= \$817.44$$

Floor Value

This is a **floor value** for the convertible bond, assuming no change in interest rates.

Minimum Value

The **minimum value** of a convertible bond is the greater of its conversion value and its straight bond value. The heavy line in Figure 15.9 illustrates the minimum value, using the example from this section. The straight bond value, shown by the horizontal line, moves up and down with changes in the interest rate. Its value also approaches the par value of $1,000 as the bond matures.

The market value for a convertible bond is greater than the minimum value.

Conversion Premium

The **conversion premium** is the amount the market value exceeds the minimum value. The conversion premium is the result of the bond holder having the option to wait before conversion. This call option gives the convertible bond holder the right to buy a number of shares (stated as the conversion ratio), at a given exercise price (the straight bond value).

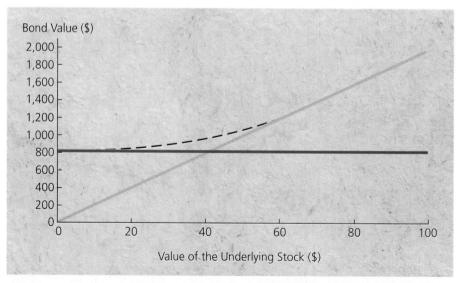

Figure 15.9 Minimum and Market Values for a Convertible Bond

Notice in Figure 15.9 that the conversion premium is at its maximum near the point where the minimum value line turns upward. If the value of the underlying stock falls below the optimum value, the conversion premium declines. This is due to the declining chance for gains through conversion. If the value of the underlying stock rises above the optimum value, the conversion premium also declines. This reflects the decreased protection of the straight bond and the greater probability of the bond being called.

Accounting for Convertibles

As stated in the section on warrants, the company income statement must disclose primary EPS and fully diluted EPS, not simple EPS, if material dilution could occur. The calculation of primary EPS and fully diluted EPS is uncomplicated for convertible bonds. The bond interest on the convertible bonds is eliminated, while the number of shares reflects the increased number of shares when the bonds are converted.

> Earnings before interest and taxes (EBIT) for Meffe Manufacturing Corporation is $10,000,000. The company has outstanding $15,000,000 of 10 percent convertible debentures with a conversion ratio of 20. Before conversion, the company has 1,200,000 shares of common stock selling at $60 per share. What is the primary EPS for the company?

McCrory Halts Payments On Debenture Issue

In a move that sparked renewed concern about its immediate future, McCrory Corporation halted principal and interest payments on its 6.5% convertible subordinated debentures. In a one-page document filed with the Securities and Exchange Commission, the company said it was "considering all of its available restructuring options." McCrory's decision to halt payment surprised some analysts. They noted that Robert Spencer said that the chain would close the fiscal year with $40.8 million in cash. It would appear, said the analysts, that McCrory had ample funds with which to make the payments. One analyst speculated that financier Meshulam Riklis, who controls the company, may have defaulted on the debentures to "create an atmosphere of uncertainty" for bondholders who own $75 million of senior subordinated exchangeable variable-rate notes. "If it can buy back $50 million at 50 cents on the dollar, there is a good chance McCrory will survive," said this analyst, who asked not to be identified. The analyst noted that last year McCrory needed to retire $75 million of bonds. Eventually Mr. Riklis was able to buy back a substantial portion of that debt at a discount.

Source: Jeffrey A. Trachtenberg, "McCrory Halts Payments of Principal And Interest on 6.5% Debenture Issue," *The Wall Street Journal,* February 18, 1992. Reprinted by permission of The Wall Street Journal, © 1992 Dow Jones & Company, Inc. All Rights Reserved Worldwide.

TABLE 15.1 Simple EPS and Primary EPS for a Convertible Bond

	SIMPLE EPS	PRIMARY EPS
Earnings before interest and taxes	$10,000,000	$10,000,000
Less: interest expense	1,500,000	0
Earnings before taxes	$ 8,500,000	$10,000,000
Less: income taxes (40%)	3,400,000	4,000,000
Earnings after taxes	$ 5,100,000	$ 6,000,000
Common shares outstanding	1,200,000	1,500,000
Earnings per share	$4.25	$4.00

The calculation of the simple EPS and the primary EPS is shown in Table 15.1. The current interest expense is $1,500,000, 0.10($15,000,000). Conversion of the debentures adds 300,000 shares, 15,000 bonds ($1,000 par value) multiplied by the conversion ratio of 20. The simple EPS is $4.25, but the primary EPS of $4.00 more accurately reflects the condition of the company. Conversion is likely with a market price of $60 per share, more than the conversion price of $50.

SUMMARY

This chapter focuses on the following learning objectives:
1. Describing call and put options, including how they are sold.
   An option is a contract giving the holder the right, but not the obligation, to buy or sell an asset at a fixed price on or before a specified expiration date. A call option gives the holder the right to buy an asset at a fixed price for a specified period of time. A put option gives the holder the right to sell an asset at a fixed price for a specified period of time.
2. Valuing call and put options.
   Five variables are important in determining the value of an American call option: (1) The value of the underlying stock is positively related to the market price of the option. (2) The exercise price is inversely related to the market price of the option. (3) The time until expiration is directly related to the market price of the option. (4) The risk-free rate of interest is positively related to the market price of the option. (5) The variability of the underlying stock price is positively related to the market price of the option.
3. Describing warrants, including the accounting treatment.
   A warrant is an option that gives the holder the right to buy a share of common stock at a fixed price for a specified period of time. Warrants are often

attached to bond and preferred stock issues as sweeteners in order to sell these securities at lower yields.

4. Valuing warrants.

   The value of a warrant when compared with its underlying stock is similar to the call option relationship. The value of underlying stock is positively related to the market price of the warrant. The value of the warrant also depends on the exercise price, the time until expiration, the risk-free rate of interest, and the variability of the underlying stock price.

5. Describing convertibles, including the accounting treatment.

   A convertible security is a bond or preferred stock that can be exchanged at the option of its holder for a specified number of common shares of the company. The conversion privilege is often included with convertible bond issues as a sweetener in order to sell these securities at lower yields. This makes the convertible bond issue similar to a straight bond issue with warrants added.

6. Valuing convertibles.

   The conversion value is the market value of the common stock if the convertible bond is converted. The market value is calculated by multiplying the conversion ratio by the market price of the common stock. The straight bond value of a convertible bond is the value of the bond without the conversion privilege.

KEY TERMS

American option, 417	Covered option, 419	Option, 417
Call option, 417	European option, 417	Primary earnings per
Conversion	Exercising the	share, 426
premium, 430	option, 417	Put option, 418
Conversion premium	Floor value, 430	Simple earnings per
ratio, 428	Fully diluted earnings	share, 426
Conversion price, 427	per share, 426	Straight bond
Conversion ratio, 427	Minimum	value, 429
Conversion value, 429	value, 430	Striking price, 417
Convertible security, 427	Naked option, 419	Warrant, 424

QUESTIONS

15.1 Explain the basics of an option, including the difference between an American and a European option.

15.2 Contrast call options with put options.

15.3 Explain by example the difference between covered and naked options.

15.4 What five variables determine the market price of an American call option?

15.5 Explain the basics of warrants.

15.6 What are the primary differences between call options and warrants?

15.7 Explain by example how the holder of a warrant might make more money by owning a similar call option.

15.8 Under what conditions can the Black-Scholes model be used in finding the value of a warrant?

15.9 What are the differences between simple EPS, primary EPS, and fully diluted EPS?

15.10 Explain the basics of convertible securities.

15.11 Explain by example what would happen if a convertible bond underwent a two-for-one stock split.

15.12 Explain by example how a company can force conversion of convertible securities through the use of the call option.

15.13 Explain by example what is meant by the minimum value of a convertible bond.

15.14 Discuss the relationship between market value and conversion premium on a convertible bond.

15.15 Who wins and who loses in the private offering of preferred stock by Chrysler Corporation?

PROBLEMS

15.1 **(Contract Valuation)** Ed Johnson purchased a European call option to buy 100 shares of common stock in the Johnson Corporation with an exercise price of $50 and an expiration date of March 15, 19X4. What is the value of the contract on the expiration date, if the underlying stock is selling for $60?

15.2 **(Contract Valuation)** Harriet Flowers purchased a European put option to sell 100 shares of common stock in the McMaster Corporation with an exercise price of $50 and an expiration date of May 15, 19X4. What is the value of the contract on the expiration date, if the underlying stock is selling for $45?

15.3 **(Upper and Lower Bounds)** Graph the upper and lower bounds for a call option with an exercise price of $40.

15.4 **(Lowest Valuation)** Kay Singley purchased an American call option to buy 100 shares of common stock in the McQuality Corporation with an exercise price of $35 and an expiration date of July 15, 19X4. If the underlying stock is selling for $40, what is the lowest possible value of the option before the expiration date?

15.5 **(Finding Option Profit)** Carlos Valdez purchased an American call option to buy 100 shares of common stock in the Eagle Transportation, Inc., for $7. The option has an exercise price of $40 and an expiration date of August 15, 19X4. If the underlying stock is selling for $50, how much profit would he make for the full contract?

15.6 **(Primary EPS)** The Howerton Lumber Company has $7,500,000 in adjusted earnings available to common shareholders and 1,000,000 common shares outstanding. Warrants to purchase 250,000 shares of common stock, with an exercise price of $30, are outstanding. The stock is currently selling for $40 per share. What is the primary EPS for that company?

15.7 **(Conversion Price and Conversion Premium Ratio)** Larry Sanders purchased a convertible bond with a par value of $1,000 and a conversion ratio of 25. The stock is currently selling for $33. What are the conversion price and the conversion premium ratio?

15.8 **(Conversion Value)** Sarah Strozier purchased a convertible bond with a conversion ratio of 25 and a stock market price of $40. What is the conversion value?

15.9 **(Conversion Value)** The conversion price for a $1,000 par value convertible debenture is $125. If the common stock is selling for $75, what is the conversion value of the bond?

15.10 **(Straight Bond Value)** Douglas Woo purchased a 10 percent, 20-year convertible bond with semiannual interest payments. What is its straight bond value if the required annual rate of return for similar non-convertible bonds is eight percent?

15.11 **(Primary EPS)** Earnings before interest and taxes (EBIT) for the Harding Corporation is $12,000,000. The company has outstanding $16,000,000 of 10 percent convertible debentures with a conversion ratio of 25. Before conversion, the company has 1,000,000 shares of common stock selling at $50 per share. Find the simple EPS and the primary EPS for the corporation.

APPENDIX 15A

Black-Scholes Option Pricing Model

Fischer Black and Myron Scholes published an article in 1970 including a set of formulas for valuing the call option. This option pricing model (OPM) is based on a number of restrictive assumptions: (1) no dividends on the stock, (2) a European option, (3) no transaction costs, (4) no taxes, (5) no restrictions on short selling, and (6) a known interest rate. Robert Merton and others have subsequently modified this model using less limiting assumptions.

The model is based on the simple idea that an investor can buy stock and write a call, thereby creating a riskless position. This allows the investor to earn a return equal to the risk-free rate. If the relationship is not holding, then demand drives the price of the option toward the equilibrium value, making it happen.

The Black-Scholes model is given by the following equations:

$$C = SN(d_1) - Ee^{-kt} N(d_2) \qquad (15A.1)$$

The terms d_1 and d_2 are given as:

$$d_1 = \frac{\ln\left(\dfrac{S}{E}\right) + \left(k_{rf} + \dfrac{\sigma^2}{2}\right)t}{\sigma(t)} \qquad (15A.2)$$

$$d_2 = d_1 - \sigma(t) \qquad (15A.3)$$

where

$$C = \text{Call value}$$
$$S = \text{Stock price}$$
$$N(d_1) = \text{Cumulative normal value of } d_1$$
$$N(d_2) = \text{Cumulative normal value of } d_2$$
$$E = \text{Exercise price}$$
$$e = 2.7183 \text{ (Base of natural logarithms)}$$
$$k_{rf} = \text{Risk-free rate of interest}$$
$$t = \text{Time to expiration}$$
$$\sigma = \text{Standard deviation of the return on the stock}$$

The calculation of Eq. 15A.1 depends on the values for d_1 and d_2 in Eq. 15.A2 and 15.A3.

> The stock of Meffe Manufacturing Corporation is selling for $25. A call option on the stock matures in exactly one year and has an exercise price of $25. The annual risk-free rate of interest is 10 percent, and the standard deviation of the return on the stock is 10 percent. What is the value of the call option?

The first step is to find the value of d_1. Substituting into Eq. 15.2,

$$d_1 = \frac{\ln\left(\frac{\$25}{\$25}\right) + \left(0.10 + \frac{0.01}{2}\right)1}{0.10(1)}$$

$$= \frac{0 + 0.105}{0.10}$$

$$= 1.05$$

The second step is to find the value of d_2 by substituting into Eq. 15.A3.

$$d_2 = 1.05 - 0.10(1)$$

$$= 0.95$$

The third step is to find the values of $N(d_1)$ and $N(d_2)$. Table 15A.1 provides the cumulative values for the standard normal distribution. This distribution has an expected value of 0 and a standard deviation of 1. We look in the table and find for $d_1 = 1.05$, $N(d_1) = 0.8531$, and for $d_2 = 0.95$, $N(d_2) = 0.8289$.

The fourth step is to calculate the call value by substituting into Eq. 15.A1.

$$= \$25(0.8531) - \$25e^{-0.10(1)}(0.8289)$$

$$= \$21.3275 - \$25(0.9048)(0.8289)$$

$$= \$2.58$$

If the call option is selling for less than $2.58, it is underpriced. Under these conditions, a trader would consider buying the call.

These equations are solved quite easily using the spreadsheet model provided with the instructor's manual. The model allows us to recalculate the call value while changing the input variables.

TABLE 15A.1 Cummulative Values for Standard Normal Distribution

z	0	1	2	3	4	5	6	7	8	9
0.0	.5000	.5040	.5080	.5120	.5160	.5199	.5239	.5279	.5319	.5359
0.1	.5398	.5438	.5478	.5517	.5557	.5596	.5636	.5675	.5714	.5753
0.2	.5793	.5832	.5871	.5910	.5948	.5987	.6026	.6064	.6103	.6141
0.3	.6179	.6217	.6255	.6293	.6331	.6368	.6406	.6443	.6480	.6517
0.4	.6554	.6591	.6628	.6664	.6700	.6736	.6772	.6808	.6844	.6879
0.5	.6915	.6950	.6985	.7019	.7054	.7088	.7123	.7157	.7190	.7224
0.6	.7257	.7291	.7324	.7357	.7389	.7422	.7454	.7486	.7517	.7549
0.7	.7580	.7611	.7642	.7673	.7703	.7734	.7764	.7794	.7823	.7852
0.8	.7881	.7910	.7939	.7967	.7995	.8023	.8051	.8078	.8106	.8133
0.9	.8159	.8186	.8212	.8238	.8264	.8289	.8315	.8340	.8365	.8389
1.0	.8413	.8438	.8461	.8485	.8508	.8531	.8554	.8577	.8599	.8621
1.1	.8643	.8665	.8686	.8708	.8729	.8749	.8770	.8790	.8810	.8830
1.2	.8849	.8869	.8888	.8907	.8925	.8944	.8962	.8980	.8997	.9015
1.3	.9032	.9049	.9066	.9082	.9099	.9115	.9131	.9147	.9162	.9177
1.4	.9192	.9207	.9222	.9236	.9251	.9265	.9278	.9292	.9306	.9319
1.5	.9332	.9345	.9357	.9370	.9382	.9394	.9406	.9418	.9430	.9441
1.6	.9452	.9463	.9474	.9484	.9495	.9505	.9515	.9525	.9535	.9545
1.7	.9554	.9564	.9573	.9582	.9591	.9599	.9608	.9616	.9625	.9633
1.8	.9641	.9648	.9656	.9664	.9671	.9678	.9686	.9693	.9700	.9706
1.9	.9713	.9719	.9726	.9732	.9738	.9744	.9750	.9756	.9762	.9767
2.0	.9772	.9778	.9783	.9788	.9793	.9798	.9803	.9808	.9812	.9817
2.1	.9821	.9826	.9830	.9834	.9838	.9842	.9846	.9850	.9854	.9857
2.2	.9861	.9864	.9868	.9871	.9874	.9878	.9881	.9884	.9887	.9890
2.3	.9893	.9896	.9898	.9901	.9904	.9906	.9909	.9911	.9913	.9916
2.4	.9918	.9920	.9922	.9925	.9927	.9929	.9931	.9932	.9934	.9936
2.5	.9938	.9940	.9941	.9943	.9945	.9946	.9948	.9949	.9951	.9952
2.6	.9953	.9955	.9956	.9957	.9959	.9960	.9961	.9962	.9963	.9964
2.7	.9965	.9966	.9967	.9968	.9969	.9970	.9971	.9972	.9973	.9974
2.8	.9974	.9975	.9976	.9977	.9977	.9978	.9979	.9979	.9980	.9981
2.9	.9981	.9982	.9982	.9983	.9984	.9984	.9985	.9985	.9986	.9986
3.0	.9987	.9990	.9993	.9995	.9997	.9998	.9998	.9999	.9999	1.0000

A Case Problem

iamond Drugs, Inc. (DDI) operated the fifth largest drug chain in the United States. The company's approximately 1,200 stores were located in 24 states in the eastern half of the country. Management believed the company held a large market share in prescription and over-the-counter drugs. It was a strategic objective of the company to retain this advantage given demographic trends, the recession-resistant nature of the business, and the importance of a pharmacy in generating customer traffic.

> *Since DDI acquired its business, it had operated under significant financial constraints, including a high debt to equity ratio and various restrictive covenants.*

Since DDI acquired its business, it had operated under significant financial constraints, including a high debt to equity ratio and various restrictive covenants. To counter this situation, management had concentrated on strong cost control measures and significant improvements in the use of working capital. The success of the company in improving cash flow had enabled it to prepay $25,000,000 of long-term debt, in addition to scheduled repayments of $49,000,000. This allowed DDI to increase stockholders' equity, reduce indebted-

ness and interest expense, and increase its financial and operating flexibility.

Management believed that opportunities existed for additional sales and earnings growth. The growth strategy was to (1) increase new store openings, (2) reduce expenses through consolidation of various administration overhead functions, (3) improve profitability through consolidation of buying and distribution activity, and (4) invest in new technology at the store level.

To take advantage of those opportunities, the company intended to implement a recapitalization plan that included the following principal components: (1) a common stock offering of 10,000,000 shares at $16.00 per share (with a market price of $16.50 per share), (2) $130,000,000 of convertible subordinated debentures, and (3) the use of substantially all of the net proceeds to redeem the company's 13% Subordinated Debentures due in 2003. The 13% debentures were callable at a redemption price of $1,065 per $1,000 principal amount of the debentures plus accrued and unpaid interest. The net proceeds were estimated at $149,100,000 from the stock offering and $126,300,000 from the convertible subordinated debentures, a total of $275,400,000.

The new convertible subordinated debentures would have an 8 percent coupon rate, a 30-year maturity, and could be sold at par. The conversion price would be set at $18.75 per share. The coupon rate on bonds of similar risk without the convertible feature was 9 percent. Interest payments were on a semiannual basis.

Leading Questions

1. What is the purpose of the recapitalization plan?
2. What is the straight value of the bond?
3. What is the conversion value of the bond when the market price of the common stock is $12.00, $14.00, $16.00, $18.00, and $20.00 per share?
4. Would you prefer to purchase the common stock or the convertible subordinated debentures? Why? Discuss.

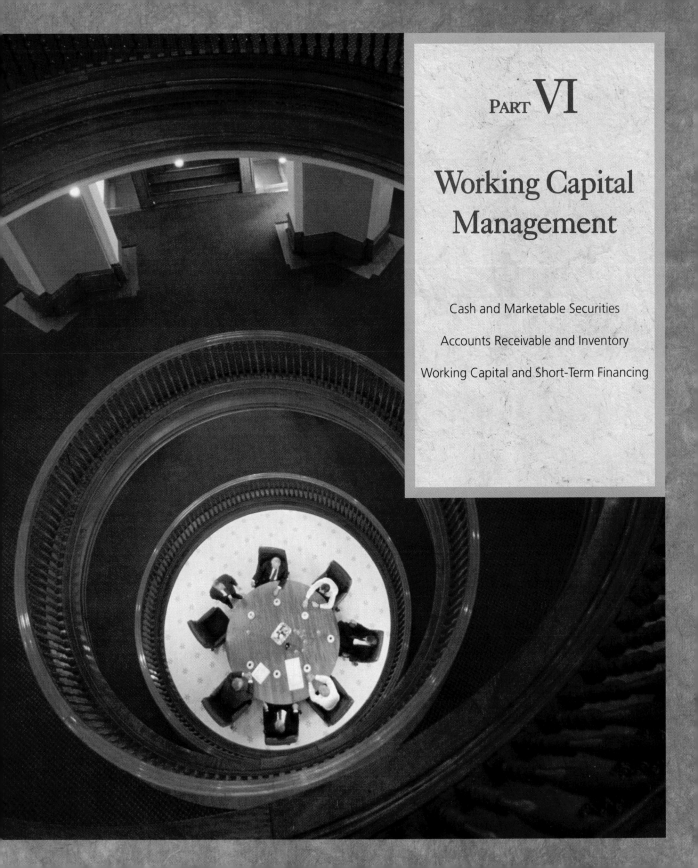

PART VI

Working Capital Management

Cash and Marketable Securities

Accounts Receivable and Inventory

Working Capital and Short-Term Financing

16 Cash and Marketable Securities

Macy Chairman Edward Finkelstein opened the door to selling some Macy stores to raise cash. He also signaled a somber new direction for Macy in other areas, including cutting advertising costs, renegotiating bank loans, and seeking new equity investors in the company. A Chapter 11 filing would be the worst case scenario. Despite the stigma of bankruptcy protection, retailers are often able to arrange new bank financing, since new lenders are given preferred status for repayment.

Macy borrows from its banks primarily through a revolving credit facility in order to buy inventory. Ordinarily, that credit line is used heavily in the buildup to the Christmas selling season; after that, the debt must be paid off almost to zero. In December, Macy favorably renegotiated its bank agreement, devising a repayment schedule it felt it could meet. Part way through last week, Macy Vice Chairman Myron Ullman realized the company wouldn't have sufficient funds to pay vendors and reduce borrowings, as promised. So Macy decided to delay payments to its suppliers.

The situation at R.H. Macy presents severe working capital management problems. Fortunately, the conditions at most companies are more favorable. Still it is important to understand the principles of cash management and marketable securities investment.

Source: Jeffrey A. Trachtenberg and George Anders, "Cash Pinch Leads Macy To Delay Paying Bills And Plan Other Steps," *The Wall Street Journal,* January 13, 1992. Reprinted by permission of The Wall Street Journal, © 1992 Dow Jones & Company, Inc. All Rights Reserved Worldwide.

CASH DISBURSEMENT AND COLLECTION

The disbursement and collection of cash results in deficits and surpluses, causing changes in the levels of debt and marketable securities. When there is a surplus, a company invests cash in marketable securities for transactions uses, for precautionary reasons, and for speculative purposes. In surplus or deficit, controlling the target cash balance involves finding methods for minimizing the total costs of maintaining cash balances.

Cash management involves control of cash outflows and cash inflows. As shown in the previous chapter with the cash budget, if cash inflows exceed cash outflows, the company builds up a cash surplus. This surplus is used to repay debt or to make an investment in marketable securities. On the other hand, if cash outflows exceed cash inflows, the company runs a deficit in cash and must borrow or sell marketable securities.

A cash manager makes payments as slowly as possible in order to maximize float. **Float** represents uncollected funds in the payment system. It is equal to the company checking account balance less the balance shown at the bank.

Float

443

Disbursement Float

Disbursement float results from checks written *by* the company requiring time to clear. For example, a company writes an average of $10,000 in checks daily, and it takes four days for these checks to clear. The resulting disbursement float is equal to $10,000 per day times four days, or $40,000. This will increase the company bank balance by that amount.

Collection Float

Collection float results from checks written *to* the company requiring time to clear. For example, a company receives an average of $8,000 in checks daily, and it takes three days for these checks to clear. The resulting collection float is equal to $8,000 per day times three days, or $24,000. This will decrease the company bank balance by that amount.

Net Float

Net float is equal to disbursement float less collection float. It is the amount by which the checking account balance at the bank exceeds the checking account balance at the company. To maximize net float, a company tries to maximize disbursement float and minimize collection float. Using the information from the two previous examples, the net float for the company is $16,000, $40,000 − $24,000.

The Disbursement of Cash

An important part of cash management is the disbursement of cash. There are two goals to be achieved in this area: maximization of net float and minimization of checking account balances. The financial manager uses remote disbursement accounts, zero-balance accounts, drafts, and overdrafts to achieve these goals.

Remote Disbursement Accounts

Remote disbursement accounts are set up at banks in relatively remote areas. This increases the time for checks to clear, thereby increasing disbursement float. An increase of one day to clear in the previous disbursement-float example would increase the float by $10,000. At an opportunity cost of 10 percent, this would increase before-tax earnings by $1,000, $10,000(0.10). A variation of this technique (the same effect as being remote) involves postmarking the envelope of a payment check and delaying mailing for a day or two.

Zero-Balance Accounts

Zero-balance accounts (ZBAs) are checking accounts in decentralized company locations, funded from a master account. Checks sent to suppliers from a ZBA are processed by the supplier, entered into the banking system, and presented at the zero-balance account for payment. At this point, funds are transferred from the master account to the ZBA. When funds in the master account reach zero, the master account is replenished by accessing a line of credit or by selling marketable securities. The process is reversed when funds in the master account build up. The ZBA system, shown in Figure 16.1, reduces excessive cash balances.

Draft

A **draft** is similar to a check but is different in that it is drawn on the issuing company rather than a bank. The issuing company benefits by not having to

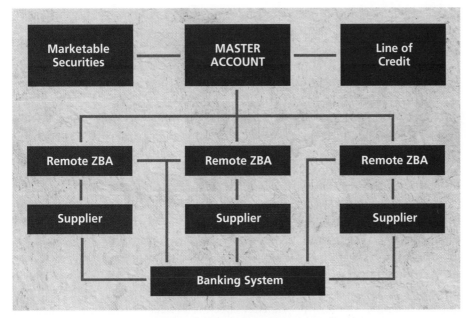

Figure 16.1 Zero-Balance Account System for Cash Disbursement
● ● ● ● ● ● ● ●

deposit funds to cover the draft until a bank presents it for payment. Bankers often charge fees for processing drafts and thereby discourage their use. Drafts are more prominently used in foreign exchange transactions.

An **overdraft** is a written direction to a bank to honor a check in excess of the funds available in an account. The amount not available becomes an automatic line of credit, subject to a predetermined limit. The use of overdraft protection allows a company to minimize the amount of cash it has on hand for cash disbursement.

Overdraft

The Collection of Cash

An equally important area in cash management is the collection of cash. The goals in the collection of cash are the same as with the disbursement of cash: maximization of net float and minimization of checking account balances. The financial manager uses lockboxes, concentration banking, and preauthorized payment to achieve these goals.

A **lockbox** is a post office box designated to receive accounts-receivable payments from customers of a particular company. A bank removes the checks from the lockbox and quickly deposits them into the company's account, immediately forwarding the accounts receivable information. The objective of the lockbox system is to clear the checks as quickly as possible, thereby reducing collection float.

Lockbox

A lockbox system for large companies normally includes lockboxes located throughout the country. The financial manager must determine the number of lockboxes, their locations, and the assignment of certain receivables to particular lockboxes. The cost of operating the lockbox system is compared with the increase in before-tax earnings resulting from reduced float. Figure 16.2 illustrates a lockbox system.

Concentration Banking

Concentration banking uses company sales offices to process customer checks. This collection process reduces the time to receive checks by mail and decreases the time for checks to clear. Using this method, sales office personnel make deposits in a local bank and forward accounts receivable information to corporate headquarters.

The company transfers excess funds from the local banks to a concentration bank near company headquarters. This is usually accomplished by a wire transfer or by a depository transfer check (DTC). A wire transfer is the fastest yet most expensive way to transfer funds. The Federal Reserve operates FedWire for domestic transfers, and the New York Clearing House Association directs the Clearing House Interbank Payments System (CHIPS) for international dollar payments. A depository transfer check is a check drawn against the local bank and deposited in the concentration bank, a slower way to transfer funds.

The Federal Reserve System also operates a system of approximately 30 automated regional clearinghouses, the National Automated Clearing House As-

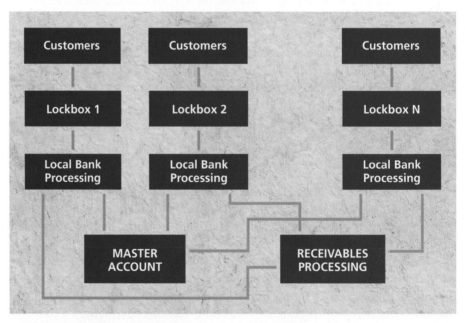

Figure 16.2　The Collection of Cash Through a Lockbox System

How To Develop Measures for Financial Work

Deciding on performance measures and gathering relevant data to determine whether much improvement is needed are preliminary steps to identifying areas for performance improvement. Typical finance performance gaps include the following: (1) the number of times internal audit reports missed the target completion date, (2) the number of vendors that complain of incorrect payment amounts, (3) the number of times an IRS audit request for information exceeds the thirty day limit, (4) the number of vendor discounts that are lost or refunded as a result of late payments, (5) amount of cash not applied as a result of poor lockbox monitoring procedures, (6) the total number of reports produced monthly and not re-quired, and (7) the number of times the same data are typed from one form to another. One suggestion for determining the importance of the performance gaps is to start by developing an Improvement Opportunities Chart. This chart shows the specific output (for example, the accounts payable system), the performance measure, the desired performance level, the actual performance level, the performance gap, and the processes affected. The objective is to close the gaps that will provide the greatest reward in the least amount of time using the least resources.

Source: "How To Develop Measures for Financial Work," *National Productivity Review,* 159–167, Spring 1992.

sociation (NACHA). These automated clearinghouses (ACHs) process transactions between financial institutions without using paper checks. This allows the concentration bank to receive one-day clearing of checks from any location in the United States.

The use of concentration banking does not preclude the use of lockboxes in combination with the local sales offices. Figure 16.3 shows a cash management system utilizing both approaches.

Preauthorized payment, or preauthorized debit, allows a company to charge the checking account of its customer, up to a predetermined limit. Since this is a checkless transaction, float due to mailing or clearing does not exist. This system seems to work best when a company has a large number of customers whose payments are fairly stable. The benefits to the company of reduced float and lower clerical costs are obvious.

Preauthorized Payment

INVESTING IN MARKETABLE SECURITIES

The investment of cash in marketable securities occurs for three reasons. First, a company needs to invest surplus cash temporarily, until required for transactions uses. The example of the Martin Corporation in the last chapter illustrates the seasonal nature of cash requirements. Second, a company needs marketable securities for precautionary reasons. It is not possible to forecast cash

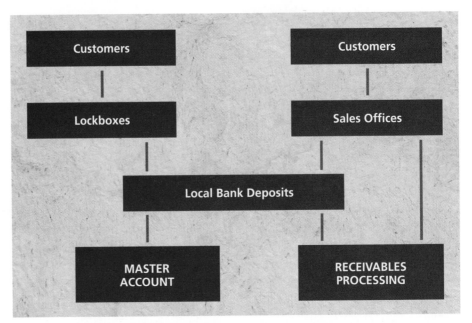

Figure 16.3 A Concentration Banking System with Lockboxes

requirements with complete accuracy; therefore, marketable securities act as a safety stock for cash. Third, a company needs marketable securities for speculative purposes. This additional liquidity allows management to take advantage of unexpected opportunities, both internal and external.

Criteria for Selection

Financial managers judge marketable securities by three major criteria: expected return, risk, and marketability. The selection of a particular security depends on the purpose for which it is chosen.

Expected return is the annual yield of an investment, but for marketable securities this return is not apparent. Most marketable securities are sold at a discount when compared with face value. The size of the discount is calculated by first multiplying the par value by the discount percentage. The result is multiplied by the time until maturity (in years) based on a 360-day year. For example, a 91-day, $10,000 par value, Treasury bill is sold at a discount of 8.50 percent. The size of the discount is $214.86, $10,000(0.0850)(91/360). The price of the Treasury bill is $9,785.14, $10,000 − $214.86. The 91-day yield is 2.20 percent, $214.86/$9,785.14.

The annual yield of the investment is the effective rate of interest using Eq. 2.10.

$$ER = \left(1 + \frac{k}{m}\right)^m - 1$$
$$= (1 + 0.0220)^{365/91} - 1$$
$$= 0.0912$$

This result was found using a financial calculator. Notice that the effective rate is calculated using a 365-day year.

Figure 16.4 is an example of Treasury bill quotations from the *Wall Street Journal*. The first entry is the maturity date, followed by the number of days until maturity. The bid quotation is the discount that the buyer receives if the seller accepts the bid price. The asked quotation is the discount that the seller delivers if the buyer accepts the asked price. For an asked quotation of 2.62 percent and 90 days until maturity, the discount is $65.50, $10,000(0.0262)(90/360).

Maturity	Days to Mat.	Bid	Asked	Chg.	Ask Yld.
Oct 07 '93	6	2.72	2.62	+0.01	2.66
Oct 14 '93	13	2.80	2.70	−0.03	2.74
Oct 21 '93	20	2.86	2.76	+0.01	2.80
Oct 28 '93	27	2.58	2.48	−0.03	2.52
Nov 04 '93	34	2.81	2.77	−0.01	2.82
Nov 12 '93	42	2.90	2.86	+0.02	2.91
Nov 18 '93	48	2.90	2.86	+0.01	2.91
Nov 26 '93	56	2.91	2.87	+0.01	2.92
Dec 02 '93	62	2.91	2.89	+0.03	2.94
Dec 09 '93	69	2.94	2.92	+0.03	2.98
Dec 16 '93	76	2.94	2.92	+0.02	2.98
Dec 23 '93	83	2.94	2.92	+0.02	2.98
Dec 30 '93	90	2.93	2.91	+0.03	2.97
Jan 06 '94	97	2.95	2.93	+0.03	2.99
Jan 13 '94	104	2.97	2.95	+0.04	3.02
Jan 20 '94	111	2.98	2.96	+0.03	3.03
Jan 27 '94	118	2.98	2.96	+0.01	3.03
Feb 03 '94	125	3.02	3.00	+0.02	3.07
Feb 10 '94	132	3.03	3.01	+0.02	3.09
Feb 17 '94	139	3.03	3.01	+0.01	3.09
Feb 24 '94	146	3.05	3.03	+0.03	3.11
Mar 03 '94	153	3.05	3.03	+0.02	3.11
Mar 10 '94	160	3.05	3.03	+0.03	3.11
Mar 17 '94	167	3.06	3.04	+0.02	3.13
Mar 24 '94	174	3.06	3.04	+0.03	3.13
Mar 31 '94	181	3.06	3.04	+0.03	3.13
Apr 07 '94	188	3.09	3.07	+0.03	3.16
May 05 '94	216	3.11	3.09	+0.02	3.18
Jun 02 '94	244	3.13	3.11	+0.03	3.21
Jun 30 '94	272	3.15	3.13	+0.03	3.23
Jul 28 '94	300	3.19	3.17	+0.02	3.28
Aug 25 '94	328	3.22	3.20	+0.03	3.32
Sep 22 '94	356	3.23	3.21	+0.04	3.33

Figure 16.4 Treasury Bill Quotations

The 90-day yield is 0.66 percent, $65.50/$9,934.50. This translates into an effective rate, or annual yield, of 2.66 percent.

The expected return on marketable securities is also affected by the taxability of the instrument and the tax status of the organization. The income from Treasury bills, for example, is not subject to state and local income taxes. Investment in a certificate of deposit requires a higher expected return to match a Treasury bill for organizations that pay taxes. Nonprofit religious, charitable, or educational foundations pay little or no taxes. For these groups, the taxability of marketable securities is of limited importance in determining expected return.

Risk in regard to marketable securities involves default risk and interest rate risk. **Default risk** refers to the perceived probability that the issuer will fail to make interest or principal payments. As mentioned in previous chapters, a number of companies publish rating information on marketable securities, with Standard & Poor's Corporation and Moody's Investors Service, Inc. being the two largest. These publications allow financial managers to avoid marketable securities with a high degree of default risk.

Default Risk

Interest rate risk involves changes in the market price of a debt security resulting from changes in the market interest rate. The variability in market price is greater for debt securities that have a longer time until maturity. For this reason, companies typically focus on short-term marketable securities.

Interest Rate Risk

Marketability, or liquidity, refers to the ease with which a marketable security may be converted to cash. This convertibility depends on the breadth and depth of the market for the security. Breadth of the market refers to the number of buyers and sellers actively interested in the security. Depth of the market refers to the amount of the security that can be sold without significantly changing the market price. Financial managers gain a measure of the breadth and depth of the over-the-counter market by observing the difference between the bid and asked prices of a marketable security. For a security traded on an organized exchange, volume traded is a corresponding proximate measure.

Marketability

Types of Money Market Securities

Years ago, companies with excess cash often chose Treasury bills for short-term investment. Today, commercial paper, negotiable certificates of deposit, and a variety of other money market instruments compete with Treasury bills to be included in short-term investment portfolios. Unlike the past, competition now includes money market securities denominated in foreign currencies.

Treasury bills are issued on a discount basis by the U.S. government in denominations from $10,000 to $1,000,000. They mature in 91 days, 182 days, and one year. The 91-day and 182-day bills are sold by auction weekly, and the yearly bills monthly.

Treasury Bills

Federal agency notes are issued, usually on a discount basis, by the Federal Home Loan bank, the Government National Mortgage Association, the Federal National Mortgage Association, and other federal agencies. The denominations and maturities vary with the issuing agency. The expected returns are higher than with corresponding government issues due to the perceived higher risk of these securities.

Federal Agency Notes

Bankers' acceptances are drafts, usually originating from foreign trade. They are backed by the bank on which they are drawn as well as on the importing company. Since the exporting company must wait up to six months to receive its money, that company may sell the acceptance on a discount basis. This instrument is less marketable than Treasury bills and not quite so safe.

Bankers' Acceptances

Negotiable certificates of deposit are issued by commercial banks in denominations of $100,000 or more. Maturities are usually for 3, 6, 9, or 12 months, with the minimum time set at 14 days. These CDs carry a rate of interest that reflects the initial investment and offer good marketability to the investing company.

Negotiable Certificates of Deposit

Eurodollar certificates of deposit are certificates of deposit originated by foreign banks. Eurodollars are U.S. dollars held by foreign banks and are loaned to companies requiring currency in dollars. Maturities range up to one year but are usually thirty days to six months. Denominations are usually for $5,000,000 or more.

Eurodollar Certificates of Deposit

Small Town Treasurers Rue the Day

Almost like Prof. Harold Hill in "The Music Man," Steven D. Wymer marched into Big Bear Lake, California, one day in 1989 and told finance director Jeffrey Brunsdon some things he was more than ready to hear. Mr. Wymer wasn't promising band uniforms or big trombones, just a quick return: a virtually risk-free way to invest the little resort town's $2 million capital-improvement fund. Mr. Brunsdon, an easygoing accountant, liked Mr. Wymer. But after the phone rang the afternoon of December 13, 1991, Mr. Brunsdon realized he had been had. Mr. Wymer was arrested four days later at his house in Newport Beach, California, and later was indicted by a federal grand jury on charges of "orchestrating a massive fraud scheme" that the U.S. government says has cost 14 cities and investment trusts more than $113 million. Federal investigators say the Wymer case is an instructive tale of how small-town treasurers can be snookered by a clever confidence game. As interest rates plunged on their Treasury securities and certificates of deposit, they frantically sought ways to keep up city income. City treasurers didn't invest their short-term cash with Mr. Wymer merely because he was charming and athletic: he didn't charge a commission on trades as other brokers do.

Commercial paper

Commercial paper is an unsecured promissory note usually issued by large, strong corporations. This short-term security is sold primarily to other corporations, pension funds, money market mutual funds, and insurance companies. Maturities range from one day up to nine months. Since there is no secondary market for these securities, marketability is low. The quality of this instrument depends on the financial strength of the particular issuer.

Repurchase Agreements

Repurchase agreements are sales of government securities, usually by a securities dealer, with an agreement to repurchase at a higher price on a specified future date. The difference in price is the effective interest paid at maturity. Maturities for repurchase agreements (repos) are usually for one business day but may range up to 180 days. Repos are highly marketable, a major reason for their popularity.

Table 16.1 summarizes some key points of these money market instruments. The focus is on comparing the marketable securities by issuer, maturity, and type of interest payment.

CONTROLLING THE TARGET CASH BALANCE

Controlling the target cash balance involves finding methods for minimizing the total costs of maintaining cash balances. In simple models, total costs are

TABLE 16.1 A Comparison of Marketable Securities

INSTRUMENT	ISSUER	MATURITY	INTEREST
Treasury bills	U.S. government	91 and 182 days; One year	Discounted
Federal agency notes	Federal Home Loan Bank, Government National Mortgage Association, etc.	Up to one year	Discounted
Bankers' acceptances	Commercial banks	Up to six months	Discounted
Negotiable CDs	Commercial banks	14 days or more	Interest paid at maturity
Eurodollar certificates of deposit	Branches of Eurobanks	Up to one year	Interest paid at maturity
Commercial paper	Large, strong corporations	Up to nine months	Discounted or interest paid at maturity
Repurchase agreements	U.S. government securities dealers	Overnight up to 180 days	Interest paid at maturity

thought of as the sum of the opportunity costs of holding too much cash plus the trading costs of holding too little cash. Simple models also require restrictive assumptions, thereby allowing uncomplicated total cost functions.

In working with the models in this section, keep in mind that companies hold excess liquidity in the form of marketable securities. So ordering cash is really the same as selling securities.

The Baumol Model

The **Baumol model,** developed by William Baumol, views cash balances as an inventory. Initially, a company with zero cash balances receives a specified quantity of cash, C. The inventory of cash at that point, time 0, is C, as shown in Figure 16.5. Through time, cash is used up until the cash balance again reaches zero. Before this happens, the company reorders a quantity of cash, C. The reordering takes place shortly before the cash balance reaches zero, in time for it not to become negative. The model assumes that cash is used up at a constant rate.

Baumol Model

To develop the model, Baumol defines the following variables:

$$C = \text{Quantity of cash delivered}$$
$$S = \text{Fixed cost of selling marketable securities}$$
$$D = \text{Cash required over the planning period}$$
$$R = \text{Opportunity cost of holding cash}$$

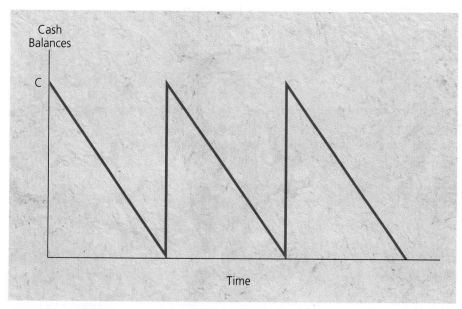

Figure 16.5 The Baumol Model for Cash Balance Management

The model assumes that the per unit cost of selling marketable securities does not depend on the quantity sold.

The total cost of controlling cash (TC) is the sum of the costs of holding cash plus the costs of ordering cash.

$$TC = \text{Holding Costs} + \text{Ordering Costs}$$

The holding costs are found by multiplying the average amount of cash on hand by the opportunity cost of holding cash. Looking at Figure 16.5, we see that the maximum cash is C and the minimum cash is zero. The average amount of cash is therefore halfway between the two extremes, C/2. Thus, the amount of holding costs is as follows:

$$\text{Holding Costs} = \frac{CR}{2}$$

The ordering costs are found by multiplying the number of orders per planning period by the fixed costs of selling marketable securities. The number of orders per planning period is the cash required over the planning period divided by the quantity of cash delivered, or D/C. Thus, the amount of ordering costs is as follows:

$$\text{Ordering costs} = \frac{DS}{C}$$

The total cost of controlling cash (TC) is the sum of the holding and ordering costs:

$$TC = \frac{CR}{2} + \frac{DS}{C} \tag{16.1}$$

Figure 16.6 is a graph of the ordering, holding, and total costs expressed in Eq. 16.1.

The optimal value for the quantity of cash delivered, C*, is found using basic calculus[1].

---

[1] First, take the first derivative of Eq. 16.1 with respect to C.

$$\frac{dTC}{dC} = \frac{R}{2} - \frac{DS}{C^2}$$

Then set the result equal to zero.

$$\frac{R}{2} - \frac{DS}{C^2} = 0$$

Next, solve for C.

$$C^* = \sqrt{\frac{2DS}{R}}$$

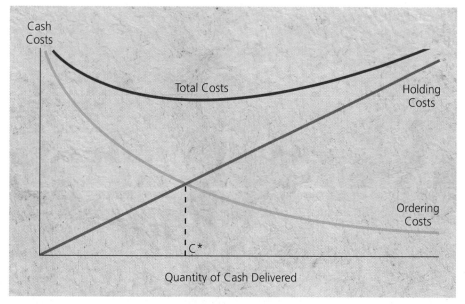

Figure 16.6 Baumol Model Ordering, Holding, and Total Costs
• • • • • • • • •

$$C^* = \sqrt{\frac{2DS}{R}} \qquad\qquad (16.2)$$

This equation represents the optimal value for the quantity of cash delivered, the amount that minimizes the total cost function.

The Ott Company has net cash outflows of a steady $2,500,000 per year. The average return on marketable securities held by the company is 10 percent on an annual basis. The fixed cost of selling the securities is $50. What is the quantity of cash delivered each time the cash balance reaches zero? What is the average level of cash?

The quantity of cash delivered is found by first finding the following values:

$$D = \$2,500,000$$
$$S = \$50$$
$$R = 0.10$$

Substitute the values into Eq. 16.2.

$$C^* = \sqrt{\frac{2DS}{R}}$$

$$= \sqrt{\frac{2(\$2,500,000)(\$50)}{0.10}}$$

$$= \$50,000$$

This is the quantity of cash delivered each time the cash balance reaches zero. The average level of cash is $C^*/2$, or $25,000.

The Baumol model is limited in one key aspect. It requires net cash flows to decline at a constant rate. Most companies have inflows and outflows that are rather random in nature, leading to variable net cash flows. Even with this limitation, it is important in the study of cash management.

The Miller-Orr Model

Miller-Orr Model

The **Miller-Orr model,** developed by Merton Miller and Daniel Orr, relaxes the assumption that net cash flows are steadily declining. Instead, this model assumes that daily net cash flows are normally distributed, a more realistic approach to cash management.

Miller and Orr designed a control limit model that allows for positive and negative cash balance changes. Figure 16.7 illustrates the process. The cash balance randomly moves up and down between two control limits. If it reaches

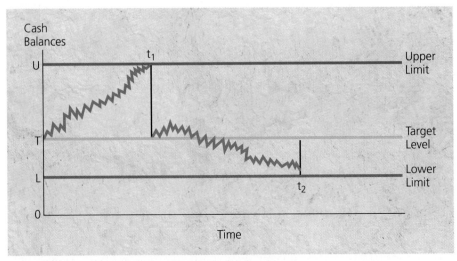

Figure 16.7 Cash Balance Changes with the Miller-Orr Model

the upper control limit, U, as it does at t_1, the cash manager buys marketable securities. The amount of the purchase is $(U - T)$, the cash balance between U and T. If it reaches the lower control limit, L, as it does at t_2, the cash manager sells marketable securities. The amount of the sale is $(T - L)$, the cash balance between L and T. In both cases, the cash balance returns to T, the target level, after the transaction.

The lower limit, L, is set by management as a safety stock of cash, the greater the value, the less likely the company will run out of cash. At a minimum, L should be equal to the compensating balance required by the bank.

The target level, T, as derived by Miller and Orr, is the following:

$$T = \sqrt[3]{\frac{3s\sigma^2}{4r}} + L \tag{16.3}$$

where

$$s = \text{Transactions cost for buying or selling}$$
$$\sigma^2 = \text{Variance of the net cash flows}$$
$$r = \text{Opportunity cost of holding cash}$$

To find T, the cash manager must first determine the variance of the net cash flows. This calculation requires data from a comparable period, if available. As in most areas of finance, finding the variance demands judgment.

The upper limit, U, as derived by Miller and Orr, is the following:

$$U = 3 \sqrt[3]{\frac{3s\sigma^2}{4r}} + L \tag{16.4}$$

$$U = 3T - 2L \tag{16.4a}$$

Notice the similarity in the expressions for T and U. As a result, the target level, T, is one-third of the distance from the lower limit, L, to the upper limit, U.

The average cash balance (ACB), as derived by Miller and Orr, is the following:

$$ACB = \frac{4T - L}{3} \tag{16.5}$$

The cash manager at the Ott Company determines that the standard deviation of net cash flows on a daily basis is $1,000. The manager also discovers that the opportunity cost of holding cash is 14.67 percent on an annual basis and the transactions cost for buying or selling securities is $256. Management sets the lower limit of the Miller-Orr model at $25,000 as a safety margin. What are the target level, upper limit, and average cash balance?

To find the key values, first you must convert the 14.67 percent annual interest to a daily basis. This is accomplished using Eq. 2.10.

$$ER = \left(1 + \frac{k}{m}\right)^m - 1$$

$$0.1467 = \left(1 + \frac{k}{365}\right)^{365} - 1$$

$$1.1467 = \left(1 + \frac{k}{365}\right)^{365}$$

Take the 365th root of both sides.

$$\sqrt[365]{1.1467} = \left(1 + \frac{k}{365}\right)$$

Calculate the 365th root with a financial calculator.

$$1.000375 = \left(1 + \frac{k}{365}\right)$$

$$0.000375 = \frac{k}{365}$$

The expression $k/365$ is the same as r, the opportunity cost of holding cash.

To find the target level, T, substitute $s = \$256$, $\sigma = \$1,000$, $r = 0.000375$, and $L = \$25,000$ into Eq. 16.3.

$$T = \sqrt[3]{\frac{3(256)(\$1,000)(\$1,000)}{4(0.000375)}} + \$25,000$$
$$= \$8,000 + \$25,000$$
$$= \$33,000$$

To find the upper limit, U, substitute $T = \$33,000$ and $L = \$25,000$ into Eq. 16.4a.

$$U = 3T - 2L$$
$$= 3(\$33,000) - 2(\$25,000)$$
$$= \$49,000$$

Notice the target level, $T = \$33,000$, is one-third of the distance from the lower limit, $L = \$25,000$, to the upper limit, $U = \$49,000$. The difference of $8,000$, $\$33,000 - \$25,000$, is one third of $\$24,000$, $\$49,000 - \$25,000$.

To find the average cash balance, substitute T = $33,000 and L = $25,000 into Eq. 16.5.

$$ACB = \frac{4(\$33,000) - \$25,000}{3}$$

$$= \$35,667$$

These calculations suggest that a cash manager should buy $16,000, $49,000 – $33,000, in marketable securities when the cash balance rises to $49,000. The manager should also sell $8,000, $33,000 – $25,000, in marketable securities when the cash balance falls to $25,000. Figure 16.8 illustrates Martin Corporation cash management using the Miller-Orr model.

The Miller-Orr model is easy to understand, but it is a bother to calculate. To make the calculations simpler, use THE FINANCIAL MANAGER (MILLORR).

The Stone Model

The **Stone model** considers information about future cash flows before the cash manager makes a decision to buy or sell securities. This contrasts with the Miller-Orr model which takes action based solely on the size of the cash balance relative to the upper and lower control limits.

Stone Model

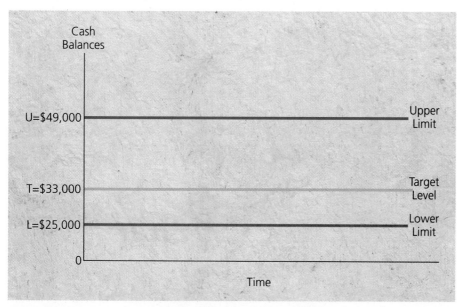

Figure 16.8 Martin Corporation Cash Management Using Miller-Orr

This model is similar to the Miller-Orr model in that it has upper (U) and lower (L) control limits and a target level (T). In addition, it has an inner set of control limits, $(U - d_U)$ and $(L + d_L)$. The two parameters, d_U and d_L, reflect the deviations from the upper and lower control limits. Figure 16.9 illustrates the structure.

The operation of the Stone model is identical to the Miller-Orr model as long as the cash balance is within the upper and lower control limits, U and L. Under these conditions, no action is taken. If the cash balance is not within the upper and lower control limits, the Stone model looks at the net cash flow forecast over the next k days. In this case, it adds the amount of the forecast to the current cash balance. If the expected total cash balance is still outside the *inner* limits, the cash manager makes a marketable securities transaction. The transaction, based on the *expected cash balance after k days*, returns the cash balance to the target level.

The parameters U, T, L, d_U, and d_L are not provided by the Stone model. It is possible, however, to employ the Miller-Orr model to specify U, T, and L while setting and varying d_U and d_L using judgment and experience.

> The cash manager at the Ott Company sets the upper limit, lower limit, and target level as shown in Figure 16.8. Based on experience, the deviations from the upper and lower control limits are each set at $3,000. The current cash balance is at the upper limit of $49,000. Over the next five days, the net cash flow forecast is expected to be -$5,000. What action, if any, should be taken? Would the answer change if the net cash flow forecast is -$1,000?

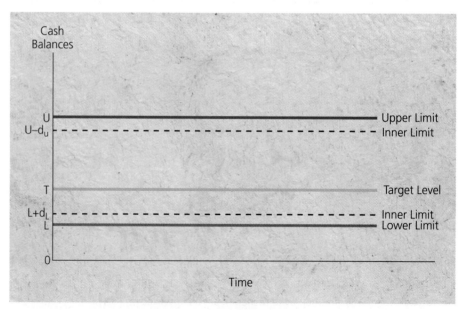

Figure 16.9 The Control-Limit Structure of the Stone Model

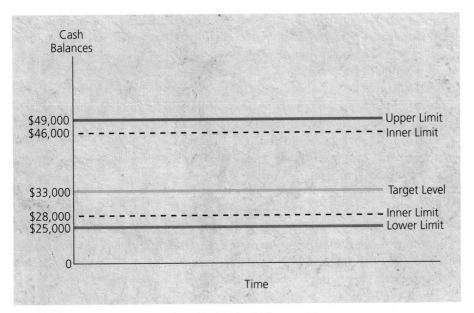

Figure 16.10 The Stone Model Limits for the Martin Corporation

The inner control limits are set by subtracting and adding the deviations of $3,000 to the upper and lower control limits from Figure 16.9. The resulting model is illustrated in Figure 16.10.

The expected cash balance after five days for a net cash flow forecast of −$5,000 is $44,000, $49,000 − $5,000. This amount is inside the *inner* limits, less than $46,000. No action is required.

The expected cash balance after five days for a net cash flow forecast of −$1,000 is $48,000, $49,000 − $1,000. This amount is outside the *inner* limits, more than $46,000. The cash manager purchases $15,000 in marketable securities, $48,000 − $33,000, returning the cash balance to the target level after five days.

The Stone model is important in that it shows that a financial manager must use all the information available. It reinforces the idea that finance is based in large measure on human judgment.

SUMMARY

This chapter focuses on the following learning objectives:
1. Managing the disbursement and collection of cash.
   There are two goals in the disbursement and collection of cash: maximization of net float and minimization of checking account balances. For disburse-

ment, remote disbursement accounts, zero-balance accounts, drafts, and overdrafts are employed; for collection, lockboxes, concentration banking, and preauthorized payment are used.

2. Explaining the criteria for selecting marketable securities.

   Financial managers judge marketable securities by three major criteria: expected return, risk, and marketability. Expected return, the annual yield of an investment, is affected by the taxability of the instrument and the tax status of the organization. Risk in regard to marketable securities involves default risk and interest rate risk. Marketability refers to the ease with which a marketable security may be converted to cash.

3. Discussing the types of money market securities.

   Commercial paper, negotiable certificates of deposit, and a variety of other money market instruments compete with Treasury bills to be included in short-term investment portfolios. Unlike the past, competition now includes money market securities denominated in foreign currencies.

4. Controlling the target cash balance through the Baumol model.

   The Baumol model views cash balances as an inventory. Initially, a company with zero cash balances receives a specified quantity of cash. Through time, cash is used up until the cash balance reaches zero. Before this happens, the company reorders a quantity of cash. The model assumes that cash is used up at a constant rate.

5. Controlling the target cash balance through the Miller-Orr model.

   The Miller-Orr model relaxes the assumption that net cash flows are steadily declining. Instead, this model assumes that daily net cash flows are normally distributed and allows for positive and negative cash balance changes. The cash balance randomly moves up and down between two control limits.

6. Controlling the target cash balance through the Stone model.

   The Stone model considers information about future cash flows before the cash manager makes a decision to buy or sell securities. This contrasts with the Miller-Orr model which takes action based solely on the size of the cash balance relative to the upper and lower control limits. This model is similar to the Miller-Orr model in that it has upper and lower control limits and a target level. In addition, it has an inner set of control limits.

Key Terms

Bankers' acceptance, 451
Baumol model, 453
Collection float, 444
Commercial paper, 452
Concentration
   banking, 446

Default risk, 450
Disbursement float, 444
Draft, 444
Eurodollar certificate of
   deposit, 451
Federal agency note, 451

Float, 443
Interest rate
   risk, 450
Lockbox, 445
Marketability, 450
Miller-Orr Model, 456

QUESTIONS

16.1 Discuss the various types of float.

16.2 Explain remote disbursement accounts.

16.3 Explain zero-balance accounts (ZBAs).

16.4 Explain the differences between drafts and checks.

16.5 How does an overdraft protection allow a company to minimize the amount of cash it has on hand for cash disbursement?

16.6 How is a lockbox used to receive accounts-receivable payments from customers?

16.7 How does a company use concentration banking to process checks?

16.8 Show how a company transfers excess funds from the local banks to a concentration bank by a wire transfer and by a depository transfer check (DTC).

16.9 What is the purpose of the National Automated Clearing House Association (NACHA)?

16.10 How is a preauthorized payment, or preauthorized debit, used by a company to charge the checking accounts of its customers?

16.11 What are the three reasons that a company invests in marketable securities?

16.12 Explain expected return in the context of marketable securities.

16.13 Explain the two types of risk involved with marketable securities.

16.14 Discuss the marketability of marketable securities, explaining breadth and depth of the market.

16.15 Discuss the following money market securities:

   (a) Treasury bills.
   (b) Federal agency notes.
   (c) Bankers' acceptances.
   (d) Negotiable certificates of deposit.
   (e) Eurodollar certificates of deposit
   (f) Commercial paper.
   (g) Repurchase agreements.

16.16 Describe the assumptions and operation of the Baumol model of cash management.

16.17   Describe the assumptions and operation of the Miller-Orr model of cash management.

16.18   How did R.H. Macy plan to improve its cash problems?

PROBLEMS

16.1   **(Float)** The Atkinson Company writes checks to its suppliers totaling $15,000, requiring four days to clear. Payments from customers of $20,000 take three days to clear. Calculate the disbursement float, the collection float, and the net float.

16.2   **(Float)** The books of Ross, Inc. show a cash balance of $500,000, but this ignores float. The company makes payments of $40,000 with a five day float and collections of $50,000 with a four day float. What is the actual cash balance?

16.3   **(Annual Yield)** The Jameson Company buys a 91-day, $10,000 par value, Treasury bill at a discount of 8.00 percent. What is the annual yield of this investment?

16.4   **(Annual Yield)** The Marks Corporation 91-day, $10,000 par value, Treasury bill is sold at a discount of 8.60 percent. What is the annual yield of this investment?

16.5   **(Baumol Model)** The Stenger Corporation has net cash outflows of a steady $3,500,000 per year. The average return on marketable securities held by the company is 11 percent on an annual basis. The fixed cost of selling the securities is $90. Using the Baumol model, what is the quantity of cash delivered each time the cash balance reaches zero? What is the average level of cash?

16.6   **(Baumol Model)** The Alice Murphy Company uses the Baumol model to control cash balances. The company has net cash outflows of a steady $2,500,000 per year. It costs $150 to sell securities, while the average annual return is nine percent. Under these conditions, what is the quantity of cash delivered each time the cash balance reaches zero? What is the average level of cash?

16.7   **(Miller-Orr Model)** The cash manager at the Zabawa Company determined that the standard deviation of net cash flows on a daily basis is $500. She also found out that the opportunity cost of holding cash is 12.33 percent on an annual basis and that the transactions cost for buying or selling securities is $350. Management sets the lower limit of the Miller-Orr model at $10,000 as a safety margin. What are the target level, upper limit, and average cash balance?

16.8 **(Miller-Orr Model)** The Padgett Roofing Company uses the Miller-Orr model to control cash balances. For this company, the standard deviation of net cash flows on a daily basis is $250. The transactions cost for buying or selling securities is $150, while the opportunity cost of holding cash is 11.34 percent on an annual basis. The company sets the lower limit of the Miller-Orr model at $5,000 as a safety margin. What are the target level, upper limit, and average cash balance?

16.9 **(Stone Model)** The cash manager at the Charta Corporation sets the upper limit, lower limit, and target level at $50,000, $20,000, and $30,000, respectively. The deviations from the control limits are each set at $2,500. The current cash balance is at the upper limit of $50,000. Over the next seven days, the net cash flow forecast is expected to be −$3,000. What action, if any, should be taken?

16.10 **(Stone Model)** The Brace Machinery Company currently is using the following Miller-Orr model:

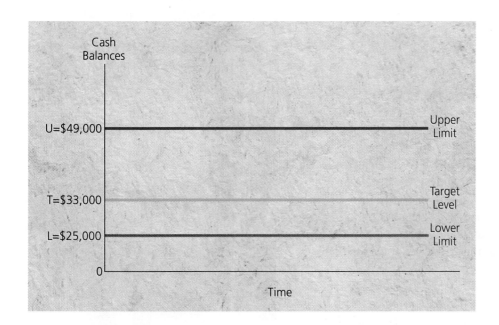

The cash manager is changing to the Stone model since he would like to use future cash flow information. Currently, he forecasts net cash flows to be −$6,000 over the next six days. He also plans to change the lower limit to $40,000 since the compensating balance requirement has been reduced. From experience he believes that each of the deviations should be $5,000. The current cash balance is $85,000. What action, if any, should he take?

A Case Problem

The FitWear Company designed and marketed swimwear, skiwear, and active fitness apparel. The SwimWear brand name was preeminent in the competition swimwear market and was widely recognized for product innovation, quality, and performance. The company's strategy was to play on its reputation in the competition swimwear market to more deeply penetrate the skiwear and fitness apparel markets. Management planned to open retail stores designed to appeal to participants in water-based and land-based activities.

The apparel industry had been subject to cyclical variation, and management was concerned that the current recession would affect long-term consumer spending habits.

The apparel industry had been subject to cyclical variation, and management was concerned that the current recession would affect long-term consumer spending habits. Several competitors had experienced financial difficulties and were having problems receiving credit. Sales in the skiwear industry had declined by 30 percent over the last 3 years. Although the company had tried to diversify into the skiwear and fitness apparel market, sales were still somewhat seasonal. The company's working capital needs peaked near the end of the third quarter of the fiscal year.

Lawrence Silver was the cash manager at FitWear. While working on his MBA, he had learned the basics of the Baumol model for controlling cash. He was considering using it to determine the new quantity of cash to receive as cash is used up. After a little research, Lawrence discovered that the company had net cash outflows of approximately $9,000,000 per year. The amount it cost to sell marketable securities depended on the quantity of securities sold:

Quantity	Amount
$ 0–$ 24,999	$100
$ 25,000–$ 74,999	$150
$ 75,000–$124,999	$200
$125,000–$174,999	$250
$175,000–$224,999	$300
$225,000–$274,999	$350

Each additional increment of $50,000 added $50 to the cost. Lawrence knew that the opportunity cost of holding cash was 10 percent.

Under these conditions, Lawrence wanted to calculate the quantity of cash that should be delivered each time the cash balance reaches zero? Lawrence had also learned about the Miller-Orr and Stone models. He wondered if these models were more appropriate. He needed to find out if the assumptions of these models applied to the situation at FitWear.

Leading Questions

1. Using the Baumol model, what is the quantity of cash to be delivered each time the cash balance reaches zero?
2. Would the Miller-Orr model or the Stone model be more appropriate?

Closely related to sales but seldom given the same attention by management decision makers, is credit. An effective business organization recognizes the interdependence of sales and credit and attempts to ensure their positive interaction. Yet most firms fail to develop an effective sales and credit interaction because the functions are usually separated into conflicting and competing groups.

17 Accounts Receivable and Inventory

The sales group is classified as a line or operating function and is supervised by line management. Its primary responsibility is generating sales. Sales unit volume and dollars are the primary performance measures used to reward sales personnel. Bad-debt losses and the time required to receive payment are, at best, given only token attention in the sales group's reward system.

Credit is classified as a staff function, managed by a staff manager, with primary responsibility for implementing credit and collection policies. Performance is measured by the amount of credit losses and the time it takes to collect credit sales. Sales volume is not part of the credit group's reward system.

With sales and credit groups operating with different objectives, performance measures, managers, reward systems, and strategies, it is difficult for them to function as a team. In addition to conflicting goals, the separation between the two groups is difficult to overcome because it usually extends beyond the organizational chart. Members of each group not only perceive themselves as different but are proud of the distinction.

Credit managers necessarily look at the credit functions from a different perspective than do sales managers. In examining each function, remember that a complete credit approach is required.

Source: David A. Kunz, "Strive for the Complete Credit Approach," *Business Credit,* June 1992. Published by the National Association of Credit Management.

CASH AND CREDIT TERMS

The shipment of a company's products requires that the customer be given either cash terms or credit terms. **Cash terms** may be in the form of cash in advance or in the form of cash on delivery. **Cash in advance** requires the customer to pay before the product is shipped, the method used with the least credit-worthy customers. **Cash on delivery (COD)** requires the customer to pay with cash or certified check before taking delivery, an approach which only involves the risk of the customer not accepting the shipment.

A company uses credit to stimulate demand for its products. The terms of a credit sale, or the **credit terms,** include the credit period, the cash discount (if any), and the kind of credit instrument.

Cash Terms

Cash in Advance

Cash on Delivery (COD)

Credit Terms

The Ferguson Company offers credit terms to its customers of 2/10, net 30. When must the customer pay, and what discount is available?

The customer must pay within 30 days. If the customer pays within 10 days, the customer receives a 2 percent discount. For example, the Ferguson Company purchases $400 in merchandise. It has the choice of paying the full $400 in 30 days or paying $392, $400(0.98), within 10 days.

Seasonal Dating

Companies with seasonal sales may use **seasonal dating.** This allows a company to receive a shipment during the winter and pay for it during the spring. The shipment could be in February, with a seasonal date of April 1. If the credit terms are 3/10, net 30, the customer has until April 30 to make the payment and would receive a 3 percent discount for paying by April 10.

Credit Period

Credit Period

The **credit period** is the length of time for which credit is extended. In the 2/10, net 30 example, the credit period is 30 days. The length of the credit period is often set by industry custom but is influenced by situational factors:

- **Account Size.** Large accounts are more important, resulting in a longer credit period.
- **Credit Worthiness.** High-risk customers receive shorter credit periods.
- **Product Perishability.** Products with a short shelf life tend to have a shorter credit period.

Increasing the credit period usually results in increased sales.

> The Morris Corporation has credit terms of net 30. It is considering changing to terms of net 60. A financial analyst for the company estimates that this will cause annual credit sales to increase by $219,000, from $1,095,000 to $1,314,000. The marginal cost of the additional sales is $154,000. The average collection period, the average time required to collect receivables, is also estimated to increase from 35 days to 68 days. The cost of financing receivables is 15 percent per year. Should this change be made?

The investment in accounts receivable (IAR) is given as follows:

$$IAR = (\text{Annual Sales}/365)(\text{Average Collection Period})$$

Calculate the IAR for the old sales.

$$IAR = (\$1,095,000/365)35$$
$$= \$105,000$$

Then, calculate the IAR for the new sales.

$$IAR = (\$1,314,000/365)68$$
$$= \$244,800$$

The additional investment in receivables is $139,800, $244,800 – $105,000.

Lengthening the credit period increases the cost of financing receivables and provides additional profit. The cost of financing receivables increases by $20,970, $139,800(0.15). The additional profit from increased sales is $65,000, $219,000 – $154,000. The incremental profit from lengthening the credit period is $44,030, $65,000 – $20,970. The Morris Corporation should make the change.

Cash Discounts

Cash discounts are price reductions given to customers for paying by a speci- **Cash Discounts** fied early date. Sellers express them as a percentage of the amount on the sales invoice. In the previous example of 2/10, net 30, the customer simply pays 2 percent less if the bill is paid within 10 days.

Customers implicitly pay interest when they pass up the opportunity to take the cash discount. In the 2/10, net 30 example, waiting 20 extra days to pay, 30 days – 10 days, the customer gives up the chance to reduce costs by 2 percent.

The annualized opportunity cost of not taking a discount (OC) is approximated by the following formula:

$$OC = \left(\frac{CD}{1-CD}\right)\left(\frac{365}{CP-DP}\right) \qquad (17.1)$$

where

$$CD = \text{Cash discount expressed as a decimal}$$
$$CP = \text{Credit period (in days)}$$
$$DP = \text{Discount period (in days)}$$

The first term of this formula, $CD/(1-CD)$ represents the opportunity cost of waiting $(CP-DP)$ days. The second term of the formula, $365/(CP-DP)$, determines the number of times the discount is foregone each year. Multiplying the two terms together annualizes the opportunity cost.

The credit terms for the Solomon Corporation are 2/10, net 30. What is the approximate annual cost of not taking the discount?

Eq. 17.1 is used to calculate the approximate annual cost of not taking the discount.

$$OC = \left(\frac{0.02}{1-0.02}\right)\left(\frac{365}{30-10}\right)$$
$$= (0.0204)(18.25)$$
$$= 0.372 \text{ or } 37.2\%$$

The opportunity cost of waiting 20 days is 2.04 percent. The number of 20-day periods in 365 days is 18.25.

The exact annual cost of not taking the discount is the effective rate of interest using Eq. 2.8.

$$ER = \left(1 + \frac{k}{m}\right)^m + 1$$
$$= (1 + 0.0204)^{18.25} - 1.0$$
$$= 0.4456 \text{ or } 44.56\%$$

Both the approximate and exact methods yield a high opportunity cost for not taking the discount.

Customers should compare the opportunity cost with the cost of borrowing and take the discount when the borrowing cost is lower. The company granting the credit terms should make sure that the opportunity cost is higher than the cost of customer borrowing to help keep the level of accounts receivable at a minimum.

The Morris Corporation has credit terms of net 30. It is considering changing to terms of 2/10, net 30. Deborah Jackson, a financial analyst for the company, estimates that this change will cause annual credit sales to increase by $146,000, from $1,095,000 to $1,241,000. The marginal cost of the additional sales is $102,700. The average collection period is estimated to decrease from 35 days to 25 days. The cost of financing receivables is 15 percent per year. Should this change be made?

The investment in accounts receivable (IAR) is given as follows:

$$IAR = (\text{Annual Sales}/365)(\text{Average Collection Period})$$

Apply this equation to the old sales.

$$IAR = (\$1,095,000/365)35$$
$$= \$105,000$$

Then, apply the equation to the new sales.

$$IAR = (\$1,241,000/365)25$$
$$= \$85,000$$

The reduced investment in receivables is $20,000, $105,000 − $85,000.

Providing the cash discount results in additional profit for the company. The cost of financing receivables decreases by $3,000, $20,000(0.15). The additional profit from increased sales is $43,300, $146,000 − $102,700. The cost of the discount is $24,820, $1,241,000(0.02). Therefore, the incremental profit from providing the discount is $21,480, $3,000 + $43,300 − $24,820. Deborah should recommend that the Morris Corporation make the change.

Credit Instruments

In the United States, most credit is offered on **open account.** Under this system, the invoice, which includes the credit terms, is the formal credit instrument. The customer signs the invoice when the shipment is received, but it is not a formal debt contract. Under open account, the cost of borrowing is implicit, based on the terms of credit to which the two parties agree. With this arrangement, both the buyer and the seller record the transaction on their books.

Open Account

In some situations, a company may require a customer to sign a **promissory note** when the product is delivered. This is an agreement to pay a certain amount at a specified future date. Companies tend to use this arrangement when the order is large or when payment may be questionable. Use of a promissory note requires the seller to use *notes receivable* on its balance sheet.

Promissory Note

Commercial drafts, which are often used in international trade, demand a credit commitment from the customer before the product is delivered. A **sight draft** requires the buyer to pay a specified amount on demand; a **time draft** allows the amount to be paid at a future date. The seller of the product sends the draft to the customer's bank, along with the invoices. After the customer signs the draft, the product is shipped.

Commercial Drafts

Sight Draft

Time Draft

A seller may require a **banker's acceptance** in lieu of accepting a time draft. With this credit instrument, the bank guarantees, for a fee, payment of the draft. Banker's acceptances are liquid instruments, allowing the holder to sell them in the money market on a discount basis.

Banker's Acceptance

A **conditional sales contract** allows the seller to retain ownership of the product until payment is complete. This credit instrument is normally used for installment sales, typically with equipment. The seller retains legal ownership of the product until all payments, including interest, are made. This arrangement makes repossession easier in the case of default.

Conditional Sales Contract

Consignment

The seller (the consignor) also retains title to product shipped to the customer (the consignee) on **consignment**. The consignee pays the consignor if the product is sold. This approach is used by grocery stores, with distributors responsible for managing specified retail space.

Optimal Credit Policy

The optimal credit policy can be defined in general terms: The optimal level of credit occurs at the point where the sum of carrying costs and opportunity costs is a minimum. Carrying costs include the incremental costs of extending credit and investing in receivables. Opportunity costs include the incremental costs of losing sales. Figure 17.1 illustrates the concept of the optimal level of credit.

CREDIT ANALYSIS

Credit analysis begins with an assessment of potential customers. The credit analyst evaluates credit capacity. The financial techniques of Chapter 4 are useful in determining how much credit each customer will receive.

The Five C's of Credit

Five C's of Credit

Traditionally, companies evaluate customers by the **five C's of credit.**

- *Character* reflects the willingness to repay debt, even under the most trying circumstances. Some customers take pride in paying bills in a timely

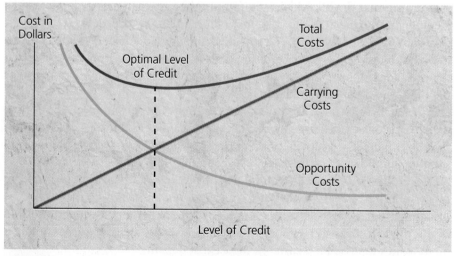

Figure 17.1 The Concept of the Optimal Level of Credit

manner. Others make a game of delaying payments and stretching their obligation to the limit. The credit analyst must be able to judge the moral makeup of each credit applicant. Bank lending officers often say that banks lend to people, not to financial statements.

- *Capacity* reflects the ability to repay debt, the financial position of the company. Credit analysts use the financial analysis techniques of Chapter 4 to make this judgment. The focus when using ratio analysis is on liquidity and profitability ratios. Liquidity ratios measure whether or not the company has the cash balances necessary to pay its bills. Profitability ratios measure whether or not a company is making enough money to pay its bills. Using both sets of ratios, the credit analyst estimates if liquidity and profitability will continue into the future.

- *Capital* reflects the degree of financial risk to which the customer is subjected. The higher the proportion of debt, the higher the level of financial risk. High risk may lead to financial distress and insolvency. Leverage ratios measure the extent to which a company uses debt rather than equity. The total debt to total assets ratio and the debt-to-net worth ratio are useful in measuring the financial risk of a company. These ratios are more valuable when compared to industry averages.

- *Collateral* reflects the assets the customer uses as security to obtain credit. Banks and other lending institutions often require customers to pledge assets when making loans. The use of collateral is less important when selling on open account. Retrieval is much more difficult with product, particularly with raw materials and services. The costs of identification and documentation are usually prohibitive in tracing individual items.

- *Conditions* reflect any circumstances that affect a particular customer as well as the general economic climate. Companies benefit or are harmed by the success or failure of lawsuits, marketing programs, contract awards, and other unique events. The general economy has an effect on all companies, to varying degrees. A credit analyst must determine how conditions will influence the particular company being analyzed.

Sources of Credit Information

Companies evaluate the financial statements of old customers and apply the five C's of credit. With new customers, companies check first with a **credit-reporting agency,** a **credit association,** or a bank. Either group can provide the basic information necessary for evaluation.

Credit-reporting agencies include Dun & Bradstreet and TRW, Inc. These agencies provide credit information on several million companies throughout the United States and Canada. Services consist of the publication of general reference books and detailed credit reports on individual companies. Most

Credit-Reporting Agency

Credit Association

credit departments subscribe to computerized services in order to receive the latest customer information.

Credit reports include a summary balance sheet and income statement, key ratios, payment information from banks and suppliers, a description of company operations, a description of the owners, and a credit rating. The most important item is the experience of other creditors with that customer.

Credit associations are local associations of credit managers who exchange information on credit customers. The National Association of Credit Managers (NACM) took this a step farther by creating Credit Interchange, a clearinghouse for information on the payment history of customers.

Banks also provide credit checks on new customers. They do this by communicating with the credit departments of other banks. Banks have a special knowledge of bank balances, loans outstanding, and payment history, as well as a general knowledge of the customer's reputation.

Credit Scoring

Credit Scoring

Credit scoring involves the use of statistical methods to predict the probability that a customer will pay on time. Companies use this approach for both consumer credit and trade credit. Factors used in computing the consumer credit score include annual income, age, home ownership, years at current address, and years at present job. Factors used in computing the trade credit score in-

How Pervasive Is Business Credit Fraud?

Few credit professionals would argue that in today's environment, credit fraud is up. Unfortunately, it happens every day. There are many individuals who make their living by going bankrupt—individuals whose sole intention is to get your company to part with merchandise or a service without having to pay. In the underworld, a planned bankruptcy is called a "bustout," and the operator of a planned bankruptcy is a "bustout artist." An average bustout will generally cost creditors several hundred thousand dollars. There are several types of bustout schemes. The type of bustout that causes the greatest losses is called the "planned insolvency." Rather than paying creditors, the operator pulls as many assets out of the business as possible, eventually leaving everyone high and dry. Another form of bustout scheme is the traditional version where an individual sets up a company from scratch, with the sole intention of eventually "busting out" in the future. They will pay all bills on time, often paying cash in advance in the beginning, if they think it will enable them to get credit later on. The final version of bustout is the "quick and dirty" bustout. None of the ordered merchandise is left when the business closes. Everything about the business is usually fake, including the name of the owner and references.

Source: "How Pervasive Is Business Credit Fraud?," *Business Credit*, 20–21, June 1992. Published by the National Association of Credit Management.

clude net worth, cash flow, as well as a variety of financial ratios. Complex calculations result in simple output, such as a score of 1, 2, or 3, for different levels of credit worthiness.

COLLECTION POLICY

Collection policy reflects the methods used to collect receivables. For most companies, this involves applying a series of progressively stronger reminders that payment has not been received. Companies usually begin with a friendly letter, and if that does not produce results, they send a second not-so-friendly letter. Next, comes a letter threatening to turn the matter over to a lawyer or collection agency. If these methods do not work, the next stage includes telephone calls or a personal visit. Finally, the company sends the overdue account to a lawyer or collection agency.

Collection Policy

Aging of Receivables

Aging of receivables involves classifying receivables by length of time outstanding. Doing this for two or more years shows the trend in the quality of receivables. Table 17.1 provides **aging schedules** for December 31, 19X4, and December 31, 19X5. Because of seasonal factors, a comparison at the same time during the year is best.

Aging of Receivables

Aging Schedules

The aging schedules show a worsening trend in receivables collection. During the 30-day payment period, the percentage has declined from 70 to 60 percent. Each of the other intervals indicates an increase in percentage. This deterioration in the quality of receivables suggests the credit manager should take immediate action.

TABLE 17.1 December 31 Aging Schedules for Markert Corporation

AGE OF RECEIVABLES	19X4 OUTSTANDING	19X4 PERCENTAGE	19X5 OUTSTANDING	19X5 PERCENTAGE
0–30 days	$17,500	70%	$18,000	60%
31–60 days	3,750	15	5,400	18
61–90 days	2,500	10	4,200	14
Over 90 days	1,250	5	2,400	8
	$25,000	100%	$30,000	100%

Factoring and Pledging Receivables

Factoring Receivables

Factor

Factoring receivables involves the sale of accounts receivable to a **factor**. A factor is a commercial finance company or the subsidiary of a commercial bank that specializes in financing receivables. This is usually done on a *nonrecourse* basis, which means that the factor bears the risk, but may also be done on a *with recourse* basis. As the company surrenders title, the receivables are removed from the balance sheet. The company avoids managing the factored receivables since payments are sent directly to the factor. The factor receives initial compensation by purchasing the receivables at a discount.

The factor may assume two other functions: credit analysis and lending. Credit analysis involves the determination of the credit worthiness of potential customers. Credit is refused if the risk exposure is too high. The factor pays the company upon collection of receivables or when a specified time period, such as 30 days, has elapsed. The company may also borrow against the receivables, with a percentage held in reserve to protect against returned product. The cost of borrowing is typically three or four percent above the prime rate.

Pledging Receivables

Pledging receivables is a method used to secure lending. In contrast to factoring, pledging is done with recourse. This means that if the customer does not pay, the company selling the product is responsible. Under this arrangement, customers normally continue to make payments to the company. It is possible, however, for the customer to pay the lender directly, an arrangement which provides the lender with greater control.

Pledging receivables protects the lender in four ways. First, the lender selects the strongest invoices. Second, the lender loans much less than the value of the pledged receivables, typically 70 to 80 percent. Third, the lender has recourse to the selling company. Fourth, the lender charges an interest rate that is greater than the rates charged on unsecured loans.

INVENTORY MANAGEMENT IN THEORY

Inventory management involves the top managers from finance, marketing, and operations, working together to formulate policy. The goals of these managers often conflict. The financial manager is interested in minimizing the investment in inventory. The marketing manager wants a large inventory to keep customers happy. The operations manager demands an inventory sized to reduce costs.

Types of Inventories

There are three types of inventories: raw materials, work-in-process, and finished goods. Raw materials inventories provide a buffer between the purchasing and production functions. By purchasing in quantity, the price is lower, the freight rate is less, and materials handling is more efficient. Work-in-process inventories uncouple the steps of the production process. This added flexibility is especially important in process-oriented, as opposed to product-oriented, systems.

Finished goods inventories provide for uncertainties in both supply and demand. It is usually more economical to produce this inventory rather than to manufacture special orders. Some industries, however, make a practice of backlogging orders, while minimizing finished goods inventory.

Economic Order Quantity Model

The basic economic order quantity (EOQ) model illustrates concepts upon which many inventory models are based. This model shows the relationship between ordering, carrying, and total costs, as well as the optimal number of units to order.

Figure 17.2 illustrates how the basic EOQ model works (without safety stock). A company receives a shipment of product it previously ordered. Through time, the production department uses up the shipment at a uniform rate. When the number of units reaches a predetermined reorder point, the inventory control section orders a new shipment. The new product arrives exactly, in this ideal case, when the number of units is zero.

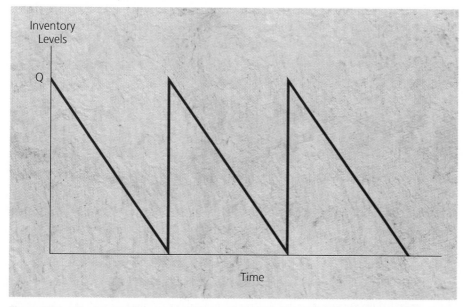

Figure 17.2   The Level of Inventory with the Basic EOQ Model (without safety stock)

Inventory Costs

The optimal order quantity is the shipment size that minimizes inventory costs. This involves both ordering and carrying costs.

Ordering costs are the costs of processing, placing, receiving, and inspecting an order. In manufacturing, ordering costs consist of the costs of setting up a production run. In the basic EOQ model, ordering costs are assumed to be constant.

Carrying costs are the costs of storing, handling, insuring, and financing inventory, as well as the costs of pilferage, spoilage, and obsolescence. Carrying costs may be expressed as a percentage of the unit price. For example, carrying costs may be 30 percent of a price of $10.00. This translates into carrying costs of $3.00 per unit.

The total ordering costs (TOC), usually calculated on a yearly basis, may be expressed by the following formula:

$$\text{TOC} = \left(\frac{D}{Q}\right)S$$

where

$$D = \text{Annual demand (units per year)}$$
$$Q = \text{Order quantity (units per order)}$$
$$S = \text{Ordering costs (dollars per order)}$$

The first term, D/Q, represents the number of orders placed per year. Multiplying by the cost of placing an order gives the total ordering costs.

The total carrying costs (TCC), usually calculated on a yearly basis, may be represented by the following formula:

$$\text{TCC} = \left(\frac{Q}{2}\right)C$$

where

$$C = \text{Carrying costs (dollars per unit per year)}$$

The first term, Q/2, represents the average number of units in stock. Multiplying by the cost of carrying one unit in inventory for one year gives the total carrying costs.

The total cost (TC) of stocking inventory, usually calculated on a yearly basis, is the sum of total ordering costs and total carrying costs.

$$\text{TC} = \left(\frac{D}{Q}\right)S + \left(\frac{Q}{2}\right)C \qquad (17.2)$$

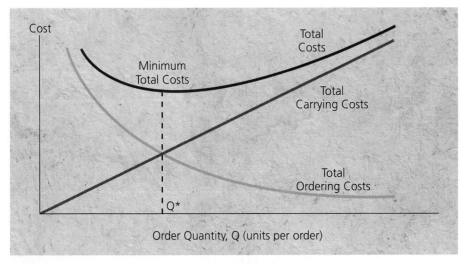

Figure 17.3 The Graphs of Carrying, Ordering, and Total Costs
•••••••••

Figure 17.3 represents for the basic EOQ model the graphs of the ordering costs, carrying costs, and total costs. Ordering costs fall as the order quantity increases, the direct result of the number of orders per year decreasing. Carrying costs rise as the order quantity increases, the consequence of the average inventory increasing. As shown by the graph in Figure 17.3, there is an optimal order quantity, Q^*, the point where the total cost curve is at a minimum[1].

$$Q^* = \sqrt{\frac{2DS}{C}} \qquad (17.3)$$

The Wilson Company purchases 20,000 units of Product X each year. The cost of placing an order is $50, and the carrying cost is $0.50 per unit per year. What is the optimal order quantity, the total yearly cost of stocking inventory, and the number of orders placed each year?

---

[1] The optimal order quantity is found initially by taking the first derivative of Eq. 17.2.

$$\frac{dTC}{dQ} = \frac{C}{2} - \frac{DS}{Q^2}$$

The result is set equal to zero.

$$\frac{C}{2} - \frac{DS}{Q^2} = 0$$

The equation is then solved for Q.

$$Q^* = \sqrt{\frac{2DS}{C}}$$

The order quantity is represented by Q^*, since this is an optimal value.

The optimal order quantity is given by Eq. 17.3.

$$Q^* = \sqrt{\frac{2DS}{C}}$$

Substitute the values into the equation.

$$Q^* = \sqrt{\frac{2(20,000)(\$50)}{\$0.50}}$$
$$= 2,000 \text{ units}$$

Each shipment contains 2,000 units of Product X.

The total cost of stocking inventory each year is given by Eq. 17.2.

$$TC = \left(\frac{D}{Q}\right)S + \left(\frac{Q}{2}\right)C$$

Again substitute the values.

$$TC = \left(\frac{20,000}{2,000}\right)\$50 + \left(\frac{2,000}{2}\right)\$0.50$$
$$= \$500 + \$500$$
$$= \$1,000$$

Notice that the total ordering costs ($500) and the total carrying costs ($500) are equal when the optimal order quantity (2,000) is ordered.

The number of orders placed each year is the annual demand, D, divided by the order quantity, Q or Q*. In this example, the calculation follows:

$$\frac{D}{Q^*} = \frac{20,000}{2,000}$$
$$= 10$$

The inventory control section reorders 2,000 units 10 times each year, a total of 20,000 units.

Reorder Point and Safety Stock

In this section, we learn how the reorder point works with and without a safety stock. The basic EOQ model described in Figure 17.2, without a safety stock, is the basis for the initial discussion.

The reorder point (RP) is the level of inventory at which the inventory control section places a new order. The amount, without safety stock, is given by the following equation:

$$RP = LT(d) \qquad (17.4)$$

where

$$LT = \text{Lead time from reorder until delivery}$$
$$d = \text{Demand per day during the lead time}$$

Without safety stock, the order arrives exactly when inventory reaches zero.

> The inventory section of the Wilson Company determines that it takes 14 days after the reorder point is reached for an order of Product X to arrive. What is the reorder point, given the information from the previous example?

The reorder point, without safety stock, is given by Eq. 17.4.

$$RP = LT(d)$$

Substitute into the equation.

$$RP = \frac{14(2,000)}{365}$$
$$= 767.12 \text{ or } 768 \text{ (rounded up)}$$

Notice that the demand per day is calculated by dividing the yearly demand (20,000 units) by the number of days in a year (365). The reordering process is triggered when the inventory level falls to 768 units.

A safety stock is a cushion of inventory provided to prevent stockouts. In practice, these additional units are necessary since demand and lead time are not constant. Figure 17.4 illustrates how the basic EOQ model works with safety stock.

The reorder point, with safety stock, is given by the following equation:

$$RP = LT(d) + SS \qquad (17.5)$$

where

$$SS = \text{Safety stock}$$

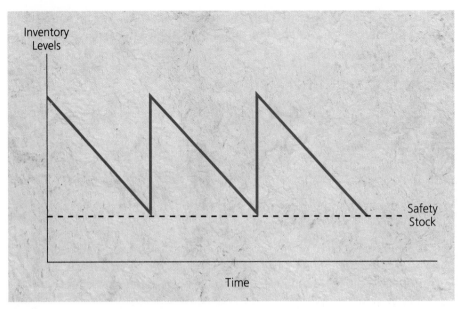

Figure 17.4 The Level of Inventory with the Basic EOQ Model (with safety stock)

With safety stock, the order arrives exactly when inventory reaches the level of the safety stock, if LT and d are constant.

The use of a safety stock allows the lead time and the daily demand to vary. If the demand during the lead time (DDLT) is less than the level of the reorder point, a stockout will not occur. If the demand during the lead time (DDLT) is greater than the level of the reorder point, a stockout will occur, causing a backorder or a lost sale.

Safety stocks are set either by using past DDLT statistics or by heuristic methods, methods based on simple rules. Production management texts focus on both approaches. In this section, safety stocks are given.

The Wilson Company sets the safety stock for Product X at 153 units. What is the reorder point? If the actual lead time is 15 or 16 days and the average demand per day during the lead time is 60 units, what is the inventory level when the new shipment arrives?

The reorder point, with safety stock, is given by Eq. 17.5.

$$RP = LT(d) + SS$$

Again, substitute into the equation.

$$RP = \frac{14(20,000)}{365} + 153$$
$$= 920.12 \text{ or } 921 \text{ (rounded up)}$$

The reordering process is triggered when the inventory level falls to 921 units.

The inventory level (IL) when the new shipment arrives is given by the following equation.

$$IL = RP - DDLT$$

Substitute 15 days.

$$IL = 921 - 15(60)$$
$$= 21 \text{ units}$$

Then, substitute 16 days.

$$IL = 921 - 16(60)$$
$$= -39$$

With the above-average daily demand, the safety stock is adequate for a lead time of 15 days. For 16 days, inventory is 39 units short.

Variations of the Basic Model

The basic economic order quantity model assumes that the unit price is independent of the quantity ordered. Relaxing this assumption makes the analysis more realistic.

The quantity discount model assumes that the price per unit is less if a specified number of units are ordered. This pricing policy occurs because it is usually less expensive to produce and ship larger quantities. In this model, more than one price break is possible.

The quantity discount model uses the formulas of the basic EOQ model but applies them in a prescribed sequence.

1. Determine the optimal order quantity using the most favorable price.
2. Find out if this order quantity is feasible. (If it is feasible, order this quantity and stop the procedure.)

3. Determine the optimal order quantity using the next most favorable price if the order quantity is not feasible. (Repeat this step until a favorable quantity is reached.)
4. Calculate the total cost of stocking inventory using the first feasible order quantity and add the yearly cost of purchasing the units.
5. Calculate the total cost of stocking inventory using the lowest quantity for all price breaks above the first feasible order quantity and add the yearly cost of purchasing the units.
6. Order the quantity associated with the lowest total cost of stocking inventory, including the purchasing costs.

The quantity discount procedure is a practical approach for dealing with the pricing structure of many suppliers.

The Wilson Company purchases 20,000 units of Product X each year. The cost of placing an order is $50, and the carrying cost is 20 percent of the unit cost, in dollars per unit per year. The price of each unit depends on the quantity ordered.

Quantity	Price
0–2,999	$2.50
3,000+	$2.25

What is the optimal order quantity?

The first step is to determine the optimal order quantity using the most favorable price of $2.25. This is accomplished using Eq. 17.3.

$$Q^* = \sqrt{\frac{2DS}{C}}$$

Substitute into the equation.

$$Q^* = \sqrt{\frac{2(20,000)(\$50)}{0.20(\$2.25)}}$$
$$= 2,108.2 \text{ units}$$

It is not feasible to order 2,108.2 units at a price of $2.25, go on to step 3.

The next step is to determine the optimal order quantity using the next most favorable price of $2.50. Using Eq. 17.3 results in the following equation:

$$Q^* = \sqrt{\frac{2(20,000)(\$50)}{0.20(\$2.25)}}$$
$$= 2,000 \text{ units}$$

This order quantity is feasible, so go on to step 4.

The total cost of stocking inventory each year, including purchasing costs, (TCP), using the first feasible order quantity, is found by modifying Eq. 17.2.

$$TCP = \left(\frac{D}{Q}\right)S + \left(\frac{Q}{2}\right)C + \text{Purchasing Costs}$$

Again, make the substitution.

$$TCP = \left(\frac{20,000}{2,000}\right)\$50 + \left(\frac{2,000}{2}\right)(0.20)(\$2.50) + 20,000(\$2.50)$$
$$= \$500 + \$500 + \$50,000$$
$$= \$51,000$$

Since there are price breaks above the first feasible order quantity, go on to step 5.

The next step is to find the total cost of stocking inventory each year, using the price break above the first feasible order quantity, including purchasing costs. Use Eq. 17.2.

$$TCP = \left(\frac{20,000}{3,000}\right)\$50 + \left(\frac{3,000}{2}\right)(0.20)(\$2.25) + 20,000(\$2.25)$$
$$= \$333 + \$675 + \$45,000$$
$$= \$46,008$$

Since $46,008 is lower than $51,000, order 3,000 units each time.

INVENTORY MANAGEMENT IN PRACTICE

Inventory management in practice is more complicated when the number of products is not small. Inventory control managers are often responsible for warehouses with as many as 500,000 inventory items. A first step for dealing with the added complexity of controlling a large inventory is to standardize as much as is practical in order to reduce the number of items.

ABC Analysis

ABC analysis involves classifying items on the basis of importance and applying management controls based on the classifications. This is necessary because of the large number of items used in most manufacturing plants. The letters A, B, and C represent the classifications, with A being the most important.

The basic idea behind ABC analysis is that about 20 percent of inventory items account for 75 to 85 percent of inventory value. Figure 17.5 illustrates the ABC classification of inventory. In this distribution, 20 percent of inventory items are A items, accounting for 75 percent of inventory value and demanding the highest level of control. Next, 30 percent of items are B items, accounting for 20 percent of inventory value and requiring a moderate level of control. Finally, 50 percent of items are C items, accounting for 5 percent of inventory value and needing a limited level of control.

The use of computerized inventory control systems impacts ABC analysis. It is now more economical to maintain records on a large number of items. It is

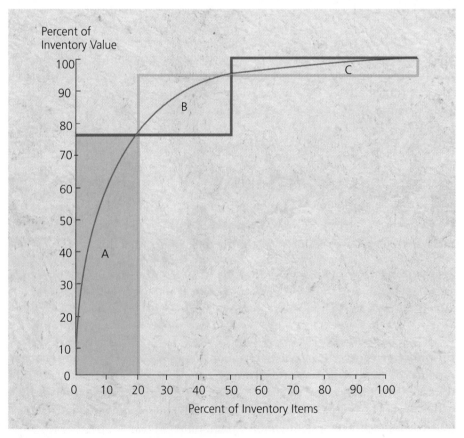

Figure 17.5 The ABC Classification of Inventory

Is JIT Really Appropriate for American Manufacturing?

Just-in-time (JIT) has become a buzzword in manufacturing organizations. The JIT system is based on the concept of maximizing profit by reducing the cost of production. That is, an organization should be producing at a higher rate while keeping the number of idle periods low and carrying little or no inventory. It implies that JIT will result in the production of quality products with little or no waste in quantity. This can be accomplished by requiring the delivery of specified quantity at the time needed. It requires the producers to work with customers and suppliers in order to know the requirements of each party. JIT also requires changes in the accounting system. That is, since the customers require frequent delivery, should the customer send a purchase order before the delivery is made, as required under the conventional accounting system, or should the goods be shipped without a standard purchase order? Further, should the customer be billed each time goods are shipped, or should the supplier wait until a certain quantity has been shipped before billing? Regardless, the accounting system has to change to allow for these changes, which might increase cost for the suppliers and customers because of increased paperwork and delayed or frequent payment.

Source: "Is JIT Really Appropriate for American Manufacturing?," *Industrial Management*, 26–28, May/June 1992. Copyright 1992, Institute of Industrial Engineers, Norcrass, Georgia.

also easier to include factors other than volume in classifying items. A complete analysis includes lead time, storage requirements, pilferage risk, stockout costs, and scarcity of material.

Material Requirements Planning

The use of computers allows for other advanced inventory control techniques. Material requirements planning (MRP) controls the quantity and timing of materials, parts, and subassemblies to production operations. The system is based on a master production schedule (MPS), a schedule showing the items produced over a planning horizon.

Production managers use MRP to improve customer service, reduce inventory investment, and increase operating efficiency. Improving customer service involves meeting the delivery date and shortening delivery time, goals that are built into the system. Reducing inventory investment results from timing materials to arrive when needed, not to remain in inventory for a long period of time. Increasing operating efficiency follows from reducing stockouts, reducing scrapped product, and increasing production capacity.

Just-In-Time Systems

Just-in-time (JIT) systems involve coordinating supplier shipments to arrive just as they are needed. The natural result of this approach, also known as a kanban system, is to reduce inventory levels. Kanban is Japanese for the card used to indicate low inventory levels.

The JIT philosophy touches every aspect of the production process: shop floor planning and control, purchasing, quality control, and maintenance. The use of JIT systems has the added benefit of uncovering production problems. Machines breaking down, product failing quality control tests, or stockouts occurring cause production to stop, forcing immediate action. In contrast, the use of in-process inventories allows problems to be ignored, at least for awhile.

SUMMARY

This chapter focuses on the following learning objectives:

1. Specifying the methods companies use to pay suppliers.
   The shipment of products requires that the customer be given cash terms or credit terms. Cash terms may be in the form of cash in advance or cash on delivery. Credit terms include the credit period, the cash discount (if any), and the kind of credit instrument. In the United States, most credit is offered on open account, a system in which the invoice is the formal credit instrument.

2. Determining the amount of credit each customer will receive.
   The optimal credit policy can be defined in general terms: The optimal level of credit occurs at the point where the sum of carrying costs and opportunity costs is a minimum. Traditionally, companies evaluate customers by the five C's of credit. Companies evaluate the financial statements of new customers with a credit-reporting agency, a credit association, or a bank. Credit scoring involves statistical methods to predict the probability that a customer will pay on time.

3. Explaining the methods companies use to collect receivables.
   Collection policy reflects the methods used to collect receivables. Aging of receivables involves classifying receivables by length of time outstanding. Factoring receivables involves the sale of accounts receivable to a factor. Pledging receivables is a method used to secure lending.

4. Describing the approaches used in inventory modeling.
   The basic economic order quantity model shows the relationship between ordering, carrying, and total costs, as well as the optimal number of units to order. A safety stock is a cushion of inventory that allows the lead time and the daily demand to vary. The quantity discount model assumes that the price per unit is less if a specified number of units are ordered.

5. Detailing the techniques inventory managers use in practice.
   Inventory management in practice is more complicated when the number of products is not small. ABC analysis involves classifying items on the basis of importance and applying management controls based on the classifications. Material requirements planning controls the quantity and timing of

materials, parts, and subassemblies to production operations. Just-in-time systems involve coordinating supplier shipments to arrive just as needed, thereby reducing inventory levels.

KEY TERMS

Aging of receivables, 477	Conditional sales contract, 473	Factoring receivables, 478
Aging schedules, 477	Consignment, 474	Five C's of credit, 474
Banker's acceptance, 473	Credit association, 475	Open account, 473
Cash discount, 471	Credit period, 470	Pledging receivables, 478
Cash in advance, 469	Credit scoring, 476	
Cash on delivery, 469	Credit terms, 469	Promissory note, 473
Cash terms, 469	Credit-reporting agency, 475	Seasonal dating, 470
Collection policy, 477		Sight draft, 473
Commercial draft, 473	Factor, 478	Time draft, 473

QUESTIONS

17.1   Explain the two forms that cash terms can take.

17.2   What are the terms of a credit sale?

17.3   Explain by example the use of seasonal dating.

17.4   What situational factors influence the length of the credit period?

17.5   Contrast offering credit on open account versus having a customer sign a promissory note.

17.6   What is a commercial draft? Explain the differences between sight drafts and time drafts.

17.7   Explain the following instruments:
   (a) Banker's acceptance.
   (b) Conditional sales contract.
   (c) Consignment.

17.8   Explain in general terms what is meant by the optimal credit policy.

17.9   Discuss how companies evaluate customers by the five C's of credit.

17.10 How does a credit-reporting agency operate?

17.11 How does a credit association function?

17.12 How do banks provide credit checks on new customers?

17.13 How do companies use credit scoring to predict the probability that a customer will pay on time?

17.14 What is the series of steps that most companies follow in handling customers that have not paid on time?

17.15 How are aging schedules used to examine the receivables of a company?

17.16 Explain what is involved in factoring receivables?

17.17 How are receivables used to secure lending?

17.18 How does the pledging of receivables protect the lender?

17.19 What are the three types of inventories, and how are they used in a manufacturing situation?

17.20 What are ordering costs and carrying costs?

17.21 Explain the concepts of ABC analysis.

17.22 How does a material requirements planning system operate?

17.23 What is a just-in-time (JIT) system, and what is the philosophy behind it?

17.24 Why is it difficult for sales and credit groups to function as a team?

17.25 What is meant by the term "bustout"?

17.26 Is just-in-time (JIT) appropriate for American manufacturing?

PROBLEMS

17.1 **(Changing Credit Terms)** The Murphy Corporation has credit terms of net 30, and is considering changing to terms of net 45. A financial analyst for the company estimates that this will cause annual credit sales to increase by $164,000, from $820,000 to $984,000. The marginal cost of the additional sales is $120,000. The average collection period is also estimated to increase from 35 days to 50 days. The cost of financing receivables is 16 percent per year. Should this change be made?

17.2 **(Changing Credit Terms)** The Manchester Company has credit terms of net 30, and is considering changing to terms of net 40. A financial analyst for the company estimates that this will cause annual credit sales to increase by $300,000, from $1,200,000 to $1,500,000. The marginal cost of the additional sales is $180,000. The cost of financing receivables is 14 percent per year. The average collection period is also estimated to increase from 35 days to 45 days. Should Manchester Company make this change?

17.3 **(Cost of Not Taking Discount)** The credit terms for customers of Harding Steel are 1/10, net 45. What is the approximate annual cost of not taking the discount?

17.4 **(Cost of Not Taking Discount)** The credit terms for Blanchard Concrete are 2/10, net 40. What is the approximate annual cost of not taking the discount?

17.5 **(Economic Order Quantity)** Wallace Corporation purchases 50,000 bicycle wheels each year. The cost of placing an order is $100, and the carrying cost is $1.00 per unit per year. What is the optimal order quantity, the total yearly cost of stocking inventory, and the number of orders placed each year?

17.6   **(Economic Order Quantity)** If the annual requirement for an item is 9,000 units, ordering costs are $30, and the cost of holding the item in inventory is $0.20 per year, what is the economic lot size to order?

17.7   **(Reorder Point)** The Marsden Bakery purchases 10,000,000 pounds of flour each year. The cost of placing an order is $150, and the carrying cost is $0.30 per pound per year. What is the optimal order quantity, the total yearly cost of stocking inventory, and the number of orders placed each year? What is the reorder point, without safety stock, if the lead time is five days?

17.8   **(Reorder Point)** The Louisville Loan Company orders $10,000,000 in cash each year to meet daily cash transactions. Each order delivered to the company costs $500. The opportunity cost of idle cash is 10 percent. What is the optimal order quantity, the total yearly cost of stocking inventory, and the number of orders placed each year? What is the reorder point, with a $25,000 safety stock, if the lead time is four days?

17.9   **(Optimal Order Quantity)** Manley Roofing, Inc. purchases 50,000 units of roofing each year. The cost of placing an order is $100, and the carrying cost is 20 percent of the unit cost, in dollars per unit per year. The price of each unit depends on the quantity ordered.

Quantity	Price
0–999	$105.00
1,000+	$103.50

What is the optimal order quantity?

17.10   **(Optimal Order Quantity)** The Mad Toy Company (MTC) produces dolls with a small computer. MTC estimates annual sales of 50,000 dolls of this type. The price of each unit depends on the quantity ordered.

Quantity	Price
0–999	$5.00
1,000–9,999	$4.75
10,000+	$4.50

If the cost of ordering is $175 and the carrying cost is 15 percent of the price paid, what is the optimal order quantity?

A Case Problem

akewood Packaging Corporation produced packaging products such as folding cartons, containerboard, and corrugated boxes. The company focused on providing packaging solutions to multinational beverage and consumer products companies.

Lakewood owned and leased timberlands to provide the primary raw material used to produce paperboard. The company designed, printed, and cut the paperboard to meet customers' specific packaging requirements. In addition, technical representatives installed proprietary packaging machines in the customers' facilities. Management believed that installation of this equipment provided a significant advantage over competitors.

The company produced approximately 1.5 million tons per year of coated and uncoated paperboard at mills located in South Carolina, Sweden, and Brazil. Forecasters at Lakewood believed that demand would continue to grow. As a result, the company entered into an agreement to purchase the assets of Savannah Kraft, a manufacturer of linerboard for corrugated box applications. This acquisition would provide the company with excess production capacity.

Lakewood currently sold on credit terms of 2/10, net 30. This policy required a letter to be sent on past due accounts after 45 days. Strong, intimidating litigation was threatened after 60 days. Currently, bad-debt expense was one percent of gross sales. Sales for the next year, after the acquisition, were forecasted at $540,000,000. Receivables turnover was currently 6.50. Customers taking discounts as measured by dollars of gross sales was 50 percent. The opportunity cost on the investment in receivables was 12 percent.

Larry Wyld, the vice-president for sales, recommended that Lakewood change both credit terms and collection policies.

Larry Wyld, the vice-president for sales, recommended that Lakewood change both credit terms and collection policies. He proposed to extend terms to 3/15, net 45, and to send a past-due letter after 75 days. Mr. Wyld believed this would increase sales for the coming year.

Calvin Close, company treasurer, agreed this change would boost sales, to an estimated $550,000,000. He further calculated that 55 percent of customers would take the discount, and that receivables turnover would decline to 6.00. He insisted that bad-debt expense would increase to two percent. In both cases, he argued that variable cost as a percentage of gross sales would remain at 75 percent. Mr. Close was sure that the internal costs of administering the credit policies would be the same for both policies.

Leading Questions

1. What are the projected net sales, after taking the discount, under the present and proposed plans?
2. What are the gross profits, after bad-debt expense, under the present and proposed plans?
3. What is the investment in receivables and the opportunity cost of that investment under the present and proposed plans?
4. What is the amount of profit after subtracting opportunity cost under the present and proposed plans?

18 Working Capital and Short-Term Financing

LOWER INTEREST RATES BRING MANY CHOICES

Low rates may not spur a rush to build new factories, but they're a silver lining in this gloomy economic climate. To make the most of them, corporate financial officers are poring over their mix of loans, bonds, notes and commercial paper in search of opportunities to refinance, switch the mix or simply count their blessings. Many of them are torn over whether to keep their debt short-term—in commercial paper, for example, where interest rates for top issuers are 4%—or to lock in more expensive, but still historically cheap, long-term debt in the 8% to 10% range. But issuing new bonds is just one of the financial officers' alternatives. Allied-Signal Corporation is doubling the amount it can prepay under sinking-fund options of some high-cost bonds.

The decision many companies face is when to go for long-term financing at the expense of the far lower rates available for one year or less. In early January, the 30-year Treasury bond dipped to 7.39%. The last time that benchmark issue, which serves as a bellwether for other long-term issues, dropped that low was in 1987. Yet the "yield curve," the arc that represents interest rates from short- to long-term maturity securities, is ex-

ceptionally steep, making it even more desirable to keep funding on the short side. For the most part, corporate bond issuers are divided into two camps: those who won't risk missing current levels by waiting to sell bonds at even lower rates and those who expect the sluggish economy to keep rates low.

Decisions of this type must be made by financial managers. The target levels for each classification of current assets and the method of financing must be specified. This involves the determination of the amounts of short-term debt and long-term capital used to finance current assets.

Source: Fred R. Bleakley, "Lower Interest Rates Bring Many Choices To Corporate Finance," *The Wall Street Journal,* January 23, 1992. Reprinted by permission of The Wall Street Journal, © 1992 Dow Jones & Company, Inc. All Rights Reserved.

WORKING CAPITAL MANAGEMENT AND POLICY

Financial managers face difficult choices when they become involved in working capital management, the administration and control of current assets and current liabilities. To make such decisions requires an understanding of the working capital cycle and short-term financing.

Working capital management is the administration and control of current assets and current liabilities. **Working capital policy** provides the target levels for each classification of current assets and specifies the method of financing. **Net working capital** is current assets less current liabilities. **Working capital,** or gross working capital, refers to current assets.

Working Capital Management

Working Capital Policy

Net Working Capital

Working Capital

Current Asset Investment Policy

A common-size balance sheet for a typical manufacturing corporation in the United States shows that current assets account for about 40 percent of total as-

497

sets. This large investment in working capital attracts the attention of managers in production and finance.

These managers are interested in finding the optimal current asset policy. As a simplification, consider three alternative investment policies: high, normal, and low levels of current assets. The levels are measured by the current assets to sales ratio.

Figure 18.1 shows the alternative current asset investment policies for varying levels of sales. The *high* level of current assets refers to an investment policy with a relatively high percentage of cash, marketable securities, accounts receivable, and inventory. Similarly, the *normal* and *low* levels relate to typical policies and to restrictive policies.

The current asset investment policy that a company chooses depends upon the situation. A company operating in a relatively riskless environment requires a *low* level of current assets. A manufacturing corporation with relatively certain demand and fixed lead times needs a *low* level of safety stocks, implying a *low* inventory. Conversely, a corporation that provides liberal credit terms experiences a *high* level of accounts receivable.

The relative size of the current asset accounts is influenced by the type of business. Manufacturing corporations invest most heavily in inventories. The manufacturing process requires raw materials, work-in-process, and finished goods inventories. In contrast, a service corporation may need a minimal inventory investment. Some corporations focus on extending credit to customers in

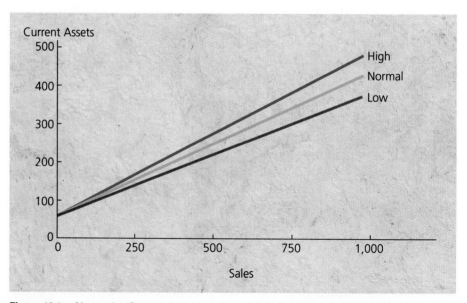

Figure 18.1   Alternative Current Asset Investment Policies (thousands of dollars)

order to profit from the interest on the unpaid balance. As a result, accounts receivable, as a percentage of current assets, is higher.

The **ideal level of current assets** is the amount that minimizes the total costs of employing the various items that make up current assets. Total costs are the sum of supply and maintenance costs. Supply costs include ordering costs (replenishment or setup costs) and stockout costs (lost sales, special handling, or cash-out costs). Maintenance costs include opportunity costs (the incremental return on the best alternative) and inventory carrying costs (storage and handling costs).

Ideal Level of Current Assets

Figure 18.2 illustrates the concept of the ideal level of current assets. Notice that maintenance costs rise and supply costs fall as the level of current assets increases. Total costs are at a minimum at the point CA*, the optimal level of current assets.

Current Asset Financing Policy

Current asset financing policy involves the determination of the amounts of short-term debt and long-term capital used to finance current assets. The discussion of this subject assumes that management has decided on the ideal level of current assets.

Figure 18.3 shows the total asset requirements for a growing company. Fixed assets increase at a steady rate, but current assets demonstrate a seasonal or cyclical pattern. Even so, there is also an upward trend for current assets.

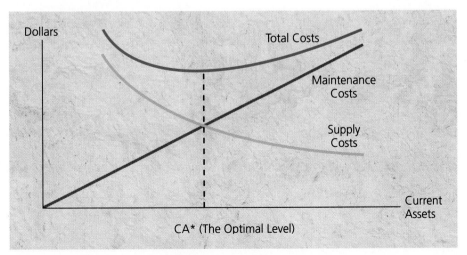

Figure 18.2   The Concept of the Ideal Level of Current Assets

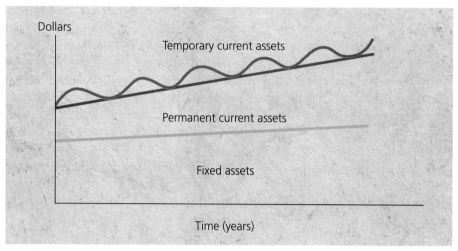

Figure 18.3 Total Asset Requirements for a Growing Company
● ● ● ● ● ● ● ●

There are three alternative policies for financing current assets: conservative, aggressive, and balanced. These policies differ in the degree to which long-term sources, equity and long-term debt, are used to finance the assets.

Conservative Working Capital Policy

Figure 18.4 demonstrates the **conservative working capital policy:** The company uses long-term sources to finance all asset requirements. This means that the maximum seasonal needs for current assets are met entirely from long-term financing. Management invests excess funds, when available, in marketable securities.

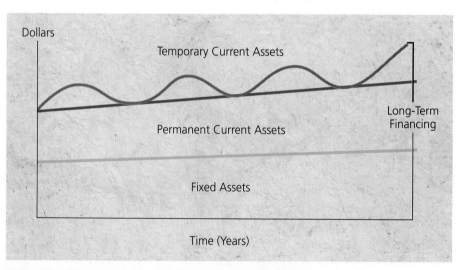

Figure 18.4 The Conservative Working Capital Financing Policy
● ● ● ● ● ● ● ●

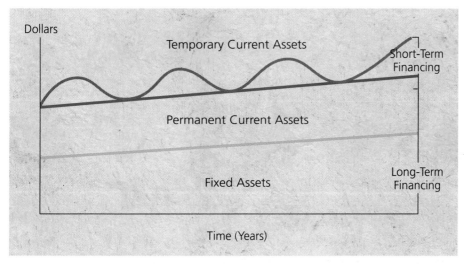

Figure 18.5 The Aggressive Working Capital Financing Policy

The conservative working capital policy reduces risk to the company. It avoids the unavailability of short-term funds and the unpredictability of short-term rates. This policy also allows the company to use short-term credit when working capital requirements are higher than expected.

Figure 18.5 demonstrates the **aggressive working capital policy:** The company uses long-term sources to finance fixed assets and most of the constant level of current assets. Management uses short-term sources to finance the temporary level of current assets and a portion of permanent current assets. This eliminates the need for investing in marketable securities. **Aggressive Working Capital Policy**

The aggressive working capital policy increases risk to the company. It requires continual renewal of maturing short-term obligations. Under unfavorable conditions, a company may have trouble securing short-term credit, and this leads to financial difficulties.

Figure 18.6 demonstrates the **balanced working capital policy:** The company uses long-term sources to finance fixed assets and permanent current assets. Management uses short-term sources to finance temporary current assets. **Balanced Working Capital Policy**

The balanced working capital policy reduces risk when compared to the aggressive approach. It requires the company to use short-term funds to cover seasonal needs while not forcing short-term borrowing to the limit. This policy also provides the company with additional short-term credit capacity when working capital requirements are higher than expected.

The **matching,** or self-liquidating, **principle** requires that management match short-term sources with short-term uses and long-term sources with long-term uses. This principle is consistent with the balanced working capital policy. **Matching**

Principle

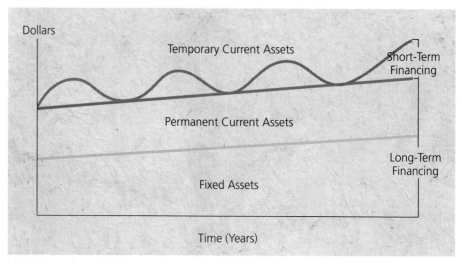

Figure 18.6 The Balanced Working Capital Financing Policy

THE WORKING CAPITAL CYCLE

Working Capital Cycle

The **working capital cycle,** or cash cycle, is the time that elapses between payment for raw materials and collection for finished product. It is equal to the length of the operating cycle less the average age of accounts payable. As we shall see in this section, the working capital cycle has a direct impact on the cash flows of the company.

The Operating Cycle

Operating Cycle

The **operating cycle** is the time that elapses between the arrival of raw materials and collection for finished product. It is equal to the average age of inventory plus the average age of receivables. Figure 18.7 illustrates the process.

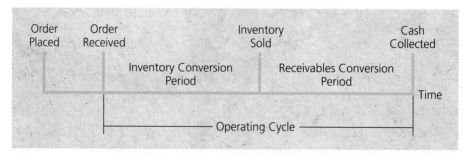

Figure 18.7 The Operating Cycle for a Manufacturing Company

The operating cycle is the time it takes for a manufacturing company to convert raw materials into sold product plus the time required to receive cash from receivables. The time spent waiting for the raw materials to arrive is not included in the operating cycle.

> It takes 14 days, on the average, for raw materials to arrive at the Jameson Corporation after an order is placed. Calculations indicate that 90 days elapse on the average from the point when an order is received until finished inventory is sold. The company collects on the average after 45 days. What is the length of the operating cycle?

The operating cycle is the length of the inventory conversion period, 90 days, plus the length of the receivables conversion period, 45 days. The length of the operating cycle, which does not include the ordering period, is 135 days. Figure 18.8 shows the process.

The Cash Cycle

The cash cycle, or working capital cycle, is equal to the length of the operating cycle less the average age of accounts payable. Figure 18.9 presents the process.

The cash cycle is the time it takes, after paying for raw materials, for a manufacturing company to collect for finished inventory. The time spent waiting to pay suppliers is not included in the cash cycle.

> The Jameson Corporation from the previous example takes 35 days on the average to pay suppliers. What is the length of the cash cycle?

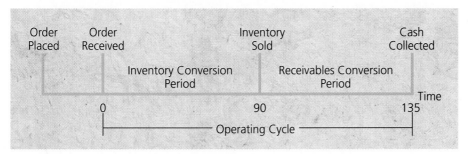

Figure 18.8 An Illustration of the Operating Cycle

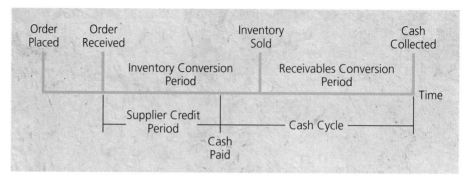

Figure 18.9 The Cash Cycle for a Manufacturing Company

The cash cycle is the length of the operating cycle, 135 days, less the average age of accounts payable, 35 days. The length of the cash cycle is 100 days. Figure 18.10 shows the process.

Cash Turnover

Cash Turnover

The higher the **cash turnover** of a company, the lower the amount of financing required. We calculate the cash turnover by dividing the cash cycle into 365.

> Richard Leigh is examining the income statements and balance sheets of the Martin Corporation for 19X4 and 19X5. These statements, first presented in Chapter 4, are repeated as Table 18.1 and 18.2. What are the cash turnovers for 19X4 and 19X5?

Calculation of the cash turnover requires the cash cycle. The cash cycle demands the average age of inventory, the average age of receivables, and the average age of accounts payable.

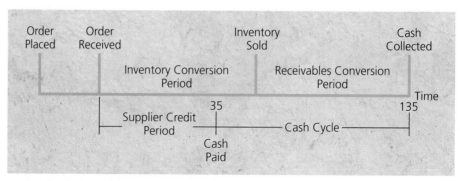

Figure 18.10 An Illustration of the Cash Cycle

TABLE 18.1 Martin Corporation: Income Statements for the Years Ended December 31
•••••••• (in thousands)

	19X4	19X5
Net sales	$1,000	$1,050
Cost of goods sold	700	756
Gross profit	$ 300	$ 294
Selling and administrative expenses	100	105
Depreciation expense	40	42
Earnings before interest and taxes	$ 160	$ 147
Interest exoense	10	21
Earnings before taxes (EBT)	$ 150	$ 126
Taxes	60	42
Earnings after taxes (EAT)	$ 90	$ 84
Preferred stock dividends	5	5
Earnings available to common shareholders	$ 85	$ 79

The average age of inventory, or days inventory, is calculated using the following formula:

$$\text{Average age of inventory} = \frac{\text{Inventory}}{\text{Costs of goods sold}/365}$$

$$\text{19X4 Average age of inventory} = \frac{120.0}{700/365} = 62.6 \text{ days}$$

$$\text{19X5 Average age of inventory} = \frac{125.8}{756/365} = 60.7 \text{ days}$$

The average age of inventory is slightly more than 60 days in both years.

The average age of receivables, or average collection period, is calculated using the following formula:

$$\text{Average age of receivables} = \frac{\text{Accounts receivable}}{\text{Net sales}/365}$$

$$\text{19X4 Average age of receivables} = \frac{80.0}{1000.0/365} = 29.2 \text{ days}$$

$$\text{19X5 Average age of receivables} = \frac{85.0}{1050.0/365} = 29.5 \text{ days}$$

The average age of receivables is slightly less than 30 days in both years.

TABLE 18.2 Martin Corporation: Balance Sheets as of December 31 (in thousands)

ASSETS		
	19X4	19X5
Current assets:		
Cash	$ 20.0	$ 21.0
Marketable securities	5.0	5.2
Accounts receivable	80.0	85.0
Inventory	120.0	125.8
Total current assets	$225.0	$237.0
Fixed assets:		
Property, plant, and equipment	$475.0	$475.0
Less: Accumulated depreciation	200.0	242.0
Net property, plant and equipment	$275.0	$233.0
Total assets	$500.0	$470.0
LIABILITIES AND STOCKHOLDERS EQUITY		
Current liabilities:		
Accounts payable	$ 40.0	$ 38.5
Notes payable	60.0	10.0
Current maturities, long-term debt	5.0	5.0
Accrued expenses	15.0	10.0
Total current liabilities	$120.0	$ 63.5
Long-term debt	40.0	30.0
Total liabilities	$160.0	$ 93.5
Stockholders' equity:		
Preferred stock	$ 50.0	50.0
Common stock ($1 par)	50.0	50.0
Capital in excess of par	100.0	100.0
Retained earnings	140.0	176.5
Total stockholders' equity	$340.0	$376.5
Total liabilities and stockholders' equity	$500.0	$470.0

The average age of accounts payable is calculated using the following formula:

$$\text{Average age of accounts payable} = \frac{\text{Accounts payable}}{\text{Costs of goods sold}/365}$$

$$\text{19X4 Average age of accounts payable} = \frac{40.0}{700/365} = 20.9 \text{ days}$$

$$\text{19X5 Average age of accounts payable} = \frac{38.5}{756/365} = 18.6 \text{ days}$$

TABLE 18.3 Tabulating the Cash Cycle of the Martin Corporation

AVERAGE AGE OF	19X4	19X5
Inventory	62.6	60.7
Receivables	29.2	29.5
Payables	20.9	18.6
Cash cycle	70.9 days	71.6 days

The cash cycle is the average age of inventory plus the average age of receivables minus the average age of accounts payable. Table 18.3 tabulates the cash cycle for the Martin Corporation.

Cash turnover is calculated using the following formula:

$$\text{Cash Turnover} = \frac{365 \text{ days}}{\text{Cash Cycle}}$$

$$19X4 \text{ Cash Turnover} = \frac{365 \text{ days}}{70.9 \text{ days}} = 5.15$$

$$19X5 \text{ Cash Turnover} = \frac{365 \text{ days}}{71.6 \text{ days}} = 5.10$$

For the Martin Corporation, the cash turnover declined slightly, indicating the financing required increases during 19X5.

As financial managers, we must pay close attention to the cash cycle. To shorten it, we must produce and sell our product faster while decreasing the collection period and increasing the payables period. Of course, we have to be careful that these actions do not lower sales or increase costs.

SHORT-TERM FINANCING

Financial managers employ several sources of short-term financing to support daily operations, with trade credit the largest source of current liabilities. Bank loans, the primary subject of this section, represent the second largest source. Commercial paper, accrued expenses, factoring, and pledging accounts for most of the remaining sources.

Unsecured Short-Term Bank Loans

Bankers extend unsecured short-term loans by a line of credit, a revolving credit agreement, or a transaction loan. The terms of such loans depend on the

Self-Liquidating Loans

needs of the company, subject to the discretion of the bank. These loans are said to be **self-liquidating loans** because companies use them to finance temporary increases in current assets.

Compensating Balances

Bankers often require borrowers to maintain deposits in low-interest or no-interest checking accounts. These **compensating balances** typically amount to 10 to 20 percent of the outstanding loan. Their purpose is to compensate the bank for services rendered. Banks also accomplish this by charging fees, in lieu of, or in addition to, compensating balances.

Line of Credit

A **line of credit** is an informal or formal agreement between a borrower and a bank to lend up to a specified amount. The interest rate is normally equal to the prime rate plus a predetermined percentage. A company uses its line of credit when funds are required and repays the loan when it has surplus cash. Financial managers use cash budgets to determine the required size of the line of credit.

Revolving Credit Agreement

Larger borrowers sometimes sign a **revolving credit agreement,** outlining the provisions of the line of credit. These contracts specify the terms of the loan. The rate of interest is often tied to the London Interbank Offer Rate (LIBOR). LIBOR is the rate six major banks in London are willing to pay to borrow dollars.

Transaction Loan

A **transaction loan,** or direct loan, is a loan made for a specific purpose and is repaid with a lump sum payment. Unlike the line of credit which is used for frequent borrowing, this type of loan is used for the occasional borrower. The cost of providing this service is higher, and consequently so is the rate of interest.

Prime Rate

The **prime rate** is the rate of interest banks charge their most credit worthy customers for large short-term loans. In recent years, however, some financially sound companies have been allowed to borrow at a rate below the stated prime. Average customers typically pay one or two percent above prime, while risky customers pay even higher.

Promissory Note

Unsecured short-term bank loans require the borrower to sign a **promissory note** outlining the conditions of the loan. Notes are usually payable in 90 days, thereby giving the bank strong control of the situation. To prevent companies from using short-term loans for long-term purposes, banks also include a **cleanup clause** forcing the company to be out of debt for a set number of days during the year.

Cleanup Clause

The interest rate on a bank loan is the result of a negotiation between the borrower and the banker. The rate charged is influenced by a number of factors. The credit worthiness of the borrower is most important. The size of the loan is significant since the cost of processing a small loan is almost as much as for a large one. Bankers normally employ a fixed interest rate in making short-term loans, in contrast to floating interest rates that are often used with longer-term loans.

Cost of Short-Term Bank Loans

The cost of short-term bank loans depends upon the timing and magnitude of the cash flows involved. The timing and magnitude of the cash flows depends upon the method of charging interest and whether or not there is a compensating balance. There are two methods of charging interest: simple interest and discount interest.

The effective interest rate (EIR) on short-term bank loans, for simple interest and discount interest, with or without a compensating balance, is as follows:

$$EIR = \left(1.0 + \frac{I}{AR}\right)^m - 1.0 \qquad (18.1)$$

where

I = Interest (Face value)(Interest rate)(Fraction of year to maturity)
AR = Amount received
m = Periods per year (1/Fraction of year to maturity)

The amount received, or net proceeds, depends upon the method of charging interest and whether or not there is a compensating balance.

Simple interest, without compensating balance (SI), provides the borrower with the face value of the loan at time 0. The borrower pays the face value plus interest at maturity.

> The First National Bank extends a $100,000 simple-interest loan to a customer at 10 percent annual interest. No compensating balance is required. What is the effective rate of interest if the loan is for one year or for 90 days?

The cash flows for the one-year loan (from the point of view of the bank) can be illustrated using a cash flow diagram:

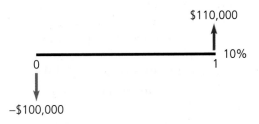

The interest, paid with the principal at time 1, is calculated as follows:

$$I = \$100,000(0.10)(1)$$
$$= \$10,000$$

The effective interest rate is found using Eq. 18.1.

$$
\begin{aligned}
EIR &= \left(1.0 + \frac{I}{AR}\right)^m - 1.0 \\
&= \left(1.0 + \frac{\$10,000}{\$100,000}\right)^1 - 1.0 \\
&= 0.1000 \text{ or } 10.00\%
\end{aligned}
$$

The effective interest rate for simple interest, without compensating balance, for one year is always the same as the nominal, or stated, rate.

The cash flows for the 90-day loan also can be illustrated using a cash flow diagram:

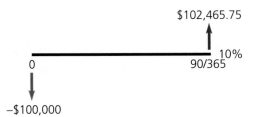

The interest, paid with the principal at 90 days, is calculated as follows:

$$I = \$100,000(0.10)(90/365)$$
$$= \$2,465.75$$

The effective interest rate is found using Eq. 18.1.

$$
\begin{aligned}
EIR &= \left(1.0 + \frac{I}{AR}\right)^m - 1.0 \\
&= \left(1.0 + \frac{\$2,465.75}{\$100,000}\right)^{365/90} - 1.0 \\
&= (1.0246575)^{4.0555555} - 1.0 \\
&= 0.1038 \text{ or } 10.38\%
\end{aligned}
$$

The calculation was made with a financial calculator.

Discount interest, without compensating balance (DI), provides the borrower with the face value of the loan less interest at time 0. The borrower pays the face value at maturity.

> The First National Bank extends a $100,000 discount-interest loan to a customer at 10 percent annual interest. No compensating balance is required. What is the effective rate of interest if the loan is for one year or for 90 days?

The cash flows for the one-year loan can be illustrated using a cash flow diagram:

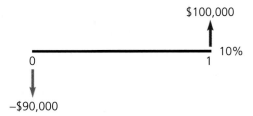

The amount of interest is the same as with simple interest, only the timing of the payment of the interest is different.

The effective interest rate is found using Eq. 18.1.

$$EIR = \left(1.0 + \frac{I}{AR}\right)^m - 1.0$$
$$= \left(1.0 + \frac{\$10,000}{\$90,000}\right)^1 - 1.0$$
$$= 0.1111 \text{ or } 11.11\%$$

The effective interest rate for discount interest, without compensating balance, for one year is always more than for simple interest.

The cash flows for the 90-day loan can also be illustrated using a cash flow diagram:

The amount of interest is the same as with simple interest, only the timing of the payment of the interest is different.

The effective interest rate is found using Eq. 18.1.

$$\begin{aligned}
\text{EIR} &= \left(1.0 + \frac{I}{AR}\right)^m - 1.0 \\
&= \left(1.0 + \frac{\$2,465.75}{\$97,534.25}\right)^{365/90} - 1.0 \\
&= (1.0252808)^{4.0555555} - 1.0 \\
&= 0.1066 \text{ or } 10.66\%
\end{aligned}$$

Notice that discount interest exacts a higher penalty on the 1-year loan than on the 90-day loan. Check this by comparing the EIR for simple and discounted interest over both time periods.

Simple interest, with compensating balance (SICB), provides the borrower with the face value of the loan, less the compensating balance, at time 0. The borrower pays the face value plus interest less the compensating balance at maturity.

> The First National Bank extends a $100,000 simple-interest loan, with a 15 percent compensating balance, to a customer at 10 percent annual interest. What is the effective rate of interest if the loan is for one year or for 90 days?

The cash flows for the one-year loan can be illustrated using a cash flow diagram:

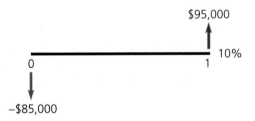

The borrower receives the $100,000 face value less the $15,000 compensating balance at time 0. The borrower pays back the $85,000 plus the $10,000 in interest at maturity.

The effective interest rate is found using Eq. 18.1.

$$\text{EIR} = \left(1.0 + \frac{I}{AR}\right)^m - 1.0$$

$$= \left(1.0 + \frac{\$10,000}{\$85,000}\right)^1 - 1.0$$

$$= 0.1176 \text{ or } 11.76\%$$

The effective interest rate with a compensating balance is always higher than without the requirement.

The cash flows for the 90-day loan can also be illustrated using a cash flow diagram:

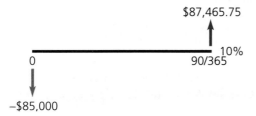

The borrower receives the same amount at time 0, but pays less interest at maturity.

The effective interest rate is found using Eq. 18.1.

$$\text{EIR} = \left(1.0 + \frac{I}{AR}\right)^m - 1.0$$

$$= \left(1.0 + \frac{\$2,465.75}{\$85,000.00}\right)^{365/90} - 1.0$$

$$= (1.0290088)^{4.0555555} - 1.0$$

$$= 0.1230 \text{ or } 12.30\%$$

Notice that the compensating balance raises the effective interest rate.

Discount interest, with compensating balance (DICB), provides the borrower with the face value of the loan, less interest and compensating balance, at time 0. The borrower pays the face value less the compensating balance at maturity.

> The First National Bank extends a $100,000 discount-interest loan, with a 15 percent compensating balance, to a customer at 10 percent annual interest. What is the effective rate of interest if the loan is for one year or for 90 days?

The cash flows for the one-year loan can be illustrated using a cash flow diagram:

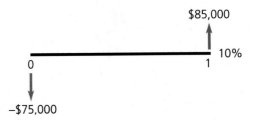

The amount of interest is the same as with simple interest, only the timing of the payment is different.

The effective interest rate is found using Eq. 18.1.

$$\text{EIR} = \left(1.0 + \frac{I}{AR}\right)^m - 1.0$$

$$= \left(1.0 + \frac{\$10,000}{\$75,000}\right)^1 - 1.0$$

$$= 0.1333 \text{ or } 13.33\%$$

The effective interest rate for discount interest, with compensating balance, for one year is always more than for simple interest.

The cash flows for the 90-day loan can also be illustrated using a cash flow diagram:

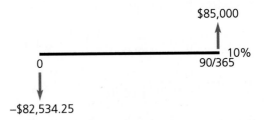

The amount of interest is the same as with simple interest, only the timing of payment is different.

The effective interest rate is found using Eq. 18.1.

$$\text{EIR} = \left(1.0 + \frac{I}{AR}\right)^m - 1.0$$

$$= \left(1.0 + \frac{\$2,465.75}{\$82,534.25}\right)^{365/90} - 1.0$$

$$= (1.0298755)^{4.0555555} - 1.0$$

$$= 0.1268 \text{ or } 12.68\%$$

CS Holding Girds for Global Competition

In Switzerland's domestic banking market, cartel arrangements have been abolished. Amid a stagnating Swiss economy, a flood of bad loans has put a severe squeeze on banking profits. A stamp tax on securities transactions has cut into the banks' domestic securities business. And a surge in inflation has caused the Swiss franc to weaken, robbing it of much of its allure. The result: a chill wind for Swiss bankers, just as Switzerland begins a process that could lead to membership in the European Community and even tougher competition. Already, the Big Three Swiss banks are girding to battle harder against their foreign rivals. Following in the footsteps of Nestle S.A. and Ciba-Geigy AG, says Hans-Dieter Vontobel, a prominent Swiss investment banker, the big Swiss banks "are becoming multinational." In what may serve as an example not only for other Swiss banks but for banks in other regions, CS Holding has evolved into a banking and financial-services group with an international flavor. Already, Credit Suisse's international project financing is run out of New York "because we have the skills and the manpower there, and it doesn't make sense to do it out of Switzerland or London," says Mr. Gut, the chairman both of Credit Suisse and its parent.

Source: Nicholas Bray, "CS Holding Girds for Global Competition Amid Changes in Swiss Banking Market," *The Wall Street Journal*, July 10, 1992. Reprinted by permission of The Wall Street Journal, © 1992 Dow Jones & Company, Inc. All Rights Reserved Worldwide.

Again the discount interest exacts a higher penalty on the 1-year loan than on the 90-day loan.

Table 18.4 summarizes the influence the method of charging interest and compensating balance has on the effective interest rate. As noted previously, the effect of discount interest is greater on longer-term loans.

SUMMARY

This chapter focuses on the following learning objectives:
1. Explaining current asset investment policy.
   A company operating in a relatively riskless environment requires a low level of current assets. A manufacturing corporation with relatively certain

TABLE 18.4 Effective Interest Rate Under Different Conditions

CONDITIONS	EIR (1 YEAR)	EIR (90 DAYS)
SI	10.00%	10.38%
DI	11.11	10.66
SICB	11.76	12.30
DICB	13.33	12.68

demand and fixed lead times needs a low inventory. A corporation that provides liberal credit terms experiences a high level of accounts receivable. The ideal level of current assets is the amount that minimizes the total costs of employing current assets.

2. Explaining current asset financing policy.

   Current asset financing policy involves the determination of the amounts of short-term debt and long-term capital used to finance current assets. There are three alternative policies for financing current assets: conservative, aggressive, and balanced. The matching, or self-liquidating, principle requires that management match short-term sources with short-term uses and long-term sources with long-term uses.

3. Calculating the operating cycle.

   The operating cycle is the time that elapses between the arrival of raw materials and collection for finished product. It is equal to the average age of inventory plus the average age of receivables. For a manufacturing company, it is the time it takes to convert raw materials into sold product plus the time required to receive cash from receivables.

4. Calculating the cash cycle and cash turnover.

   The cash cycle is equal to the length of the operating cycle less the average age of accounts payable. For a manufacturing company, it is the time it takes, after paying for raw materials, to collect for finished inventory. The higher the cash turnover of a company, the lower the amount of financing required. The cash turnover is calculated by dividing the cash cycle into 365.

5. Discussing unsecured short-term bank loans.

   Bankers extend unsecured short-term loans by a line of credit, a revolving credit agreement, or a transaction loan. To compensate the bank for services rendered, bankers often require borrowers to maintain compensating balances in low-interest or no-interest checking accounts. Unsecured short-term bank loans require the borrower to sign a promissory note outlining the conditions of the loan.

6. Computing the cost of short-term bank loans.

   The cost of short-term bank loans depends upon the timing and magnitude of the cash flows involved, which depend upon the method of charging interest and whether or not there is a compensating balance. There are two methods of charging interest: simple interest and discount interest.

KEY TERMS

Aggressive working capital policy, 501

Balanced working capital policy, 501

Cash turnover, 504

Cleanup clause, 508

Compensating balance, 508

Conservative working capital policy, 500

Ideal level of current assets, 499

QUESTIONS

18.1 Explain working capital management and working capital policy.

18.2 What is the difference between net working capital and working capital?

18.3 What does the current asset investment policy that a company chooses depend upon?

18.4 Discuss the relative size of the current asset accounts.

18.5 What are the components of the total costs of employing current assets?

18.6 What is involved in current asset financing policy?

18.7 Explain the three alternative policies for financing current assets.

18.8 Describe the matching, or self-liquidating, principle.

18.9 What is the rationale for using short-term sources rather than long-term sources to finance current assets?

18.10 Describe the working capital or cash cycle?

18.11 What is the operating cycle, and how does it relate to the cash cycle?

18.12 What is cash turnover, and why is it important?

18.13 What are the major sources of short-term financing?

18.14 What are self-liquidating loans?

18.15 Describe the three major types of short-term loans extended by banks.

18.16 What is the prime rate, and how is it used?

18.17 What are compensating balances, and why are they used?

18.18 What is a cleanup clause in a promissory note?

18.19 Why is it advantageous to borrow short term when the yield curve is especially steep?

18.20 How is Swiss banking affected by global competition?

PROBLEMS

18.1 **(Operating Cycle)** On the average it takes 17 days for raw materials to arrive at the Johnson Company after an order is placed. It requires on the average 100 days from the point when an order is received until finished inventory is sold. The average collection period is 40 days. What is the length of the operating cycle?

18.2 **(Operating Cycle)** Emil Roy Publishing collects on the average after 120 days. For raw materials to arrive after placing an order requires 25 days. It takes 180 days from the point when an order is received. What is the length of the operating cycle?

18.3 **(Cash Cycle)** The Johnson Company from Problem 18.1 takes 30 days on the average to pay suppliers. What is the length of the cash cycle?

18.4 **(Cash Cycle)** Emil Roy Publishing from Problem 18.2 takes 40 days on the average to pay suppliers. What is the length of the cash cycle?

18.5 **(Cash Turnovers)** The income statements and balance sheets for the Singley Corporation follow:

SINGLEY CORPORATION: INCOME STATEMENTS FOR THE YEARS ENDED DECEMBER 31 (IN THOUSANDS)

	19X4	19X5
Net Sales	$ 1,380	$ 1,318
Cost of goods sold	969	963
Gross profit	$ 411	$ 355
Selling and administrative expenses	229	248
Depreciation expense	36	41
Earnings before interest and taxes	$ 146	$ 66
Interest expense	16	18
Earnings before taxes (EBT)	$ 130	$ 48
Taxes	52	19
Earnings after taxes (EAT)	$ 78	$ 29
Preferred stock dividends	6	6
Earnings available to common shareholders	$ 72	$ 23
Shares outstanding	50,000	50,000
Earnings per share	$1.44	$0.46
Dividends per share	$0.80	$0.80
Market price per share	$18.750	$10.250

SINGLEY CORPORATION: BALANCE SHEETS AS OF DECEMBER 31 (IN THOUSANDS)

ASSETS

	19X4	19X5
Current assets		
Cash	$ 24.0	$ 36.5
Marketable securities	6.0	9.1
Accounts receivable	220.2	188.3
Inventory	206.1	186.0
Prepaid expenses	9.3	7.0
Total current assets	$465.6	$426.9

	19X4	19X5
Fixed assets:		
Property, plant, and equipment	$353.2	$376.8
Less: Accumulated depreciation	163.9	204.9
Net property, plant, and equipment	$189.3	$171.9
Total assets	$654.9	$598.8

LIABILITIES AND STOCKHOLDERS' EQUITY

	19X4	19X5
Current liabilities:		
Accounts payable	$149.6	138.5
Notes payable	40.0	20.0
Current maturities, long-term debt	10.0	10.0
Accrued taxes	20.2	21.4
Total current liabilities	$219.8	$189.9
Long-term debt	129.8	120.6
Total liabilities	$349.6	$310.5
Stockholders' equity:		
Preferred stock	60.0	60.0
Common stock ($1 par)	14.0	14.0
Capital in excess of par	32.6	32.6
Retained earnings	198.7	181.7
Total stockholders' equity	$305.3	$288.3
Total liabilities and stockholders' equity	$654.9	$598.8

What are the cash turnovers for 19X4 and 19X5?

18.6 **(Effective Interest Rate)** The Martinez Corporation is negotiating with several banks for a $200,000 loan. Which loan alternative has the lowest effective interest rate (EIR), assuming a one-year loan?

(a) Simple interest, without compensating balance (SI), annual interest of 14 percent.

(b) Discount interest, without compensating balance (DI), annual interest of 13 percent.

(c) Simple interest, with 15 percent compensating balance (SICB), annual interest of 12 percent.

(d) Discount interest, with 15 percent compensating balance (DICB), annual interest of 11 percent.

18.7 **(Effective Interest Rate)** Griffin Machinery is considering several alternatives for a $450,000 loan. Which loan alternative has the lowest effective interest rate (EIR), assuming a 100-day loan?

(a) Simple interest, without compensating balance (SI), annual interest of 12 percent.

(b) Discount interest, without compensating balance (DI), annual interest of 11 percent.

(c) Simple interest, with 20 percent compensating balance, annual interest of 10 percent.

(d) Discount interest, with 20 percent compensating balance, annual interest of 9 percent.

18.8 **(Face Value)** Manchester Corporation is planning to borrow $100,000. What is the face value of the loan under each of the following methods of calculation:

(a) Simple interest, without compensating balance (SI), annual interest of 14 percent.

(b) Discount interest, without compensating balance (DI), annual interest of 13 percent.

(c) Simple interest, with 20 percent compensating balance, annual interest of 12 percent.

(d) Discount interest, with 20 percent compensating balance, annual interest of 11 percent.

18.9 **(Face Value)** Orange Park Industries is planning to borrow $500,000. What is the face value of the loan under each of the following methods of calculation:

(a) Simple interest, without compensating balance (SI), annual interest of 12 percent.

(b) Discount interest, without compensating balance (DI), annual interest of 11 percent.

(c) Simple interest, with 15 percent compensating balance (SICB), annual interest of 10 percent.

(d) Discount interest, with 15 percent compensating balance (DICB), annual interest of 9 percent.

A Case Problem

Security Electronics Corporation (SEC) was a supplier of electronic security systems to retail and non-retail customers. The company manufactured, marketed, and serviced surveillance systems, microprocessor-controlled closed circuit television systems, and exception monitoring systems. These loss prevention systems were used to deter shoplifting, or other theft, in retail stores, industrial plants, and government facilities.

During the last five years, Security Electronics had gained a controlling interest in the distributor in Great Britain and had established an Asia/Pacific headquarters in Singapore.

SEC marketed its products throughout the United States, Canada, Europe, and certain Asia/Pacific countries. During the last fiscal year, 40 percent of revenues were derived from foreign countries. The company had strengthened its global presence to a large degree through acquisition. During the last five years, Security Electronics had gained a controlling interest in the distributor in Great Britain and had established an Asia/Pacific headquarters in Singapore. During the same period, SEC acquired American Cable Company, a manufacturer of closed circuit television systems.

Melissa Manley was hired by Security Electronics as a financial analyst. She had an undergraduate degree in business administration from the University of Georgia. Melissa had just completed the company training pro-

gram, and was ready to apply what she had learned in her finance concentration. In her six months with SEC, she had already gained a new perspective as to how the business world really works.

Melissa's first assignment was to study the working capital cycle, with the goal of reducing the minimum operating cash requirements. She remembered from her basic finance class three approaches for decreasing the amount of cash necessary for operations: (1) pay bills as late as possible without damaging the credit rating of the company, (2) manage the inventory-production cycle efficiently to maximize the turnover rate, and (3) collect accounts receivables quickly. She knew that improvement in these areas would produce a shorter cash cycle, a higher cash turnover, and a lower minimum level of operating cash.

Melissa planned to use all three approaches to cash management. The first approach required that she stretch the average age of accounts payable from 30 to 35 days. Her boss assured her that this small increase would be possible without damaging the company's credit rating. The second approach involved reduction in the raw materials, work-in-process, and finished goods inventories. In discussions with operations personnel, she determined that the 50-day level of raw material could be reduced to 30 days, and the work-in-process inventory must remain at its current 5 days. The sales department admitted, after some questioning, that finished goods inventory could be reduced from 60 days to the industry average of 40 days. The average age of receivables would decrease from 50 to 45 days.

Security Electronics spent approximately $46 million per year on operating costs. With an opportunity cost of 10 percent, a significant reduction in the level of cash required would lead to a large annual savings. The cash saved could be converted immediately to short-term marketable securities.

Leading Questions

1. What are the number of days in the old cash cycle and the new cash cycle?
2. What are the old cash turnover rate and the new cash turnover rate?
3. What are the old minimum level and new minimum level of cash?
4. What is the downside of implementing this plan?

AVERY DENNISON DUSTS ITSELF OFF AFTER ROUGH MERGER

hairman Charles D. Miller admits the timing of the
October 1990 marriage that created Avery Dennison Corporation "wasn't ideal." Not only did it
come on the eve of a recession, it also was held up at the
altar by a U.S. antitrust review. Still, the rocky relationship
so far for the combined Avery International Corporation
and Dennison Manufacturing Company hasn't dampened
the executive's ardor for the global office-products giant

19 Business Combinations and Failure

he now runs. "I don't want to sound cocky, but I believe it is already beginning to bear fruit," Mr. Miller says.

But analysts are wary. The timetable for recovering from the merger has slipped by a year, to 1994 at the earliest. And Mr. Miller's goal of more than doubling profits by that year, and increasing return on capital to 13% from the current level of 6.7%, wouldn't achieve much more than restoring the capital ratio and per-share earnings to where they were in 1989—the year before the merger.

The merger agreement gave Dennison holders 1.12 shares of Avery for each Dennison share. Prior to the announcement, Avery shares were trading at $28.50, and Dennison shares at $19. But by the time the merger closed, Avery's share price had plunged 43% to $16.25. "Dennison shareholders got creamed," says Stuart Pulvirent, an analyst at Shearson Lehman Brothers Inc. To settle related shareholder lawsuits, an agreement was reached for Avery Dennison to increase the quarterly dividend to 20 cents from 18 cents.

Business combinations create winners and losers. In the case of Avery Dennison, it may take some time to determine who wins and who loses. That determination is usually difficult, especially as economic conditions change, since it requires a knowledge of the basics, formation, and evaluation of mergers, consolidations, and acquisitions. Business combinations in the worst case may lead to business failure, causing financial difficulty, voluntary settlements, bankruptcy legislation, reorganization, and liquidation.

Source: Rhonda L. Rundle, "Avery Dennison Dusts Itself Off After Rough Merger," *The Wall Street Journal,* March 11, 1992. Reprinted by permission of The Wall Street Journal, © 1992 Dow Jones Company, Inc. All Rights Reserved Worldwide.

THE BASICS OF COMBINATIONS

Business combinations are either mergers, consolidations, or acquisitions. In each of these forms, keep in mind that the objective is to maximize the value of the common stock. A company should seek a combination only if it satisfies this goal.

Characteristics of Combinations

A **merger** is a combination of two or more companies in which the acquiring company retains its name and identity, while the acquired company ceases to exist as a business entity. The assets and liabilities of the acquired company are

Merger

525

Consolidation

merged with those of the acquiring company. The shareholders of each company must approve the merger, usually by a vote of two-thirds of the shares.

A **consolidation** is a combination of two or more companies in which a completely new company is created, while both the acquiring and acquired companies no longer exist as business entities. As with mergers, the assets and liabilities of the companies are combined, a move which requires 100 percent ownership of the acquired company. In practice, the term *merger* includes combinations which are actually consolidations.

Acquisition

An **acquisition** occurs from a legal perspective when one company acquires a majority of the common stock of another company, not just a controlling interest. A controlling interest means the company has control of a majority share of the votes. This is accomplished either by owning more than 50 percent of the stock or by obtaining enough votes from outside shareholders to make up the difference. In widely-held corporations, a controlling interest may require as little as 10 percent of the outstanding shares.

A holding company is a corporation that has a controlling interest in the common stock of one or more other corporations. A pure holding company has no business operations, while a holding-operating company has business operations and has controlling interests in other companies. Most holding companies are of the latter form. Figure 19.1 illustrates the two forms.

Financial managers also classify business combinations by type. A horizontal combination occurs when two companies in the same line of business combine. The companies combine into one larger company or compete with each other as separate entities. A vertical combination results when a company acquires either a customer or a supplier. This provides the acquiring company with greater control over finished goods or raw materials, an economic advantage.

A congeneric combination happens when two companies in the same industry combine, without having a customer/supplier relationship. This allows both companies to use the same sales and distribution channels. A conglomerate combination exists when the companies are not related to each other. Risk is reduced by combining companies with different patterns of sales and earnings, a portfolio effect.

Accounting and Tax Considerations

The acquisition of a company has accounting and tax considerations for the companies involved, and tax consequences for the shareholders of the acquired company. The accounting and tax treatment for the companies involved depends upon the amount of stock acquired and whether or not there is a merger or consolidation. The tax consequences for the shareholders of the acquired company depend on whether or not cash is exchanged.

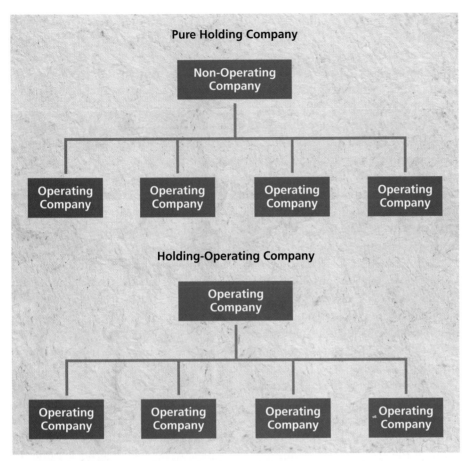

Figure 19.1 Pure Holding and Holding-Operating Companies

The acquisition of between 20 and 50 percent of the outstanding shares of another company requires the acquiring company to use the equity method of accounting. This rule also applies if a company has effective control with less than 20 percent of the shares. Under the equity method, the acquiring company must recognize the income or losses of the acquired company, whether or not dividends are paid.

The Harrison Corporation owns 30 percent of the outstanding shares of the McAllister Company. McAllister reports $100,000 in net income for the year and pays $40,000 in dividends. How would this affect the financial statements of the Harrison Corporation?

The Harrison Corporation recognizes $30,000 in income from the McAllister Company, 30 percent of $100,000, and reports it on the income statement. The investment account on the balance sheet also increases by $30,000. The dividends of $12,000, 30 percent of $40,000, increase cash but reduce the investment account by $12,000. The net increase in the investment account is $18,000, $30,000 − $12,000.

The acquisition of more than 50 percent of the outstanding shares of another company creates a new relationship. In this case, the acquiring company is known as the **parent company,** and the acquired company is referred to as the **subsidiary company.** Both companies prepare individual financial statements and must present consolidated financial statements, unless the parent company does not exercise operational control over the subsidiary (FASB 94). For example, a service company that acquires a manufacturing company is generally required to furnish consolidated statements, even though they are in dissimilar businesses.

Transactions between a parent company and its subsidiaries are eliminated before preparing the consolidated financial statements. The use of elimination entries allows account balances to be presented as if they were from a single economic unit. This action prevents double counting of resources in the preparation of the consolidated statements.

Consolidated financial statements, as a result of merger, consolidation, or acquisition, are treated as either a purchase or a pooling of interests. The purchase method requires the assets and liabilities of the acquired company to be revalued at their fair market values as of the combination date. Goodwill is the excess of the purchase price over the fair market value of the net assets.

The pooling of interests method requires all assets and liabilities, including those of the acquired and acquiring companies, to be valued at book value. In this case, goodwill is not created. To use the pooling of interests method, twelve criteria must be satisfied (APB Opinion No. 16). As a result, less than 20 percent of business combinations use the pooling method.

The tax treatment of the shareholders of the acquired company depends upon whether or not the acquiring company pays cash for the acquired company. If cash is paid, the normal rules for gains and losses immediately apply to the shareholders. If stock in the acquiring company is exchanged for stock of the acquired company, no gain or loss is recognized until the new shares are sold. Thus, shareholders normally benefit from an exchange of stock by having their taxes deferred.

Leveraged Buyouts

The managers of a publicly-owned company, or a small group of investors, may acquire that company through a **leveraged buyout (LBO).** Under this arrangement, a new company is formed, with the equity provided by the man-

Parent Company

Subsidiary Company

Leveraged Buyout

agers or other investors. To have enough capital for the purchase of the publicly-owned company, junk bonds are sold through an investment banking firm. After the issue is sold, the investing group makes a cash tender offer for the shares of the publicly-owned company at a premium price. If the LBO is successful, the new company and the old company merge as a privately-owned company. In this process, typically 90 percent or more of the capital raised is through the issuance of the junk bonds.

The privately-owned company therefore has a high debt-to-net worth ratio, such as 10 to 1. This level of leverage motivates the managers, who are usually also the owners, to find ways to meet the interest payments and to reduce the amount of debt. This often leads to cost reduction programs and elimination of management perquisites, as well as to the sale of unnecessary assets and unrelated businesses. Failure to do so can bring legal action, possibly resulting in reorganization or bankruptcy.

The managers of the privately-owned company are also motivated to work hard and to produce, as new owners of the company. In a publicly-owned company, the ownership may be quite diverse, in contrast to the new concentrated ownership. This fact alone leads to more careful monitoring of management practices.

Attractive LBO candidates share certain characteristics: (1) a balance sheet with little debt, (2) predictable cash flows that are adequate to cover interest and principal payments, (3) unnecessary assets that can be sold to retire debt, (4) a strong management group, and (5) limited needs for capital expenditures over the next several years. Possession of these characteristics provides the best chance for the LBO to create an increase in value.

THE FORMATION OF COMBINATIONS

The formation of business combinations is usually handled by investment bankers. This group finds a suitable candidate and then negotiates with its management. In the process, the company that plans to secure another company is called the **acquiring company,** and the company it seeks is called the **target company.**

Acquiring Company

Target Company

The Negotiation Process

Negotiations may lead to an agreement between the two management groups. In this case, the companies issue statements recommending that the shareholders approve the merger. If this occurs, the process is a **friendly merger.** The acquiring company pays the shareholders of the target company with its

Friendly Merger

own stock, bonds, or cash. This negotiation process usually takes more than one offer.

Negotiations may break down, or management of the target company may choose to fight the merger. If the acquiring company wishes to pursue a **hostile takeover,** it must deal directly with the shareholders of the target company.

In a hostile takeover, the acquiring company uses a **tender offer** to secure the stock of the target company. This is a formal offer to purchase a specified number of shares at a set price. The announcement of the tender offer is made through financial newspapers or through a mailing to the target shareholders. The price for each share of the target company is stated in dollars, in shares of stock, or in bonds of the acquiring company. An acquiring company makes the tender offer at a premium above the market price of the stock before the announcement. Sometimes the acquiring company makes a two-tier tender offer, a proposal offering a more favorable price for shares tendered early in the process.

Takeover Defenses

Target companies that do not favor a merger or acquisition may employ a wide variety of **takeover defenses.** Basic strategies include suing the acquiring company or simply advising shareholders of the negative effects of the takeover. If the acquiring company is interested in the liquid assets of a target company, the target company may eliminate the liquidity by paying dividends, repurchasing stock, purchasing fixed assets, or making a cash acquisition.

There are a number of other strategies for avoiding hostile takeover attempts. Using the white knight strategy, the target company attempts to negotiate a friendly merger with a more compatible company. While negotiations are going on, management of the target company can secure golden parachutes, a form of severance pay should the takeover be successful. Corporate charters also may contain a shark repellent, a provision making it more difficult to transfer managerial control. Poison pills are used to make the company less valuable to the acquiring company, often by offering current shareholders new shares at bargain prices.

Greenmail is the strategy of repurchasing a large block of stock by paying one or more shareholders a premium price for the shares, a form of blackmail. The board of directors of the target company may employ the crown jewel strategy, a plan to sell its most valuable assets to its own shareholders. The target company may amend its charter to include a supermajority provision, thereby requiring a large vote, such as three-fourths, to approve a merger. Under a leveraged recapitalization, the company pays a large cash dividend financed by debt, a strategy designed to increase financial leverage. A target company may also use staggered terms for its board of directors, increasing the time to replace the current board.

Lloyds Bank Drops Midland Bid

Lloyds Bank PLC bowed out of the bidding war for Midland Bank PLC, a surprise retreat that cleared the way for HSBC Holdings PLC's recently sweetened offer. Following a two-hour board meeting, Lloyds said its directors had concluded that any new offer should be pitched between 520 pence and 550 pence a share, or 4.1 billion British pounds. That would be an 11% to 18% premium over Lloyds' previous conditional bid, very likely too rich for Lloyds' shareholders to accept. "At that price, most of the benefits would have gone to Midland Bank shareholders rather than Lloyds Bank shareholders," said a Lloyds' spokesman. "The feeling of the board was, 'What's in it for Lloyds Bank?'" HSBC's bid has already cleared regulatory hurdles in the U.K., Europe and the U.S.; by contrast, Lloyds' offer last month was referred to U.K. competition authorities. The uncertainty caused by the review, which wouldn't have been completed until after the HSBC offer closed, meant Lloyds had to produce a huge incentive for Midland shareholders just to stave off an early HSBC win. "I think it was a very brave decision the board made," said Robert Law, an analyst for Lehman Brothers International in London. "It's to their credit that they realized Midland had moved just beyond their reach."

Source: Laurence Hooper, "Lloyds Bank Drops Midland Bid, Clearing Way for HSBC's Offer," *The Wall Street Journal*, June 8, 1992. Reprinted by permission of The Wall Street Journal, © 1992 Dow Jones Company, Inc. All Rights Reserved Worldwide.

Purchase and Sale of Assets

As an alternative to merger or acquisition, a company may purchase all of the assets of a target company. This action avoids problems with minority stockholders, who may attempt to block a merger. Although the transfer of title to the assets is expensive, the process only requires approval by a majority of the target company shareholders.

A company may also sell its assets, a **divestiture.** There are several ways of doing this: (1) selling an operating unit to another company, either for cash or for stock of the acquiring company, (2) selling an operating unit to existing management, often by using a leveraged buyout, (3) converting an operating unit into an independent corporation, while transferring ownership on a pro rata basis to the shareholders of the parent company, a **spin-off,** and (4) liquidating an operating unit by sale of individual assets.

Divestiture

Spin-Off

Divestiture often takes place after merger or acquisition, but it also occurs anytime a company wishes to raise cash, discontinue unprofitable operations, or restructure itself in line with corporate strategy. The last possibility may be an **operational restructuring,** where the assets of the corporation are changed, or a **financial restructuring,** where the capital structure is changed.

Operational Restructuring
Financial Restructuring

THE EVALUATION OF COMBINATIONS

The evaluation of business combinations requires an examination of why the proposed business combination is beneficial, including a quantitative analysis of the proposal. This section focuses on the motives involved and the use of net present value analysis.

The Motive for Forming Combinations

Synergy

The primary economic motive for forming business combinations is **synergy.** Synergy exists when the value of the combined enterprise is greater than the sum of the individual company values before combination. This increase in value results from four factors: (1) revenue growth, (2) cost reduction, (3) tax benefits, and (4) cost of capital decline. The first three factors increase the cash flows of the combination, while the fourth factor increases the present value of the cash flows. During the 1980s, there were other motives by the deal makers, which prevented the economic advantages from occurring.

Revenue growth results from improved marketing, expanded product opportunities, and increased market power. Improved marketing involves advertising, customer relations, distribution, and product mix. Expanded product opportunities suggests products developed as a result of the new combination of creative and technical ability. Increased market power refers to decreased competition in the marketplace. Combinations that lessen competition are examined by the antitrust division of the Justice Department and the Federal Trade Commission.

Cost reduction results from economies of scale, vertical combinations, elimination of managers, and technical information sharing. Economies of scale implies greater efficiency by combining facilities, projects, and operations. Vertical combinations ensure stable suppliers and customers, thereby lowering costs. Elimination of managers involves reducing the number of managers necessary for operations. Technical information sharing refers to technology transfers that would have been unavailable in the absence of the combination.

Tax benefits result by avoiding taxes on dividends and by taking advantage of net operating losses of the acquired company. Companies that have extra cash after taking advantage of investment opportunities may pay dividends or repurchase their own stock. Paying dividends forces shareholders to pay taxes immediately. Repurchase may be challenged by the IRS if the purpose is to avoid paying dividends. Using surplus cash to acquire another company has no immediate tax effect and is therefore a motivation for forming business combinations.

A company receives a tax benefit from acquiring the shares of a company with a tax loss carryforward. This allows an acquiring company to use the net operating losses of the acquired company to reduce taxes. This benefit is a consideration only if the acquiring company believes it can turn the acquired company around or sell its assets at a profit.

The Tax Reform Act of 1986, however, sets limitations on the amount of the carryover. For example, Section 381(c)(1)(B) limits the net operating loss carryover to the percentage of days remaining in the tax year times the taxable income of the acquiring corporation. Even with these limitations, tax loss carryforwards are an important consideration in business combinations.

The Asbury Corporation merges with the Bentley Company on October 19, 19X4, which is 73 days from December 31, 19X4, the end of the tax year for both companies. For the year, Asbury has taxable income of $100,000, while Bentley has $75,000 in tax loss carryforwards. In 19X5 and 19X6, Asbury expects earnings before taxes of $125,000 and $150,000, respectively. If the marginal tax rate is 40 percent, what are the earnings after taxes for Asbury without and with the merger?

The net operating loss carryover for 19X4 is $20,000, 73/365($100,000). The remainder of the loss carryover, $75,000 − $20,000 = $55,000, is carried forward to 19X5. Table 19.1 provides the calculations of earnings after taxes, without and with the merger, for each of the three years. Notice that with the merger, taxes are reduced each year by the amount of the tax loss carryforward times the tax rate.

TABLE 19.1 Earnings After Taxes Without and With the Merger

	WITHOUT MERGER		
	19X4	**19X5**	**19X6**
Earnings before taxes	$100,000	$125,000	$150,000
Taxes (40%)	40,000	50,000	60,000
Earnings after taxes	$ 60,000	$ 75,000	$ 90,000

	WITH MERGER		
	19X4	**19X5**	**19X6**
Earnings before losses	$100,000	$125,000	$150,000
Tax loss carryforward	20,000	55,000	0
Earnings before taxes	$ 80,000	$ 70,000	$150,000
Taxes (40%)	32,000	28,000	60,000
Earnings after taxes	$ 48,000	$ 42,000	$ 90,000

Economies of scale in issuing securities reduces the cost of capital. It is simply less expensive to issue large amounts of debt and equity. Smaller companies also have little access to long-term capital sources and must rely on shorter-term sources such as bank loans. Under these conditions, a larger company may have a lower cost of capital after a business combination.

Net Present Value Analysis

Companies often use net present value analysis when evaluating a business combination. This requires knowledge of the cash flows involved, as well as the appropriate discount rate. Before making these estimations, consider the thought processes involved when the values of the companies are known, before and after a merger. There are two situations: (1) an acquisition for cash, and (2) an acquisition for shares of the parent company.

The net present value of a merger (NPV_M) to the acquiring company is given by the following equation:

$$NPV_M = V_{AT} - V_A - P_T \qquad (19.1)$$

where

$$V_{AT} = \text{Value of combined company}$$
$$V_A = \text{Value of acquiring company before merger}$$
$$P_T = \text{Amount paid for the target company}$$

If the net present value of the merger is positive, synergy exists, and the acquiring company should make the acquisition.

The price paid for the target company includes a premium over and above the market price of the stock before negotiations begin. Investors expect the value of the target company to rise, and will bid up the price of the stock.

The value of the acquiring company before the merger is the market value *before* investors have knowledge of a possible merger. When merger information becomes available, the price of the stock of the Asbury Company will rise. This occurs even if a relatively small group of investors believes the merger will take place.

The Asbury Company, with 50,000 shares outstanding, is considering acquiring and merging with the Thomas Company. The value of the Asbury Company before the merger is $1,000,000, the value of the combined companies is $1,500,000. The cash price paid for the Thomas Company is $400,000. What is the net present value of the merger, and what is the market value of each share of stock, before and after the merger?

The net present value of the merger is given by Eq. 19.1.

$$NPV_M = V_{AT} - V_A - P_T$$
$$= \$1,500,000 - \$1,000,000 - \$400,000$$
$$= \$100,000$$

The value of the stock of the Asbury Company is $100,000 higher after the merger.

The value of a share of stock (V_s) is given by the following formula:

$$V_s = \frac{\text{Total Market Value}}{\text{Shares Outstanding}} \qquad (19.2)$$

Substitute the values before the merger.

$$V_s = \frac{\$1,000,000}{50,000}$$
$$= \$20$$

Then, substitute the values after the merger.

$$V_s = \frac{\$1,100,000}{50,000}$$
$$= \$22$$

The market value of the combined company decreases by the amount of cash paid for the target company. The shareholders of the Asbury Company benefited by the $2 increase in the price of the stock.

Acquiring companies also purchase target companies with shares of stock instead of cash. In this situation, the acquiring company issues a specified number of new shares in exchange for each share of the target company. The value of a share of stock in the new company should be the same after the merger if cash is paid or if shares are exchanged.

The Asbury Company from the previous example plans to offer a specified number of shares of its stock in exchange for each share of the stock of the Thomas Company. The Thomas Company has 10,000 shares outstanding. What is the exchange ratio for The Asbury Company?

The value of a share of stock (V_s) is given by Eq. 19.2. Substitute the value of each share after the merger, letting X equal the number of new shares.

$$V_s = \frac{\text{Total Market Value}}{\text{Shares Outstanding}}$$

$$\$22 = \frac{\$1,500,000}{50,000 + X}$$

Solve the equation for X.

$$X = 18,181.8 \text{ new shares}$$

Since the Thomas Company has 10,000 old shares, shareholders of the Thomas Company should receive 1.818 shares of the Asbury Company, 18,181.8/10,000. The exchange ratio is 1.818:1. Notice that the total market value of the new company after merger is higher since cash is not used for the purchase.

BUSINESS FAILURE

Businesses that cannot meet their recurring obligations as they come due may become bankrupt. Before this happens, the debtor company and creditors should meet to solve their problems through a voluntary settlement. If this is not possible, the bankruptcy laws are used. In that case, the company reorganizes, or if that is not possible, liquidates.

Financial Difficulty

Business failure from an economic standpoint exists when a company continually earns a rate of return on its investments less than its cost of capital. The resulting degree of financial difficulty depends upon how long this condition is allowed to continue.

Technical Insolvency   **Technical insolvency** occurs when a company is unable to meet its current obligations as they come due. Even though the value of assets are greater than the value of liabilities, the company is suffering from a liquidity crisis. This may be caused by low sales, slow payment from customers, or an unusual financial obligation. If the conditions are temporary, it may be worked out with creditors. A sale of assets within a reasonable length of time may serve the purpose. If the conditions are permanent, the company may become legally insolvent.

Legal Insolvency   **Legal insolvency** occurs when the total liabilities exceed the total assets, as recorded on the balance sheet. Absolute insolvency is similarly defined, but in this case, assets are shown at their fair market value. The latter suggests a more critical stage of financial difficulty, possibly leading to bankruptcy.

Bankruptcy is a legal term indicating a company has begun a legal proceeding under the control of a bankruptcy court. The Bankruptcy Act of 1938, amended in 1978 and 1984, allows a company to petition into bankruptcy using technical insolvency, legal insolvency, or absolute insolvency as a basis. This action leads to reorganization or liquidation.

Bankruptcy

Voluntary Settlements

A company in financial difficulty may arrange a **voluntary settlement** with its creditors. This approach is faster and avoids the high costs of bankruptcy proceedings. Under this arrangement, the company meets with a committee of creditors to draw up a plan for resolving the situation.

Voluntary Settlement

The informal plan may include an extension, a composition, an assignment, or some combination of the three methods. An extension postpones the payment of debt obligations while requiring that the full amount be paid. Usually during this period the company is required to make cash payments. This is a practical approach when the creditors view the financial difficulty as temporary. A composition is an agreement in which the creditors accept a pro rata cash settlement. The company, however, must have sufficient liquidity to enter into such an arrangement. Creditors accept composition if they believe this is their best alternative given the high costs of a bankruptcy proceeding.

An assignment is the appointment of a trustee to manage the assets of the company. The trustee usually replaces management and guides the operation until either the assets are liquidated or, in a few cases, profitable operation returns.

Bankruptcy Legislation

The Bankruptcy Act of 1938, amended in 1978 and 1984, is the primary legislation governing bankruptcy. This act contains several chapters, with Chapter 7 and Chapter 11 the most important. Chapter 7 deals with the procedures followed in liquidation, the sale of assets and the distribution of cash to creditors. Chapter 11 details the procedures for reorganizing a failing company such that creditors are treated fairly.

Under the Bankruptcy Act, a petition is filed with the federal district bankruptcy court. This petition may be filed voluntarily by the management of the debtor company or involuntarily by its creditors. The court then appoints a committee of unsecured creditors to negotiate with management regarding a reorganization of the debtor company. If this action fails, the debtor company is liquidated.

Reorganization

Voluntary Reorganization

Involuntary Reorganization

The management of a company in financial difficulty, or an outside party, may file a reorganization petition under Chapter 11 of the Bankruptcy Act. If the petition is filed by the debtor company, it is a **voluntary reorganization.** If the petition is filed by an outside party such as a creditor, it is an **involuntary reorganization.** An involuntary petition may be challenged by the debtor company at a hearing held to determine if the company is in fact insolvent. If the petition is accepted by the court, it issues an order of relief barring creditors from enforcing claims.

Reorganization Plan

The debtor company must present a **reorganization plan** to the court and to the Securities and Exchange Commission (SEC). A hearing is then held to review the plan for fairness and feasibility. Fairness means that the claims of creditors, preferred stockholders, and common shareholders are settled in the order of their priority. Feasibility means that the reorganization plan has a good chance of working. For example, the plan must include sufficient working capital and have a high probability of covering fixed charges.

The reorganization plan is submitted to the creditors for approval after acceptance by the bankruptcy court and the SEC. Voting occurs by class: unsecured creditors, secured creditors, preferred stockholders, and common shareholders. The plan must be approved in each class by creditors representing a simple majority and two-thirds of the dollar amount of the claims. The plan must also be approved in each class by two-thirds of the preferred stockholders and common shareholders voting by number of shares.

The debtor company and the creditors may reach an impasse. In this case, the court through a trustee can impose a solution. This is done after deciding if the company is worth more dead than alive. To make this decision, the value of the company as a going concern is compared with the net liquidation value. The value as a going concern is found by discounting the future cash flows. The net liquidation value is found by adding the liquidation values of each of the assets and subtracting the administrative costs. Technical insolvency normally leads to reorganization under Chapter 11. Absolute insolvency often leads to liquidation under Chapter 7.

Liquidation

Liquidation

Liquidation normally occurs when the bankruptcy court determines that reorganization is not indicated. This happens when no reorganization petition is filed, when the reorganization petition is denied, and/or when the reorganization plan is disapproved.

A company that has been adjudged bankrupt requires a trustee to administer the liquidation. The trustee is responsible for safeguarding the assets from the owners of the bankrupt company and for distributing the assets equitably. This process begins by a meeting with creditors to explain what is likely to happen in the liquidation.

The trustee must follow the priority of claims specified in the Bankruptcy Act. Secured creditors, with specific assets pledged as collateral, have priority over other claimants. If the proceeds from liquidation are insufficient to meet their claims, then the secured creditors become unsecured creditors for the amount remaining. In the reverse situation, excess funds from the sale of secured assets are distributed according to the priority of claims schedule.

The proceeds from the sale of assets are distributed in the following order:

1. Secured creditors.
2. Costs of administering the bankruptcy.
3. Interim costs in an involuntary proceeding.
4. Wages, salaries, and commissions within 90 days of the bankruptcy petition.
5. Claims for contributions to employee benefit plans.
6. Customer deposits.
7. Taxes due to federal, state, county, and any other government.
8. Unfunded pension plan liabilities.
9. Unsecured creditors.
10. Preferred stockholders.
11. Common shareholders.

The Martin Corporation must be liquidated. Table 19.2 summarizes claims against the Martin Corporation, not including unsecured creditors. The balance sheet before liquidation is shown in Table 19.3. The trustee obtained $400,000 from current assets and $600,000 from fixed assets. How is the $1,000,000 distributed?

TABLE 19.2 Summary of Claims Against the Martin Corporation

First mortgage	$500,000
Second mortgage	300,000
Costs of administration	200,000
Wages due workers	80,000
Unpaid taxes	20,000

TABLE 19.3 Balance Sheet Before Liquidation of Assets

ASSETS	
Current assets:	
Cash	$ 40,000
Marketable securities	20,000
Accounts receivable	300,000
Inventory	440,000
Total current assets	$ 800,000
Land	$ 300,000
Net plant	500,000
Net equipment	400,000
Total fixed assets	$1,200,000
Total assets	$2,000,000

LIABILITIES AND STOCKHOLDERS' EQUITY	
Current liabilities:	
Accounts payable	$ 200,000
Notes payable	300,000
Accrued wages	80,000
Accrued taxes	20,000
Total current liabilities	$ 600,000
First mortgage	$ 500,000
Second mortgage	300,000
Unsecured bonds	300,000
Total long-term debt	$1,100,000
Preferred stock (1,000 shares)	$ 100,000
Common stock (20,000 shares)	20,000
Capital in excess of par	130,000
Retained earnings	50,000
Total stockholders' equity	$ 300,000
Total liabilities and stockholders' equity	$2,000,000

Table 19.4 summarizes the distribution of liquidation proceeds of the Martin Corporation. Notice, the second mortgage holder receives only $100,000 initially, the amount left of the $600,000 received from selling the fixed assets, after paying the $500,000 first mortgage. The amount received is 33 percent of the amount claimed, $100,000/$300,000 = 0.33. The second mortgage holder then receives an additional $20,000 as an unsecured creditor. Since unsecured creditors are not fully paid, preferred stockholders and common shareholders receive nothing.

Columbia Gas Restructuring On Schedule

espite a number of financial and procedural hurdles, Columbia Gas System Inc. said it expects to complete its reorganization plan one to two years after last July's bankruptcy filing. Although one analyst speculated that the company was prepared to file such a plan without debtors' consent, a company spokesman Friday said he didn't know whether a plan would be filed. Separately, in the annual report, the company's independent accountant, Arthur Anderson & Company, said that uncertainties related to the bankruptcy proceedings, shareholder litigation against the company and other matters may force the company to sell assets or settle liabilities for undetermined amounts. That prospect creates "substantial doubt about the corpo-

ration's ability to continue as a going concern," it said. Also in its annual report, the natural gas and energy company said it is likely to take a first-quarter after-tax write-down of about $100 million. The item will be necessary under Securities and Exchange Commission rules to write down the carrying value of its oil and gas properties to reflect the recent decline in natural gas prices. The company filed for Chapter 11 protection as a way to get the contracts renegotiated.

Source: Suein L. Hwang, "Columbia Gas Restructuring On Schedule," *The Wall Street Journal,* March 30, 1992. Reprinted by permission of the Wall Street Journal, © 1992 Dow Jones & Company, Inc. All Rights Reserved Worldwide.

TABLE 19.4 Liquidation Proceeds of the Martin Corporation

Proceeds from liquidation		$1,000,000
First mortgage	$ 500,000	
Second mortgage	100,000	
Costs of administration	200,000	
Wages due workers	80,000	
Unpaid taxes	20,000	900,000
Available for unsecured creditors		$ 100,000

TYPE OF UNSECURED CLAIM	AMOUNT CLAIMED	AMOUNT RECEIVED
Accounts payable	$ 200,000	$ 20,000
Notes payable	300,000	30,000
Second mortgage	200,000	20,000
Unsecured bonds	300,000	30,000
Totals	$1,000,000	$ 100,000

SUMMARY

. . . .

This chapter focuses on the following learning objectives:

1. Describing the characteristics of business combinations.

   A merger is a combination of two or more companies in which the acquiring company retains its name and identity, while the acquired company ceases to exist as a business entity. A consolidation is a combination of two or more companies in which a completely new company is created, while both the acquiring and acquired companies no longer exist as business entities. An acquisition occurs from a legal perspective when one company acquires a majority of the common stock of another company, not just a controlling interest.

2. Discussing accounting and tax considerations of business combinations.

   The accounting and tax treatment for the companies involved in a business combination depends upon the amount of stock acquired and whether or not there is a merger or consolidation. The tax consequences for the shareholders of the acquired company depend on whether or not cash is exchanged.

3. Explaining leveraged buyouts.

   The managers of a publicly-owned company, or a small group of investors, may acquire a company through a leveraged buyout. Under this arrangement, a new company is formed, with the equity provided by the managers or other investors. To have enough capital, junk bonds are sold through an investment banking firm.

4. Demonstrating the formation of business combinations.

   The formation of business combinations is usually handled by investment bankers. The securing company is called the acquiring company, and the company it seeks is called the target company. As an alternative to merger or acquisition, a company may purchase all of the assets of a target company.

5. Evaluating business combinations.

   The primary motive for forming business combinations is synergy. Synergy exists when the combined value is greater than the sum of the individual company values. Net present value analysis is used when evaluating a business combination.

6. Illustrating the processes involved in business failure.

   Business failure from an economic standpoint exists when a company earns a rate of return less than its cost of capital. A company in financial difficulty may arrange a voluntary settlement with its creditors. The Bankruptcy Act of 1938, amended in 1978 and 1984, is the primary legislation governing bankruptcy.

Key Terms

Acquiring company, 529	Legal insolvency, 536	Synergy, 532
Acquisition, 526	Leveraged buyout, 528	Takeover defense, 530
Bankruptcy, 537	Liquidation, 538	Target company, 529
Consolidation, 526	Merger, 525	Technical
Divestiture, 531	Operational	insolvency, 536
Financial	restructuring, 531	Tender offer, 530
restructuring, 531	Parent company, 528	Voluntary
Friendly merger, 529	Reorganization	reorganization, 538
Hostile takeover, 530	plan, 538	Voluntary
Involuntary	Spin-off, 531	settlement, 537
reorganization, 538	Subsidiary company, 528	

Questions

19.1   What are mergers and consolidations?

19.2   What are the characteristics of acquisitions and holding companies?

19.3   How are business combinations classified?

19.4   When is the equity method of accounting required for an acquisition?

19.5   When does a parent company file consolidated statements with a subsidiary?

19.6   What are elimination entries?

19.7   Contrast the purchase method and the pooling of interest method of accounting.

19.8   Describe how a leveraged buyout is accomplished.

19.9   Describe what happens in a friendly merger.

19.10 Describe what happens in a hostile takeover.

19.11 What takeover defenses are used to fight a hostile takeover?

19.12 How does a company accomplish a divestiture?

19.13 What is the difference between an operational restructuring and a financial restructuring?

19.14 What is synergy, and what factors cause it?

19.15 What is a tax loss carryforward?

19.16 What are the differences between technical insolvency, legal insolvency, and absolute insolvency?

19.17   Explain how a voluntary settlement works.

19.18   Explain the key points of bankruptcy legislation.

19.19   What are the differences between a voluntary reorganization and an involuntary reorganization?

19.20   Who must approve a reorganization plan?

19.21   When does liquidation occur?

19.22   How are the proceeds from the sale of assets in a liquidation distributed?

19.23   Who wins and who loses in the Avery Dennison merger?

19.24   Why did Lloyds Bank drop the Midland Bank bid?

19.25   Why did Columbia Gas file for Chapter 11 protection?

PROBLEMS

19.1   **(Combination Accounting)** The McGriff Company owns 40 percent of the outstanding shares of McMichael Corporation. McMichael reports $500,000 in net income for the year and pays $200,000 in dividends. How would this affect the financial statements of the McGriff Company?

19.2   **(Combination Accounting)** Jane Masden is evaluating the financial statements of the Folsom Corporation. She knows that Folsom owns 40 percent of the outstanding shares of the Vyas Company. Vyas had $410,000 in net income for the year and paid $200,000 in dividends. What changes would she make on the financial statements of the Folsom Corporation?

19.3   **(Merger Earnings)** The Mansville Company plans to merge with the Hawkes Company 146 days from the end of the 19X4 tax year for both companies. Over the year, Mansville has taxable income of $250,000, while Hawkes has $150,000 in tax loss carryforwards. In 19X5 and 19X6, Mansville expects earnings before taxes of $250,000 and $350,000. If the marginal tax rate is 40 percent, what are the earnings after taxes for Mansville for each of the three years, without and with the merger?

19.4   **(Merger Earnings)** The planned merger between the Greene Company and the Redd Company will occur 180 days from the end of the tax year. During the year, Redd has $400,000 in tax loss carryforwards, while Greene has taxable income of $575,000. For the next two years, Greene expects earnings before taxes of $750,000 and $950,000. If the marginal tax rate is 40 percent, what are the earnings after taxes for Greene for each of the three years, without and with the merger?

19.5   **(Market Value)** The Weed Corporation, with 100,000 shares outstanding, is considering acquiring and merging with the Knox Corporation.

The value of the Weed Company before merger is $2,100,000; the value of the combined companies is $3,500,000. The cash price paid for the Knox Corporation is $800,000. What is the net present value of the merger, and what is the market value of each share of stock before and after the merger?

19.6 **(Exchange Ratio)** The Weed Corporation from the previous problem plans to offer a specified number of shares of its stock in exchange for each share of the stock of the Knox Corporation. The Knox Corporation has 25,000 shares outstanding. What is the exchange ratio for the Weed Corporation?

19.7 **(Market Value)** The Marceau Company plans to acquire and merge with the Siddons Company. The value of the 500,000 shares of the Marceau Company before merger is $5,000,000; the value of the combined companies is $6,500,000. The cash price paid for the Siddons Company is $1,000,000. What is the net present value of the merger, and what is the market value of each share of stock before and after the merger?

19.8 **(Exchange Ratio)** The Siddons Company from the previous problem has 100,000 shares outstanding. The Marceau Company will offer a specified number of shares of its stock in exchange for each share of the stock of the Siddons Company. What is the exchange ratio for the Marceau Company?

19.9 **(Asset Distribution)** The Stanley Corporation must be liquidated. The balance sheet before liquidation is shown below. The trustee obtained $1,000,000 from current assets and $1,500,000 from fixed assets. Claims against the Stanley Corporation, not including unsecured creditors, are also shown. How is the $2,500,000 distributed?

ASSETS	
Current assets:	
Cash	$ 100,000
Marketable securities	50,000
Accounts receivable	750,000
Inventory	1,100,000
Total current assets	$2,000,000
Land	$ 750,000
Net plant	1,250,000
Net equipment	1,000,000
Total fixed assets	$3,000,000
Total assets	$5,000,000

LIABILITIES AND STOCKHOLDERS' EQUITY

Current liabilities:	
Accounts payable	$ 500,000
Notes payable	750,000
Accrued wages	200,000
Accrued taxes	50,000
Total current liabilities	$1,500,000
First mortgage	$1,250,000
Second mortgage	750,000
Unsecured bonds	750,000
Total long-term debt	$2,750,000
Preferred stock (1,000 shares)	250,000
Common stock (20,000 shares)	50,000
Capital in excess of par	325,000
Retained earnings	125,000
Total stockholders' equity	$ 750,000
Total liabilities and stockholders' equity	$5,000,000

SUMMARY OF CLAIMS

First mortgage	$1,250,000
Second mortgage	750,000
Costs of administration	500,000
Wages due workers	200,000
Unpaid taxes	50,000

A Case Problem

Billy's, Inc. operated and franchised a chain of quick-service restaurants in seven states in the southeastern United States. The company had been in the business since 1952 and had begun franchising in 1992. Billy's tried to differentiate itself from its competitors by focusing on offering its small oval-shaped hamburgers and breakfast biscuits at low prices.

In 1990, Sammie Brodie, then Chairman of the Board and a shareholder of the company, organized Billy's Shares, Inc. (BSI), a Delaware corporation, to acquire all of the shares of the company in a leveraged buyout transaction. BSI's sole function was to issue subordinated debentures to former shareholders of the company and to hold the acquired shares of the company. These debentures had a principal balance of approximately $20,000,000 as of March 31, 1993, at 10% per annum, and matured June 30, 2005.

In 1993, Billy's, Inc. offered 2,000,000 shares of common stock to the public at a price per share of $12.00. The net proceeds from the sale were estimated to be approximately $22,000,000. The company would use $20,000,000 from this amount to repay the subordinated debentures issued in connection with the acquisition. The remaining balance, together with $10.1 million of cash and short-term marketable securities, would primarily be used to finance the development of additional company-owned restaurants.

> *Billy's, Inc. had paid dividends to BSI, its parent corporation, in order to provide BSI with funds to pay the interest on the subordinated debentures.*

Billy's, Inc. and Billy's Shares, Inc., the holder of the debentures, entered into a merger agreement, in which Billy's, Inc. would merge with BSI. The agreement provided that the current shareholders of BSI would receive ten shares of Billy's common stock for each share of BSI stock owned, while the former shares of BSI would be canceled. The merger agreement was conditioned upon consummation of the stock offering.

Billy's, Inc. had paid dividends to BSI, its parent corporation, in order to provide BSI with funds to pay the interest on the subordinated debentures. Otherwise, Billy's had not paid any cash dividends since the acquisition. After the repayment of the subordinated debentures and merger, the Board of Directors of the company planned initially to retain all earnings for the growth and development of the business. The payment of dividends was limited under credit and long-term note agreements to an amount equal to 50 percent of the cumulative net income from the date of repayment of the debentures. The level of dividend payments was also restricted by certain financial ratio limitations.

Leading Questions

1. Why did Sammie Brodie enter into the leveraged buyout transaction?
2. What is the downside risk of this arrangement?

There are many reasons offered why industries in one country become internationally competitive. Yet debaters of all stripes seem to agree on one fact: The U. S. trails its global economic rivals in Germany and Japan when it comes to the good old-fashioned art of making things. If you want high quality, super productivity, great engineering and fine craftsmanship, the models to follow are in Stuttgart or

20 International Financial Management

Osaka, not Cleveland. Or so goes the conventional wisdom.

My colleagues and I recently put this wisdom to the test by actually examining labor productivity in nine representative manufacturing industries in Germany, Japan and the U. S.: autos, auto parts, metalworking, steel, computers, consumer electronics, soap and detergent, beer, and processed food. We adjusted both for differences in product quality and for fluctuations in the business cycle. The results of this study by McKinsey's Global Institute are illuminating—not only for the facts they debunk and establish, but for the explanations that lie beneath those facts. Put simply, global competitiveness is a bit like tennis: You get better by playing against people who are better than you.

The mechanism for transferring these productivity improvements from company to company and nation to nation is notable as well. Foreign direct investments—transplant factories—play the pivotal role in moving them around the world. In fact, foreign direct investment has been far more powerful than trade as a force for improving productivity, especially in Germany and the U.S.

The secret to competitiveness begins with a willingness to learn about the global environment. One aspect of this environment is international financial management.

Source: William Lewis, "The Secret to Competitiveness," *The Wall Street Journal,* October 22, 1993. Reprinted by permission of The Wall Street Journal, © 1993 Dow Jones & Company Inc. All Rights Reserved Worldwide.

FOREIGN EXCHANGE RATES AND MARKETS

The foreign exchange market includes large domestic and foreign banks, a small number of exchange brokers, domestic and foreign multinational companies, central banks, small foreign-exchange businesses, and speculators. Within this framework, multinational finance emphasizes the differences between foreign and domestic firms and specifies how these differences should be treated.

Exchange Rate Quotations

The **exchange rate** is the price of a currency in terms of another currency. Market forces are the primary determinant of this price. This section focuses on the mechanics of exchange rate quotations and the functioning of exchange markets.

Exchange Rate

Exchange Rate Quotation

The **exchange rate quotation** for a particular currency may be expressed in terms of any other currency. The reverse is also true: Any other currency may be quoted in terms of the particular currency. For example, if the exchange rate for a British pound is $2.00, then the exchange rate for a U.S. dollar is £0.50. A reciprocal relationship exists between the two currencies and any other two currencies as well.

Figure 20.1 shows the foreign exchange quotations from *The Wall Street Journal* for Monday, January 28, 1991. This listing represents the conventional way of reporting quotations, U.S. dollars per unit of foreign currency. The reciprocal approach, foreign currency per U.S. dollar, is referred to as the European system.

The quotations in Figure 20.1 represent the *asked price*, the rate charged by Banker's Trust Company for providing foreign currency. These wholesale prices apply to transactions of $1,000,000 or more. For example, a customer receives 508,800 British pounds for $1,000,000, $1,000,000(0.5088). Smaller retail exchanges provide smaller quantities of foreign currency. Dealers also purchase foreign currency at the *bid price*, a rate not shown in Figure 20.1. In that situation, customers receive a smaller amount of foreign currency than is shown by the asked price.

Spot Rate

Currencies are bought and sold for immediate delivery or for delivery at some future time. The **spot rate** is the price for immediate delivery, normally

EXCHANGE RATES

Monday, January 28, 1991

The New York foreign exchange selling rates below apply to trading among banks in amounts of $1 million and more, as quoted at 3 p.m. Eastern time by Bankers Trust Co. Retail transactions provide fewer units of foreign currency per dollar.

Country	U.S. $ equiv. Mon.	U.S. $ equiv. Fri.	Currency per U.S. $ Mon.	Currency per U.S. $ Fri.
Argentina (Austral) ...	.0001479	.0001563	6762.00	6399.00
Australia (Dollar)	.7825	.7770	1.2780	1.2870
Austria (Schilling)	.09553	.09501	10.47	10.52
Bahrain (Dinar)	2.6525	2.6525	.3770	.3770
Belgium (Franc)				
Commercial rate	.03264	.03251	30.64	30.76
Brazil (Cruzeiro)	.00510	.00518	196.23	193.13
Britain (Pound)	1.9655	1.9530	.5088	.5120
30-Day Forward	1.9545	1.9417	.5116	.5150
90-Day Forward	1.9337	1.9215	.5171	.5204
180-Day Forward	1.9079	1.8963	.5241	.5273
Canada (Dollar)	.8606	.8587	1.1620	1.1645
30-Day Forward	.8576	.8557	1.1661	1.1687
90-Day Forward	.8530	.8509	1.1724	1.1752
180-Day Forward	.8478	.8453	1.1795	1.1830
Chile (Official rate)	.002892	.003057	345.84	327.13
China (Renmimbi)	.191205	.191205	5.2300	5.2300
Colombia (Peso)	.001777	.001779	562.62	562.19
Denmark (Krone)	.1747	.1740	5.7246	5.7457
Ecuador (Sucre)				
Floating rate	.001050	.001073	952.50	932.00
Finland (Markka)	.27766	.27705	3.6015	3.6095
France (Franc)	.19796	.19714	5.0515	5.0725
30-Day Forward	.19746	.19662	5.0642	5.0860
90-Day Forward	.19646	.19562	5.0900	5.1120
180-Day Forward	.19495	.19410	5.1295	5.1520
Germany (Mark)	.6725	.6702	1.4870	1.4920
30-Day Forward	.6714	.6691	1.4894	1.4945
90-Day Forward	.6689	.6667	1.4950	1.5000
180-Day Forward	.6651	.6629	1.5035	1.5086
Greece (Drachma)	.006309	.006289	158.50	159.00
Hong Kong (Dollar) ...	.12830	.12834	7.7945	7.7920
India (Rupee)	.05423	.05435	18.44	18.40
Indonesia (Rupiah)	.0005305	.0005305	1885.01	1885.01
Ireland (Punt)	1.7930	1.7830	.5577	.5609
Israel (Shekel)	.4965	.5050	2.0139	1.9803
Italy (Lira)	.0008961	.0008921	1116.00	1121.00
Japan (Yen)	.007605	.007536	131.50	132.70
30-Day Forward	.007598	.007528	131.62	132.83
90-Day Forward	.007584	.007515	131.85	133.07
180-Day Forward	.007573	.007504	132.04	133.26
Jordan (Dinar)	1.4995	1.4995	.6669	.6669
Kuwait (Dinar)	z	z	z	z
Lebanon (Pound)	.000955	.001013	1047.50	987.50
Malaysia (Ringgit)	.3708	.3705	2.6970	2.6990
Malta (Lira)	3.3784	3.3613	.2960	.2975
Mexico (Peso)				
Floating rate	.0003396	.0003418	2945.00	2926.00
Netherland (Guilder) .	.5966	.5942	1.6763	1.6830
New Zealand (Dollar) .	.5980	.5970	1.6722	1.6750

Source: The Wall Street Journal, January 29, 1991. Reprinted by permission of The Wall Street Journal, © 1991 Dow Jones & Company, Inc. All Rights Reserved Worldwide.

Figure 20.1 Foreign Exchange Quotations for January 28, 1991

within two business days. This exchange occurs through cable, wire, or electronic transfer. The **forward rate** is the price for delivery at some point in the future. The time is usually 30, 90, or 180 days, but may range up to two years. Figure 20.1 lists forward rates for currencies where a forward market exists.

Forward Rate

If the forward rate is higher than the spot rate, the currency is trading at a premium. If the forward rate is lower, the currency is trading at a discount. Figure 20.1 shows that the British pound is quoted at a **forward discount,** which means that market participants expect that currency to depreciate versus the U.S. dollar.

Forward Discount

The **forward premium,** FP, is expressed on an annual percentage basis by using the following equation:

Forward Premium

$$FP = \left(\frac{FR - SR}{SR}\right)\left(\frac{12}{n}\right)(100\%) \qquad (20.1)$$

where

$$FR = \text{Forward rate}$$
$$SR = \text{Spot rate}$$
$$n = \text{Number of months forward}$$

Eq. 20.1 is applied to the British pound in Figure 20.1, for 30 days.

$$FP = \left(\frac{1.9545 - 1.9655}{1.9655}\right)\left(\frac{12}{1}\right)(100\%)$$
$$= -6.72\%$$

Then, apply it for 180 days.

$$FP = \left(\frac{1.9079 - 1.9655}{1.9655}\right)\left(\frac{12}{6}\right)(100\%)$$
$$= -5.86\%$$

The negative values reflect a forward discount and suggest that market participants expect the spot rate to decrease in the future.

Forward to Spot Rate Relationship

Theorists and practitioners in international finance are interested in determining if the forward rate is a predictor of the future spot rate. Theorists say markets are efficient and the forward rate is an accurate predictor, if the following conditions are met: interest-rate parity and purchasing-power parity.

Interest-Rate Parity

Interest-rate parity implies that the forward premium on currency X is equal to the interest rate differential between countries X and Y, with the lower interest rate quoted at a forward premium. This suggests that if domestic interest rates are lower than a particular foreign rate, the foreign currency sells at a discount, and vice versa. For example, in the previous section, the 180-day forward discount for the British pound is –5.86 percent. Interest-rate parity requires the annual interest rate in Great Britain to be approximately 13.86 percent if the annual interest rate in the United States is 8.00 percent. An arbitrage opportunity exists when interest-rate parity does not hold.

> The interest rate in the United States is 8 percent, the interest rate in Great Britain is 16 percent, and the 180-day forward premium for the British pound is –5.86 percent. How is an arbitrage profit made?

The following activities allow an investor to pursue an arbitrage profit:

1. Borrow U.S. dollars at 8 percent.
2. Exchange the U.S. dollars for British pounds, at the spot rate.
3. Invest the British pounds at 16 percent for 180 days in the British money market.
4. Sell the British pounds at the 180-day forward rate.
5. Accept U.S. dollars in 180 days by delivering the British pounds invested in the British money market.
6. Repay loan of U.S. dollars, pocketing the profit.

Covered-Risk Arbitrage

This set of transactions is called **covered-risk arbitrage** since risk is covered by the forward market.

This arbitrage process produces interest-rate parity by causing the forward discount on the British pound to widen and the interest rate differential to narrow. The forward discount widens because (1) buying the British pound in the spot market increases the spot rate, and (2) selling the British pound at the forward rate depresses the forward rate. The interest rate differential narrows because (1) borrowing in the United States raises U.S. interest rates, and (2) investing in Great Britain lowers British interest rates.

Purchasing-Power Parity

Purchasing-power parity implies that the exchange rates between two countries depend on the rates of inflation in the two countries. This principle suggests that as the inflation rate for a country increases, the relative value of its currency decreases. If this were not so, then arbitrageurs would buy commodities in one market and sell in the other market, thereby reaping a profit. As a result, the difference in inflation rates is approximately equal to the decline in the exchange rate of the higher-interest country. For example, if the rate of inflation per year in the United States is 6 percent and is 10 percent in Great Britain, the British Pound would depreciate at a rate of 4 percent per year.

Foreign Exchange Participants

Foreign exchange market participants include large domestic and foreign banks, a small number of exchange brokers, domestic and foreign multinational companies, central banks, small foreign-exchange businesses, and speculators. The large commercial banks operate in the foreign exchange market to meet the needs of their customers: large multinational companies and small retail clients. Exchange brokers work quietly with these banks and other brokers to arrange deals, without disclosing if the bank plans to buy or to sell.

The foreign exchange market does not have a central meeting place to conduct business as do the stock exchanges. It is therefore comparable to the over-the-counter markets discussed in Chapter 12. The exchange market physically consists of trading desks at large commercial banks and the offices of foreign exchange brokers. These facilities are connected by wire and by electronic communication systems. Transactions made with these means are later confirmed in writing.

The large banks in the foreign exchange markets usually avoid taking positions in the market. This means that they attempt to square their positions—maintaining equality in their commitments to buy and sell. If the bank commits to buy more than it commits to sell, it establishes a long position. The reverse of this is a short position. Speculators, in contrast to banks, deliberately take long and short positions.

Central banks, such as the Federal Reserve System, try to maintain or influence exchange rates by buying and selling currencies. This is accomplished by maintaining a reserve of foreign currencies.

Currency Futures and Options

Future exchange contracts are bought and sold at the International Monetary Mart (IMM), part of the Chicago Mercantile Exchange. The trading is similar to commodity futures contracts on the Chicago Board of Trade. Currency futures traded include the British pound, Canadian dollar, Dutch guilder, French franc, German mark, Japanese yen, Mexican peso, and Swiss franc.

Hedgers and speculators take part in the currency futures market. Hedgers try to minimize risk, whereas speculators attempt to maximize profit. Hedgers sell a futures contract with the goal of buying it back at a lower price. Speculators buy futures contracts with the hope of selling at a higher price.

Options on currency futures are bought and sold on the Chicago Mercantile Exchange. Options traded include the British pound, German mark, and Swiss

Currency Futures Option

franc. The Philadelphia Exchange also trades the British pound, Canadian dollar, French franc, German mark, Japanese yen, and Swiss franc. A **currency futures option** gives the holder the right, but not the obligation, to buy or sell a futures contract at a fixed price on or before a specified expiration date. Figure 20.2 shows futures and options quotations from *The Wall Street Journal* for Monday, January 28, 1991.

The foreign exchange futures market and the forward exchange market are similar, but there are important differences. The futures market operates at a few locations and serves small businesses trying to avoid exchange risk as well as speculators. The forward market functions on a worldwide basis with large banks and brokers primarily serving multinational companies. Also, currency futures contracts are rarely exercised, whereas currency forward contracts are usually exercised at the maturity date.

Foreign Exchange Rate Risk

Multinational companies are exposed to exchange rate risk in their daily operations. These companies reduce such exposure by hedging. Hedging allows a future cost to be known, thus eliminating the variability of the market.

Forward Market Hedge

A **forward market hedge** requires a U.S. company to execute a contract in the forward exchange market to buy a fixed amount of foreign currency at the

FUTURES

	Open	High	Low	Settle	Change	Lifetime High	Lifetime Low	Open Interest
JAPANESE YEN (IMM)–12.5 million yen; $ per yen (.00)								
Mar	.7544	.7588	.7544	.7587	+ .0065	.8040	.6315	43,455
June	.7537	.7578	.7537	.7572	+ .0065	.8010	.6645	1,623
Sept		....	....	.7564	+ .0065	.7995	.7346	202
Dec		....	....	.7562	+ .0065	....	....	100
Est vol 13,326; vol Fri 18,609; open int 45,380, –716.								
DEUTSCHEMARK (IMM)–125,000 marks; $ per mark								
Mar	.6705	.6711	.6689	.6705	+ .0022	.6800	.5820	48,808
June	.6665	.6672	.6662	.6668	+ 0022	.6777	.6163	1,486
Est vol 16,982; vol Fri 23,614; open int 50,366, +527.								
CANADIAN DOLLAR (IMM)–100,000 dlrs.; $ per Can $								
Mar	.8555	.8563	.8550	.8555	+ .0014	.8665	.7990	22,927
June	.8504	.8504	.8492	.8495	+ .0013	.8601	.7995	2,797
Sept	.8450	.8455	.8449	.8446	+ .0012	.8545	.7985	1,691
Est vol 2,9765; vol Fri 11,067; open int 27,453, +227.								
BRITISH POUND (IMM)–62,500 pds.; $ per pound								
Mar	1.9450	1.9494	1.9432	1.9476	+.0122	1.9520	1.6580	23,386
June	1.9170	1.9200	1.9170	1.9198	+.0124	1.9310	1.7660	1,144
Est vol 8,219; vol Fri 10,024; open int 24,571, –190.								
SWISS FRANC (IMM)–125,000 francs; $ per franc								
Mar	.7919	.7929	.7895	.7915	+ .0019	.8055	.6500	31,650
June	.7900	.7905	.7872	.7894	+ .0021	.8050	.7065	658
Sept		....	....	.7874	+ .0022	.8015	.6916	141
Est vol 18,432; vol Fri 19,074; open int 32,453, +747.								
AUSTRALIAN DOLLAR (IMM)–100,000 dlrs.; $ per A.$								
Mar	.7775	.7784	.7760	.7777	+ .0062	.8200	.7500	1,782
Est vol 462; vol Fri 252; open int 1,855, +9.								

OPTIONS

PHILADELPHIA EXCHANGE

Option & Underlying	Strike Price	Calls–Last			Puts–Last		
		Feb	Mar	Jun	Feb	Mar	Jun
50,000 Australian Dollars-cents per unit.							
ADollr	...76	2.35	2.43	r	r	r	r
78.25	...77	1.37	r	r	r	r	r
78.25	...81	r	r	0.62	r	r	r
31,250 British Pounds-cents per unit.							
BPound	170	s	r	r	s	r	0.30
196.48	.180	r	r	r	r	r	1.25
196.48	.185	r	r	r	r	0.33	2.46
196.48	187½	8.80	r	r	0.05	r	r
196.48	.190	6.48	6.40	r	r	1.23	r
196.48	192½	r	4.42	r	0.60	r	r
196.48	.195	2.08	r	r	1.35	3.05	r
196.48	197½	0.98	1.77	r	2.70	r	r
196.48	.200	r	1.08	r	r	r	r
196.48	202½	r	0.61	r	r	r	r
196.48	.205	r	0.30	1.43	r	r	r
50,000 Canadian Dollars-cents per unit.							
CDollr	...84	r	r	r	r	0.15	r
86.02	...85	r	r	r	r	0.39	r
86.02	.85½	r	r	r	r	0.58	r
86.02	...86	r	r	r	0.46	r	r

Source: The Wall Street Journal, January 29, 1991. Reprinted by permission of The Wall Street Journal, © 1991 Dow Jones & Company, Inc. All Rights Reserved Worldwide.

Figure 20.2 Foreign Exchange Futures and Options Quotations

forward rate. The cost of this transaction is known, in contrast to an exchange based on a future spot rate which is variable.

> The Connelly Corporation must pay a British company 1,000,000 pounds in 180 days. Based on Monday's quote in Figure 20.1, what is the fixed amount the Connelly Corporation must pay using a forward market hedge?

The Connelly Corporation must pay $1,907,900, £1,000,000(1.9079), based on the 180-day forward rate. Thus, the corporation knows the amount with certainty. The spot rate in 180 days is unknown.

A **money market hedge** requires a U.S. company to borrow funds from a U.S. bank, exchange the funds for foreign currency, and invest in the foreign money market until needed for a transaction. The net cost of this arrangement depends upon the loan interest rate and the yield on the money market securities.

Money Market Hedge

> The Connelly Corporation must pay a British company 1,000,000 pounds in 180 days. Assume that money may be borrowed in the United States at 10 percent and invested on a short-term basis in Great Britain at 9 percent. Based on Figure 20.1, what is the cost of this transaction, using a money market hedge?

EC Debates Opening Telephone Market

The next big step in the dismantling of Europe's national telephone monopolies is under discussion in Brussels. At stake, proponents say, is faster economic growth and lower charges for telephoning from one European country to another. Later this month the European Community Commission will resume deliberations on a plan to end state monopolies over telephone traffic between one EC state and another and to let private companies offer competing services. If adopted, the plan would be a bombshell in the hyper-regulated, high-priced world of European telecommunications. Currently, in every EC country except Britain, a single state-owned company or organization has a legal monopoly over most telecommunications services, international and do-mestic. The plan under consideration by EC Commissioners represents the biggest challenge yet to those monopoly profits. An economic study ordered by the EC Commission concluded that extensive liberalization of telecommunications would more than triple the overall European market for telecommunications services in 20 years and generate 1.2 trillion European currency units of cash to modernize the continent's phone systems.

The Connelly Corporation must borrow $1,965,500, £1,000,000(1.9655), based on the spot rate. This amount of money is exchanged for 1,000,000 British pounds. This foreign currency is then invested in the money market of Great Britain. The cost to the Connelly Corporation is $9,692.88, $1,965,500(180/365)(0.10 − 0.09).

WORKING CAPITAL MANAGEMENT

The principles of working capital management discussed earlier in this text apply to multinational as well as domestic corporations. Most decisions involve a risk-return tradeoff. There are, however, important differences for financial managers: (1) more options for funds (parent versus local sources), (2) greater risks (political and exchange rate risk), (3) more diversity in local conditions (geographical dispersion, not necessarily a matter of distance), and (4) varying tax considerations (differential tax rates).

The Transfer of Corporate Funds

Unbundling

Unbundling is the policy of dividing the transfer of corporate funds into separate cash flows. Typically, multinational corporations classify funds from an affiliate to the parent as (1) royalties, the compensation for specialized knowledge, (2) fees, the compensation for services, (3) prices, the compensation for product shipped, (4) debt payments, the compensation for loans, and (5) dividends, the compensation for ownership. The practice of unbundling reduces tax liabilities in the host country, avoids limitations on dividends, and allows the effective use of transfer pricing.

Transfer Pricing

Transfer pricing is the establishment of intracorporate prices for inputs, services, and technology in such a way as to meet corporate objectives. Multinational corporations often use reinvoicing centers located in tax havens to control transfer pricing policy. This arrangement allows the company to realize profits in a low-taxed country and to move funds to countries with more stable currencies. Certain practical matters limit the use of transfer pricing. Multinational companies must consider their relationships with the host company, and tax regulations at home and in the host country limit the usefulness of this mechanism.

In less-developed countries, the host government may attempt to block the transfer of funds. This action is often motivated by a shortage of foreign exchange but may be rationalized as necessary to promote local investment. The strategy for dealing with blocked funds depends upon the severity of the situation. Strategies range from unbundling and transfer pricing to making investments in the host country that are unrelated to the primary business of the affiliate.

Receivables Management

A multinational company that exports its products must determine the currency of invoicing and whether to offer cash terms or credit terms. The currency-of-invoicing decision controls which company will accept the exchange rate risk. The exporter shifts the risk to the other party by invoicing in the currency of the exporter. Cash terms may be in the form of cash in advance or in the form of cash on delivery. Credit terms include the credit period, the cash discount (if any), and the kind of credit instrument.

International financial managers make the decision on credit terms by comparing incremental profits with incremental costs. This is the approach used by the domestic financial manager as well, but the international situation includes another wrinkle: foreign exchange losses on credit sales by a subsidiary.

A subsidiary of a U.S. corporation in Great Britain is considering relaxing its credit terms to include customers who were previously denied credit. Financial analysts estimate this action will cause sales to increase by 1,000,000 British pounds per year. The contribution to profit on these sales is 20 percent. Bad debt expense for the new customers is 2 percent. The cost of carrying the additional accounts receivable is 14 percent per year. Credit terms are net 30. What is the maximum depreciation of the British pound against the U.S. dollar that would allow extending credit to the new customers?

The maximum depreciation of the British pound against the U.S. dollar occurs at the point where incremental profits equal incremental costs. In this example, incremental profit, IP, is given by increased sales multiplied by contribution to profit.

$$IP = £1,000,000(0.20)$$
$$= £200,000$$

Incremental costs, IP, is given by bad debt losses (increased sales multiplied by bad debt ratio) *plus* the cost of financing additional receivables (increased sales multiplied by variable costs as a percentage of sales multiplied by annual rate for carrying receivables multiplied by fraction of a year) *plus* the foreign exchange losses on credit sales (increased sales multiplied by one minus bad debt ratio multiplied by expected rate of depreciation of the foreign currency, D). In this example, D is the percent depreciation in the British pound.

$$
\begin{aligned}
IC &= £1,000,000(0.02) + £1,000,000(0.80)(0.14)(30/365) + £1,000,000(1 - .02)D \\
&= £20,000 + £9,205.4794 + £980,000D \\
&= £29,205.4794 + £980,000D
\end{aligned}
$$

Set incremental profits equal to incremental costs.

$$£200,000 = £29,205.4794 + £980,000D$$

Then, solve for D.

$$D = 0.174 \text{ or } 17.4 \text{ percent}$$

Since this level of depreciation over the period of a month is unlikely, the granting of the additional credit is indicated.

Inventory Management

Inventory management in a multinational environment presents many of the challenges found in the domestic climate. The inventory models studied in Chapter 17 apply equally well to international operations. There are, however, complicating factors that make practical application more difficult. Geographically diverse locations, longer or unpredictable lead times, supply disruption due to political strife, and varying import controls add a new dimension to the problem. As with receivables management, the financial manager must consider currency exchange risk.

Multinational corporations stockpile their products throughout the world to counter unpredictable circumstances. Key variables in this decision to stockpile are (1) the rate of depreciation of the local currency against the U.S. currency, (2) forecasted increases of inputs in terms of the local currency, (3) inventory carrying costs, and (4) the availability of alternate sources of supply. As with many areas of finance, the final decision is largely a matter of judgment.

Cash Management

Centralization is the most important concept in cash management. This involves centralizing the decision-making process involving the movement of cash. A centralized system allows (1) minimum levels of cash, (2) investment of excess cash, (3) liquidity throughout the organization, (4) transfer pricing, (5) hedging strategies, and (6) system netting. The following paragraphs discuss the last item.

System netting consists of netting out receivables and payables of company units throughout the world in order to minimize the net amounts transferred. This reduces transactions costs by decreasing the number of transfers and currency conversions.

The McDonnell Corporation has affiliates in Canada, India, and Japan. Table 20.1 shows the payables/receivables matrix for the company. What are the net transfers required to remove the imbalance of payments?

Table 20.2 summarizes the net payments and net receipts for the McDonnell Corporation. The required transfers include a $300,000 payment from Canada to the United States and a $200,000 payment from Japan to India.

FINANCING THE MULTINATIONAL

A multinational corporation finances foreign projects in the home country, in the host country, or in a third country. If the parent corporation raises funds at home, it may hedge the risk by selling a contract in the forward exchange market. If the company raises funds in the host country, it acquires an effective hedge against foreign exchange risk. If the parent raises funds in a third country, it may enjoy lower rates while inviting the risks of inflation.

TABLE 20.1 McDonnell Corporation Payables/Receivables Matrix (thousands of dollars)

| | PAYING UNITS | | | | |
RECEIVING UNITS	UNITED STATES	CANADA	INDIA	JAPAN	TOTAL RECEIPTS
United States	—	500	300	600	1,400
Canada	400	—	200	300	900
India	200	300	—	500	1,000
Japan	500	400	300	—	1,200
Total payments	1,100	1,200	800	1,400	4,500

TABLE 20.2 McDonnell Corporation Net Payments and Net Receipts

	TOTAL PAYMENTS	TOTAL RECEIPTS	NET PAYMENT	NET RECEIPT
United States	1,100	1,400	—	300
Canada	1,200	900	300	—
India	800	1,000	—	200
Japan	1,400	1,200	200	—
Total	4,500	4,500	500	500

Short-Term Financing

Eurodollars

Eurocurrency Markets

Eurodollars are U.S. dollars deposited in foreign banks or foreign branches of U.S. banks. The foreign bank then lends these funds as Eurodollar loans, primarily to foreign subsidiaries of U.S. multinational companies. **Eurocurrency markets** are markets in which Eurobanks conduct transactions in currencies foreign to the banking location.

Eurobanks make loans on a floating-rate basis. The interest rate is tied to the London Interbank Offered Rate (LIBOR), a rate published daily in *The Wall Street Journal*. Large multinational corporations borrow about 0.5 percent above LIBOR, a borrowing rate normally below the stated U.S. bank prime rates. Eurocurrency loans range from $500,000 to $500,000,000 and include maturities from overnight to 10 years.

International Bond Markets

International Bond

Foreign Bond

Eurobond

An **international bond** is a bond initially issued outside the country of the borrower, and it is classified as either a foreign bond or a Eurobond. A **foreign bond** is an international bond denominated in the currency of the country in which it is issued. For example, if a U.S. multinational corporation issues bonds in Japan denominated in yen, they are foreign bonds. A **Eurobond** is an international bond denominated in a currency other than the country in which it is issued. For example, if a U.S. multinational corporation issues bonds in Germany, they are Eurobonds, or specifically a Euromark bond issue.

The U.S. dollar dominates the Eurobond market. This is primarily explained by the lower capital cost for borrowers. These bonds are not subject to SEC registration, thereby reducing disclosure requirements. The majority of the issues are the result of a public offering, although some are privately placed. Unlike most foreign bonds, companies issue Eurobonds in bearer form, allowing ownership to be established by possession.

The Swiss franc dominates the foreign bond market. This is the result of the low interest rates and the stability of the currency. Foreign bonds issued in the United States are called Yankee bonds and are often listed on the New York Stock Exchange.

International Equity Markets

Multinational corporations find that it is often possible to raise equity capital at a lower cost by using foreign markets. In many countries, the equity markets are simply too small to accommodate the needs of large multinational corporations. This has led to the emergence of the **Euro-equity market,** the world market that deals in international issues. London is the center of this market.

The New York Stock Exchange and other regional exchanges list a limited number of foreign stocks, the number kept small by the standards required by the exchange and the SEC. Most foreign stock trading in the United States is in the form of **American Depository Receipts (ADRs).** ADRs are certificates denominated in U.S. dollars issued by a U.S. bank. Since the bank holds the underlying security, investors do not exchange currencies and do not take possession of the stock certificates. Investors buy ADRs in an attempt to secure international diversification.

Multinational corporations also offer nonvoting stocks, which allow investors to receive dividends while sacrificing control. The participation certificate (PC), primarily offered by the Swiss, is a form of nonvoting stock. Institutional investors often purchase these securities. In some countries such as Germany and Austria, the dividends from nonvoting stocks are fully or partially deductible from income, as is interest.

Euro-Equity Market

American Depository Receipts

Multinational Banking

Multinational banking takes place in many forms. The simplest approach is **correspondent banking,** where a domestic bank keeps a correspondent account with a bank in another country. The foreign bank makes the necessary transactions upon request.

A domestic bank may also have foreign branches, foreign subsidiary banks, or Edge Act Corporations. A **foreign branch** functions according to the rules of the foreign country while operating under the total control of the domestic bank. A **foreign subsidiary bank** is incorporated in the foreign country, and this clouds the issue of control due to the separate board of directors. An **Edge Act corporation** is an American banking subsidiary with wider latitude than other foreign subsidiaries in conducting business.

Correspondent Banking

Foreign Branch

Foreign Subsidiary Bank

Edge Act Corporation

MULTINATIONAL CAPITAL BUDGETING

Multinational capital budgeting in a basic sense is no different from domestic capital budgeting: Incremental domestic cash flows are discounted at an appropriate rate. The project is accepted if the resultant net present value (NPV) is positive and rejected if it is negative.

Calculation of Net Present Value

The procedure for calculating NPV involves a four step process. (1) Estimate cash flows in terms of the foreign currency. (2) Convert the cash flows to the domestic equivalents. (3) Determine the appropriate discount rate. (4) Calculate the net present value using the information in steps 2 and 3.

The estimation of cash flows is not the same as with domestic capital budgeting. The process of unbundling previously discussed in this chapter complicates the cash flow forecast. The financial analyst must consider the following factors: royalties, fees, transfer prices, and debt payments, in addition to host country taxes. In less-developed countries, the analyst must judge if the host government plans to block the transfer of funds.

The conversion of the cash flows to the domestic equivalents may be done in two ways: (1) by forecasting exchange rates for the future years, or (2) by using interest-rate parity and purchasing-power parity to predict the future exchange rates. The first method ties acceptance or rejection of the project to estimates of future exchange rates, a practice that may encourage analysts to be overly optimistic. The second method is more procedural and detached.

The expected exchange rate, EER_N, N years in the future, is given by the following formula:

$$EER_N = SR \left[\frac{(1 + i_d)^N}{(1 + i_f)^N} \right]$$
(20.2)

where

$$SR = \text{Spot rate}$$
$$i_d = \text{Domestic interest rate}$$
$$i_f = \text{Foreign interest rate}$$
$$N = \text{Number of years in the future}$$

This equation is developed using concepts of interest-rate parity and purchasing-power parity.

The determination of the appropriate marginal cost of capital involves the marginal cost of capital of the parent company adjusted for the level of risk of the project. The risk depends on the political risk in the host country and the diversification from international investment. Political risk involves major changes in the form of the government as well as the attack on a specific industry through nationalization. With international diversification, systematic risk is reduced thereby reducing the cost of capital of the parent company.

The calculation of net present value is illustrated using a cash flow diagram:

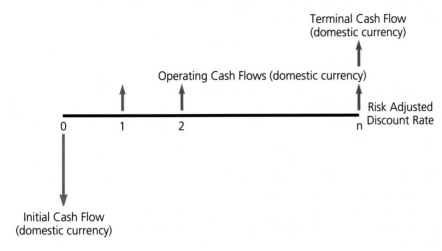

The procedures of Chapter 7 apply when the cash flows and discount rate are known.

The Carlton Corporation is considering a new project in Great Britain. A financial analyst for the company, after studying the effects of unbundling and transfer pricing, estimates the cash flows (in British pounds) as follows:

Year	Cash Flow
0	−£100,000
1	£ 30,000
2	£ 30,000
3	£ 30,000
4	£ 30,000
5	£ 50,000

The interest rate is 8 percent in the United States and 13 percent in Great Britain. The spot rate for the British pound is given in Figure 20.1. The marginal cost of capital is 12 percent for the Carlton Corporation, and considering the effects of international diversification, the risk-adjusted discount rate is 3 percent higher. What is the net present value of the project in U.S. dollars?

Since the project cash flows are already known, the first step is to convert the cash flows to their domestic equivalents. This requires calculation of the expected exchange rates for each of the five years, using Eq. 20.2. For year 1, use a spot rate from Figure 20.1 of $1.9655,

$$EER_N = SR\left[\frac{(1 + i_d)^N}{(1 + i_f)^N}\right]$$

$$EER_1 = \$1.9655\left[\frac{(1 + 0.08)^1}{(1 + 0.13)^1}\right]$$

$$= \$1.8785$$

Apply the equation to year 2.

$$EER_2 = \$1.9655\left[\frac{(1 + 0.08)^2}{(1 + 0.13)^2}\right]$$

$$= \$1.7954$$

Then, apply the equation to year 3.

$$EER_3 = \$1.9655\left[\frac{(1 + 0.08)^3}{(1 + 0.13)^3}\right]$$

$$= \$1.7160$$

Next, apply the equation to year 4.

$$EER_4 = \$1.9655\left[\frac{(1 + 0.08)^4}{(1 + 0.13)^4}\right]$$

$$= \$1.6400$$

Finally, apply the equation to year 5.

$$EER_5 = \$1.9655\left[\frac{(1 + 0.08)^5}{(1 + 0.13)^5}\right]$$

$$= \$1.5675$$

The British cash flows are converted to their domestic equivalents by multiplying by the expected exchange rates.

Year	British Cash Flow	Expected Exchange Rate	U.S. Cash Flow
0	−£100,000	$1.9655	−$196,550
1	£ 30,000	$1.8785	$ 56,355
2	£ 30,000	$1.7954	$ 53,862
3	£ 30,000	$1.7160	$ 51,480
4	£ 30,000	$1.6400	$ 49,200
5	£ 50,000	$1.5675	$ 78,375

The net present value is calculated by applying the U.S cash flows and the risk-adjusted discount rate of 15 percent to Eq. 7.1.

$$NPV = -\$196,550 + \frac{\$56,355}{(1+0.15)^1} + \frac{\$53,862}{(1+0.15)^2}$$

$$+ \frac{\$51,480}{(1+0.15)^3} + \frac{\$49,200}{(1+0.15)^4} + \frac{\$78,375}{(1+0.15)^5}$$

$$= -\$196,550 + \$56,355(PVF_{15\%,1}) + \$53,862(PVF_{15\%,2})$$

$$+ \$51,480(PVF_{15\%,3}) + \$49,200(PVF_{15\%,4}) + \$78,375(PVF_{15\%,5})$$

$$= -\$5,873$$

The negative net present value indicates rejection. The internal rate of return is 13.78 percent. This implies the project would have been accepted if 12 percent were used instead of the risk-adjusted value of 15 percent.

The complete cash flow diagram follows.

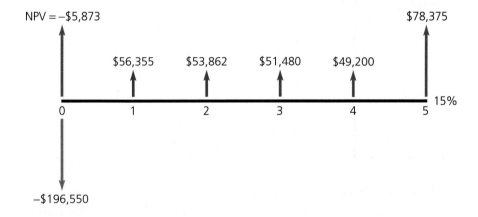

Tax Considerations

A multinational company from the United States may take a tax credit for taxes paid to foreign governments. The amount is limited to what would be charged had U.S. rates been applied to that income. Since the Tax Reform Act of 1986 reduced the highest marginal corporate tax rate to 34 percent, multinational companies in high-tax countries may not be able to take advantage of the entire credit. As a result, U.S. multinationals look carefully at the level of foreign taxes.

The Tax Reform Act of 1986 contained other changes directed specifically at multinational companies. Included were provisions applying to tax deferrals on foreign income, capital gains from stock sales, and withholding taxes. Since many states base their taxes on the federal system, these modifications affect state taxes on foreign income as well.

RJR, Ingersoll-Rand Join Growing List

At a recent banquet with several hundred business executives, Russia's acting prime minister, Yegor Gaidar, made a little joke: While xenophobic conservatives criticize the government for selling out the country to Western capitalists, he said, little do they know how hard it is to persuade those same capitalists to buy in. Everybody laughed. But European capitalists have been sniffing out investments in Russia for some time, and now even Americans are starting to buy the official pitch that communism is dead and a free market is being born. A small but steady stream of U.S. investment has begun to flow into Russian manufacturing. R.J. Reynolds Tobacco International, a division of RJR Nabisco Inc., announced its purchase of a 52% stake in St. Petersburg's Uritski Tobacco factory. Also, Ingersoll-Rand Company announced a joint stock company in which it will have majority control. Neither U.S. company has manufactured before in the huge and largely untapped Russian market, though Ingersoll-Rand has sold tools in Russia since 1903. Both will sell their products for rubles, and figure the currency will become convertible by the time their operations become profitable, in four years or so.

Source: Laurie Hayes, "RJR, Ingersoll-Rand Join Growing List of U.S.-Russia Manufacturing Ventures," *The Wall Street Journal*, July 16, 1992. Reprinted by permission of The Wall Street Journal, © 1992 Dow Jones & Company, Inc. All Rights Reserved Worldwide.

SUMMARY

This chapter focuses on the following learning objectives:

1. Describing the mechanics of foreign exchange rate quotations and the functioning of foreign exchange markets.

   The exchange rate is the price of a currency in terms of another currency. The quotation of U.S. dollars per unit of foreign currency is the conventional way of reporting; foreign currency per U.S. dollar is the European system. Markets are efficient, and the forward rate is an accurate predictor under the following conditions: interest-rate parity and purchasing-power parity. The large banks in the foreign exchange markets attempt to square their positions—maintaining equality in their commitments to buy and sell.

2. Explaining the principles of multinational working capital management.

   The principles of working capital management apply to multinational as well as domestic corporations. Most decisions involve a risk-return tradeoff. There are, however, important differences for financial managers: (1) more options for funds (parent versus local sources), (2) greater risks (political and exchange rate risk), (3) more diversity in local conditions (geographical dispersion, not necessarily a matter of distance), and (4) varying tax considerations (differential tax rates).

3. Discussing how to finance foreign projects using hedging techniques to reduce risk.

   Multinational corporations find that it is often possible to raise equity capital at a lower cost by using foreign markets. This has led to the Euro-equity market, the world market that deals in international issues, with London the center. Most foreign stock trading in the United States is in the form of American Depository Receipts. Since the bank holds the underlying security, investors do not exchange currencies and do not take possession of the stock certificates.

4. Applying capital budgeting techniques to multinational projects.

   Multinational capital budgeting involves four steps. (1) Estimate cash flows in terms of the foreign currency. (2) Convert cash flows to the domestic equivalents. (3) Determine the appropriate discount rate. (4) Calculate net present value using the information in steps 2 and 3. The conversion of the cash flows to the domestic equivalents may be done in two ways: (1) by forecasting exchange rates for the future years, or (2) by using interest-rate parity and purchasing-power parity to predict the future exchange rates.

KEY TERMS

American Depository Receipts, 561
Correspondent banking, 561
Covered-risk arbitrage, 552
Currency futures option, 554
Edge Act corporation, 561
Eurobond, 560
Eurocurrency market, 560

Eurodollars, 560
Euro-equity market, 561
Exchange rate, 549
Exchange rate quotation, 550
Foreign bond, 560
Foreign branch, 561
Foreign subsidiary bank, 561
Forward discount, 551
Forward market hedge, 554

Forward premium, 551
Forward rate, 551
Interest-rate parity, 552
International bond, 560
Money market hedge, 555
Purchasing-power parity, 552
Spot rate, 550
Transfer pricing, 556
Unbundling, 556

QUESTIONS

20.1 Explain how exchange rates are quoted.

20.2 What are the differences between the terms spot rate and forward rate?

20.3 Explain trading at a premium and trading at a discount in relation to forward rates.

20.4   What is interest-rate parity, and how does this relate to differences in interest rates between countries?

20.5   What is covered-risk arbitrage, and how does this cause interest-rate parity?

20.6   What is purchasing-power parity, and how does this relate to currency depreciation?

20.7   Who are the participants in the foreign exchange market?

20.8   Where does the foreign exchange market meet, and what physical facilities does it have?

20.9   What are long and short positions in the foreign exchange market, and what does it mean to square a position?

20.10   Where are currency futures traded, and how do hedgers and speculators participate in this market?

20.11   What is a currency option, and where are they traded?

20.12   What are the differences between the foreign exchange futures market and the forward exchange market?

20.13   What are the differences between a forward market hedge and a money market hedge?

20.14   What are the important differences between domestic and multinational working capital management?

20.15   In the process of unbundling, in what categories do multinational corporations classify funds from an affiliate to the parent?

20.16   How do multinational corporations use transfer pricing to control cash flows?

20.17   In receivables management, how does the currency-of-invoicing decision control which company will accept the exchange rate risk?

20.18   What additional factor must a credit manager consider when deciding on credit terms in an international situation?

20.19   How is inventory management in a multinational environment different from that of a domestic climate, and how does this affect the lead time and reorder point?

20.20   What are the key variables in the decision of a multinational corporation to stockpile products?

20.21   How is centralization important in cash management?

20.22   How does system netting reduce transactions costs?

20.23   Define the following terms: Eurodollars, Eurodollar loans, Eurocurrency markets, and Eurobanks.

20.24   Explain the basis on which Eurobanks make loans.

20.25   How do foreign bonds and Eurobonds differ?

20.26 Explain how American Depository Receipts (ADRs) are used to invest in foreign securities.

20.27 What are the forms in which multinational banking takes place?

20.28 What is the procedure for calculating the net present value of a multinational project?

20.29 What effect did the Tax Reform Act of 1986 have on foreign tax credits?

20.30 What *is* the secret to global competitiveness?

20.31 How would opening the telephone market in Europe increase the demand for telecommunications services?

20.32 Why are companies such as Ingersoll-Rand interested in investment in Russia?

PROBLEMS

20.1 **(U.S. Equivalent)** The Hart corporation received 512,000 French francs (FF). Using Figure 20.1 for currency quotations, what is the U.S. equivalent in dollars?

20.2 **(Forward Premium)** Calculate the forward premium for the French franc at 30, 90, and 180 days, based on Figure 20.1.

20.3 **(Arbitrage Profit)** The interest rate in the United States is 8 percent and 15 percent in France. Based on the 180-day forward rate for the French franc in Figure 20.1, would it be possible to make an arbitrage profit? If so, explain the steps.

20.4 **(Forward Market Hedge)** The Hamilton Company must pay a French company 10,000,000 French francs in 180 days. Based on Figure 20.1, what is the fixed amount the Hamilton Company must pay, using a forward market hedge?

20.5 **(Money Market Hedge)** The Hamilton Company must pay a French company 10,000,000 French francs in 90 days. Assume that money may be borrowed in the United States at nine percent and invested on a short-term basis in France at seven percent. Based on Figure 20.1, what is the cost of this transaction, using a money market hedge?

20.6 **(Maximum Depreciation)** A subsidiary of a U.S. corporation in France is considering relaxing its credit terms to include customers who were previously denied credit. Financial analysts estimate this action will cause sales to increase by 10,000,000 French francs per year. The contribution to profit on these sales is 25 percent. Bad debt expense for the new customers is three percent. The cost of carrying the additional accounts receivable is 15 percent per year. Credit terms are net 40. What is the maximum depreciation of the French franc against the U.S. dollar that would allow extending credit to the new customers?

20.7 **(Net Transfers)** The Bush Corporation has affiliates in the United States, Mexico, Peru, and Spain. The table below shows the payables/receivables matrix for the company. What are the net transfers required to remove the imbalance of payments?

BUSH CORPORATION PAYABLES/RECEIVABLES MATRIX (THOUSANDS OF DOLLARS)

	PAYING UNITS				
RECEIVING UNITS	**UNITED STATES**	**MEXICO**	**PERU**	**SPAIN**	**TOTAL RECEIPTS**
Brazil	—	600	400	500	1,500
Mexico	400	—	300	500	1,200
Peru	300	400	—	300	1,000
Spain	500	300	500	—	1,300
Total Payments	1,200	1,300	1,200	1,300	5,000

20.8 **(Net Present Value)** The Matlock Company plans a new project in France. A financial analyst for the company, after studying the effects of unbundling and transfer pricing, estimates the cash flows (in French francs) as follows:

Year	Cash Flow
0	−FF1,000,000
1	FF350,000
2	FF350,000
3	FF350,000
4	FF350,000
5	FF500,000

The interest rate is 8 percent in the United States and 12 percent in France. The spot rate for the French franc is given in Figure 20.1. The marginal cost of capital is 11 percent for the Carlton Corporation, and considering the effects of international diversification, the risk-adjusted discount rate is three percent higher. What is the net present value of the project in U.S. dollars?

A Case Problem

NorPharm was engaged in the research, development, production, and distribution of medical imaging contrast media. Contrast media enhanced the effectiveness of medical imaging techniques in viewing and analyzing soft tissues in the human body. In addition, the company developed, manufactured, and distributed prescription and other therapeutic drugs. The company, based in Norway, derived approximately 75 percent of its operating revenues from foreign sources.

NorPharm's foreign operating revenues were subject to the impact of currency fluctuations. The results of operations were most sensitive to exchange rate fluctuations of the U.S. dollar, since the United States represented the most significant market for the company's products and services. In the past, there had been great volatility in the exchange rate between the Norwegian kroner and the U.S. dollar.

> *To reduce exposure to foreign currency exchange even more, NorPharm hedged through borrowing in foreign currencies and forward exchange contracts.*

Since 1990, the Norwegian kroner had been linked to the European Monetary System, and this tended to reduce overall exchange rate volatility. To reduce exposure to foreign currency exchange even more, NorPharm hedged through borrowing in foreign currencies and forward exchange contracts. These methods were used to hedge receivables and liabilities denominated in foreign currencies and to manage the currency composition of the company's loan portfolio.

Under the Norwegian Tax Reform Act, in 1992 the nominal tax rate was reduced from 50.8% to 28.0%, an apparent major reduction of taxes. However, other aspects of the Tax Reform Act actually increased the effective tax rate of the company: (1) rates under the declining balance method of accelerated depreciation were reduced, (2) the provision to postpone 23% of taxable profit each year was abolished, and (3) dividends which were previously deductible in computing taxes were now taxed at the 28% tax rate.

In accordance with Norwegian law, NorPharm established a Corporate Assembly with 18 members. The shareholders elected 12 members while NorPharm employees elected 6 members. Major investments and changes that affect the number or allocation of employees were subject to approval by the Assembly. The overall control of policy and management of the company was vested in the Board of Directors.

NorPharm had paid an annual dividend on its equity capital for over 50 years. Under Norwegian law, the payment of dividends must be proposed by the Board of directors, reviewed by the Corporate Assembly, and approved by the shareholders at the annual meeting. Interim dividends were not permitted. Under Norwegian foreign exchange controls, a non-Norwegian resident could receive dividend payments, provided that such payment was made through a licensed bank.

Leading Questions

1. What problems would NorPharm encounter in working in a multinational environment?
2. How does management at NorPharm differ from management in a U.S. domestic corporation?

Appendix A

$$\text{Present Value Factor } PVF_{k\%,n} = \frac{1}{(1 + k)^n}$$

n	1%	2%	3%	4%	5%	6%	7%	8%	9%	10%	11%
1	.9901	.9804	.9709	.9615	.9524	.9434	.9346	.9259	.9174	.9091	.9009
2	.9803	.9612	.9426	.9246	.9070	.8900	.8734	.8573	.8417	.8264	.8116
3	.9706	.9423	.9151	.8890	.8638	.8396	.8163	.7938	.7722	.7513	.7312
4	.9610	.9238	.8885	.8548	.8227	.7921	.7629	.7350	.7084	.6830	.6587
5	.9515	.9057	.8626	.8219	.7835	.7473	.7130	.6806	.6499	.6209	.5935
6	.9420	.8880	.8375	.7903	.7462	.7050	.6663	.6302	.5963	.5645	.5346
7	.9327	.8706	.8131	.7599	.7107	.6651	.6227	.5835	.5470	.5132	.4817
8	.9235	.8535	.7894	.7307	.6768	.6274	.5820	.5403	.5019	.4665	.4339
9	.9143	.8368	.7664	.7026	.6446	.5919	.5439	.5002	.4604	.4241	.3909
10	.9053	.8203	.7441	.6756	.6139	.5584	.5083	.4632	.4224	.3855	.3522
11	.8963	.8043	.7224	.6496	.5847	.5268	.4751	.4289	.3875	.3505	.3173
12	.8874	.7885	.7014	.6246	.5568	.4970	.4440	.3971	.3555	.3186	.2858
13	.8787	.7730	.6810	.6006	.5303	.4688	.4150	.3677	.3262	.2897	.2575
14	.8700	.7579	.6611	.5775	.5051	.4423	.3878	.3405	.2992	.2633	.2320
15	.8613	.7430	.6419	.5553	.4810	.4173	.3624	.3152	.2745	.2394	.2090
16	.8528	.7284	.6232	.5339	.4581	.3936	.3387	.2919	.2519	.2176	.1883
17	.8444	.7142	.6050	.5134	.4363	.3714	.3166	.2703	.2311	.1978	.1696
18	.8360	.7002	.5874	.4936	.4155	.3503	.2959	.2502	.2120	.1799	.1528
19	.8277	.6864	.5703	.4746	.3957	.3305	.2765	.2317	.1945	.1635	.1377
20	.8195	.6730	.5537	.4564	.3769	.3118	.2584	.2145	.1784	.1486	.1240
21	.8114	.6598	.5375	.4388	.3589	.2942	.2415	.1987	.1637	.1351	.1117
22	.8034	.6468	.5219	.4220	.3418	.2775	.2257	.1839	.1502	.1228	.1007
23	.7954	.6342	.5067	.4057	.3256	.2618	.2109	.1703	.1378	.1117	.0907
24	.7876	.6217	.4919	.3901	.3101	.2470	.1971	.1577	.1264	.1015	.0817
25	.7798	.6095	.4776	.3751	.2953	.2330	.1842	.1460	.1160	.0923	.0736
26	.7720	.5976	.4637	.3607	.2812	.2198	.1722	.1352	.1064	.0839	.0663
27	.7644	.5859	.4502	.3468	.2678	.2074	.1609	.1252	.0976	.0763	.0597
28	.7568	.5744	.4371	.3335	.2551	.1956	.1504	.1159	.0895	.0693	.0538
29	.7493	.5631	.4243	.3207	.2429	.1846	.1406	.1073	.0822	.0630	.0485
30	.7419	.5521	.4120	.3083	.2314	.1741	.1314	.0994	.0754	.0573	.0437
32	.7273	.5306	.3883	.2851	.2099	.1550	.1147	.0852	.0634	.0474	.0355
34	.7130	.5100	.3660	.2636	.1904	.1379	.1002	.0730	.0534	.0391	.0288
36	.6989	.4902	.3450	.2437	.1727	.1227	.0875	.0626	.0449	.0323	.0234
38	.6852	.4712	.3252	.2253	.1566	.1092	.0765	.0537	.0378	.0267	.0190
40	.6717	.4529	.3066	.2083	.1420	.0972	.0668	.0460	.0318	.0221	.0154
42	.6584	.4353	.2890	.1926	.1288	.0865	.0583	.0395	.0268	.0183	.0125
44	.6454	.4184	.2724	.1780	.1169	.0770	.0509	.0338	.0226	.0151	.0101
46	.6327	.4022	.2567	.1646	.1060	.0685	.0445	.0290	.0190	.0125	.0082
48	.6203	.3865	.2420	.1522	.0961	.0610	.0389	.0249	.0160	.0103	.0067
50	.6080	.3715	.2281	.1407	.0872	.0543	.0339	.0213	.0134	.0085	.0054
52	.5961	.3571	.2150	.1301	.0791	.0483	.0297	.0183	.0113	.0070	.0044
54	.5843	.3432	.2027	.1203	.0717	.0430	.0259	.0157	.0095	.0058	.0036
56	.5728	.3229	.1910	.1112	.0651	.0383	.0226	.0134	.0080	.0048	.0029
58	.5615	.3171	.1801	.1028	.0590	.0341	.0198	.0115	.0067	.0040	.0024
60	.5504	.3048	.1697	.0951	.0535	.0303	.0173	.0099	.0057	.0033	.0019

12%	13%	14%	15%	16%	17%	18%	19%	20%	25%	30%	35%
.8929	.8850	.8772	.8696	.8621	.8547	.8475	.8403	.8333	.8000	.7692	.7407
.7972	.7831	.7695	.7561	.7432	.7305	.7182	.7062	.6944	.6400	.5917	.5487
.7118	.6931	.6750	.6575	.6407	.6244	.6086	.5934	.5787	.5120	.4552	.4064
.6355	.6133	.5921	.5718	.5523	.5337	.5158	.4987	.4823	.4096	.3501	.3011
.5674	.5428	.5194	.4972	.4761	.4561	.4371	.4190	.4019	.3277	.2693	.2230
.5066	.4803	.4556	.4323	.4104	.3898	.3704	.3521	.3349	.2621	.2072	.1652
.4523	.4251	.3996	.3759	.3538	.3332	.3139	.2959	.2791	.2097	.1594	.1224
.4039	.3762	.3506	.3269	.3050	.2848	.2660	.2487	.2326	.1678	.1226	.0906
.3606	.3329	.3075	.2843	.2630	.2434	.2255	.2090	.1938	.1342	.0943	.0671
.3220	.2946	.2697	.2472	.2267	.2080	.1911	.1756	.1615	.1074	.0725	.0497
.2875	.2607	.2366	.2149	.1954	.1778	.1619	.1476	.1346	.0859	.0558	.0368
.2567	.2307	.2076	.1869	.1685	.1520	.1372	.1240	.1122	.0687	.0429	.0273
.2292	.2042	.1821	.1625	.1452	.1299	.1163	.1042	.0935	.0550	.0330	.0202
.2046	.1807	.1597	.1413	.1252	.1110	.0985	.0876	.0779	.0440	.0254	.0150
.1827	.1599	.1401	.1229	.1079	.0949	.0835	.0736	.0649	.0352	.0195	.0111
.1631	.1415	.1229	.1069	.0930	.0811	.0708	.0618	.0541	.0281	.0150	.0082
.1456	.1252	.1078	.0929	.0802	.0693	.0600	.0520	.0451	.0225	.0116	.0061
.1300	.1108	.0946	.0808	.0691	.0592	.0508	.0437	.0376	.0180	.0089	.0045
.1161	.0981	.0829	.0703	.0596	.0506	.0431	.0367	.0313	.0144	.0068	.0033
.1037	.0868	.0728	.0611	.0514	.0433	.0365	.0308	.0261	.0115	.0053	.0025
.0926	.0768	.0638	.0531	.0443	.0370	.0309	.0259	.0217	.0092	.0040	.0018
.0826	.0680	.0560	.0462	.0382	.0316	.0262	.0218	.0181	.0074	.0031	.0014
.0738	.0601	.0491	.0402	.0329	.0270	.0222	.0183	.0151	.0059	.0024	.0010
.0659	.0532	.0431	.0349	.0284	.0231	.0188	.0154	.0126	.0047	.0018	.0007
.0588	.0471	.0378	.0304	.0245	.0197	.0160	.0129	.0105	.0038	.0014	.0006
.0525	.0417	.0331	.0264	.0211	.0169	.0135	.0109	.0087	.0030	.0011	.0004
.0469	.0369	.0291	.0230	.0182	.0144	.0115	.0091	.0073	.0024	.0008	.0003
.0419	.0326	.0255	.0200	.0157	.0123	.0097	.0077	.0061	.0019	.0006	.0002
.0374	.0289	.0224	.0174	.0135	.0105	.0082	.0064	.0051	.0015	.0005	.0002
.0334	.0256	.0196	.0151	.0116	.0090	.0070	.0054	.0042	.0012	.0004	.0001
.0266	.0200	.0151	.0114	.0087	.0066	.0050	.0038	.0029	.0008	.0002	.0001
.0212	.0157	.0116	.0086	.0064	.0048	.0036	.0027	.0020	.0005	.0001	.0000
.0169	.0123	.0089	.0065	.0048	.0035	.0026	.0019	.0014	.0003	.0001	.0000
.0135	.0096	.0069	.0049	.0036	.0026	.0019	.0013	.0010	.0002	.0000	.0000
.0107	.0075	.0053	.0037	.0026	.0019	.0013	.0010	.0007	.0001	.0000	.0000
.0086	.0059	.0041	.0028	.0020	.0014	.0010	.0007	.0005	.0001	.0000	.0000
.0068	.0046	.0031	.0021	.0015	.0010	.0007	.0005	.0003	.0001	.0000	.0000
.0054	.0036	.0024	.0016	.0011	.0007	.0005	.0003	.0002	.0000	.0000	.0000
.0043	.0028	.0019	.0012	.0008	.0005	.0004	.0002	.0002	.0000	.0000	.0000
.0035	.0022	.0014	.0009	.0006	.0004	.0003	.0002	.0001	.0000	.0000	.0000
.0028	.0017	.0011	.0007	.0004	.0003	.0002	.0001	.0001	.0000	.0000	.0000
.0022	.0014	.0008	.0005	.0003	.0002	.0001	.0001	.0001	.0000	.0000	.0000
.0018	.0011	.0007	.0004	.0002	.0002	.0001	.0001	.0000	.0000	.0000	.0000
.0014	.0008	.0005	.0003	.0002	.0001	.0001	.0000	.0000	.0000	.0000	.0000
.0011	.0007	.0004	.0002	.0001	.0001	.0000	.0000	.0000	.0000	.0000	.0000

Present Value Factor of an Annuity

$$PVFA_{k\%,N} = \frac{1 - \dfrac{1}{(1+k)^N}}{k}$$

N	1%	2%	3%	4%	5%	6%	7%	8%	9%
1	0.9901	0.9804	0.9709	0.9615	0.9524	0.9434	0.9346	0.9259	0.9174
2	1.9704	1.9416	1.9135	1.8861	1.8594	1.8334	1.8080	1.7833	1.7591
3	2.9410	2.8839	2.8286	2.7751	2.7232	2.6730	2.6243	2.5771	2.5313
4	3.9020	3.8077	3.7171	3.6299	3.5460	3.4651	3.3872	3.3121	3.2397
5	4.8534	4.7135	4.5797	4.4518	4.3295	4.2124	4.1002	3.9927	3.8897
6	5.7955	5.6014	5.4172	5.2421	5.0757	4.9173	4.7665	4.6229	4.4859
7	6.7282	6.4720	6.2303	6.0021	5.7864	5.5824	5.3893	5.2064	5.0330
8	7.6517	7.3255	7.0197	6.7327	6.4632	6.2098	5.9713	5.7466	5.5348
9	8.5660	8.1622	7.7861	7.4353	7.1078	6.8017	6.5152	6.2469	5.9952
10	9.4713	8.9826	8.5302	8.1109	7.7217	7.3601	7.0236	6.7101	6.4177
11	10.3676	9.7868	9.2526	8.7605	8.3064	7.8869	7.4987	7.1390	6.8052
12	11.2551	10.5753	9.9540	9.3851	8.8633	8.3838	7.9427	7.5361	7.1607
13	12.1337	11.3484	10.6350	9.9856	9.3936	8.8527	8.3577	7.9038	7.4869
14	13.0037	12.1062	11.2961	10.5631	9.8986	9.2950	8.7455	8.2442	7.7862
15	13.8651	12.8493	11.9379	11.1184	10.3797	9.7122	9.1079	8.5595	8.0607
16	14.7179	13.5777	12.5611	11.6523	10.8378	10.1059	9.4466	8.8514	8.3126
17	15.5623	14.2919	13.1661	12.1657	11.2741	10.4773	9.7632	9.1216	8.5436
18	16.3983	14.9920	13.7535	12.6593	11.6896	10.8276	10.0591	9.3719	8.7556
19	17.2260	15.6785	14.3238	13.1339	12.0853	11.1581	10.3356	9.6036	8.9501
20	18.0456	16.3514	14.8775	13.5903	12.4622	11.4699	10.5940	9.8181	9.1285
21	18.8570	17.0112	15.4150	14.0292	12.8212	11.7641	10.8355	10.0168	9.2922
22	19.6604	17.6580	15.9369	14.4511	13.1630	12.0416	11.0612	10.2007	9.4424
23	20.4558	18.2922	16.4436	14.8568	13.4886	12.3034	11.2722	10.3711	9.5802
24	21.2434	18.9139	16.9355	15.2470	13.7986	12.5504	11.4693	10.5288	9.7066
25	22.0232	19.5235	17.4131	15.6221	14.0939	12.7834	11.6536	10.6748	9.8226
26	22.7952	20.1210	17.8768	15.9828	14.3752	13.0032	11.8258	10.8100	9.9290
27	23.5596	20.7069	18.3270	16.3296	14.6430	13.2105	11.9867	10.9352	10.0266
28	24.3164	21.2813	18.7641	16.6631	14.8981	13.4062	12.1371	11.0511	10.1161
29	25.0658	21.8444	19.1885	16.9837	15.1411	13.5907	12.2777	11.1584	10.1983
30	25.8077	22.3965	19.6004	17.2920	15.3725	13.7648	12.4090	11.2578	10.2737
32	27.2696	23.4683	20.3888	17.8736	15.8027	14.0840	12.6466	11.4350	10.4062
34	28.7027	24.4986	21.1318	18.4112	16.1929	14.3681	12.8540	11.5869	10.5178
36	30.1075	25.4888	21.8323	18.9083	16.5469	14.6210	13.0352	11.7172	10.6118
38	31.4847	26.4406	22.4925	19.3679	16.8679	14.8460	13.1935	11.8289	10.6908
40	32.8347	27.3555	23.1148	19.7928	17.1591	15.0463	13.3317	11.9246	10.7574
42	34.1581	28.2348	23.7014	20.1856	17.4232	15.2245	13.4524	12.0067	10.8134
44	35.4555	29.0800	24.2543	20.5488	17.6628	15.3832	13.5579	12.0771	10.8605
46	36.7272	29.8923	24.7754	20.8847	17.8801	15.5244	13.6500	12.1374	10.9002
48	37.9740	30.6731	25.2667	21.1951	18.0772	15.6500	13.7305	12.1891	10.9336
50	39.1961	31.4236	25.7298	21.4822	18.2559	15.7619	13.8007	12.2335	10.9617
52	40.3942	32,1449	26.1662	21.7476	18.4181	15.8614	13.8621	12.2715	10.9853
54	41.5687	32.8383	26.5777	21.9930	18.5651	15.9500	13.9157	12.3041	11.0053
56	42.7200	33.5047	26.9655	22.2198	18.6985	16.0288	13.9626	12.3321	11.0220
58	43.8486	34.1452	27.3311	22.4296	18.8195	16.0990	14.0035	12.3560	11.0361
60	44.9550	34.7609	27.6756	22.6235	18.9293	16.1614	14.0392	12.3766	11.0480

10%	11%	12%	13%	14%	15%	16%	17%	18%	19%
0.9091	0.9009	0.8929	0.8850	0.8772	0.8696	0.8621	0.8547	0.8475	0.8403
1.7355	1.7125	1.6901	1.6681	1.6467	1.6257	1.6052	1.5852	1.5656	1.5465
2.4869	2.4437	2.4018	2.3612	2.3216	2.2832	2.2459	2.2096	2.1743	2.1399
3.1699	3.1024	3.0373	2.9745	2.9137	2.8550	2.7982	2.7432	2.6901	2.6386
3.7908	3.6959	3.6048	3.5172	3.4331	3.3522	3.2743	3.1993	3.1272	3.0576
4.3553	4.2305	4.1114	3.9975	3.8887	3.7845	3.6847	3.5892	3.4976	3.4098
4.8684	4.7122	4.5638	4.4226	4.2883	4.1604	4.0386	3.9224	3.8115	3.7057
5.3349	5.1461	4.9676	4.7988	4.6389	4.4873	4.3436	4.2072	4.0776	3.9544
5.7590	5.5370	5.3282	5.1317	4.9464	4.7716	4.6065	4.4506	4.3030	4.1633
6.1446	5.8892	5.6502	5.4262	5.2161	5.0188	4.8332	4.6586	4.4941	4.3389
6.4951	6.2065	5.9357	5.6869	5.4527	5.2337	5.0286	4.8364	4.6560	4.4865
6.8137	6.4924	6.1944	5.9176	5.6603	5.4206	5.1971	4.9884	4.7932	4.6105
7.1034	6.7499	6.4235	6.1218	5.8424	5.5831	5.3423	5.1183	4.9095	4.7147
7.3667	6.9819	6.6282	6.3025	6.0021	5.7245	5.4675	5.2293	5.0081	4.8023
7.6061	7.1909	6.8109	6.4624	6.1422	5.8474	5.5755	5.3242	5.0916	4.8759
7.8237	7.3792	6.9740	6.6039	6.2651	5.9542	5.6685	5.4053	5.1624	4.9377
8.0216	7.5488	7.1196	6.7291	6.3729	6.0472	5.7487	5.4746	5.2223	4.9897
8.2014	7.7016	7.2497	6.8399	6.4674	6.1280	5.8178	5.5339	5.2732	5.0333
8.3649	7.8393	7.3658	6.9380	6.5504	6.1982	5.8775	5.5845	5.3162	5.0700
8.5136	7.9633	7.4694	7.0248	6.6231	6.2593	5.9288	5.6278	5.3527	5.1009
8.6487	8.0751	7.5620	7.1016	6.6870	6.3125	5.9731	5.6648	5.3837	5.1268
8.7715	8.1757	7.6446	7.1695	6.7429	6.3587	6.0113	5.6964	5.4099	5.1486
8.8832	8.2664	7.7184	7.2297	6.7921	6.3988	6.0442	5.7234	5.4321	5.1668
8.9847	8.3481	7.7843	7.2829	6.8351	6.4338	6.0726	5.7465	5.4509	5.1822
9.0770	8.4217	7.8431	7.3300	6.8729	6.4641	6.0971	5.7662	5.4669	5.1951
9.1609	8.4881	7.8957	7.3717	6.9061	6.4906	6.1182	5.7831	5.4804	5.2060
9.2372	8.5478	7.9426	7.4086	6.9352	6.5135	6.1364	5.7975	5.4919	5.2151
9.3066	8.6016	7.9844	7.4412	6.9607	6.5335	6.1520	5.8099	5.5016	5.2228
9.3696	8.6501	8.0218	7.4701	6.9830	6.5509	6.1656	5.8204	5.5098	5.2292
9.4269	8.6938	8.0552	7.4957	7.0027	6.5660	6.1772	5.8294	5.5168	5.2347
9.5264	8.7686	8.1116	7.5383	7.0350	6.5905	6.1959	5.8437	5.5277	5.2430
9.6086	8.8293	8.1566	7.5717	7.0599	6.6091	6.2098	5.8541	5.5356	5.2489
9.6765	8.8786	8.1924	7.5979	7.0790	6.6231	6.2201	5.8617	5.5412	5.2531
9.7327	8.9186	8.2210	7.6183	7.0937	6.6338	6.2278	5.8673	5.5452	5.2561
9.7791	8.9511	8.2438	7.6344	7.1050	6.6418	6.2335	5.8713	5.5482	5.2582
9.8174	8.9774	8.2619	7.6469	7.1138	6.6478	6.2377	5.8743	5.5502	5.2596
9.8491	8.9988	8.2764	7.6568	7.1205	6.6524	6.2409	5.8765	5.5517	5.2607
9.8753	9.0161	8.2880	7.6645	7.1256	6.6559	6.2432	5.8781	5.5528	5.2614
9.8969	9.0302	8.2972	7.6705	7.1296	6.6585	6.2450	5.8792	5.5536	5.2619
9.9148	9.0417	8.3045	7.6752	7.1327	6.6605	6.2463	5.8801	5.5541	5.2623
9.9296	9.0509	8.3103	7.6789	7.1350	6.6620	6.2472	5.8807	5.5545	5.2625
9.9418	9.0585	8.3150	7.6818	7.1368	6.6631	6.2479	5.8811	5.5548	5.2627
9.9519	9.0646	8.3187	7.6841	7.1382	6.6640	6.2485	5.8815	5.5550	5.2628
9.9603	9.0695	8.3217	7.6859	7.1393	6.6647	6.2489	5.8817	5.5552	5.2629
9.9672	9.0736	8.3240	7.6873	7.1401	6.6651	6.2492	5.8819	5.5553	5.2630

Future Value Factor $FVF_{k\%,n} = (1 + k)^n$

n	1%	2%	3%	4%	5%	6%	7%	8%	9%	10%
1	1.0100	1.0200	1.0300	1.0400	1.0500	1.0600	1.0700	1.0800	1.0900	1.1000
2	1.0201	1.0404	1.0609	1.0816	1.1025	1.1236	1.1449	1.1664	1.1881	1.2100
3	1.0303	1.0612	1.0927	1.1249	1.1576	1.1910	1.2250	1.2597	1.2950	1.3310
4	1.0406	1.0824	1.1255	1.1699	1.2155	1.2625	1.3108	1.3605	1.4116	1.4641
5	1.0510	1.1041	1.1593	1.2167	1.2763	1.3382	1.4026	1.4693	1.5386	1.6105
6	1.0615	1.1262	1.1941	1.2653	1.3401	1.4185	1.5007	1.5869	1.6771	1.7716
7	1.0721	1.1487	1.2299	1.3159	1.4071	1.5036	1.6058	1.7138	1.8280	1.9487
8	1.0829	1.1717	1.2668	1.3686	1.4775	1.5938	1.7182	1.8509	1.9926	2.1436
9	1.0937	1.1951	1.3048	1.4233	1.5513	1.6895	1.8385	1.9990	2.1719	2.3579
10	1.1046	1.2190	1.3439	1.4802	1.6289	1.7908	1.9672	2.1589	2.3674	2.5937
11	1.1157	1.2434	1.3842	1.5395	1.7103	1.8983	2.1049	2.3316	2.5804	2.8531
12	1.1268	1.2682	1.4258	1.6010	1.7959	2.0122	2.2522	2.5182	2.8127	3.1384
13	1.1381	1.2936	1.4685	1.6651	1.8856	2.1329	2.4098	2.7196	3.0658	3.4523
14	1.1495	1.3195	1.5126	1.7317	1.9799	2.2609	2.5785	2.9372	3.3417	3.7975
15	1.1610	1.3459	1.5580	1.8009	2.0789	2.3966	2.7590	3.1722	3.6425	4.1772
16	1.1726	1.3728	1.6047	1.8730	2.1829	2.5404	2.9522	3.4259	3.9703	4.5950
17	1.1843	1.4002	1.6528	1.9479	2.2920	2.6928	3.1588	3.7000	4.3276	5.0545
18	1.1961	1.4282	1.7024	2.0258	2.4066	2.8543	3.3799	3.9960	4.7171	5.5599
19	1.2081	1.4568	1.7535	2.1068	2.5270	3.0256	3.6165	4.3157	5.1417	6.1159
20	1.2202	1.4859	1.8061	2.1911	2.6533	3.2071	3.8697	4.6610	5.6044	6.7275
21	1.2324	1.5157	1.8603	2.2788	2.7860	3.3996	4.1406	5.0338	6.1088	7.4002
22	1.2447	1.5460	1.9161	2.3699	2.9253	3.6035	4.4304	5.4365	6.6586	8.1403
23	1.2572	1.5769	1.9736	2.4647	3.0715	3.8197	4.7405	5.8715	7.2579	8.9543
24	1.2697	1.6084	2.0328	2.5633	3.2251	4.0489	5.0724	6.3412	7.9111	9.8497
25	1.2824	1.6406	2.0938	2.6658	3.3864	4.2919	5.4274	6.8485	8.6231	10.835
26	1.2953	1.6734	2.1566	2.7725	3.5557	4.5494	5.8074	7.3964	9.3992	11.918
27	1.3082	1.7069	2.2213	2.8834	3.7335	4.8223	6.2139	7.9881	10.245	13.110
28	1.3213	1.7410	2.2879	2.9987	3.9201	5.1117	6.6488	8.6271	11.167	14.421
29	1.3345	1.7758	2.3566	3.1187	4.1161	5.4184	7.1143	9.3173	12.172	15.863
30	1.3478	1.8114	2.4273	3.2434	4.3219	5.7435	7.6123	10.063	13.268	17.449
32	1.3749	1.8845	2.5751	3.5081	4.7649	6.4534	8.7153	11.737	15.763	21.114
34	1.4026	1.9607	2.7319	3.7943	5.2533	7.2510	9.9781	13.690	18.728	25.548
36	1.4308	2.0399	2.8983	4.1039	5.7918	8.1473	11.424	15.968	22.251	30.913
38	1.4595	2.1223	3.0748	4.4388	6.3855	9.1543	13.079	18.625	26.437	37.404
40	1.4889	2.2080	3.2620	4.8010	7.0400	10.286	14.974	21.725	31.409	45.259
42	1.5188	2.2972	3.4607	5.1928	7.7616	11.557	17.144	25.339	37.318	54.764
44	1.5493	2.3901	3.6715	5.6165	8.5572	12.985	19.628	29.556	44.337	66.264
46	1.5805	2.4866	3.8950	6.0748	9.4343	14.590	22.473	34.474	52.677	80.180
48	1.6122	2.5871	4.1323	6.5705	10.401	16.394	25.729	40.211	62.585	97.017
50	1.6446	2.6916	4.3839	7.1067	11.467	18.420	29.457	46.902	74.358	117.39
52	1.6777	2.8003	4.6509	7.6866	12.643	20.697	33.725	54.706	88.344	142.04
54	1.7114	2.9135	4.9341	8.3138	13.939	23.255	38.612	63.809	104.96	171.87
56	1.7458	3.0312	5.2346	8.9922	15.367	26.129	44.207	74.427	124.71	207.97
58	1.7809	3.1536	5.5534	9.7260	16.943	29.359	50.613	86.812	148.16	251.64
60	1.8167	3.2810	5.8916	10.520	18.679	32.988	57.946	101.26	176.03	304.48

11%	12%	13%	14%	15%	16%	17%	18%	19%	20%
1.1100	1.1200	1.1300	1.1400	1.1500	1.1600	1.1700	1.1800	1.1900	1.2000
1.2321	1.2524	1.2769	1.2996	1.3225	1.3456	1.3689	1.3924	1.4161	1.4400
1.3676	1.4049	1.4429	1.4815	1.5209	1.5609	1.6016	1.6430	1.6852	1.7280
1.5181	1.5735	1.6305	1.6890	1.7490	1.8106	1.8739	1.9388	2.0053	2.0736
1.6851	1.7623	1.8424	1.9254	2.0114	2.1003	2.1924	2.2878	2.3864	2.4883
1.8704	1.9738	2.0820	2.1950	2.3131	2.4364	2.5652	2.6996	2.8398	2.9860
2.0762	2.2107	2.3526	2.5023	2.6600	2.8262	3.0012	3.1855	3.3793	3.5832
2.3045	2.4760	2.6584	2.8526	3.0590	3.2784	3.5115	3.7589	4.0214	4.2998
2.5580	2.7731	3.0040	3.2519	3.5179	3.8030	4.1084	4.4355	4.7854	5.1598
2.8394	3.1058	3.3946	3.7072	4.0456	4.4114	4.8068	5.2338	5.6947	6.1917
3.1518	3.4786	3.8359	4.2262	4.6524	5.1173	5.6240	6.1759	6.7767	7.4301
3.4985	3.8960	4.3345	4.8179	5.3503	5.9360	6.5801	7.2876	8.0642	8.9161
3.8833	4.3635	4.8980	5.4924	6.1528	6.8858	7.6987	8.5994	9.5964	10.699
4.3104	4.8871	5.5348	6.2613	7.0757	7.9875	9.0075	10.147	11.420	12.839
4.7846	5.4736	6.2543	7.1379	8.1371	9.2655	10.539	11.974	13.590	15.407
5.3109	6.1304	7.0673	8.1372	9.3576	10.748	12.330	14.129	16.172	18.488
5.8951	6.8660	7.9861	9.2765	10.761	12.468	14.426	16.672	19.244	22.186
6.5436	7.6900	9.0243	10.575	12.375	14.463	16.879	19.673	22.901	26.623
7.2633	8.6128	10.197	12.056	14.232	16.777	19.748	23.214	27.252	31.948
8.0623	9.6463	11.523	13.743	16.367	19.461	23.106	27.393	32.429	38.338
8.9492	10.804	13.021	15.668	18.822	22.574	27.034	32.324	38.591	46.005
9.9336	12.100	14.714	17.861	21.645	26.186	31.629	38.142	45.923	55.206
11.026	13.552	16.627	20.362	24.891	30.376	37.006	45.008	54.649	66.247
12.239	15.179	18.788	23.212	28.625	35.236	43.297	53.109	65.032	79.497
13.585	17.000	21.231	26.462	32.919	40.874	50.658	62.669	77.388	95.396
15.080	19.040	23.991	30.167	37.857	47.414	59.270	73.949	92.092	114.48
16.739	21.325	27.109	34.390	43.535	55.000	69.345	87.260	109.59	137.37
18.580	23.884	30.633	39.204	50.066	63.800	81.134	102.97	130.41	164.84
20.624	26.750	34.616	44.693	57.575	74.009	94.927	121.50	155.19	197.81
22.892	29.960	39.116	50.950	66.212	85.850	111.06	143.37	184.68	237.38
28.206	37.582	49.947	66.215	87.565	115.52	152.04	199.63	261.52	341.82
34.752	47.143	63.777	86.053	115.80	155.44	208.12	277.96	370.34	492.22
42.818	59.136	81.437	111.83	153.15	209.16	284.90	387.04	524.43	708.80
52.756	74.180	103.99	145.34	202.54	281.45	390.00	538.91	742.65	1020.7
65.001	93.051	132.78	188.88	267.86	378.72	533.87	750.38	1051.7	1469.8
80.088	116.72	169.55	245.47	354.25	509.61	730.81	1044.8	1489.3	2116.5
98.676	146.42	216.50	319.02	468.50	685.73	1000.4	1454.8	2109.0	3047.7
121.58	183.67	276.44	414.59	619.58	922.71	1369.5	2025.7	2986.5	4388.7
149.80	230.39	352.99	538.81	819.40	1241.6	1874.7	2820.6	4229.2	6319.7
184.56	289.00	450.74	700.23	1083.7	1670.7	2566.2	3927.4	5988.9	9100.4
227.40	362.52	575.54	910.02	1433.1	2248.1	3512.9	5468.5	8480.9	13105
280.18	454.75	734.91	1182.7	1895.3	3025.0	4808.8	7614.3	12010	18871
345.21	570.44	938.41	1537.0	2506.6	4070.5	6582.8	10602	17007	27174
425.34	715.56	1198.3	1997.5	3314.9	5477.3	9011.1	14762	24084	39130
524.06	897.60	1530.1	2595.9	4384.0	7370.2	12335	20555	34105	56348

Future Value Factor of an Annuity

$$FVFA_{k\%,N} = \frac{(1+k)^N - 1}{k}$$

N	1%	2%	3%	4%	5%	6%	7%	8%	9%	10%
1	1.0000	1.0000	1.0000	1.0000	1.0000	1.0000	1.0000	1.0000	1.0000	1.0000
2	2.0100	2.0200	2.0300	2.0400	2.0500	2.0600	2.0700	2.0800	2.0900	2.1000
3	3.0301	3.0604	3.0909	3.1216	3.1525	3.1836	3.2149	3.2464	3.2781	3.3100
4	4.0604	4.1216	4.1836	4.2465	4.3101	4.3746	4.4399	4.5061	4.5731	4.6410
5	5.1010	5.2040	5.3091	5.4163	5.5256	5.6371	5.7507	5.8666	5.9847	6.1051
6	6.1520	6.3081	6.4684	6.6330	6.8019	6.9753	7.1533	7.3359	7.5233	7.7156
7	7.2135	7.4343	7.6625	7.8983	8.1420	8.3938	8.6540	8.9228	9.2004	9.4872
8	8.2857	8.5830	8.8923	9.2142	9.5491	9.8975	10.260	10.637	11.028	11.436
9	9.3685	9.7546	10.159	10.583	11.027	11.491	11.978	12.488	13.021	13.579
10	10.462	10.950	11.464	12.006	12.578	13.181	13.816	14.487	15.193	15.937
11	11.567	12.169	12.808	13.486	14.207	14.972	15.784	16.645	17.560	18.531
12	12.683	13.412	14.192	15.026	15.917	16.870	17.888	18.977	20.141	21.384
13	13.809	14.680	15.618	16.627	17.713	18.882	20.141	21.495	22.953	24.523
14	14.947	15.974	17.086	18.292	19.599	21.015	22.550	24.215	26.019	27.975
15	16.097	17.293	18.599	20.024	21.579	23.276	25.129	27.152	29.361	31.772
16	17.258	18.639	20.157	21.825	23.657	25.673	27.888	30.324	33.003	35.950
17	18.430	20.012	21.762	23.698	25.840	28.213	30.840	33.750	36.974	40.545
18	19.615	21.412	23.414	25.645	28.132	30.906	33.999	37.450	41.301	45.599
19	20.811	22.841	25.117	27.671	30.539	33.760	37.379	41.446	46.018	51.159
20	22.019	24.297	26.870	29.778	33.066	36.786	40.995	45.762	51.160	57.275
21	23.239	25.783	28.676	31.969	35.719	39.993	44.865	50.423	56.765	64.002
22	24.472	27.299	30.537	34.248	38.505	43.392	49.006	55.457	62.873	71.403
23	25.716	28.845	32.453	36.618	41.430	46.996	53.436	60.893	69.532	79.543
24	26.973	30.422	34.426	39.083	44.502	50.816	58.177	66.765	76.790	88.497
25	28.243	32.030	36.459	41.646	47.727	54.865	63.249	73.106	84.701	98.347
26	29.526	33.671	38.553	44.312	51.113	59.156	68.676	79.954	93.324	109.18
27	30.821	35.344	40.710	47.084	54.669	63.706	74.484	87.351	102.72	121.10
28	32.129	37.051	42.931	49.968	58.403	68.528	80.698	95.339	112.97	134.21
29	33.450	38.792	45.219	52.966	62.323	73.640	87.347	103.97	124.14	148.63
30	34.785	40.568	47.575	56.085	66.439	79.058	94.461	113.28	136.31	164.49
32	37.494	44.227	52.503	62.701	75.299	90.890	110.22	134.21	164.04	201.14
34	40.258	48.034	57.730	69.858	85.067	104.18	128.26	158.63	196.98	245.48
36	43.077	51.994	63.276	77.598	95.836	119.12	148.91	187.10	236.12	299.13
38	45.953	56.115	69.159	85.970	107.71	135.90	172.56	220.32	282.63	364.04
40	48.886	60.402	75.401	95.026	120.80	154.76	199.64	259.06	337.88	442.59
42	51.879	64.862	82.023	104.82	135.23	175.95	230.63	304.24	403.53	537.64
44	54.932	69.503	89.048	115.41	151.14	199.76	266.12	356.95	481.52	652.64
46	58.046	74.331	96.501	126.87	168.69	226.51	306.75	418.43	574.19	791.80
48	61.223	79.354	104.41	139.26	188.03	256.56	353.27	490.13	684.28	960.17
50	64.463	84.579	112.80	152.67	209.35	290.34	406.53	573.77	815.08	1163.9
52	67.769	90.016	121.70	167.16	232.86	328.28	467.50	671.33	970.49	1410.4
54	71.141	95.673	131.14	182.85	258.77	370.92	537.32	785.11	1155.1	1708.7
56	74.581	101.56	141.15	199.81	287.35	418.82	617.24	917.84	1374.5	2069.7
58	78.090	107.68	151.78	218.15	318.85	472.65	708.75	1072.6	1635.1	2506.4
60	81.670	114.05	163.05	237.99	353.58	533.13	813.52	1253.2	1944.8	3034.8

11%	12%	13%	14%	15%	16%	17%	18%	19%	20%
1.0000	1.0000	1.0000	1.0000	1.0000	1.0000	1.0000	1.0000	1.0000	1.0000
2.1100	2.1200	2.1300	2.1400	2.1500	2.1600	2.1700	2.1800	2.1900	2.2000
3.3421	3.3744	3.4069	3.4396	3.4725	3.5056	3.5389	3.5724	3.6061	3.6400
4.7097	4.7793	4.8498	4.9211	4.9934	5.0665	5.1405	5.2154	5.2913	5.3680
6.2278	6.3528	6.4803	6.6101	6.7424	6.8771	7.0144	7.1542	7.2966	7.4416
7.9129	8.1152	8.3227	8.5355	8.7537	8.9775	9.2068	9.4420	9.6830	9.9299
9.7833	10.089	10.405	10.730	11.067	11.414	11.772	12.142	12.523	12.916
11.859	12.300	12.757	13.233	13.727	14.240	14.773	15.327	15.902	16.499
14.164	14.776	15.416	16.085	16.786	17.519	18.285	19.086	19.923	20.799
16.722	17.549	18.420	19.337	20.304	21.321	22.393	23.521	24.709	25.959
19.561	20.655	21.814	23.045	24.349	25.733	27.200	28.755	30.404	32.150
22.713	24.133	25.650	27.271	29.002	30.850	32.824	34.931	37.180	39.581
26.212	28.029	29.985	32.089	34.352	36.786	39.404	42.219	45.244	48.497
30.095	32.393	34.883	37.581	40.505	43.672	47.103	50.818	54.841	59.196
34.405	37.280	40.418	43.842	47.580	51.660	56.110	60.965	66.261	72.035
39.190	42.753	46.672	50.980	55.717	60.925	66.649	72.939	79.850	87.442
44.501	48.884	53.739	59.118	65.075	71.673	78.979	87.068	96.022	105.93
50.396	55.750	61.725	68.394	75.836	84.141	93.406	103.74	115.27	128.12
56.939	63.440	70.749	78.969	88.212	98.603	110.28	123.41	138.17	154.74
64.203	72.052	80.947	91.025	102.44	115.38	130.03	146.63	165.42	186.69
72.265	81.699	92.470	104.77	118.81	134.84	153.14	174.02	197.85	225.03
81.214	92.503	105.49	120.44	137.63	157.41	180.17	206.34	236.44	271.03
91.148	104.60	120.20	138.30	159.28	183.60	211.80	244.49	282.36	326.24
102.17	118.16	136.83	158.66	184.17	213.98	248.81	289.49	337.01	392.48
114.41	133.33	155.62	181.87	212.79	249.21	292.10	342.60	402.04	471.98
128.00	150.33	176.85	208.33	245.71	290.09	342.76	405.27	479.43	567.38
143.08	169.37	200.84	238.50	283.57	337.50	402.03	479.22	571.52	681.85
159.82	190.70	227.95	272.89	327.10	392.50	471.38	566.48	681.11	819.22
178.40	214.58	258.58	312.09	377.17	456.30	552.51	669.45	811.52	984.07
199.02	241.33	293.20	356.79	434.75	530.31	647.44	790.95	966.71	1181.9
247.32	304.85	376.52	465.82	577.10	715.75	888.45	1103.5	1371.2	1704.1
306.84	384.52	482.90	607.52	765.37	965.27	1218.4	1538.7	1943.9	2456.1
380.16	484.46	618.75	791.67	1014.3	1301.0	1670.0	2144.6	2754.9	3539.0
470.51	609.83	792.21	1031.0	1343.6	1752.8	2288.2	2988.4	3903.4	5098.4
581.83	767.09	1013.7	1342.0	1779.1	2360.8	3134.5	4163.2	5529.8	7343.9
718.98	964.36	1296.5	1746.2	2355.0	3178.8	4293.0	5799.0	7833.0	10577
887.96	1211.8	1657.7	2271.5	3116.6	4279.5	5878.9	8076.8	11094	15234
1096.2	1522.2	2118.8	2954.2	4123.9	5760.7	8049.8	11248	15713	21939
1352.7	1911.6	2707.6	3841.5	5456.0	7753.8	11022	15664	22253	31594
1668.8	2400.0	3459.5	4994.5	7217.7	10436	15090	21813	31515	45497
2058.2	3012.7	4419.6	6493.0	9547.6	14044	20658	30375	44631	65518
2538.0	3781.3	5645.5	8440.5	12629	18900	28281	42296	63204	94348
3129.2	4745.3	7210.8	10971	16704	25434	38716	58895	89506	135864
3857.6	5954.7	9209.7	14261	22093	34227	53001	82008	126751	195646
4755.1	7471.6	11762	18535	29220	46058	72555	114190	179495	281733

Using Calculators for Financial Analysis

You can solve any time value of money problem with this appendix. The examples use the Texas instruments BA-II Plus, but you may adapt any financial calculator to these methods.

Solving problems requires three steps: (1) Express the problem in terms of a cash flow diagram. (2) Enter the cash flows into the calculator. (3) Find the present value of the cash flows, an equivalent cash flow, and/or the rate of return of the cash flows. Let's try this approach on problems involving the time value of money.

Management at the Baxley Company analyzed a proposal and determined the following cash flow stream:

Year	Cash Flow	Year	Cash Flow
0	−$10,000	3	+$2,000
1	+$ 2,000	4	+$4,000
2	+$ 2,000	5	+$5,000

Find the internal rate of return and net present value for a marginal cost of capital of 10 percent.

I. Express the problem in terms of a cash flow diagram.

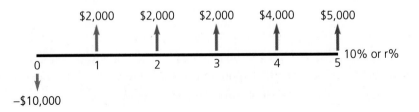

II. Enter the cash flows into the calculator.

Procedure	Keystrokes	Display	
Select Cash Flow worksheet.	CF	CF_0 (old contents)	
Clear worksheet.	2nd [CLR Work]	$CF_0 =$	0.0000
Enter initial cash flow.	−10,000 ENTER	$CF_0 = -10,000.0000$	
Enter cash flows for years one through three.	↓ 2,000 ENTER ↓ 3 ENTER	C01 = F01 =	2,000.0000 3.0000
Enter cash flow for year four.	↓ 4,000 ENTER ↓	C02 = F02 =	4,000.0000 1.0000
Enter cash flow for year five.	↓ 5,000 ENTER ↓	C03 = F03 =	5,000.0000 1.0000

III. Find the present value of the cash flows, an equivalent cash flow, and/or the rate of return of the cash flows.

Find the internal rate of return.

Procedure	Keystrokes	Display	
Access IRR portion of Cash Flow worksheet.	IRR	IRR =	0.0000
Compute internal rate of return.	CPT	IRR =	12.6179

Find the net present value.

Procedure	Keystrokes	Display	
Access NPV portion of Cash Flow worksheet.	NPV	I =	0.0000
Enter interest rate per period.	10 ENTER	I =	10.0000
Compute net present value.	↓ CPT	NPV =	810.3644

Jamie Richards finds a 30-year semiannual bond that pays total interest of $120 each year and has a $1,000 par value. The bond was issued five years ago by the Cameron Corporation. What is the value of this bond if the required annual rate of return is now 10 percent?

I. Express the problem in terms of a cash flow diagram.

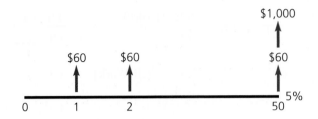

II. Enter the cash flows into the calculator.

Procedure	Keystrokes	Display	
Select Cash Flow worksheet.	CF	CF_0 (old contents)	
Clear worksheet.	2nd [CLR Work]	$CF_0 =$	0.0000
Move to period one.	↓	$C01 =$	0.0000
Enter cash flows	↓ 60 ENTER	$C01 =$	60.0000
for periods one	↓ 49 ENTER	$F01 =$	49.0000
through 49.			
Enter cash flow	↓ 1060 ENTER	$C02 =$	1060.0000
for 50th period.	↓	$F02 =$	1.0000

III. Find the present value of the cash flows, an equivalent cash flow, and/or the rate of return of the cash flows.

Find the value of the bond.

Procedure	Keystrokes	Display	
Access NPV portion of Cash Flow worksheet.	NPV	$I =$	0.0000
Enter interest rate per period.	5 ENTER	$I =$	5.0000
Compute net present value.	↓ CPT	$NPV =$	1182.5593

Using the net present value portion of the cash flow worksheet produces the value of the bond.

John Franklin purchases a 12 percent, $1,000 par value, semiannual payment bond, with 25 years to maturity, for the current price of $1,182.55. What is the yield to maturity of the bond?

I. Express the problem in terms of a cash flow diagram.

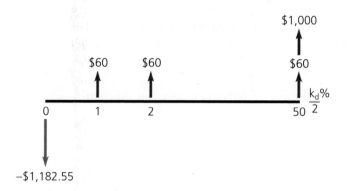

II. Enter the cash flows into the calculator.

Procedure	Keystrokes	Display	
Select Cash Flow worksheet.	CF	CF_0 (old contents)	
Clear worksheet.	2nd [CLR Work]	$CF_0 =$	.0000
Enter initial	−1182.55		
cash flow.	ENTER	$CF_0 =$	−1182.5500
Enter cash flows	↓ 60 ENTER	C01 =	60.0000
for periods one	↓ 49 ENTER	F01 =	49.0000
through 49.			
Enter cash flow	↓ 1060 ENTER	C02 =	1060.0000
for 50th year.	↓	F02 =	1.0000

III. Find the present value of the cash flows, an equivalent cash flow, and/or the rate of return of the cash flows.

   Find the yield to maturity.

Procedure	Keystrokes	Display	
Access IRR portion of Cash Flow worksheet.	IRR	IRR =	0.0000
Compute internal rate of return.	CPT	IRR =	5.0000

Using the internal rate of return portion of the cash flow worksheet produces the yield to maturity.

John Franklin purchases a 12 percent annual coupon interest rate, $1,000 par value, semiannual payment bond, with five years remaining before the bond can be called. He pays the current price of $980.55 for the bond, knowing that if the bond is called, he will receive $1,100. What is the yield to call of the bond?

I. Express the problem in terms of a cash flow diagram.

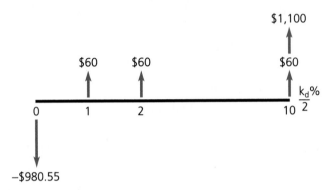

II. Enter the cash flows into the calculator.

Procedure	Keystrokes	Display	
Select Cash Flow worksheet.	CF	CF$_0$ (old contents)	
Clear worksheet.	2nd [CLR Work]	CF$_0$ =	.0000
Enter initial cash flow.	−980.55 ENTER	CF$_0$ =	−980.5500
Enter cash flows for periods one through nine.	↓ 60 ENTER ↓ 9 ENTER	C01 = F01 =	60.0000 9.0000
Enter cash flow for 10th period.	↓ 1160 ENTER ↓	C02 = F02 =	1160.0000 1.0000

III. Find the present value of the cash flows, an equivalent cash flow, and/or the rate of return of the cash flows.
    Find the yield to call.

Procedure	Keystrokes	Display	
Access IRR portion of Cash Flow worksheet.	IRR	IRR =	0.0000
Compute internal rate of return.	CPT	IRR =	7.0007

Using the internal rate of return portion of the cash flow worksheet produces the yield to call.

The industrial engineers at the Addison Company studied a new project and determined the following cash flow stream:

Year	Cash Flow	Year	Cash Flow
0	−$10,000	4	+$3,000
1	+$ 2,000	5	+$3,000
2	+$ 2,000	6	+$3,000
3	+$ 3,000	7	+$4,000

What is the equivalent cash flow at time 10, assuming a 10 percent interest rate?

I. Express the problem in terms of a cash flow diagram.

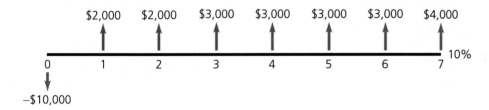

II. Enter the cash flows into the calculator.

Procedure	Keystrokes	Display
Select Cash Flow worksheet.	CF	CF_0 (old contents)
Clear worksheet.	2nd [CLR Work]	CF_0 = .0000
Enter initial cash flow.	−10,000	
	ENTER	CF_0 = −10,000.0000
Enter cash flows for years one through two.	↓ 2,000 ENTER	C01 = 2,000.0000
	↓ 2 ENTER	F01 = 2.0000
Enter cash flow for years three through six.	↓ 3,000 ENTER	C02 = 3,000.0000
	↓ 4 ENTER	F02 = 4.0000
Enter cash flow for seventh year.	↓ 4,000 ENTER	C03 = 4,000.0000
	↓	F03 = 1.0000

III. Find the present value of the cash flows, an equivalent cash flow, and/or the rate of return of the cash flows.

Find the net present value.

Procedure	Keystrokes	Display		
Access NPV portion of Cash Flow worksheet.	NPV	I	=	0.0000
Enter interest rate per period.	10 ENTER	I	=	10.0000
Compute net present value.	↓ CPT	NPV =		3382.8774

Find the equivalent cash flow at time 10.

Procedure	Keystrokes	Display	
Multiply by $(1 + k)^n$	X 1.10 y^x		1.1000
for k equal to 0.10 and	10		10
n equal to 10.	=	NPV =	8774.3127

Using the net present value portion of the cash flow worksheet produces the equivalent cash flow at time 10.

Using the Financial Manager

System Requirements:

Use THE FINANCIAL MANAGER on any IBM PC compatible microcomputer. Minimum system resources:

- 640KB of RAM
- DOS 2.1 or greater
- Hard disk
- Color or monochrome display

Description:

- THE FINANCIAL MANAGER is a powerful, easy-to-use, standalone spreadsheet program. It does not require another spreadsheet program to use the models.
- THE FINANCIAL MANAGER does not demand knowledge of programming or spreadsheet design by the instructor or student. The models are completely menu driven and use a common menu system.
- THE FINANCIAL MANAGER is not tied to specific chapter problems. The models perform a broad range of financial analysis (for example net present value, yield to maturity, cash budgets, ratio analysis).
- THE FINANCIAL MANAGER programs, such as PROJECT, allow the user to change input variables and simultaneously compare the effects on several output variables. This makes it easy to perform sensitivity analysis.

Installation:

Insert the program diskette into a 3.5" floppy drive, change to that drive, and type "install". This creates a subdirectory named FM and copies THE FINANCIAL MANAGER to that subdirectory.

Starting the Financial Manager:

Change to the FM subdirectory. (For example, at the prompt C:\> type "CD\FM". Then, at the prompt: C:\FM\> Type "FM".)

THE FINANCIAL MANAGER will load and take you to the Main Menu. Simply select the model you wish to use from the menu. As you move the cursor down the list, a box will appear on the right side of the screen indicating the uses of that model.

Using the Models:

Understanding the distinction between data, commands, and help is basic to using THE FINANCIAL MANAGER.

- Data is information typed in response to questions or empty cells within the spreadsheet model. (Choose the appropriate command after entering data into the spreadsheet,.)
- Commands tell the computer what the user wants to do. Commands are available for solving, printing, saving, and retrieving spreadsheets. (Access commands from the menu or a function key.)
- Help is available for all of THE FINANCIAL MANAGER models. (Press the F1 function key to access instructions, definitions, and handy tips.)

THE FINANCIAL MANAGER is not designed to replace the knowledge necessary for analysis. But it makes it much easier to solve complex problems.

Answers to Chapter Problems

Chapter 1

1.1 A variety of responses.
1.2 Income Tax Liability = $17,222.00
The marginal tax rate is 31%.
1.3 Income Tax Liability = $14,803.00
The marginal tax rate is 28%.
1.4 Income Tax Liability = $46,728.50
The marginal tax rate is 36%.
1.5 Income Tax Liability = $41,750.00
The marginal tax rate is 39%.

Chapter 2

2.1 $V_0 = \$10,000$
2.2 $V_5 = \$176,230$
2.3 $V_0 = \$3,104,500$
2.4 (a) $V_3 = \$1,404.90$
(b) $V_8 = \$1,593.80$
(c) $V_{60} = \$1,816.70$
2.5 $V_{10} = \$14,487$
2.6 ER = 0.1255 or 12.55%
2.7 $V_0 = \$497,503.25$
2.8 $V_0 = \$185,136$
2.9 k = 10%
2.10 $V_{10} = \$10,174.40$
2.11 X = $1765.54
2.12 P = $2,224.45
2.13 k = 9%
2.14 k = 26%
2.15 $V_0 = \$2,581.40$

2.16 Machine A, $V_0 = \$5,971.63$
Machine B, $V_0 = \$5,713.30$
2.17 k = 12%
2.18 k = 8%
2.19 $V_0 = \$7,429$
2.20 k = 15%
2.21 $V_0 = \$2,605.93$
2.22

Year	Interest
1	$6,500.00
2	$5,159.76
3	$3,645.29
4	$1,933.93

2.23 The rate of return is 7 percent.
2.24 D = $5,437.53
2.25 $V_{10} = \$2225.54$
2.26 W = $9330.89
2.27 D = $627.47
2.28 D = $442.20
2.29 (a) Project A, $V_0 = \$6,862$
Project B, $V_0 = \$7,892$
(b) Project A, $V_0 = \$11,124$
Project B, $V_0 = \$7,892$
2.30 k = 0.069315 or 6.9315%
2.31 At age 25, N = 26 years
(The money will run out at age 91.)
2.32 P = $1,734.72
2.33 $V_{0,11.0\%} = \$6,407.75$
$V_{0,11.5\%} = \$4,311.32$
$V_{0,12.0\%} = \$2,280.08$
$V_{0,12.5\%} = \$311.51$
$V_{0,13.0\%} = -\$1,596.78$
2.34 $V_0 = \$58,822.33$

Chapter 3

3.1 $V = \$57,045.75$
3.2 $V = \$5,618.97$
3.3 $V_b = \$1,098.26$
3.4 $V_b = \$919.08$
3.5 $V_b = \$936.68$
3.6 The yield to maturity is 4%.
3.7 The yield to call is 7%.
3.8 The yield to call is 4%.
3.9 $k_d = 6\%$
3.10 The yield to maturity is 6%.
3.11 $V_b = \$833.33$
3.12 $I_5 = \$1,079.87 - \$927.88 = \$151.99$
      $I_{10} = \$1,134.21 - \$887.02 = \$247.19$
3.13 The yield to maturity is 4%.
3.14 $V_p = \$90$
3.15 $V_p = \$137.50$
3.16 $ER = 0.2011$ or 20.11%
      $V_p = \$150$
3.17 $V_s = \$39.22$
3.18 $V_s = \$33.33$
3.19 $V_s = \$15.00$
3.20 $V_s = \$32.00$
3.21 $V_s = \$16.625$
3.22 $V_s = \$40.00$
3.23 $V_s = \$45.57$
3.24 $V_s = \$58.16$
3.25 $g = 8\%$

Chapter 4

4.1 19X3 Current ratio = 1.88
     19X4 Current ratio = 2.00
     19X5 Current ratio = 2.10
     19X3 Quick ratio = 1.25
     19X4 Quick ratio = 1.26
     19X5 Quick ratio = 1.31
4.2 19X3 Total asset turnover ratio = 2.14
     19X4 Total asset turnover ratio = 2.27
     19X5 Total asset turnover ratio = 2.32
4.3 Debt-to-net worth ratio = 0.500

4.4 Cash flows from operating activities:

$84,000	Net income in 19X5
42,000	Depreciation in 19X5
(5,000)	Negative of $85,000 – $80,000
(5,800)	Negative of $125,800 – $120,000
(1,500)	Difference of $38,500 – $40,000
(5,000)	Difference of $10,000 – $15,000
$108,700	Summation of cash flows

Cash flows from investing activities:

$ (200)	Negative of $5,200 – $5000

Cash flows from financing activities:

$(50,000)	Difference of $10,000 – $60,000
(10,000)	Difference of $30,000 – $40,000
(47,500)	Negative of $47,500 in 19X5
$(107,500)	Summation of cash flows
$ 1,000	Summation of all activities

4.5 Times interest earned ratio = 16.9
     Net return on total assets = 0.215 or 21.5%
4.6 Report varies.
4.7 (a)

	19X4	19X5
Liquidity:		
Current ratio	1.88	1.85
Quick ratio	1.05	1.00
Activity:		
Total asset turnover ratio	1.98	1.89
Average collection period	57.8	60.9
Days inventory	69.8	75.1
Leverage:		
Debt ratio (%)	47.1	46.7
Debt-to-net worth ratio	0.9	0.9
Coverage:		
Times interest earned ratio	7.2	3.9
Cash flow-to-current		
maturities ratio	6.8	4.4
Profitability:		
Net return on total assets (%)	9.8	5.2
Net return on common equity	18.5	9.7
Market:		
Price-to-earnings ratio	8.6	9.9
Market-to-book value ratio	1.6	1.0

(b) Analysis varies.

4.8 (a)

	19X4	19X5
Liquidity:		
Current ratio	2.12	2.25
Quick ratio	1.18	1.27
Activity:		
Total asset turnover ratio	2.11	2.20
Average collection period	58.2	52.1
Days inventory	77.6	70.5
Leverage:		
Debt ratio (%)	53.4	51.9
Debt-to-net worth ratio	1.4	1.4
Coverage:		
Times interest earned ratio	9.1	3.7
Cash flow-to-current maturities ratio	6.8	2.4
Profitability:		
Net return on total assets (%)	11.0	3.8
Net return on common equity	29.4	10.1
Market:		
Price-to-earnings ratio	13.0	22.3
Market-to-book value ratio	3.8	2.2

(b) Analysis varies.

Chapter 5

5.1 $Y_{19X6} = \$2,326.6$
5.2 $Y_{19X7} = \$1,397.4$
5.3 $Y_{19Y0} = \$11,792,000$
5.4 Additional funds required = $48,125
5.5 Additional funds required = $(63,542)
5.6 Earnings available to common
    shareholders = $30.2
    Additional funds required = $106.725
5.7 Total receipts $2,360, $2,160, $2,100
    Total payments $1,400, $1,470, $2,324
5.8 Total receipts $4,630, $3,740, $3,630
    Total payments $2,584, $2,888, $3,888
5.9 Surplus $229,500, ($17,100), ($46,700)
5.10 Surplus $34,500, ($ 38,800), ($ 19,400)

Chapter 6

6.1 Initial cash flow = −$35,300
6.2 Initial cash flow = −$87,000
6.3 Initial cash flow = −$51,600
6.4 Initial cash flow = −$200,200
6.5 Initial cash flow = −$377,400
6.6 $CF_n = \$42,600$, $EAT_n = \$33,600$
6.7 $CF_n = \$27,000$, $EAT_n = \$19,500$
6.8 1-5, $CF_n = \$32,000$, $EAT_n = \$27,000$
    6-15, $CF_n = \$34,000$, $EAT_n = \$24,000$
6.9 1-4, $CF_n = \$130,000$, $EAT_n = \$105,000$
    5-10, $CF_n = \$136,000$, $EAT_n = \$96,000$

6.10

Period	CF_n	EAT_n
1	$66,130	−$ 9,195
2	$77,250	−$25,875
3	$47,610	$18,585
4	$40,210	$29,685
5	$32,800	$40,800
6	$36,000	$36,000
7	$36,000	$36,000
8	$36,000	$36,000
9	$36,000	$36,000
10	$36,000	$36,000

6.11

Period	CF_{add}	CF_n	EAT_n
0	−$769,000	0	0
1	0	$211,200	$133,200
2	0	$211,200	$133,200
3	0	$211,200	$133,200
4	0	$211,200	$133,200
5	0	$211,200	$133,200
6	0	$211,200	$133,200
7	0	$211,200	$133,200
8	0	$211,200	$133,200
9	0	$211,200	$133,200
10	$4,000	$211,200	$133,200

6.12

Period	CF_{add}	CF_n	EAT_n
0	−$1,148,000	0	0
1	0	$336,000	$246,000
2	0	$336,000	$246,000
3	0	$336,000	$246,000
4	0	$336,000	$246,000

Period	CF$_{add}$	CF$_n$	EAT$_n$
5	0	$336,000	$246,000
6	0	$336,000	$246,000
7	0	$336,000	$246,000
8	0	$336,000	$246,000
9	0	$336,000	$246,000
10	$350,000	$336,000	$246,000

6.13

Period	CF$_{add}$	CF$_n$	EAT$_n$
0	–$894,000	0	0
1	0	$212,000	$132,000
2	0	$212,000	$132,000
3	0	$212,000	$132,000
4	0	$212,000	$132,000
5	0	$212,000	$132,000
6	0	$212,000	$132,000
7	0	$212,000	$132,000
8	0	$212,000	$132,000
9	0	$212,000	$132,000
10	$100,000	$212,000	$132,000

6.14

Period	CF$_{add}$	CF$_n$	EAT$_n$
0	–$440,000	0	0
1	0	$128,800	$106,800
2	0	$137,800	$ 93,300
3	0	$135,900	$ 96,150
4	0	$134,200	$ 98,700
5	0	$132,660	$101,010
6	0	$131,260	$103,110
7	0	$130,600	$104,100
8	0	$130,600	$104,100
9	0	$130,620	$104,070
10	0	$130,600	$104,100
11	0	$131,820	$102,270
12	0	$131,800	$102,300
13	0	$131,820	$102,270
14	0	$131,800	$102,300
15	0	$131,820	$102,270
16	0	$125,900	$111,150
17	0	$120,000	$120,000
18	0	$120,000	$120,000
19	0	$120,000	$120,000
20	$85,000	$120,000	$120,000

Chapter 7

7.1	NPV = $7,659, r = 12%, PI = 1.06
7.2	NPV = –$8,556, r = 7%, PI = 0.87
7.3	NPV = $18,118, r = 13%, PI = 1.07
7.4	PB = 3.64 years, ARR = 0.296 or 29.6%
	NPV = $530,260, r = 24%, PI = 1.69
7.5	PB = 3.25 years
7.6	ARR = 0.240 or 24.0%
7.7	ARR = 0.146 or 14.6%
7.8	PB = 3.42 yrs, ARR = 0.3075 or 30.75%
	NPV = $954,041, r = 27%, PI = 1.83
7.9	PB = 4.22 yrs, ARR = 0.264 or 26.4%
	NPV = $336,042, r = 20%, PI = 1.38
7.10	PB = 2.50 years, DPB = 3.02 years
7.11	PB = 3.39 yrs, ARR = 0.5769 or 57.69%
	NPV = $492,341, r = 30%, PI = 2.12
7.12	From 0 to 300 percent. At 150 percent.

Chapter 8

8.1	NPV$_A$ = $13,554, NPV$_B$ = $21,947
8.2	Incremental r = 15% to 16%
	Model 3581 r = 14% to 15%
	NPV$_{3402}$ = $11,445, NPV$_{3581}$ = $20,244
8.3	Incremental r = 25% to 26%
	NPV$_R$ = $24,069, NPV$_S$ = $18,062
8.4	Incremental r = 7% to 8%, Model 1
	r = 17% to 18%, Incremental PI = 0.82
	Model 1 PI = 1.26, NPV$_1$ = $32,652
	NPV$_2$ = $27,590
8.5	NPV$_C$ = $19,712, NPV$_{A'}$ = $21,973
	NPV$_{B'}$ = $35,575, For C, X = $3,208
	For A, X = $3,575, For B, X = $5,790
8.6	NPV$_Z$ = $19,223, NPV$_{K'}$ = $21,966
	For Z, X = $3,128, For K, X = $13,551
8.7	E(R) = 9.05%, σ = 9.05%, 20 percent
8.8	EV$_A$ = $20,000, EV$_B$ = $20,000
	σ_A = 5,477, σ_B = 3,536, Project B
8.9	E(R) = 12.97%, σ = 2.25%

8.10 $r_p = 11.79\%$, $\sigma_p = 3.42\%$

8.11 $NPV_{3402} = \$11,445$, $NPV_{3581} = -\$3,113$

8.12 $NPV_{8\%} = \$15,687$, $NPV_{9\%} = \$11,577$
$NPV_{10\%} = \$7,659$, $NPV_{11\%} = \$342$
$NPV_{12\%} = -\$6,339$

8.13

Change	R_n	OC_n	MCC
+10%	$114,192	$41,408	$61,364
0%	$ 68,702	$68,702	$68,702
−10%	$ 23,212	$95,996	$76,376

Chapter 9

9.1 $ATCD_{12\%} = 7.20\%$

9.2 $ATCD_{9.60\%} = 5.76\%$

9.3 $ATCD_{12.91\%} = 7.75\%$

9.4 $k_p = 0.1275$ or 12.75%

9.5 $k_s = 0.1500$ or 15.00%

9.6 $k_s = 0.1500$ or 15.00%

9.7 $k_s = 15.00\%$

9.8 $k_s = 11.40\%$

9.9 $k_e = 0.1641$ or 16.41%

9.10 $k_e = 0.2096$ or 20.96%

9.11

Component	Book Weight	Market Weight
Long-term debt	36.4%	32.4%
Preferred stock	9.1%	7.2%
Common equity	54.5%	60.4%

9.12

Project	Cumulative	IRR
B	$1,000,000	18%
C	$1,500,000	15%
D	$2,300,000	13%
A	$2,900,000	12%

9.13 $0 to $1,250,000, MCC = 11.70%
$1,250,000 to $3,000,000, MCC = 12.18%
$3,000,000 to $3,750,000, MCC = 12.66%
$3,750,000+, MCC = 13.14%

9.14 Accept Projects B, C, and D. Reject Project A. Optimal capital budget, $2,300,000.

Chapter 10

10.1 $Q_{BE} = 600$ units, $Q = 1,600$ units

10.2 $Q_{BE} = 500$ units, $S_{BE} = \$425,000$

10.3 $Q_{BE} = 10,000$ units, $DOL = 3.00$

10.4 $DOL = 2.67$

10.5 $DOL = 2.00$, $DFL = 1.50$,
$DTL = 3.00$, $S_{BE} = \$425,000$

10.6 (a) EPS: $4.20, $6.60, $5.10
(b) $DOL = 2.00$, $DFL = 1.43$, $DTL = 2.86$
$DOL = 1.75$, $DFL = 1.82$, $DTL = 3.18$
$DOL = 1.75$, $DFL = 1.18$, $DTL = 2.06$
(c) $S_{BE} = \$5,000,000$, $S_{BE} = \$4,285,714$

10.7 $V = \$7,142,857$ (both companies)
$S = \$2,142,857$, $k_{sl} = 23.33\%$

10.8 $V_u = \$10,000,000$, $V_l = \$12,400,000$
$S = \$6,400,000$, $k_{sl} = 14.25\%$

Chapter 11

11.1 Retention Ratio = 0.40
Payout Ratio = 0.60

11.2 Retention Ratio = 0.60
Retained Earnings = $27,000

11.3 Dividend Yield = 0.0400 or 4.00%

11.4 Monday, December 7, 1992

11.5 Approximately $47.50

11.6 $D_5 = \$2.58$

11.7 EACS = $2,800,000, EPS = $2.80
Dividend yield = 0.0500 or 5.00%
Payout ratio = 0.50, Retention ratio = 0.50

11.8 Based on retained earnings-DPS = $4.50
Based on available cash-DPS = $3.00
Dividends = $66,000

11.9 Price = $20.83

11.10 Price = $25.00

11.11

Common stock	$2,200,000
Capital in excess of par	19,800,000
Retained earnings	8,000,000

Before EPS = $2.20, After EPS = $2.00

11.12
Common stock	$600,000
Capital in excess of par	5,000,000
Retained earnings	3,400,000

Before EPS = $1.50, After EPS = $0.50

11.13
Current assets	= $48,950,000
Common stock	= $10,500,000
Paid-in capital	= $44,500,000
Retained earnings	= $143,950,000

11.14   (a)
Year	EPS	DPS	Year	EPS	DPS
1983	$1.00	$0.40	1988	$1.40	$0.56
1984	1.20	0.48	1989	1.40	0.56
1985	1.30	0.52	1990	1.50	0.60
1986	2.00	0.80	1991	2.00	0.80
1987	1.20	0.48	1992	1.60	0.64

(b)
Year	EPS	DPS	Year	EPS	DPS
1983	$1.00	$0.40	1988	$1.40	$0.56
1984	1.20	0.44	1989	1.40	0.56
1985	1.30	0.48	1990	1.50	0.60
1986	2.00	0.52	1991	2.00	0.64
1987	1.20	0.52	1992	1.60	0.64

(c)
		Extra			Extra
Year	DPS	DPS	Year	DPS	DPS
1983	$0.40	$0.00	1988	$0.50	$0.00
1984	0.42	0.00	1989	0.52	0.00
1985	0.44	0.00	1990	0.54	0.00
1986	0.46	0.34	1991	0.56	0.24
1987	0.48	0.50	1992	0.58	0.00

11.15   Dividends = $11,440,000, Payout Ratio = 0.55, Retention Ratio = 0.45

11.16   Accept Projects A,B,D. Reject Project C Optimal capital budget = $1,900,000. Dividends = $860,000, Ratio = 0.43

11.17   Accept Projects B,C,D. Reject Project A Optimal capital budget = $2,300,000. Dividends = $1,620,000, Ratio = 0.54

Chapter 12

12.1   TEY = 16.67%

12.2   X = $450,000 shares

12.3   Responses will vary.

Chapter 13

13.1
Common stock	$ 600,000
Capital in excess of par	4,900,000
Retained earnings	6,600,000

13.2
Common stock ($1 par)	$ 900,000
Capital in excess of par	3,600,000
Retained earnings	5,560,000

13.3   Majority, zero. Cumulative, two.

13.4   Majority, zero. Cumulative, three.

13.5   Rights = 2, TMV = $7,000,000 P_{ex} = $23.33 per share

13.6   R = $0.83. Price ex-rights is $29.17.

13.7   Preferred ($340,000), Bonds ($384,000)

13.8   Preferred ($600,000), Bonds ($744,000)

13.9   ATPY = 11.04%, ATBY = 7.20%

13.10   ATPY = 11.00%, ATBY = 6.60%

Chapter 14

14.1   PV = $4,598,678

14.2   PV = $1,628,685

14.3   PV = $6,296,882

14.4 PV_L = −$1,137,348 PV_O = −$1,035,708

14.5   PV = $146,470

14.6 PV_L = −$2,143,248 PV_O = −$2,051,776

14.7   PV = −$313,030

Chapter 15

15.1 $1,000 for the 100 shares

15.2 $500 for the 100 shares

15.3   Upper bound begins at $0 stock value. Lower bound begins at $40 stock value

15.4 $500 for 100 shares

15.5   The profit is $300.

15.6   Primary EPS = $7.06

15.7   Conversion Price = $40, Conversion Premium Ratio = 0.21 or 21%

15.8 Conversion Value = $1,000

15.9 Conversion Value = $600

15.10 V_b = $1,197.94

15.11 Simple EPS = $6.24
Primary EPS = $5.14

Chapter 16

16.1 Disbursement float is $60,000.
Collection float is $60,000.
Net float for the company is $0.

16.2 Actual cash balance is $500,000.

16.3 ER = 0.0854 or 8.54%

16.4 ER = 0.09215 or 9.215%

16.5 C* = $75,679, Average level of cash is $37,839.5.

16.6 C* = $91,287, Average level of cash is $45,643.5.

16.7 T = $15,897, U = $27,691
ACB = $17,863

16.8 T = $7,894, U = $13,682
ACB = $8,859

16.9 No action is required.

16.10 Purchase $31,000 in marketable securities.

Chapter 17

17.1 Incremental profit is $35,014.

17.2 Incremental profit is $110,219.

17.3 OC = 0.105 or 10.5%

17.4 OC = 0.248 or 24.8%

17.5 Q* = 3,162 units, TC = $3,162
Orders = 15.8

17.6 Q* = 1,643 units

17.7 Q* = 100,000 units, TC = $30,000
Orders = 100, RP = 136,987

17.8 Q* = 316,228 units, TC = $31,623
Orders = 31.6, RP = 134,590

17.9 Order 1,000 units each time.

17.10 Order 10,000 units each time.

Chapter 18

18.1 Length of the operating cycle, 140 days.

18.2 Length of the operating cycle, 300 days.

18.3 Length of the cash cycle, 110 days.

18.4 Length of the cash cycle, 260 days.

18.5 19X4 Cash Turnover = 4.60
19X5 Cash Turnover = 5.21

18.6 (a) EIR = 0.1400 or 14.00%
(b) EIR = 0.1494 or 14.94%
(c) EIR = 0.1412 or 14.12%
(d) EIR = 0.1486 or 14.86%

18.7 (a) EIR = 0.1253 or 12.53%
(b) EIR = 0.1182 or 11.82%
(c) EIR = 0.1308 or 13.08%
(d) EIR = 0.1211 or 12.11%

18.8 (a) Face Value = $100,000
(b) Face Value = $114,943
(c) Face Value = $125,000
(d) Face Value = $144,928

18.9 (a) Face Value = $500,000
(b) Face Value = $561,798
(c) Face Value = $588,236
(d) Face Value = $657,895

Chapter 19

19.1 Recognize $200,000 of income. Increase investment account by $200,000. Dividends of $80,000 increase cash but reduce investment account by $80,000. Net increase in investment account is $120,000.

19.2 Recognize $164,000 of income. Increase investment account by $164,000. Dividends of $80,000 increase cash but reduce investment account by $80,000. Net increase in investment account is $84,000.

19.3 Without, $150,000, $150,000, $210,000
With, $ 90,000, $120,000, $210,000

19.4 Without, $345,000, $450,000, $570,000
With, $174,863, $380,137, $570,000

19.5 $NPV_M = \$600,000$, Before, $V_s = \$21$
After, $V_s = \$27$

19.6 Exchange ratio is 1.185:1.

19.7 $NPV_M = \$500,000$, Before, $V_s = \$10$
After, $V_s = \$11$

19.8 Exchange ratio is 0.909:1.

19.9

First mortgage	$1,250,000
Second mortgage	250,000
Costs of administration	500,000
Wages due workers	200,000
Unpaid taxes	50,000
Accounts payable	50,000
Notes payable	75,000
Second mortgage	50,000
Unsecured bonds	75,000

Chapter 20

20.1 $100,722.05

20.2 30 days, FP = -3.03%
90 days, FP = -3.03%
180 days, FP = -3.04%

20.3 An arbitrage opportunity exists since interest-rate parity does not hold.

20.4 $1,949,500

20.5 $9,762.41

20.6 D = 0.214 or 21.4 percent

20.7

	Payments	Receipts	Payment	Receipt
United States	1,200	1,500	—	300
Mexico	1,300	1,200	100	—
Peru	1,200	1,000	200	—
Spain	1,300	1,300	—	—

20.8 NPV = 30,482

APPENDIX E

Glossary

Accelerated Cost Recovery System (ACRS) The depreciation system required by the Internal Revenue Service under the provisions of the Economic Recovery Tax Act of 1981.

Accounting rate of return The average earnings after tax for a project divided by the average book value.

Acquiring company The company that plans to secure another company.

Acquisition Occurs from a legal perspective when one company acquires a majority of the common stock of another company, not just a controlling interest.

Activity ratios Measure how efficiently a company is using its assets by relating sales to total assets, accounts receivable, and inventory.

Advisement The consulting function of investment banking.

After-tax cost of new debt The cost of the debt component adjusted for taxes since interest from debt is tax deductible.

Aging of receivables Involves classifying receivables by length of time outstanding.

Aging schedule A compilation of accounts receivable according to the age of the account.

Agency costs The costs of trying to minimize the agency problem.

Agency problem The tendency of management to choose goals other than share-price maximization, the result of management placing personal goals ahead of the goal of maximizing share value.

Agency relationships The relationships between management and shareholders and between shareholders and creditors resulting in agency costs.

Aggressive working capital policy The policy of using long-term sources to finance fixed assets and most of the constant level of current assets, using short-term sources to finance the temporary level of current assets and a portion of permanent current assets.

Alternate method The method under accelerated cost recovery systems that applies straight line depreciation over the recovery period while using a half-year convention.

American Depository Receipts Certificates denominated in U.S. dollars issued by a U.S. bank, providing the form of most foreign stock trading in the United States.

American option An option that can be exercised at any time until, but not after, the expiration date.

American Stock Exchange This exchange is similar to the New York Stock Exchange, but most of its listed firms are smaller and newer since listing requirements are less stringent.

Amortized loan Equal loan payments over the life of the loan , thereby providing a stated interest rate to the lender.

Amortization schedule Shows how a loan payment is divided between interest and principal.

Authorized stock The maximum number of shares that a corporation can issue without an amendment to the charter.

Annuity A series of identical cash flows spaced at equal intervals.

Annuity due A series of identical, equally-spaced cash flows with the cash flows received at the beginning of each period.

Asymmetric information Assumes managers often have more and better information than investors.

Balance sheet Provides a financial representation of the assets of and claims against a company at a given point in time.

Balanced working capital policy The policy of using long-term sources to finance fixed assets and permanent current assets, using short-term sources to finance temporary current assets.

Bankers' acceptances Drafts usually originating from foreign trade that are backed by the bank on which they are drawn as well as on the importing company.

Bankruptcy A legal term indicating a company has begun a legal proceeding under the control of a bankruptcy court.

Baumol model Views cash balances as an inventory in which a company reorders a quantity of cash when the amount of cash reaches a certain level.

Beta Measures the volatility of an asset relative to the market.

Bird-in-the-hand approach The theory that investors prefer the certainty of dividends to the uncertainty of receiving income in the form of capital gains.

Blue chip stocks Stocks of highly regarded, established corporations such as General Motors, IBM, and Xerox.

Bond indenture A contract between the company issuing the bonds and the bondholder.

Bond ratings Reflect the probability that the issuing corporation will default on the bond.

Bond refunding The replacement of all or part of a bond issue with another bond issue, normally when interest rates decline.

Book value The value of an asset as shown on a balance sheet.

Book value weights Capital structure weights based on historical costs, the book values found on company balance sheets.

Breakeven analysis Used to find the output or sales level which generates earnings before interest and taxes of zero.

Business risk Measured by the variability in earnings before interest and taxes for a company.

C corporations Corporations treated for tax purposes as regular corporations, resulting in a double taxation of income: corporate earnings are taxed and then dividends are taxed after they have been distributed to the individual shareholders.

Call feature Specifies conditions under which a bond may be retired by the issuer prior to its stated maturity.

Call option Gives the holder the right to buy an asset at a fixed price for a specified period of time.

Callable preferred stock Preferred stock that may be retired at the discretion of the issuing corporation by paying the preferred stockholder a stated amount, usually a sum slightly higher than the par value.

Capital asset pricing model Shows the relationship between diversification, risk, and the required rate of return of an asset.

Capital Budgeting The process of allocating funds among competing long-term investment opportunities.

Capital expenditures Expenditures that provide future benefits beyond the period in which they are incurred.

Capital impairment rule A regulation that prevents a company from paying dividends out of its shareholder capital.

Capital in excess of par The account representing the difference between what the new shareholders paid and the par value.

Capital markets Financial markets involving securities with maturities greater than one year.

Cash budget A statement prepared on a cash rather than on an accrual basis that details the future cash inflows and cash outflows of a company over a specified period of time.

Cash budget worksheet Represents the cash inflows from sales and the cash outflows from purchases.

Cash discounts Price reductions given to customers for paying by a specified early date.

Cash flow diagram A visual method of indicating the magnitude and timing of cash flows and showing the appropriate interest rate.

Cash in advance Requires the customer to pay before the product is shipped, the method used with the least creditworthy customers.

Cash on delivery (COD) Requires the customer to pay with cash or certified check before taking delivery, an approach which only involves the risk of the customer not accepting the shipment.

Cash terms The conditions under which cash is paid, either in the form of cash in advance or in the form of cash on delivery.

Cash turnover Calculated by dividing the cash cycle into 365.

Characteristic line The regression line of the returns of an asset and the market over time.

Charter Two documents, the articles of incorporation and the certificate of incorporation, which grant a corporation its legal existence.

Cleanup clause A provision in a promissory note forcing a company to be out of debt for a set number of days during the year in order to prevent the company from using short-term loans for long-term purposes.

Clearinghouses Use computerized records instead of embossed certificates to avoid the procedures of transfer agents and registrars.

Closely held corporation A corporation owned by a few shareholders who play an active role in management.

Collateral trust bonds Bonds secured by financial securities such as stocks and bonds deposited with the trustee.

Collection float Results from checks written to the company requiring time to clear.

Collection policy Reflects the methods used to collect receivables.

Commercial draft A credit instrument which demands a credit commitment from the customer before the product is delivered.

Commercial paper An unsecured promissory note usually issued by large, strong corporations with maturities ranging from one day up to nine months.

Commission brokers Act as agents for brokerage firms and execute orders on the floor of the stock exchange.

Common-size balance sheet A balance sheet in which all components are divided by total assets and are expressed as percentages, allowing comparisons in financial performance from year to year.

Common-size income statement All components in this income statement are divided by sales and are expressed as percentages, allowing comparisons in financial performance from year to year.

Compensating balance Balance required by a bank to compensate the bank for services rendered, thereby increasing the effective rate of interest.

Compound growth rate technique Determines the compound growth rate of sales over a period of time and applies the growth rate to one or more future periods.

Compound interest Interest earned on cash flows plus interest earned on prior interest.

Compounding The process of finding an equivalent cash flow in the future.

Concentration banking Uses company sales offices to process customer checks, thereby reducing the time to receive checks by mail and decreasing the time for checks to clear.

Conditional sales contract Allows the seller to retain ownership of the product until payment is complete.

Conservative working capital policy The policy of using long-term sources to finance all asset requirements while investing excess funds, when available, in marketable securities.

Consignment A system of credit in which the seller (the consignor) retains title to product shipped to the customer (the consignee), with payment made by the consignee to the consignor if the product is sold.

Consolidation A combination of two or more companies in which a completely new company is created while both the acquiring and acquired companies no longer exist as business entities.

Constant dividend growth model A stock valuation model developed by Myron J. Gordon that assumes dividends grow at a constant rate indefinitely.

Constant dividend payout ratio policy Requires a company to pay out a fixed percentage of earnings each year.

Constant dividends with extras policy Requires a company to pay a small quarterly dividend plus an occasional extra year-end dividend in order to signal investors that a high dividend, when it occurs, may not continue.

Constant dividends with growth policy Requires a company to pay low dividends, increasing the amount of the dividends when it appears that the increase can be sustained.

Continuous probability distribution. A probability distribution that includes an unlimited number of possibilities.

Control The design of systems to ensure that the company achieves objectives that lead to attainment of the primary goal.

Conventional projects Projects that begin with one or more negative cash flows followed by one or more positive cash flows and include only one sign change in the sequence.

Covered option Writing a call option when the investor owns the underlying stock.

Conversion premium The amount the market value exceeds the minimum value for a convertible bond.

Conversion premium ratio The conversion price of a convertible bond less the current stock price divided by the current stock price.

Conversion price The par value of the convertible security divided by the conversion ratio.

Conversion ratio The number of common shares into which a convertible security converts.

Conversion value The market value of the common stock if a convertible bond is converted.

Convertible preferred stock Preferred stock that is convertible into a fixed number of shares of common stock at the discretion of the preferred stockholder.

Convertible security A bond or preferred stock that can be exchanged at the option of its holder for a specified number of common shares of the company.

Corporation A legal entity created by a state that is separate from the owners of the organization thereby providing the shareholders with limited liability.

Correlation coefficient Measures the relationship between two series of numbers.

Correspondent banking A form of multinational banking where a domestic bank keeps a correspondent account with a bank in another country that makes transactions upon request.

Cost of capital The rate of return a company must earn on its average-risk investments in order to leave the market value of its equity unchanged.

Cost of new common stock The cost of equity when new common stock is used to supply that capital component.

Cost of perpetual preferred stock The cost of the perpetual preferred stock capital component, not adjusted for taxes since dividends from preferred stock are not tax deductible.

Cost of retained earnings The cost of equity when retained earnings are used to supply that capital component.

Coupon interest rate The percentage of par value of a bond that a company or governmental unit promises to pay the bondholder each interest period.

Coupon payment The interest payment paid to the bondholder each period.

Covenants Restrictions in an indenture which limit the risk to the bondholder or preferred shareholder.

Coverage ratios Measure the extent to which the current debt obligations of a company are covered by the funds flowing from operations.

Covered-risk arbitrage A set of transactions in which risk is covered by the forward market.

Credit associations Local associations of credit managers who exchange information on credit customers.

Credit period The length of time for which credit is extended.

Credit scoring Involves the use of statistical methods to predict the probability that a customer will pay on time.

Credit terms The terms of a credit sale, including the credit period, the cash discount (if any), and the kind of credit instrument.

Credit-reporting agencies Provide credit information on several million companies throughout the United States and Canada, including general reference books and detailed credit reports on individual companies.

Cumulative preferred stock Requires that all unpaid preferred dividends be paid before dividends are paid on common stock.

Currency option Gives the holder the right but not the obligation to buy or sell a futures contract at a fixed price on or before a specified expiration date.

Cyclical stocks Stocks which experience price changes greater than the overall market.

Debenture An unsecured bond normally with a life of more than 15 years.

Declaration date The date the board of directors meets to declare the regular dividend.

Default risk Refers to the perceived probability that the issuer of marketable securities will fail to make interest or principal payments.

Defensive stocks Stocks with prices that remain stable or possibly increase during periods of recession.

Degree of financial leverage The percentage change in earnings per share for a given percentage change in earnings before interest and taxes.

Degree of operating leverage The percentage change in earnings before interest and taxes for a given percentage change in sales.

Degree of total leverage The percentage change in earnings per share for a given percentage change in sales.

Disbursement float Results from checks written by the company requiring time to clear.

Discount bond A bond selling below par value.

Discounted payback period The number of years necessary to recover the initial project investment using cash flows discounted to time 0 using the marginal cost of capital.

Discounting The process of finding an equivalent cash flow in the past.

Discrete probability distribution A probability distribution that includes a limited number of possible outcomes.

Diversification The process of reducing risk by combining assets into a portfolio.

Divestiture The selling of a portion of the assets of a company as a strategic move.

Dividend clientele effect The theory that a company which increases dividends attracts investors who prefer immediate income, thereby increasing the demand for the stock and pushing prices upward.

Dividend decision The determination of how earnings after taxes are distributed to preferred and common shareholders or retained for investment.

Dividend reinvestment plans Allow shareholders to reinvest their dividends in the stock of the company paying the dividends.

Dividend Signalling The theory that an increase in dividends is a signal from management that better earnings are forecast, resulting in increases in stock prices.

Dow Jones Industrial Average An average of the market prices of 30 industrial common stocks.

Draft An instrument similar to a check but different in that the issuing company does not have to deposit funds to cover the draft until a bank presents it for payment.

Earnings after taxes Earnings before taxes less corporate income taxes, the bottom line of the income statement.

Earnings before interest and taxes Gross profit less the various operating expenses.

Edge Act corporation An American banking subsidiary with wider latitude than other foreign subsidiaries in conducting business.

Effective rate of interest The rate of interest for any compounding period compounded on an annual basis.

Equipment trust certificates Bonds secured by equipment such as railroad rolling stock.

Equivalent annual annuity approach The method of spreading net present value over the lives of mutually exclusive projects, while selecting the project which provides the greater yearly value increase.

Euro-equity market The world market that deals in international issues, with London the center of this market.

Eurobond An international bond denominated in a currency other than the country in which it is issued.

Eurocurrency markets Markets in which Eurobanks conduct transactions in currencies foreign to the banking location.

Eurodollar certificates of deposit Certificates of deposit originated by foreign banks.

Eurodollars U.S. dollars deposited in foreign banks or foreign branches of U.S. banks.

European option An option that can only be exercised on the expiration date

Equivalent cash flow A single cash flow that represents one or more cash flows while allowing for the time value of money.

Ex-dividend date The date the right to dividends no longer remains with the stock, four business days before the holder-of-record date.

Exchange rate The price of a currency in terms of another currency.

Exercising the option Involves buying or selling an asset through the option contract.

Expected rate of return The average return a project will bring.

Expected return of a portfolio The weighted average of the expected returns of the individual assets in the portfolio.

External rationing Occurs when lenders restrict the amount of borrowing a company can do by making the cost of credit prohibitively high.

Factor A commercial finance company or the subsidiary of a commercial bank that specializes in financing receivables.

Factoring receivables Involves the sale of accounts receivable to a factor.

Federal agency notes Notes usually issued on a discount basis by the Federal Home Loan bank, the Government National Mortgage Association, the Federal National Mortgage Association, and other federal agencies.

Five C's of credit The five keys used by credit managers to analyze creditworthiness: character, capacity, capital, collateral, and conditions.

Financial risk The additional risk, above business risk, resulting from substituting debt into the capital structure.

Financing decision The determination of how a company's assets are financed, including decisions that result in the best mix of debt and equity.

Financial leverage The extent to which debt is used in the capital structure.

Financial lease A lease with the following characteristics: (1) The lease is fully amortized, (2) The lessee is responsible for maintenance, property taxes, and insurance, (3) The lease is noncancelable, and (4) The lessee may renew the lease at expiration.

Financial institutions Financial intermediaries that collect money from individuals, businesses, and governments and use the funds to make loans or investments.

Financial markets The markets in which financial assets are bought and sold, with short-term markets called money markets and long-term markets called capital markets.

Financial restructuring Restructuring of a corporation where the capital structure is changed.

Financial services The delivery of financial products through means such as banking, financial planning, investments, real estate, and insurance.

Float Represents uncollected funds in the payment system and is equal to the company checking account balance less the balance shown at the bank.

Floor brokers Assist commission brokers when there are too many orders to handle and receive part of the commission paid to the commission broker.

Floor traders Buy and sell for their own accounts, do not handle public orders, and make money by speculating on trading imbalances.

Floor value for a convertible bond The straight bond value of a convertible bond.

Foreign branch Functions according to the rules of the foreign country while operating under the total control of the domestic bank.

Foreign bond An international bond denominated in the currency of the country in which it is issued.

Foreign subsidiary bank A subsidiary of a domestic bank that is incorporated in the foreign country, clouding the issue of control due to the separate board of directors.

Forward discount The currency trading situation where the forward rate is lower than the spot rate.

Forward market hedge Requires a company to execute a contract in the forward exchange market to buy a fixed amount of foreign currency at the forward rate.

Forward premium The currency trading situation where the forward rate is higher than the spot rate.

Forward rate The price for delivery of currency at some point in the future, usually a time of 30, 90, or 180 days, but it may range up to two years.

Friendly merger A merger endorsed by the management and approved by the shareholders of the target company.

Fully diluted earnings per share Adjusted earnings available to common shareholders divided by the average number of shares outstanding based on all warrants, rights, and convertible securities being exercised or converted.

Future value The equivalent cash flow at a specified point in the future.

Future value factor The multiplier used to calculate the future value.

Future value of an annuity An equivalent cash flow located at the end of the annuity.

Gross profit Net sales less cost of goods sold.

Gross profit margin Gross profit divided by sales.

Growth stocks Stocks that are expected to experience in the future a substantial growth in earnings per share and price while retaining a high proportion of earnings.

Holder-of-record date The date on which shareholders who are registered as the owners of a stock are declared recipients of dividends.

Hostile takeover A merger not supported by the management of the target company, forcing the acquiring company to deal directly with the shareholders of the target company.

Ideal level of current assets The amount that minimizes the total costs of employing the various items that make up current assets.

Improper earnings accumulation A finding by the Internal Revenue Service that a company has paid too small a dividend in order to allow shareholders to defer personal taxes on the dividends.

Income bonds Unsecured bonds with interest paid from the projects the bonds finance.

Income statement Shows the total revenues and total expenses for a company, including income taxes, over a stated period of time.

Income stocks Stocks that have a long-term record of steady, large cash dividends.

Incremental cash flows. The additional after-tax cash flows expected when a project is accepted.

Independent projects Projects whose cash flows do not depend on one another.

Industry average ratios Show ratios for a particular industry over a period of time.

Initial cash flows One-time expenditures made near the beginning of a project.

Internal rationing Occurs when company management chooses not to accept all projects indicated by the optimal capital budget.

International bond A bond initially issued outside the country of the borrower and classified as either a foreign bond or a Eurobond.

Interest-rate parity Implies that the forward premium on currency X is equal to the interest rate differential between countries X and Y, with the lower interest rate quoted at a forward premium.

Interest rate risk The variability in the value of a debt security due to changes in market interest rates.

Internal rate of return (IRR) The discount rate which causes the present value of the cash flows of a project to be equal to 0.

Investment bankers Bankers who serve as financial middlemen in the process of raising long-term funds for businesses and government.

Investment decision The determination of the size and composition of company assets, including investment in new assets and removal of assets that are no longer productive.

Investment grade bonds Require a rating in the top four classifications, AAA through BBB for Standard & Poor's and Aaa through Baa for Moody's.

Investment opportunity schedule The schedule that arranges investment opportunities from the highest to the lowest ranking (using IRR), while summing the required initial investments, displayed with a tabular presentation or with an investment opportunity curve.

Investment tax credit A reduction in the federal income tax liability that encourages companies to make capital investments.

Involuntary reorganization The filing of a reorganization petition under Chapter 11 of the Bankruptcy Act by an outside party such as a creditor.

Junk bonds High-risk, high-yield subordinated debentures rated BB or lower by Standard & Poor's and Ba by Moody's.

Lease A contract in which the owner, called the lessor, grants to the user, called the lessee, the right to use an asset for a given time in return for periodic payments.

Legal insolvency Occurs when the total liabilities exceed the total assets, as recorded on the balance sheet.

Leverage ratios Measure the extent to which a company uses debt rather than equity to finance the company's assets, the higher the proportion of debt, the higher the chance of financial distress.

Leveraged buyout Takeover of a company using the assets of the target company as security for the loan, repaying the loan out of cash flow from the acquired company.

Leveraged lease A financial lease with the following properties: (1) The lessee makes periodic payments for use of the assets, (2) The lessor purchases the assets but only provides 20 to 50 percent of the capital necessary for the purchase, and (3) A lender, possibly an insurance company or pension fund, provides the remainder of the financing.

Line of credit An informal or formal agreement between a borrower and a bank to lend up to a specified amount.

Liquidation Occurs when the bankruptcy court determines that reorganization is not indicated such as when no reorganization petition is filed, when the reorganization petition is denied, and when the reorganization plan is disapproved.

Liquidation value The current market value of company assets less the total of liabilities, preferred stock, and liquidating expenses.

Liquidity ratios Measure the ability of a company to meet its short-term obligations as they come due.

Loan projects Projects that begin with one or more positive cash flows followed by one or more negative cash flows and include only one sign change in the sequence.

Lockbox A post office box designated to receive accounts-receivable payments from customers of a particular company.

Managerial finance Relates to duties of the financial manager in private companies, governmental operations, and not-for-profit institutions.

Marginal cost of capital The cost of the last dollar of capital that a company raises for its capital budget.

Marginal cost of capital schedule The schedule showing the relationship between the size of the capital budget and the cost of capital, displayed with a tabular presentation or with a marginal cost of capital curve.

Marginal tax rate The rate applied to each incremental amount of taxable income, important in finance since it shows the marginal effect of a decision.

Market ratios Associate the market price of a share of stock with its earnings per share or its book value per share, with high values reflecting investor confidence in the company.

Market value weights Capital structure weights based on the market values of the securities of a company.

Marketability Refers to the ease with which a marketable security may be converted to cash.

Matching principle Requires that management match short-term sources with short-term uses and long-term sources with long-term uses, a principle consistent with the balanced working capital policy.

Maturity date The time when the last payment and the lump sum of a bond are paid.

Merger A combination of two or more companies in which the acquiring company retains its name and identity while the acquired company ceases to exist as a business entity.

Miller-Orr model Assumes that daily net cash flows are normally distributed and includes control limits that allow for positive and negative cash balance changes.

Minimum value of a convertible bond The greater of the conversion value and the straight bond value for a convertible bond.

Modified Accelerated Cost Recovery System (MACRS) The depreciation system required by the Internal Revenue Service under the provisions of the Tax Reform Act of 1986.

Modified internal rate of return The discount rate which causes the absolute value of the present value of the negative cash flows to equal the present value of the terminal value of the positive cash flows

Modigliani and Miller model with corporate taxes States that the value of the company increases and the cost of capital of the company decreases as debt is added to the capital structure.

Modigliani and Miller model without corporate taxes States that the value of the company and the cost of capital are independent of its capital structure.

Money market hedge Requires a company to borrow funds from a bank, exchange the funds for foreign currency, and invest in the foreign money market until needed for a transaction.

Money markets A financial market involving securities with maturities of one year or less

Mortgage bonds Bonds secured by liens on real property such as buildings and land.

Mutually exclusive projects Acceptance of one project precludes acceptance of the other project.

Naked option Writing a call option when the investor does not own the underlying stock.

Negotiable certificates of deposit Issued by commercial banks in denominations of $100,000 or more with maturities of 3, 6, 9, or 12 months with a minimum time of 14 days.

Net float Equal to disbursement float less collection float.

Net present value (NPV) The present value of the cash flows of a project discounted at the marginal cost of capital.

Net present value profile The graph of the relationship of the net present value to the discount rate used in the calculation.

Net profit margin Earnings after taxes divided by sales.

Net working capital Current assets minus current liabilities.

New York Stock Exchange The largest and most important stock exchange in the United States, dominating the American Stock Exchange and the regional exchanges.

Nonconventional projects Projects that begin with either positive or negative cash flows followed by no fixed order of cash flows and include more than one sign change in the sequence.

Off-balance-sheet financing. Financial leases not included on the right hand side of the balance sheet and, instead, reported in footnotes to the financial statements.

Open account A system of credit where the invoice, which includes the credit terms, is the formal credit instrument.

Operating cash flows The change in cash flows caused by changes in operating revenues, operating costs, and depreciation, the result of acceptance of a capital project.

Operating lease A lease with the following characteristics: (1) The lease is not fully amortized, (2) The lessor is responsible for maintenance, property taxes, and insurance, and (3) The lease is cancelable at the option of the lessee.

Operating leverage The extent to which operating costs are fixed as opposed to variable.

Operating cycle The time that elapses between the arrival of raw materials and collection for finished product, equal to the average age of inventory plus the average age of receivables.

Operational restructuring Restructuring of a corporation where the assets are changed.

Opportunity costs The cash flows foregone when a capital project is accepted.

Optimal capital structure The capital structure that maximizes the value of the common stock of the company.

Option A contract giving the holder the right but not the obligation to buy or sell an asset at a fixed price on or before a specified expiration date.

Over-the-counter market A network of securities dealers linked by computer terminals, telephones, and teletypes.

Ordinary annuity A series of identical, equally spaced cash flows with the cash flows received at the end of each period.

Origination Preliminary discussions with an investment banker as to the amount of new capital to be raised, the timing of the offering, the type of securities to be issued, the characteristics of the issue, and the price of the security.

Overdraft A written direction to a bank to honor a check in excess of the funds available in an account, with the amount not available becoming an automatic line of credit.

Par value of a bond The face value of a bond to be repaid at maturity

Par value of stock An arbitrary face value set in the charter by the organizers of the corporation.

Parent company The acquiring company in an acquisition.

Participating preferred stock Allows preferred stockholders to receive dividends above the stated rate of the preferred stock.

Partnership A business operated by two or more persons working under a written or oral agreement as either a general partnership or as a limited partnership.

Payback period The number of years necessary to recover the initial investment of a project.

Payment date The date when dividend checks are mailed out.

Percentage of sales forecasting method A method of preparing a pro forma balance sheet that assumes certain balance sheet accounts are proportional to the level of sales and are currently optimal.

Perpetual Bond A bond that offers annual or semiannual interest payments forever (an infinite sequence) and does not provide a lump sum at any point.

Perpetual preferred stock A preferred stock that pays a fixed dividend forever (an infinite sequence).

Perpetuity An annuity that continues forever (an infinite sequence).

Pledging receivables A method used to secure lending.

Portfolio A collection of assets.

Preauthorized payment Allows a company to charge the checking account of its customer up to a predetermined limit, a checkless transaction resulting in zero float.

Preemptive right The right to purchase any new shares sold by the corporation, a right often provided by the corporate charter.

Premium bond A bond selling above par value.

Present value The equivalent cash flow at a specified point in the past.

Present value factor The multiplier used to calculate the present value.

Present value of an annuity An equivalent cash flow located one time period before the first of the equal cash flows.

Primary earnings per share Adjusted earnings available to common shareholders divided by the average number of shares outstanding based on warrants, rights, and convertible securities likely to be exercised or converted.

Primary goal The principal objective for management in a public corporation: To maximize the value of its common stock by maximizing the present value of future returns to its shareholders.

Primary market The market for the issuance of new securities.

Prime rate The rate of interest banks charge their most creditworthy customers for large short-term loans.

Pro forma balance sheet Balance sheet projected for a future date.

Pro forma income statement Income statement projected for a future period.

Probability The likelihood that an event will occur.

Probability distribution The description of all possible outcomes and probabilities of a distribution.

Profitability index The ratio of the present value of the positive cash flows of a project to the absolute value of the present value of the negative cash flows.

Profitability index profile The graph of the relationship of the profitability index to the discount rate used in the calculation.

Profitability ratios Measure the ability of a company to grow and to repay debt.

Promissory note An agreement to pay a certain amount at a specified future date, requiring the seller to use notes receivable on its balance sheet.

Prospectus A document providing investors with enough information to make an informed buying decision, including the purpose and use of the funds that result from the sale of the securities.

Protective covenants Provisions in bond indentures designed to reduce the possibility that the company will default on the bonds.

Purchasing-power parity Implies that the exchange rates between two countries depend on the rates of inflation in the two countries and suggests that as the inflation rate for a country increases, the relative value of its currency decreases.

Put option Gives the holder the right to sell an asset at a fixed price for a specified period of time.

Qualitative forecasting Projections based on judgments as to the factors that will cause sales, or any other financial variable, to be different in the future from what they were in the past.

Quantitative forecasting The projection of current trends using methods such as regression analysis and the compound growth rate technique.

Rate of interest The compensation the demander of funds pays to the supplier, consisting of a real risk-free rate of interest plus premiums reflecting inflation, risk, and marketability.

Recovery percentages The percentages applied under accelerated cost recovery systems to the unadjusted basis of an asset over the specified recovery period.

Recovery period The depreciation term required under accelerated cost recovery systems.

Regional exchanges List popular New York Stock Exchange and American Stock Exchange securities as well as securities of regional interest and include the Pacific Coast Stock Exchange located in San Francisco and Los Angeles and the Midwest Stock Exchange located in Chicago.

Registration statement Documents providing formal disclosure of the financial condition and future plans of a company issuing securities.

Regression analysis Considers one or more independent variables to forecast the dependent variable.

Reinvestment rate risk. The risk that interest rates will decline by the time a short-term bond matures.

Remote disbursement accounts Accounts set up at banks in relatively remote areas, thereby increasing the time for checks to clear and disbursement float.

Reorganization plan A plan of reorganization the debtor company must present to the court and to the Securities and Exchange Commission.

Replacement chain approach The method of comparing projects over a common useful life and selecting the project with the higher net present value.

Repurchase agreements Sales of government securities, usually by a securities dealer, with an agreement to repurchase at a higher price on a specified future date.

Residual dividend theory Requires that earnings be used to provide the amount of equity needed for capital budgeting purposes and any residual earnings to be paid as dividends.

Revolving credit agreement A contract outlining the provisions of a line of credit.

Required rate of return The minimum expected rate of return that would cause an investor to make an investment when assets are priced competitively.

Right The document authorizing the holder to subscribe to new shares according to the terms of a rights offering.

Rights offering An offering of common stock to existing shareholders normally at a price lower than the price later offered to the public.

Risk The probability of a loss when making an investment.

Risk-adjusted discount rate approach Allows for risk by controlling the discount rate used for capital budgeting decisions.

Risk-free rate of return The real rate of interest plus the inflation premium.

S corporation. This status allows the income of a corporation to be taxed to the individual shareholders thereby avoiding the double taxation of the C corporation.

Sale-and-leaseback arrangement A financial lease with the following properties: (1) The lessee sells an asset to the lessor for cash and immediately leases it back, and (2) The lessee keeps the asset and makes periodic payments to the lessor.

Sales forecast A projection of future sales using quantitative and qualitative techniques.

Sales multiplier The forecast sales level divided by the sales from the previous year.

Seasonal dating Allows a company to receive a shipment one season and pay for it during the next season.

Secondary market The market for existing securities.

Secured bonds Bonds which have specific assets pledged to protect the bondholder in the event of default.

Security market line Shows the relationship between an asset's required rate of return and its beta coefficient.

Self-liquidating loans Loans used to finance temporary increases in current assets that repay by providing cash as current assets are reduced.

Sensitivity analysis An approach used to determine the effect on the output variable of increasing or decreasing one input variable, all other input variables held constant.

Serial bonds Bonds which have various maturity dates allowing the entire issue to be retired over a period of time.

Sight draft A commercial draft that requires the buyer to pay a specified amount on demand.

Simple earnings per share Earnings available to common shareholders divided by the average number of shares outstanding.

Sinking fund provision Requires that bonds be retired in a systematic fashion.

Sole proprietorship A business owned by one person who assumes unlimited liability and applies the net income or net loss of the company to his or her personal income tax return.

Specialists Execute orders for other brokers, receiving part of the customer commission, and act as dealers, buying and selling stocks in which they specialize, accepting the risk of price changes.

Speculative grade bonds Bonds assigned ratings below investment grade, also known as junk bonds.

Speculative stocks Stocks with high risk and high potential return.

Spin-off Converting an operating unit into an independent corporation while transferring ownership on a pro rata basis to the shareholders of the parent company.

Spot rate The price for immediate delivery of a currency, normally within two business days.

Spreadsheet A ledger sheet that records the financial statements of a company in a column and row format.

Standard & Poor's 500 Index An index made up of 400 industrials, 40 public utilities, 20 transportations, and 40 financial stocks.

Standard deviation Measures the risk, or variability, of a probability distribution.

Standard deviation of portfolio return Measures the risk or variability of a portfolio.

Statement of cash flows Shows over an accounting period the cash flows from operating, investing, and financing activities as well as how these activities have affected liquidity.

Stock dividend A dividend payment in the form of additional shares of stock to the common shareholders of a corporation.

Stock repurchase The repurchase of its own stock instead of paying a cash dividend by a company that has excess cash.

Stock certificate Represents ownership of the stock of the company and shows the name of the company, the state of incorporation, the number of shares owned by the shareholder, and the signatures of the corporate president and secretary.

Stock market average The arithmetic average of the market prices of a given set of stocks at a specified point in time.

Stock split A proportionate increase in the number of common shares owned.

Stone model Considers information about future cash flows before the cash manager makes a decision to buy or sell securities.

Straight bond value of a convertible bond The value of a convertible bond without the conversion privilege.

Strategic planning The setting of objectives and the design of strategies to meet the primary goal of maximizing the value of the common stock of the corporation.

Subordinated debentures Debentures that are subordinate to other creditors named in the bond indenture.

Subsidiary company The acquired company in an acquisition.

Sunk costs Capital costs that do not depend on acceptance or rejection of the project.

Supernormal dividend growth Dividend growth that exceeds the required annual rate of return.

Symmetric information Assumes that managers and investors have the same information about the operations and future prospects of the company.

Synergy Exists when the value of the combined enterprise is greater than the sum of the individual company values before combination.

Systematic risk The nondiversifiable risk that cannot be eliminated by having a diversified portfolio.

Takeover defenses Basic strategies used when target companies do not favor a merger or acquisition.

Target capital structure The proportions of debt, preferred stock, and common equity a company will use in the future.

Target company The company an acquiring company seeks.

Technical insolvency Occurs when a company is unable to meet its current obligations as they come due.

Tender offer This is a formal offer to purchase a specified number of shares of the target company at a set price.

Term structure of interest rates The relationship between the interest rate and the time to maturity for a given class of securities.

Terminal cash flows Cash flows that result when a capital project is terminated.

Time draft A commercial draft that allows the amount to be paid at a future date.

Total leverage The combined effect of using operating and financial leverage.

Traditional approach Assumes that the cost of debt and the cost of equity remain fairly constant up to a point and then begin to rise at higher levels of debt, indicating that the amount of debt in the capital structure is relevant.

Transaction loan A loan made for a specific purpose, repaid with a lump sum payment.

Transfer pricing The establishment of intracorporate prices for inputs, services, and technology in such a way as to meet corporate objectives.

Treasury bills Treasury Department securities issued on a discount basis in denominations from $10,000 to $1,000,000 which mature in 91 days, 182 days, and one year.

Treasury bonds Treasury Department securities with maturities of more than ten years.

Treasury notes Treasury Department securities with maturities greater than one year and less than ten years.

Unbundling The policy of dividing the transfer of corporate funds into separate cash flows to reduce tax liabilities in the host country, avoid limitations on dividends, and allow the effective use of transfer pricing.

Uncertainty, The probabilities of outcomes are not known (and cannot be estimated) as opposed to risk where the probabilities of outcomes are known (or can be estimated).

Underwriting The process of forming an underwriting syndicate.

Underwriting syndicate. An underwriting group composed of an originating house or manager and a group of investment bankers.

Unsecured bonds Bonds backed by the general credit of the company issuing them and not secured by any specific property.

Unsystematic risk The diversifiable risk that can be reduced by adding projects to a portfolio.

Value additivity principle The net present value of a group of independent projects is the sum of the net present values of the individual projects.

Voluntary reorganization The filing by the debtor company of a reorganization petition under Chapter 11 of the Bankruptcy Act.

Voluntary settlement A company in financial difficulty meets with a committee of creditors to draw up a plan for resolving the situation in order to avoid the high costs of bankruptcy proceedings.

Warrant An option that gives the holder the right to buy a share of common stock at a fixed price for a specified period of time.

Weighted average cost of capital The weighted average of the capital component costs, the costs of debt, preferred stock, and common equity.

Working capital Refers to current assets.

Working capital cycle (cash cycle) The time that elapses between payment for raw materials and collection for finished product, equal to the length of the operating cycle less the average age of accounts payable.

Working capital management The administration and control of current assets and current liabilities.

Working capital policy Provides the target levels for each classification of current assets and specifies the method of financing.

Worksheet A document that records after-tax cash flows and the relationships with operating revenues, operating costs, and depreciation.

Yield curve Shows the term structure of interest rates, with a normal yield curve indicating that short-term borrowing costs are less than long-term borrowing costs.

Yield to call The market rate of return the bondholder receives when the bond is called at its earliest call date.

Yield to maturity The interest rate that causes the cash flows of a bond when discounted to time 0 to equal the current price.

Zero-balance accounts Checking accounts in decentralized company locations funded from a master account which is replenished by accessing a line of credit or by selling marketable securities.

Zero coupon bond. A bond that does not pay interest during the life of the bond yet pays the par value of the bond at maturity.

Index